IMAGES
of America

CHICOT COUNTY

ON THE COVER: The Lake Village Water Carnival was first held on July 4, 1920. Celebrating Independence Day and the town's place on Lake Chicot, the event incorporated swimming and diving competitions, a parade, baseball, dancing, and, by 1921, boat races. Fireworks were added in 1923. Sponsored by the W.T. Conkley Post of the American Legion, the carnival attracted visitors from across the region—an estimated 8,000 to 10,000 in 1926. The event ended following the flood of 1927 and the Great Depression, only to be revived in 1947. (Courtesy of the Museum of Chicot County, Arkansas.)

IMAGES
of America

CHICOT COUNTY

Blake Wintory
on behalf of the Lakeport Plantation

ARCADIA
PUBLISHING

ISBN 978-1-4671-1405-9

Published by Arcadia Publishing
Charleston, South Carolina

Printed in the United States of America

Library of Congress Control Number: 2015937929

For all general information, please contact Arcadia Publishing:
Telephone 843-853-2070
Fax 843-853-0044
E-mail sales@arcadiapublishing.com
For customer service and orders:
Toll-Free 1-888-313-2665

Visit us on the Internet at www.arcadiapublishing.com

To Marvin Buffington, William Sessions, Clara Henry, Elbert Cashion Sr., John C. Hammock, George Kelley, Sheila Brannon, Libby Borgognoni, and all other Chicot County historians.

Contents

Acknowledgments		6
Introduction		7
1.	Chicot County, the Early Years	9
2.	Lake Village	31
3.	Dermott	65
4.	Eudora	81
5.	Lake Chicot and Recreation	97
6.	Scenes from around Chicot County	109
Bibliography		127

ACKNOWLEDGMENTS

The photographs in this book are only a slice of Chicot County's history. I know that many stories are not told, and some people, places, and groups are underrepresented. However, the stories and images here, I believe, do offer a glimpse of Chicot County's places, times, and people—its history. Everyone has a story, a family, and history. Write it down, share it, and preserve it. It makes my job easier, but your kids and grandkids will appreciate it even more.

The selected bibliography includes many of the valuable sources on Chicot County's history that were used to write this book. I made efforts to correct past errors and verify facts. I regret any errors that I might have made.

Everyone who shared an image used in the book is credited, but I would like to offer special thanks to those who went out of their way to share their knowledge and find photographs for this project—Libby Borgognoni, Cathy Cannatella, Annie Paden, LaRhonda Mangrum, Jimmy Parkerson, and the Arkansas Historic Preservation Program.

INTRODUCTION

Created in the Arkansas Territory in 1823, Chicot County is situated along the Mississippi River in Southeast Arkansas. In the 16th and 17th centuries, Europeans explored the region, meeting, trading, and sometimes fighting with Native Americans like the Quapaw and Tunica. Spanish explorer Hernando de Soto died at the village of Guachoya on May 31, 1542, in what is likely now Chicot County. Frenchman René-Robert Cavelier Sieur de La Salle claimed the region for France in 1682. Under La Salle's authority, Henri de Tonti established Arkansas Post at the mouth of the Arkansas River in 1686. With the area now part of New France, French fur traders descended the Mississippi River. When they encountered snags and tree stumps in the waterway that could damage boats or skiffs, they called them *chicots*—French for "teeth" or "stumps." Chicot County derived its name from a particularly dangerous passage along the route down the Mississippi. Georges-Henri-Victor Collot, a French government official writing during a 1796 expedition, described the "Island aux Chicots" as one of two passages "encumbered with drift-wood, heaped up sixty feet high" that impeded navigation. In the early 19th century, Point Chicot became the county's earliest point of trade. John James Audubon stopped there in 1820 and commented in his journal, "Point Chico is a handsome spot on this river that never overflows—and answers well for the Growth of Cotton Corn etc."

Upon Arkansas statehood in 1836, Chicot County's population reached only 2,471 (white and enslaved), but wealthy planters attracted to the county's rich frontier lands were already investing in cotton plantations along the Mississippi River. The tale of the "Arkansas Traveler," told (possibly as early as 1840) by Chicot County planter Sanford C. Faulkner, illustrated the tensions between the rural poor who squatted on the frontier and the elite planters. Cotton agriculture and slavery soon dominated the county's economy. In 1860, Chicot County produced more cotton (40,948 bales) than any county in the state. Chicot County also had the distinction of having the highest percentage of slaves in the state, 81 percent of the county's total population of 9,234.

Chicot County's support for secession beamed bright after the election of Pres. Abraham Lincoln and the formation of the Confederate States of America in the fall and winter of 1860. In January 1861, candidates vying to represent the county in Arkansas's secession convention unanimously favored a "Southern Confederacy" of "Slave States." However, the Civil War almost immediately disrupted planters' control of enslaved labor and cotton production. After Federal gunboats appeared on the Mississippi River in June 1862, Confederates began burning cotton and sending some slaves away from the river, as far away as Texas. During 1863, Union troops frequently raided resource-rich plantations to supply the ongoing siege at Vicksburg, and, in the process, freed slaves. Confederate resistance continued, especially in the Greenville Bends, where slow moving Union gunboats and transports could easily be attacked. After Confederates successfully disrupted traffic in the river, Union action was forced at the Battle at Ditch Bayou on June 6, 1864. The battle, the last major battle in Arkansas, removed the Confederate threat along the river in Chicot County.

In 1865, at war's end, Chicot County was not the wealthy garden spot it was before the conflict. Cotton production by 1870 was only a quarter of production in 1860. Thousands of slaves were now free, but many former Confederates (planters and their families) maintained control of the county's plantations. Many freedmen and their descendants, until mechanization, became tied to the land and cotton through the cycles of sharecropping and debt.

The town of Dermott, located in the northwest corner of Chicot County, emerged on the trade route between Gaines Landing on the Mississippi River and the western interior of the state. In 1851, the route claimed the first railroad charter in Arkansas. By 1861, the incomplete Mississippi, Ouachita, and Red River Railroad extended seven miles inland from Eunice on the Mississippi River. Destroyed by Union troops in 1863, it was rebuilt and reached the town by 1872. The post office, initially known as Bartholomew in 1838, was renamed Bend by 1875 and renamed again in 1877 to honor longtime resident Charles McDermott (1808–1884). Another earlier settler, John J. Bowie (1785–1859), the brother of the famous Jim Bowie, also settled nearby, giving townships in Chicot and Desha Counties their names.

By 1887, two railroads crossed through Dermott, bringing industry and people. Incorporated in 1890, the town boasted a population of 500, two steam grist mills and cotton gins, four churches, and a school. By 1912, the prosperous town neared 2,000 residents and businesses on Iowa Street flourished. Dermott's new industries focused on hardwoods. Firms like Bimel-Ashcroff Manufacturing produced spokes, handles, and staves. As a regional center of industry and agriculture, the town remained the largest in the county throughout the 20th century.

Lake Village, in anticipation of becoming the new county seat, was first platted in 1856. Centrally located and situated along Lake Chicot (known as Old River Lake until 1866), a Union soldier described Lake Village in 1864 as a "gem . . . as fair a picture as one could wish" from which "county roads [led] to various landings along the river bank." Despite its beauty, Lake Village was an unfinished place. In the spring of 1857, a traveler described Lake Village as "quite a pleasant place," but discovered the local meeting house had "no glass in the windows."

Before the Civil War, a two-story brick courthouse along with a brick jail were constructed, but Lake Village did not grow quickly. Woodie Streett arrived in 1896 and noted, "not a nail had been driven or a house painted" since the town was completed. When Lake Village incorporated in 1898, the population had reached only 250. Growth finally came with the arrival of the railroad in 1903. Four years later, the city could finally boast three saw mills, two stave manufacturers, and a cotton gin. By 1912, manufacturing remained stable, while the number of businesses grew with demand from the farm trade. The town proclaimed itself "Home of the Big Black Bass" and sportsmen and tourists arrived to fish and swim in Lake Chicot. Tourists could stay at the new Lake Shore Hotel and eat at one of five restaurants. Tourism and the beauty of Lake Chicot helped sustain Lake Village into the 20th century.

Eudora, incorporated in 1904, is located in the Bayou Macon Hills in southern Chicot County. A post office named Eudora operated from 1856 to 1867 near the Eudora Plantation, founded by E.C. James in 1851. A second post office took the name Carmel in 1888, and the town was platted under that name in 1903. However, when the Memphis, Helena, & Louisiana Railroad established a station around 1903, it opted to call the stop Eudora. Reflecting the power of the railroad, the town soon changed its name.

Once the railroad opened at Eudora, the town became a successful trading point for southern Chicot County and northeastern Louisiana. Merchants with operations on the Mississippi River, first at Grand Lake, and later Carriola and Barnard, moved their businesses into Eudora. In 1906, with a population of 450, Eudora was a collection of a dozen general and grocery stores, three livery stables, and one bank, hotel, restaurant, hardware, and drug store. Industry was virtually nonexistent, with a single barrel maker in town, J.T. Jackson. Six years later, the town had grown slightly, to around 650. Businesses had expanded modestly and now included two banks, five physicians, a dentist, a cotton gin, a tailor, and a blacksmith. Industry had also arrived, with a stave manufacturer, Akin, Shannon and Ward, and the Imperial Wheel Company. Today, Eudora is home to Superior Uniforms' distribution center, the single largest employer in Chicot County.

One

Chicot County, the Early Years

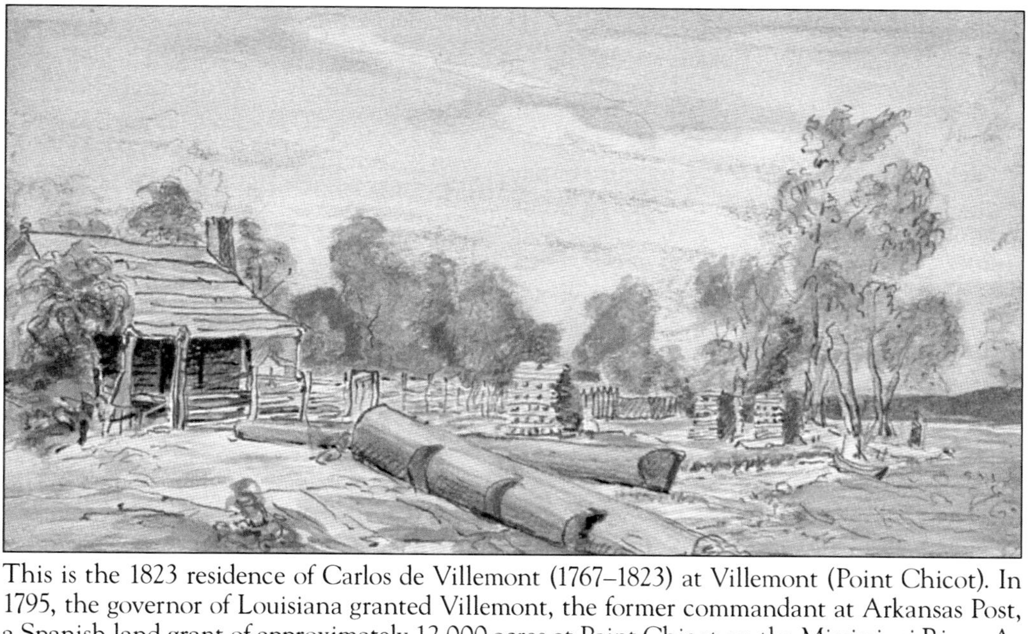

This is the 1823 residence of Carlos de Villemont (1767–1823) at Villemont (Point Chicot). In 1795, the governor of Louisiana granted Villemont, the former commandant at Arkansas Post, a Spanish land grant of approximately 12,000 acres at Point Chicot on the Mississippi River. As early as 1816, the Isle of Chicot and Point Chicot provided cordwood (stacks of which can be seen here) to passing steamboats. Villemont served as the county's first seat until 1833, when it was moved north to Columbia. Flooding in 1840 destroyed the town; however, Villemont's wife and family still resided in Chicot County in 1850. This watercolor painting, completed in the 1940s by Arkansas artist Adrian Brewer, is based on an 1823 sketch of Villemont by Charles Alexandre Lesueur, a French artist who lived and traveled in the United States from 1815 to 1837. (Courtesy of the Butler Center for Arkansas Studies, Central Arkansas Library System.)

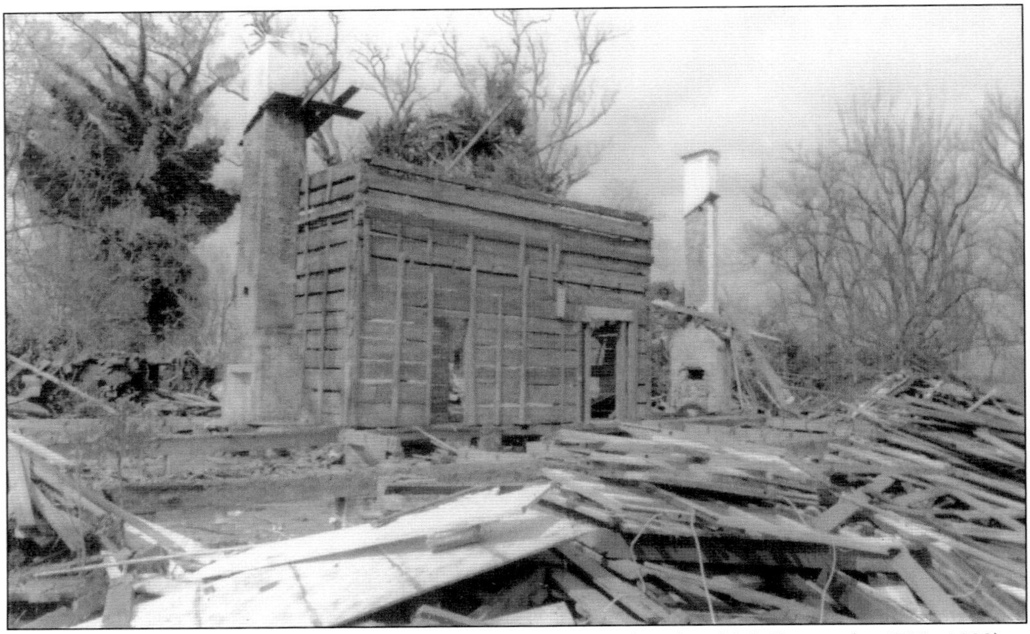

This log house, built around 1830, was likely the home of Richard M. Rotan (c. 1780–1833), a planter who moved to the east side of Lake Chicot from Mississippi around 1827. After his death in 1833, his wife, Susannah, daughter, and two sons maintained the plantation, later called Myrtle Grove. In 1840, the plantation included 157 acres and 10 slaves. (Courtesy of the Arkansas Historic Preservation Program.)

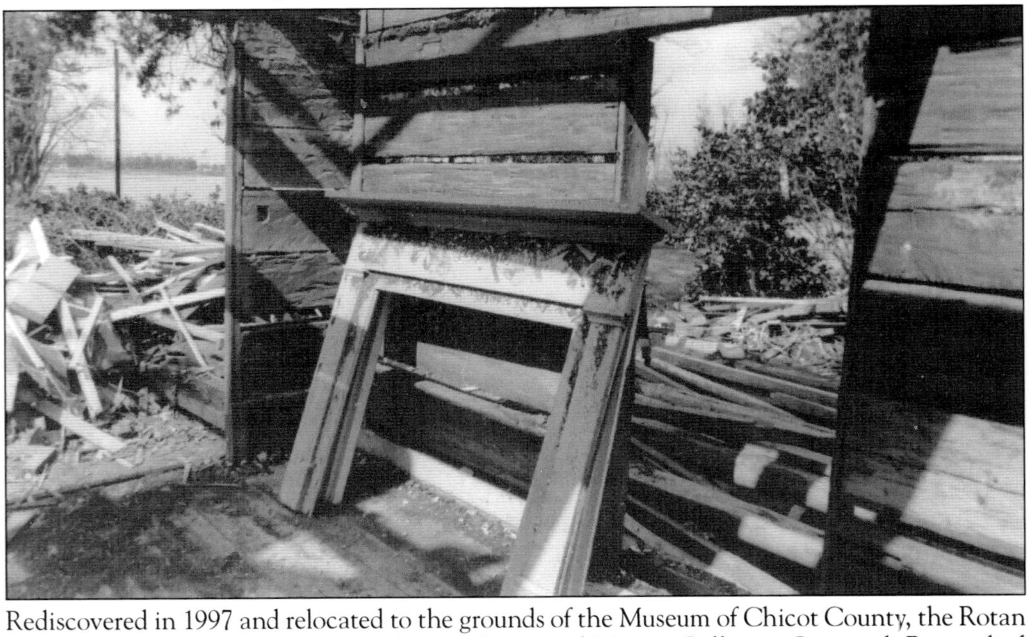

Rediscovered in 1997 and relocated to the grounds of the Museum of Chicot County, the Rotan house was hidden inside the former home of Don and Marion Calloway. Susannah Rotan died in 1858; headstones for her and other Rotan family members were documented by the Daughters of the American Revolution at Myrtle Grove in the 1960s. Since then, some Rotan headstones, but not Susannah's, were moved to the Lake Village City Cemetery. The fate of her headstone is unknown. (Courtesy of the Arkansas Historic Preservation Program.)

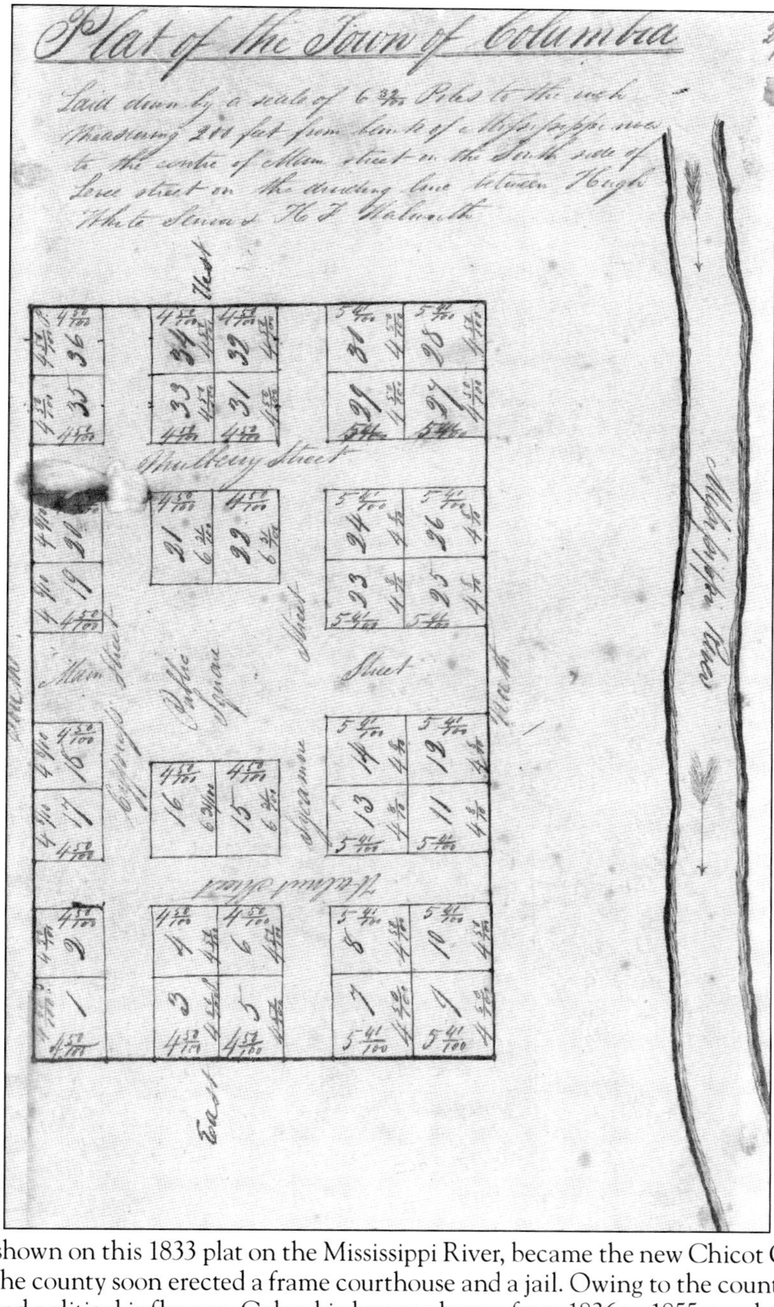

Columbia, shown on this 1833 plat on the Mississippi River, became the new Chicot County seat that year. The county soon erected a frame courthouse and a jail. Owing to the county's growing prosperity and political influence, Columbia became home, from 1836 to 1855, to a branch of the Real Estate Bank of Arkansas. While river towns like Columbia and Desha County's Napoleon gained reputations for gambling, drinking, and violence, the *James' River Guide* wrote that Columbia in 1856 was "a very pleasant place, containing a number of stores, a court-house, and a population of about 400. Here commences the great cotton growing region, and the banks of the river are almost one succession of plantations." As the river threatened the town, the county seat was moved inland, first to Masona in 1855 and then to Lake Village in 1857. A traveler at Columbia in 1857 noted, "There is no town here; only a decay and little perishing wreck of a town." It is believed the river overtook the town in the 1870s. (Courtesy of the Chicot County Courthouse.)

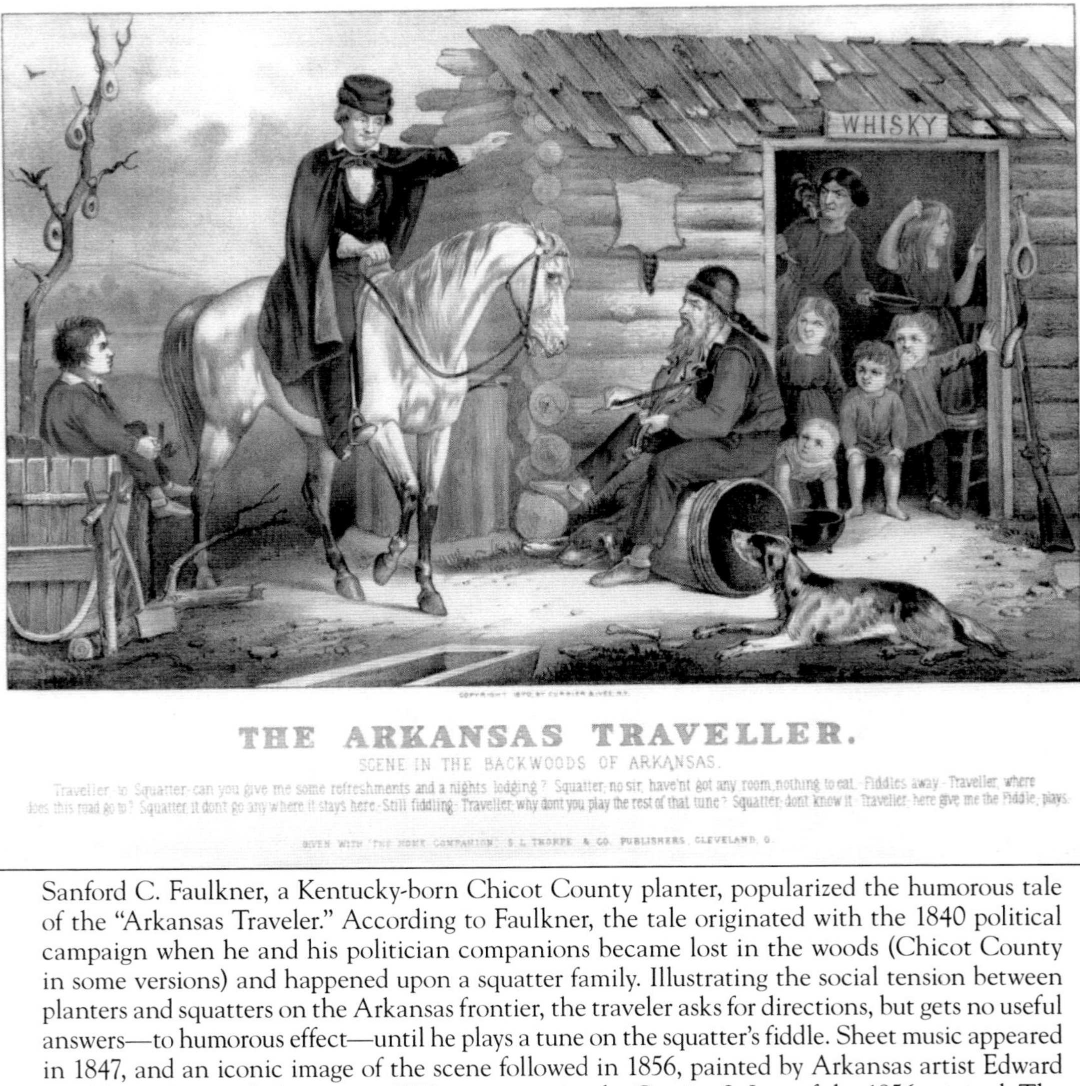

Sanford C. Faulkner, a Kentucky-born Chicot County planter, popularized the humorous tale of the "Arkansas Traveler." According to Faulkner, the tale originated with the 1840 political campaign when he and his politician companions became lost in the woods (Chicot County in some versions) and happened upon a squatter family. Illustrating the social tension between planters and squatters on the Arkansas frontier, the traveler asks for directions, but gets no useful answers—to humorous effect—until he plays a tune on the squatter's fiddle. Sheet music appeared in 1847, and an iconic image of the scene followed in 1856, painted by Arkansas artist Edward Washburn. Pictured above is an 1870 interpretation by Currier & Ives of the 1856 original. The tune, story, and image continued their popularity into the 20th century, often defining outsiders' views of the state. (Courtesy of the Permanent Collection of the Historic Arkansas Museum.)

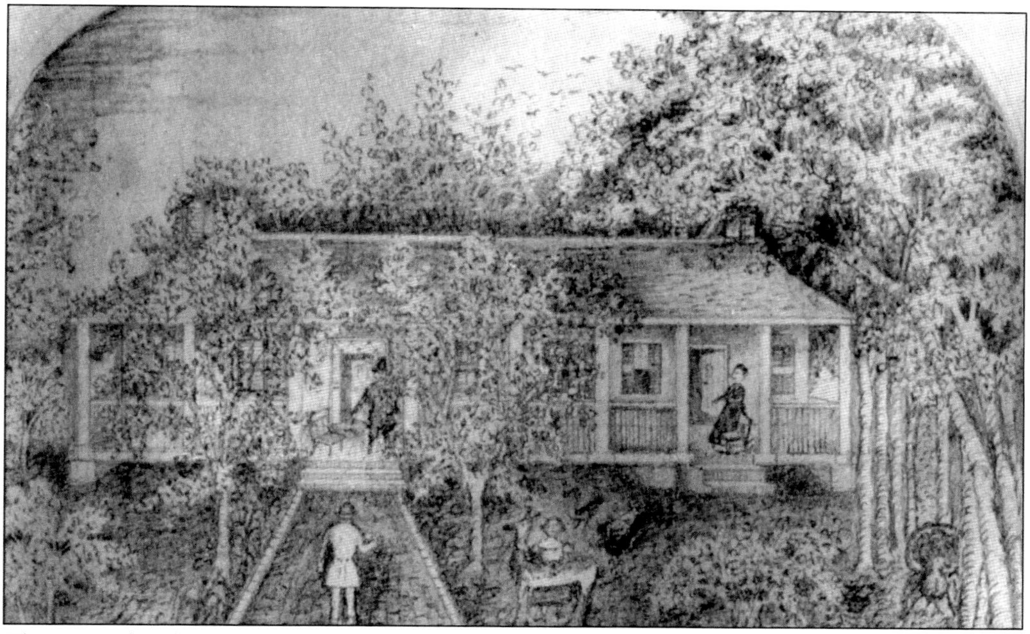

This 1853 sketch of the Lake Hall plantation house (built around 1850) shows a pet deer and turkeys roaming the ornamental front lawn. Standing in the walkway is, perhaps, Frances W. Davies, the artist and 10-year-old daughter of Anthony Harpin Davies (1798–1862) and Mildred Pollard Gaines Davies (1815–1900). The house stood until the early 1980s, when it was consumed by fire. (Courtesy of the Permanent Collection of the Historic Arkansas Museum.)

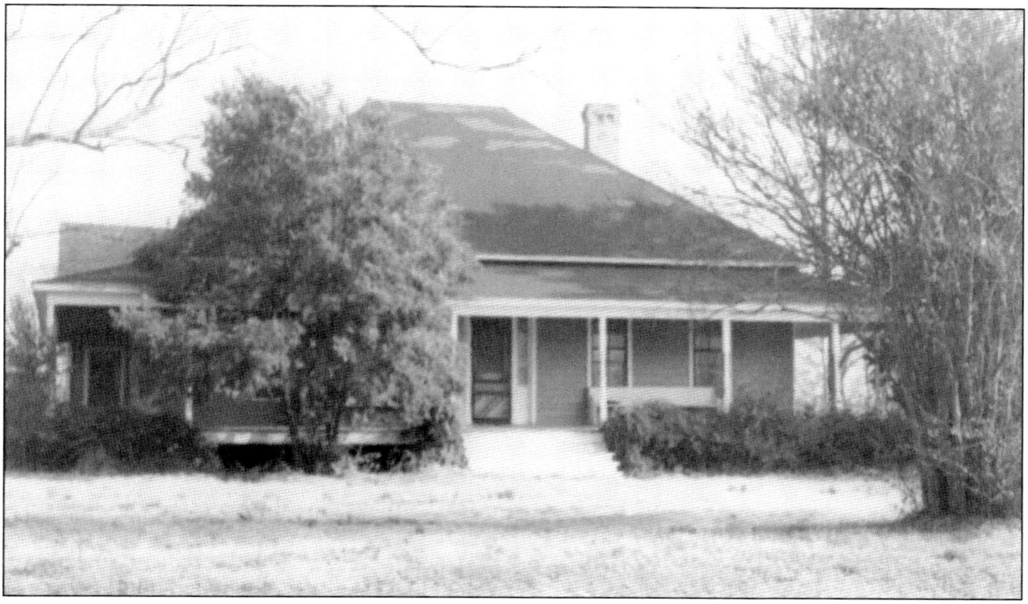

The Lake Hall Plantation, pictured in 1979, had a modified roof and other changes. Last occupied in the late 1970s, it was remembered to have a large entryway with a parlor to the right and two bedrooms to the left. At the back was a large dining room, butler's pantry, and an attached kitchen. In the late 1970s, the house still had some original furniture: large dining room table, chifforobes, chairs, a bed, and a piano. Two outbuildings, a commissary and a log structure, also remained intact in 1979. (Courtesy of the Arkansas Historic Preservation Program.)

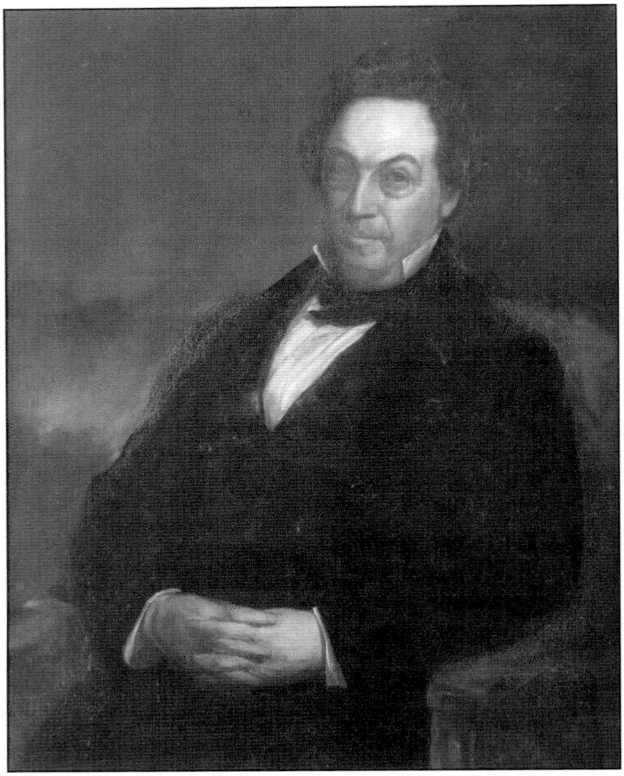

Anthony Harpin Davies and his wife, Mildred Pollard Davies, married in Natchez in 1841 and sat for St. Louis portrait artist William C. Cogswell around 1858. Davies, a native of Connecticut, worked as a bookkeeper in Nashville, Tennessee, before he arrived in Chicot County around 1832. He had a business at Columbia and a plantation on the east side of Lake Chicot he named Lake Hall. Mildred Davis, sister of Chicot County planter Richard Gaines, was a native of Kentucky. Anthony Davies died during the Civil War in 1862, and Mildred Davies fled to Texas but returned to Chicot County following the end of the conflict. (Both, courtesy of the Permanent Collection of the Historic Arkansas Museum.)

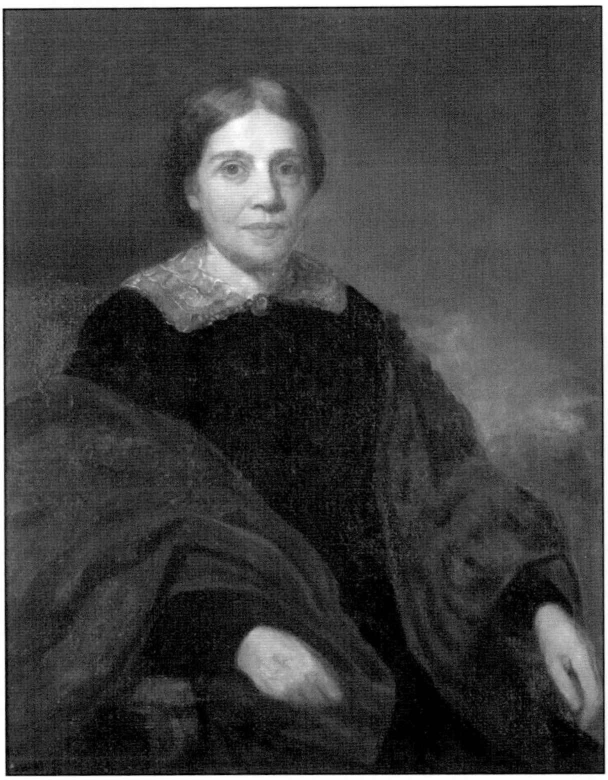

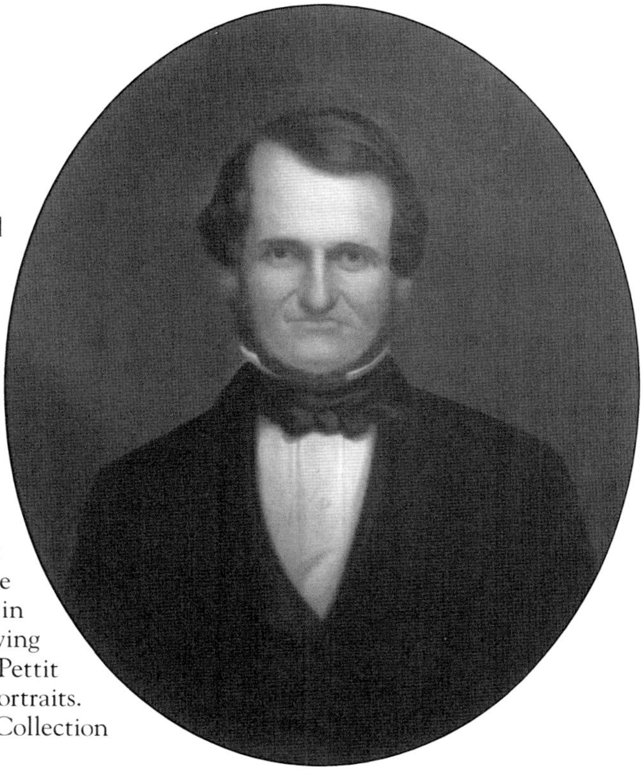

William McDowell Pettit settled in Chicot County in 1830 along the west bank of Lake Chicot, near where Lake Village is today. By 1850, his estate was valued at $300,000 and included 109 slaves. Pettit married his third wife, Eliza Bulloch Pettit, in Shelby County, Kentucky, in 1842. Reportedly, Pettit met portrait artist William C. Cogswell in the East and encouraged him to come to Chicot County. Cogswell is believed to have painted at least 10 portraits while in the county during the 1850s. Following the death of Pettit in 1853, Eliza Pettit returned to Kentucky with these portraits. (Both, courtesy of the Permanent Collection of the Historic Arkansas Museum.)

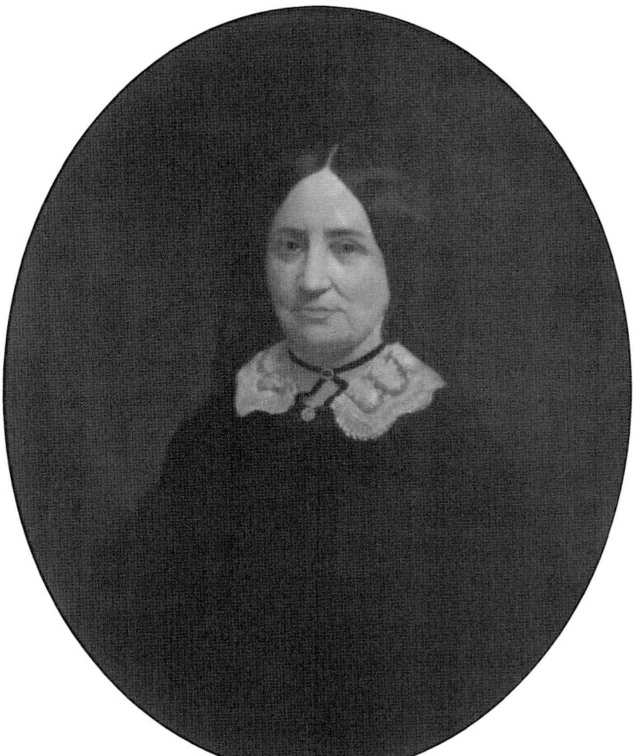

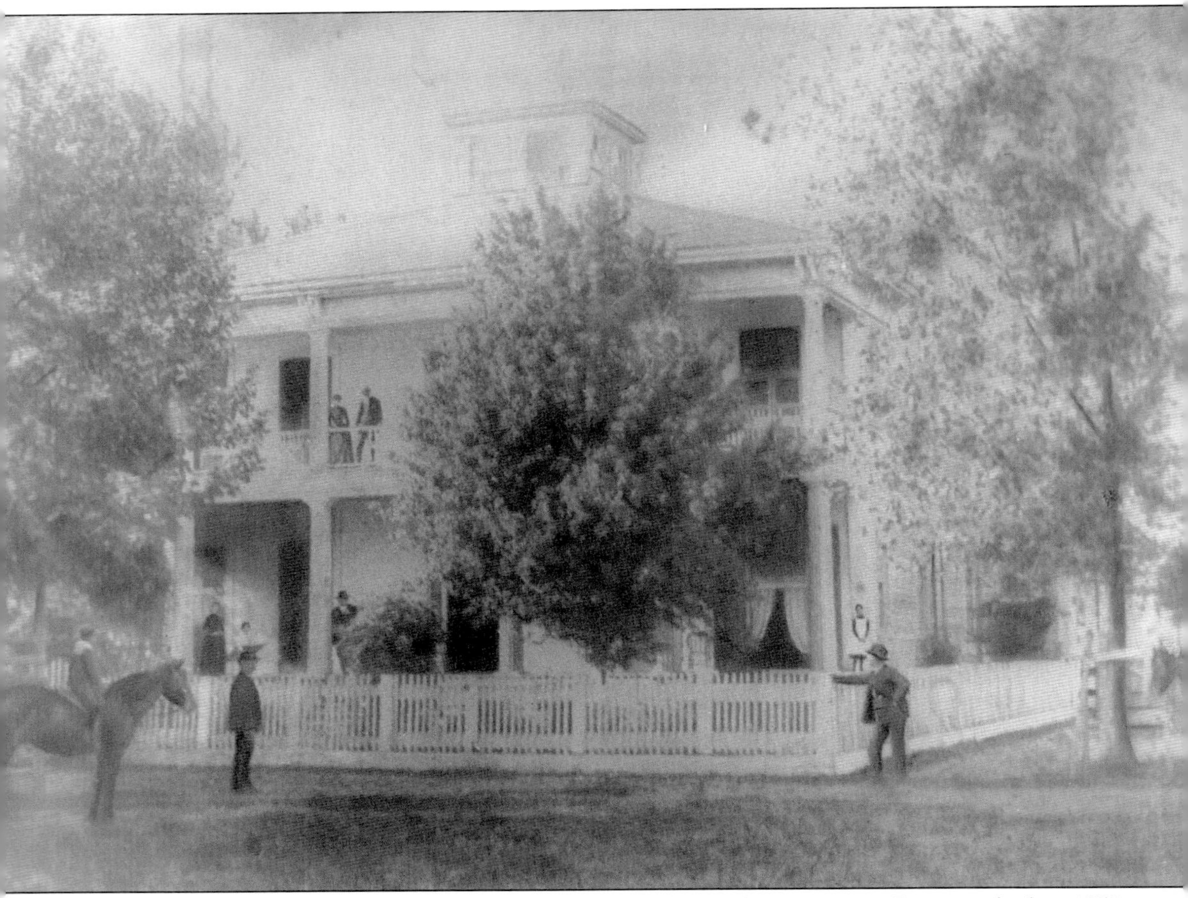

James McMurray's Patria Plantation house was built facing the Mississippi River in the late 1850s near Luna Landing in the Greenville Bends. During the Civil War, according to McMurray family tradition, Union gunboats shelled the house, damaging the roof. Confederates used the Greenville Bends to attack Union boats in 1863, and planters like the McMurrays were suspected as accomplices. The home survived the war, only to be torn down later under threat from the Mississippi River. (Courtesy of Madeline Warick.)

Peakland, later known as the Warfield House (1896–1943), was a plantation house on Grand Lake built around 1850 in the Italianate style for James Peak. Peak came to Chicot County from Kentucky around 1829. In 1860, the plantation boasted 2,700 acres and 90 slaves. During the Civil War, most of Peak's neighbors fled, while he remained at Grand Lake; however, a resident reported he "was reduced to the necessity of cooking and washing for himself." The third floor, it is claimed, had a secret room where Confederates were hidden. The 27-room structure was lost to fire on August 12, 1958. The 1840 date listed on this postcard seems unlikely, given that Italianate architecture was not popular until the late 1840s, and few, if any, large homes like this were built in Chicot County until the 1850s. (Courtesy of JoAnne Coleman.)

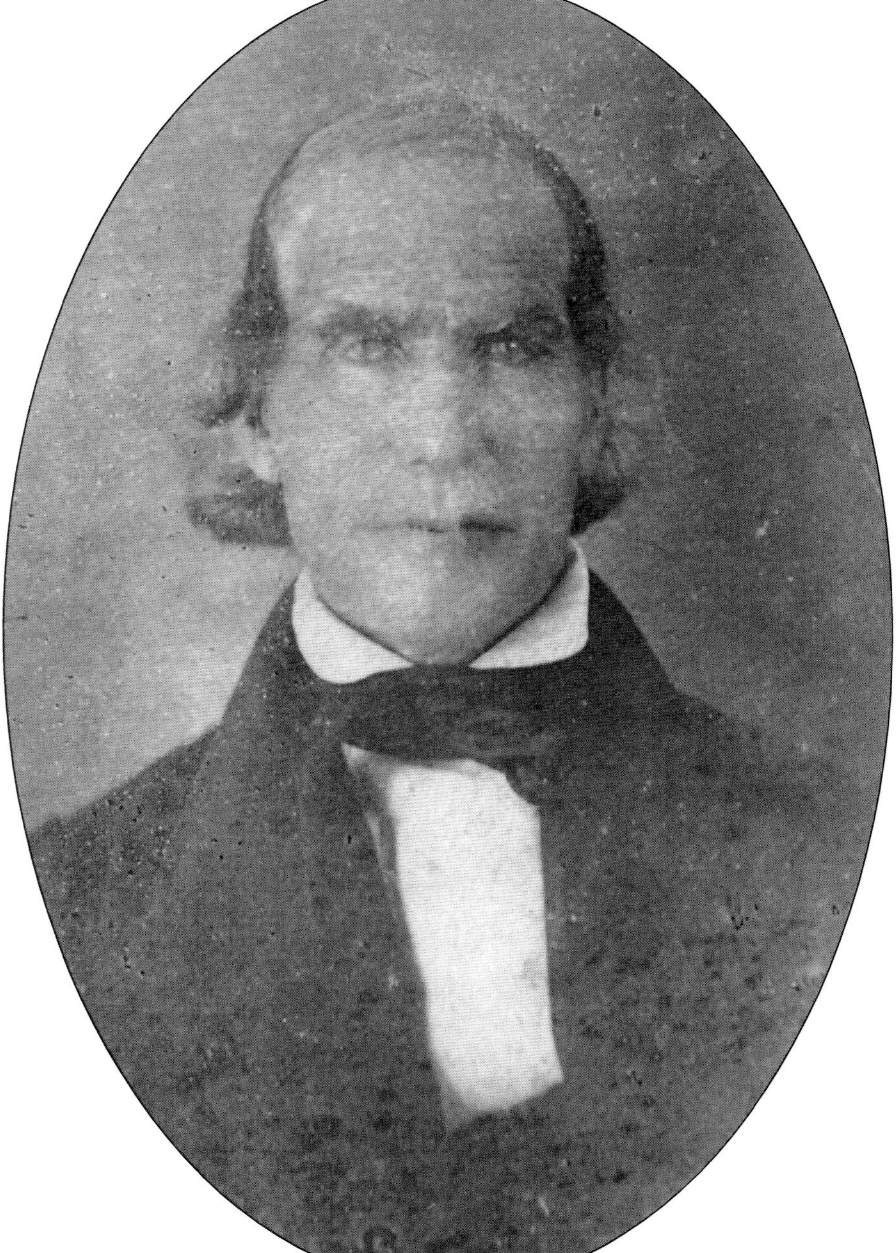

Elisha Worthington (1818–1872) was Chicot County's largest planter and Arkansas's largest slaveholder. His three brothers settled across the river in Washington County, Mississippi. Worthington owned substantial land holdings: Sunnyside, Eminice, Red Leaf, and So-So Plantations. On his prized Sunnyside Plantation, Worthington maintained a magnificent home with a 5,000-volume library, greenhouse for his prized camellia japonicas, and brass and string band composed of his slaves. During the Civil War, Worthington fled with most of his slaves to Tarrant County, Texas, and left his two Oberlin-educated mulatto children, James and Martha Mason, in charge at Sunnyside. (Courtesy of Annie Paden.)

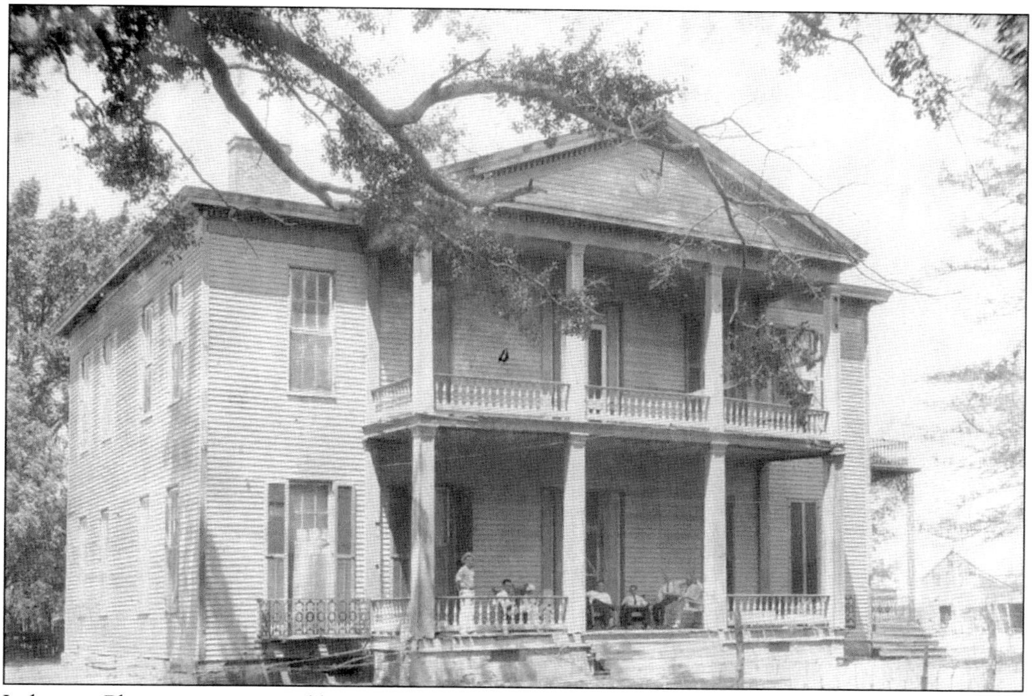

Lakeport Plantation, pictured here in 1925, was built around 1859 for Lycurgus and Lydia Johnson. In 1860, the plantation raised 1,300 bales of cotton and 10,000 bushels of corn with the labor of 155 slaves. The house survives today and has been restored by Arkansas State University. (Courtesy of Doris Johnson.)

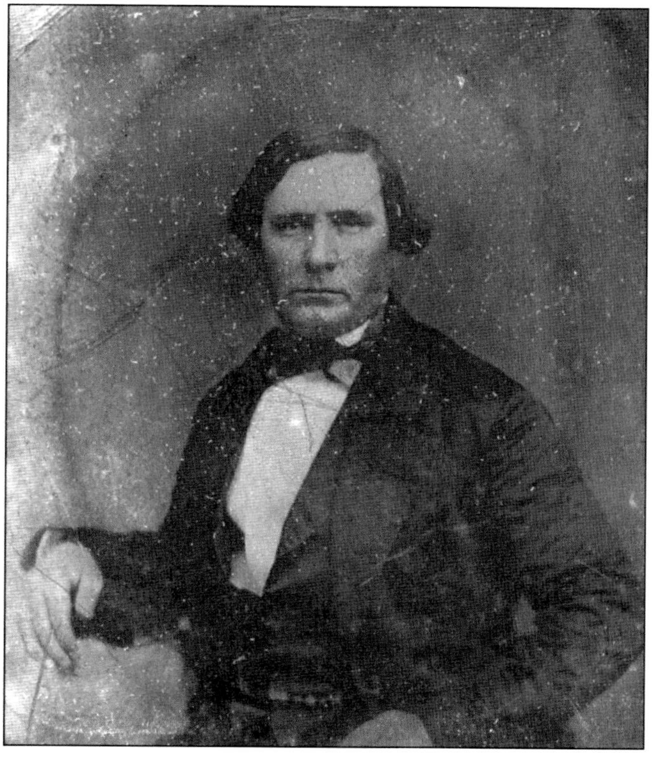

Lycurgus L. Johnson, pictured here around 1850, was born in Georgetown, Scott County, Kentucky, in 1818. His father, Joel, left Georgetown in 1831 and arrived at Lakeport in Chicot County with 23 slaves. Lycurgus arrived by 1837 and married Lydia Taylor in 1842 in Chicot County. Their marriage was officiated by Lycurgus's uncle Judge Benjamin Johnson. Lycurgus and Lydia first lived at the Florence Plantation; when his father's estate was settled in 1858, they began construction on their grand house at Lakeport. (Courtesy of Annie Paden.)

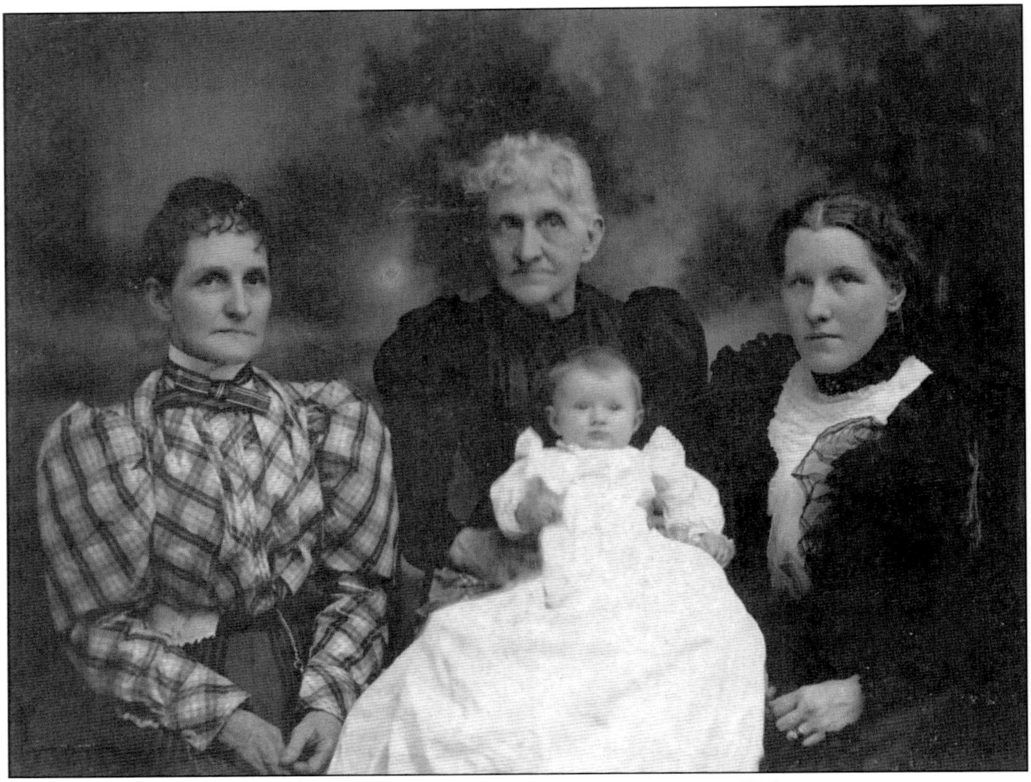

Four generations of Johnson women pose for this photograph in 1897. From left to right are May (Johnson) Worthington, Lydia (Taylor) Johnson, baby May Worthington Spencer, and Annie Taylor (Worthington) Spencer. (Courtesy of Annie Paden.)

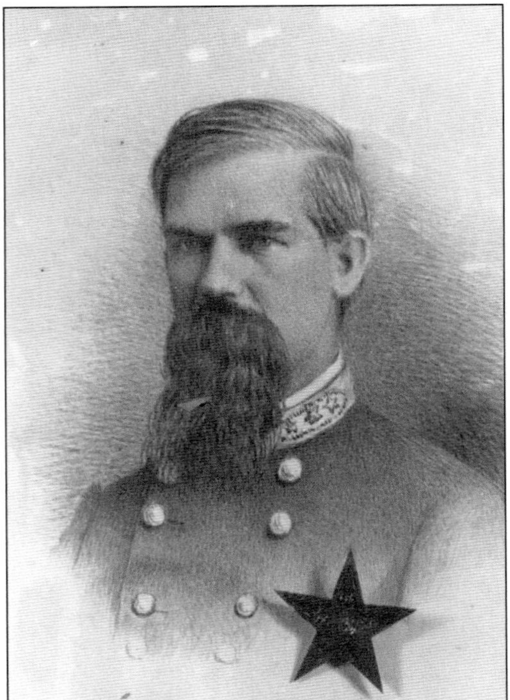

Daniel Harris Reynolds arrived in Chicot County from Ohio in 1858 and practiced law in the new county seat, Lake Village. When the Civil War began in 1861, he raised a company of men, the Chicot Rangers, to support the Confederacy. During the war, he rose to the rank of general and fought in both the Trans-Mississippi West and in the East. Chicot County contributed two other companies to the Confederacy: the Chicot Guards and Chicot Rebels. (Courtesy of Richard and Connie Cox.)

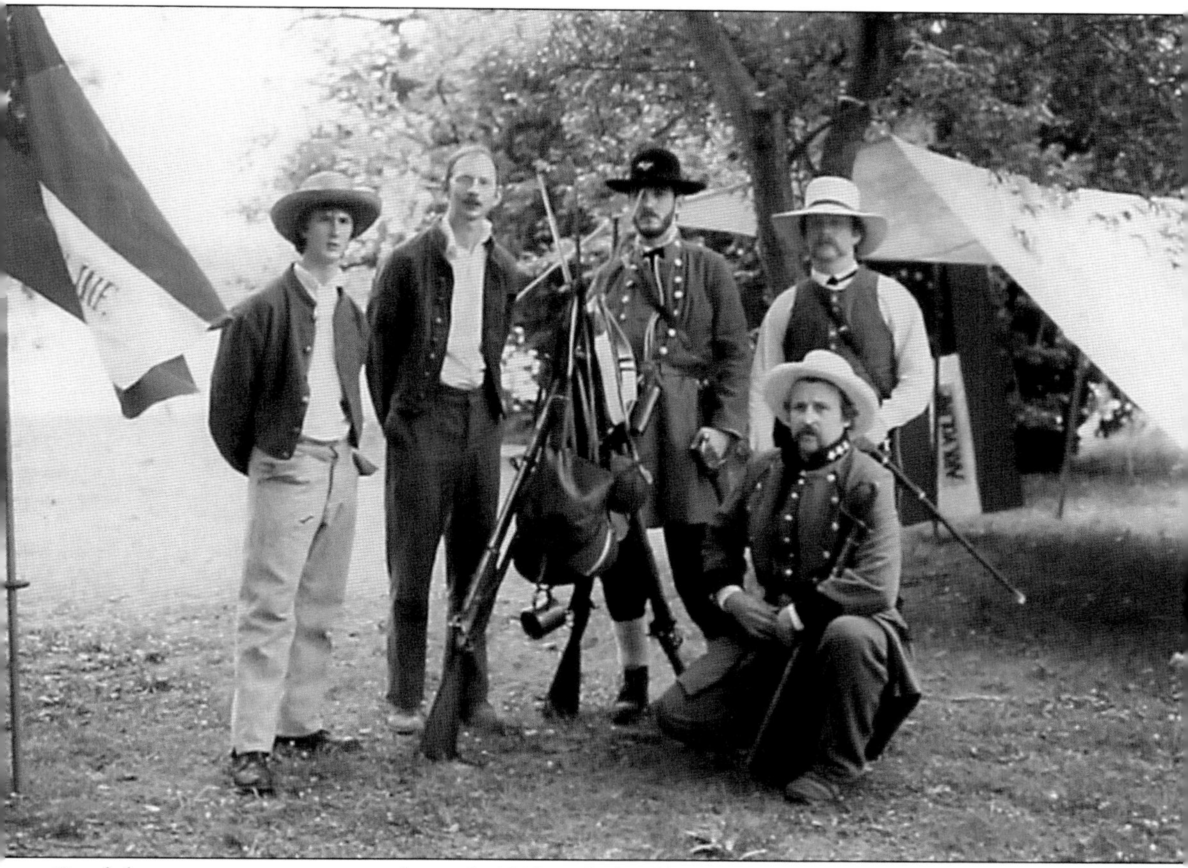

Confederate reenactors pose in the early 1980s at Lake Chicot State Park during the Civil War Days event commemorating the Battle at Ditch Bayou, which took place on June 6, 1864, in Chicot County. The engagement was the largest in Southeast Arkansas and the last major battle of the Civil War in Arkansas. Union action was forced in the spring of 1864; Confederates disrupted "illegal" cotton trading and Union river traffic in the Greenville Bends. A Union force landed at Sunnyside and planned to sweep around Lake Chicot and either engage the enemy or force them away from the Mississippi River. After skirmishes at Red Leaf, the smaller Confederate force made a stand behind Ditch Bayou. Surprised by the obstacle, Union troops were forced to engage at the edge of the bayou. Confederates finally retreated when supplies ran low. However, it was a strategic victory; Union forces lost at least 50 men to the Confederates' four. (Courtesy of Don R. Simons.)

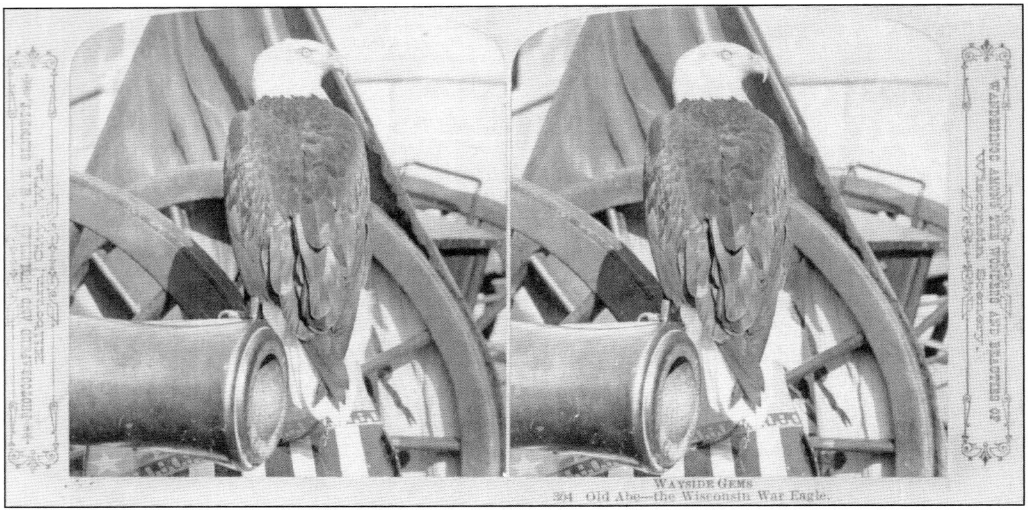

The 8th Wisconsin Volunteer Infantry were among the Midwesterners who fought at the Battle at Ditch Bayou. An American bald eagle named Old Abe in honor of Pres. Abraham Lincoln served as the unit's mascot and was present at all of the 8th's battles. Old Abe lived out the remainder of his life in the Wisconsin capitol building. (Courtesy of the Old State House Museum.)

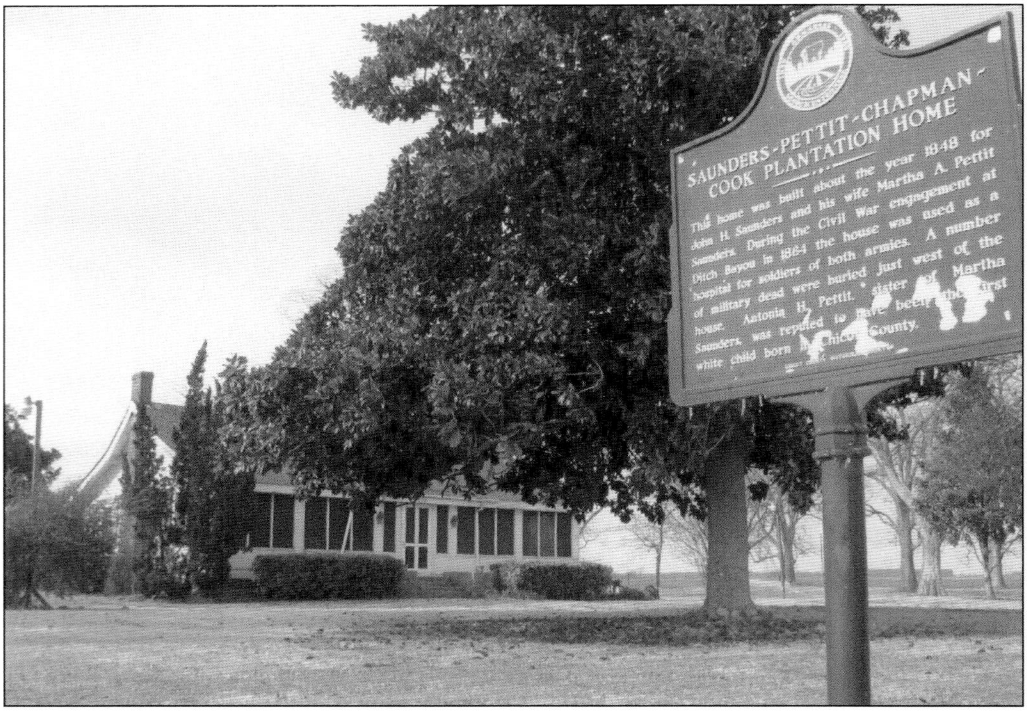

Following the Union victory at Ditch Bayou, Union troops reportedly occupied the Saunders-Pettit (Cook) House and used it as a hospital. As they made their sweep around Lake Chicot, Union troops occupied Lake Village for the evening. Union officers headquartered in the Hunnicutt Hotel, while soldiers looted the town, destroyed livestock, and threw the equipment of the *Chicot Press* into Lake Chicot. Reportedly, only one building was burned—a community building that served as a school during the week and a church on Sundays. (Courtesy of Lakeport Plantation.)

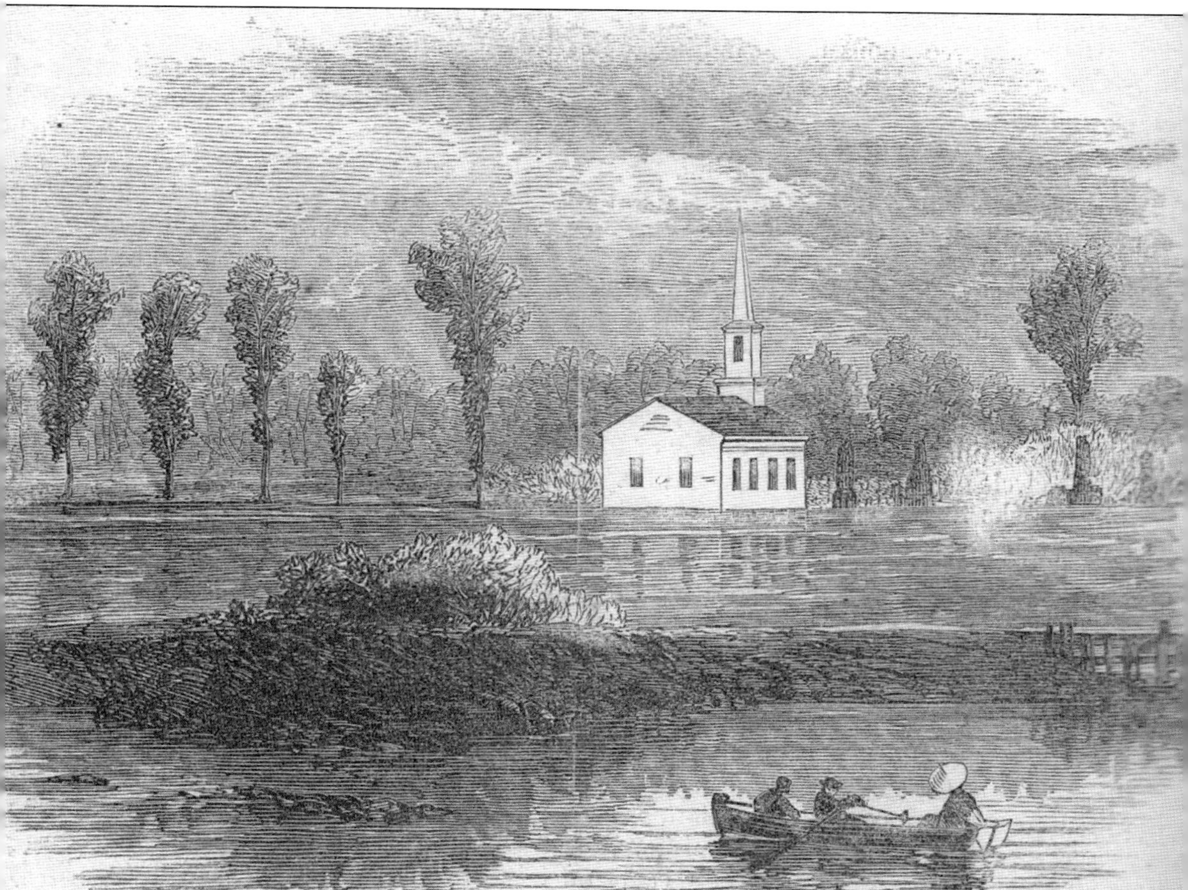

This illustration, titled "Grand Lake on the Mississippi," appeared in *Harper's Weekly* on June 2, 1866. It shows post-war destruction and flooding in Chicot County and may show the Mount Carmel Presbyterian Church. *Harper's* described the scene: "On a Sabbath morning our boat reached at the land-place of Grand Lake, on the Mississippi. Here was the only church we had seen thus far. It was located away from any considerable town, and how the inhabitants reach it at this stage of the water without boats is a problem. Near the church were many burnt chimney, the remains of buildings destroyed in the war. Ruins of this sort were quite frequent all along the river." Mount Carmel Presbyterian Church was organized around 1845 as the Grand Lake Presbyterian Church and changed its name to Mount Carmel around 1850. In 1861, when the church joined the Presbyterian Church in the Confederate States of America, it had 67 members, but only 28 the next year. The church was dissolved by the end of the Civil War. (Courtesy of Lakeport Plantation.)

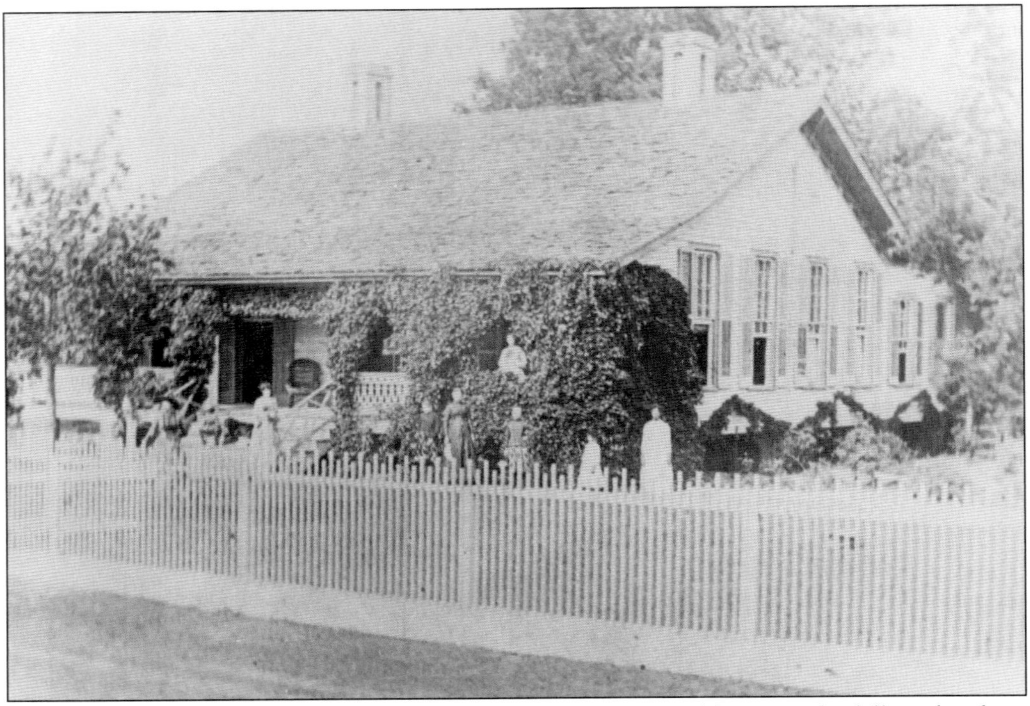

Returning to Lake Village after the Civil War, Gen. D.H. Reynolds received a full pardon from Pres. Andrew Johnson in 1866 and was soon elected to the Arkansas Senate. In 1872, he built his residence, "Lakeside," with his law office next door. Built by another Ohio native, Nelson Bunker, the house still has a view of Lake Chicot and was remodeled in the 1890s. General Reynolds died in 1902, but his descendants occupied the house until the 1940s. (Above, courtesy of Richard and Connie Cox; below, courtesy of the Arkansas Historic Preservation Program.)

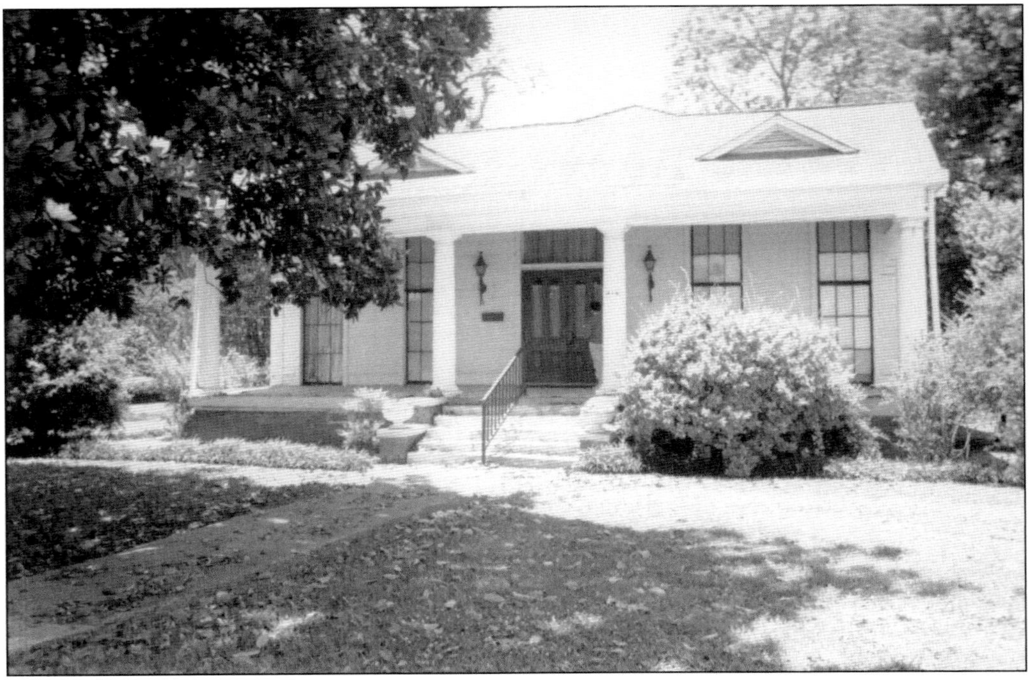

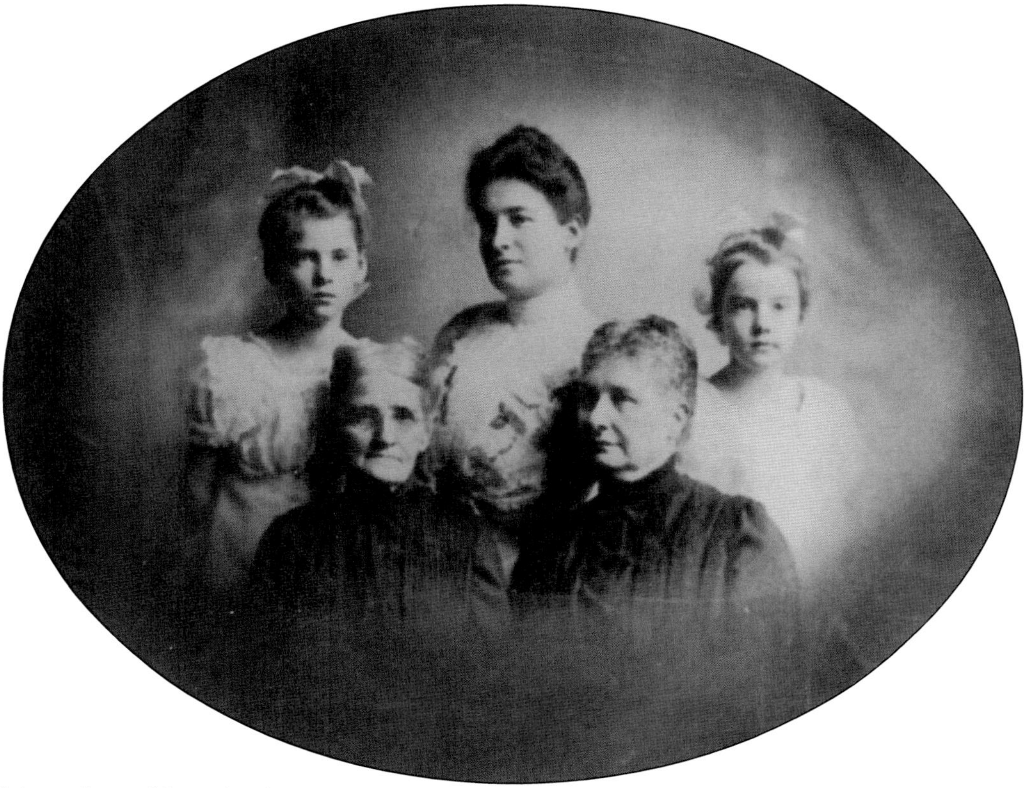

Mattie Reynolds, wife of D.H. Reynolds, is pictured here around 1915 in the first row at right next to her mother, Eleanor Avent. Behind them are, from left to right, granddaughter Isabel, daughter Ruth (Reynolds) Bull, and granddaughter Eleanor Bull. In 1910, Mattie Reynolds lived with her mother, two daughters, and two granddaughters at the Lakeside house. They also took in several boarders, including Morris E. Rosenzweig, a longtime Lake Village merchant. (Courtesy of Richard and Connie Cox.)

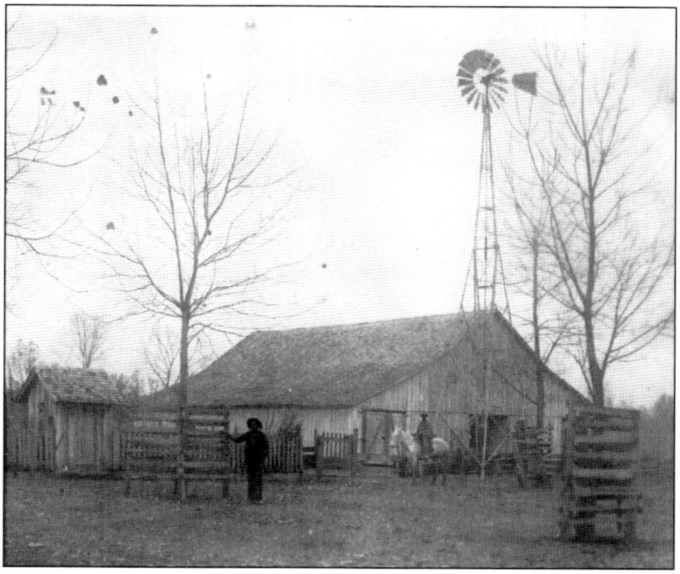

The Hilliard Plantation headquarters barn, pictured here around 1890, was part of a complex of farm buildings that included a cotton gin, cotton house, and commissary. The plantation was passed to Isaac Hilliard III and his brother Edwin after their father's death in 1868. Isaac died in 1882, and Edwin, who had an acrimonious relationship with his sister-in-law, managed the plantation. The Hilliard papers are held by the Louisiana State University Libraries. (Courtesy of Carol T. Meyer.)

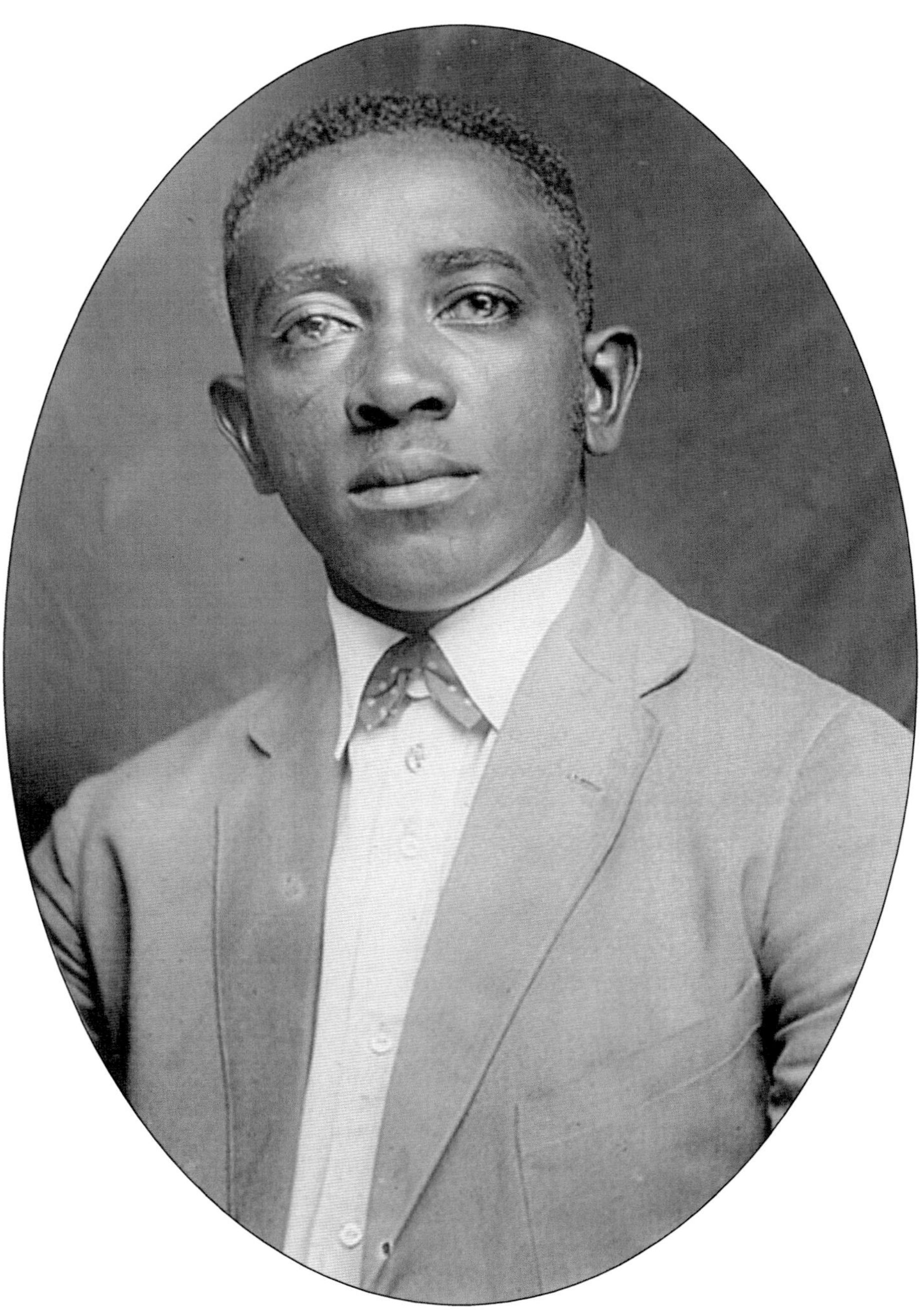

In 1868, James A. Herod, then a nine-year-old Memphis orphan, found himself "on a great cotton plantation with its large quarters and hundreds of hands" near Lakeport. After three and a half years of "brutal treatment" under an overseer, he partnered to make a crop and planned to return to Memphis. He fell into a deep despair after his leg was crushed by a farm wagon and had to be amputated. A teacher from the American Missionary Association encouraged him to apply to Straight University in New Orleans in 1885. He attended the university for nine years, traveling back to Chicot County to earn money. Herod eventually settled in Abbeville, Louisiana, where he had a long and respected career as an educator and minister. (Courtesy of the American Missionary Association Archives, Amistad Research Center at Tulane University.)

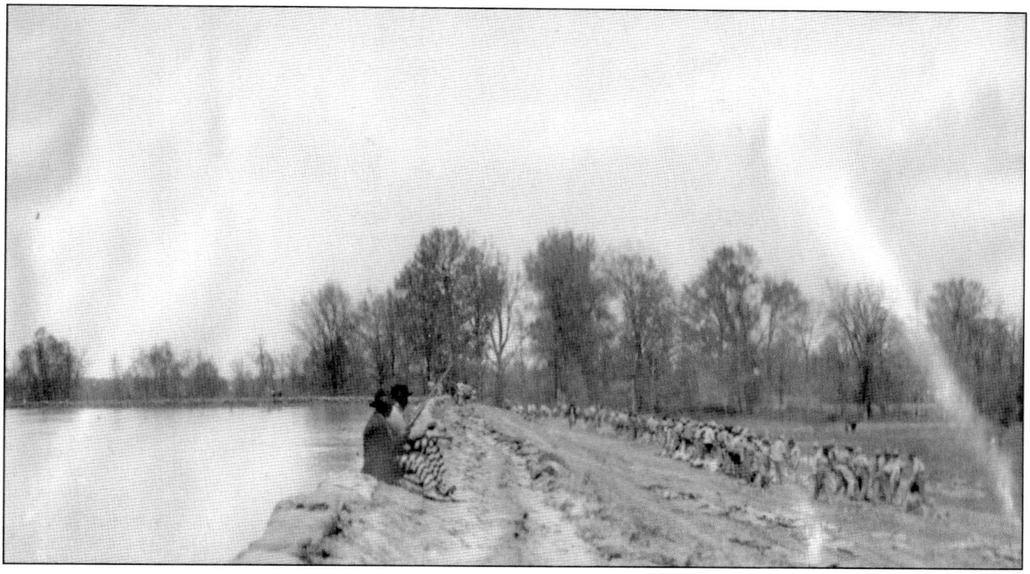

The flood of 1912 is often forgotten. On April 11, the levee at Panther Forest, about five miles north of Luna Landing, began to weaken. With just eight inches of earth above the flooding Mississippi, the 32-foot levee began to slough. The dangerous work of repairing the levee was abandoned the next day and Chicot County Levee Board president I.M. Worthington asked the US government to scuttle barges at the point. The request fell on deaf ears and the levee broke later that day, flooding Chicot County. While the *Verne Swain* took refugees from Lake Village, others were stranded in a cotton gin at Bellaire and along the levee. (Both, courtesy of the Special Collections of the William Alexander Percy Memorial Library.)

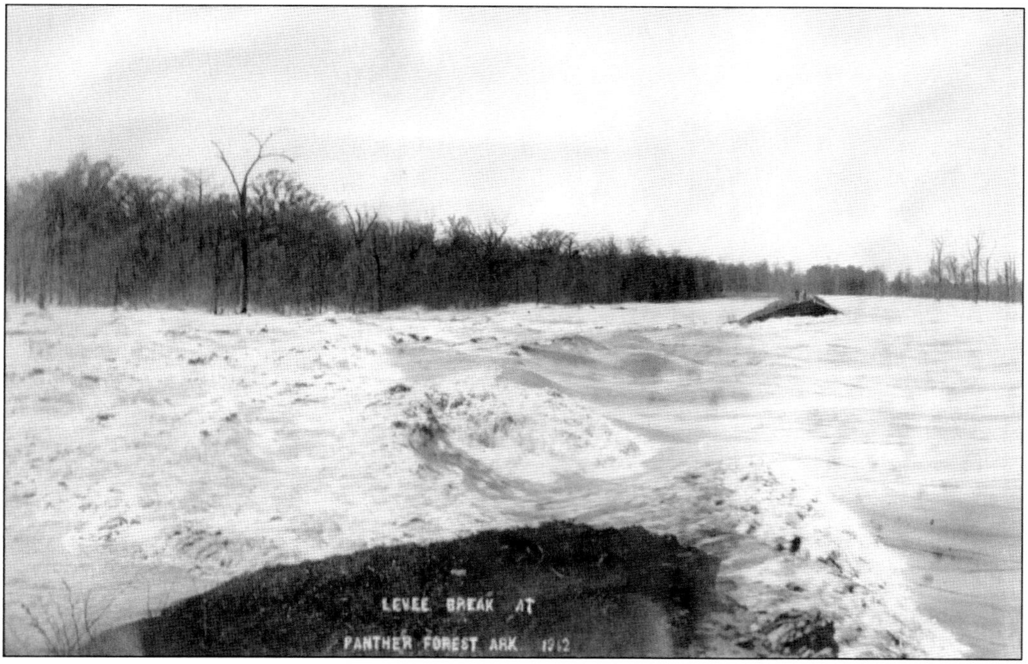

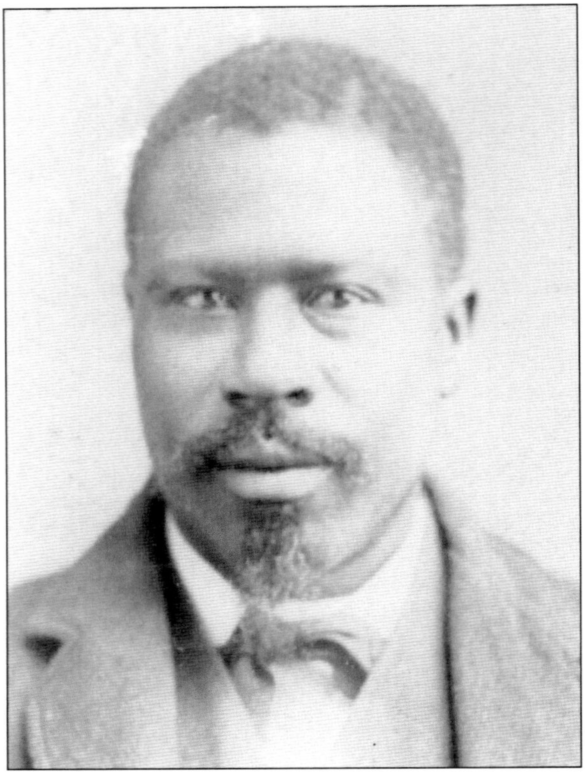

From 1868 until 1893, a dozen African American men represented Chicot County in the Arkansas General Assembly. With the exception of James W. Mason, the mulatto son of planter Elisha Worthington, none were native to Chicot County. Representatives Green Hill Jones (left) and Nathan E. Edwards (below) were likely born into slavery in Tennessee and Georgia, in 1845 and 1855, respectively. Both likely arrived in the county in the 1870s. Jones, a minister, sharecropper, and farm laborer, served two terms in the Arkansas House (1885 and 1889), and also served as Chicot County treasurer from 1874 to 1876. He died in 1924 and is buried in Mason Cemetery. Edwards, a farmer and pastor at First Baptist Church near Eudora, served in the House in 1893, when only two African Americans remained in the General Assembly. He died in 1908. (Both, courtesy of the Arkansas History Commission.)

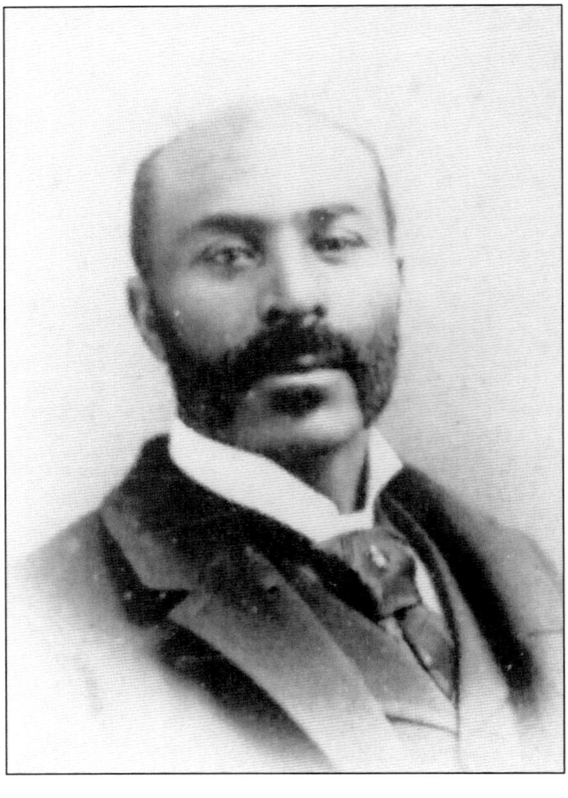

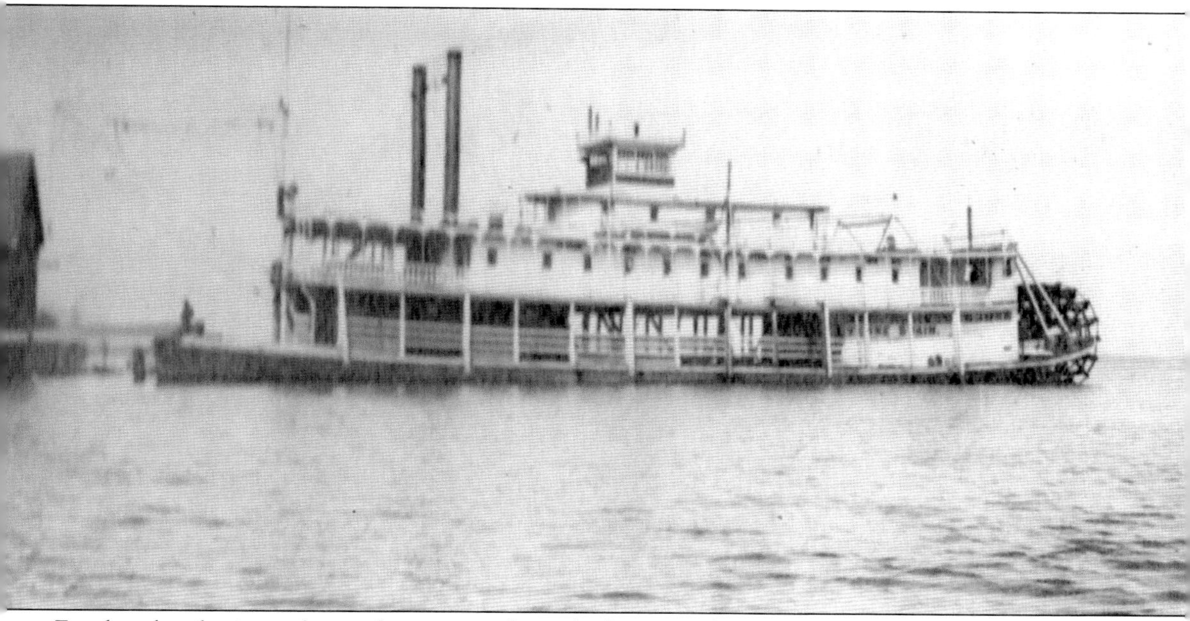

For decades, ferries and steamboats were the only direct method of travel between Greenville, Mississippi, and Chicot County. Pictured here around 1908 is the *Verne Swain*. Owned by the Lyon Packet Company, the vessel transported passengers, cotton, and plantation supplies during its daily trips from Greenville to Luna Landing and Sunnyside. (Courtesy of the Special Collections of the William Alexander Percy Memorial Library.)

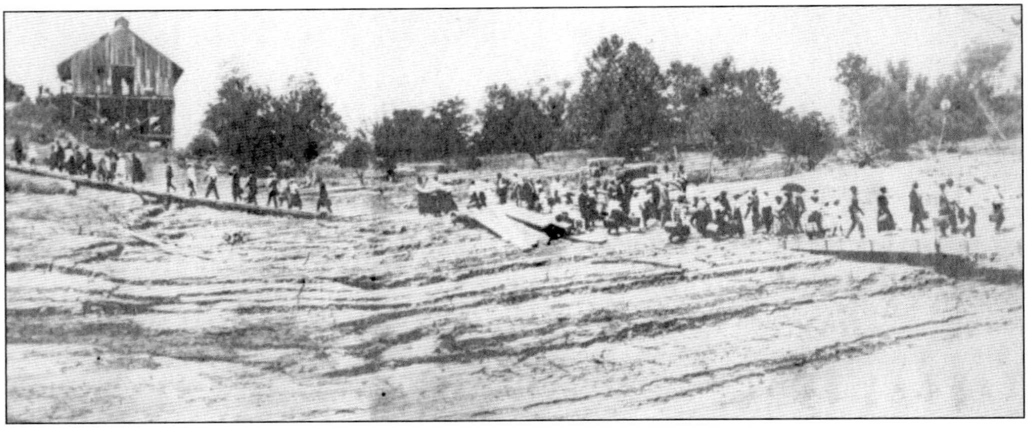

The Mississippi River, Hamburg, and Western Railway finished construction on a railroad and depot at Luna Landing in 1901. The rail connection linked the interior of the state and the Mississippi River with the county's agricultural and natural resources. The scene above shows passengers being exchanged between steamboats and the railroad. Below, a train is waiting at the depot. (Both, courtesy of the Special Collections of the William Alexander Percy Memorial Library.)

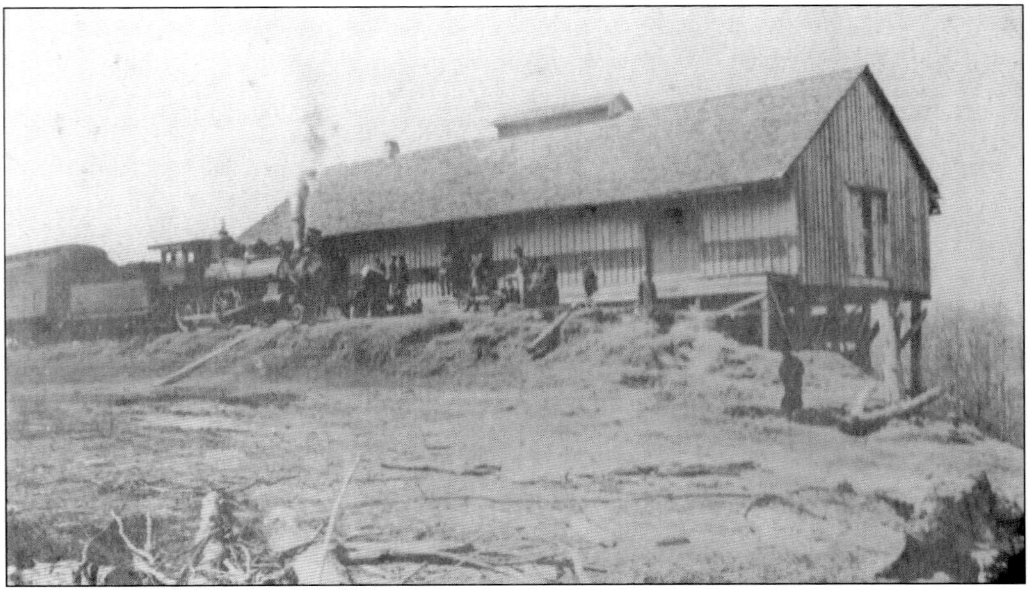

Two

Lake Village

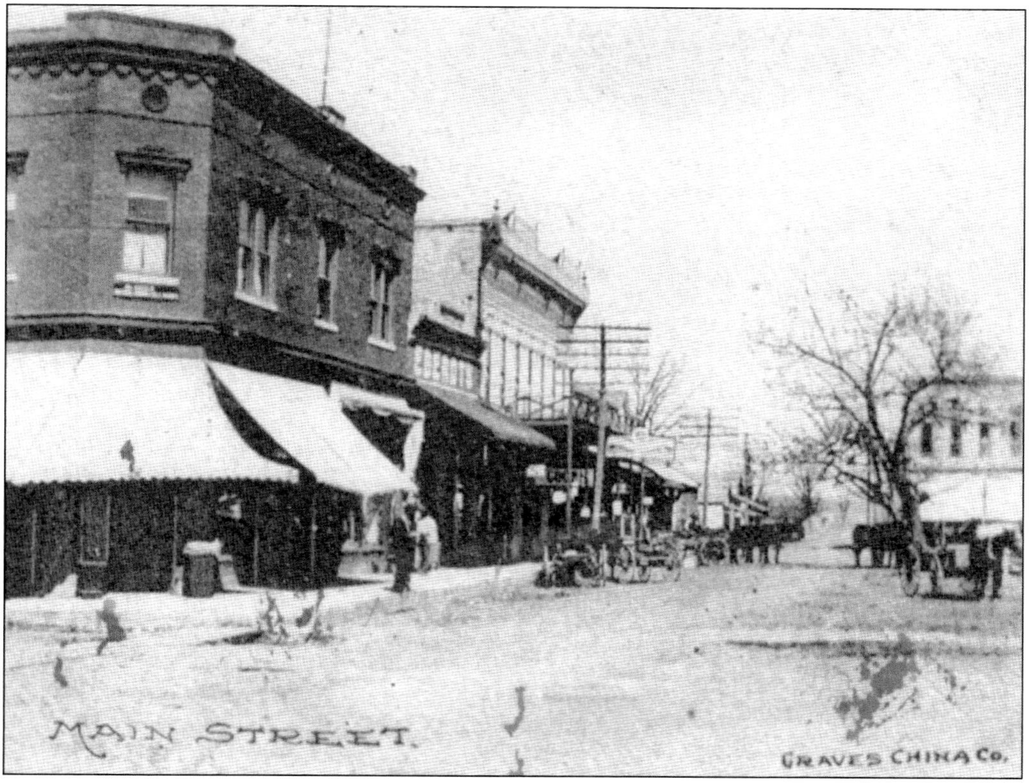

Built by Austro-Hungarian immigrant John Tushek in 1906, the Tushek Building served as his jewelry store for many years. Tushek also practiced as an optometrist. Later, the building housed the law office of Carneal Warfield and the Epstein Department Store. Glenn and Beverly Rowe donated the building to the city in 2008. Restored in 2011–2012 under Mayor JoAnne Bush, the LEED-certified building now serves as Lake Village City Hall. (Courtesy of Blake Wintory.)

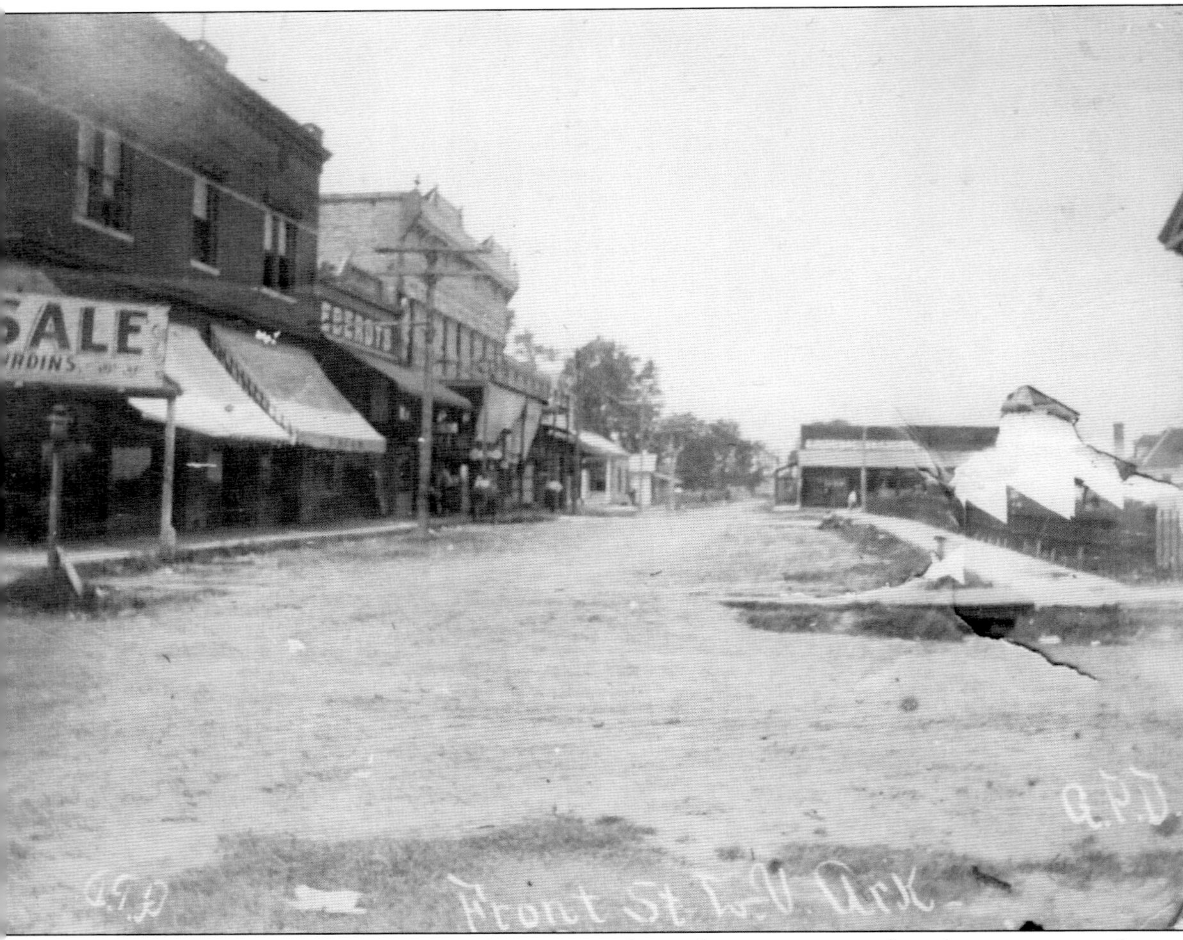

In the image on the previous page, the 1907 courthouse does not appear to have been constructed. In this photograph, taken from a similar angle, the courthouse's west columns are visible. North of the courthouse is a drugstore and a movie theater. West of the courthouse are several dry-goods, drug, and grocery stores, including Gus Eberdt's. His son Frank continued business as Eberdt's Seed & Feed on Main Street. (Courtesy of Carol T. Meyer.)

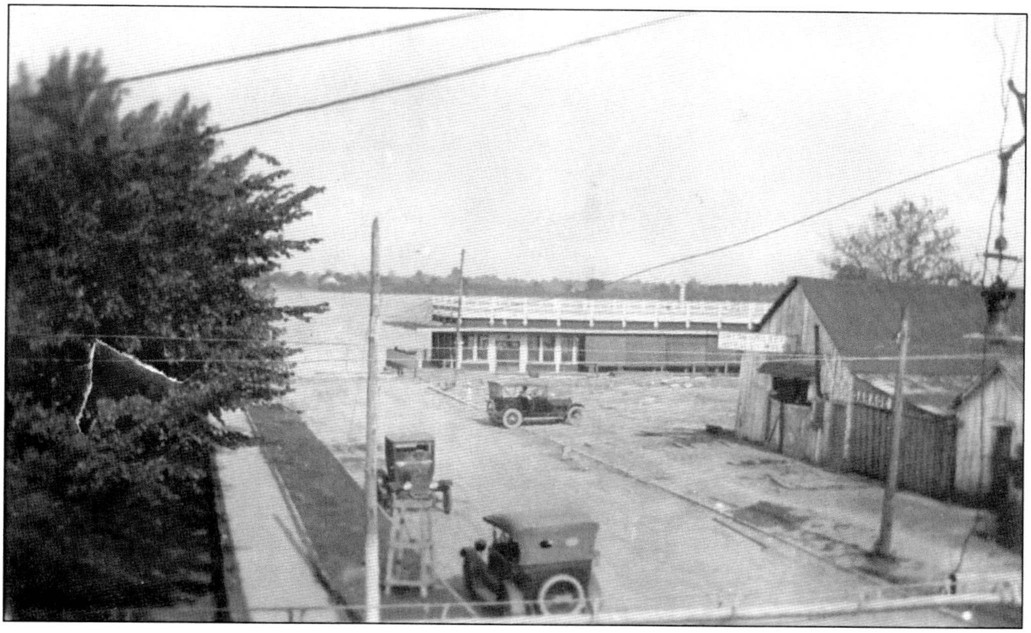

Lake Village, first platted in 1856, initially developed along the lakeshore and around the courthouse. These two photographs show Lake Village's downtown and lakefront around 1920. Gaines Cafeteria and Bathing Pavilion is visible in both images along Lake Chicot; the first photograph appears to have been taken from the second floor of the Tushek Building and shows a newly cleared lot on the southwest corner of Lakeshore Drive and Main Street. Also visible is Watt Orton's Livery Stable and a building labeled "Garage." From the water, the 1907 courthouse and Lake Village's downtown are visible. (Both, courtesy of the Bill and Jeanine Sessions Collection, Lakeport Plantation.)

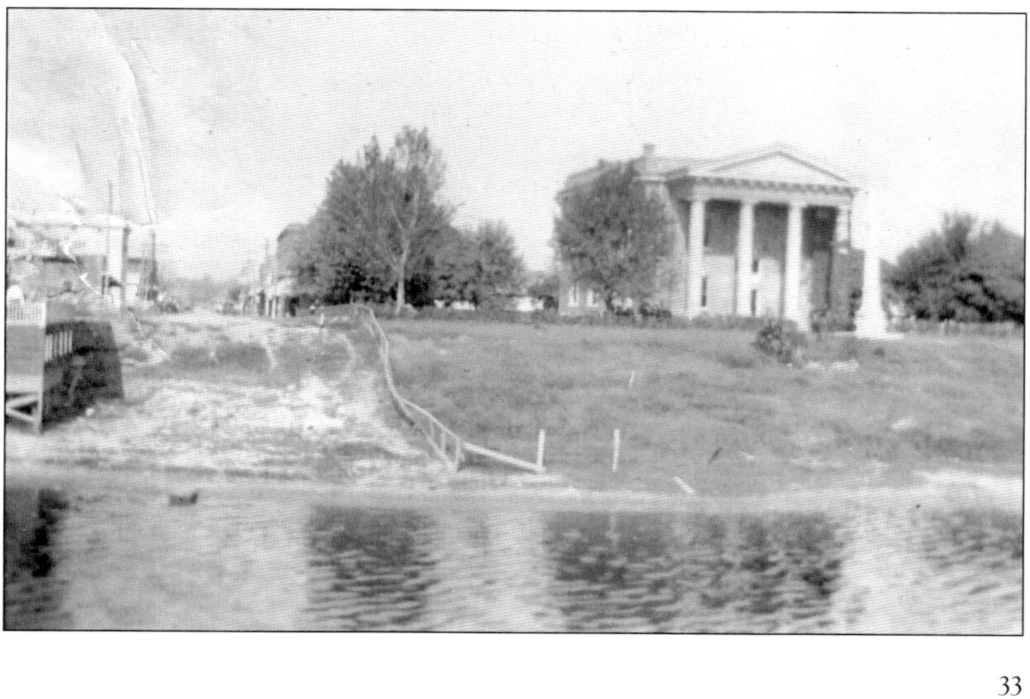

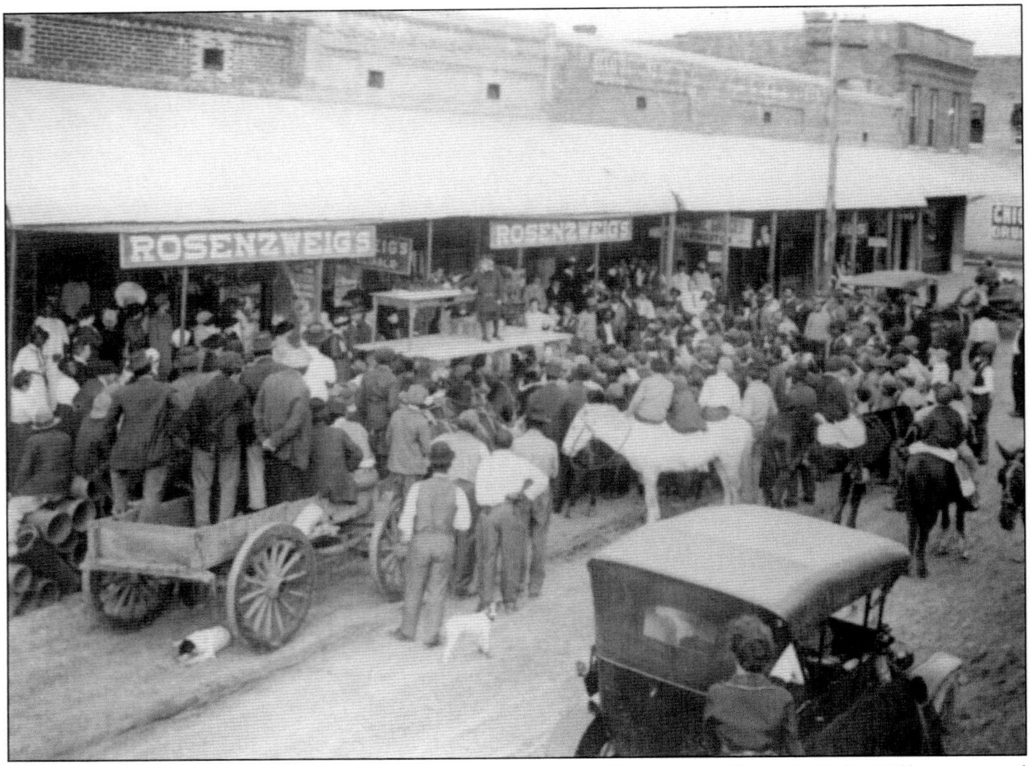

Buster Brown and his dog Tige made an appearance at the Rosenzweig Store in Lake Village around 1915 for the Brown Shoe Company. Morris E. Rosenzweig, born in Russia, started out as a peddler and owned his own dry-goods store in Lake Village as early as 1906. (Courtesy of the Carolyn LeMaster Collection, Butler Center for Arkansas Studies, Central Arkansas Library System.)

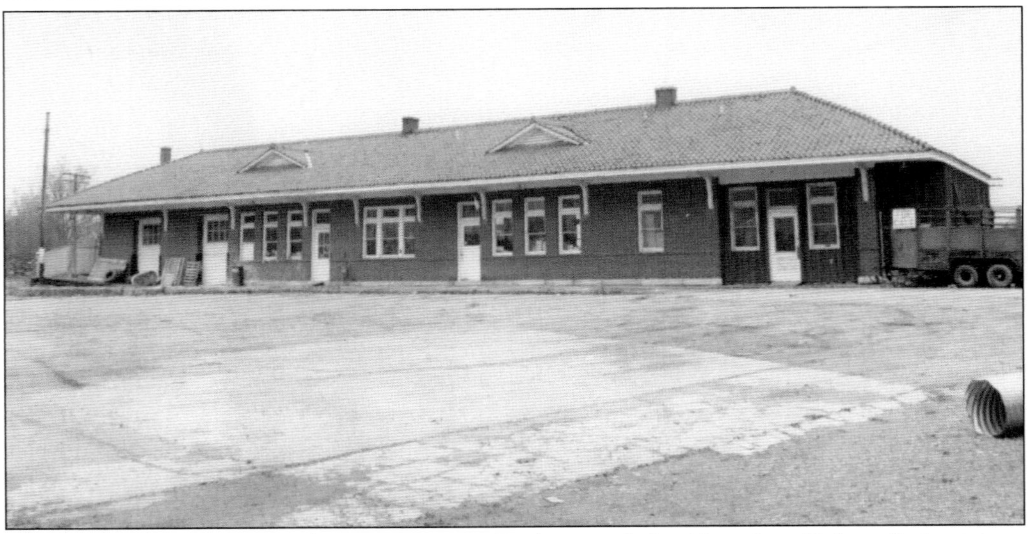

The Mississippi River, Hamburg & Western Railway and the Memphis, Helena & Louisiana Railroad came to Lake Village in 1901 and 1903, respectively. A depot constructed at the west end of Main Street encouraged new businesses away from the lakefront. The Lake Village Missouri Pacific Depot, photographed here in 1990, was built by 1917 and burned in the early 1990s. (Courtesy of the Arkansas Historic Preservation Program.)

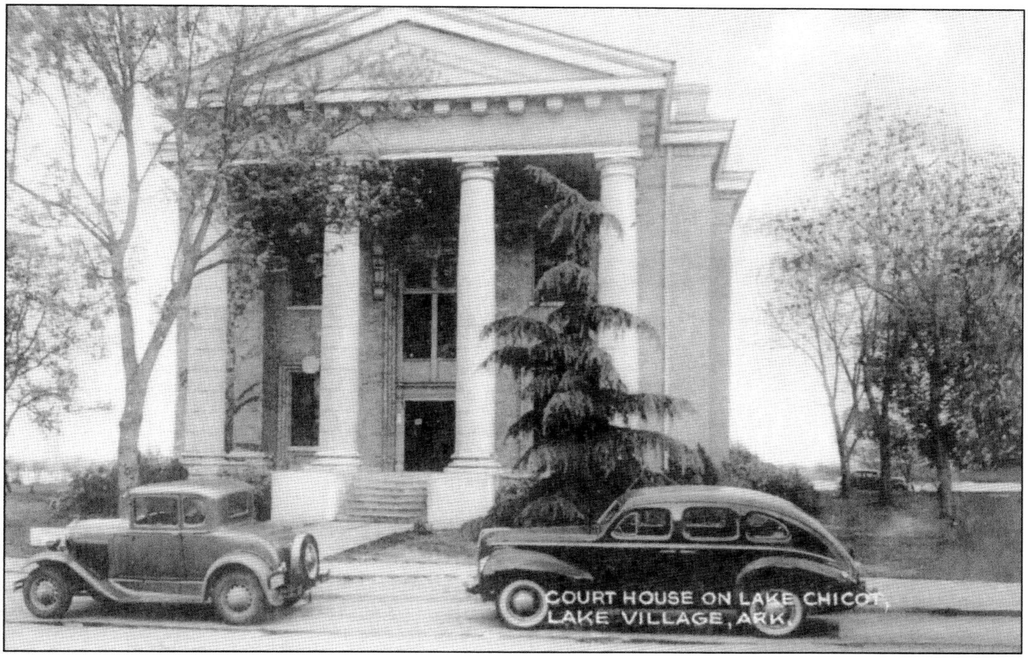

When Lake Village became the county seat in 1857, the county erected a courthouse and jail. In 1907, a new Classical Revival courthouse replaced the 1857 structure. Built by Lake Village contractor Albert G. Simms, the building featured a pediment and columns on both the east and west façades. In 1956, the courthouse was torn down after many years of foundation problems. (Courtesy of Blake Wintory.)

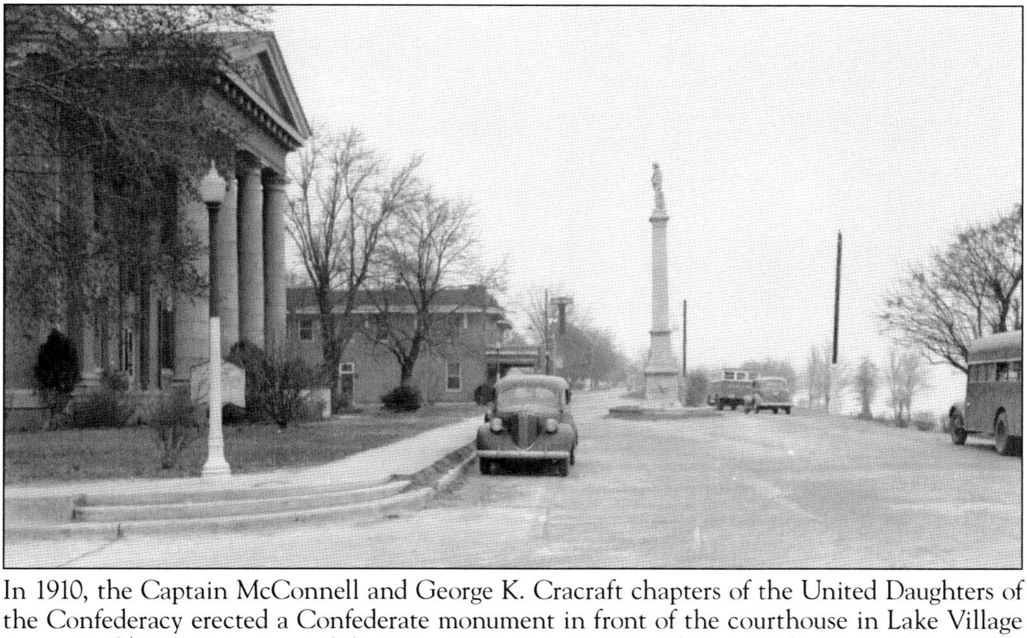

In 1910, the Captain McConnell and George K. Cracraft chapters of the United Daughters of the Confederacy erected a Confederate monument in front of the courthouse in Lake Village at a cost of $3,000. Many Confederate monuments were erected across Arkansas and the South in honor of the "Lost Cause." Local historian LaRhonda Mangrum has identified 37 burials of Confederate veterans in Chicot County cemeteries. Mangrum has also identified two African American Union burials in Chicot County. (Courtesy of Blake Wintory.)

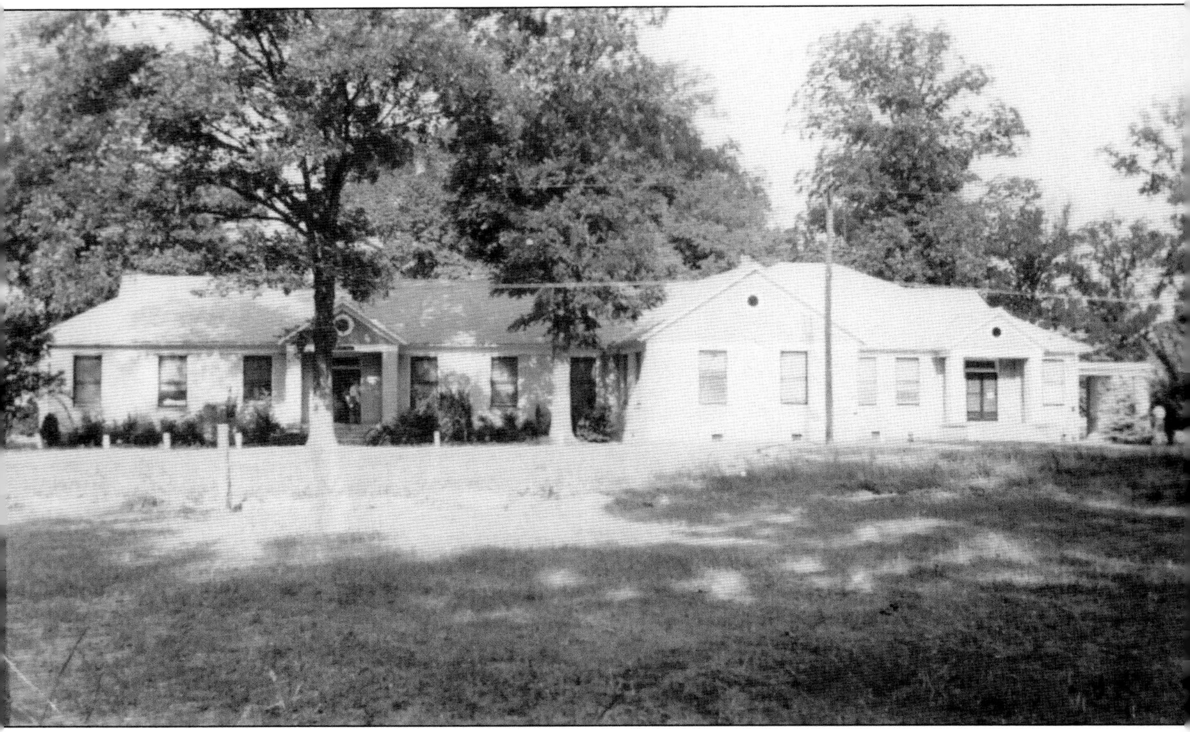

In 1825, a Dr. Prine of Point Chicot treated "invalids who get sick travelling on the Mississippi river" and may well have been the county's earliest physician, according to the *Natchez Gazette*. Several physicians practiced in Lake Village around 1900, including Dr. Robert Henry and Dr. Frank L. Connelly. A few years later, Dr. Marion M. Norton had a general practice in Lake Village, and by 1917, his Lakeside Sanitarium operated south of downtown. In 1911, Dr. Edward P. McGehee founded the Lake Village Infirmary. McGehee expanded the infirmary in the late 1920s, and it became a well-known surgical center. In 1967, a new 50-bed Chicot Memorial Hospital replaced the infirmary. From 1996 to 2015, the infirmary housed the Museum of Chicot County. (Courtesy of the Museum of Chicot County, Arkansas.)

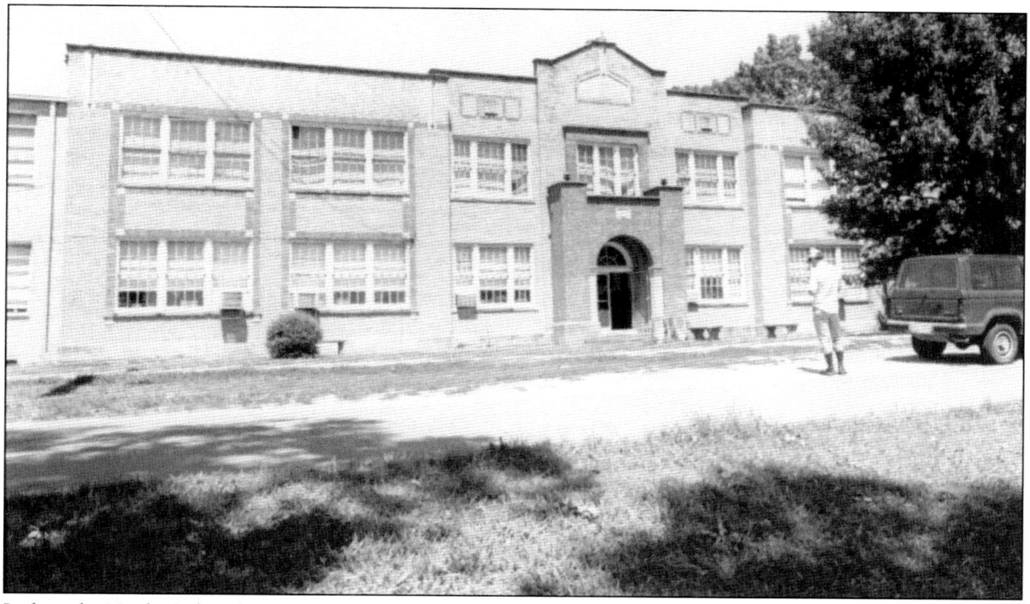

Lakeside High School in Lake Village was first constructed along Lakeshore Drive by Albert G. Simms in 1906 and remodeled in 1910. Central, a separate school for African Americans, was constructed about 1910 as well. Lakeside, photographed here in 1990, had several additions in the 80 years that followed. The structure was razed around 2000. (Courtesy of the Arkansas Historic Preservation Program.)

The first jail in Lake Village was a wrought iron plate building constructed in 1857 by the firm of Valleau & Jacobs of Cincinnati, Ohio. The 1857 jail was demolished during the construction of the 1907 courthouse. Around 1908, a new county jail was constructed on the corner of Main and Duvall Streets. Pictured here in 1969, water marks from the 1927 flood were still visible on the walls. (Courtesy of Lake Village Public Library.)

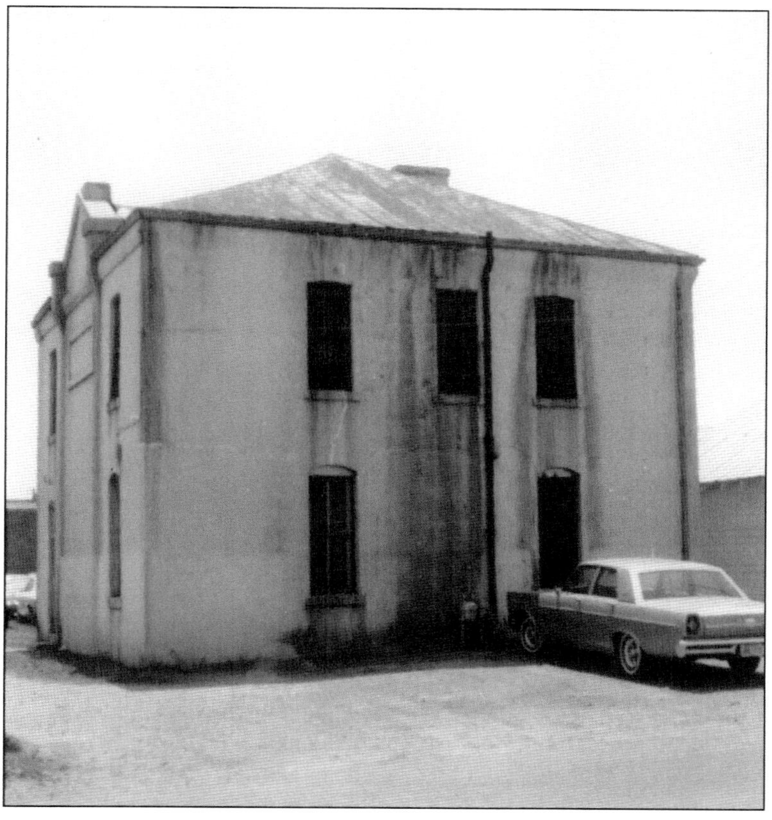

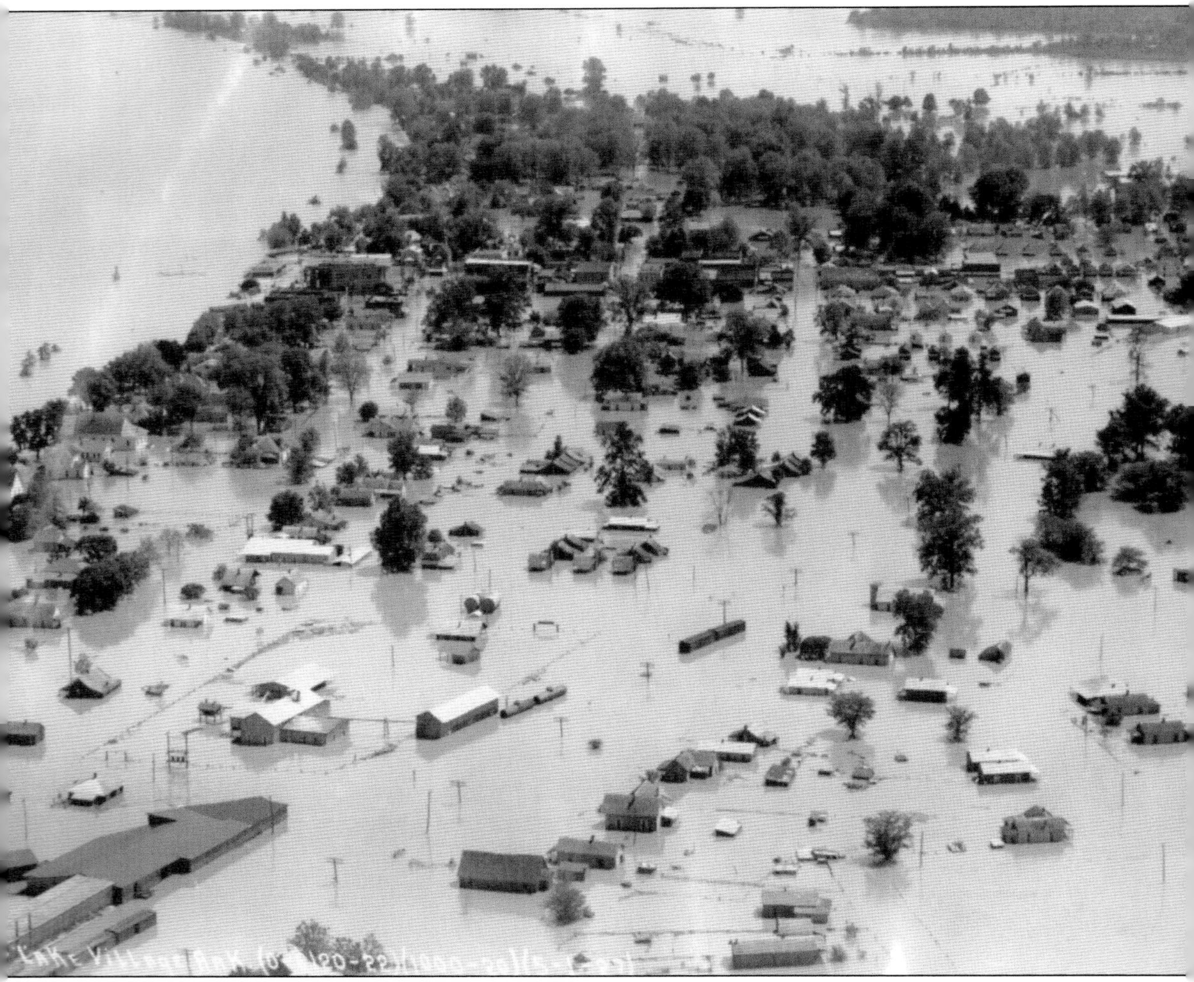

The Great Flood of 1927 was one of the worst natural disasters in American history. On April 21, about 47 miles north of Lake Village, the Arkansas River levee broke at Pendleton. The break quickly brought floodwaters to Southeast Arkansas. After a visit to Lake Village, George M. Moreland, columnist for the Memphis *Commercial Appeal*, wrote, "There is a high strip of land along the lakeshore dividing the waters of Lake Chicot from the 'sea of Arkansas,' which extends 13 miles westward." (Courtesy of Butler Center for Arkansas Studies, Central Arkansas Library System.)

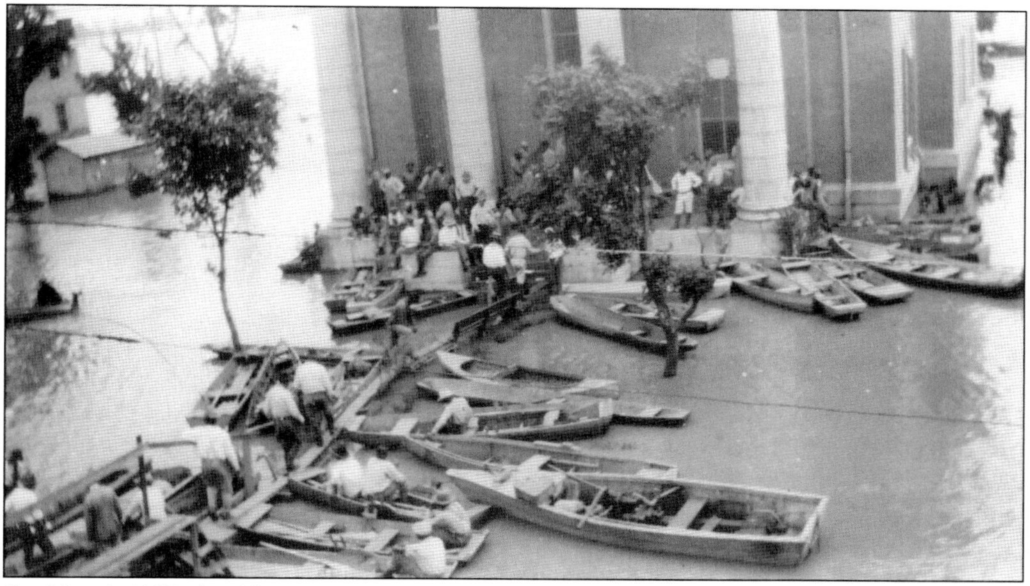

On May 6, 1927, the *Chicot Spectator* reported, "The courthouse is becoming more and more a community and industrial center." A week earlier, Lake Village mayor J.C. Gillison stated 700 to 1,000 people were marooned in the flooded lowlands "clinging to small rafts and floating trees . . . or packed like sardines in barn lofts." (Courtesy of Libby Borgognoni.)

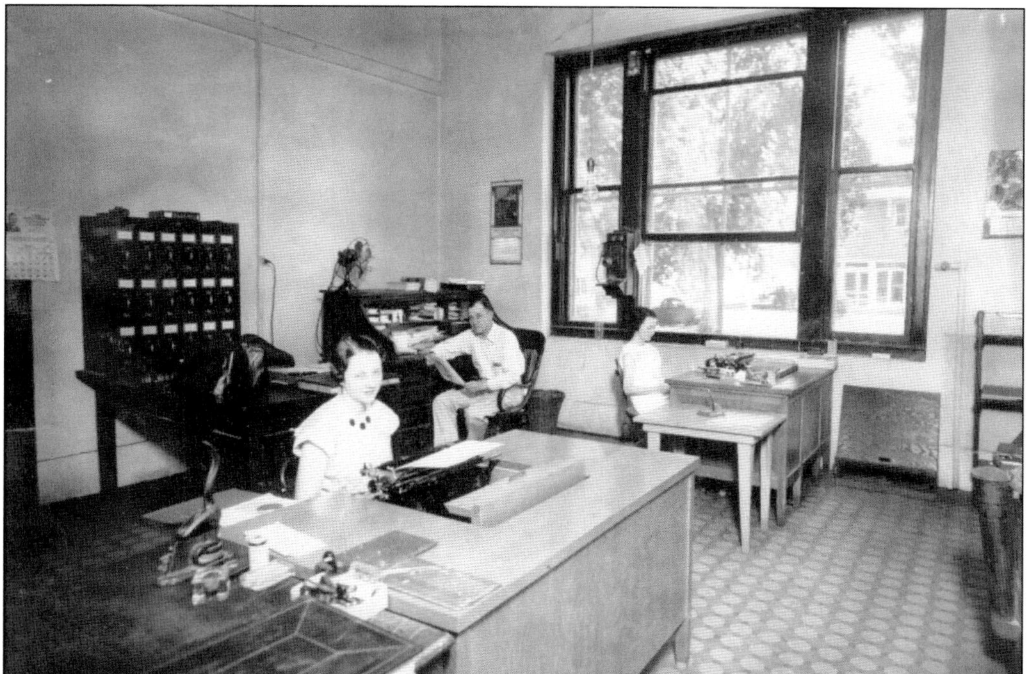

Circuit clerk Dixon T. Gaines sits inside his office in the Chicot County Courthouse in 1937, according to the calendar on the wall. Gaines served as circuit clerk from 1937 to 1944. His father, Abner Gaines, served in the same position from 1919 to 1925. Also pictured are Mattie Haynes (left) and Irene Turpin. (Courtesy of Chicot County Courthouse.)

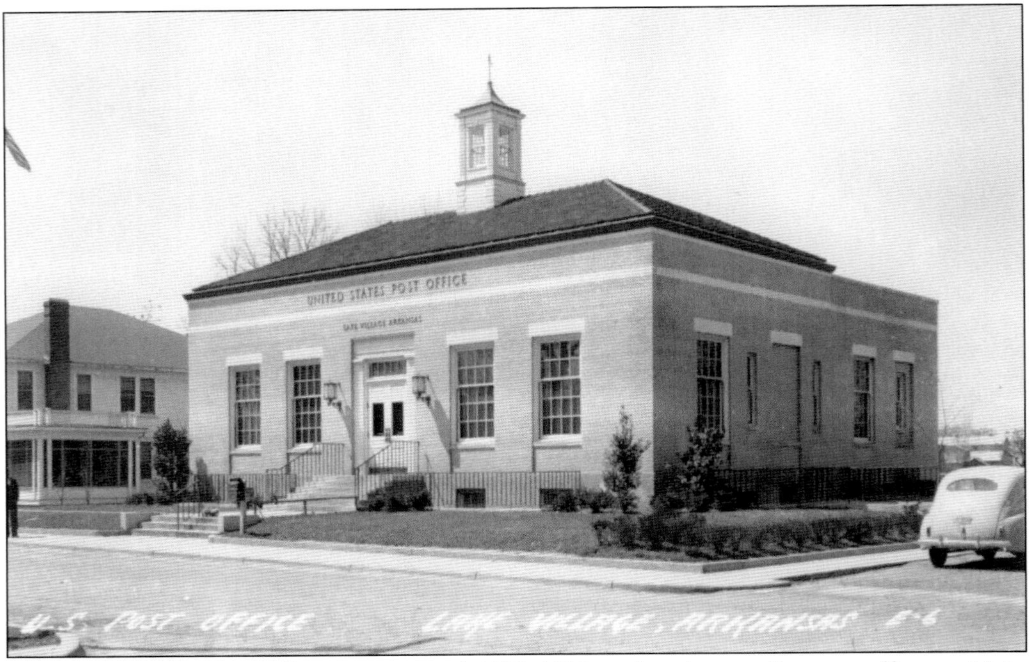

The Lake Village Post Office, constructed 1938–1939, replaced an earlier post office on Main Street. In 1941, a mural financed by the US Treasury Fine Arts section, titled *Lake Country Wild Life*, was painted by New Jersey artist Avery Johnson. (Courtesy of Blake Wintory.)

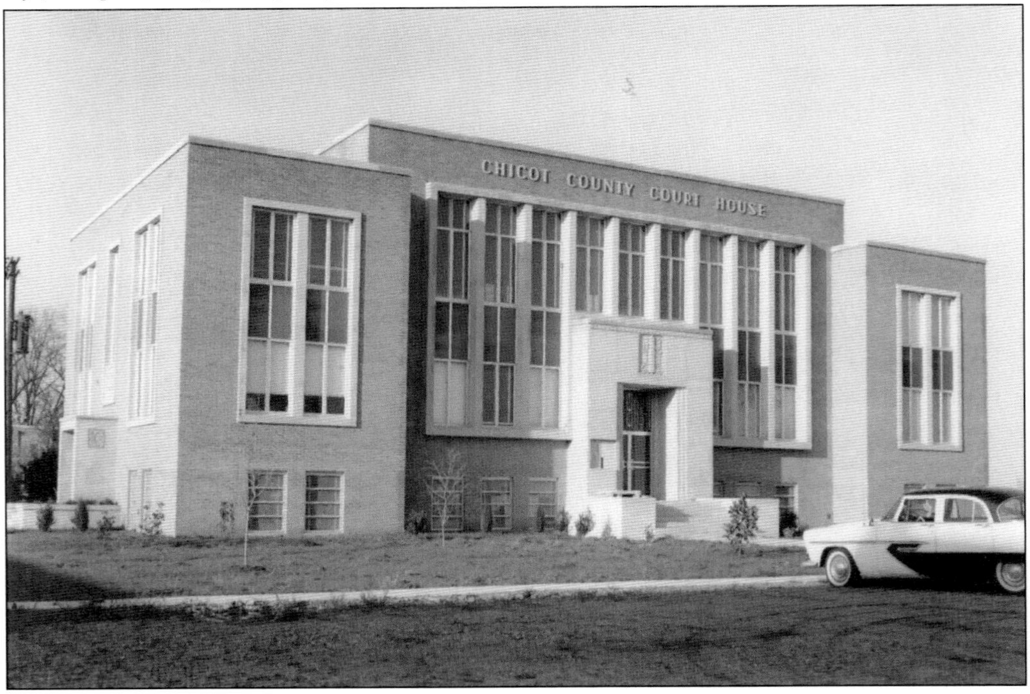

Architect Herbert Voelker of Texas designed Chicot County's 1956 courthouse in the Art Deco style. The structure is still in use as the county's seat of government. The parking lot of the 1956 courthouse is the site of the old 1907 courthouse. (Courtesy of the Bill and Jeanine Sessions Collection, Lakeport Plantation.)

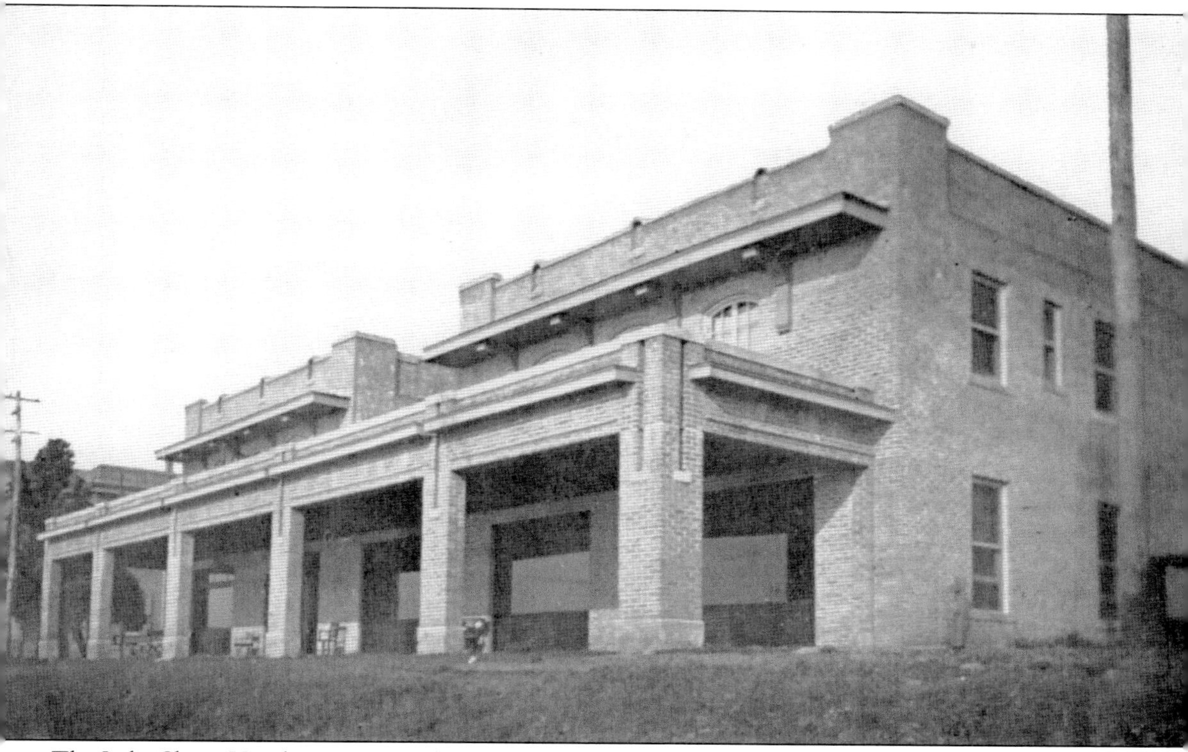

The Lake Shore Hotel, incorporated on December 22, 1910, and constructed by local contractor Albert G. Simms, featured 34 rooms, a dancing hall, and hot and cold running water. In the 1910s, the hotel advertised special weekly rates for fishing and hunting parties and a free electric fan. It was under the management of R.M. Gaines, and, by the 1920s, Mollie H. Smith. In 1986, the building was converted to apartments. (Courtesy of Lakeport Plantation.)

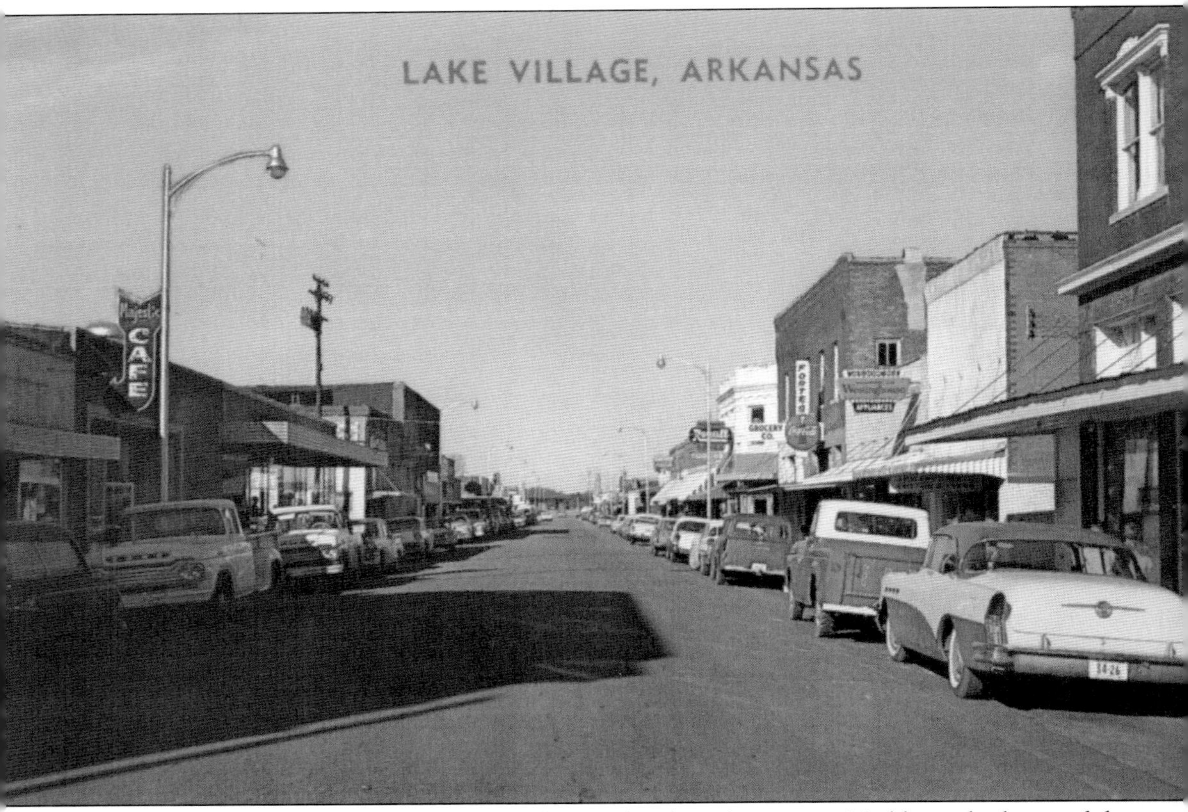

By the 1950s, Lake Village had matured into a bustling downtown. Visible in the heart of the town's commercial district are the Majestic Cafe, Epstein Department Store, and Sam Forte's Grocery Store. (Courtesy of Blake Wintory.)

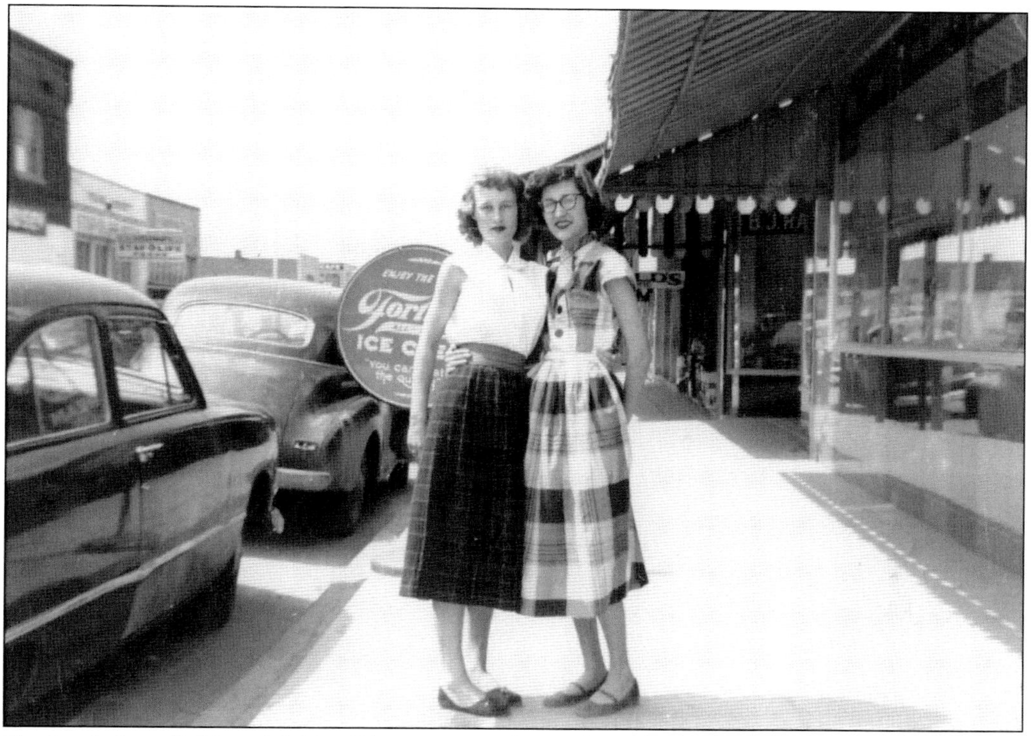

Shirley Jarboe (left) and Libby Olivi pose in the early 1950s in front of Holloway Drugstore downtown on a busy Saturday afternoon. The primary hangout for school kids in the 1950s, Holloway had a soda fountain with booths in the front and a pharmacy in back. (Courtesy of Libby Borgognoni.)

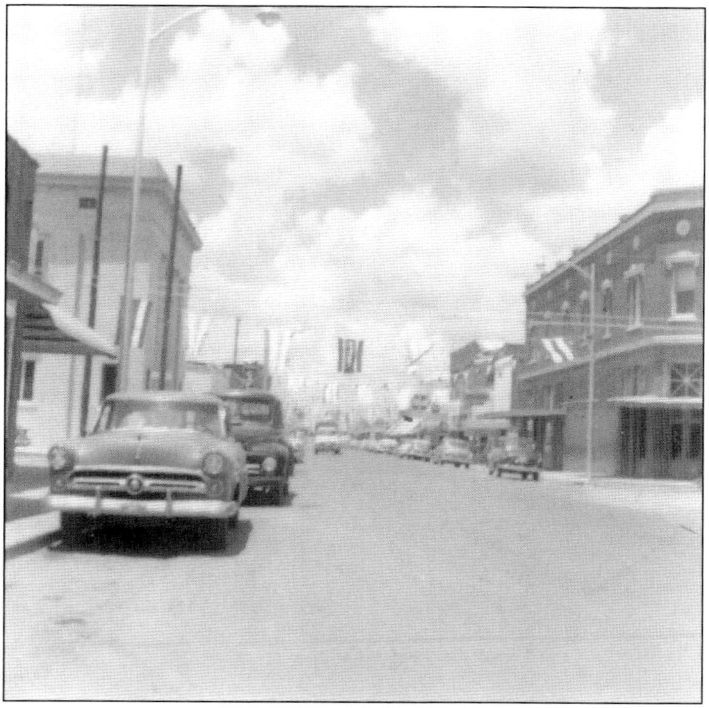

The inscription on the back of this photograph from about 1955 reads, "Lake Village goes all out for July 4th. Main street and the lake front is decorated with flags. 50,000 franks given away—Boat racing is main feature." (Courtesy of Blake Wintory.)

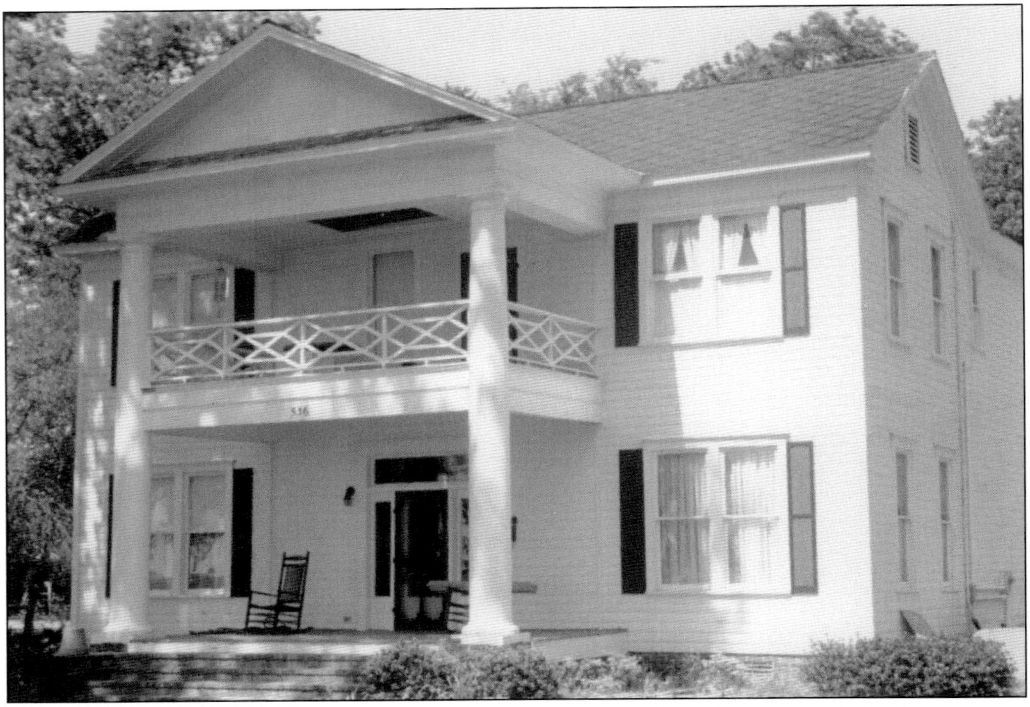

The Haynes House, built for John R. and Ida Haynes around 1904, is one of Lake Village's iconic homes along Lakeshore Drive. Reportedly, when the columns arrived by train, they attracted a large crowd, which followed them to the construction site. The Haynes family owned Haynes Hardware Store downtown, which also included a funeral business. (Courtesy of the Arkansas Historic Preservation Program.)

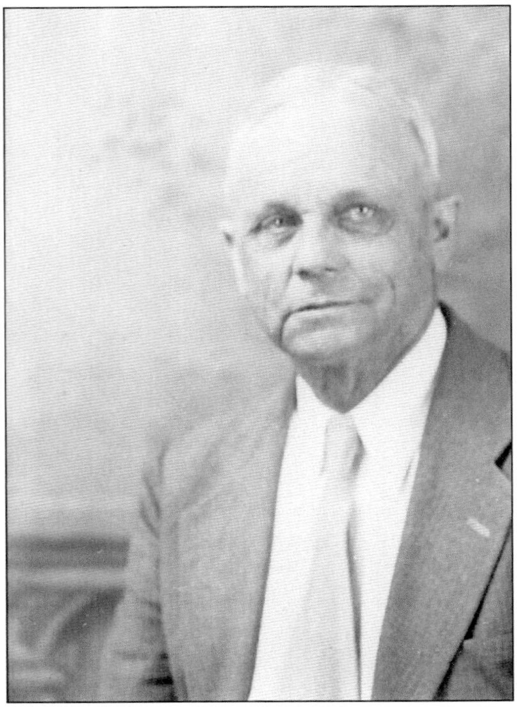

Albert G. Simms (1875–1945), a contractor and owner of Chicot Building Supply, constructed many important buildings in the county, including the 1907 courthouse, Lake Shore Hotel (c. 1911), Lakeside High School (1906), government buildings at Jerome, and many Lake Village residences. (Courtesy of Sadie Crouse.)

The Henry House was constructed in 1910 for Dr. Robert N. Henry, possibly by Albert G. Simms. Dr. Henry, a native of Hinds County, Mississippi, received his medical education at the Louisville College of Medicine and came to Lake Village in 1898. During his practice, he made house calls on horseback. His daughter Clara Henry served as Chicot County circuit clerk from 1961 to 1978. (Courtesy of the Arkansas Historic Preservation Program.)

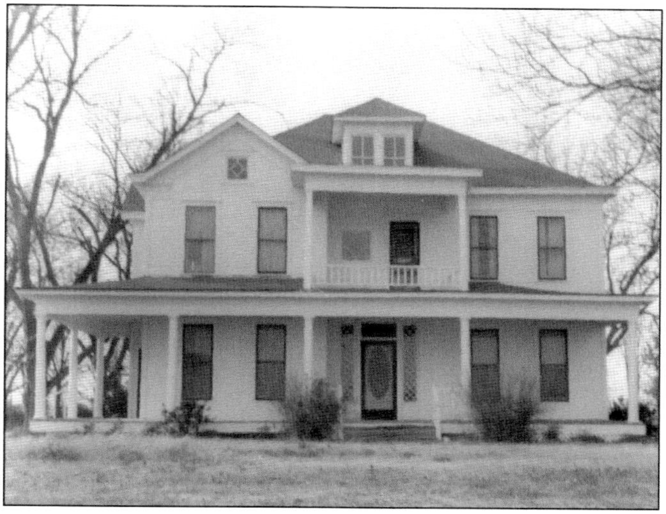

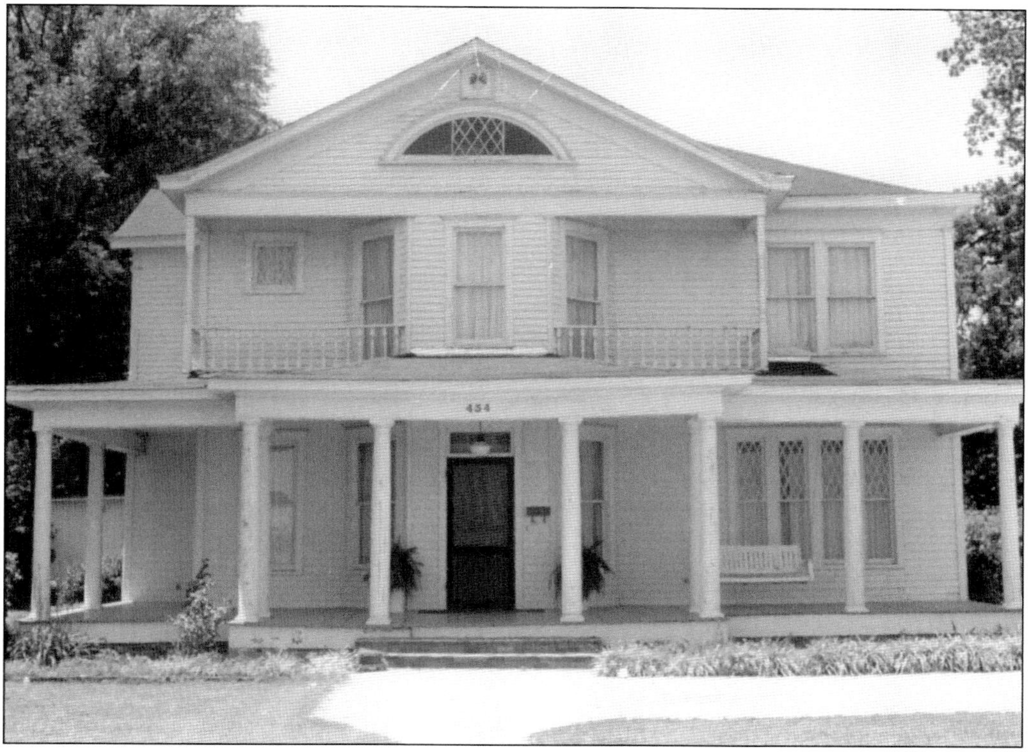

The Carlton House was built by Albert G. Simms around 1905 for his cousin Herman Carlton Sr., a native of Chicot County who served as postmaster at Sunnyside in the early 1890s and was appointed to that position in Lake Village in 1914 and again in 1918. Widowed at 46 in 1929, his wife, Gertrude, lived in the house for many years after his death, converting several rooms into apartments during the Great Depression. Restored by Jerry and Sadie Crouse in the 1980s, the Carlton House was listed in the National Register of Historic Places in 1991 as "one of the best examples of the Colonial Revival style architecture in Lake Village." (Courtesy of the Arkansas Historic Preservation Program.)

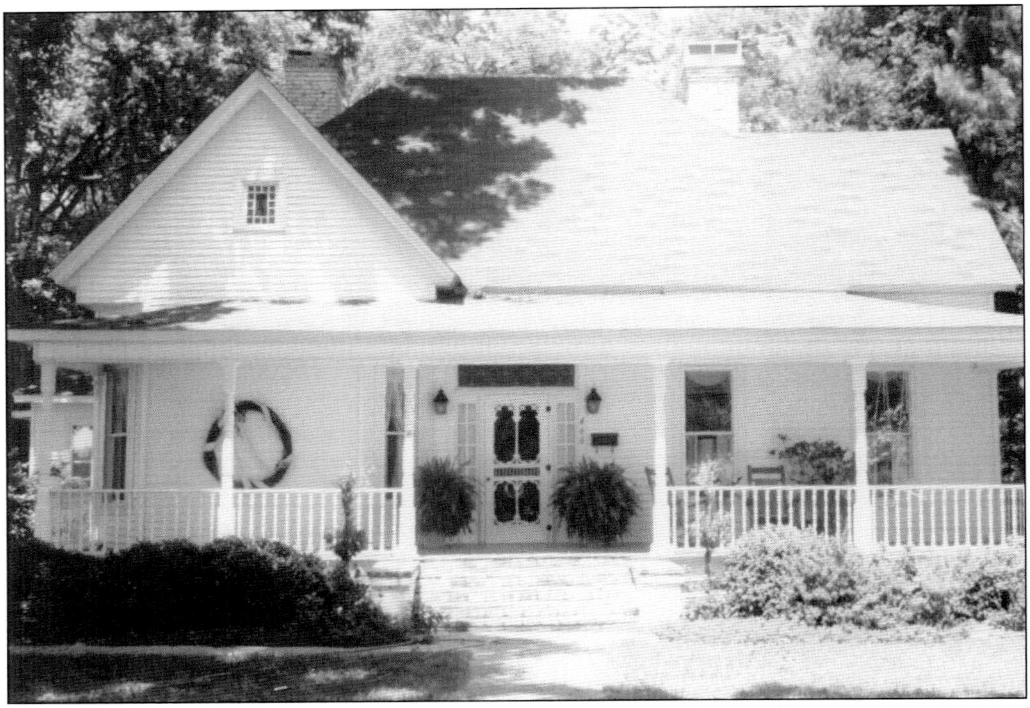

The Mulligan House was constructed about 1915 for Peter and Mary Mulligan. Peter, a native of North Carolina, came to Lake Village around 1900. A 1909 directory shows him as a saloon owner; later, he operated a grocery and wholesale business. Jim and Linda Haddock purchased the house in 1976 and began its restoration. (Courtesy of the Arkansas Historic Preservation Program.)

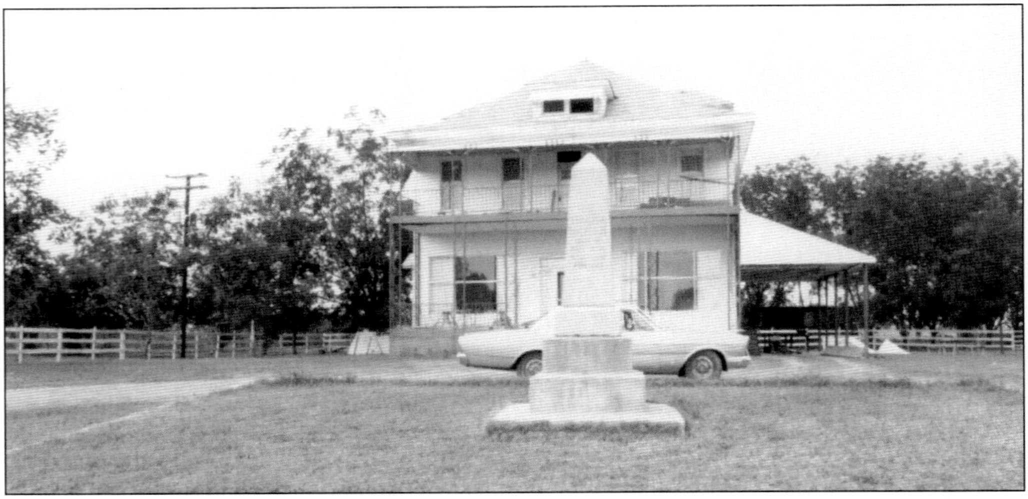

The Lewis house, built around 1912, served as a country club in April 1923 when a young and not yet famous Charles Lindbergh landed nearby. The innkeeper, a Mr. Henry, offered him accommodations. Lindbergh, who had been offering rides for $5, gave Henry a night flight over Lake Village. Lindbergh later claimed that this was his first night flight. In 1934, the Chicot Delphian Society memorialized the event with a monument. Leading up to World War II, Lindbergh gave speeches touting Germany's military prowess. His popularity nosedived during World War II, and the monument was painted yellow and toppled over. Lindbergh's popularity later revived, and the monument was restored. (Courtesy of the Arkansas Historic Preservation Program.)

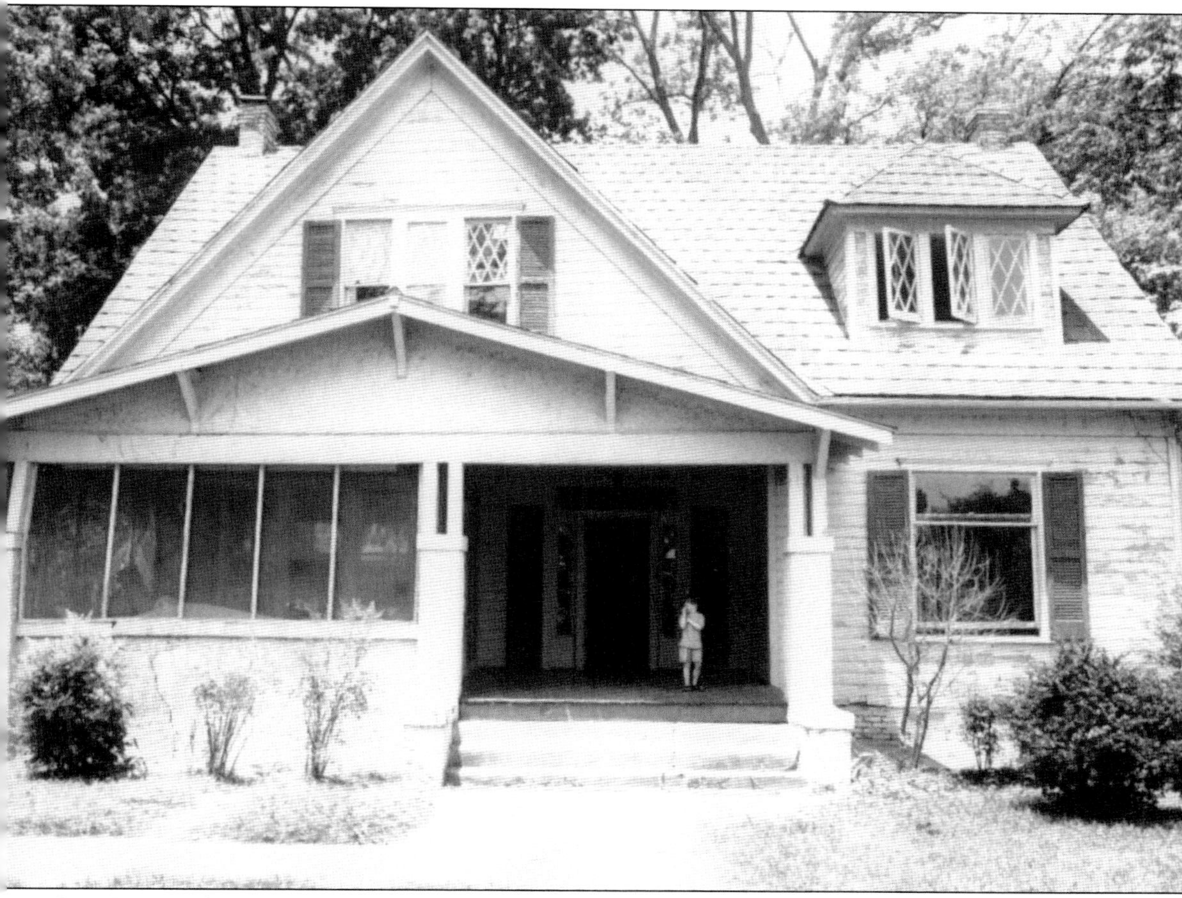

Sam Epstein (1875–1944), a Jewish merchant and immigrant from Russia, constructed this house around 1910. Starting out as a peddler out of Memphis, Tennessee, in the late 1890s, he and his brother Nathan established a store at Luna Landing on the Mississippi River. By 1900, Epstein had his own dry-goods store in Lake Village, and by 1917, he operated the successful Epstein Gin as well. His obituary in the *Delta Democrat-Times* described him as "one of the community's most influential business and political leaders." (Courtesy of the Arkansas Historic Preservation Program.)

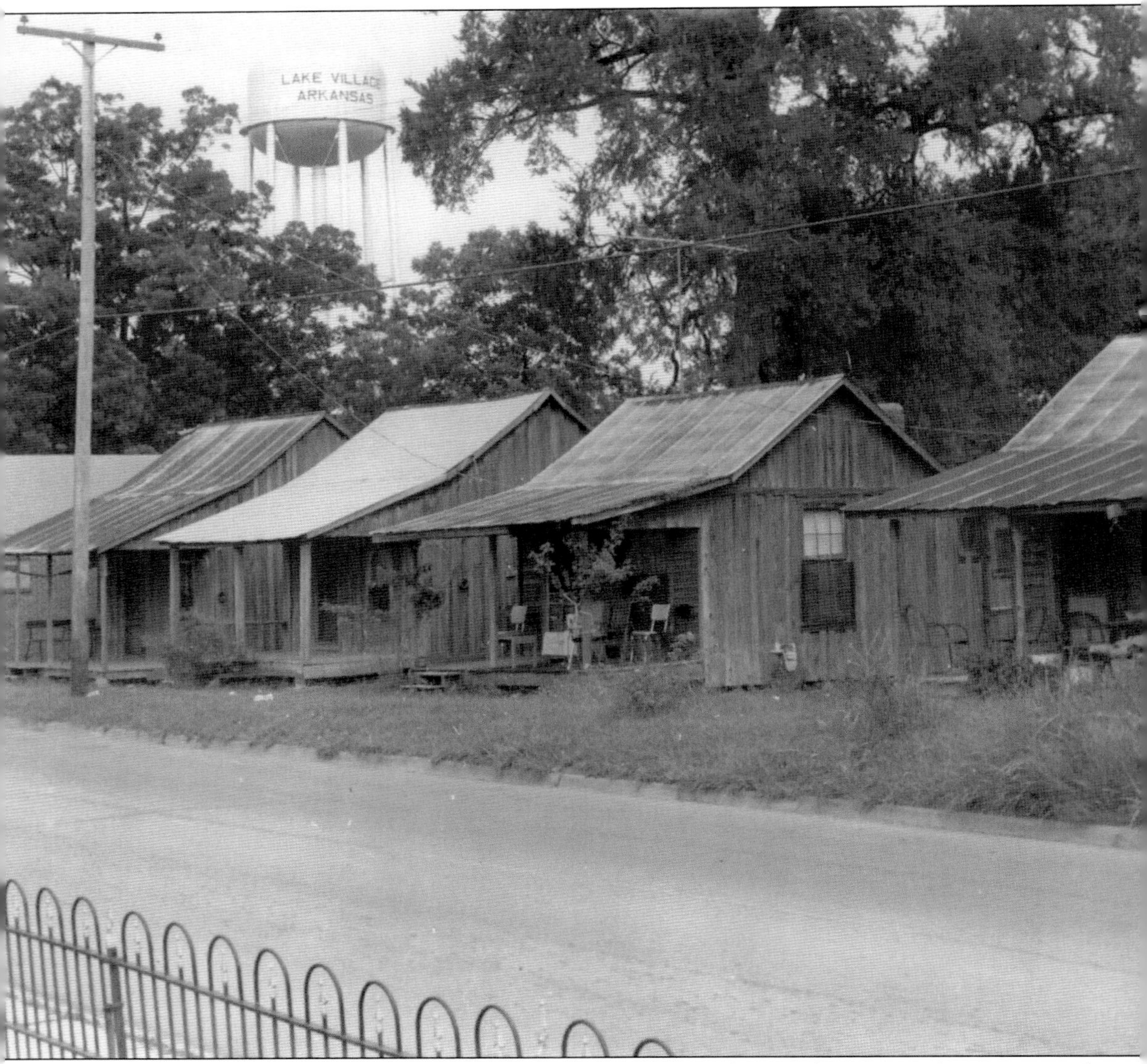

The population of Chicot County peaked in 1940 with a population of 27,454. Mechanization and the loss of farm jobs encouraged residents (black and white) to move; the population declined to 18,990 in 1960. Sallie (Lewis) Lightfoot, born about 1866, is one example. The daughter of former slaves, she married George Lightfoot in 1888, raised 11 children on a cotton farm outside of Lake Village, and was widowed in 1939. After a lifetime in Chicot County, she left for Chicago in 1947 to live with her daughter. Lightfoot celebrated her 100th birthday there in 1966. (Courtesy of the Museum of Chicot County, Arkansas.)

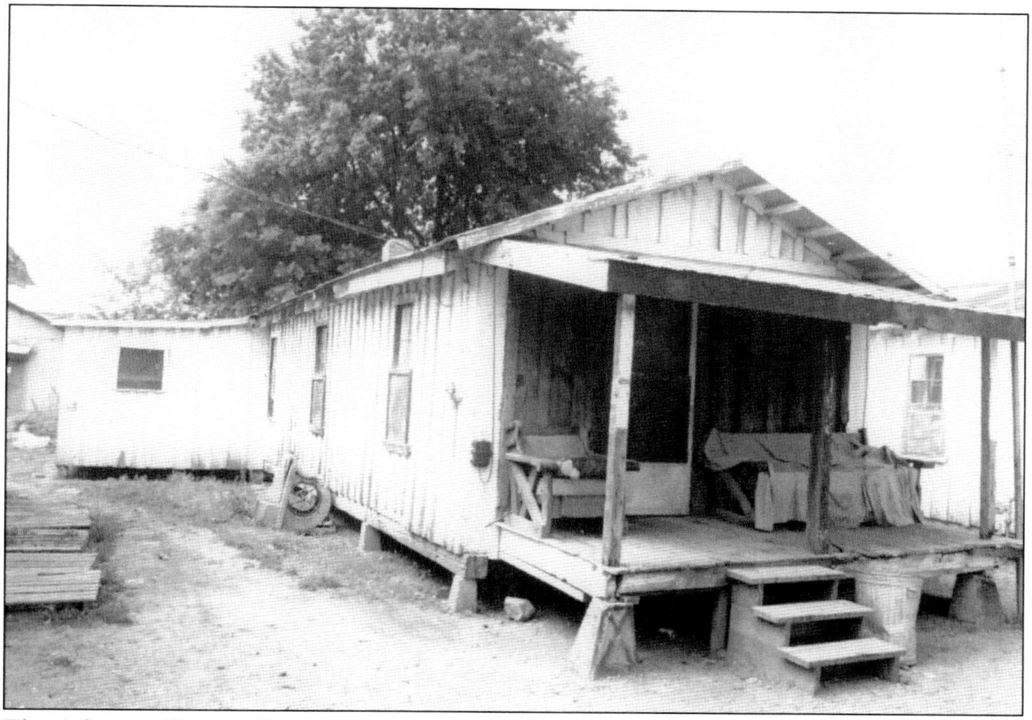

The Arkansas Historic Preservation Program documented several frame shotgun houses along Beadle (now Carter) Street in 1990. Built around 1915, shotgun houses like this were common in Lake Village on Beadle Street, Church Street, and north of Confederate Street in the 1920s and 1930s. Shotgun houses were first built in New Orleans by Haitian immigrants in the early 1800s. The style spread throughout the Southeast in both rural and urban settings. (Courtesy of the Arkansas Historic Preservation Program.)

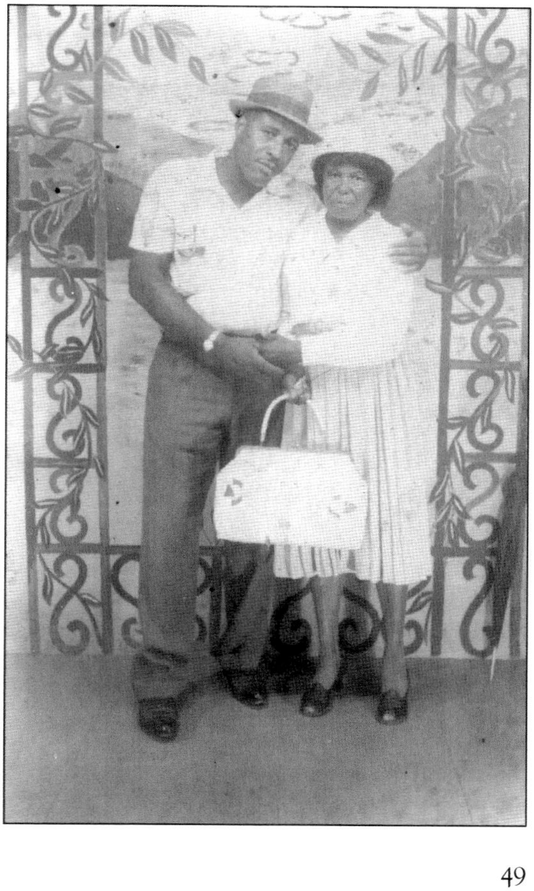

Isaiah McGehee of Jennie stopped to take a photograph with family friend Mandy Moore on the street during a Saturday trip to shop in Lake Village in the late 1940s. McGehee's wife, Jeanetta, remembers catching a cab and coming to town to buy "buffalo fish, eggs and carp." Photographers stationed on busy Main Street would capture moments like this between neighbors for 40¢. (Courtesy of Jeanetta McGehee.)

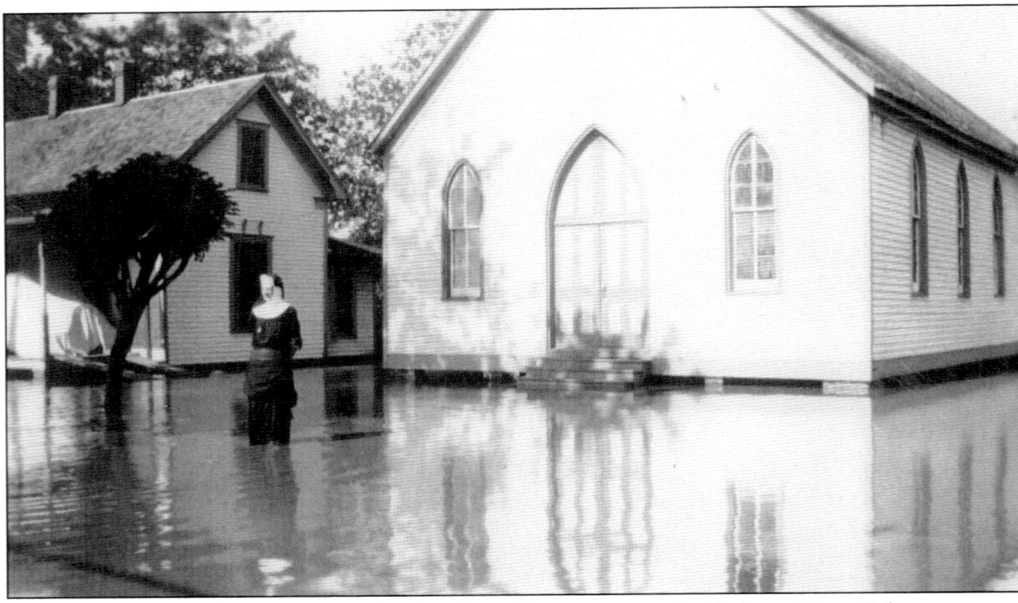

Katherine Kiernan Johnson arrived in Lake Village as a new bride from New Orleans around 1857. Missing her Catholic faith, she started the first Catholic mission in Chicot County in 1866. St. Mary's of the Lake Catholic Church built its first structure in 1869, pictured here in 1927 during the flood. In 1896, the church was renamed Our Lady of the Lake Catholic Church. The original sanctuary, replaced in 1939, was used as a parish hall and cafeteria until 1965. (Courtesy of Libby Borgognoni.)

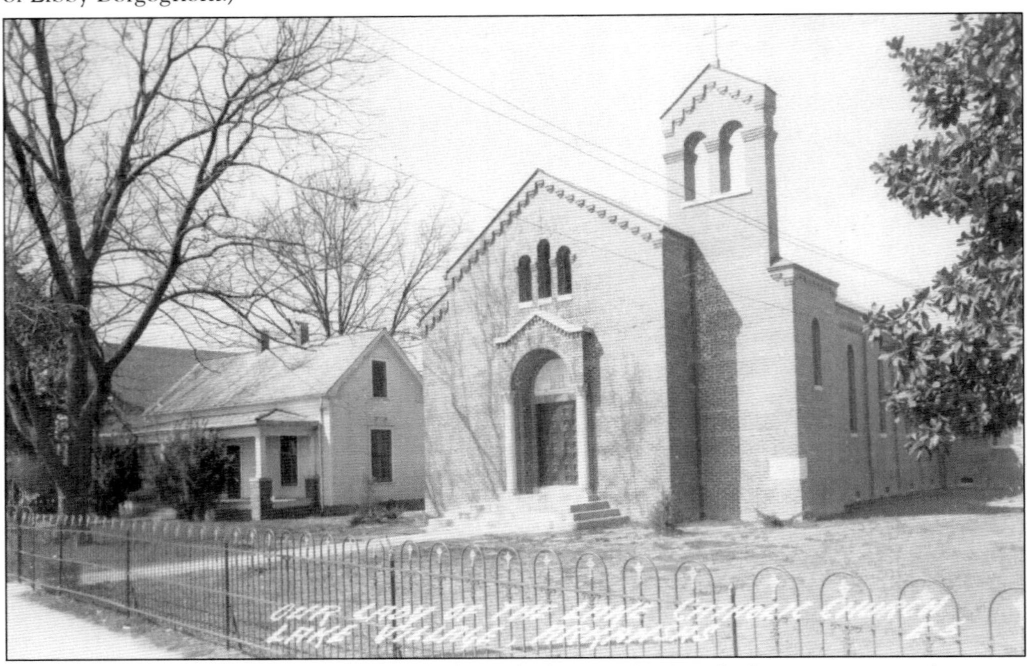

Our Lady of the Lake Catholic Church thrived after 1895, when Italian immigrants began to arrive to work on the nearby Sunnyside Plantation. This photograph shows the 1912 rectory and the new 1939 sanctuary. In the mid-1960s, a new rectory was built to replace the 1912 structure. (Courtesy of Libby Borgognoni.)

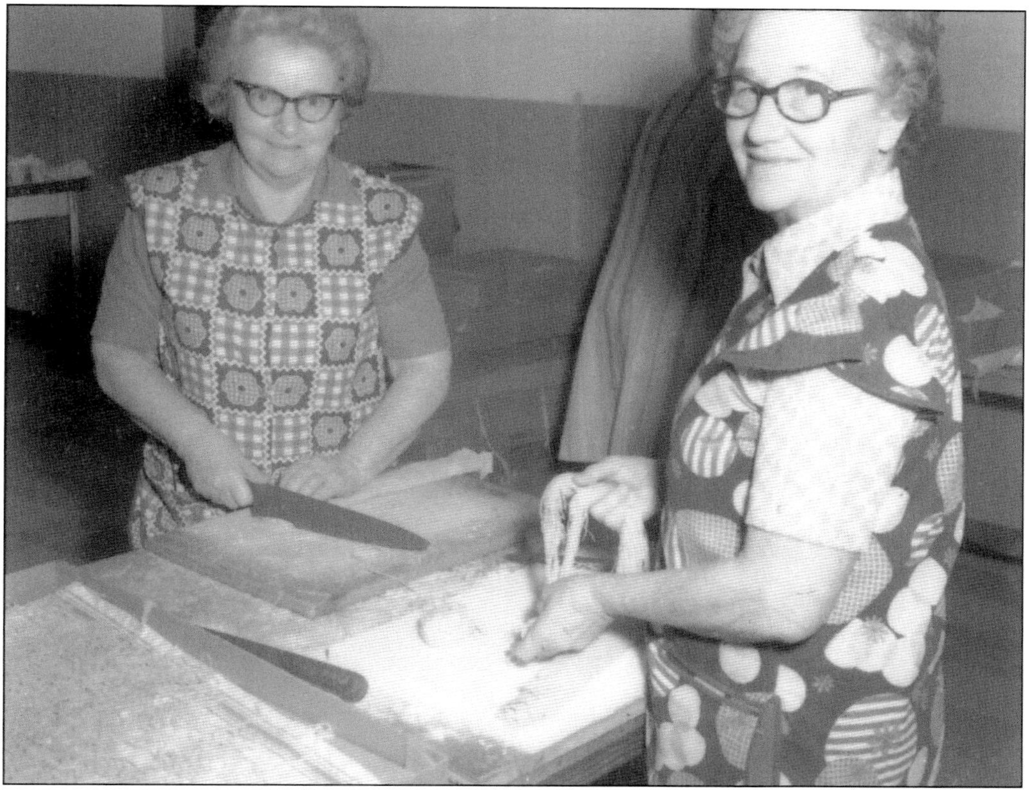

An annual spaghetti dinner sponsored by Our Lady of the Lake Catholic Church started in 1910. Mary J. Grassi (left) and Stella Alpe, pictured here around 1960, are cutting traditional spaghetti. (Courtesy of Libby Borgognoni.)

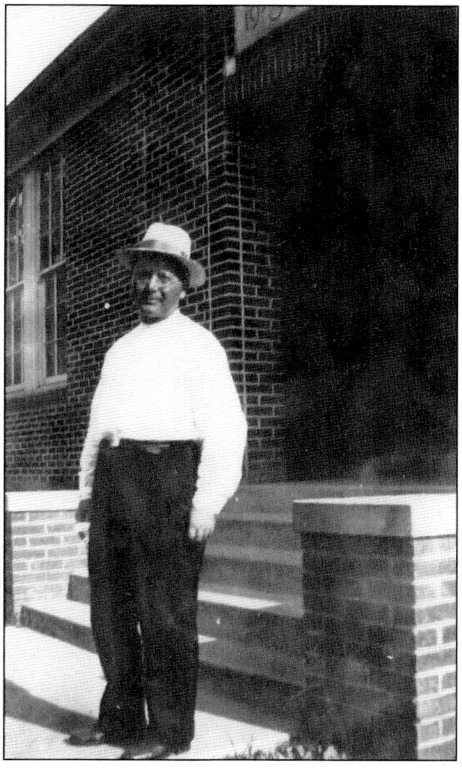

Fr. Matthew Saettele founded the parochial school of St. Mary's in 1908. Benedictine sisters from Jonesboro and later Fort Smith taught classes in the church and then in a converted house. Fr. Joachim Galloni, pictured here on the steps of St. Mary's, supervised the construction of a new brick building with classrooms and an auditorium in 1925. Lay teachers replaced the sisters beginning in 1963. St. Mary's closed in 2015. (Courtesy of Libby Borgognoni.)

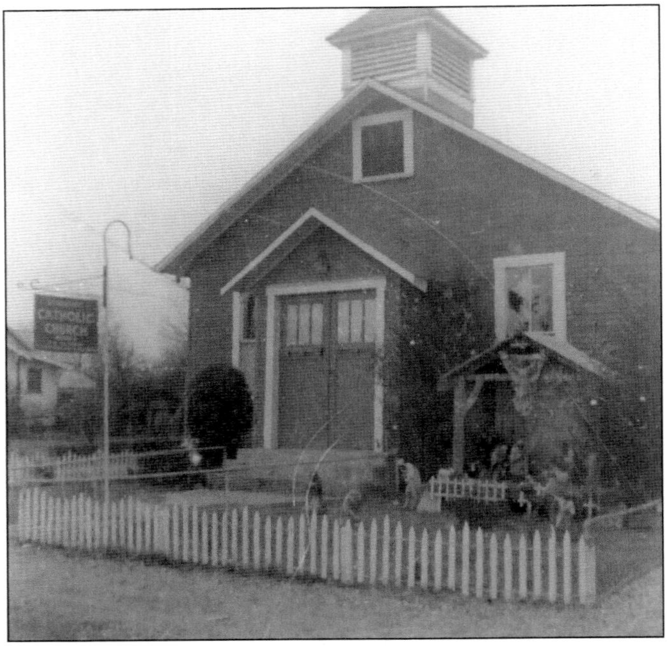

St. John's Colored Catholic Church was started in 1943 as a mission of the Franciscan order by Fr. Angelus Schaffer. Each summer, Benedictine sisters from St. Scholastica in Fort Smith taught two-week classes in Catholicism. In 1963, St. John's was folded into the congregation at Our Lady of the Lake Catholic Church. (Both, courtesy of Libby Borgognoni.)

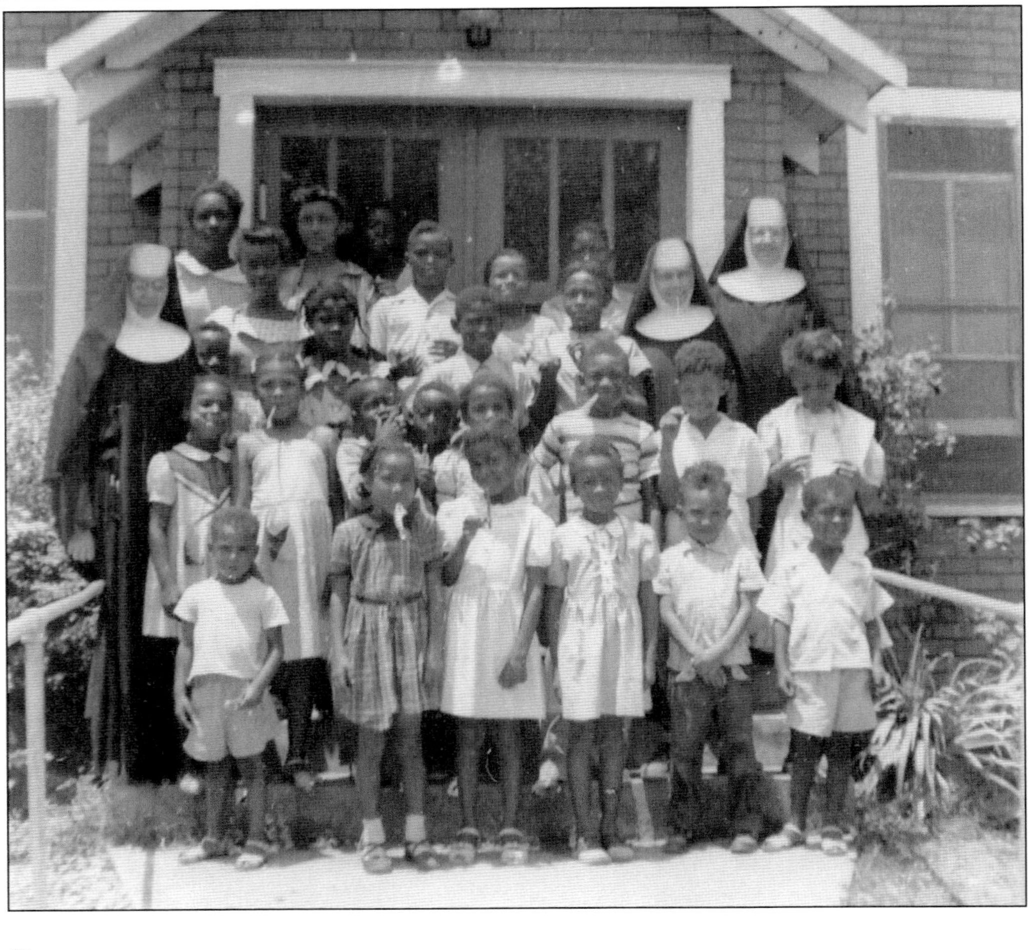

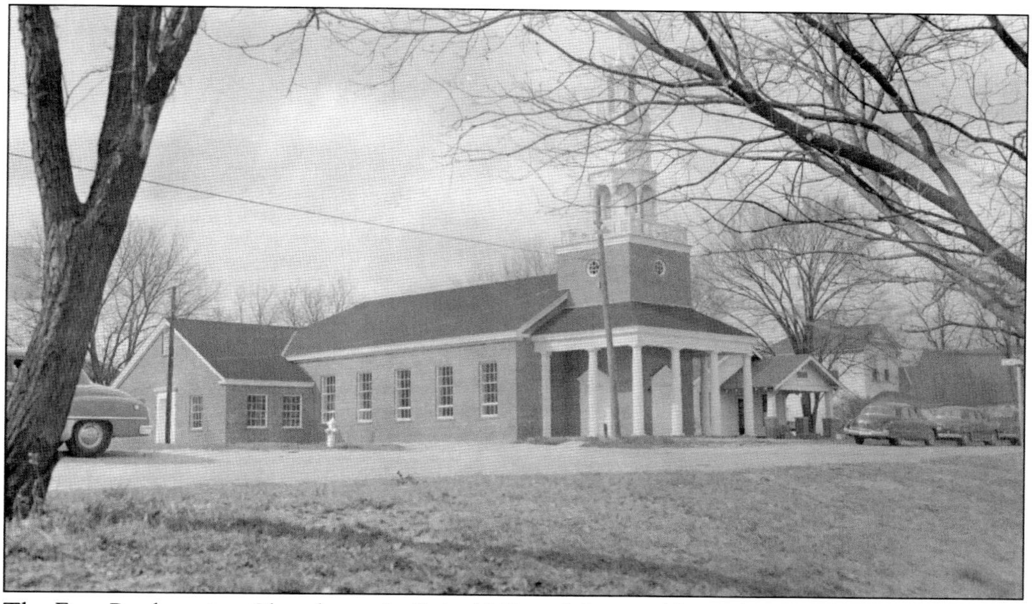

The First Presbyterian Church was built in 1949 and designed by architect John Parks Almand of Little Rock. First recognized in 1899 by the Presbyterian Church, the original church building was on Main Street. By 1917, the congregation had moved to North Lakeshore Drive. A second Presbyterian church, Smith's Chapel, held services between 1934 and 1954. (Courtesy of the Museum of Chicot County.)

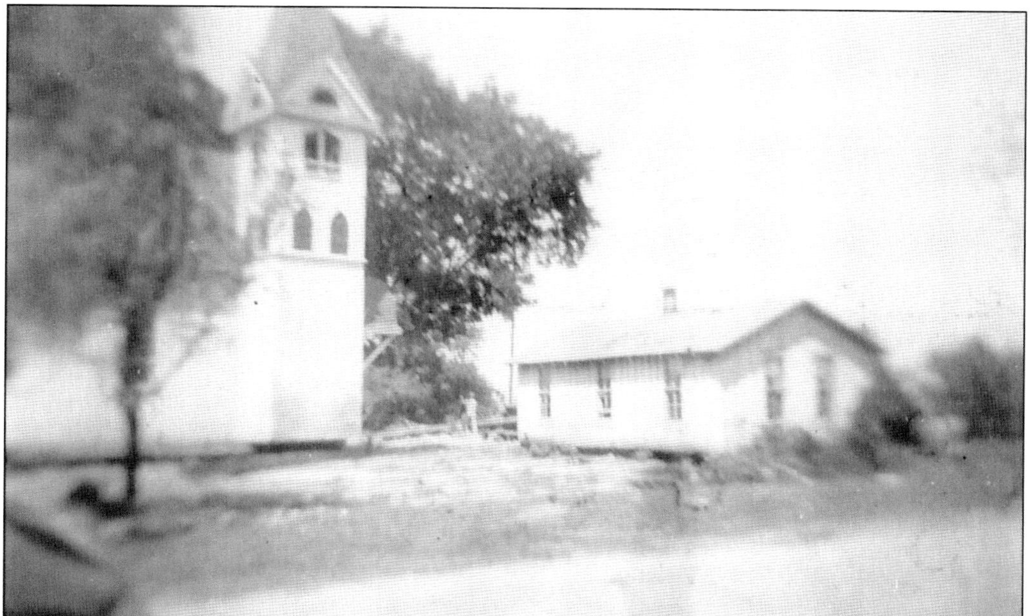

The Lakeside Methodist Church was organized in 1884 by Elenor Avent. Avent carried the church for many years, holding services in her home and convincing her son-in-law Gen. D.H. Reynolds to donate land for the church building. The first structure, 34 by 40 feet with a bell tower, was built in 1891. In 1900, the church added a three-room frame parsonage. Both buildings can be seen in this photograph from about 1946. (Courtesy of the Bill and Jeanine Sessions Collection, Lakeport Plantation.)

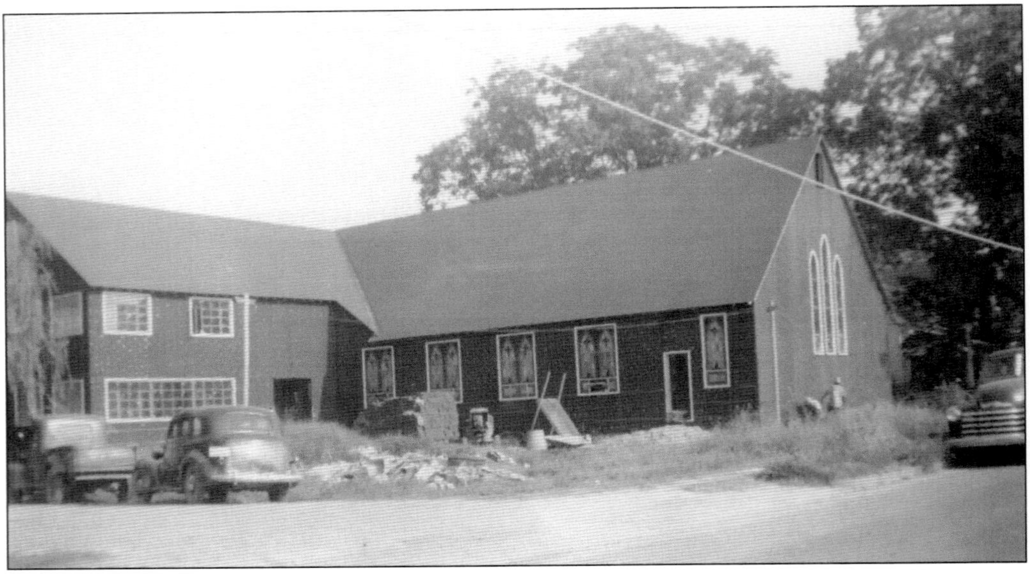

In 1946, Rev. Ralph Clayton led the Lakeside Methodist Church to construct a new sanctuary. As construction began, the 1891 structure was moved and torn down. This photograph shows construction around 1948. Designed by Reverend Clayton, the building was dedicated on January 9, 1949. (Courtesy of the Bill and Jeanine Sessions Collection, Lakeport Plantation.)

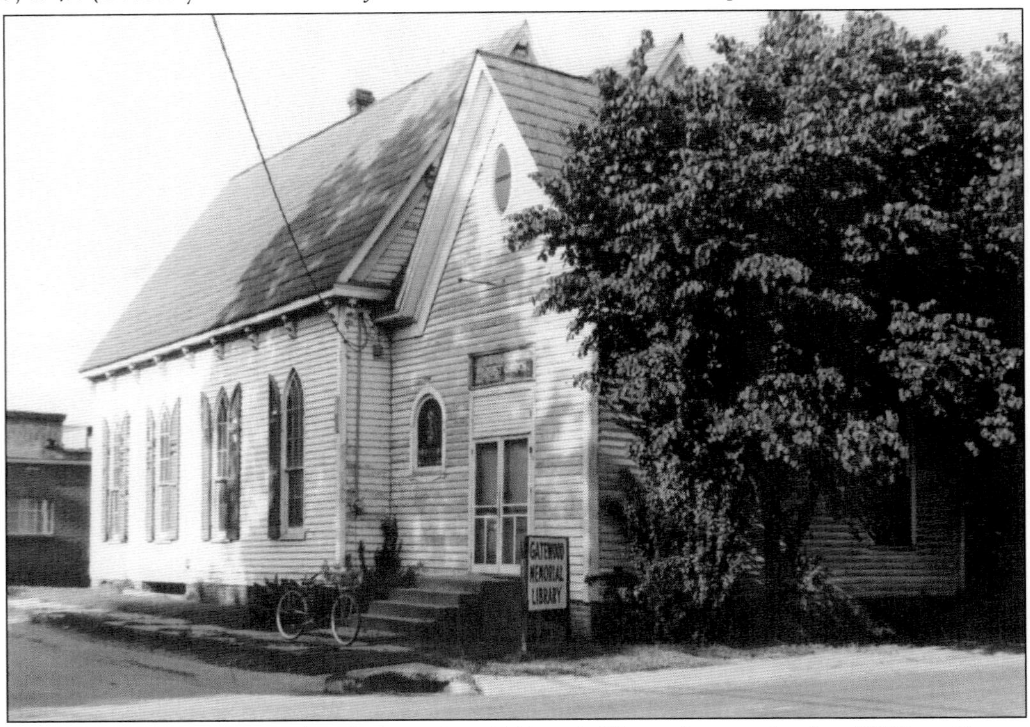

The Lake Village Baptist Church formed in 1861 with 22 members under Rev. William Green. Meeting first in the Chicot County Courthouse, the church built its first building in 1871 under Rev. George B. Eager. After the church moved to a new building in 1931, the structure housed the Gatewood Memorial Library, pictured here around 1945. (Courtesy of Lake Village Public Library.)

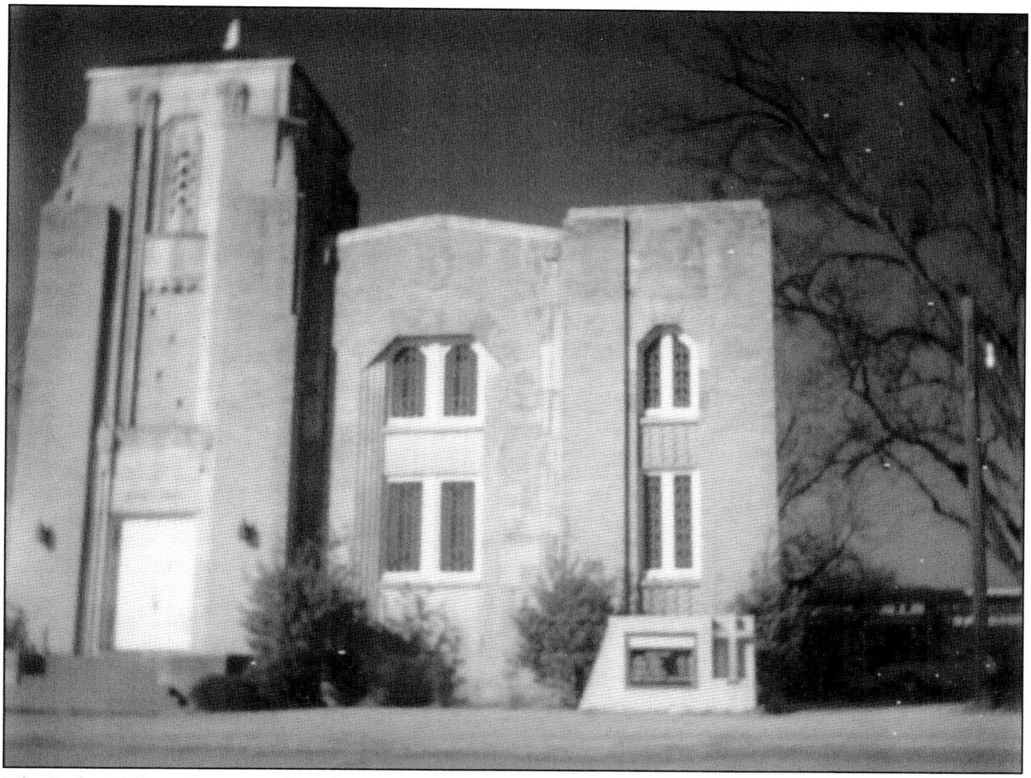

The Lake Village Baptist Church, seen here in 1969, was erected in 1931. Noah Webster Overstreet, a Jackson, Mississippi–based architect, designed the church, and Henry Price Chastang constructed the building. (Courtesy of Lake Village Public Library.)

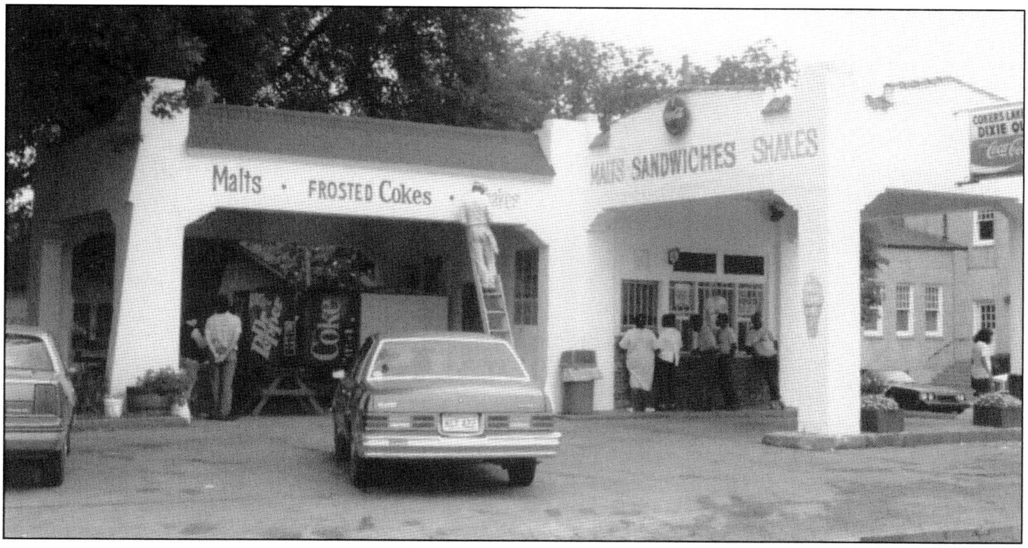

Coker's Lakeside Dixie Queen (pictured here in 1990) was a popular hangout serving all-American hamburgers and ice cream from 1953 through the 1990s. Originally a service station built in the Mission Revival style around 1935, the building was demolished in 2011, leaving a hole along Lakeshore Drive between the 1911 Lake Shore Hotel and the 1931 First Baptist Church. (Courtesy of the Arkansas Historic Preservation Program.)

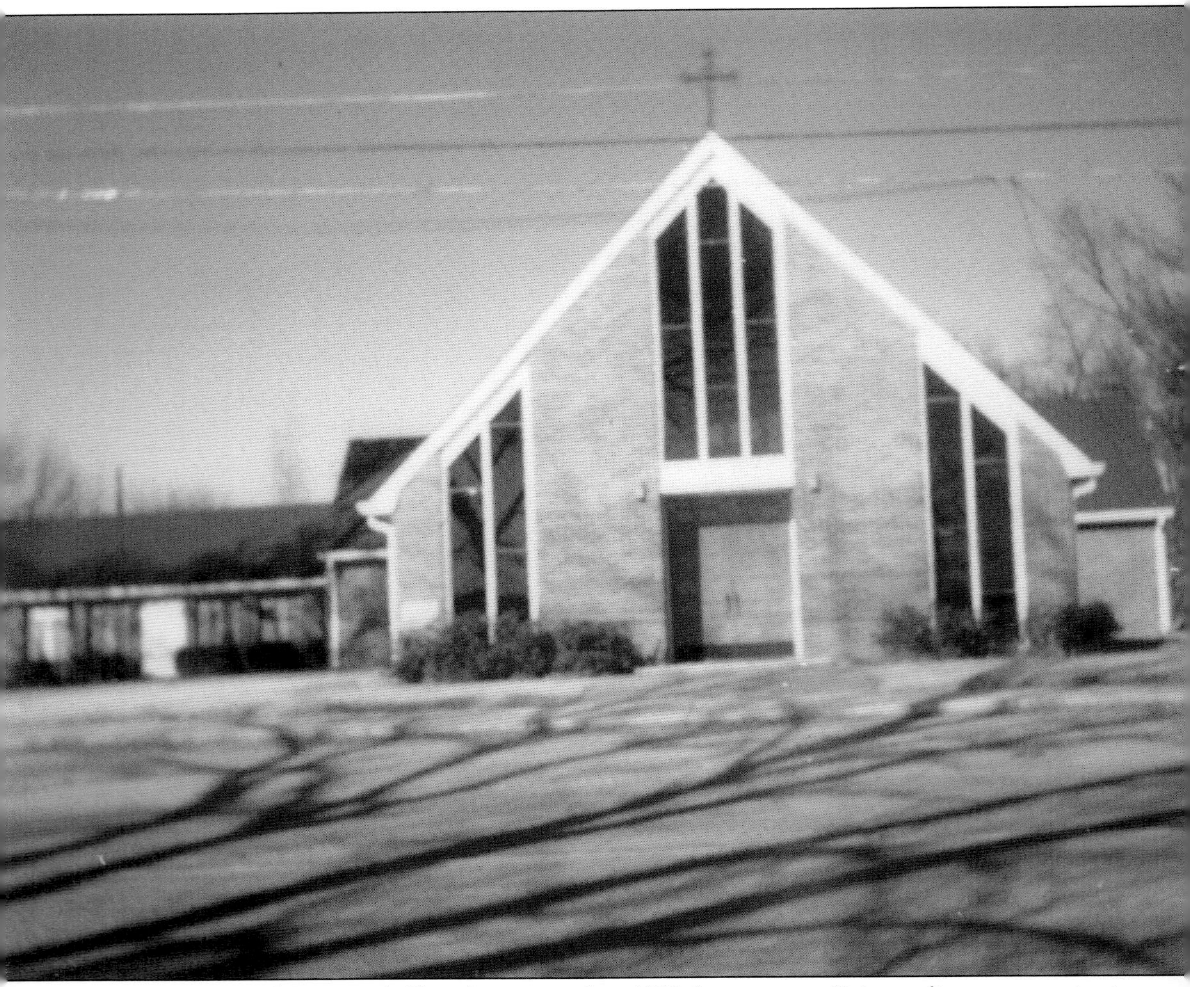

The Emmanuel Episcopal Church organized in 1901; however, an Episcopalian community in Chicot County grew from some of the earliest settlers, which included the Gaines, Davies, and Chapman families. The Episcopal church acquired land from John and Nancy Sumner in 1858 and finished construction on a church building in 1870. Still without fulltime clergy, the congregation suffered a setback around 1890 when it lost its church building. In 1901, Emmanuel claimed its first full-time minister, Rev. J.W. Barker, and built a Gothic Revival church. The new church seated 150 and was finished and furnished in natural pine. The current home of Emmanuel, photographed here in 1969, was constructed in 1964. (Courtesy of Lake Village Public Library.)

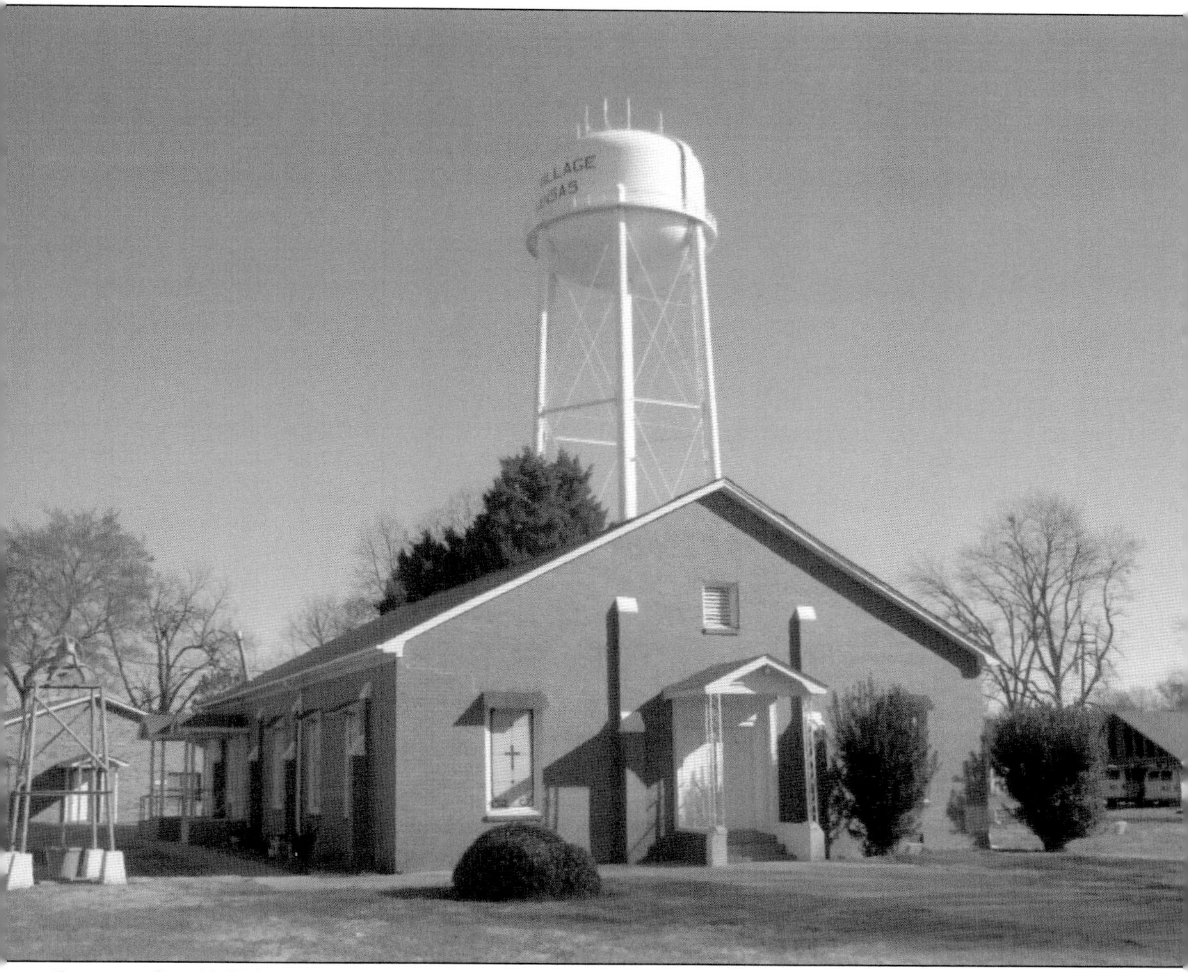

Organized in 1860, New Hope Missionary Baptist Church is one of the oldest African American churches in Arkansas. With permission, Jim Kelley, a slave, began the church at its current location. In 1873, the church officially acquired the deed to the land from William and Julia Streett. Having outgrown the original building by 1941, the church enlarged it; in 1959, it was encased in brick. The cemetery on the church grounds, noted for a number of fraternal markers, was listed in the National Register of Historic Places in 1992 as a "historic resource directly associated with the historic black community within Lake Village" during the early 20th century. (Courtesy of Lakeport Plantation.)

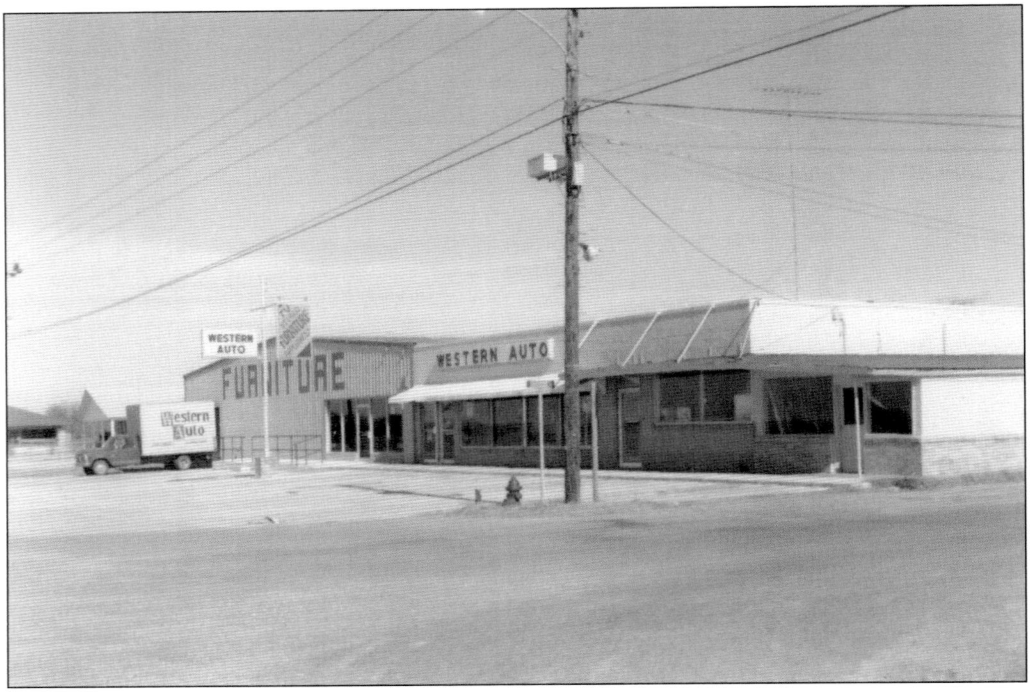

Bob and Patricia Reinhardt opened the Western Auto store in Lake Village in June 1970. Following a fire in May 1981, the Reinhardts rebuilt their business and reopened that September. Since 1982, the store has been a True Value Hardware selling everything from appliances to pencils. (Both, courtesy of Bob and Patricia Reinhardt.)

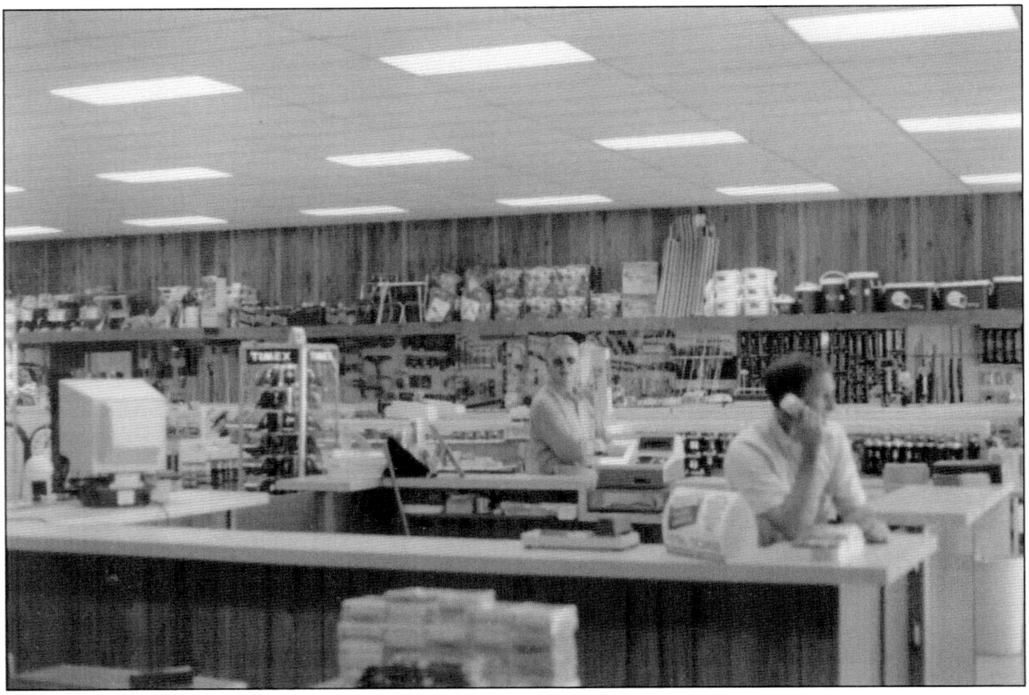

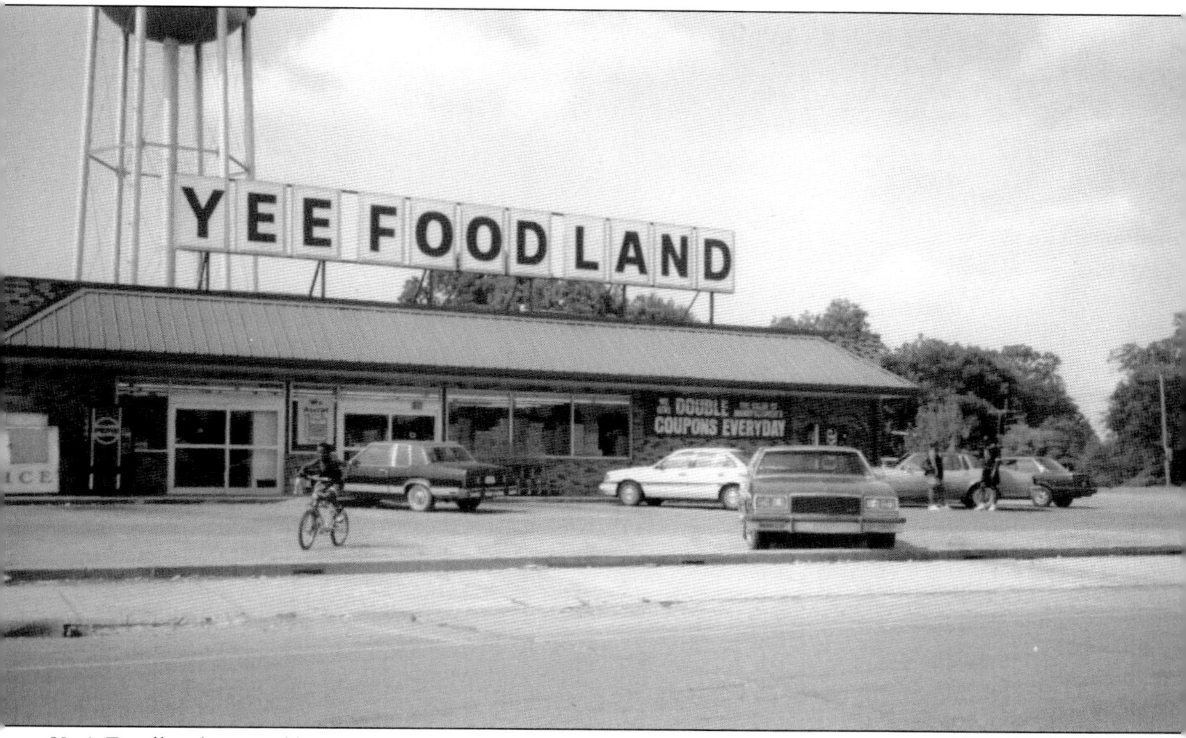

Yee's Foodland, started by Tin Bow and Shuey Gene Yee about 1959, was the last of many Chinese grocery stores in Lake Village. Tin Bow arrived in the United States about 1940 and worked at relatives' grocery stores in Dermott and Dumas. He briefly returned to China and married Shuey Gene. As early as 1910, there were four Lake Village grocery stores operated by men native to China. In the 1920s and 1930s, Yum Gee and his family owned the N.G. Food Market. (Courtesy of Libby Borgognoni.)

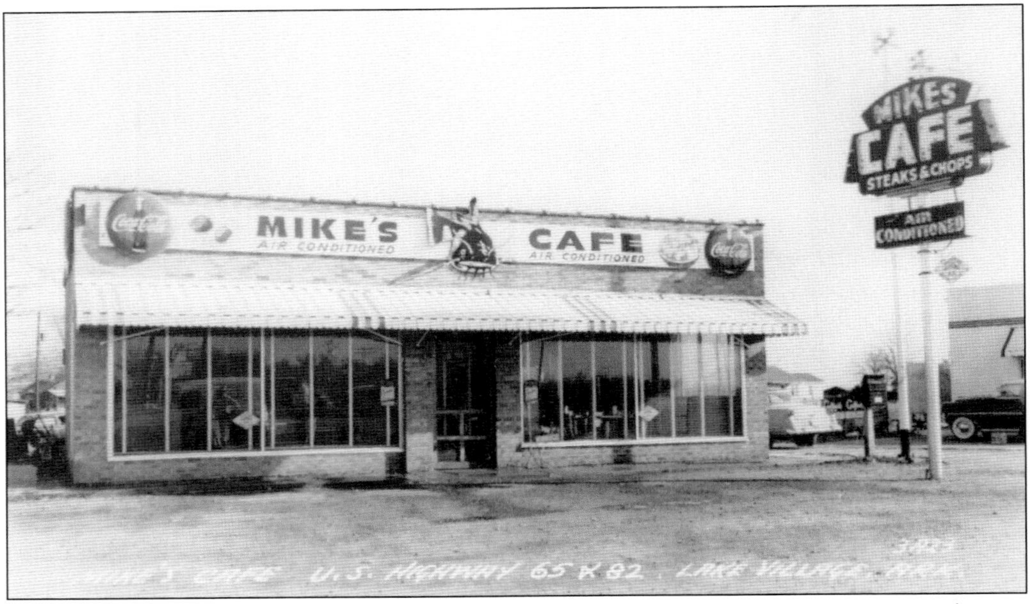

Mike's Cafe was a staple of Southern and Italian food in Lake Village from 1946 until 1998. Marino "Mike" Pesaresi immigrated from Italy to Bridgeport, Connecticut, in 1912. By January 1920, he met and married Mary Reginelli at the Sunnyside Plantation. Pesaresi farmed for a few years before he started Mike's Cafe on Main Street in 1946. The restaurant soon moved near the train depot and finally to the highway in 1952. (Courtesy of Mike Pesaresi Jr.)

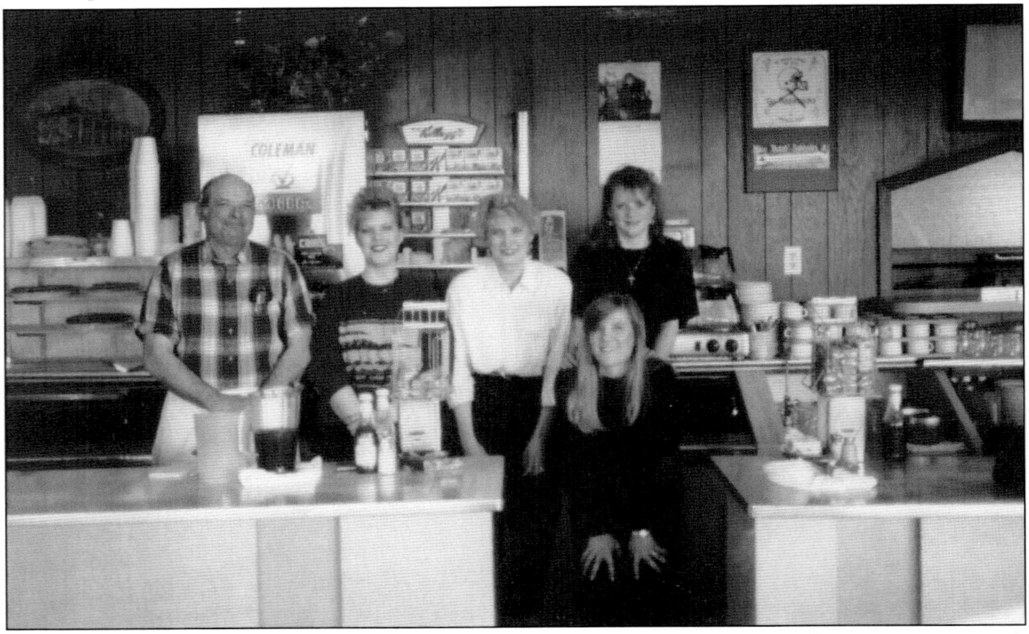

Mike Pesaresi Jr. took over Mike's Cafe from his father starting in 1957. After a stint as a cook in the National Guard, he returned to the café. The restaurant was known for its coconut and chocolate pies, making a dozen every day. Mike's Cafe closed in 1998, but Mike is still known to cook up some of the best spaghetti in Chicot County. Pictured here around 1990 are staff members, from left to right, Mike Jr., Terry McAffery, Ellen Lou, Dawn Ann Ogelvie, and Terry Scarborough. (Courtesy of Mike Pesaresi Jr.)

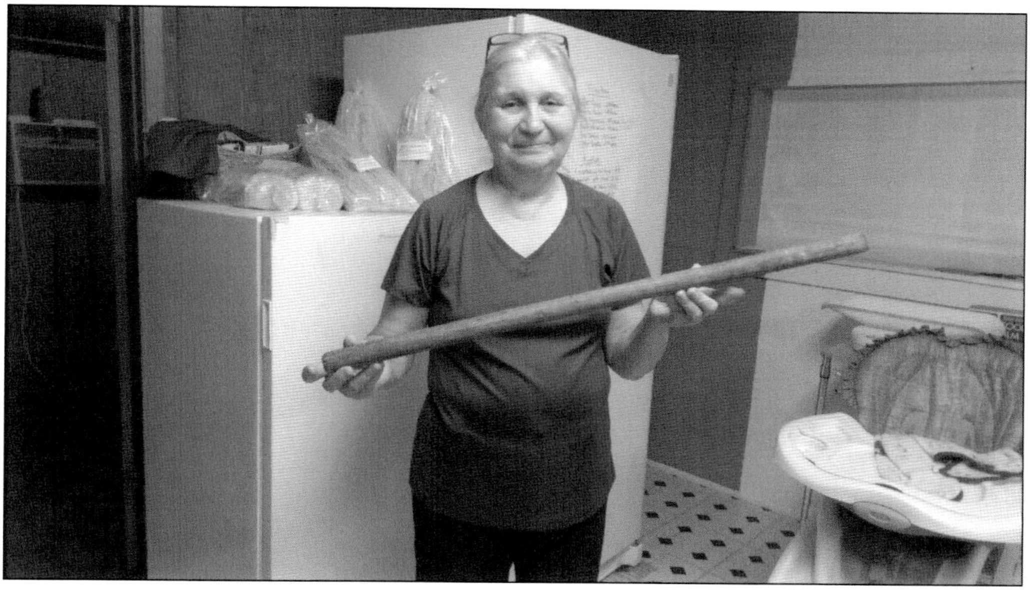

Regina Moyer opened Regina's Pasta Shop in 2014 after cooking from her home for 20 years. Moyer cooks traditional homemade Italian food like meatballs, sauces, and tortellini. She still has her mother's rolling pin made from an old broomstick by her father, Angelo DeAngelo, who arrived in the United States from Italy in 1906 at 18 months old. (Both, courtesy of Lakeport Plantation.)

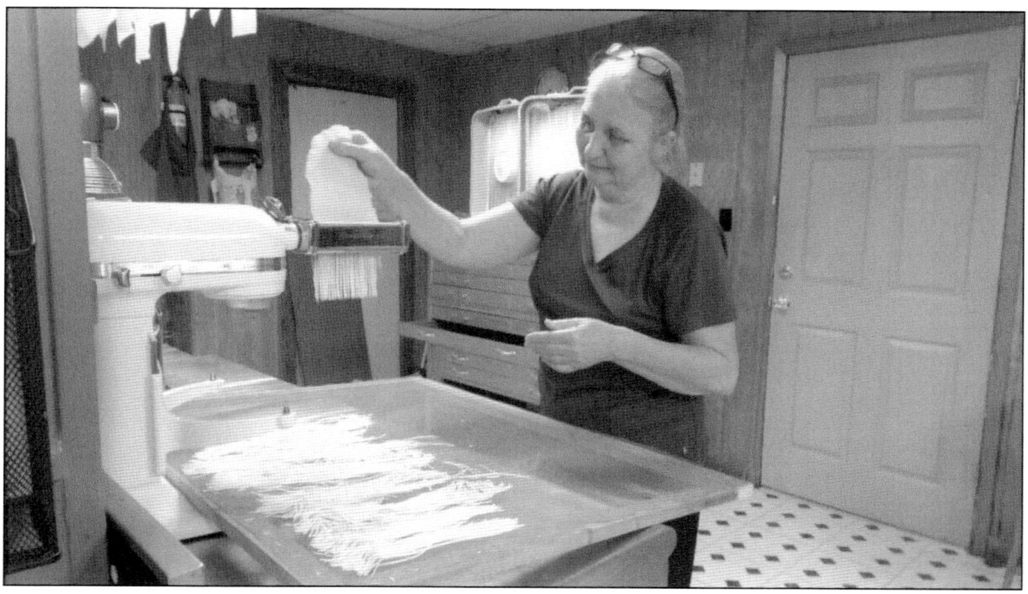

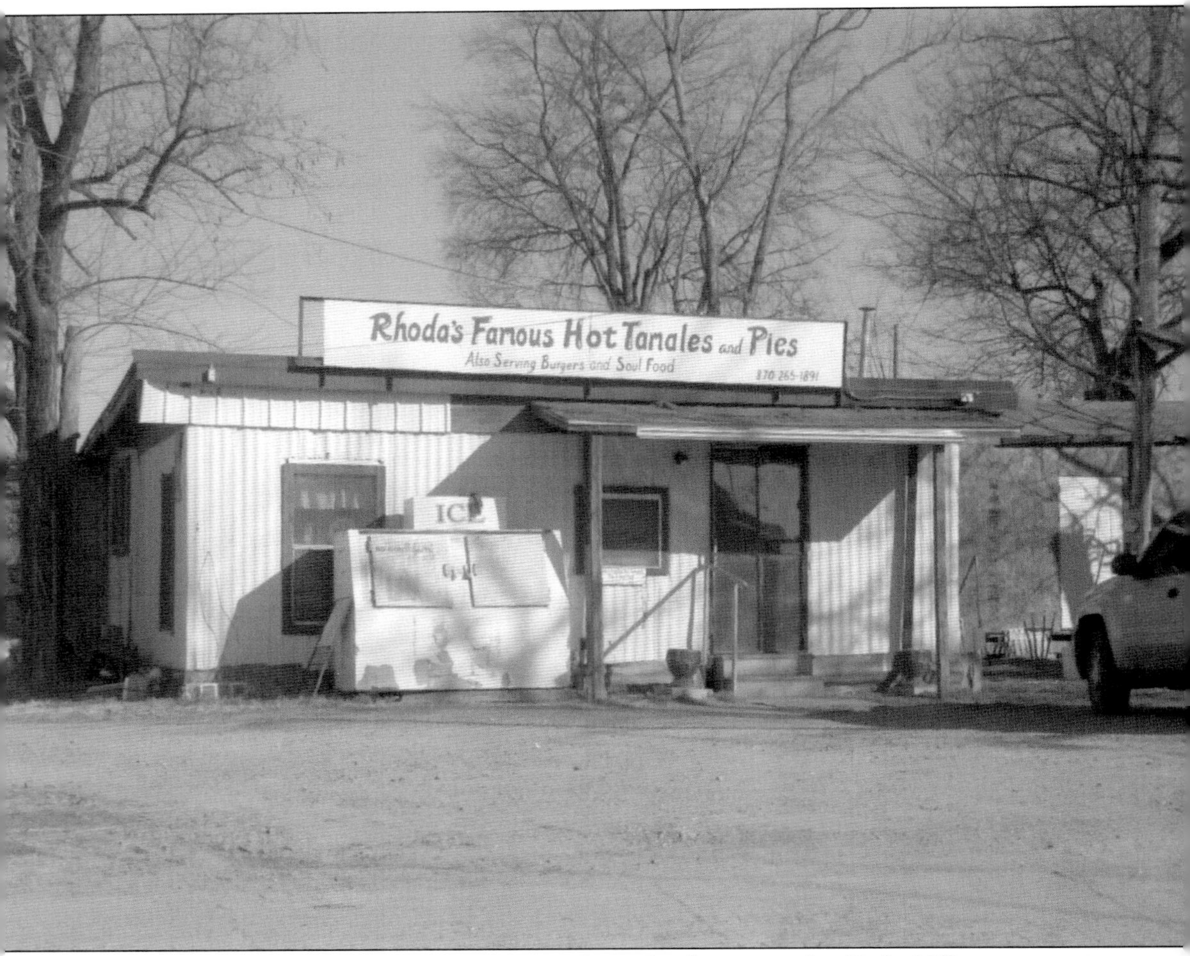

Rhoda's Famous Hot Tamales on St. Mary's Street has been a staple of Lake Village cuisine since the early 1980s. Rhoda Adams began cooking pies from her home in the early 1970s for her church. Later, with encouragement from her husband, James, and an aunt, she started cooking Delta-style hot tamales. (Courtesy of Lakeport Plantation.)

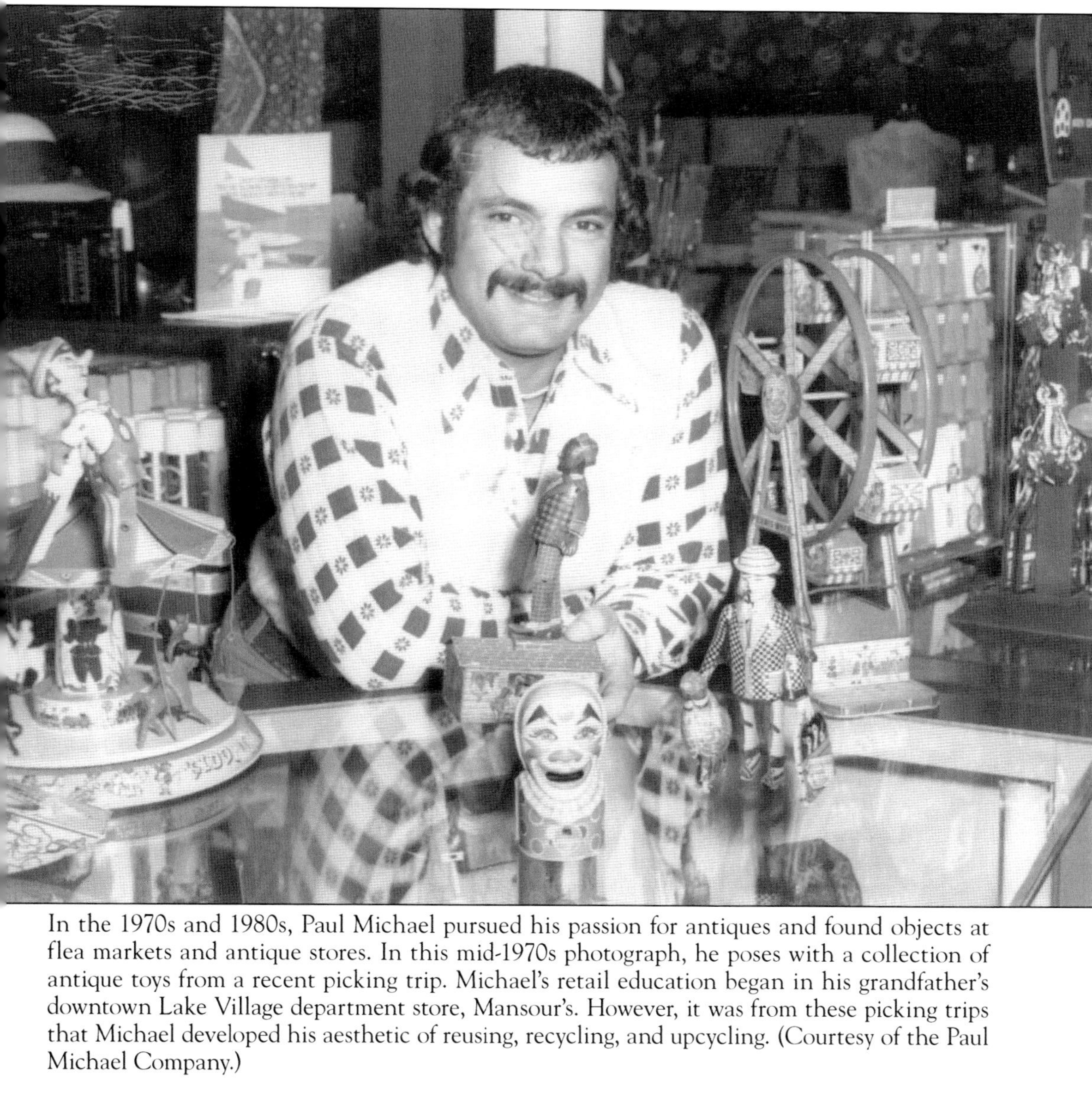

In the 1970s and 1980s, Paul Michael pursued his passion for antiques and found objects at flea markets and antique stores. In this mid-1970s photograph, he poses with a collection of antique toys from a recent picking trip. Michael's retail education began in his grandfather's downtown Lake Village department store, Mansour's. However, it was from these picking trips that Michael developed his aesthetic of reusing, recycling, and upcycling. (Courtesy of the Paul Michael Company.)

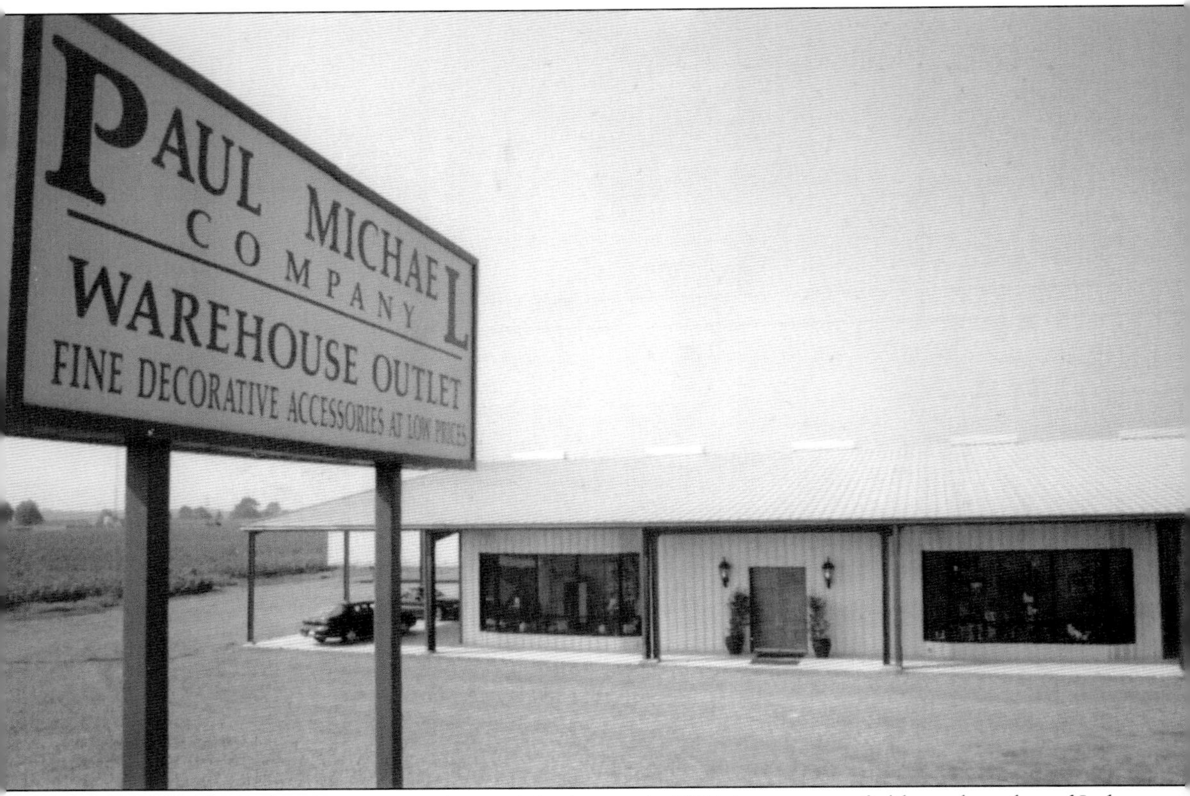

Paul Michael Company opened its original store in 1993 in a cotton field on the edge of Lake Village. Having evolved out of a wholesale jewelry business in downtown, the 36,000-square-foot home-decor store sells furniture and other collections. The company also has a workshop in Dermott that manufactures (or upcycles) furniture and other products. Between 2003 and 2009, the company expanded with three new locations: Monroe, Louisiana; Canton, Texas; and Lafayette, Louisiana. (Courtesy of Paul Michael Company.)

Three

Dermott

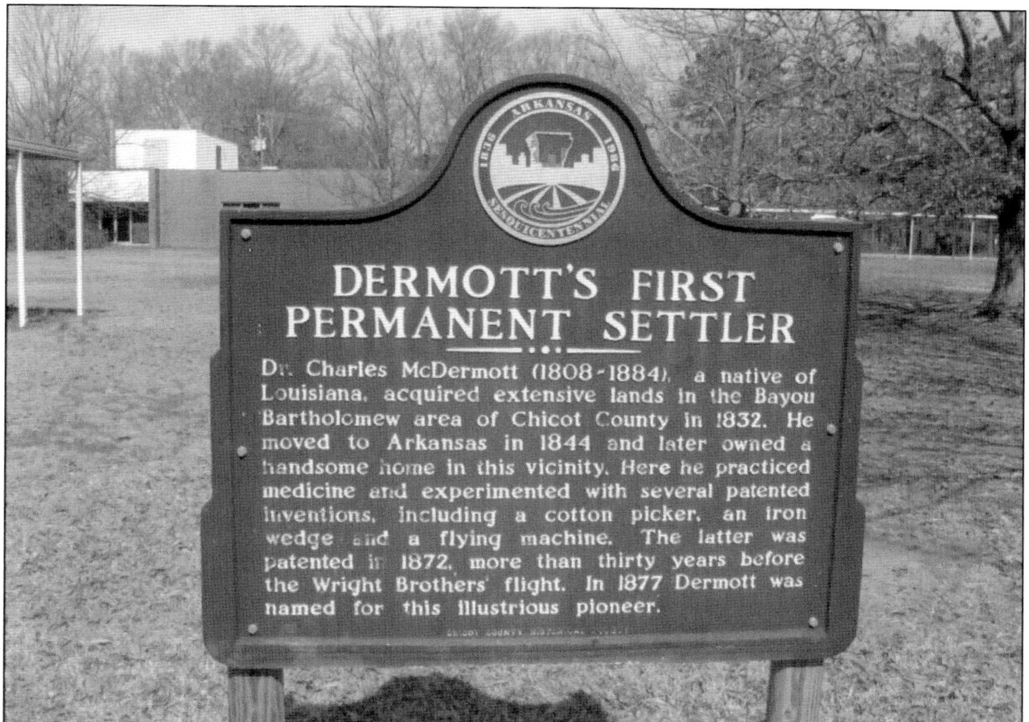

Charles McDermott (1808–1884) arrived in the county from Louisiana around 1844, about a decade after his brother Edward; both settled near Bayou Bartholomew. Travelers headed west from Gaines Landing in the 1850s knew to stop at the McDermott plantation, which boasted a 16-room house named "Bois d'Arc." Following the war, Charles, an avowed and unrepentant secessionist, fled with his family to British Honduras, but returned to his Chicot County plantation by 1870. Also an inventor with several patents, he is best remembered for his flying machine, patented in 1872. (Courtesy of Lakeport Plantation.)

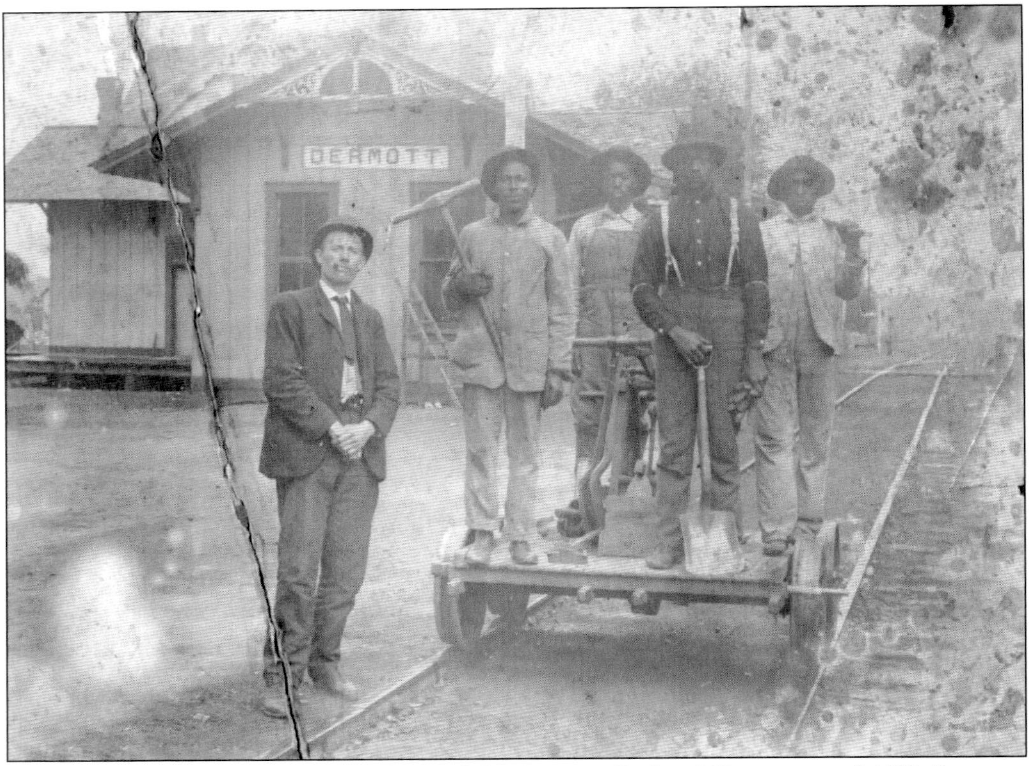

Members of a section crew pose in front of the Dermott Railroad Depot around 1910. Foreman Alva Lee Lusk (left), and his crew traveled along a section of the railroad making repairs. A downtown fire in February 1913 halted construction on a new brick depot. It was completed later in 1913 and razed in 1973. (Courtesy of Nancy and Robert Jolly.)

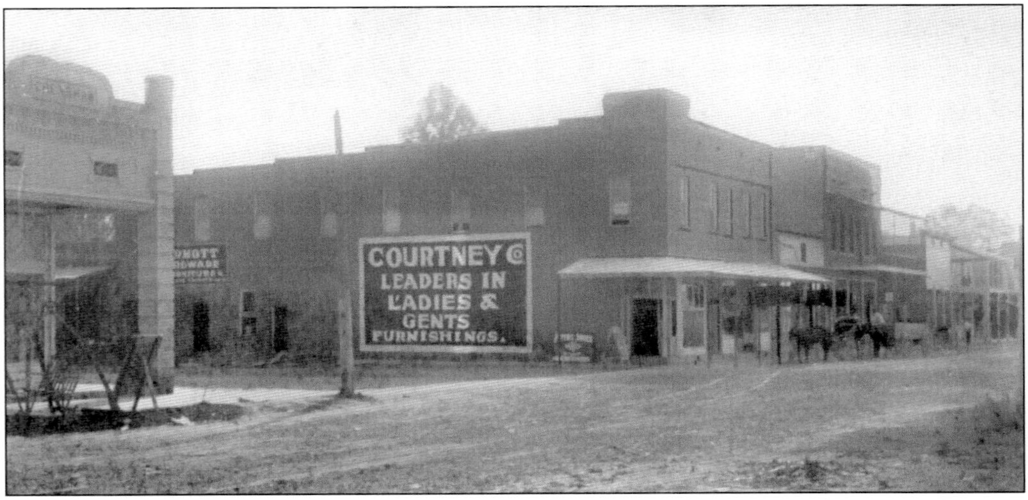

In the early 20th century, many businesses fronting the railroad sprang up along Iowa Avenue. In this photograph from about 1914 are the Courtney Dry Goods and Clothing store and the Crenshaw Building, then serving as a variety or "racket store." Anna Crenshaw operated a drugstore at the location as early as 1906. Henry E. Courtney owned a butcher and grocery store at the location from around 1904 until 1912, when the family expanded into dry goods. (Courtesy of Lakeport Plantation.)

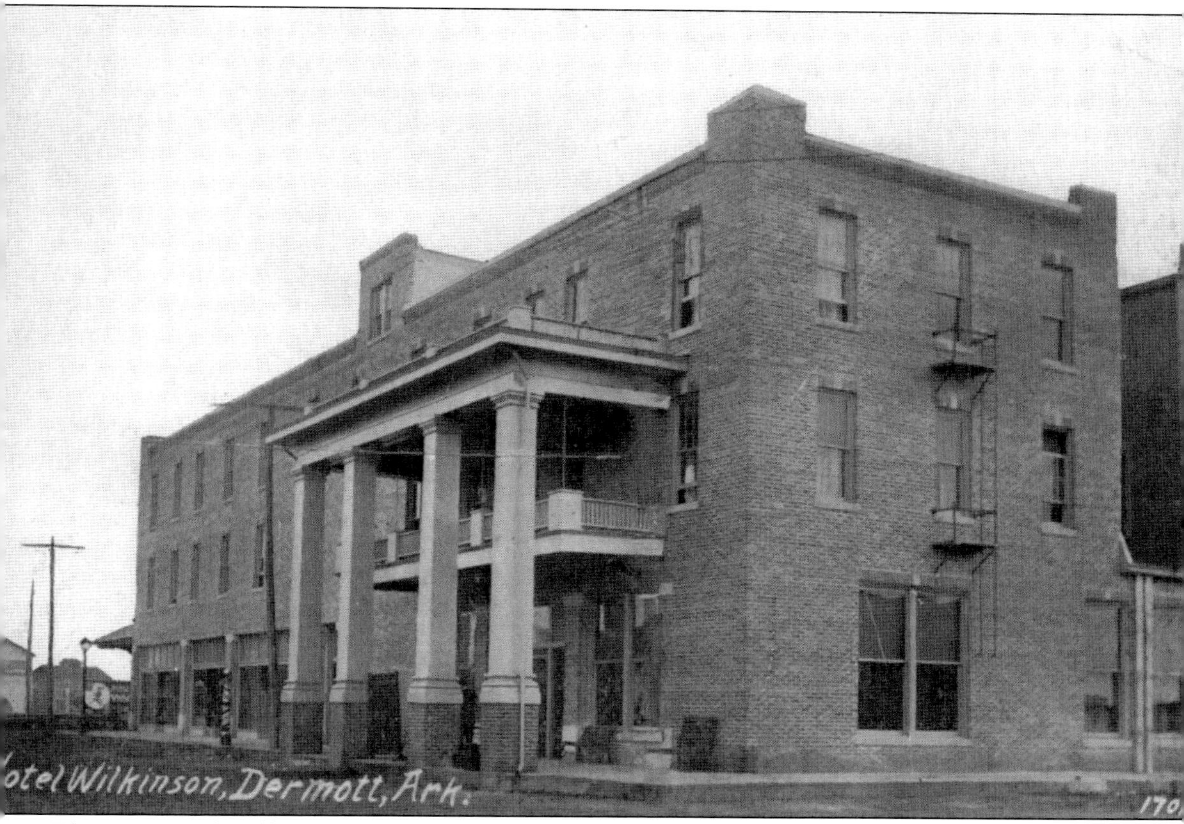

The New Hotel Wilkinson, pictured here around 1915, was built following a devastating fire in February 1913 that destroyed several businesses and the unfinished brick railroad station. In 1906, the Hotel Wilkinson, operated by T.A. Wilkinson at the corner of Iowa Avenue and Pythian (later Arkansas) Street, advertised as the "Headquarters for Commercial Men." "Fine rooms" ran $2 per day and included electric lights. At the nearby Hotel Bruce, Maude Skipper and Ellen Denson offered the same rates and amenities, plus "Fine Baths—Hot and Cold Water." The Reed House, also nearby on Iowa Street, offered accommodations for African American travelers in 1908. (Courtesy of the Butler Center for Arkansas Studies, Central Arkansas Library System.)

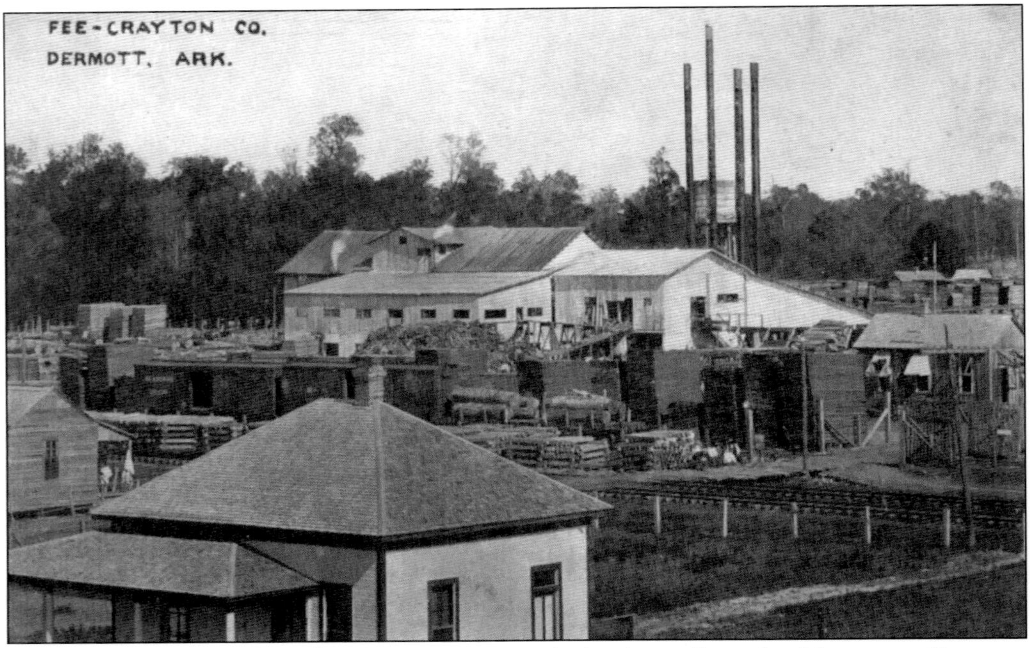

Fee-Crayton Hardwood Lumber Company operated a lumber mill north of downtown Dermott. In 1908, the mill could produce 22,000 board feet per day. By 1915, about when this photograph was taken, Fee-Crayton kept an average of three million board feet of lumber in its yard. (Courtesy of the Butler Center for Arkansas Studies, Central Arkansas Library System.)

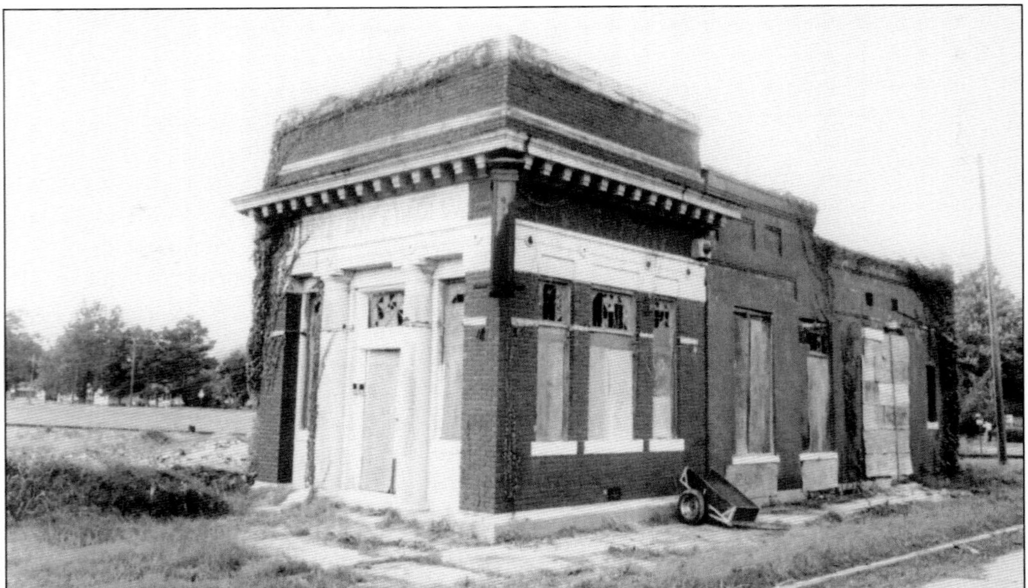

Dermott Bank & Trust was incorporated on December 20, 1910, and constructed this Classical Revival structure. In 1914, H. Thane served as bank president and E.P. Remley as vice president. The bank failed on December 1921 and reorganized the next year. After another failure during the Great Depression, the building was used as a building-supply store and warehouse. It was listed in the National Register of Historic Places in 1994, but unfortunately has been torn down. (Courtesy of the Arkansas Historic Preservation Program.)

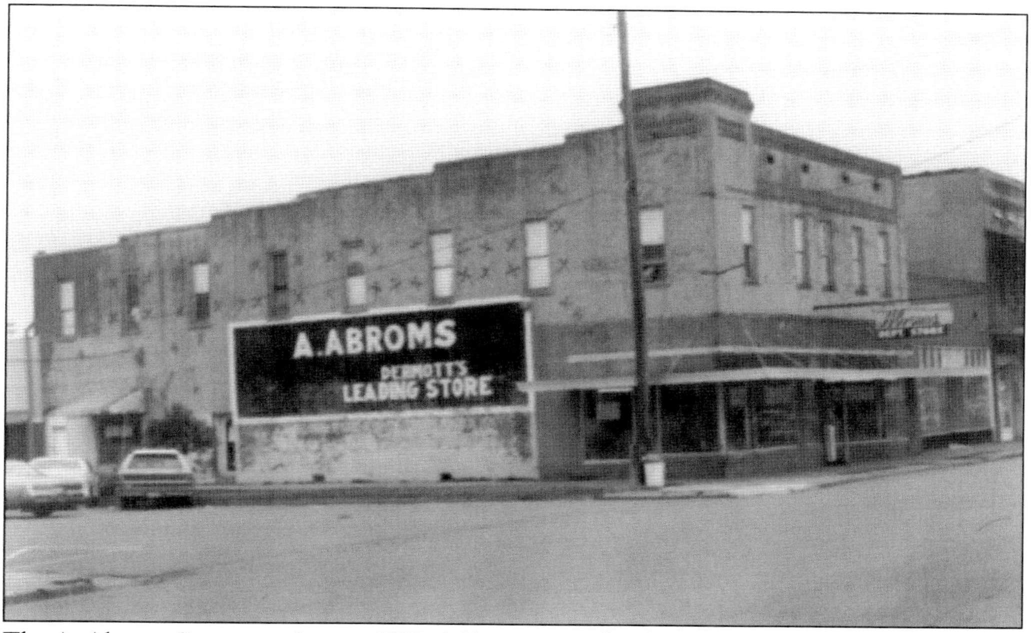

The A. Abroms Store, seen here in 1979, did business in the old Courtney building. Abe Abroms, a Jewish merchant, arrived in Dermott around 1920 from Kentucky via Shaw, Mississippi. Abroms retired in 1972 and sold the business to his niece DeVera and her husband, Joe Goldstein. In later years, the Goldsteins' daughter Margie and her husband, Barry Brunner, took over the operation. (Courtesy of the Arkansas Historic Preservation Program.)

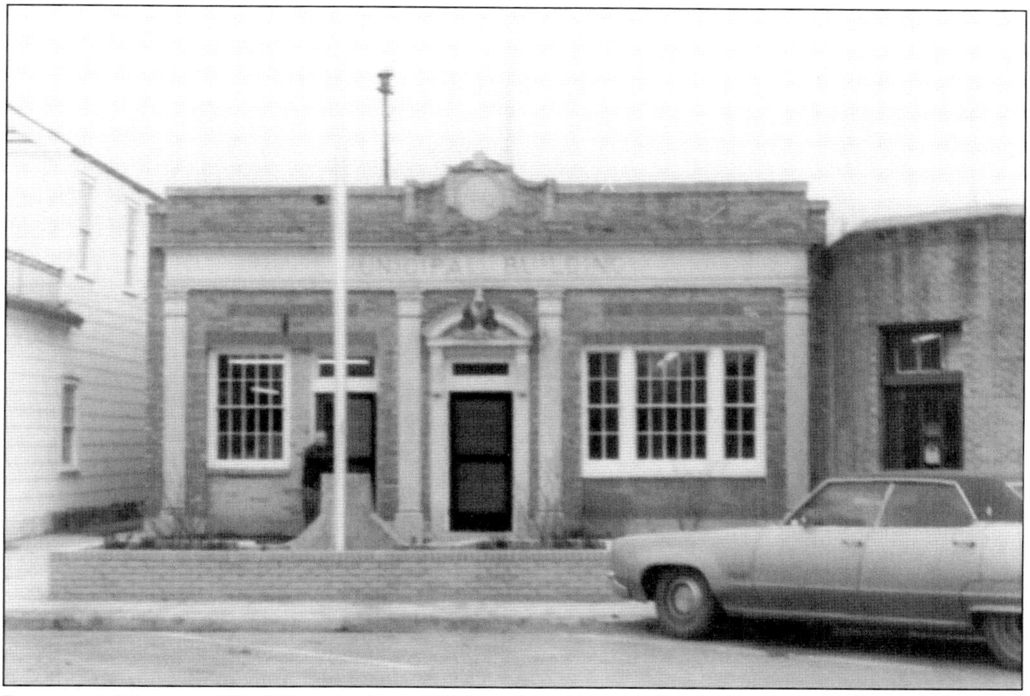

Dermott's Municipal Building, built in 1928 in the Classical Revival style, stands apart from its commercial neighbors. The building housed city offices until 2004 and now holds the police department. (Courtesy of the Arkansas Historic Preservation Program.)

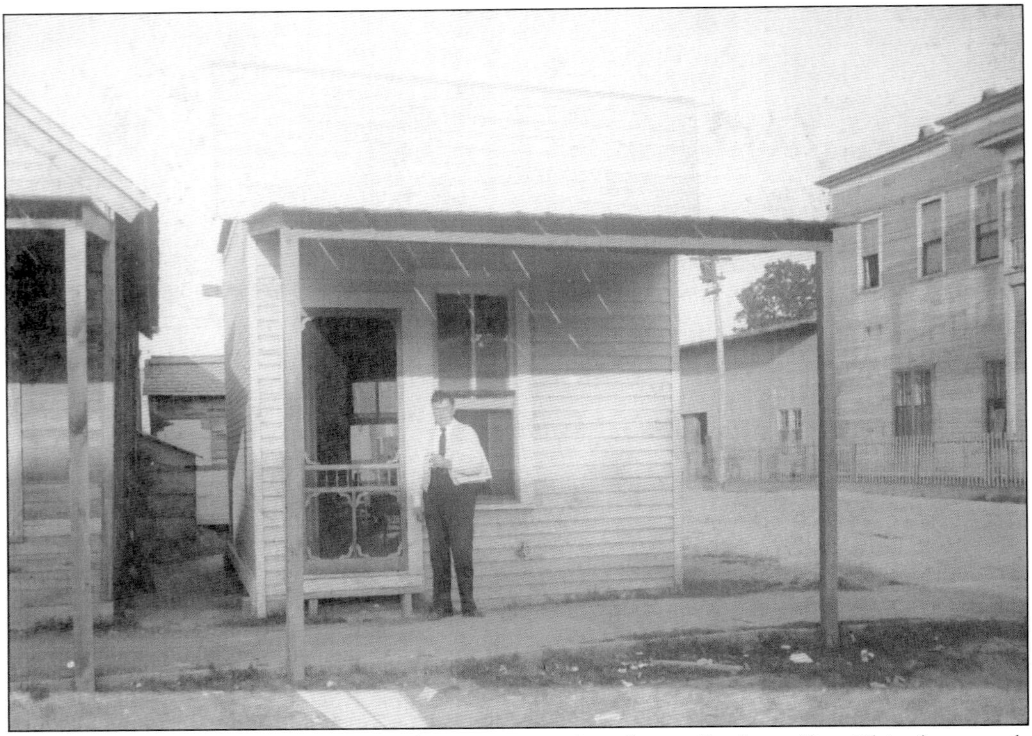

Ernest G. Hammock, a former mayor of Dermott, stands in front of his law office. This photograph was taken before the 1912 fire that consumed several downtown businesses. (Courtesy of Dermott Historical Museum.)

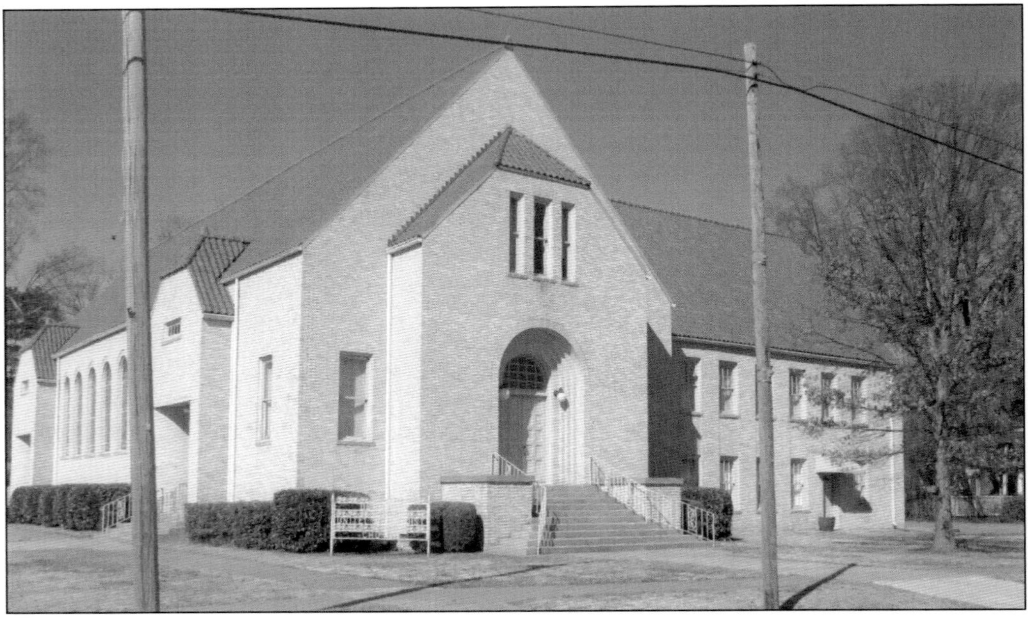

The Dermott Methodist Church was founded by John Crenshaw and Hattie Peddicord in 1886. Three denominations shared a Union church building on Freeman Street in the 1880s and 1890s. The Methodists moved to their current location at Main and Peddicord Streets in 1913. The present building was erected in 1925. (Courtesy of Lakeport Plantation.)

The Dermott Presbyterian Church began in 1868 as the New Bethany Church. Founding members Charles McDermott and William Daniels had previously been members of the Monticello Presbyterian Church. In 1894, the church changed its name to Dermott Presbyterian Church. A Gothic wood-frame structure was erected around 1899 and subsequently remodeled in 1957 to its current appearance. (Courtesy of Lakeport Plantation.)

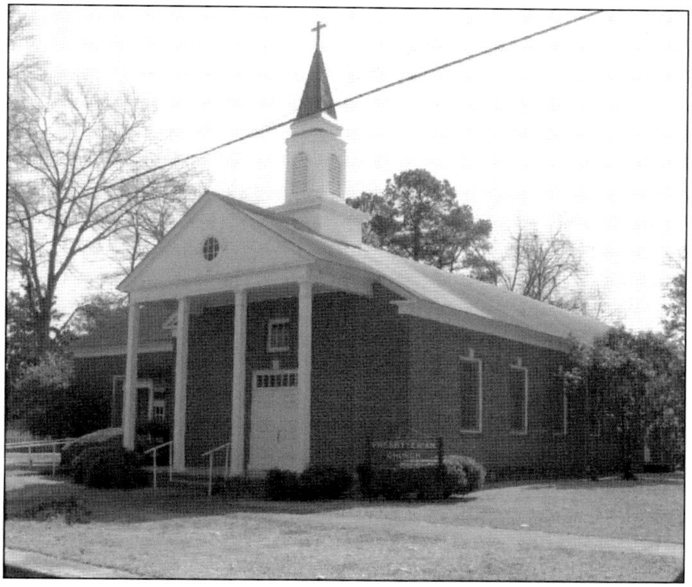

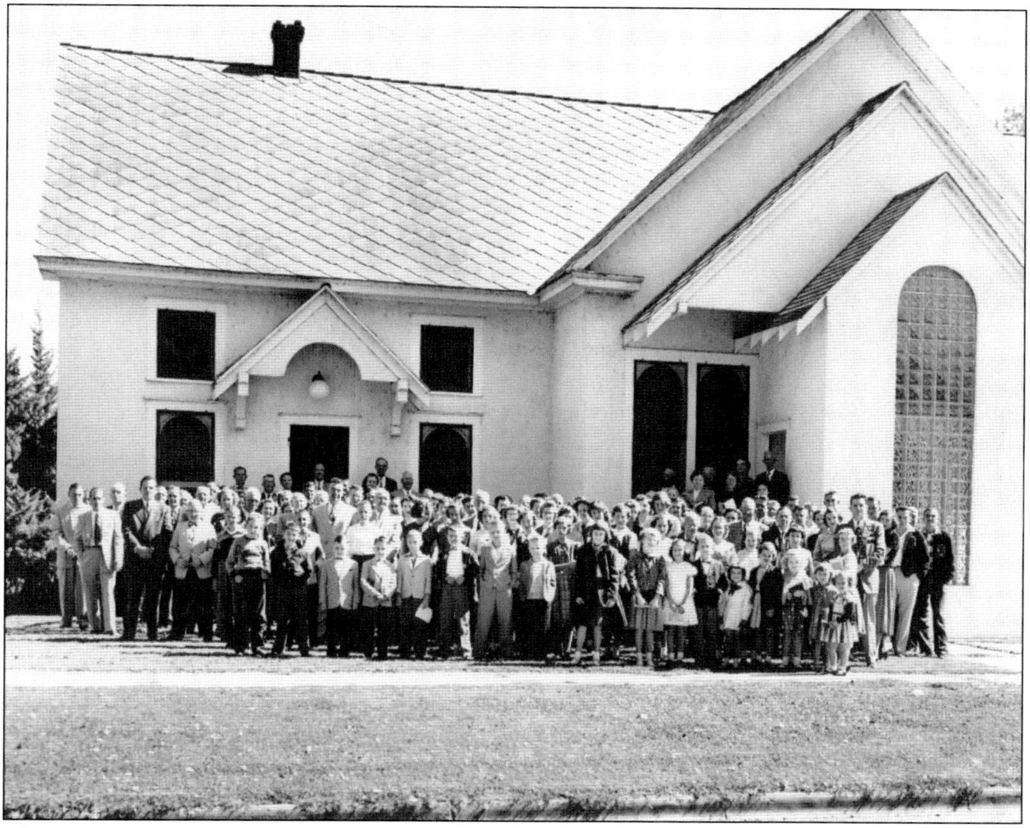

The Dermott Baptist Church was founded in 1904 by Rev. N.C. Denson, and a one-room house for worship was constructed in 1906. In the 1920s, the church moved locations and built the sanctuary pictured here in 1954. (Courtesy of Dermott Baptist Church.)

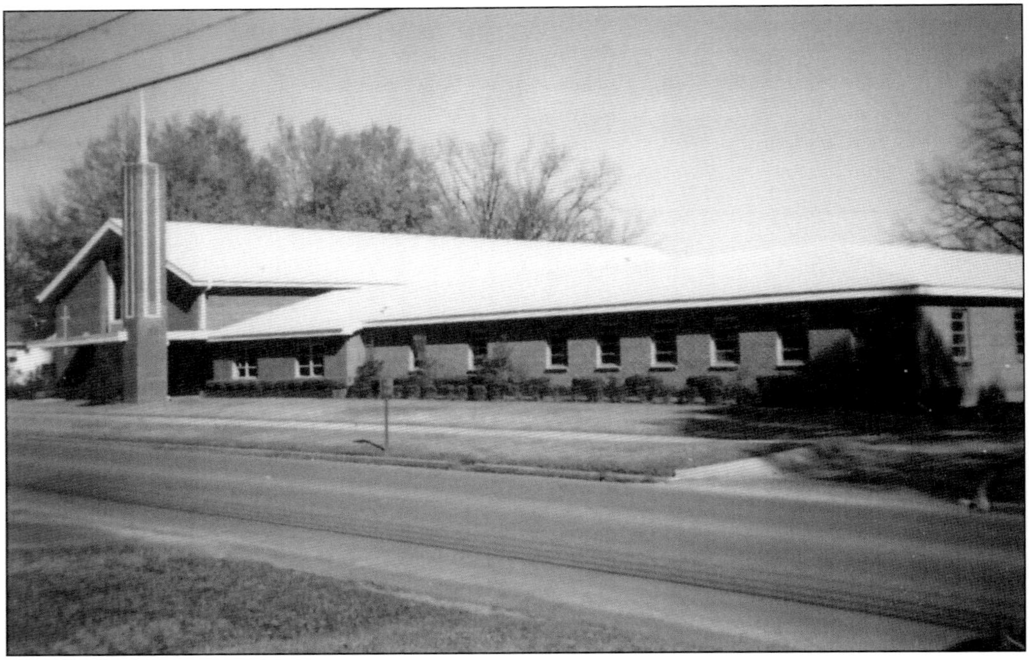

The new Dermott Baptist Church, designed by architect Marvin Frank of El Dorado, Arkansas, was dedicated in 1962. Described by the *Dermott News* as "contemporary," architectural historians today call this style Midcentury Modern. Its use of new materials, clean lines, and abstract stained glass reflect postwar optimism. (Courtesy of Dermott Baptist Church.)

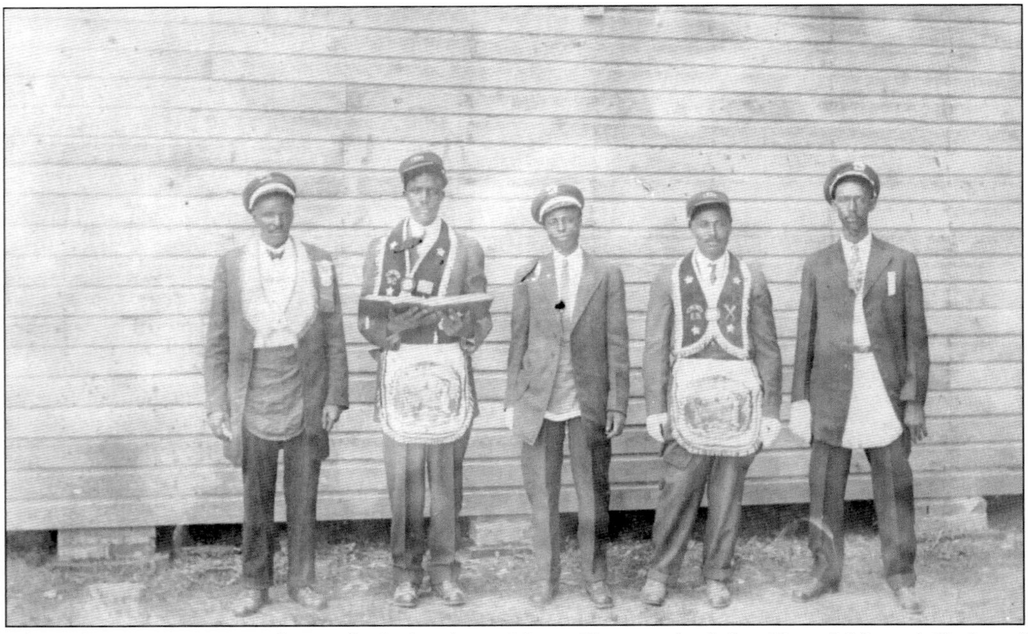

These five men are members of a lodge (possibly in Dermott) of the Grand United Order of Odd Fellows (GUOOF), an African American fraternal organization. The Chicot Lodge of the GUOOF was established in Lake Village in 1878. In 1915, about when this photograph was taken, members were eligible for a $300 death benefit. By 1920, over 13,000 black Arkansans were Odd Fellows members. (Courtesy of Dermott Historical Museum.)

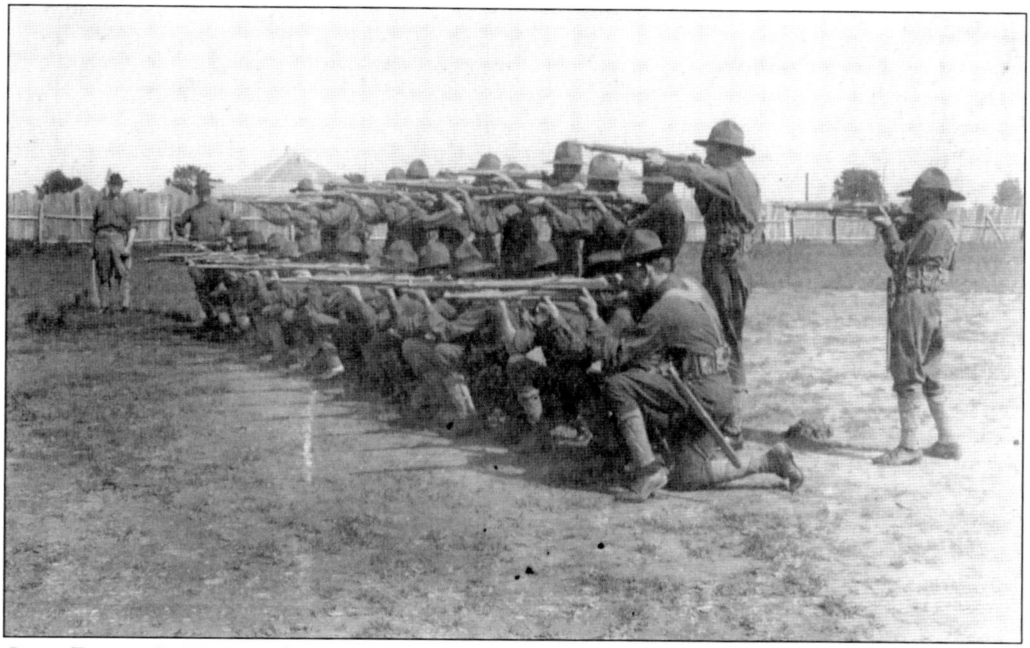

Capt. Ernest G. Hammock commanded Dermott's Company K, Arkansas National Guard, in this 1914 photograph. In preparation for entry into World War I, all Arkansas guardsmen were federalized and reported to Fort Roots in Little Rock. By 1918, most of Arkansas's guard had been shipped to France. Most returned in 1919 and demobilized that year. (Courtesy of Dermott Historical Museum.)

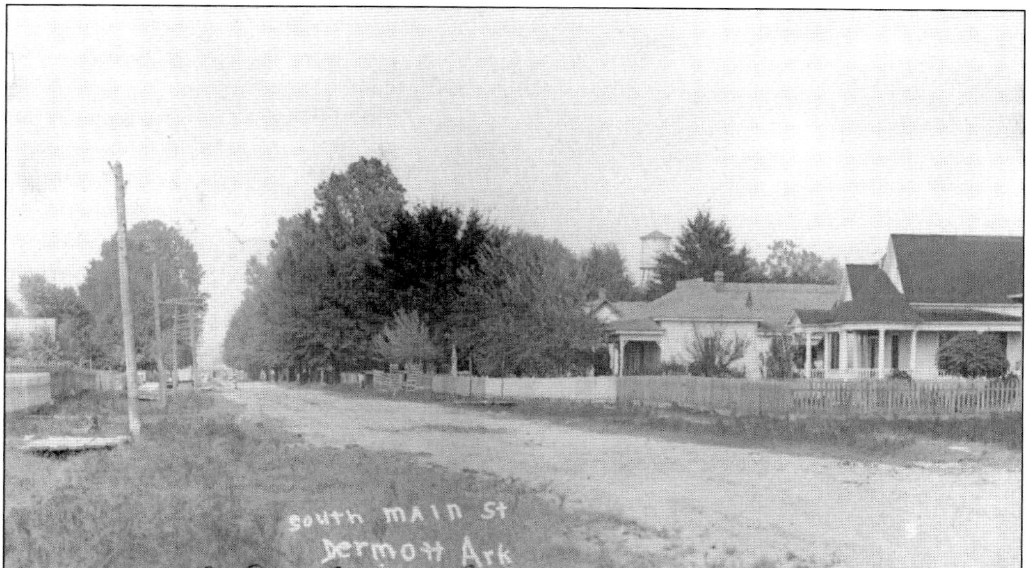

In 1908, South Main Street was lined with residences and trees. According to John J. Hammock, writing in 1973, "trees were . . . carefully planted [in the 1890s] to line the streets—great oak and pecan trees." (Courtesy of the Butler Center for Arkansas Studies, Central Arkansas Library System.)

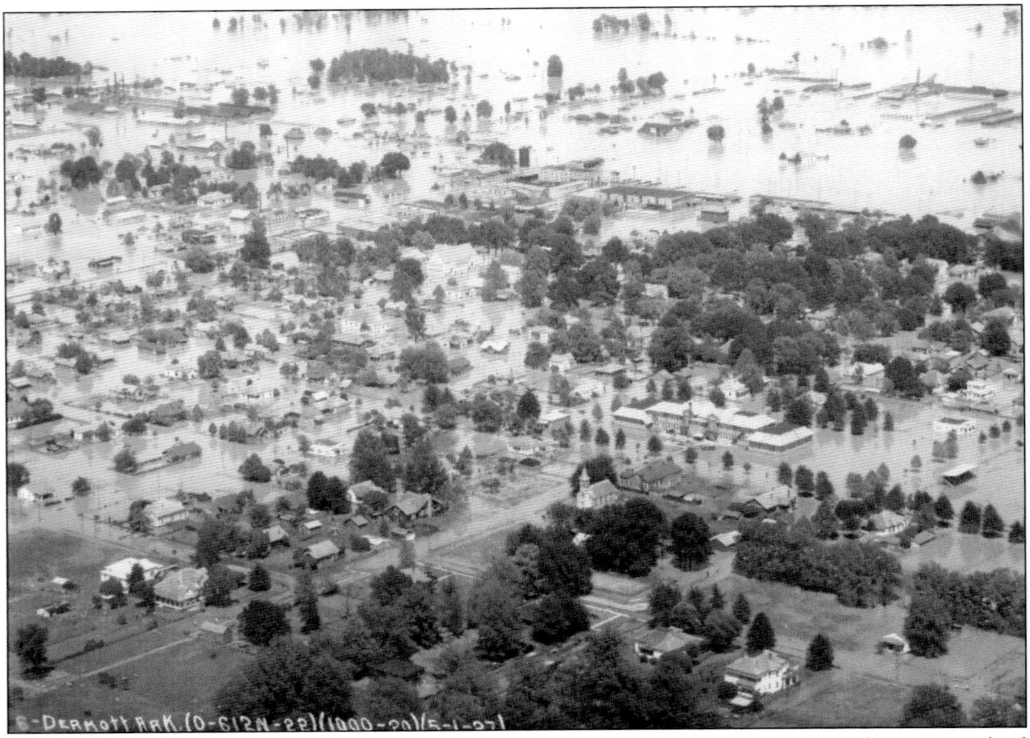

After the levee broke on the Arkansas River at Pendleton on April 21, 1927, floodwaters reached Dermott on April 25. The Red Cross reported 2,431 persons cared for at Dermott, pictured here on May 1. Many refugees headed west to Monticello, where the Red Cross reported 4,060. (Courtesy of the Butler Center for Arkansas Studies, Central Arkansas Library System.)

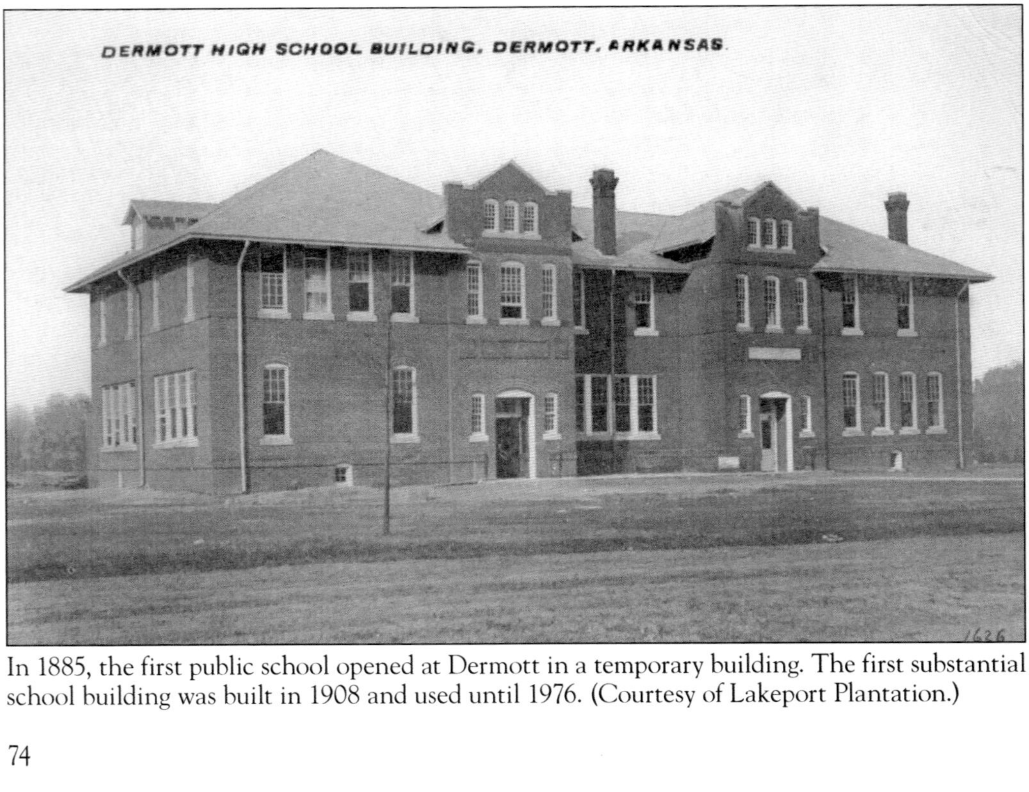

In 1885, the first public school opened at Dermott in a temporary building. The first substantial school building was built in 1908 and used until 1976. (Courtesy of Lakeport Plantation.)

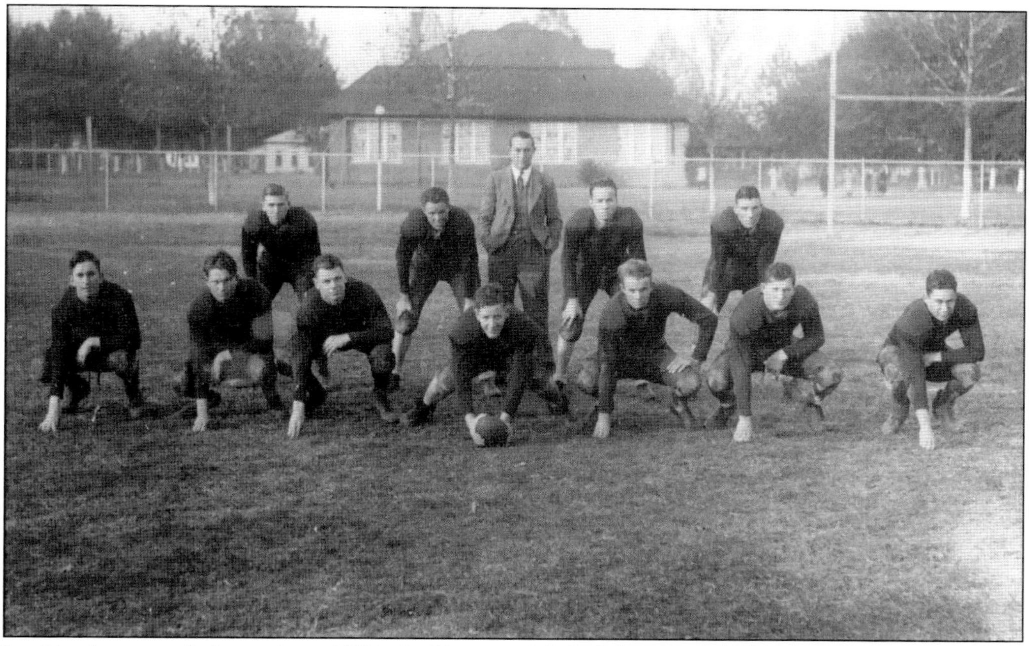

In this photograph from about 1920, the Dermott High School Football team is coached by Zebe Perry. The team was composed of, from left to right, (first row) Demp Buffalo, unidentified, Buddy Walker, unidentified, Joe Jeffers, J.W. Shockley, and Frank Dennington; (second row) Robert Gibson, Pete Lowry, Harry Daniels, and Tom Cokely. (Courtesy of Dermott Historical Museum.)

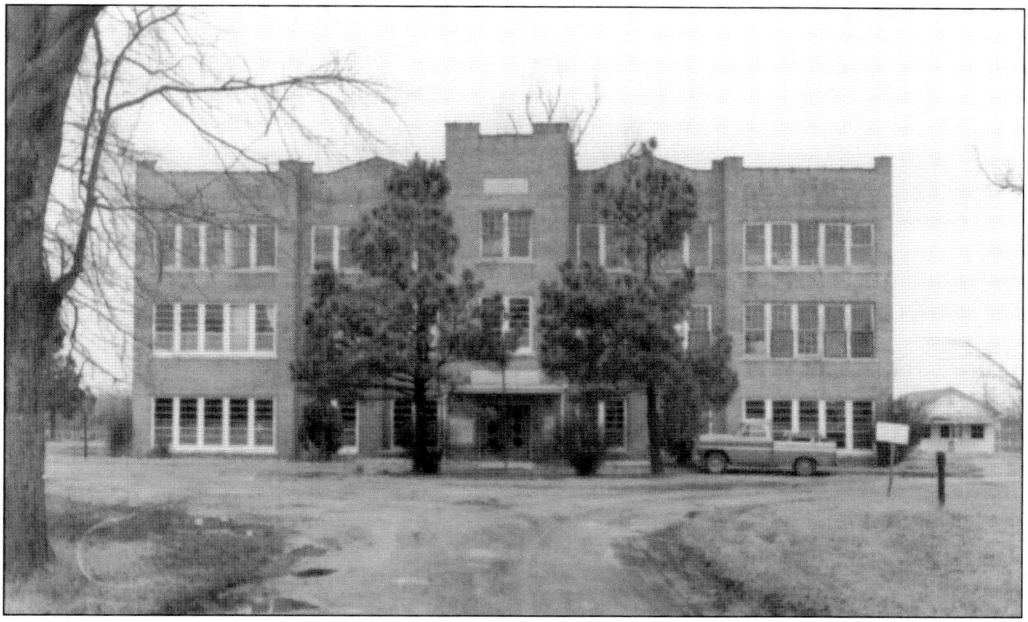

Morris Booker Memorial Baptist College was founded in 1899 as Southeast Baptist Academy and renamed in 1934. The building, seen here in 1979, was built in 1921. Dr. Samuel Lee Kountz Jr., a renowned transplant surgeon, was a graduate. Nearby was another school for African Americans, the Chicot County Training School. Originally constructed in 1924 and rebuilt in 1929, the Rosenwald-funded school operated as a public school until 1975. (Courtesy of the Arkansas Historic Preservation Program.)

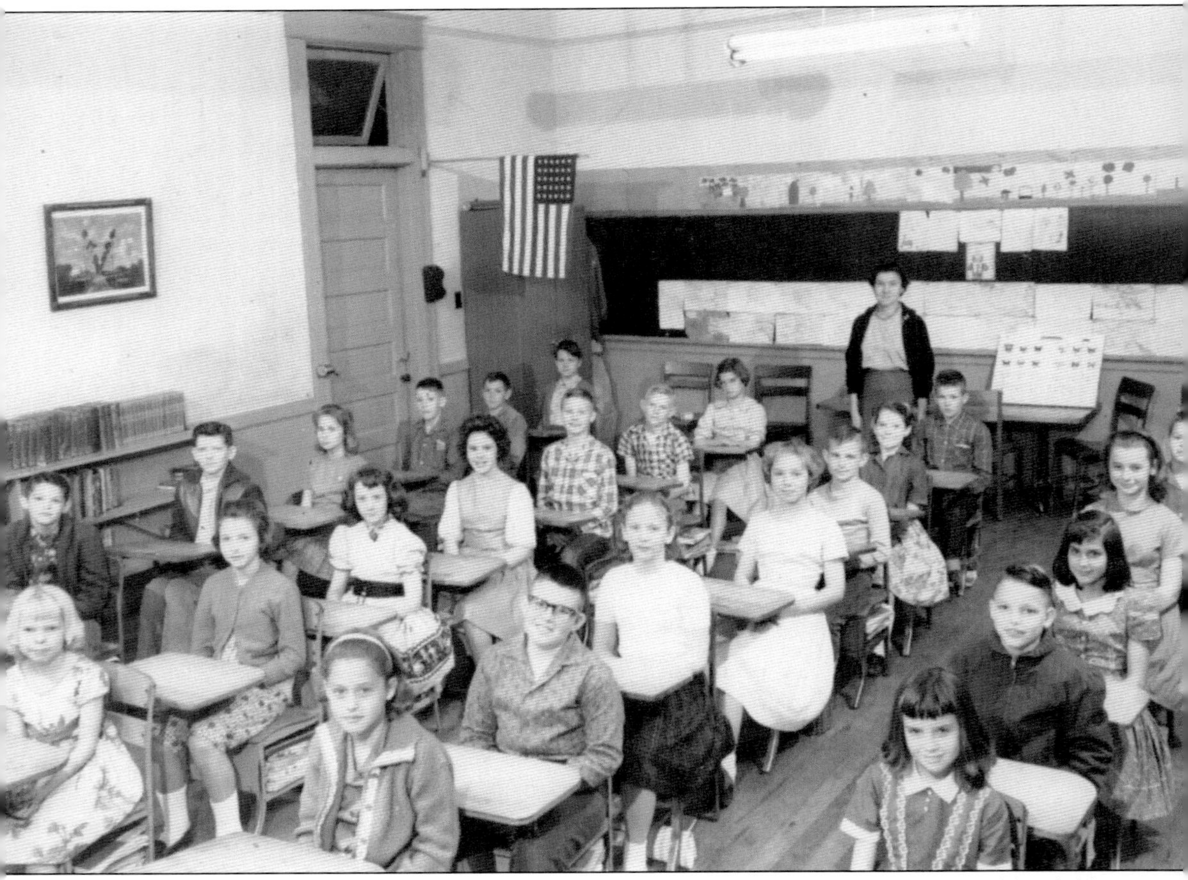

Marie Gray's fifth grade class poses at Dermott Elementary School in 1961–1962. None of the children are identified. While Eudora schools consolidated with Lake Village following a 2006 mandate, Dermott's schools have remained independent. (Courtesy of Dermott Historical Museum.)

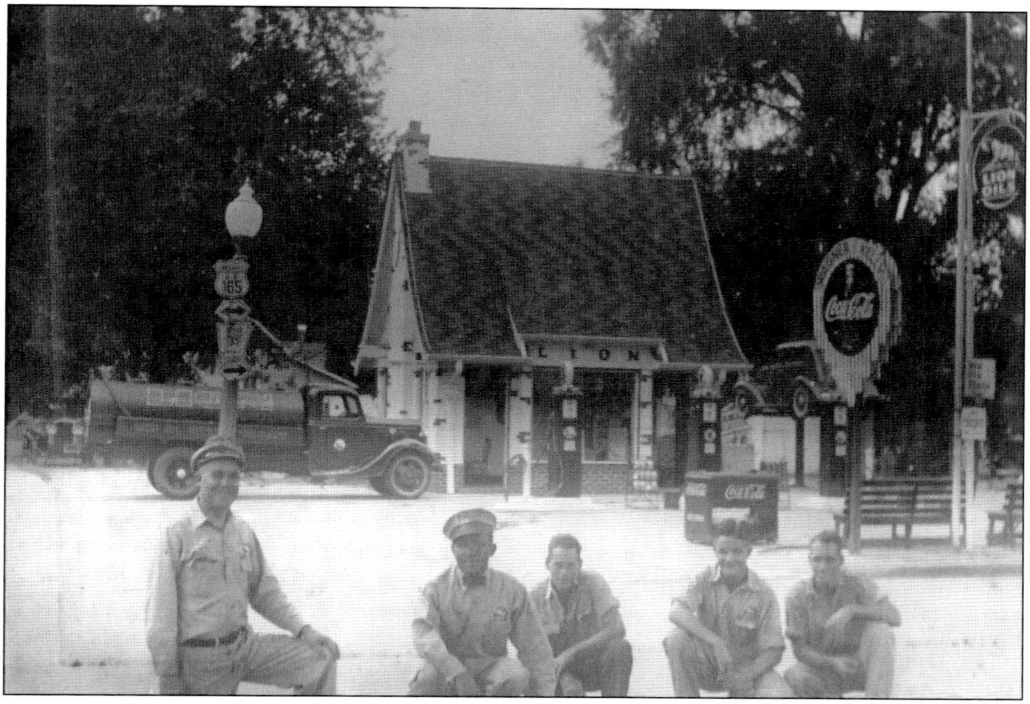

Wagner's Lion Oil Service Station, a franchise of the El Dorado–based oil refiner, opened hundreds of service stations by the 1930s. Wagner's trucks hauled gas to Arkansas City for riverboats. The top photograph is believed to have been taken before the 1927 flood. From left to right are Ed Wagner, Roosevelt Smith, Fritz Ellis, James Wagner, and Bill Ellis. Below is a 1938 close-up of the quaint building and its employees. V.M. Tyler, an African American photographer in Dermott, took this picture. (Both, courtesy of Dermott Historical Museum.)

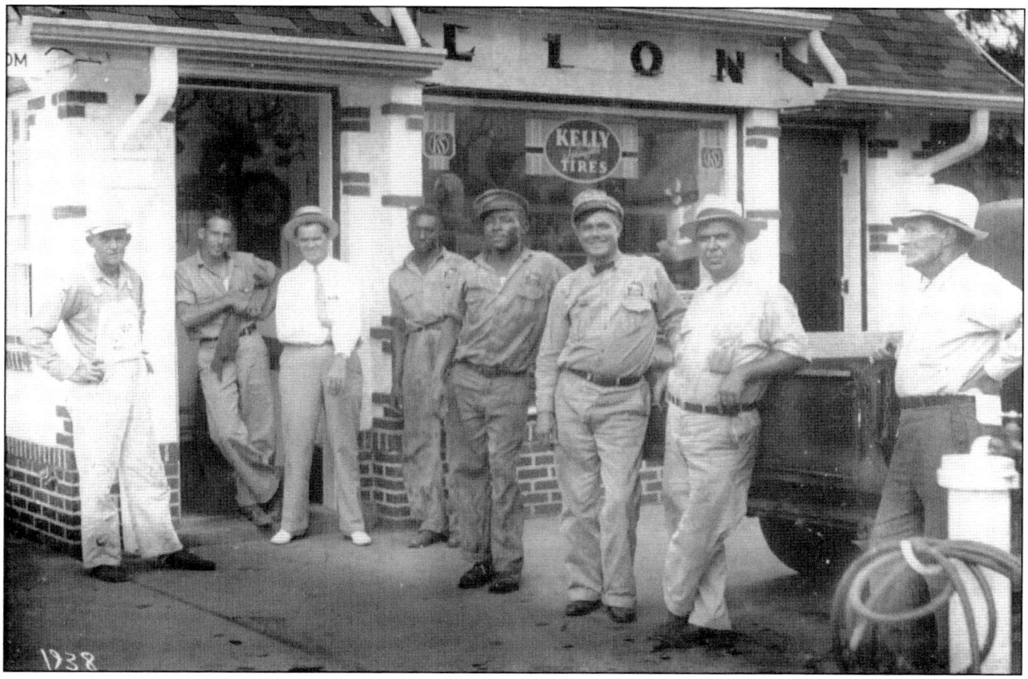

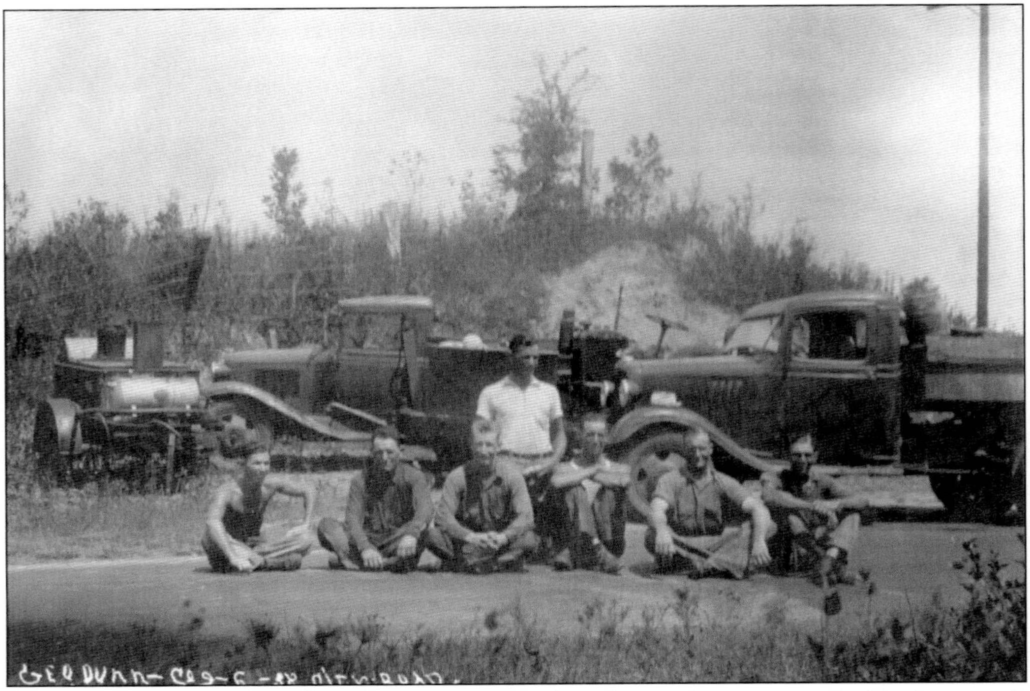

George R. Dunn, a Dermott-based contractor, owned a redi-mix plant in town. In this photograph from about 1938 by V.M. Tyler, Dunn (white shirt) poses with a construction crew while paving a road in Southeast Arkansas. (Courtesy of Nancy and Robert Jolly.)

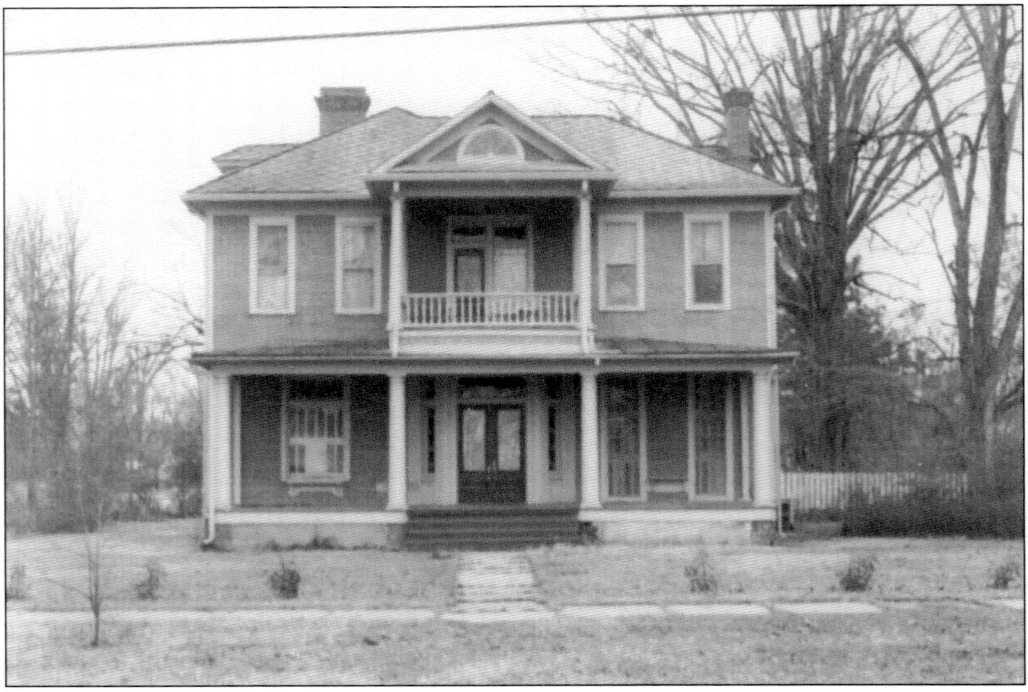

This house was built for James A. Bennett in the Classical Revival style around 1910. Bennett served as city marshal and as mayor of Dermott from 1916 to 1926. He and his wife, Eula, had two sons. (Courtesy of the Arkansas Historic Preservation Program.)

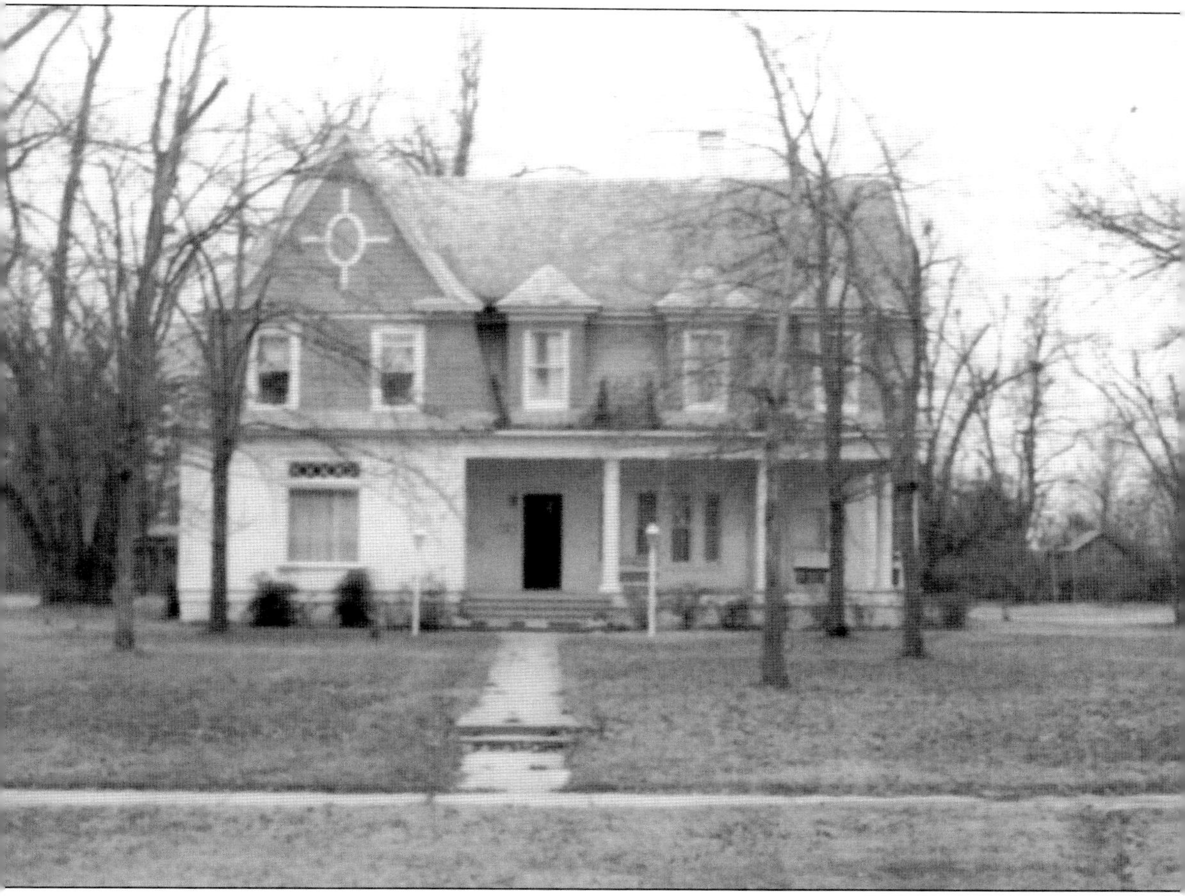

The Crenshaw-Burleigh house was constructed around 1905 in the Classical Revival style. Seen here in 1979, the house was built for Anna Crenshaw and her family. The home is associated with James and Mattie (Crenshaw) Burleigh, owners of a sawmill that made axe handles and other hardwood products. The house was listed in the National Register of Historic Places in 2012 as "an excellent example of a house constructed in the Colonial Revival style." The nomination noted the house's "asymmetrical plan, a rarer house plan that was popular during the later decades of the nineteenth century and the first decade of the twentieth century." (Courtesy of the Arkansas Historic Preservation Program.)

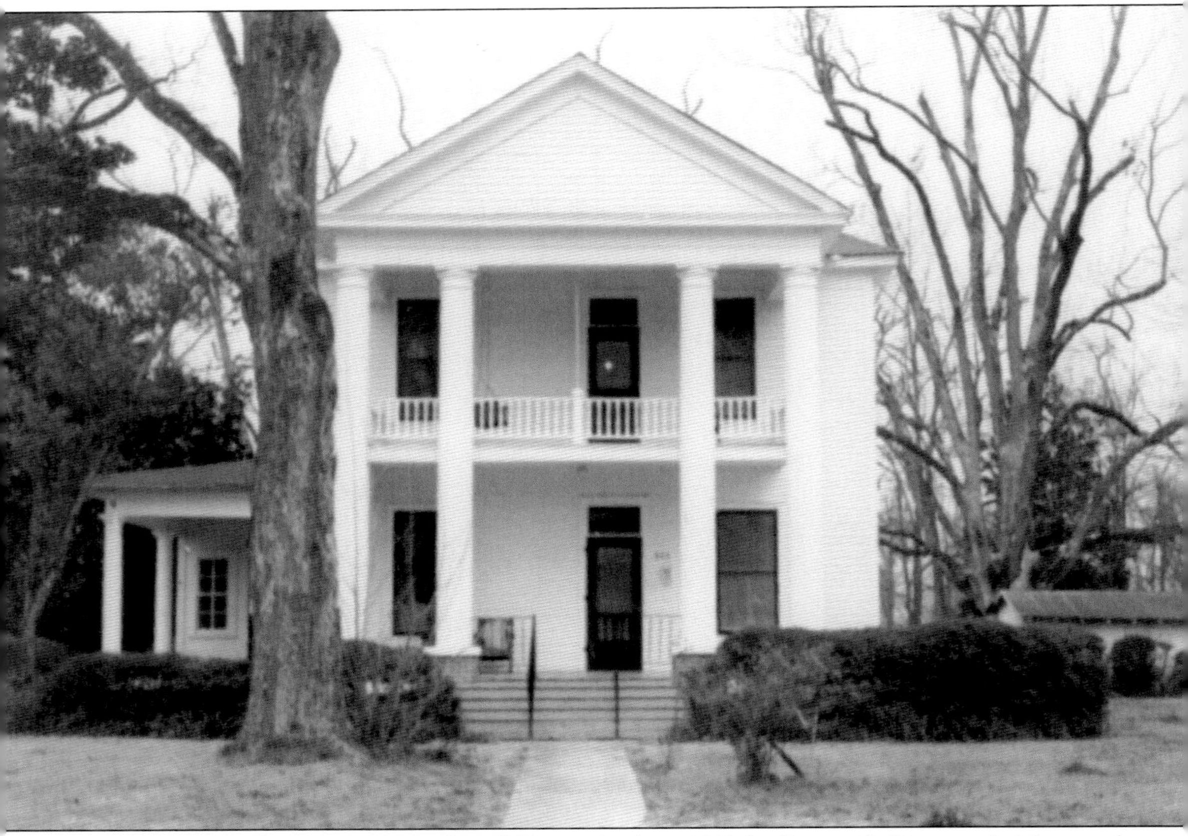

The Hammock House, pictured in 1979, was built in 1911 for Ernest G. Hammock. Hammock served as mayor in 1898 and also worked as a lawyer in Monticello and Little Rock before returning to Dermott in 1911 to practice law and construct this residence. Since the mid-1990s, the Hammock house has been owned by the Dermott Chamber of Commerce. (Courtesy of the Arkansas Historic Preservation Program.)

Four

EUDORA

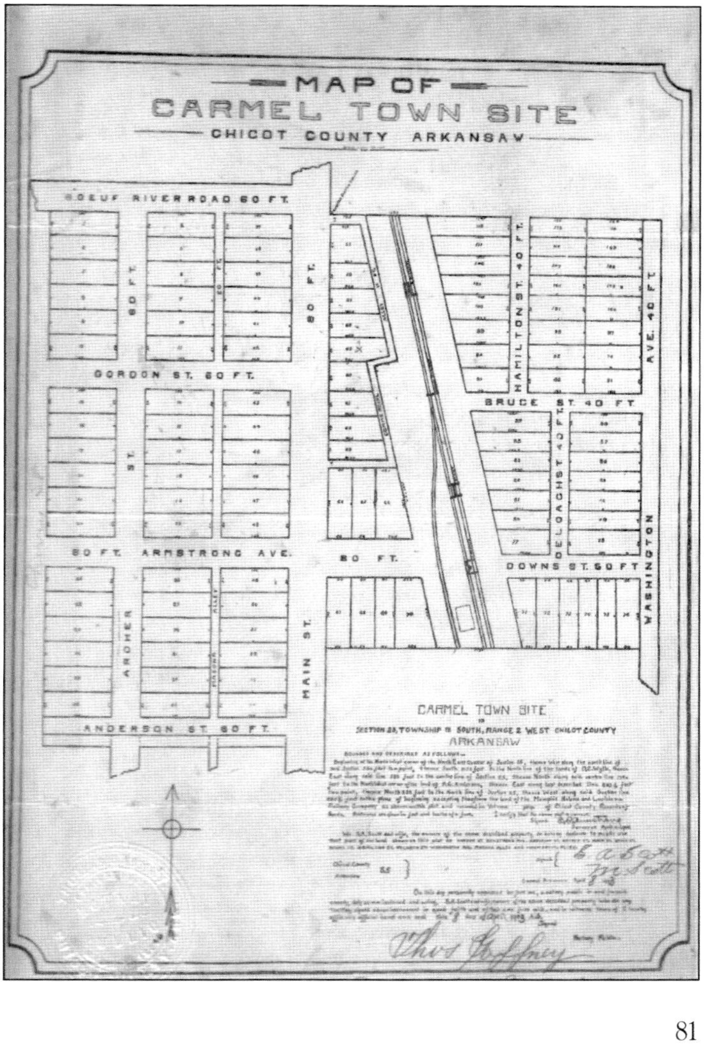

On August 13, 1903, S.A. Scott registered the plat for the town of Carmel in the Chicot County Courthouse. Scott registered another plat on January 4, 1905, under the name Eudora after the Iron Mountain Railway arrived and chose to call its station Eudora. (Courtesy of the Chicot County Courthouse.)

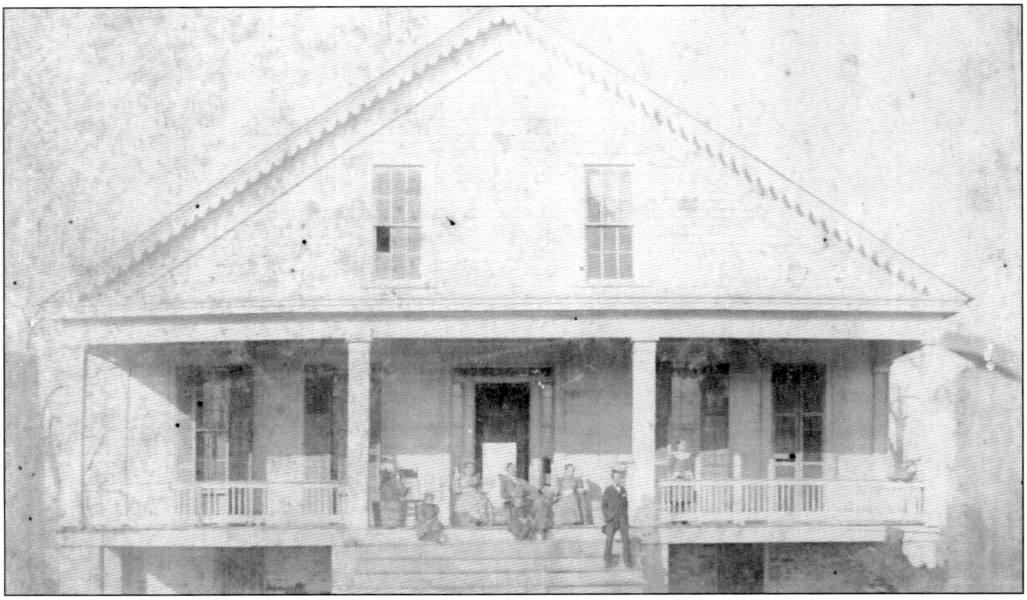

The Sweet House is believed to be the earliest house built in the Eudora area. S.E. Sweet, a merchant and builder from Rhode Island, built the structure around 1858. By 1900, it was the home of another merchant, William H. Stephenson. The antebellum home stood as late as 1936. (Courtesy of Carol T. Meyer.)

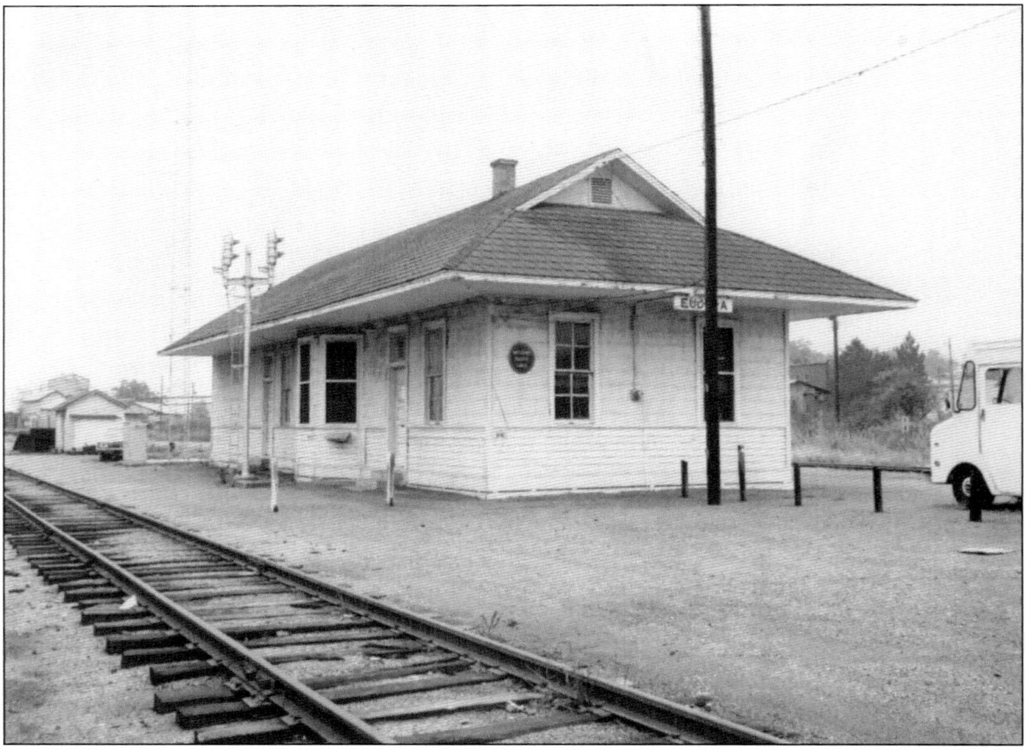

The Eudora Depot, pictured here in 1976, was likely built around 1903 for the Iron Mountain Railway. The new railroad gave the town its name and sparked growth. (Courtesy of the Arkansas Historic Preservation Program.)

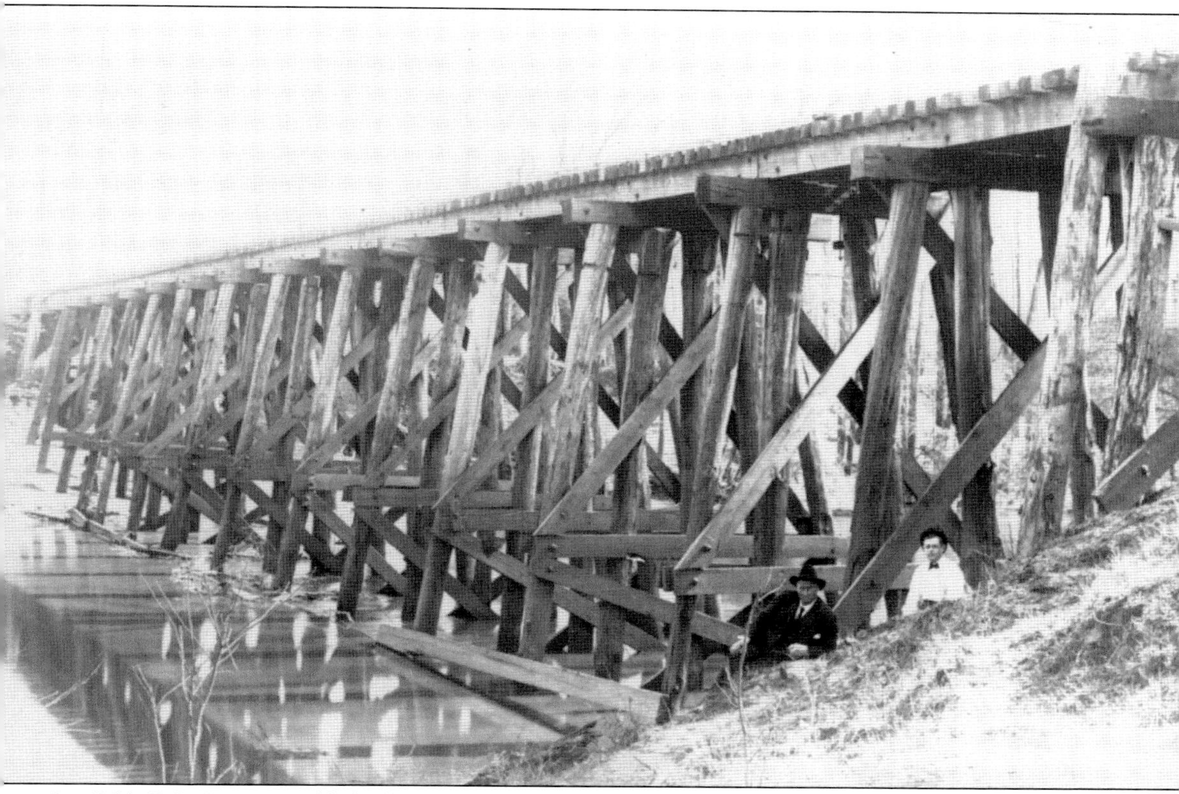

In 1856, E.C. James established a ferry across Bayou Macon, east of Eudora. In use until 1886, the ferry was replaced by a wooden bridge across the bayou. The wooden bridge was replaced in 1912. This 1908 photograph shows the Iron Mountain Railroad's bridge over Bayou Macon. (Courtesy of Carol T. Meyer.)

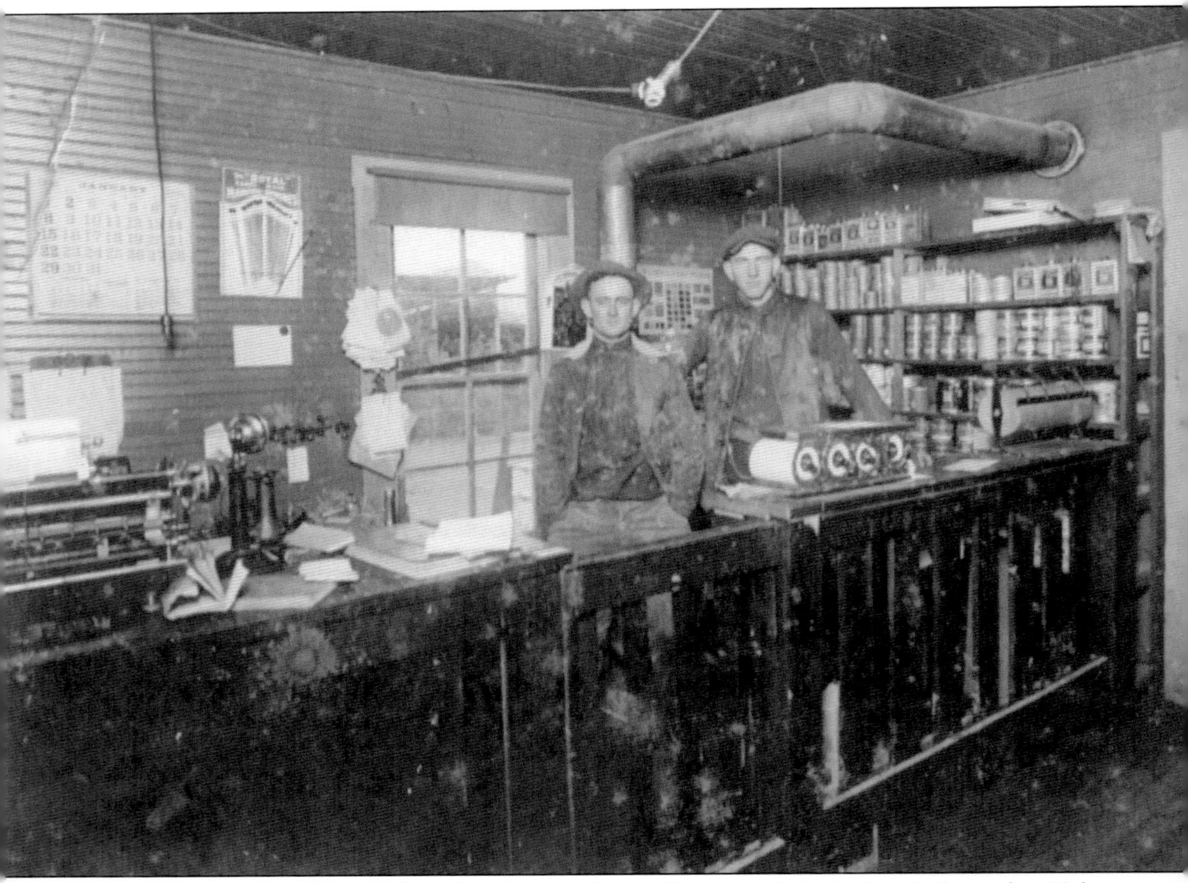

Lumber operations like the Leslie Lumber and Supply Company thrived after the Memphis, Helena, & Louisiana Railroad entered the county in 1903. In this 1922 image, Mip and Fred Pierce stand at the counter of the company's Eudora operations. In 1921, the Eudora yard kept an average of 75,000 board feet on hand. The Leslie Lumber and Supply Company also had operations in Lake Village and Pine Bluff. (Courtesy of Lakeport Plantation.)

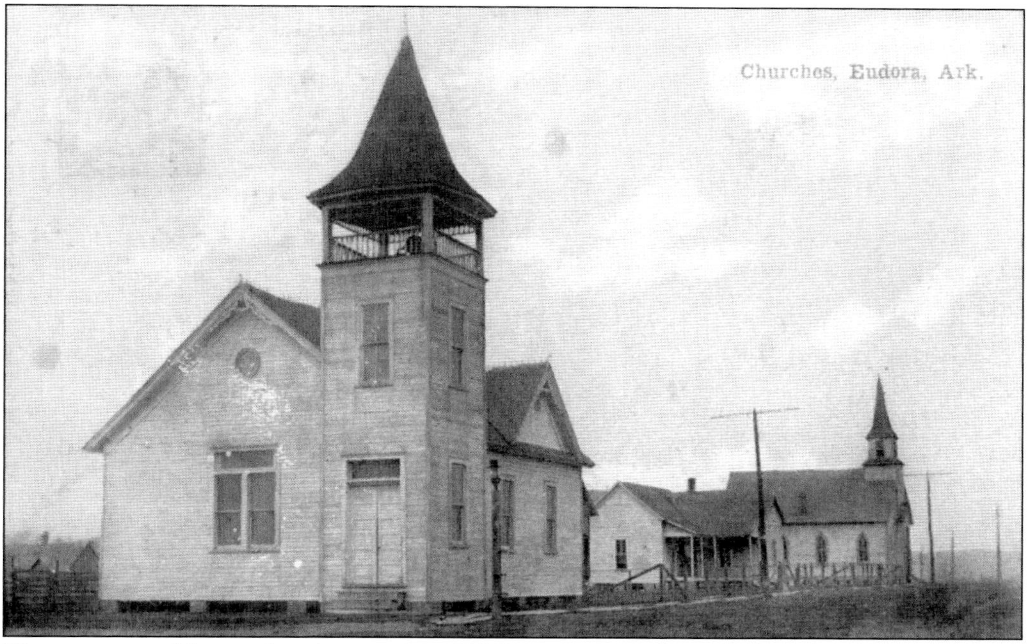

These two wood-frame churches are the 1905 Scott Memorial Methodist Church and the 1904 Baptist church along Main Street between Beouff and Hunter Streets. The Baptist church, constructed by an African American contractor, Elder Williams of Pine Bluff, was razed in 1924 when the Baptists erected a new brick house of worship on Archer Street. (Courtesy of Lakeport Plantation.)

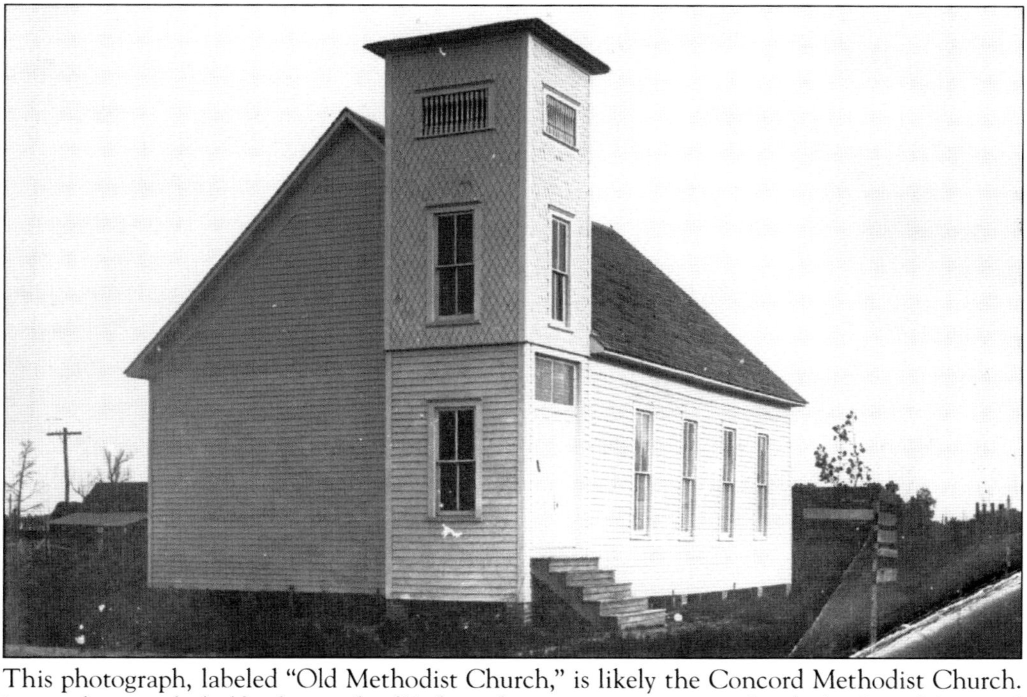

This photograph, labeled "Old Methodist Church," is likely the Concord Methodist Church. Located two and a half miles north of Eudora, the congregation merged with the Scott Memorial Methodist Church in 1924. (Courtesy of Carol T. Meyer.)

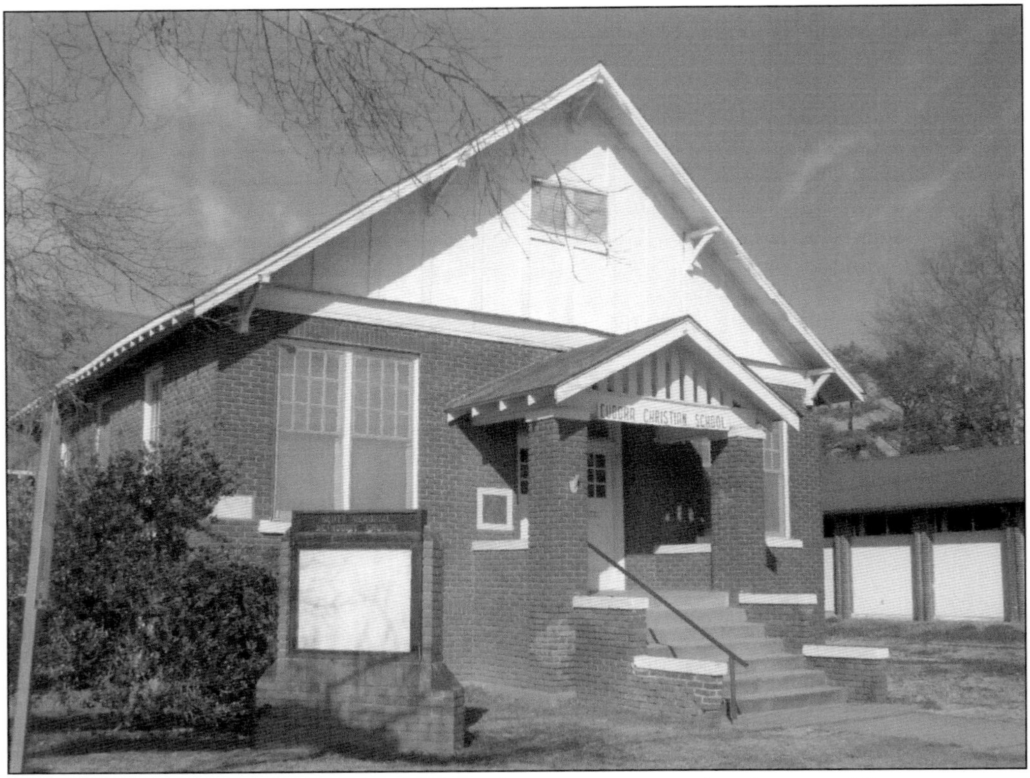

In 1922, the Scott Memorial Methodist Church congregation replaced its wood-frame structure with a new brick building (above). A third sanctuary (below) was built in 1969 and is still in use. (Both, courtesy of Lakeport Plantation.)

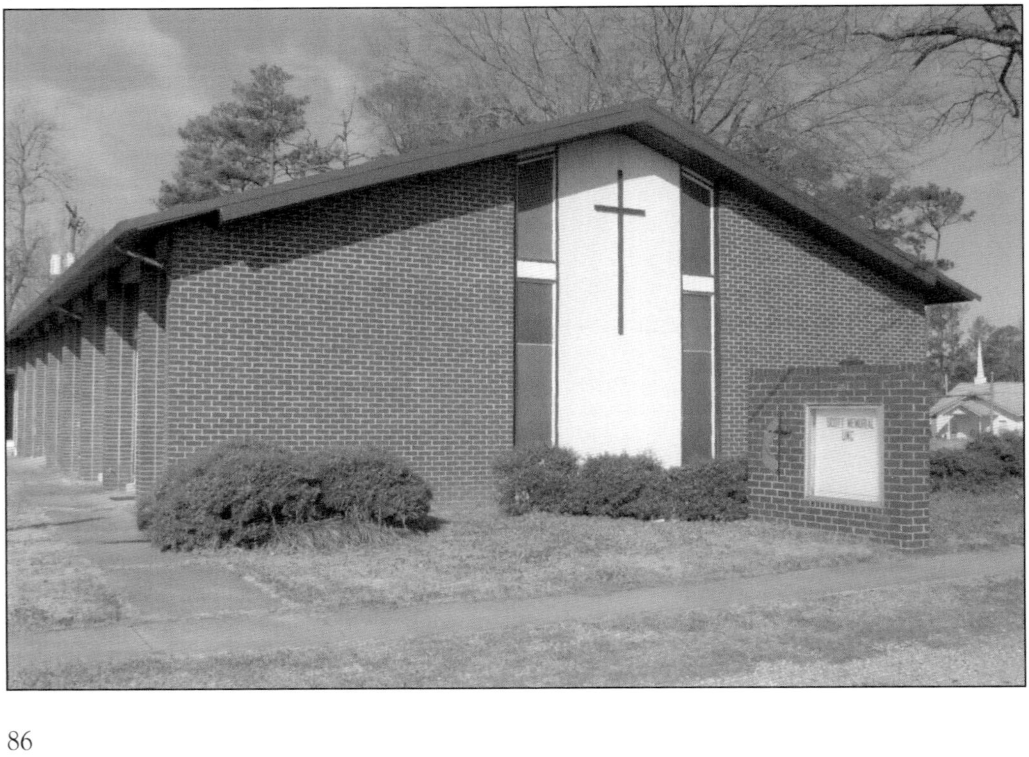

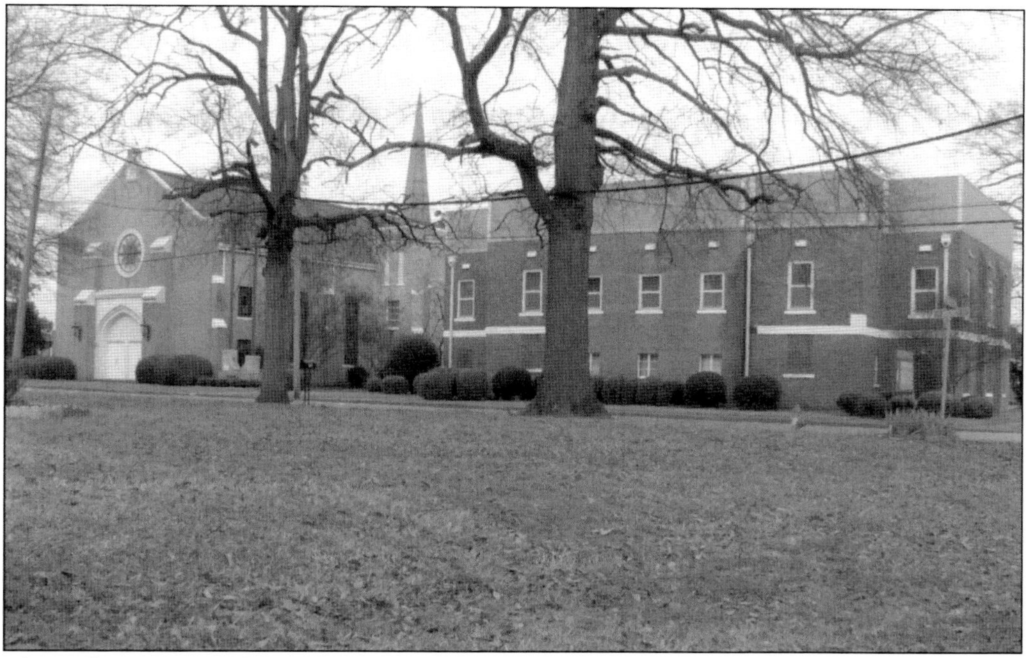

The Eudora Baptist Church, organized in 1903 by Rev. N.C. Denson, erected its first building on Main Street. In 1924, the church built a new three-story brick building on Archer Street. (Courtesy of Lakeport Plantation.)

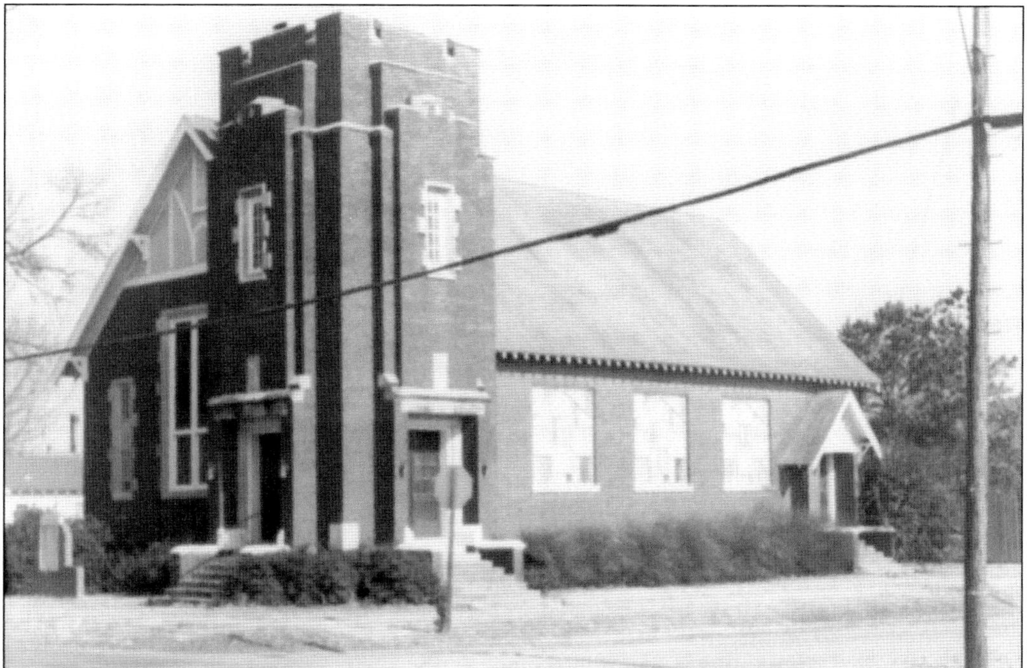

An early Presbyterian church and girls' seminary formed at Mount Carmel around 1846, but disbanded during the Civil War. The Presbyterian church congregation reformed in 1916, and the First Presbyterian Church erected this brick building in 1922. Shown in 1979, the congregation disbanded on March 3, 2001. (Courtesy of the Arkansas Historic Preservation Program.)

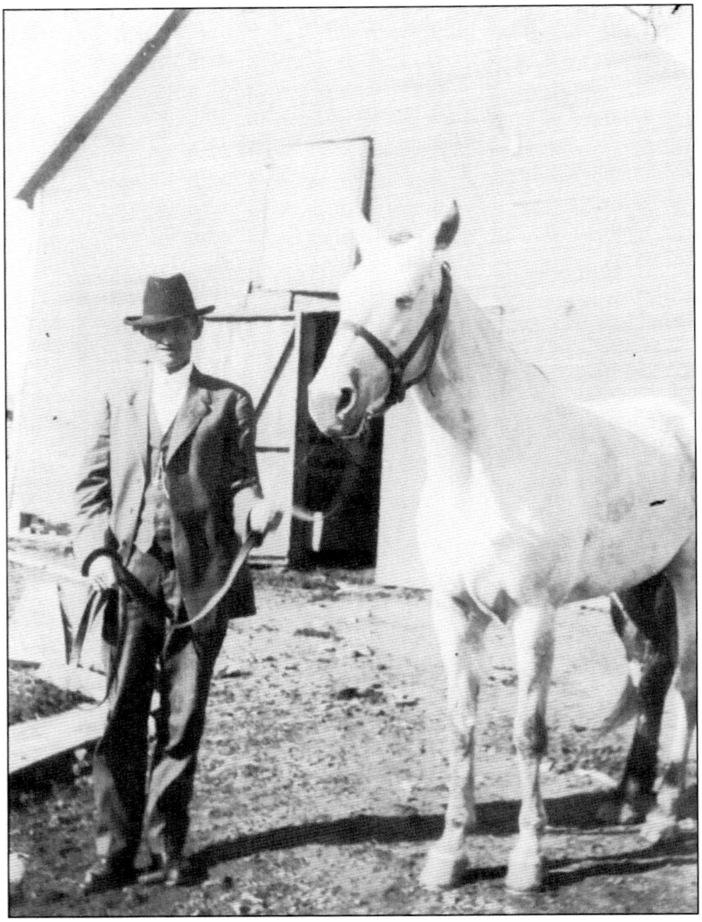

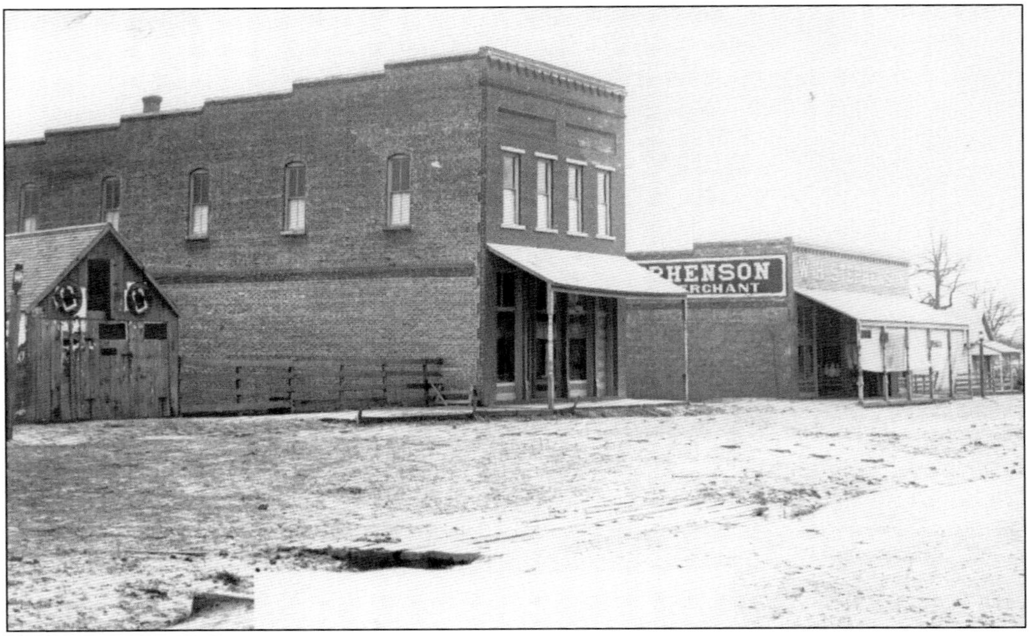

William Hardy Stephenson, born in 1860, was a successful merchant and gin owner. His store, built in 1904, was the first brick building in Eudora. Soon after, the Masonic Lodge and Knights of Pythias erected a two-story lodge next door. (Both, courtesy of Carol T. Meyer.)

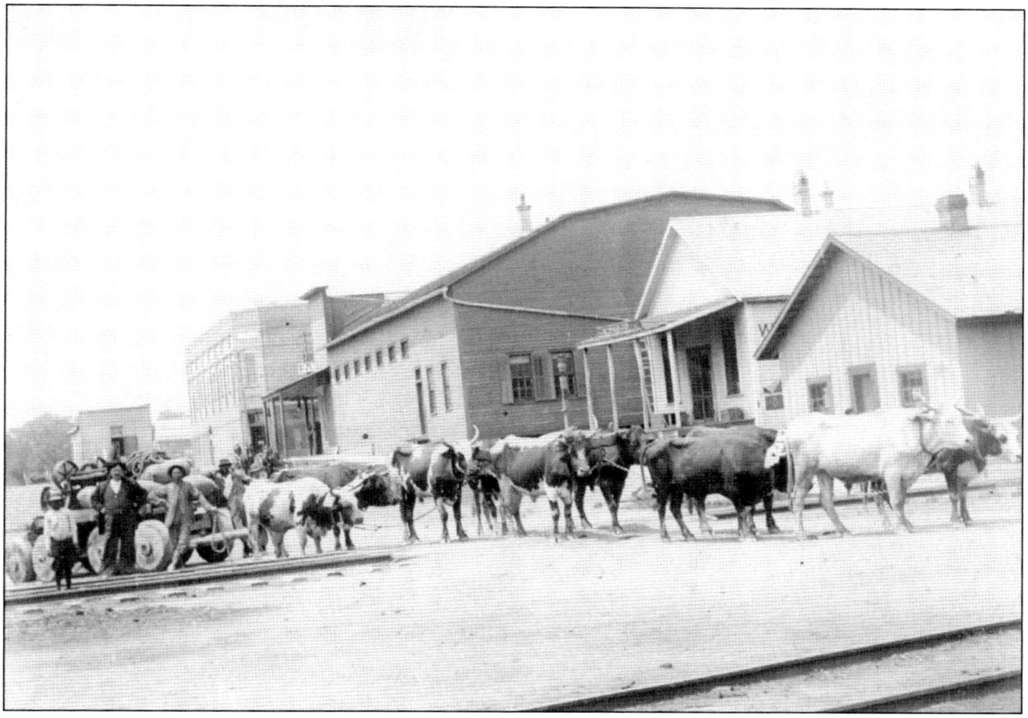

Henry Francis Brooks is pictured here around 1907 with a team of oxen moving grain through downtown Eudora. To the right is a restaurant, possibly W.A. Farmer's. Brooks, a native of Louisiana, lived and farmed most of his life at Ross Vanness near Eudora. (Courtesy of Mary Jane Dodson.)

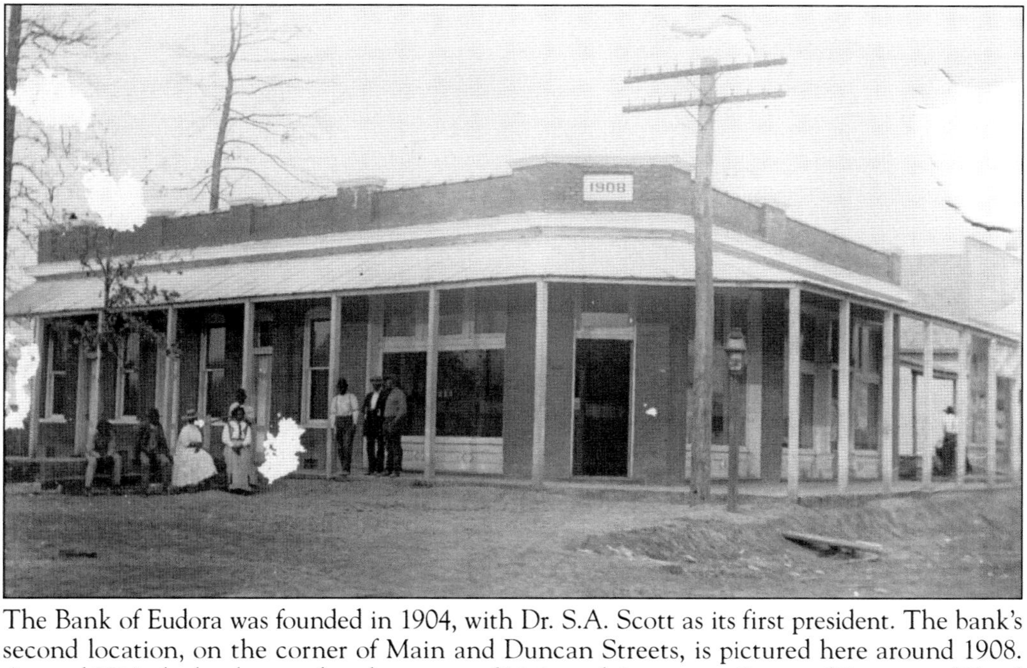

The Bank of Eudora was founded in 1904, with Dr. S.A. Scott as its first president. The bank's second location, on the corner of Main and Duncan Streets, is pictured here around 1908. Around 1914, the bank moved to the corner of Main and Armstrong Streets. (Courtesy of Carol T. Meyer.)

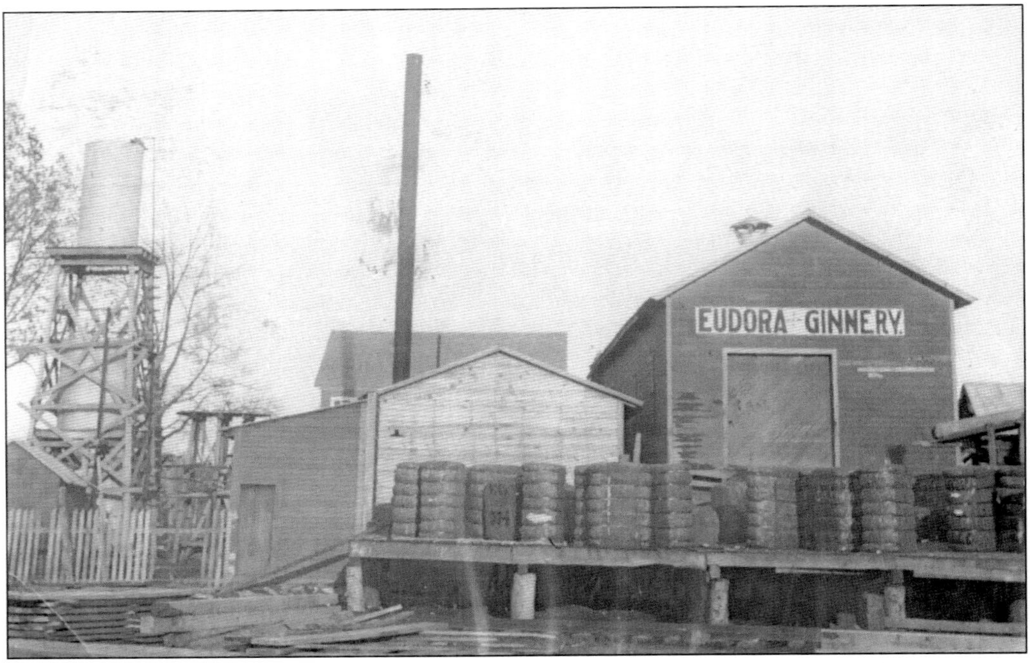

The Eudora Ginnery pictured here around 1920 is likely the Eudora Gin and Mill Company. It began business around 1915 and was one of several cotton gins in the town. (Courtesy of the Butler Center for Arkansas Studies, Central Arkansas Library System for Arkansas Studies.)

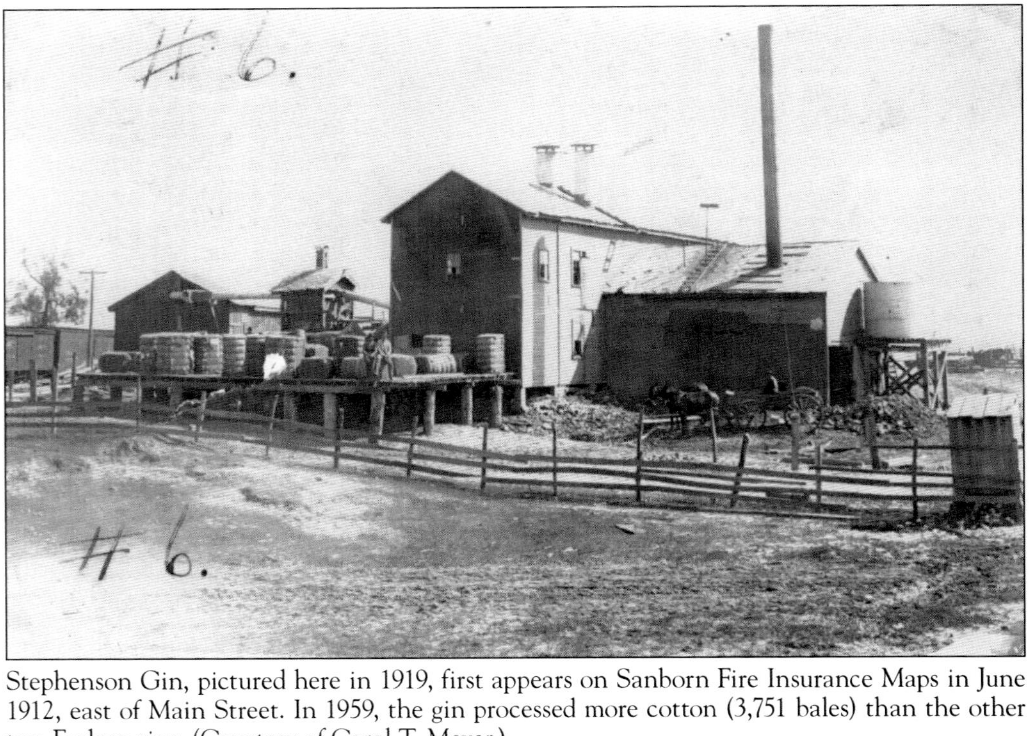

Stephenson Gin, pictured here in 1919, first appears on Sanborn Fire Insurance Maps in June 1912, east of Main Street. In 1959, the gin processed more cotton (3,751 bales) than the other two Eudora gins. (Courtesy of Carol T. Meyer.)

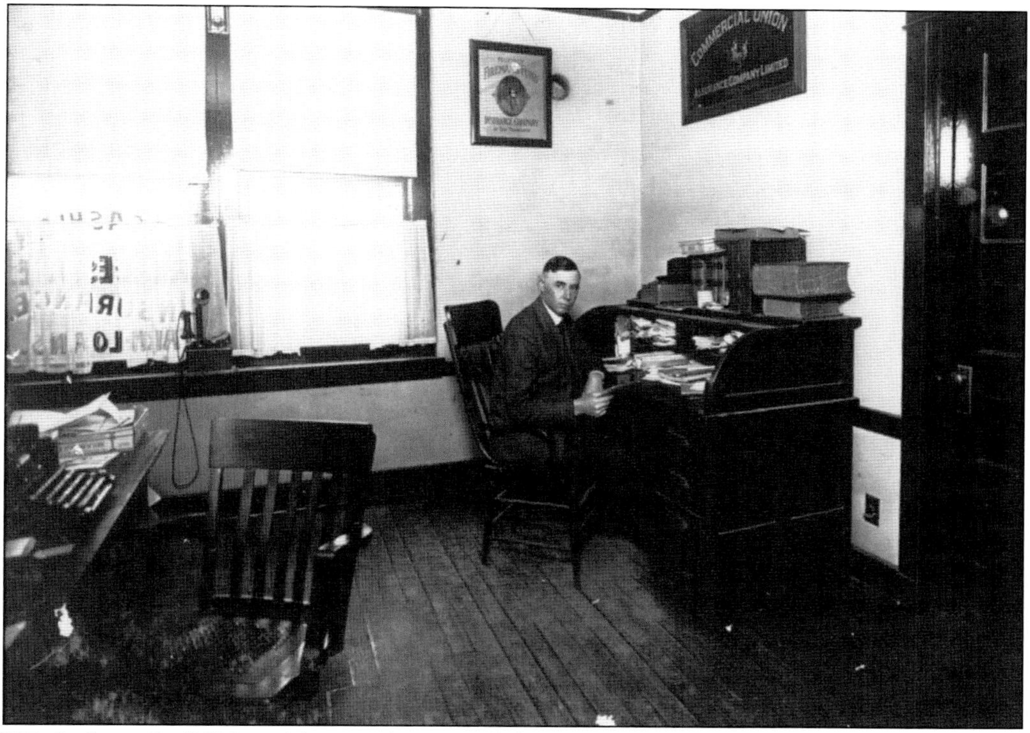

E.T. Cashion Sr. (1890–1961) sits in his second-floor office in the Liberto Building around 1925. Cashion, a banker with the Bank of Eudora and president of the Eudora Chamber of Commerce, authored *A History of Eudora, Arkansas* in 1937. (Courtesy of Carol T. Meyer.)

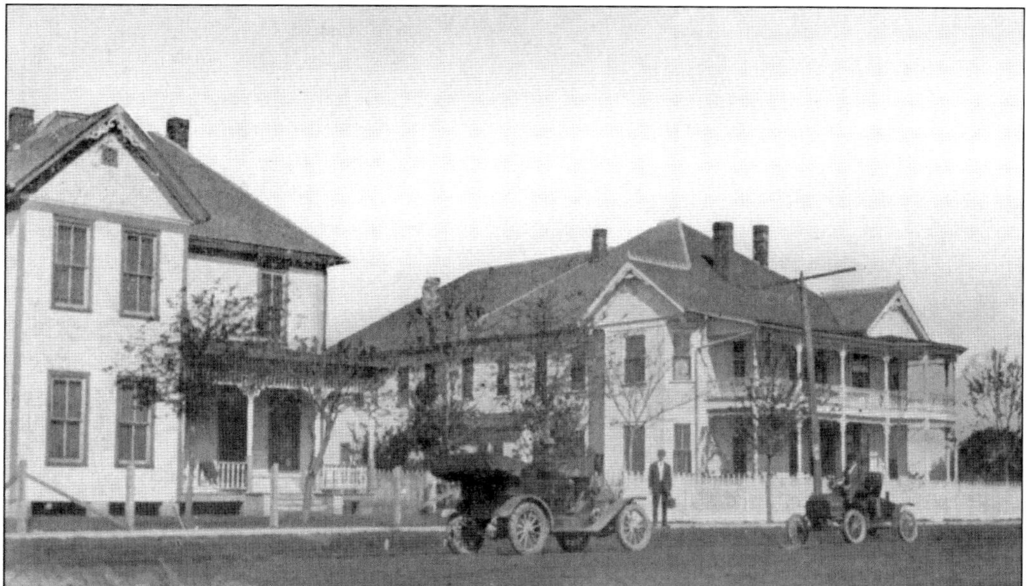

In 1912, the Parkman Hotel, located at the corner of Main and Boueff Streets, was managed by M.L. Parkman. The hotel charged $2 per day and advertised, "We Cater to Commercial Travelers." (Courtesy of the Butler Center for Arkansas Studies, Central Arkansas Library System for Arkansas Studies.)

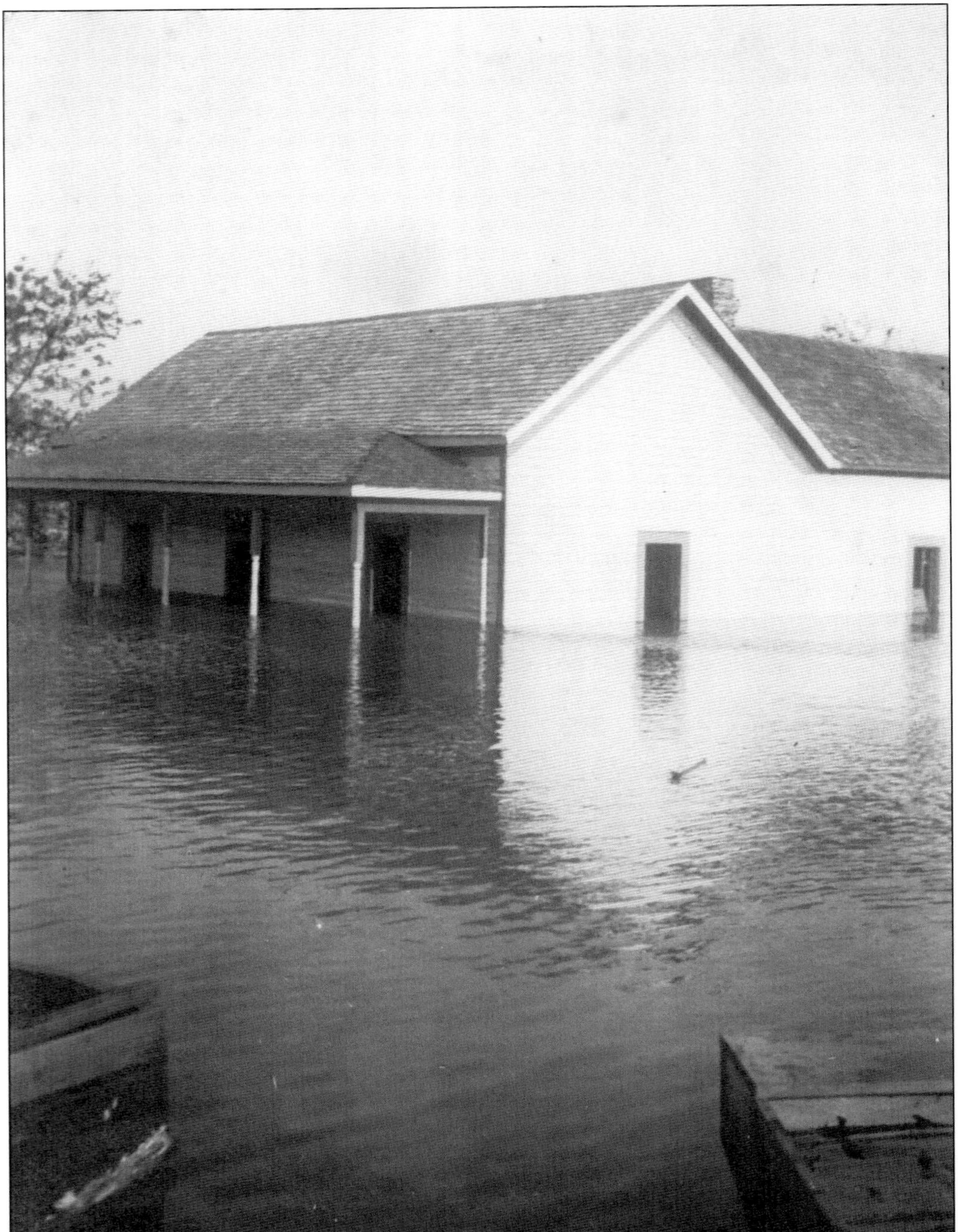

Macon Hills remained dry during the flood of 1927, but sections of Eudora in the lowlands, like this house on Downs Street, suffered. The Red Cross set up segregated camps in the hills, and the town absorbed 1,586 refugees. (Courtesy of Carol T. Meyer.)

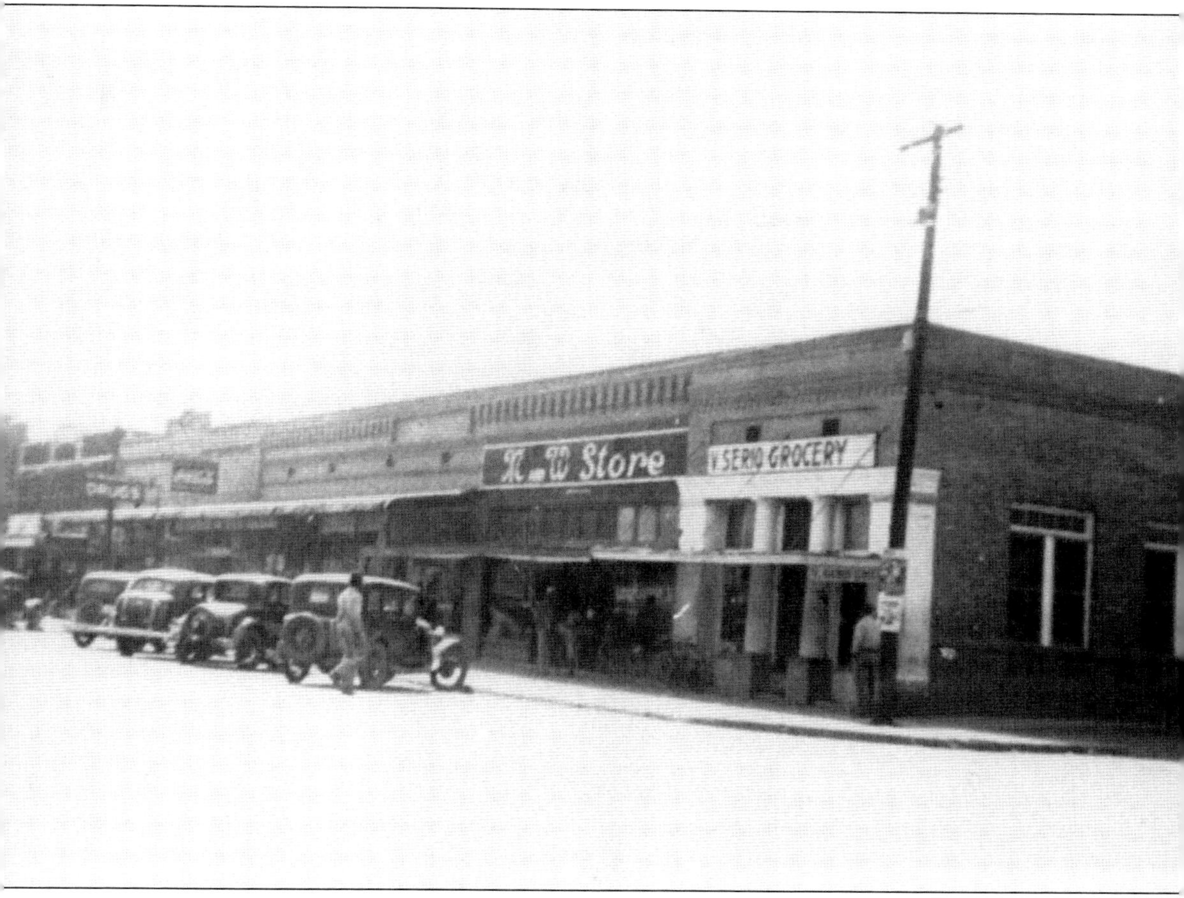

In 1928, Carroll Meyer and Ewell Weinberg partnered to open the M and W Store, pictured here on October 22, 1936. Carroll Meyer was the youngest son of Adolph Meyer. The older Meyer opened his first store at Grand Lake around 1869 after peddling wares in the Delta. He is also credited with naming Cariola Landing after his wife, Carrie, and the wife of his partner, Eola Ford. He moved his store to Eudora around 1905. (Courtesy of the Carolyn LeMaster Collection, Butler Center for Arkansas Studies, Central Arkansas Library System.)

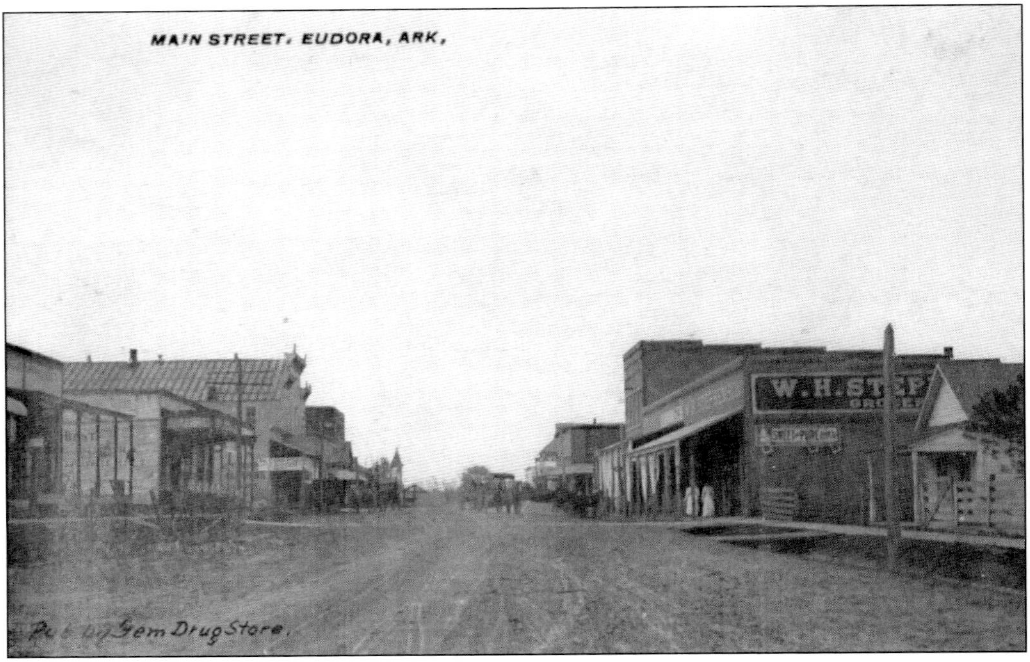

Eudora grew from a population of just over 600 in 1910 to 1,808 in 1940. A telephone system was added in 1906 and by 1913 had over 40 subscribers. Electricity and electric lights were available beginning in 1914 and a sewage system in 1917. Main Street was paved in 1919 as a section of the Arkansas-Louisiana Highway. (Both, courtesy of the Butler Center for Arkansas Studies, Central Arkansas Library System.)

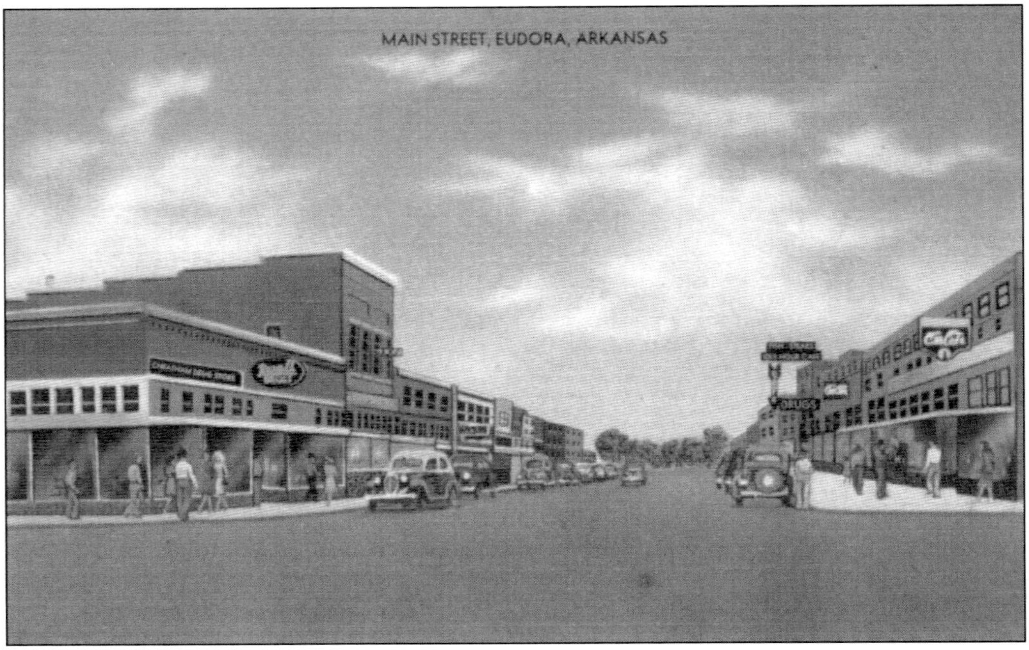

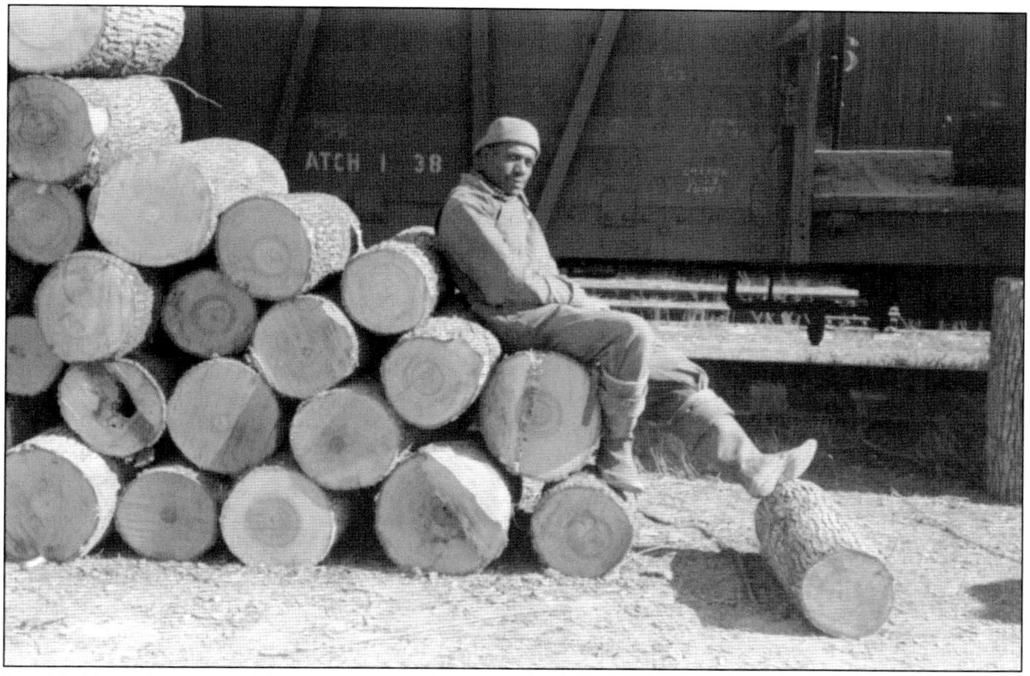

In this Farm Security Administration photograph dated January 1939, a man rests on a pile of logs to be loaded into a boxcar at Eudora. These logs were shipped to Tallulah, Louisiana, and made into barrel staves. (Courtesy of the Library of Congress.)

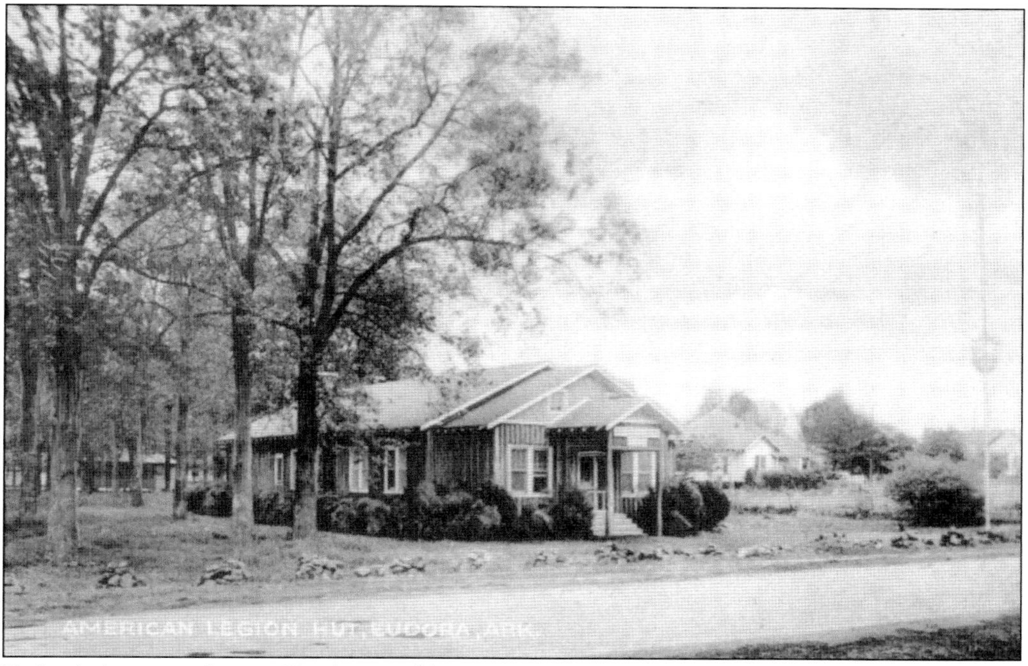

Eudora's American Legion Hut (pictured here in 1942) was constructed by the Wilson Burnett Post in 1934. The Eudora Garden Club restored the log structure in 1986. Today it is a private residence. (Courtesy of the Butler Center for Arkansas Studies, Central Arkansas Library System.)

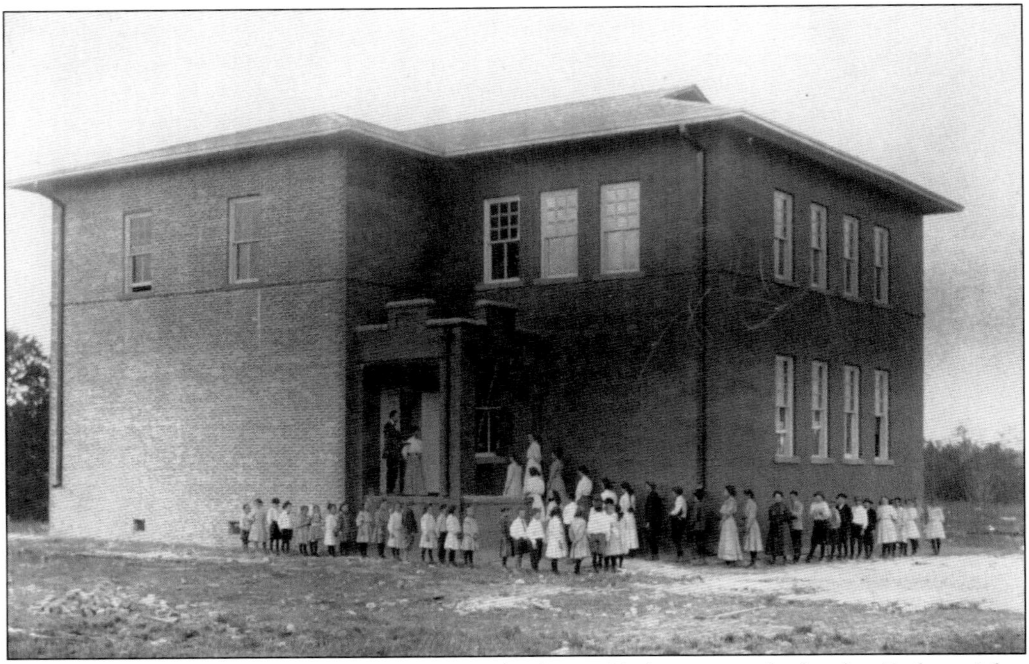

A wood-frame schoolhouse, built in 1903, was the first publicly supported school in Eudora. After rapid growth, the impressive Eudora High School was constructed in 1928 at Franklin (now Mabry) and Gaffney Streets. Eudora's public school for African Americans was located at what is now Baker and Swanigan Streets. (Courtesy of Carol T. Meyer.)

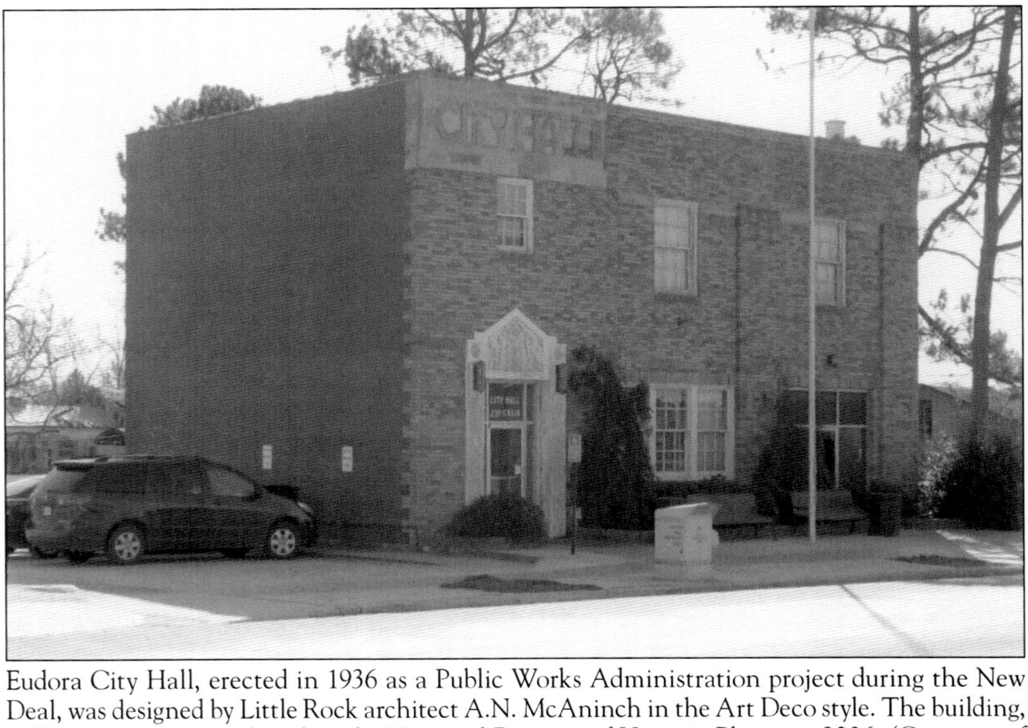

Eudora City Hall, erected in 1936 as a Public Works Administration project during the New Deal, was designed by Little Rock architect A.N. McAninch in the Art Deco style. The building, still in use today, was listed in the National Register of Historic Places in 2006. (Courtesy of Lakeport Plantation.)

Five

Lake Chicot and Recreation

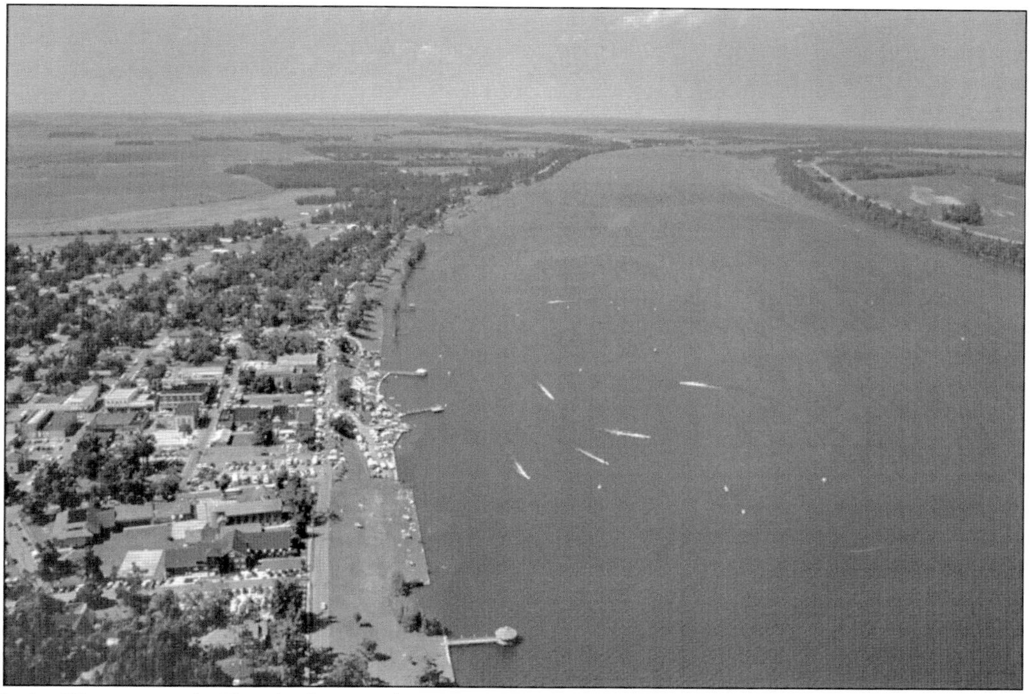

Lake Chicot, nearly 22 miles long and covering over 5,000 acres, is Arkansas's largest natural lake and the largest oxbow lake in North America. In 1866, the county court petitioned to change the name from Old River Lake to Lake Chicot. Formed by the meandering path of the Mississippi River about 500 years ago, its banks may have been the temporary burial place of Hernando de Soto, who died in the area on May 31, 1542. (Courtesy of the Arkansas Department of Parks and Tourism.)

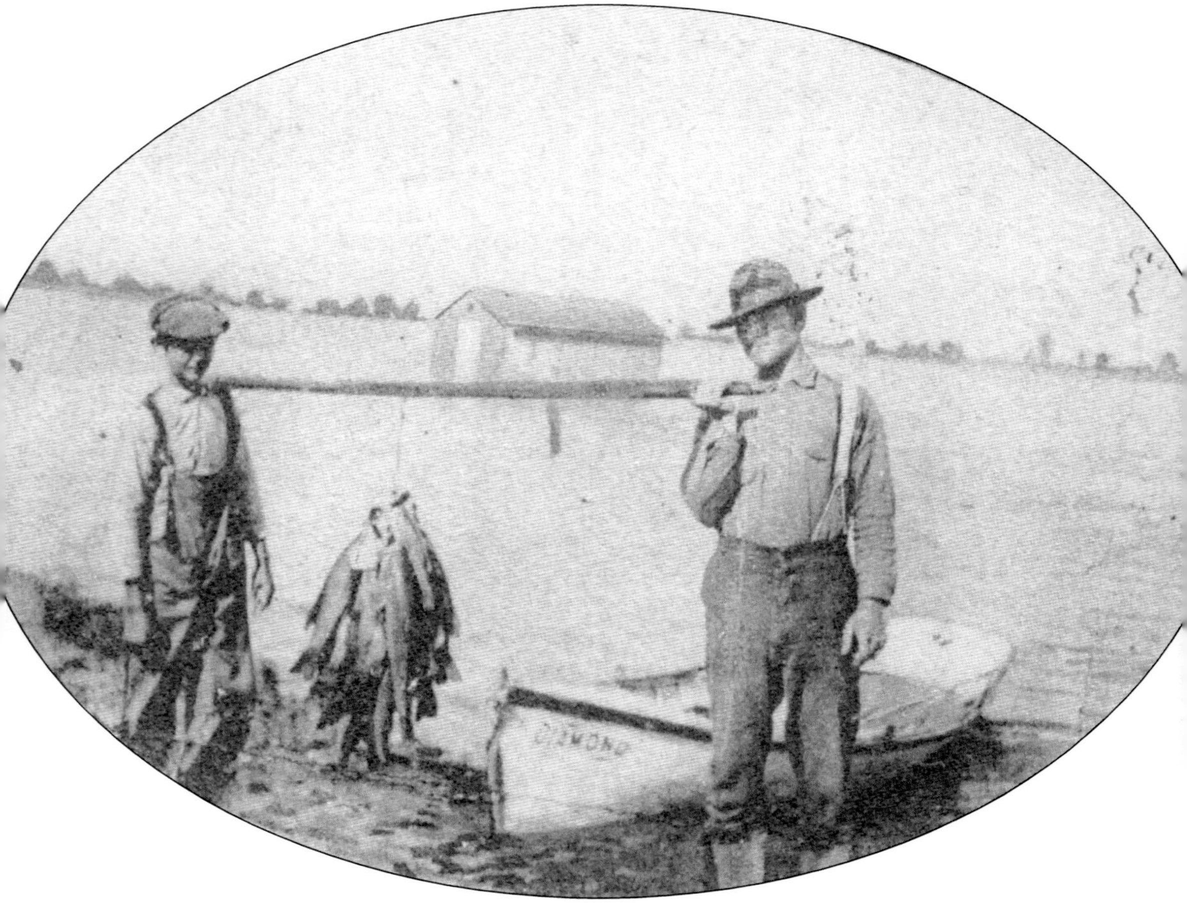

In 1888, the *Chicot Chronicle* reported the bounty to be had fishing in Lake Chicot. Isaac M. Worthington and his son Lycurgus "caught 117 bass, which weighed 135 pounds, and made a string seventeen feet long." The paper stated Worthington "gave away fish enough to supply, including his own [at Lakeport], twenty-two families—six white and sixteen colored." (Courtesy of Blake Wintory.)

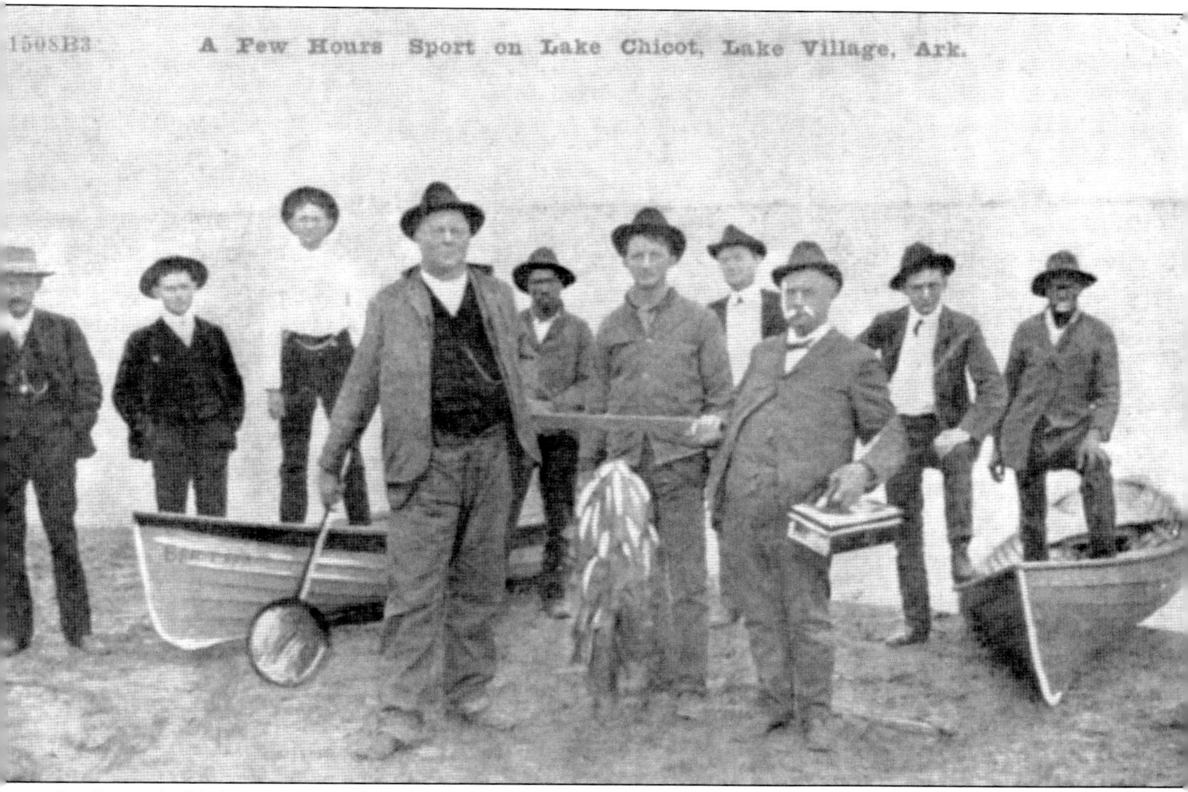

In the early 20th century, Lake Chicot and Lake Village were known as the "Home of the Black Bass." Pictured here around 1910 is a day's haul for a group of sportsmen, who apparently intended to cook and eat the fish, judging by the frying pan. In 1919, the *Arkansas Gazette* reported, "An average of more than 5,000 lbs. of iced fish are daily shipped to Little Rock, Memphis, St. Louis, Chicago and even New York" from Lake Village. (Courtesy of Blake Wintory.)

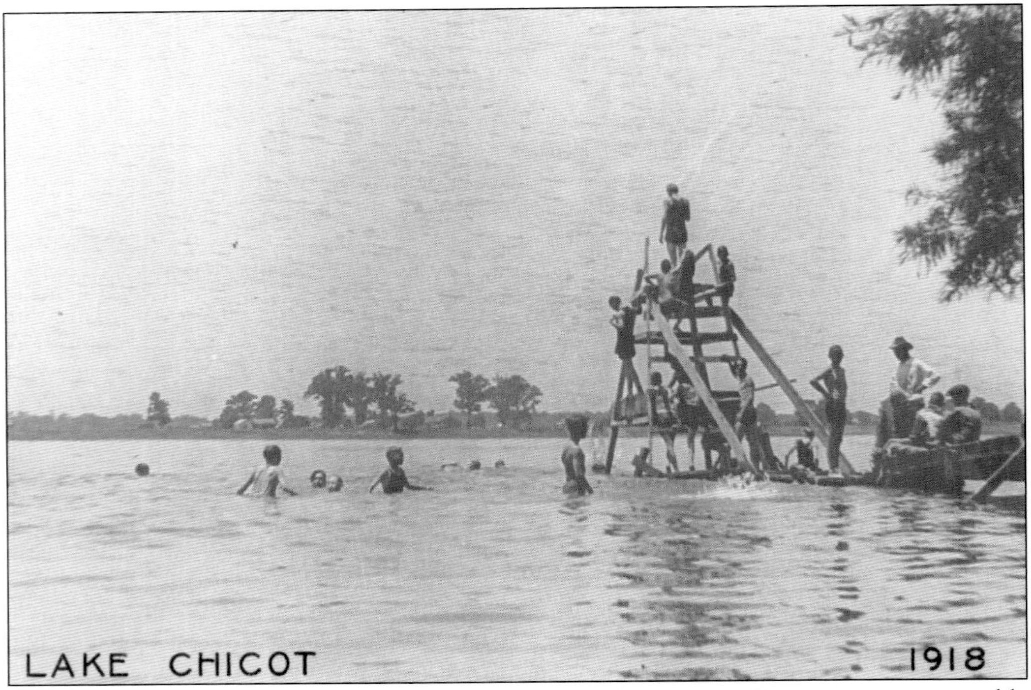

In the 1910s and 1920s, Lake Village boomed as a tourist destination. Transportation was readily available by rail, boat, and two paved highways, both finished in the early 1920s: the Chicot-Ashley Highway and Arkansas-Louisiana Highway; even Main Street was paved in 1912. Chicot Beach on the edge of downtown Lake Village was a popular swimming spot, as seen in these two photographs. Of course, swimming was segregated, with a "colored" swimming area north of Lake Village that was never mentioned in promotional brochures or booster newspaper articles. (Above, courtesy of the Special Collections of the William Alexander Percy Memorial Library; below, courtesy of Blake Wintory.)

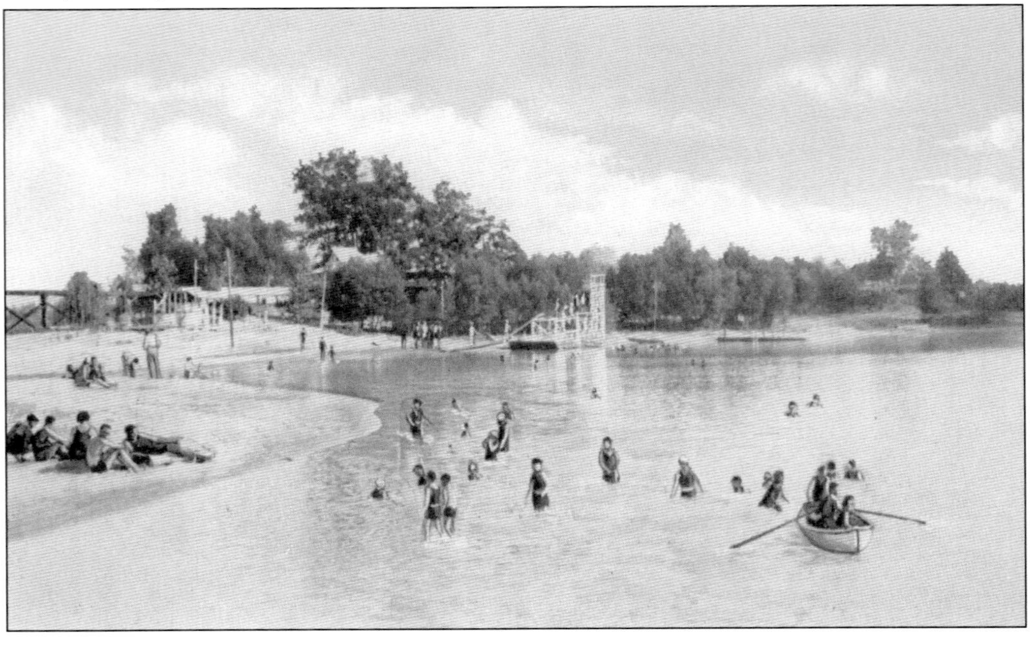

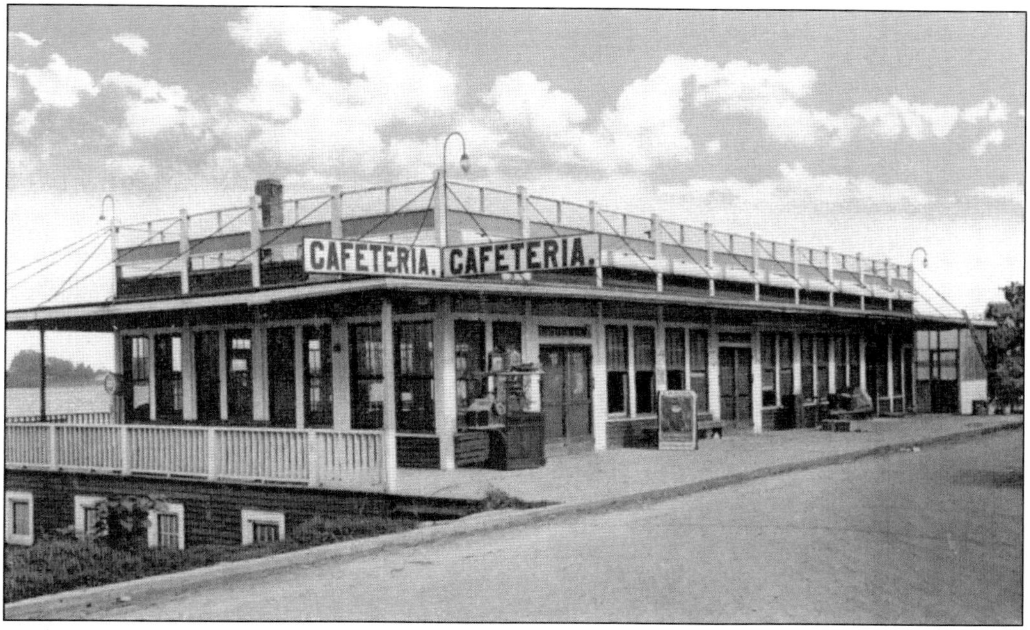

In the 1920s, the Gaines Cafeteria and Bathing Pavilion catered to conventions, tourists, and sunbathers, all with a view of beautiful Lake Chicot. The upstairs (street level) served fish like black bass in the dining room. While downstairs, at the lake level, the bathing pavilion catered to swimmers. (Courtesy of Blake Wintory.)

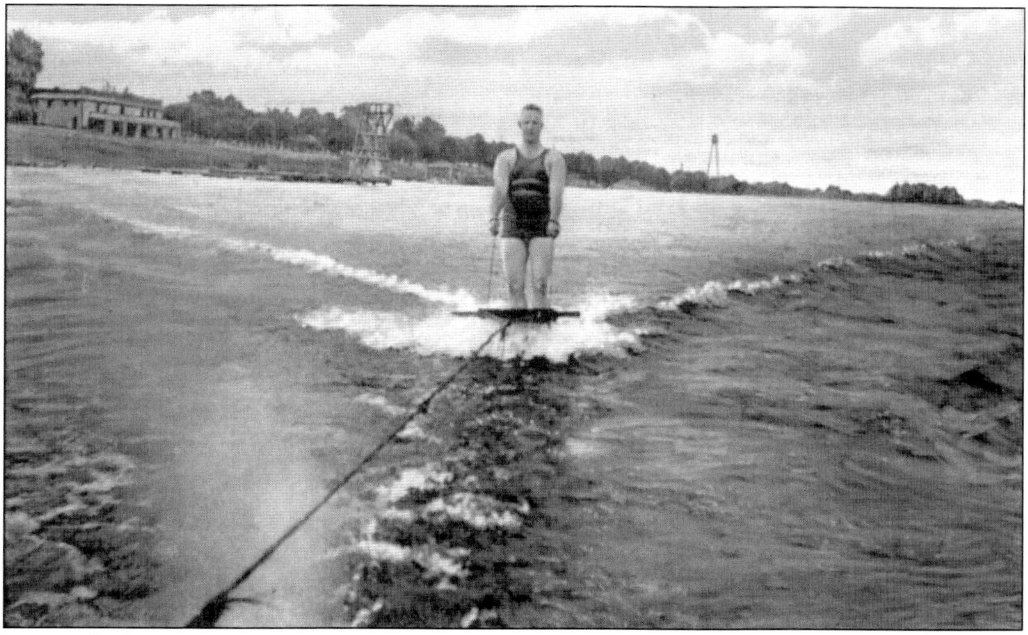

Postmarked June 1931, a woman named Esther sent this postcard to her friend Harriett Tuttle in Kansas City: "I am down in Lake Village having the time of my life . . . I am having a swell time going swimming every day in Lake Chicot. It is awful hot here." (Courtesy of Blake Wintory.)

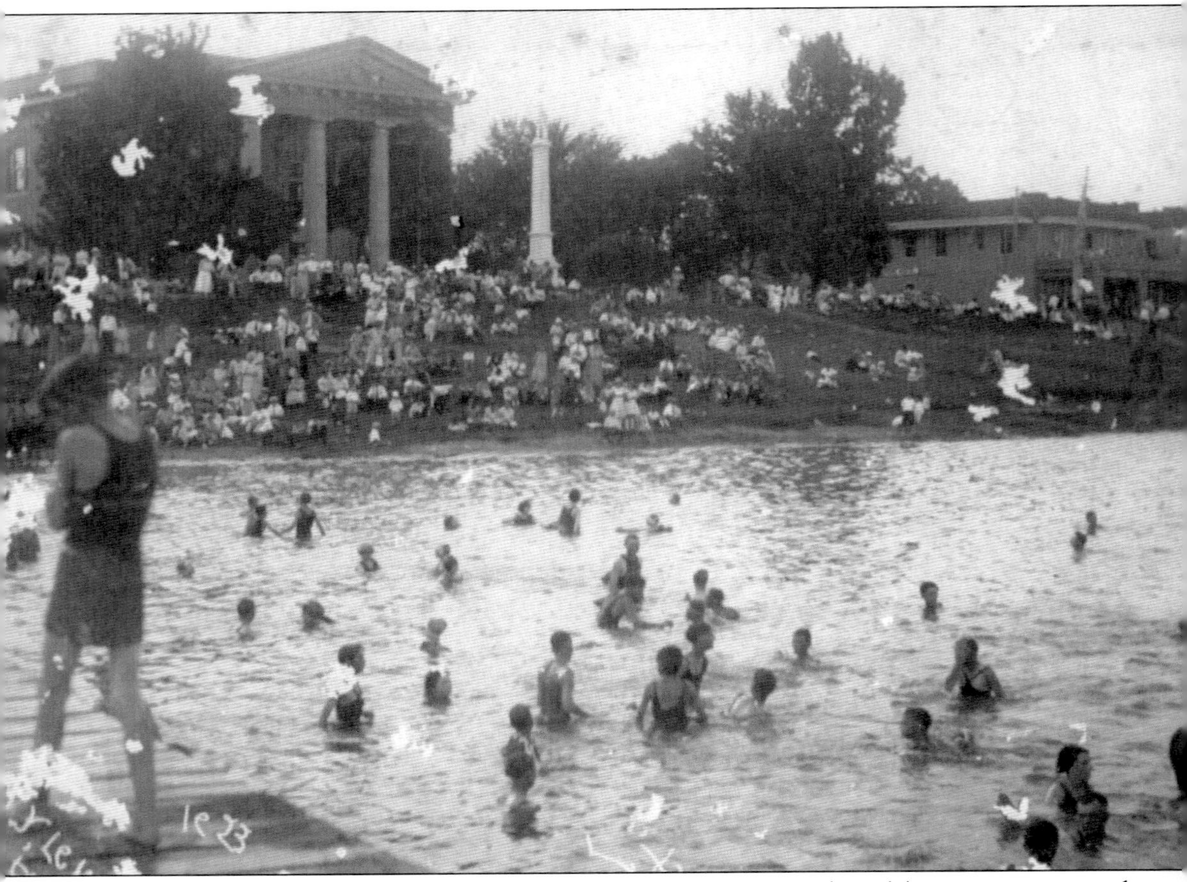

The first Lake Village Water Carnival was held on July 4, 1920. The celebration incorporated water sports (swimming and diving) a parade, a baseball game, and, by 1921, boat races. Fireworks were added in 1923. Sponsored by the W.T. Conkley Post of the American Legion, the carnival attracted visitors from across the region—an estimated 8,000 to 10,000 in 1926. However, the event ended following the flood of 1927 and the Great Depression, only to be revived in 1947. (Courtesy of the Museum of Chicot County.)

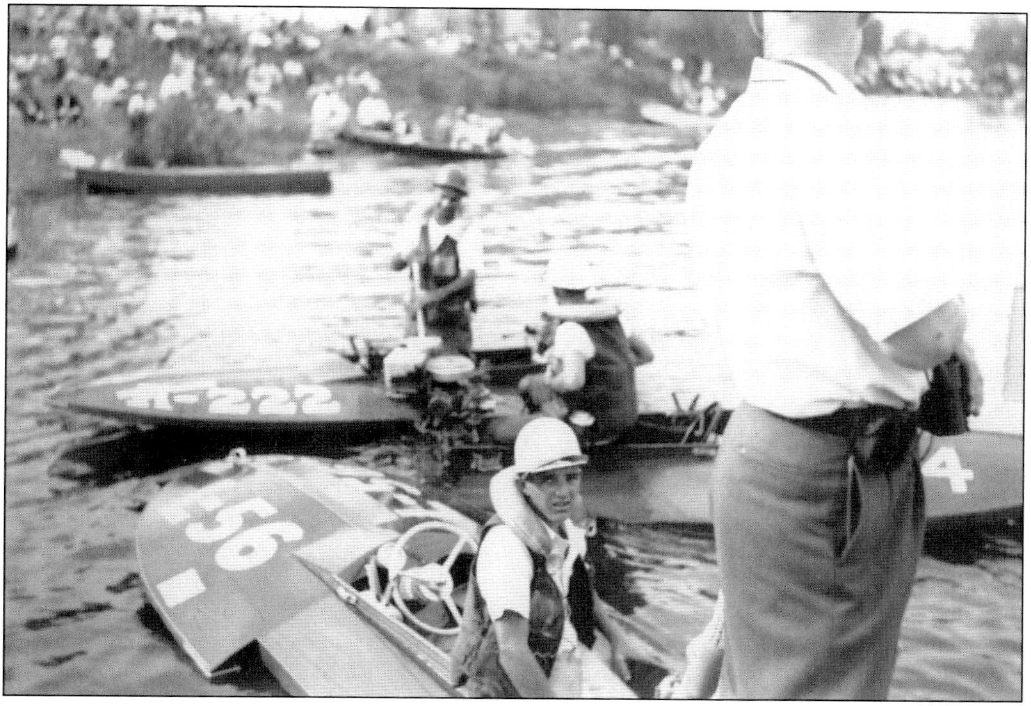

David Livingston (No. 56) began racing at the age of 13 in 1946. At the fourth annual Lake Village Water Carnival held on July 4, 1950, Livingston won the 22-horsepower runabout race in front of 17,000 spectators. In 1951 he was crowned again, setting a speed record. The next year, at the National Boat Races held in Lake Chicot, he successfully defended his National Outboard Racing title. (Both, courtesy of the Museum of Chicot County.)

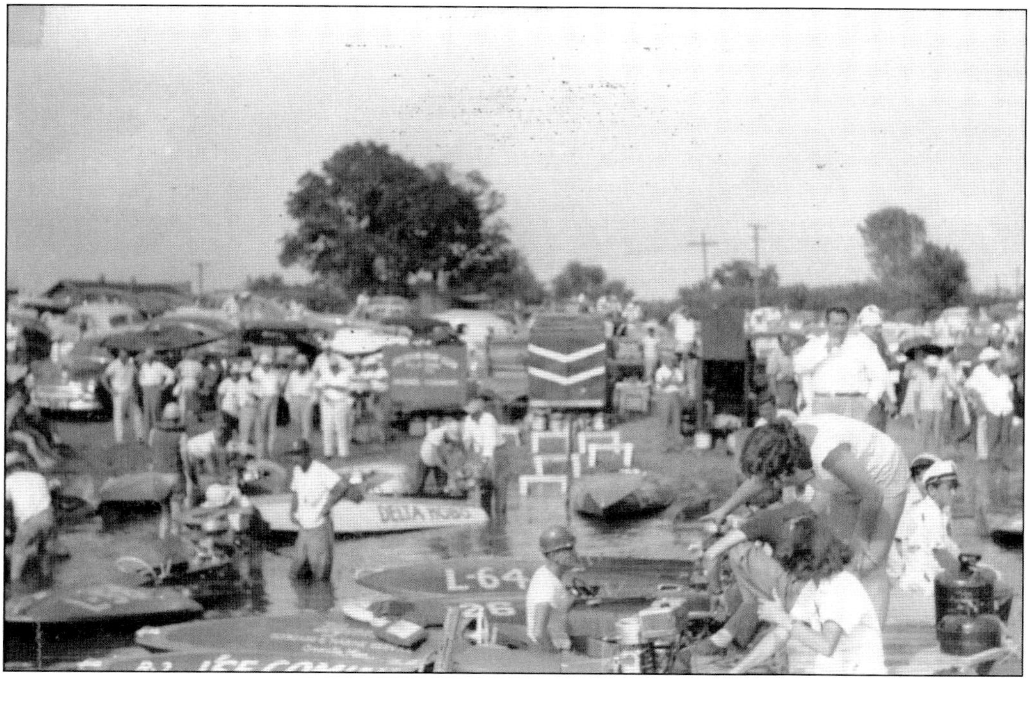

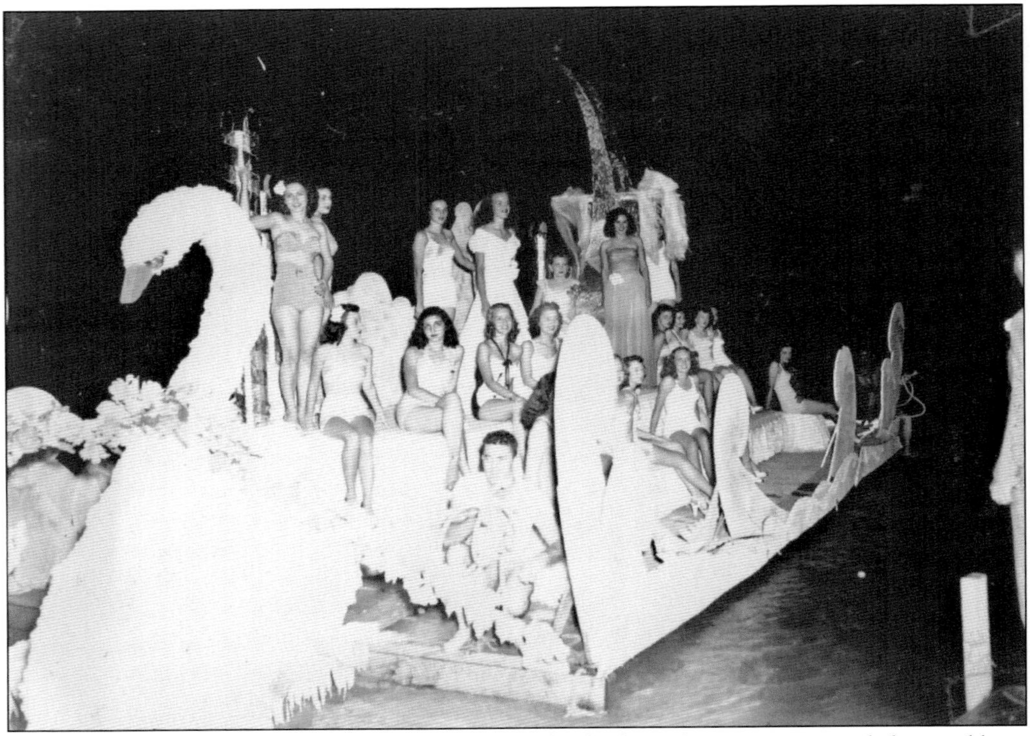

The Lake Village Water Carnival, held each Fourth of July in the postwar period, featured boat races, water floats, a parade, fireworks, baseball, hot dogs, and the Bathing Beauty Revue. While the 1948 carnival was dedicated to the "Restoration of Lake Chicot," the carnival was canceled in 1956, and Lake Chicot's water quality discouraged its continuation. Boat races were held periodically, but the event was not revived until 1979, once construction began on the Lake Chicot Pumping Plant. The event was called Whiskey Shoot in 1979. In 1980, the name was changed to the family-friendly Lake Village Annual Festival. (Above, courtesy of the Museum of Chicot County; below, courtesy of Libby Borgognoni.)

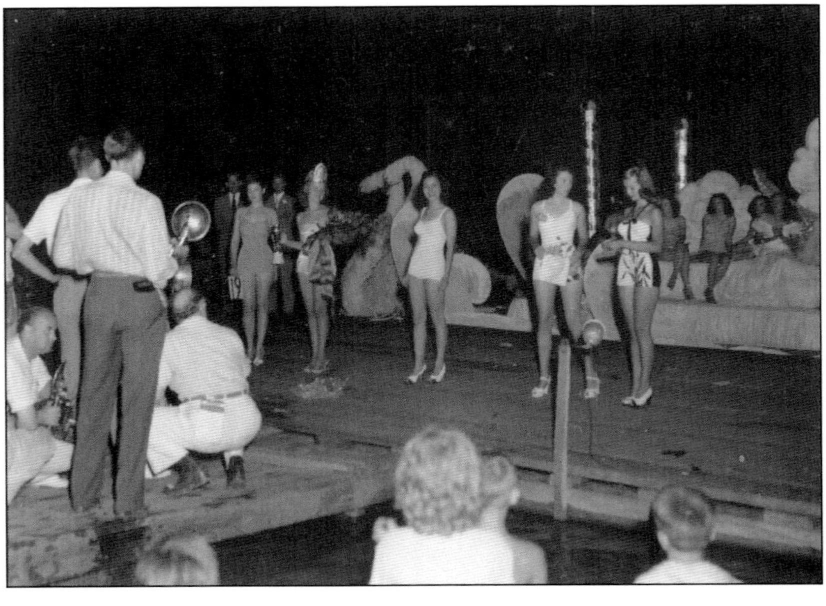

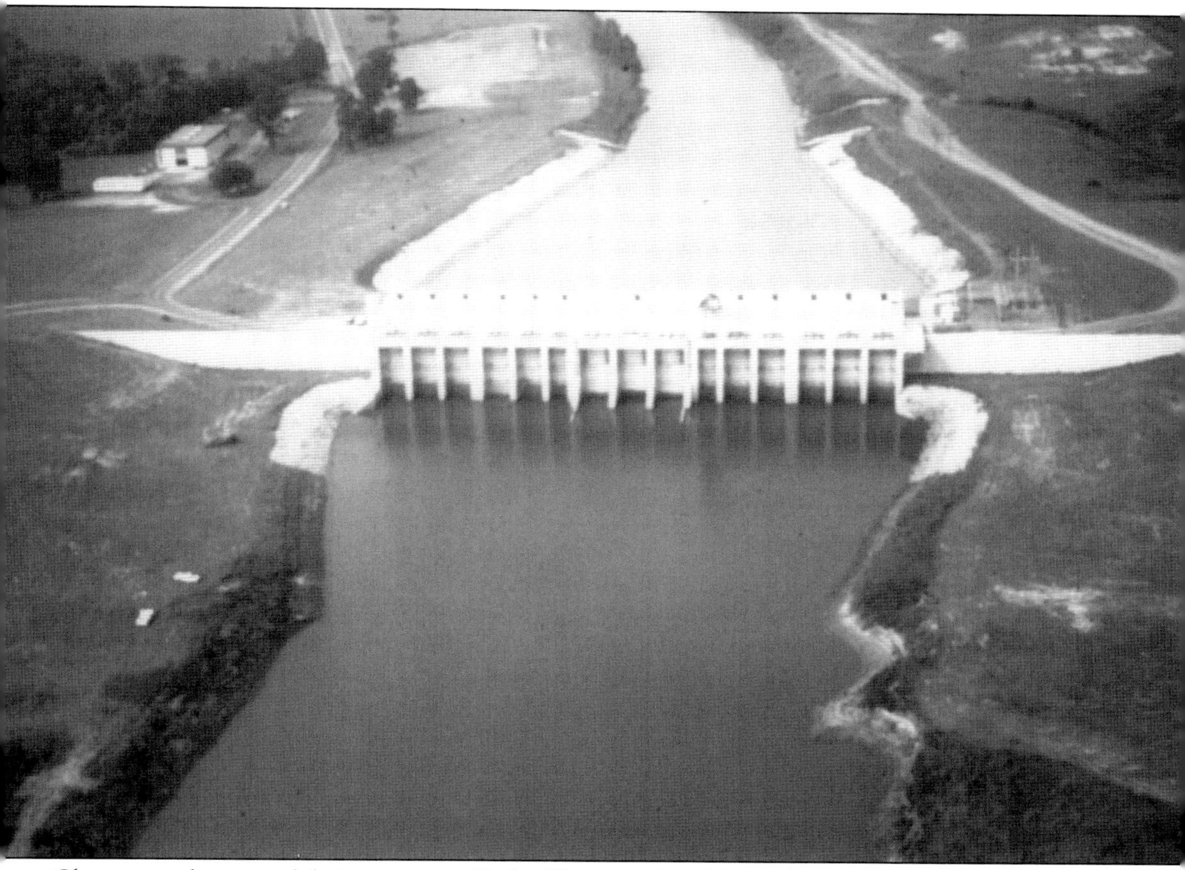

Changes to the natural drainage around Lake Chicot in the 1920s and extensive land clearing in the 1940s destroyed the lake's water quality with silt and pollution. By the 1960s, locals complained of the economic losses, bemoaning Lake Chicot as an "oversized drainage ditch." Studies showed the lake was filling in at the rate of two or three inches per year and would be completely filled within 200 years. In 1968, Congress authorized the Lake Chicot Project to divert undesirable runoff into the Mississippi River through a new pumping plant and other control structures. The Lake Chicot Pumping Plant, pictured here, began diverting runoff from Macon Lake in 1985. (Courtesy of the Museum of Chicot County.)

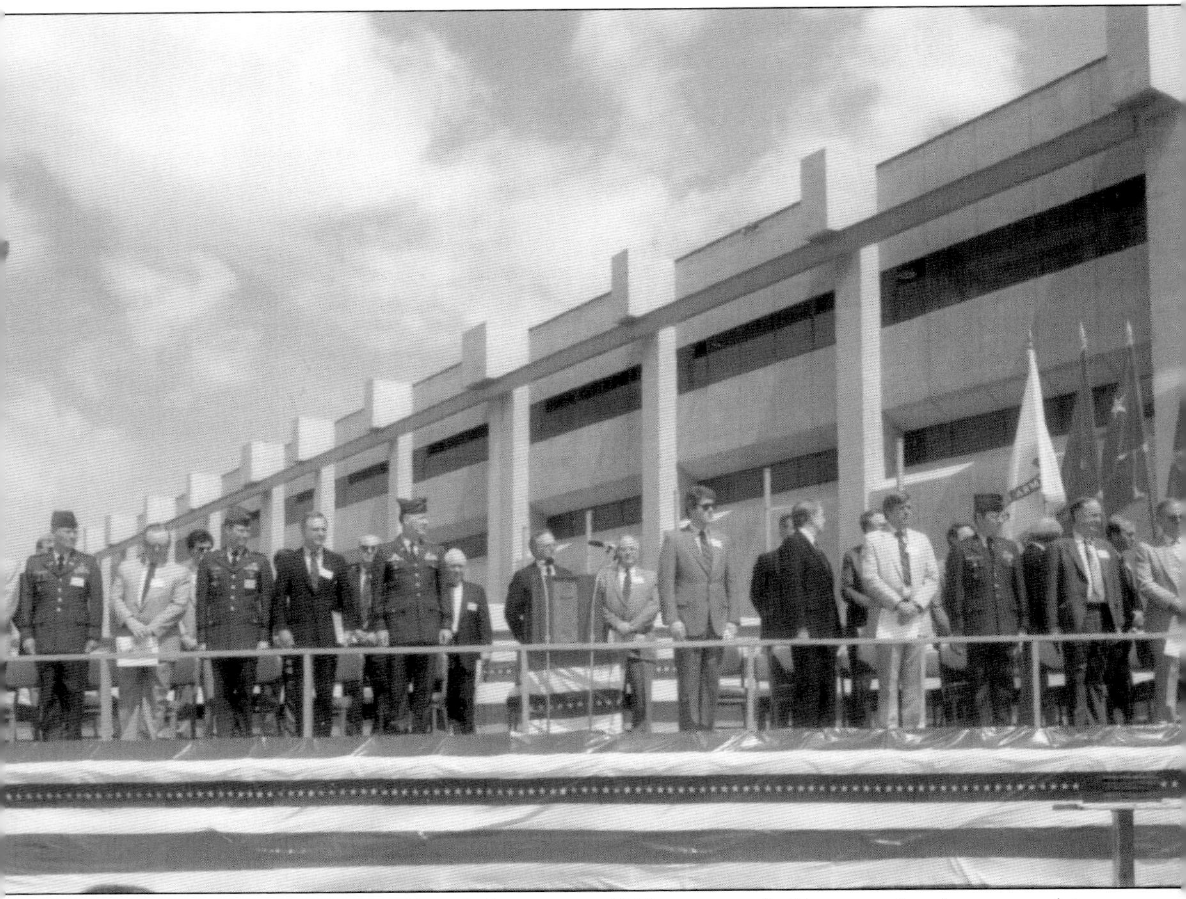

The Lake Chicot Pumping Plant dedication in 1984 was attended by many local, state, and Army Corps dignitaries, including Arkansas governor Bill Clinton and Senators Dale Bumpers and David Pryor. In 1966, then a candidate for the US House of Representatives, Pryor campaigned to make the Lake Chicot Project a "top priority challenge." (Courtesy of the David Hampton Pryor Papers, Special Collections, University of Arkansas Libraries.)

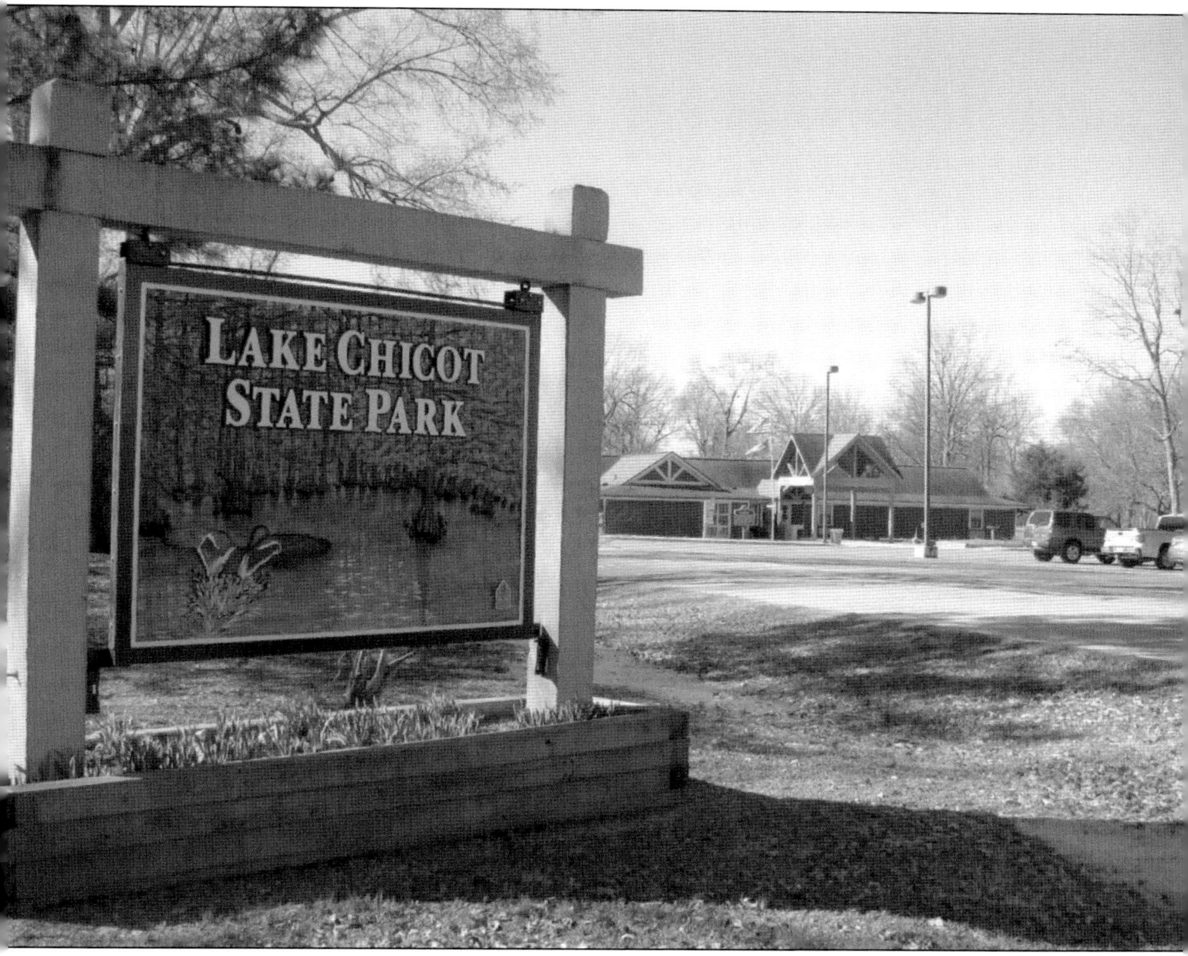

Lake Chicot State Park opened in April 1957, giving the public access to Arkansas's largest natural lake. The park, located on the former Letrobe Plantation, was made possible after citizens raised $6,000 to purchase the 43-acre tract, which was then donated to the state. Today the park has a visitor center with exhibits on the lake and Chicot County's history, 122 campsites, 14 cabins, and a popular swimming pool. (Courtesy of Lakeport Plantation.)

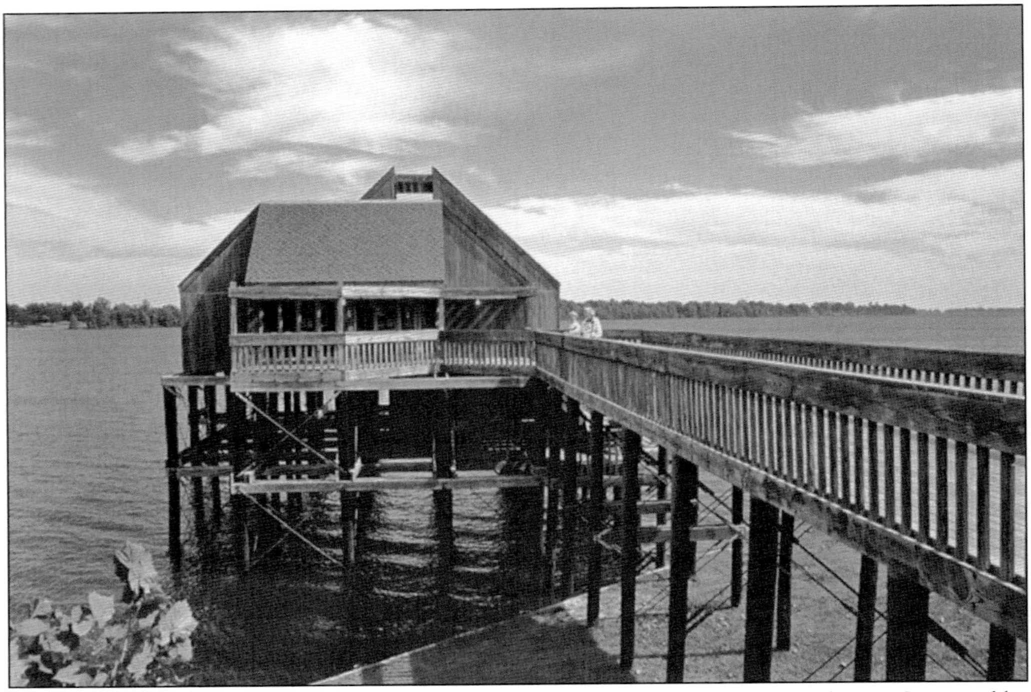

The first Lake Village welcome center was built in 1980 on piers over Lake Chicot. Operated by the Arkansas Department of Parks and Tourism, it was the state's first solar powered welcome center. In 2009, a new welcome center was constructed and dedicated by Gov. Mike Beebe in January 2010. The new center, built on land with a three level dock for viewing the lake and fishing, saw 55,000 visitors in 2014. (Above, courtesy of the Arkansas Department of Parks and Tourism; below, courtesy of Lakeport Plantation.)

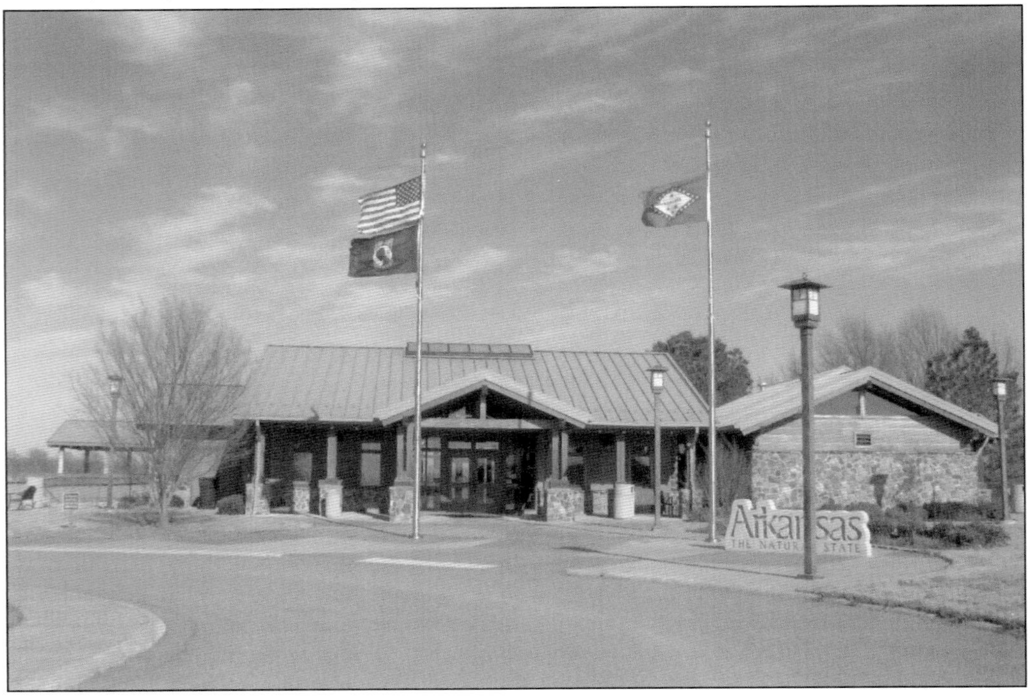

Six

Scenes from around Chicot County

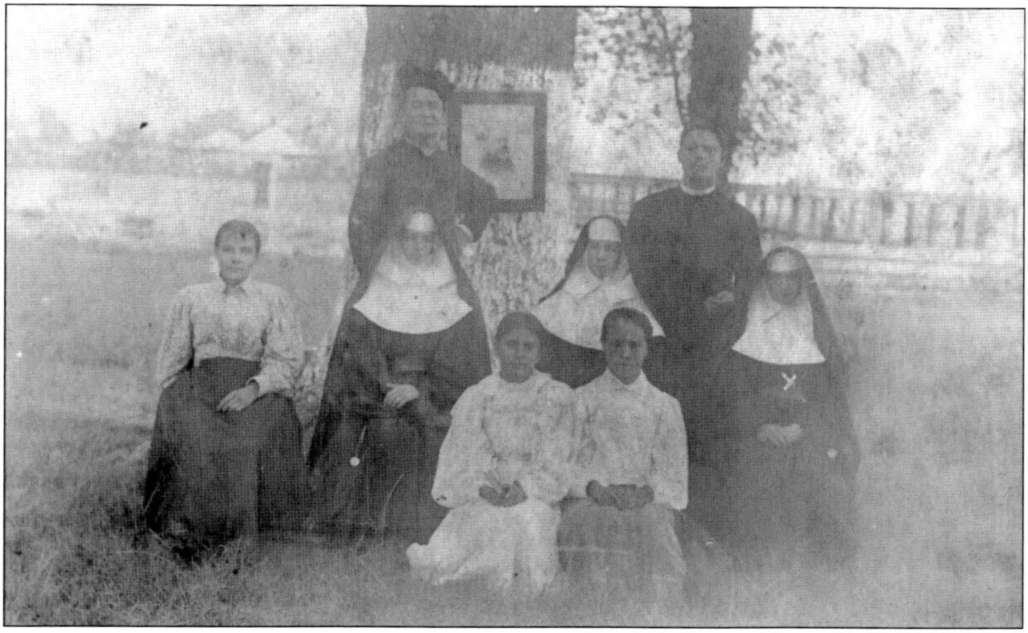

In 1895, Austin Corbin, a New York financier, planned to settle 100 Italian families onto small farms at his Sunnyside Plantation; 73 families arrived in New Orleans from Italy in November 1895 with contracts in hand. Fr. Pietro Bandini, assigned as chaplain to the new immigrants in early 1896, led a sizable group of Italians in 1898 to the Tontitown settlement in northwestern Arkansas after they found conditions at Sunnyside difficult (climate, disease, water supply, and contract disputes). Father Bandini is pictured here around 1896 standing next to a portrait of Corbin, who had recently died in a carriage accident. (Courtesy of Tontitown Historical Museum, Bastianelli Collection.)

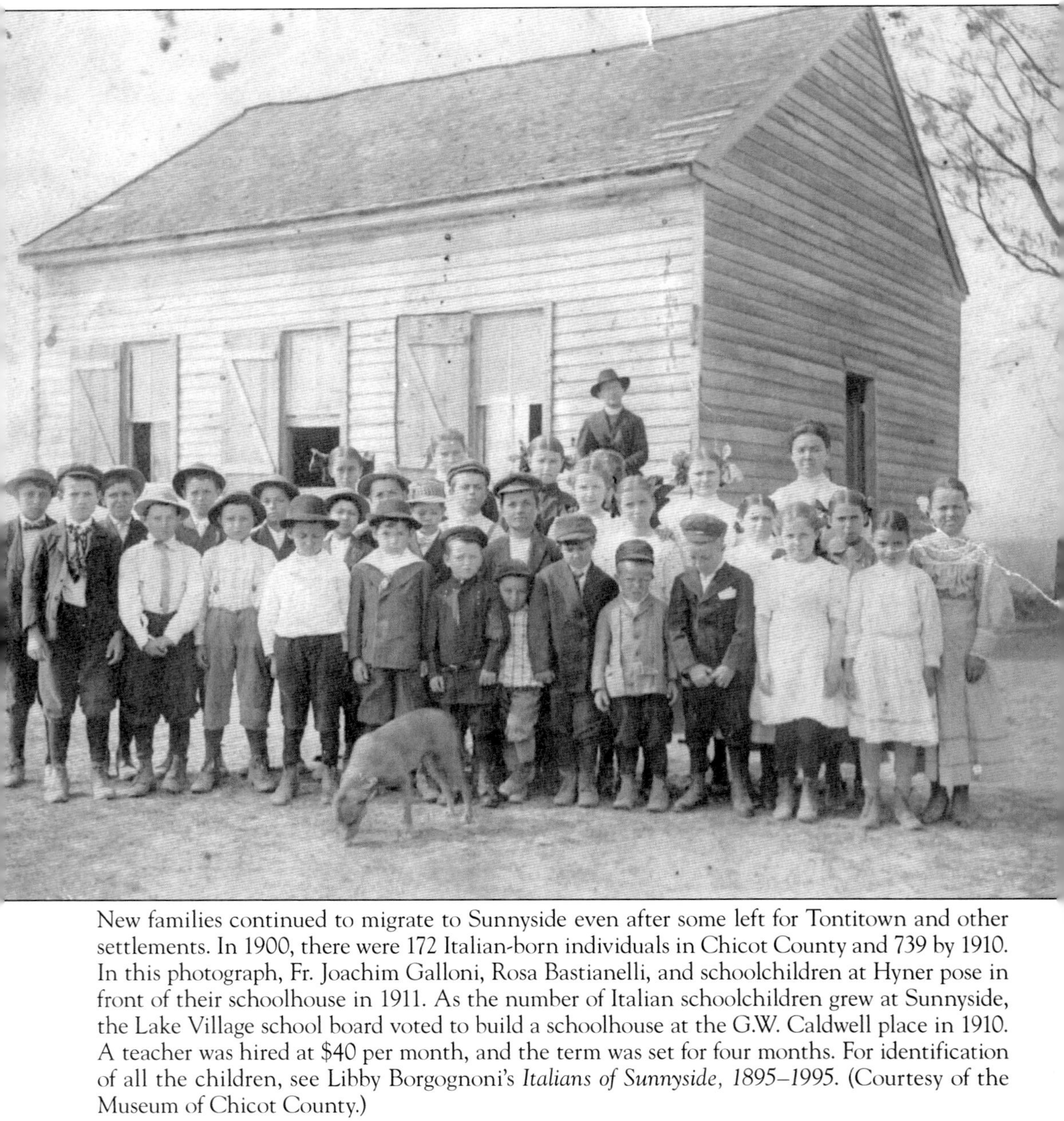

New families continued to migrate to Sunnyside even after some left for Tontitown and other settlements. In 1900, there were 172 Italian-born individuals in Chicot County and 739 by 1910. In this photograph, Fr. Joachim Galloni, Rosa Bastianelli, and schoolchildren at Hyner pose in front of their schoolhouse in 1911. As the number of Italian schoolchildren grew at Sunnyside, the Lake Village school board voted to build a schoolhouse at the G.W. Caldwell place in 1910. A teacher was hired at $40 per month, and the term was set for four months. For identification of all the children, see Libby Borgognoni's *Italians of Sunnyside, 1895–1995*. (Courtesy of the Museum of Chicot County.)

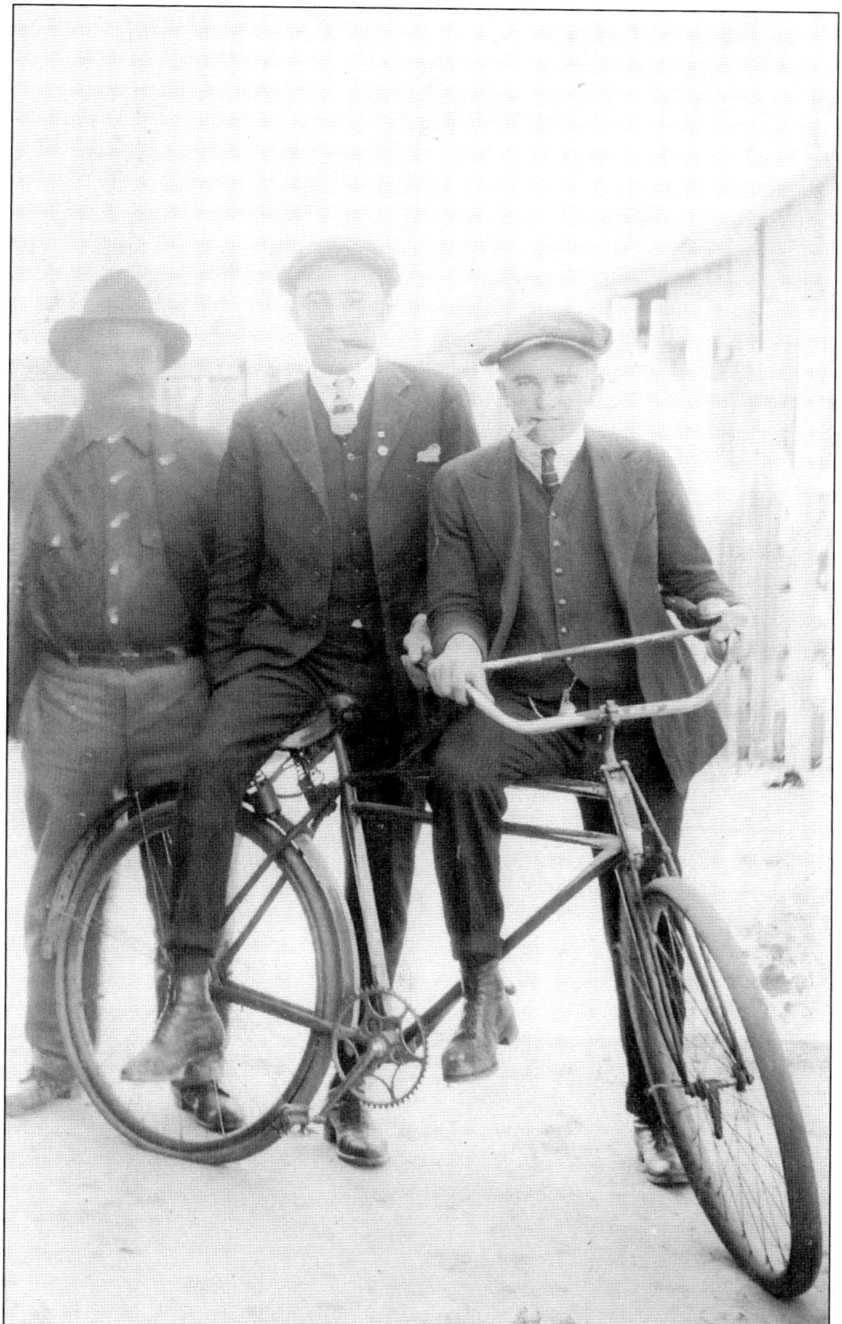

From left to right, Italian-born neighbors Florio Cingolani, Santo Rossini, and Primo Nicolini are pictured around 1920. Florio Cingolani arrived in the United States in September 1908 and married Anna Catalani in August 1909. Santo Rossini arrived from Italy with his parents in 1902. Rossini, well known in the Delta for his Old World–style wines, married Elvira Sampoalesi in 1922 and later wed Isola Carletti in 1948. Primo Nicolini became a citizen in 1906; he married Bernice Turner in 1938, worked as a carpenter, and resided in Lake Village until his death in 1973. (Courtesy of Libby Borgognoni).

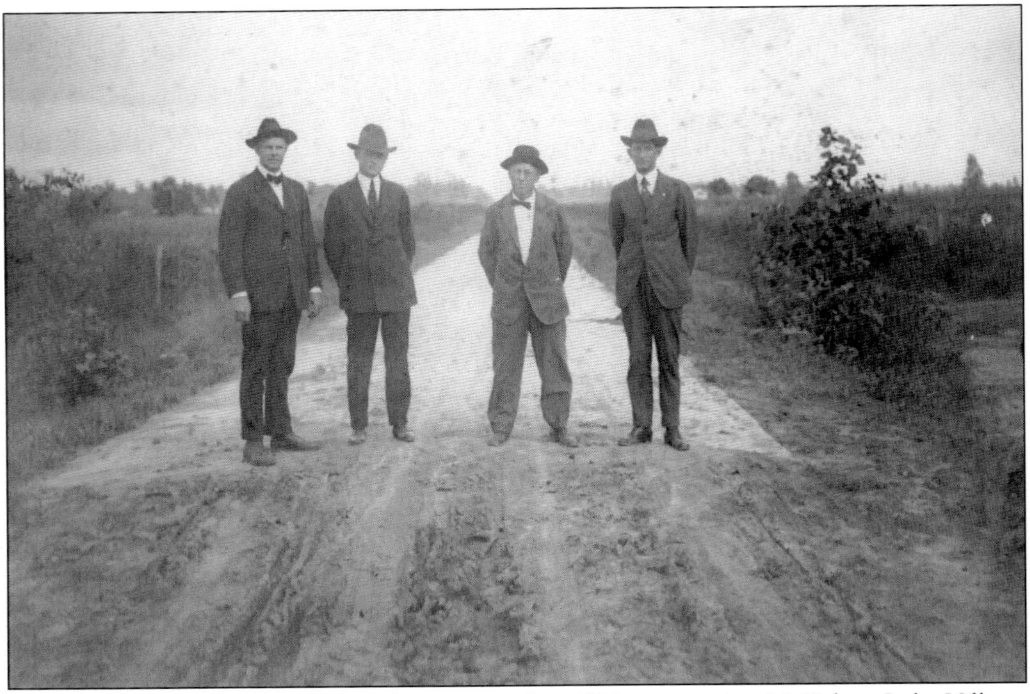

The paved Arkansas-Louisiana Highway opened in 1922, connecting McGehee, Lake Village, and Eudora to Louisiana's paved road. Before its unveiling, unpaved roads in buckshot soil were the norm and difficult to traverse and maintain. These two photographs show officials from Dermott, Lake Village, McGehee, and Little Rock standing ceremoniously on the highway in 1919 (above) and in 1922 (below), when it was completed. (Both, courtesy of Desha County Historical Society.)

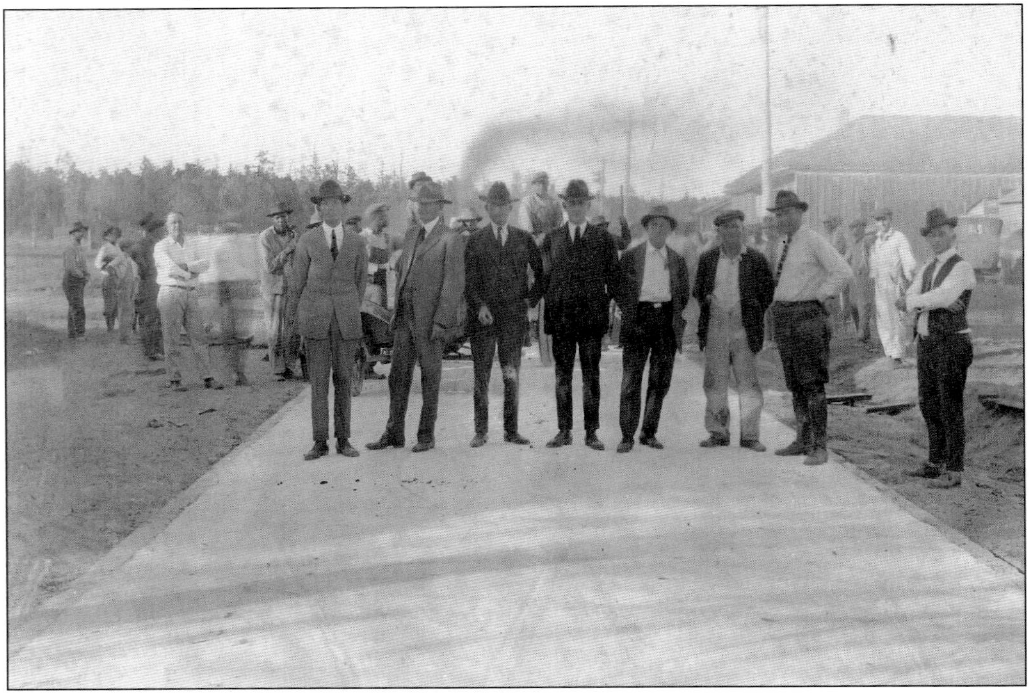

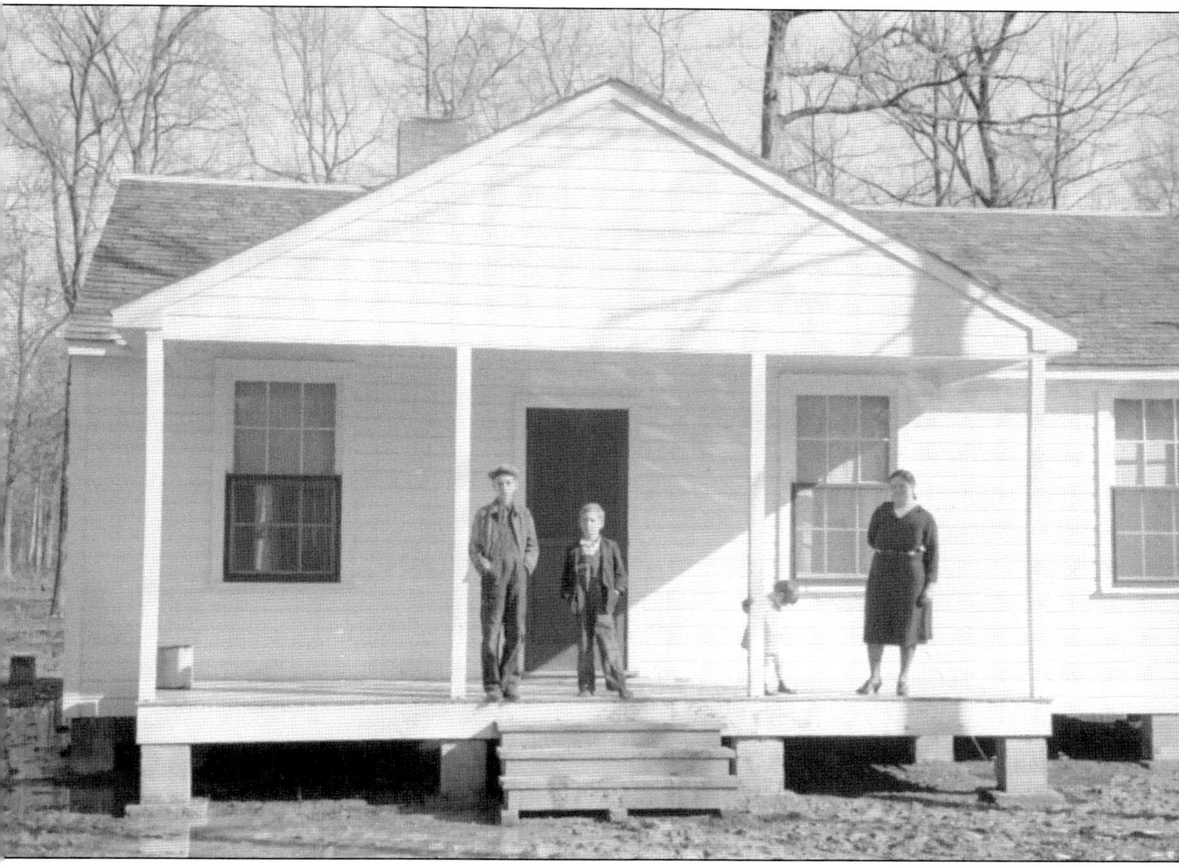

This Farm Security Administration photograph, dated January 1939, shows a house at Chicot Farms, a New Deal resettlement community. Chicot Farms spanned 13,781 acres in Chicot and Drew Counties and was divided into 53-acre plots. According to historian Donald Holley, it was one of dozens of Depression-era "model rural communities, complete with neat, white-frame houses, picket fences, red barns, vegetable gardens, flower beds, and fruit trees" meant to "rebuild rural life through the use of good sense and scientific planning." Leased to the War Relocation Authority during World War II, Chicot Farms became a Japanese American internment camp and then a German POW camp. (Courtesy of the Library of Congress.)

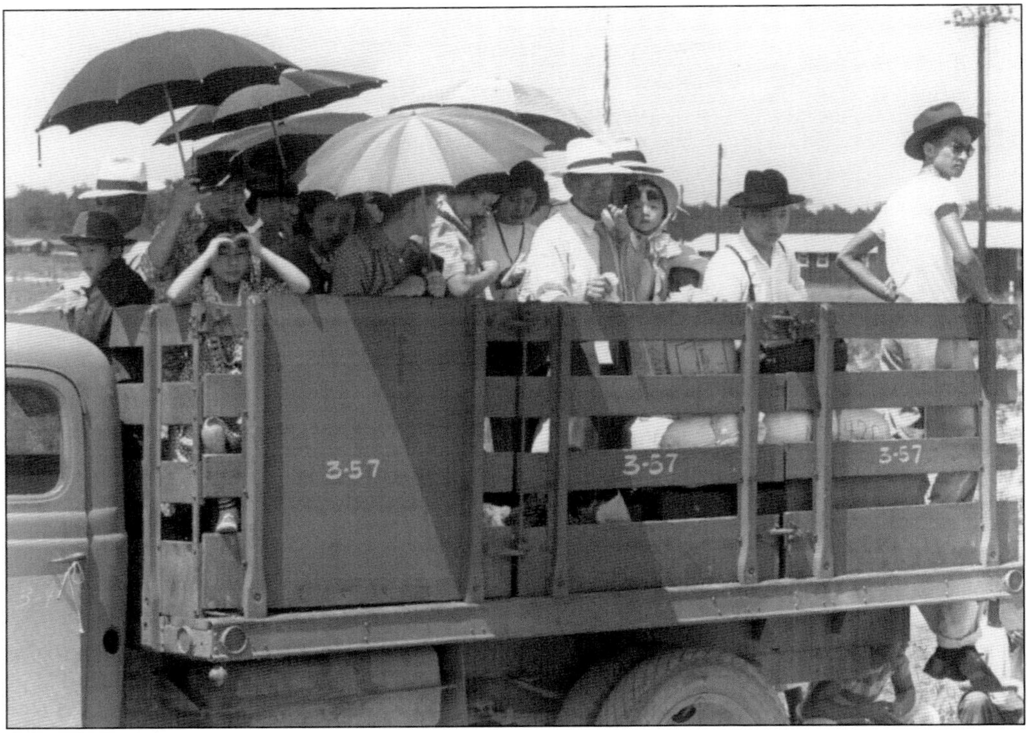

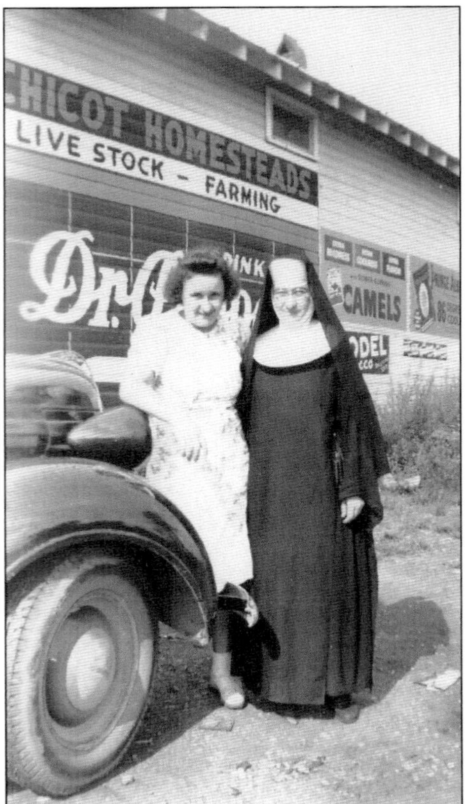

The World War II Japanese American internment camp at Jerome operated from October 6, 1942, to June 30, 1944, when it reached a peak population of 8,497 internees. The internees, American citizens mostly from the West Coast, were rounded up during the hysteria following the bombing of Pearl Harbor. When Jerome became a German POW camp, internees were transferred to Rohwer in Desha County, and other camps. (Courtesy of the Jerome Relocation Center Records, Special Collections, University of Arkansas Libraries.)

Sr. Patrick Cingolani and a friend pose at Chicot Homesteads, a Farm Security Administration project for African American farmers. The project leased farmland for 30 families in 1939. (Courtesy of Libby Borgognoni.)

These photographs from April 22, 1927, show the flood fight at Lakeport. The US Army Corps of Engineers marshaled barges, sandbags, revetments made of timbers, and local labor in an attempt to reinforce the levees that held the Mississippi River's floodwaters. Lakeport, which can be seen in the distance at right, suffered no direct flood damage. (Both, courtesy of the Library of Congress.)

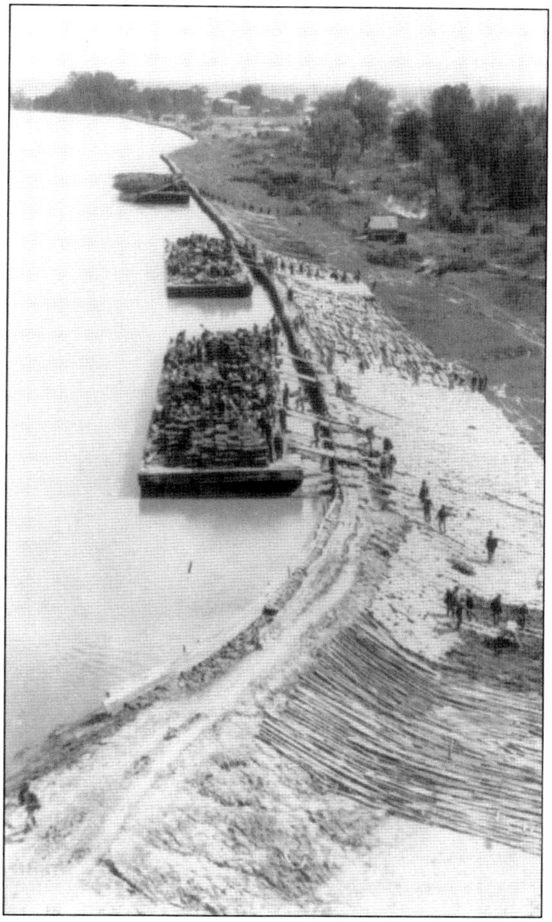

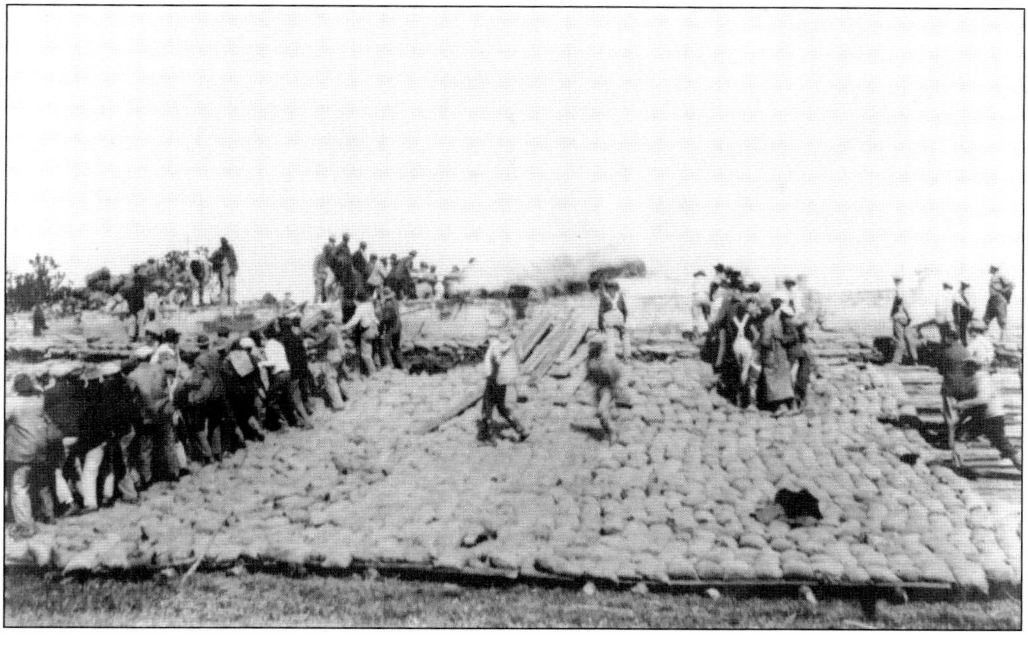

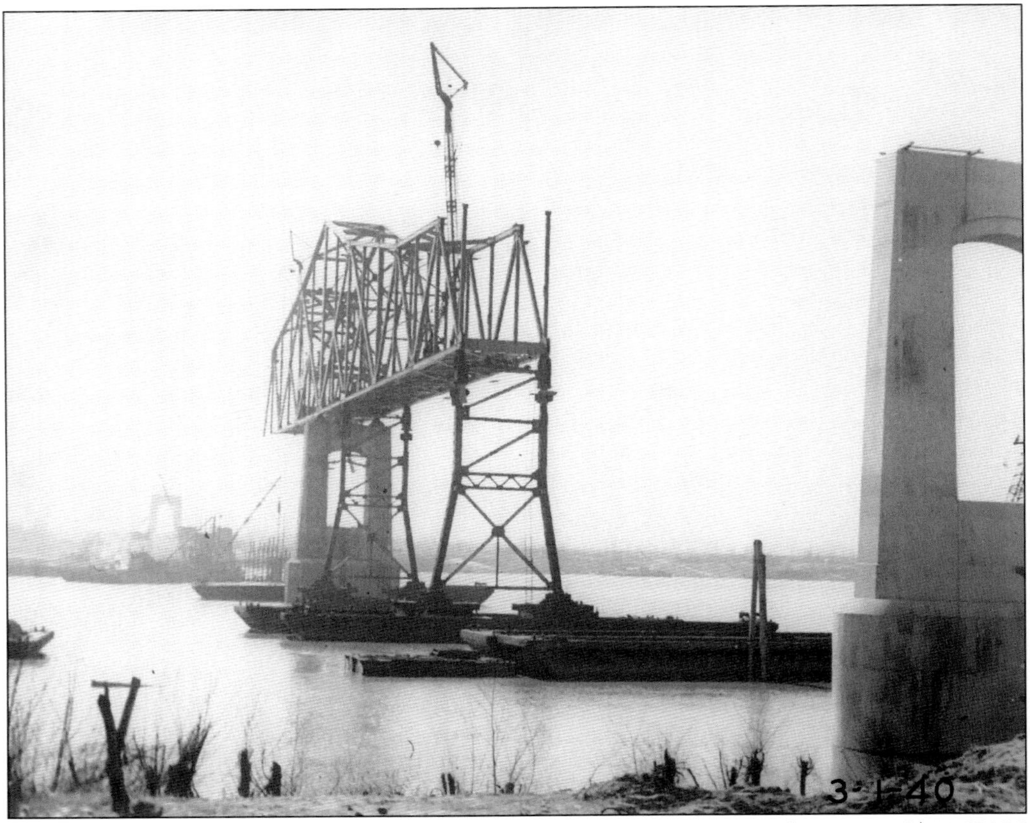

The B.G. Humphrey's Bridge (Greenville–Lake Village Bridge), constructed at a cost of $4,447,000 over five years, opened on September 17, 1940. Before the bridge, ferries were the primary transportation across the Mississippi River. In 1940, Greenville Bridge & Ferry Co. transported 200 to 300 cars, plus trucks and buses each day. (Both, courtesy of the Special Collections of the William Alexander Percy Memorial Library.)

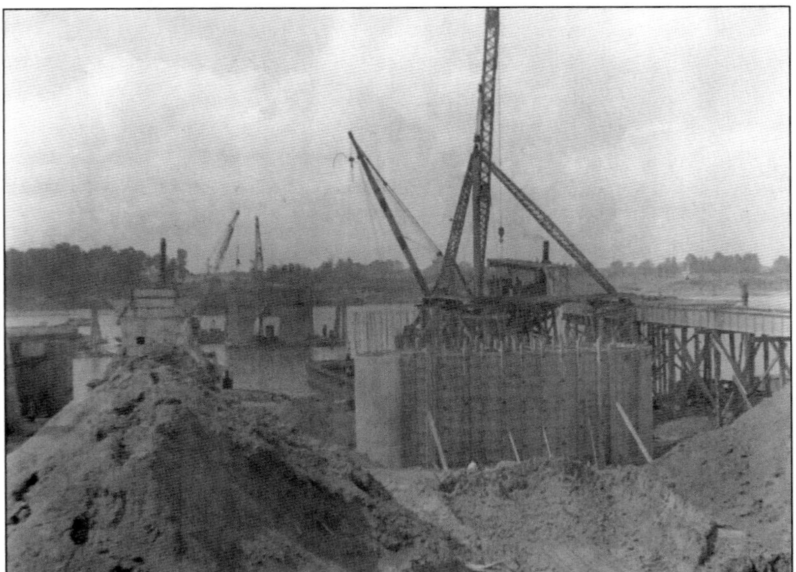

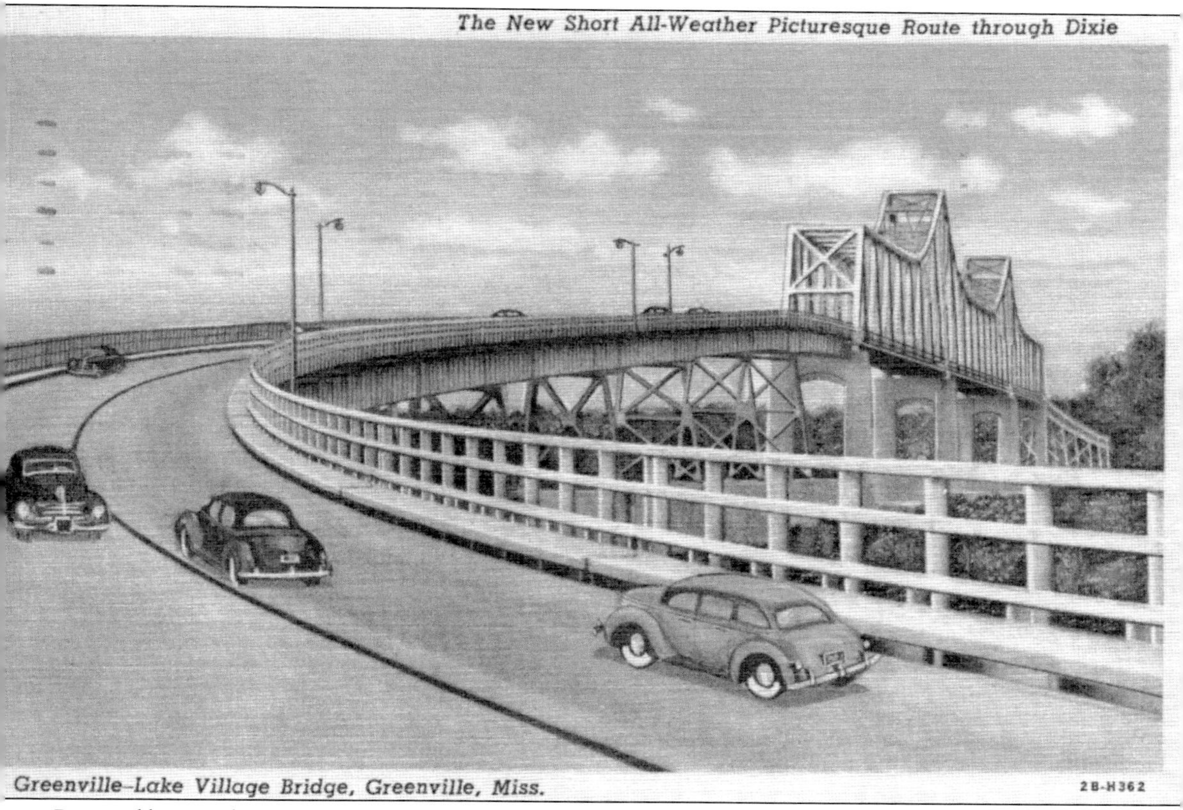

Pictured here is the B.G. Humphrey's Bridge, a two-lane steel through-truss bridge linking Chicot County, Arkansas, with Washington County, Mississippi. The bridge opened an all-weather route from coast to coast and was expected to be a boon for the local economy. Operated by the City of Greenville, the bridge originally charged a toll for cars, buses (by the passenger), trucks (by the axle), pedestrians, and livestock. Rates were slowly reduced until the bridge became free in November 1950. The city allowed the Tennessee Gas Transmission Company to place gas lines under the bridge, which generated enough revenue to pay for it. (Courtesy of Blake Wintory.)

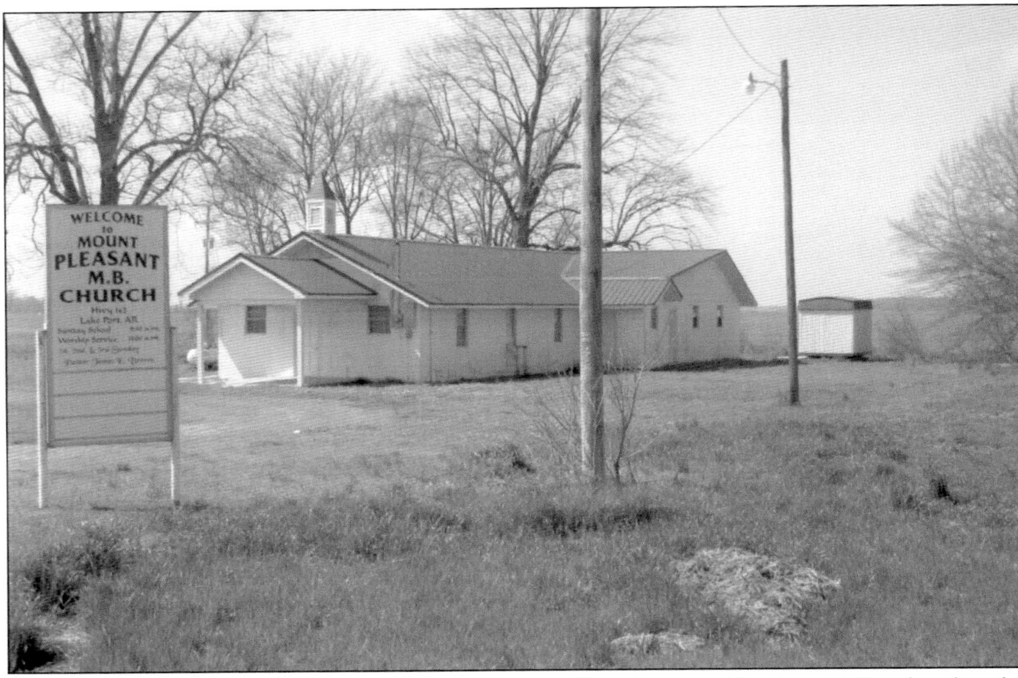

Records for the Mount Pleasant Missionary Baptist Church extend back to 1889. The church's original location was at the grudge ditch near the Old Lakeport Cemetery. The cemetery is believed to date to slavery and has over 200 graves, many of them unmarked. (Courtesy of Lakeport Plantation.)

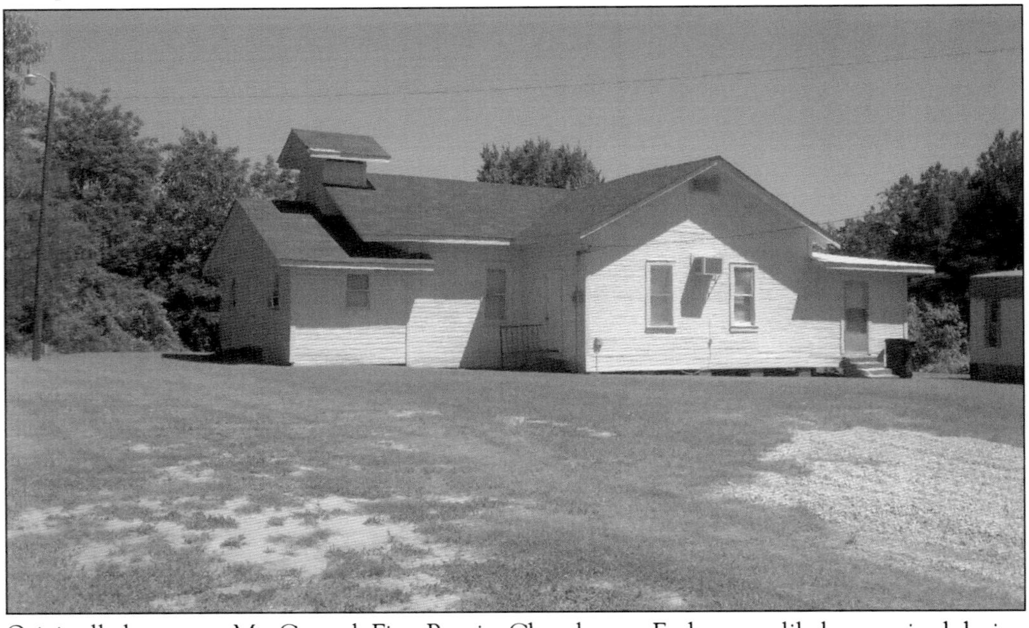

Originally known as Mt. Carmel, First Baptist Church near Eudora was likely organized during Reconstruction. Its first pastor, Nathan E. Edward, arrived in Chicot County in the early 1870s. This wood-frame building was constructed in 1946, replacing an earlier structure erected in 1900. The First Baptist Church was listed in the National Register of Historic Places in 1998 for its significance to local African American history. (Courtesy of Lakeport Plantation.)

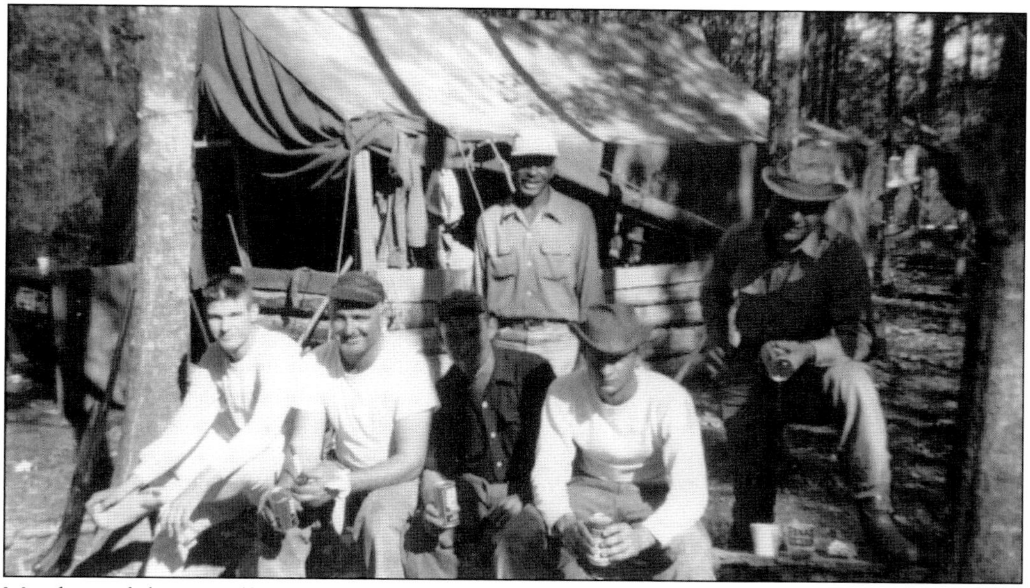

Members of the Boueff River Hunting Club pictured here are, from left to right, Fred Zieman, Emillo Grassi, Guy McDill Jr., Mike Pesaresi Jr., Henry Tolliver, and Frank Pesaresi, at camp around 1953. The men hunted and tracked deer on horseback, a technique Mike Pesaresi described as "riding the dogs." (Courtesy of Mike Pesaresi Jr.)

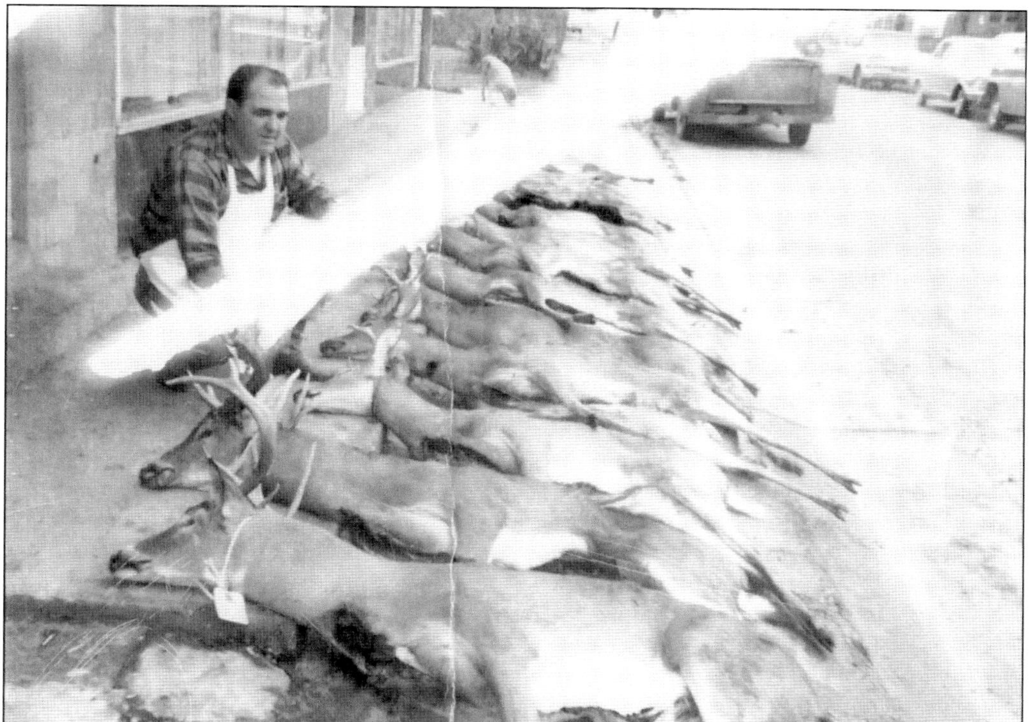

Johnny's Food Bank in downtown Lake Village processed meat for hunters and, in some years, offered "cash for squirrel tails." Johnny Grassi is pictured here with several kills from the 1963 season. In 1965, Grassi reported 95 deer had been killed in the Lake Village area, a smaller number than the 125 the previous year. (Courtesy of Mike Pesaresi Jr.)

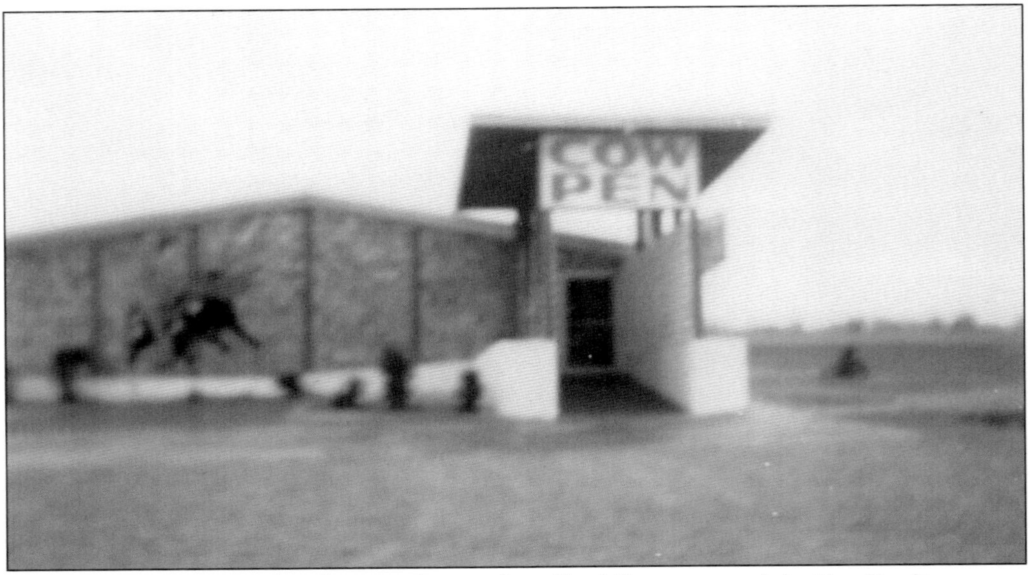

In 1967, two years before this photograph was taken, Floyd Owens opened the Cow Pen Restaurant in a former cattle-inspection station. Ownership passed to Gene and Juanita Grassi in 1977 and to the Faulk family in 2007. After a fire in 2007, the Faulks rebuilt and opened in 2008, still serving steaks and seafood as well as Mexican and Italian food. (Courtesy of Lake Village Public Library.)

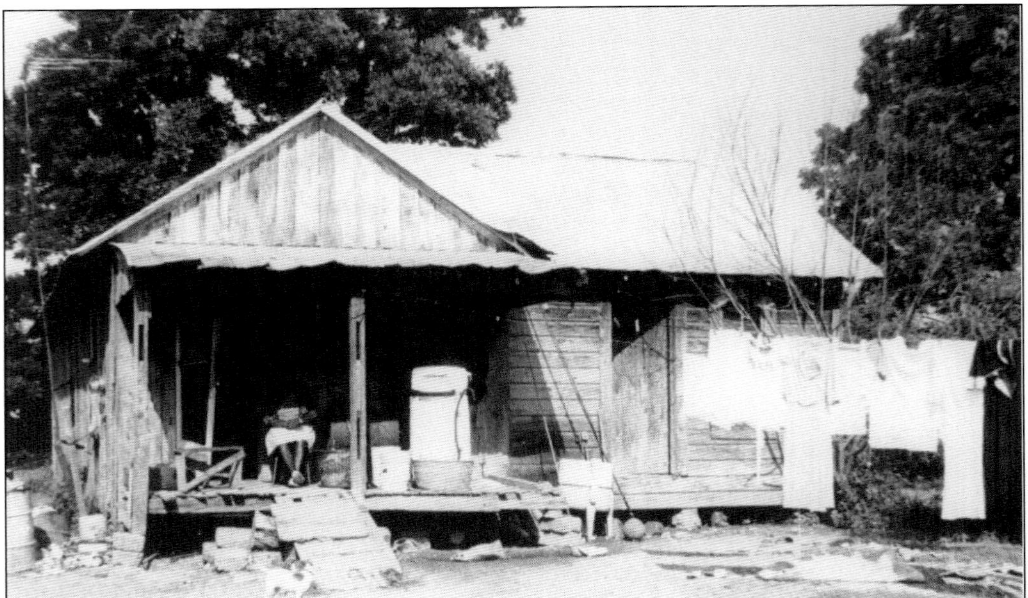

Plantations in Chicot County used to be dotted with houses like Elizabeth Brown's, pictured here in 1984. In the 1950s, the house was moved from the Blackwater Plantation to behind the Lakeport Plantation house; Della Cartwright, who worked for the Ford family at Lakeport, occupied it. After Cartwright moved to Eudora in 1972, Elizabeth and Willie Brown lived in the house. Elizabeth Davis first arrived at Lakeport around 1936 to farm for Frank Dantzler. In her marriage to Brown in 1938, Dantzler was listed as a surety. (Courtesy of the Arkansas Historic Preservation Program.)

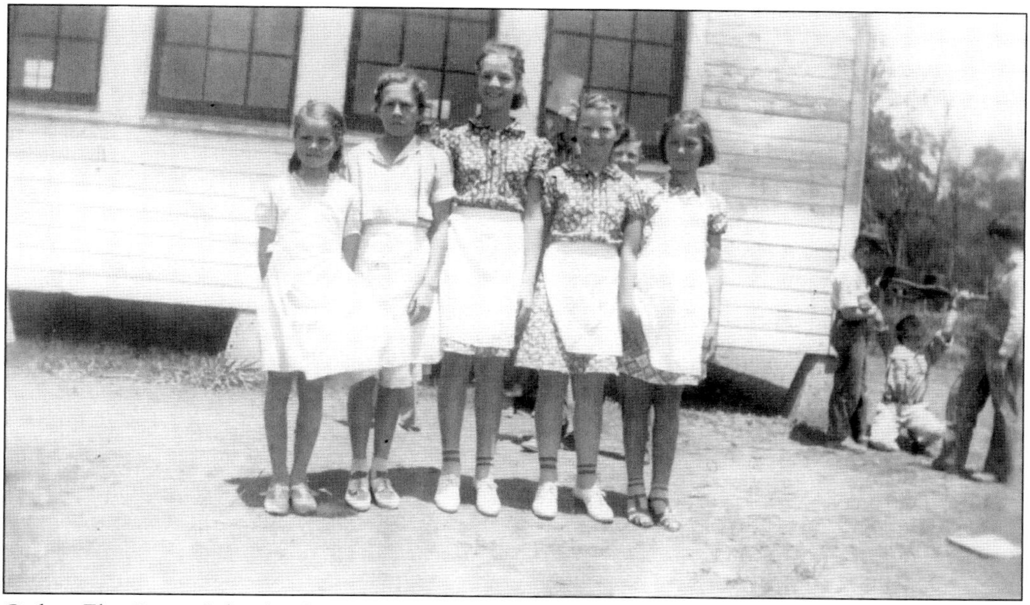

Girls at Elm Grove School at Jennie pose after a home economics lesson given by Amelia Arensman on how to make cream of tomato soup. From left to right are Elssie Smith, Flossie Steadman, Martha and Mildred Bennett, and Alice Prosell. The boys in the corner are, from left to right, Bobby Scarborough, Bobby Merrill, and Gerald Hendrix. (Courtesy of Alice Arensman.)

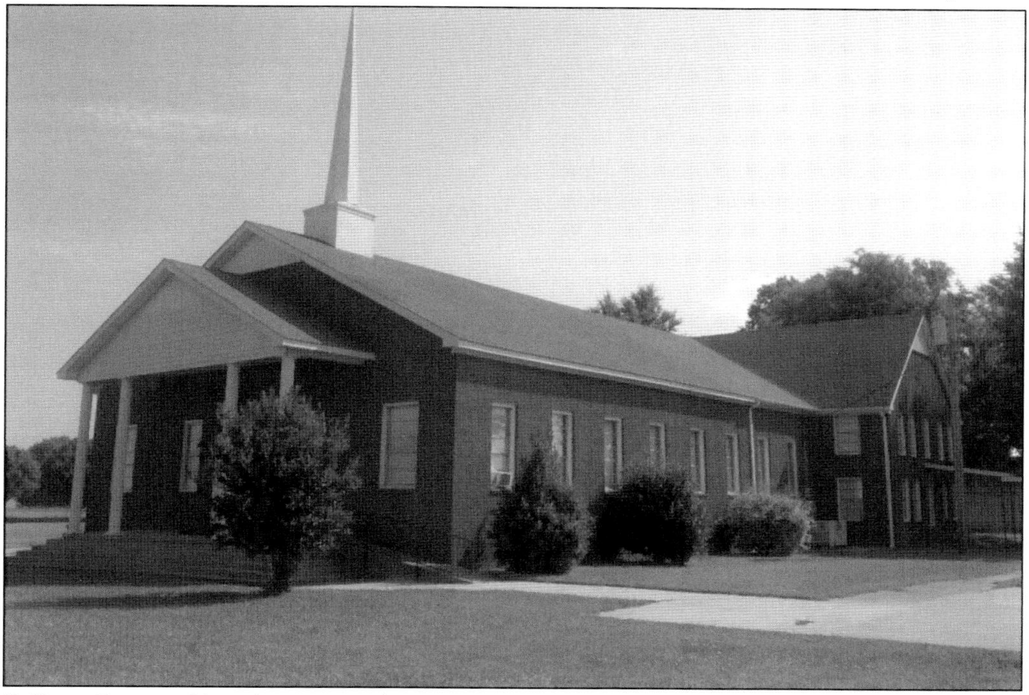

Bellaire Baptist Church, organized in 1917, constructed a new church building in 1950 and dedicated it in January 1951. The new structure, built under the guidance of foreman G.W. Roberts, featured asbestos siding and an interior finished with pine and a celotex ceiling. Since 1950, brick has replaced asbestos siding, and the turret has been replaced with a spire. (Courtesy of Lakeport Plantation.)

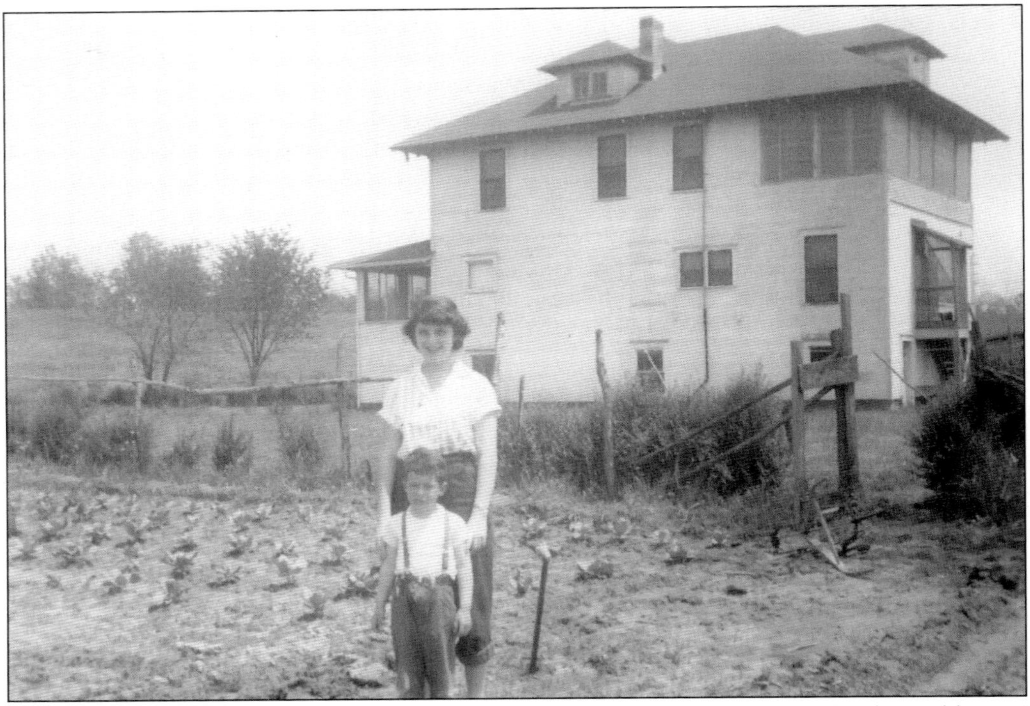

Goldstein House at Lakeport on the Chicot Plantation was built about 1914 for the Goldsteins' farm managers. Nathan Goldstein II moved into the house in 1947, farmed there for 17 years, and then owned a bookstore in Greenville until 1989. Here JoAnne Sachs and Nicky Goldstein stand in the garden at the back of the house. The home burned in the late 1990s. (Courtesy of Nelken Archives, Greenville History Museum.)

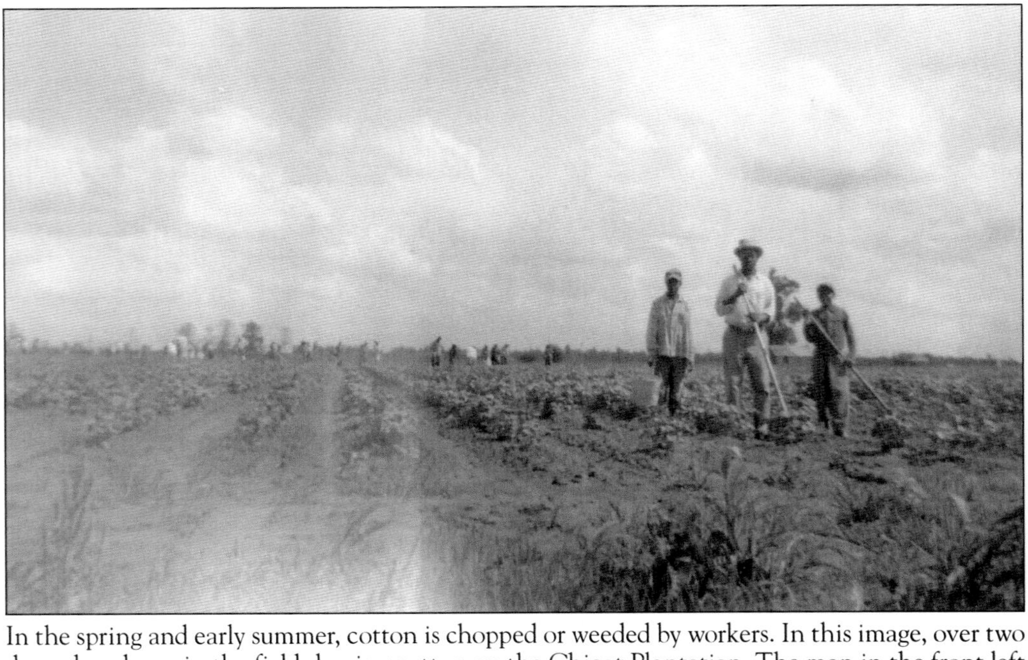

In the spring and early summer, cotton is chopped or weeded by workers. In this image, over two dozen hands are in the fields hoeing cotton on the Chicot Plantation. The man in the front left is holding a water pail. (Courtesy of Nelken Archives, Greenville History Museum.)

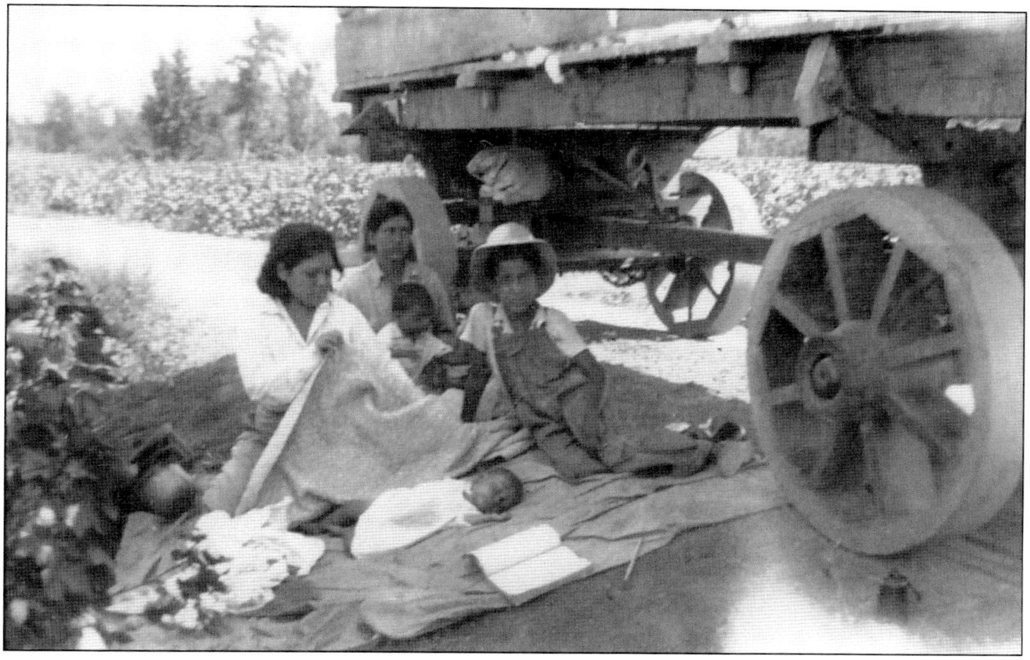

Cotton-picking season in September and October required hundreds of hands. It was common for buses to pick up hands in Greenville and Eudora and bring them to farms to chop or pick cotton. Some farmers, like Nathan Goldstein, brought Hispanic labor from Texas and the Southwest in the 1940s. (Courtesy of Nelken Archives, Greenville History Museum.)

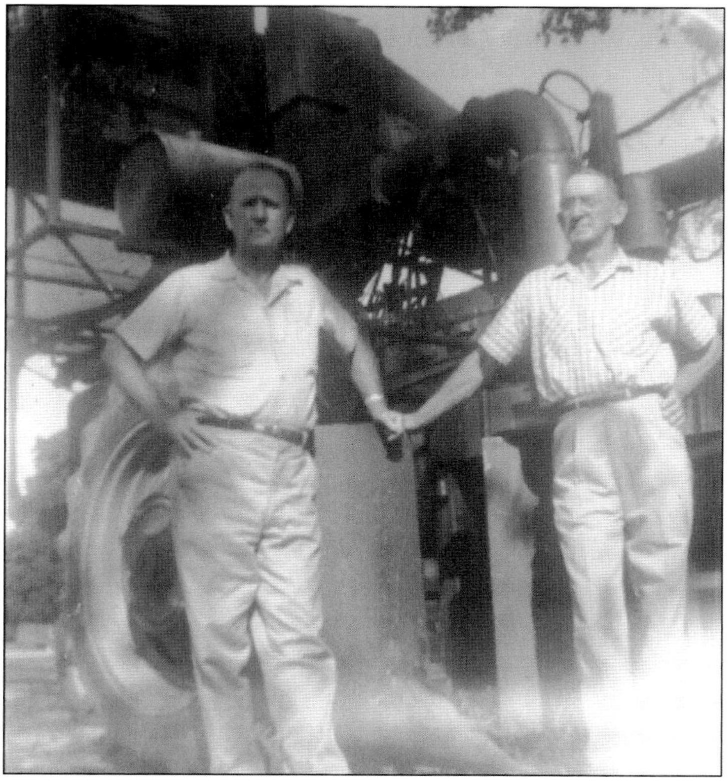

Alvin Ford Sr. and John Henbest pose with a two-row John Deere mechanical cotton picker at the Lakeport Plantation in November 1959. Lakeport's first mechanical picker was a one-row International Harvester picker from about 1955 that attached to a tractor and ran in reverse. The first commercial mechanical cotton pickers were produced by International Harvester in 1949; Deere and Company followed in 1950. (Courtesy of Jerry and Susie Ford.)

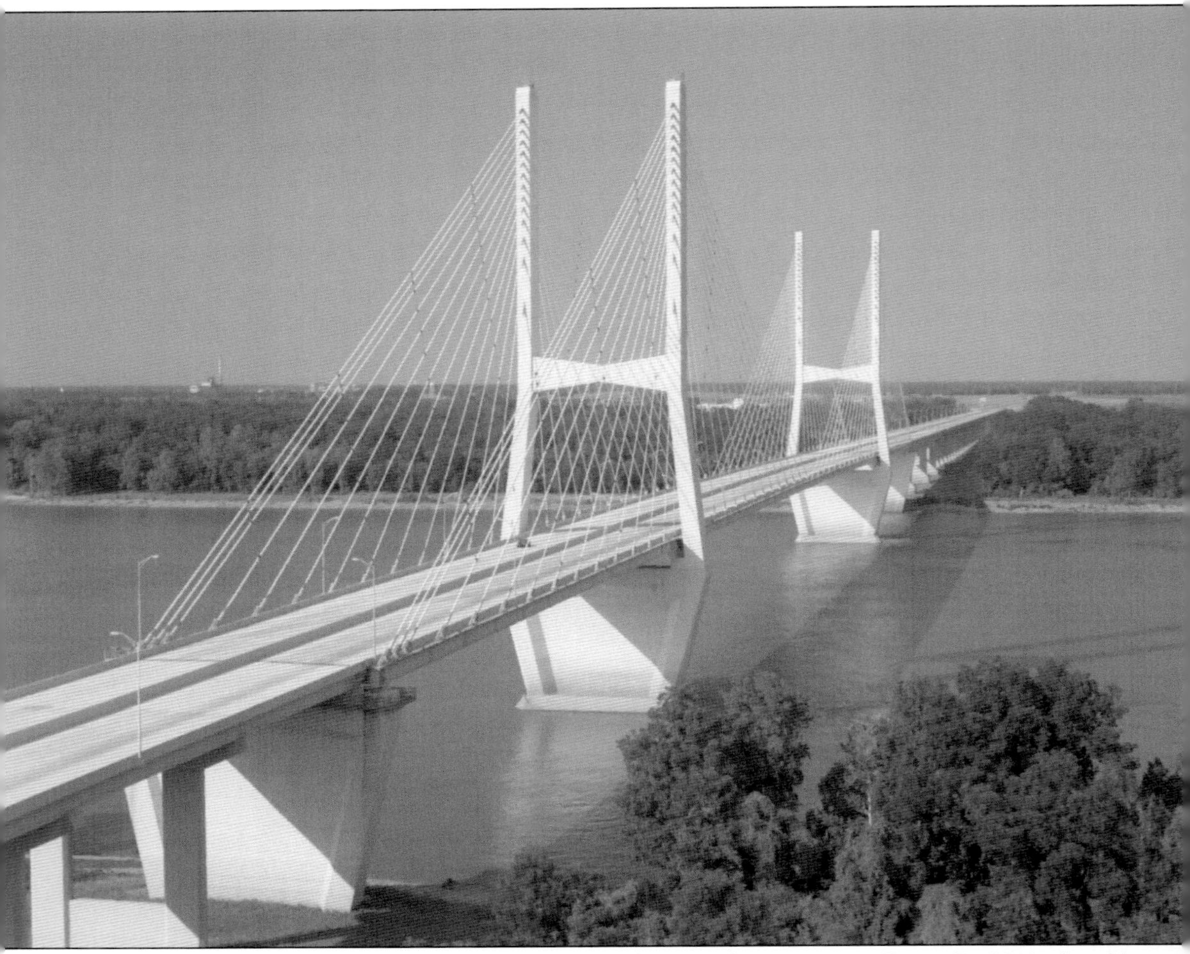

In 2010, a new cable-span four-lane bridge opened across the Mississippi River. By 2012, the old bridge had been dismantled after 80 years of use. (Courtesy of the Arkansas Department of Parks and Tourism.)

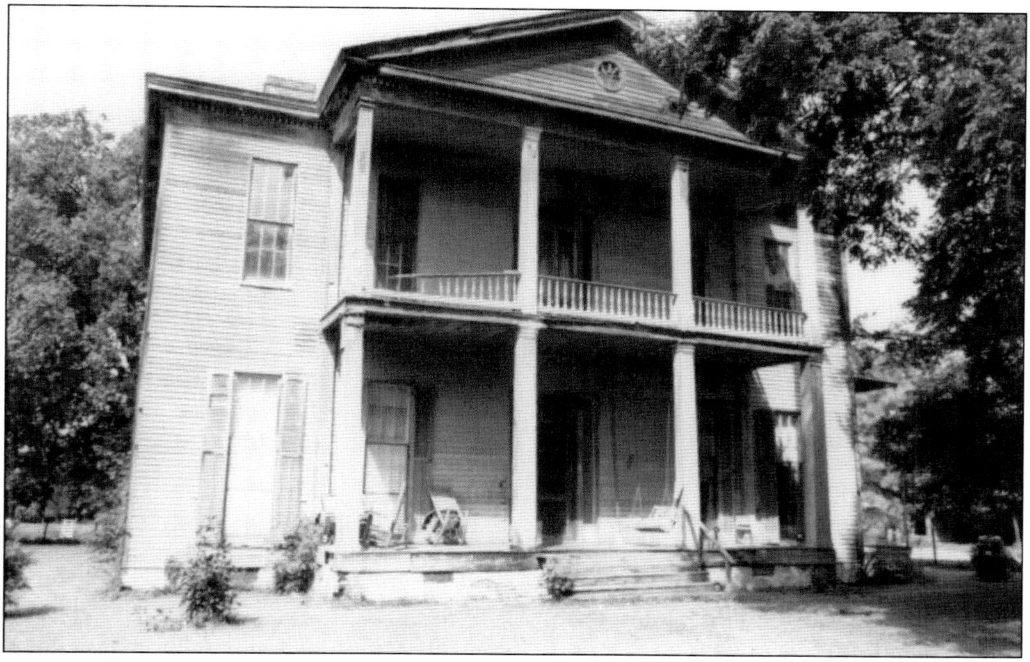

Lakeport Plantation house, built for Lycurgus and Lydia Johnson in 1859, is one of the few remaining antebellum plantation homes in Arkansas. The plantation house, pictured above in 1973 for the National Register of Historic Places survey, is one of Arkansas's premier historic structures and a model of preservation. Gifted to Arkansas State University in 2001 by the Sam Epstein Angel family, the house was restored between 2003 and 2007 and opened to the public as an Arkansas State University Heritage Site. (Above, courtesy of the Arkansas Historic Preservation Program; below, courtesy of the Arkansas Department of Parks and Tourism.)

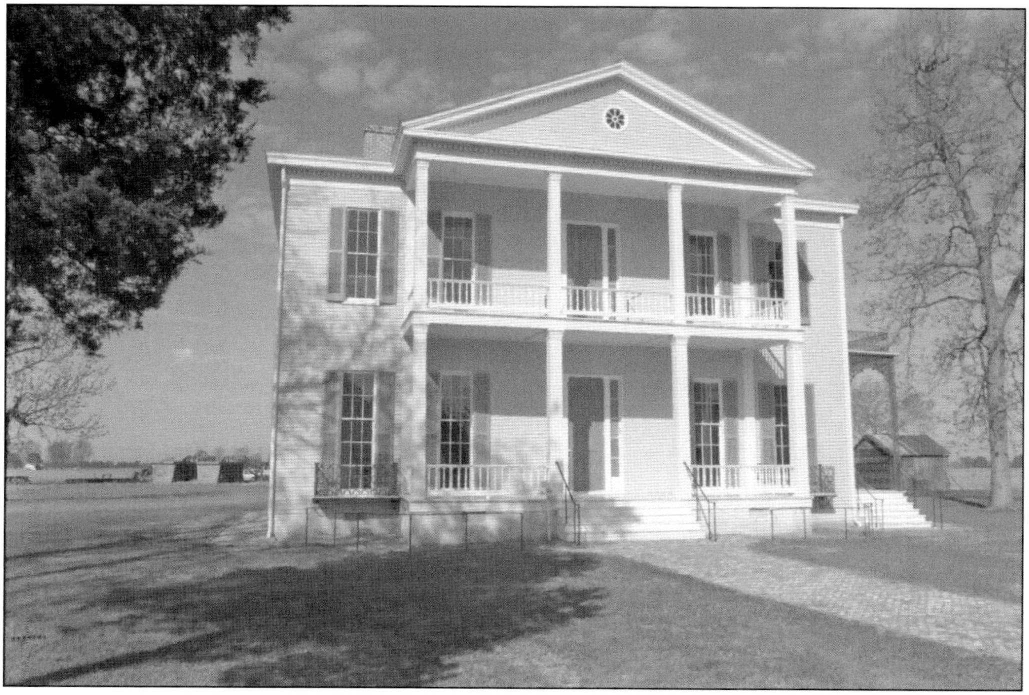

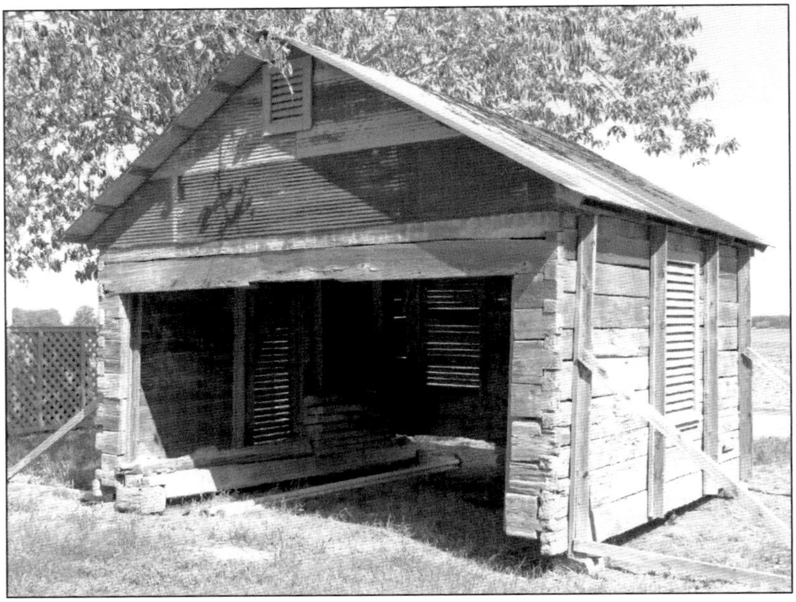

This log structure at the Lakeport Plantation is believed to be the last of 15 slave quarters that were on the plantation in 1860. The number of slaves at Lakeport fell from 155 in 1860 to 24 in 1864. As Union forces gained control of the Mississippi River in 1863 and 1864, the slaves who remained in the county were liberated. Lucretia Alexander, a slave at Rossmere Plantation, remembered in her WPA interview how freedom came: "One time I saw the Yankee a long way off. They had on blue uniforms and was on coal black horses . . . I heard them tell the slaves they were free. A man named Captain Barkus . . . called for the three near-by plantations to meet at our place. Then he got up on a platform with another man beside him and declared peace and freedom. He p'nted to a colored man and yelled, 'You're free as I am.' Old colored folks, old as I am now, that was on stick, throwed them sticks away and shouted." (Courtesy of Lakeport Plantation.)

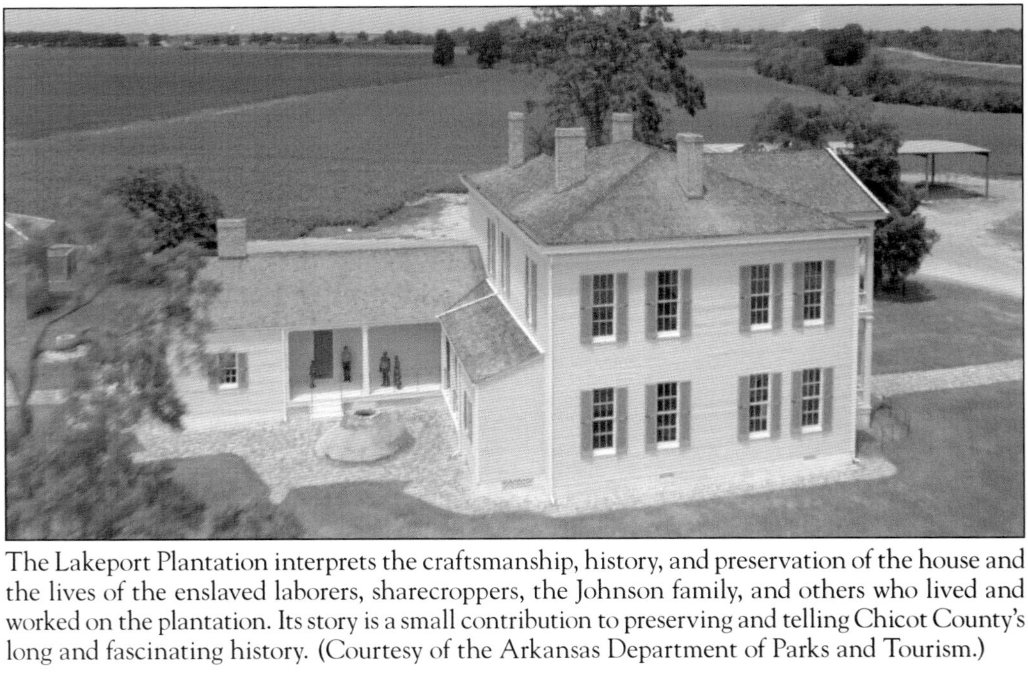

The Lakeport Plantation interprets the craftsmanship, history, and preservation of the house and the lives of the enslaved laborers, sharecroppers, the Johnson family, and others who lived and worked on the plantation. Its story is a small contribution to preserving and telling Chicot County's long and fascinating history. (Courtesy of the Arkansas Department of Parks and Tourism.)

Bibliography

Bender, Robert Patrick, ed. *Worthy of the Cause for Which They Fight: The Civil War Diary of Brigadier General Daniel Harris Reynolds, 1861–1865*. Fayetteville, AR: University of Arkansas Press, 2011.

Biographical and Historical Memoirs of Southern Arkansas. Chicago, Nashville, and St. Louis: Goodspeed Publishing Co., 1890.

Borgononi, Libby. *Italians of Sunnyside, 1896–1995: A People of Faith, of Hope, and of Love*. Lake Village, AR: privately printed, 1995.

Brannon, Sheila, ed. *A Tribute to Chicot County Arkansas*: Dermott, AR: privately printed, 2000.

Cashion, Elbert Thomas Sr. *A History of Eudora, Arkansas, Chicot County*. Eudora, AR: 1937.

Chicot County Sesquicentennial Edition, 1823–1973. Supplement to *Dermott News*, *Chicot Spectator*, and *Eudora Enterprise*. November 14–15, 1973.

Chicot County Spectator. Centennial Edition, June 26, 1936.

DeBlack, Thomas A. "A Garden in the Wilderness: The Johnsons and the Making of Lakeport Plantation, 1831–1876." PhD dissertation, University of Arkansas, 1995.

Jones, J. Wayne. "Seeding Chicot: The Isaac H. Hilliard Plantation and the Arkansas Delta." *Arkansas Historical Quarterly* 59 (Summer 2000): 147–185.

Leslie, James. "Jefferson and Chicot Counties' Connection Many Over the Years." *Pine Bluff News*, March 24, 1986.

Polk's Arkansas State Gazetteer and Business Directory, 1884–1885, 1888–1889, 1892–1893, 1898–1899, 1906–1907, 1912–1913. Memphis, Detroit, and Chicago: R.L. Polk & Co.

Sanborn Fire Insurance Maps. Dermott (1908, 1912, 1915, 1924), Eudora (1912, 1921, 1932), and Lake Village (1908, 1912, 1917, 1928, 1943).

Shea, William L. "The Battle at Ditch Bayou." *Arkansas Historical Quarterly* 39 (Autumn 1980): 195–207.

Simons, Don R. *In Their Words: A Chronology of the Civil War in Chicot County, Arkansas and Adjacent Waters of the Mississippi River*. Sulphur, LA: Wise Publications, 1999.

Sutton, Keith. "The Death and Rebirth of Lake Chicot." *Arkansas Game and Fish* 16 (September/October 1985): 5–9.

Whyane, Jeannie M., ed. *Shadows Over Sunnyside: An Arkansas Plantation in Transition, 1830–1945*. Fayetteville, AR: University of Arkansas Press, 1993.

Wintory, Blake J. "African-American Legislators in the Arkansas General Assembly, 1868–1893." *Arkansas Historical Quarterly* 54 (Winter 2006): 385–434.

Young, Susan. *"So Big, This Little Place": The Founding of Tontitown, Arkansas, 1898–1917*. Tontitown, AR: Tontitown Historical Museum, 2009.

IMAGES
of America

Berkeley Township

Alfred T. Stokley

ARCADIA
PUBLISHING

ISBN 978-1-4671-2293-1

Published by Arcadia Publishing
Charleston, South Carolina

Printed in the United States of America

Library of Congress Control Number: 2014946974

For all general information, please contact Arcadia Publishing:
Telephone 843-853-2070
Fax 843-853-0044
E-mail sales@arcadiapublishing.com
For customer service and orders:
Toll-Free 1-888-313-2665

Visit us on the Internet at www.arcadiapublishing.com

This book is dedicated to my father, Fred Stokley (1911–1990), who moved his family to Bayville to enjoy living by Barnegat Bay.

Contents

Acknowledgments 6

Introduction 7

1. Homesteads 9

2. By the Bay 19

3. Pinewald 53

4. In the Pines 61

5. Along Route 9 73

6. Community 119

ACKNOWLEDGMENTS

This book was made possible, first and foremost, with the assistance of the Berkeley Township Historical Society (BTHS), which contributed most of these photographs. Unless otherwise noted, images appear courtesy of BTHS. Special thanks go to members Jerry Beer and Larry, Fran, and Larry F. Casele who have helped both to contribute and document the many old photographs and postcards. Appreciation is also extended to Arcadia Publishing and Katie Owens, the Ocean County Historical Society and Janis Gibson, the Ocean County Library, the Ocean County Cultural and Heritage Commission and Tim Hart, the New Jersey Preservation Office and Andrea Tingey, Barbara and Bud Magahan, Dale Cottrell, Jim Fosbre, John Enggren, Don Stilwell, Pat Hamilton, Marian Wick, Bob Coar, Charles Hall, Ernest and Rose Gruenzburger, Jean Baldwin and Gary Castildi, Mary Corrigan, Pat Newman, Annegret Specht, Pamela Karcheski, Betty Cramer, Gary Madden, John Brinckman, Bob Farrell, Lois Morris, Judy LaTorre, the McIntyre family, Margaret Kehoe, E.H. Weber, and all the other individuals who have generously donated photographs and information to the Berkeley Museum.

INTRODUCTION

Berkeley Township, named after Lord John Berkeley of England, was originally part of Dover Township. It later became a separate municipality and incorporated on March 31, 1875. Created from Berkeley were six separate boroughs: Seaside Park, in 1898; Beachwood, in 1917; Ocean Gate, in 1918; Pine Beach, in 1925; South Toms River, in 1927; and Island Beach, in 19331, but reabsorbed as a state park in 1965. The total area now is 42 square miles with a population of 44,000. It is located in the central part of Ocean County, bordering the New Jersey Pinelands Reserve on the west and Barnegat Bay on the east. Sections include Bayville, Pinewald, Manitou Park, Pelican Island, and South Seaside Park.

The Lenni-Lenape Indians first inhabited Berkeley. In 1609, Sir Henry Hudson, sailing in the *Half Moon*, cruised its coastline. Early industries included bog iron, lumber, cranberries, salt hay, farming, pound fishing, and shipbuilding. There were quaint homesteads and shops along the old shore road, now Route 9.

Bayville became the populated section of Berkeley along the five-mile Route 9 corridor between Toms River and Forked River. In 1850, the post office established the area as Potters Creek; in 1868, as Chaseford; and finally, in 1870, as Bayville or Cape Bayville. In 1871, a Central Jersey Railroad train station was established in Pinewald. In the 1970s, with the spreading population and the advent of senior housing west of the Garden State Parkway, the entire municipality was, and still is, generally referred to as Berkeley.

In 1887, Lt. Edward Farrow developed Barnegat Park for retired military officers. In the 1920s, B.W. Sangor purchased the property and established what is now Pinewald. The mammoth project included several hundred lots, but it failed during the Depression.

Bayville later offered many water-based recreational activities at fishing camps and marinas found at Cedar Creek, Sloop Creek, Mill Creek, and Barnegat Pier. From Barnegat Pier, there was boating access from Barnegat Bay to the Atlantic Ocean. Lagoon housing development along the bay's shoreline would spark commercial growth. In the pines, Double Trouble State Park had a small village of workers to operate the cranberry bogs, packaging plant, and sawmill. It was dedicated in 1995 and reopened to the public.

Berkeley Township's diversified geographic regions provide for an interesting and colorful history. This information has been recorded and saved in the unique photograph collection presented here.

One

Homestead

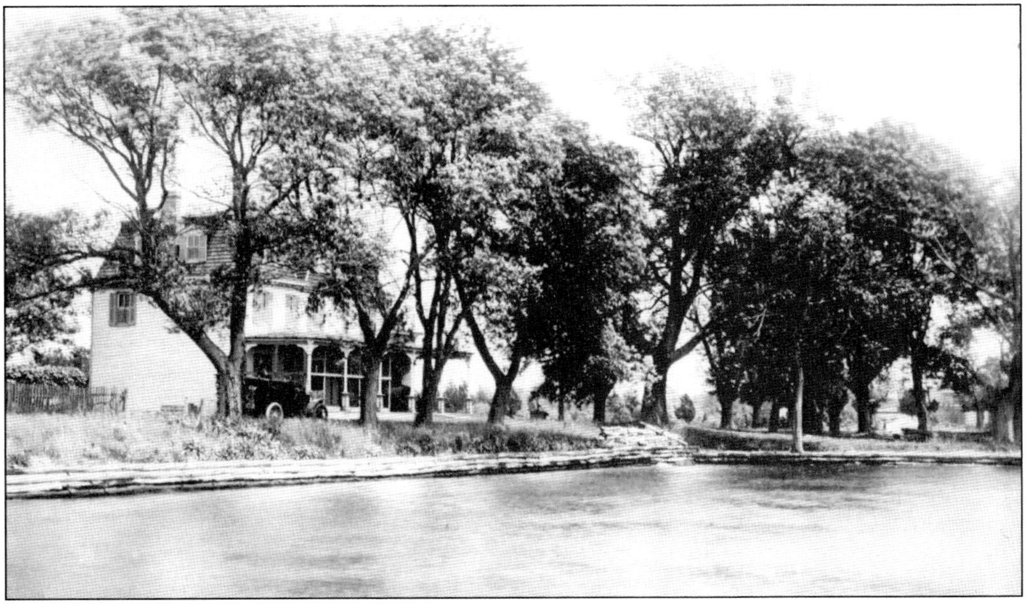

The three-story, Victorian-style Harbor Inn, with a mansard roof, was built around 1860. It is located at Harbor Inn Road and Neary Avenue overlooking Cedar Creek. It served as an inn for the many travelers and sportsmen who visited the Barnegat Bay area to hunt and fish. A two-story addition was added on the east side in 1909 to offer a total of 30 rooms for the inn. In 1925, Percival Grant, a Bayville native, became the owner and proprietor. His wife, Nettie Grant, used to serve chicken dinners for 50¢. The Thomas McIntyre family owned the property from 1929 to 1969 and used it as both a residence and business office for the nearby Cedar Beach development. Today, it continues to be a private residence. (Courtesy of Charles Hall.)

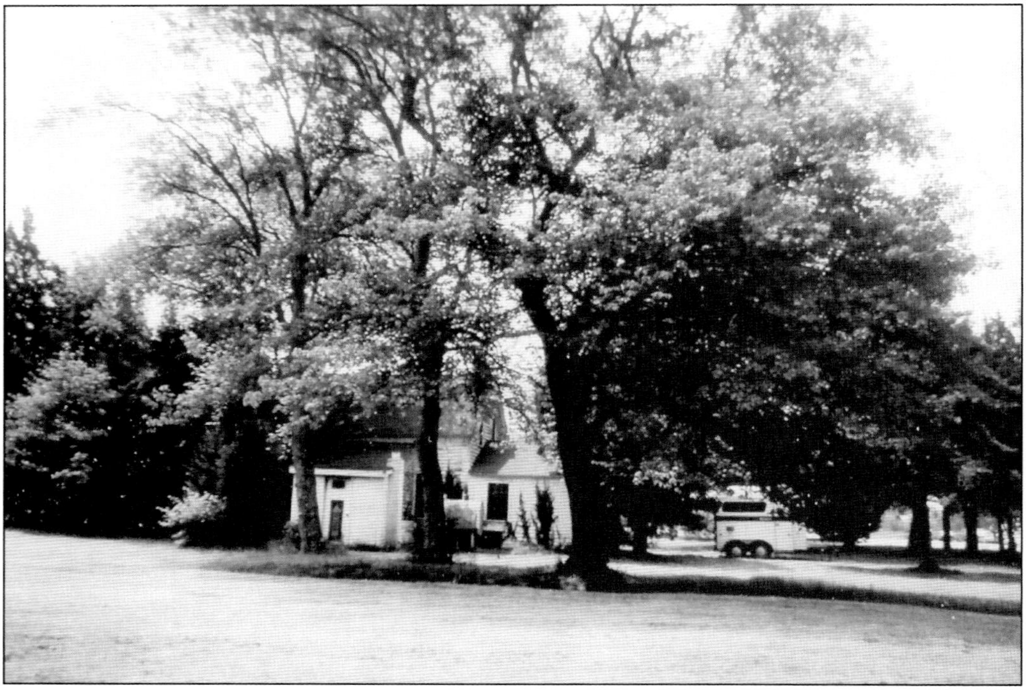

This cottage was nestled on a large lot overlooking Cedar Creek on East Harbor Inn Road. Members of the Grant family, who were listed as "mariners" on Barnegat Bay, owned the homestead around 1850. This location was known as Horne's Point, with Lois Horne as the last sole occupant. The historic house was demolished around 2005 and replaced by a larger house.

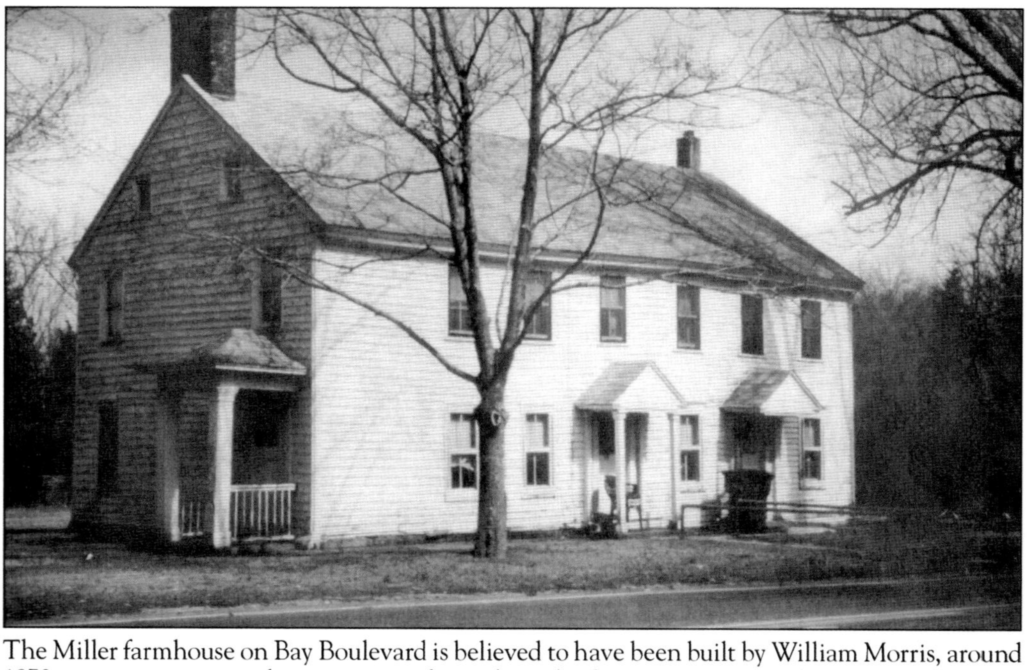

The Miller farmhouse on Bay Boulevard is believed to have been built by William Morris, around 1870, in two sections with an entrance for each in the front. In 1926, Frank Miller purchased it from the Holly Park on Barnegat Bay Corporation. There have been several owners since then. Today, the house is vacant.

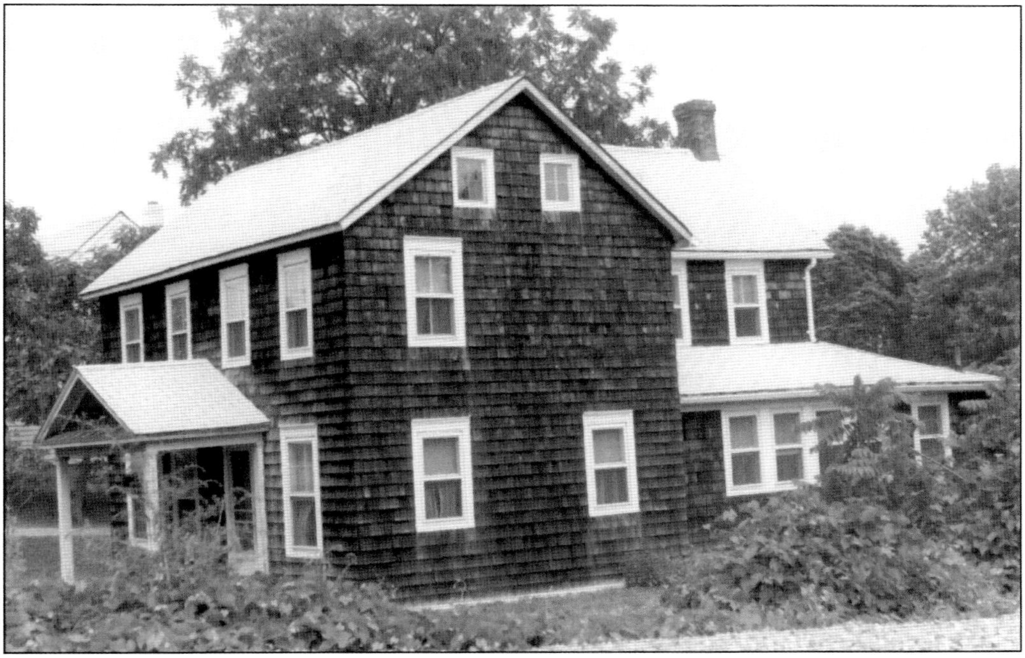

Clara B. Worth, the former principal of Bayville Grade School, once owned the house at 76 Route 9; it was built in the 1890s. Clara lived here for most of her 88 years. A single light from the back room at night would usually indicate that she was still doing schoolwork. The house has maintained its original size and integrity. Today, Quality Medical Transport occupies it. (Courtesy of New Jersey Historic Preservation Office.)

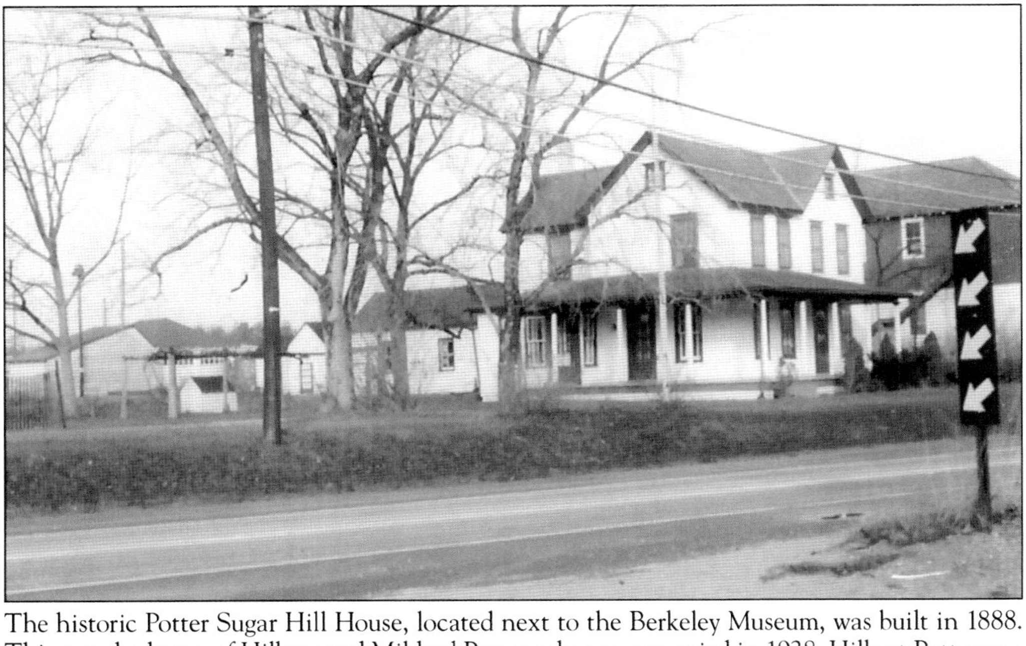

The historic Potter Sugar Hill House, located next to the Berkeley Museum, was built in 1888. This was the home of Hilbert and Mildred Potter, who were married in 1928. Hilbert Potter was the former Berkeley Township clerk and died in 1973. Mildred Potter was a teacher and principal of the Bayvi1le Grade School for many years. She lived in the home until her death in 2007 at age 101. Today, the house is utilized for commercial purpose.

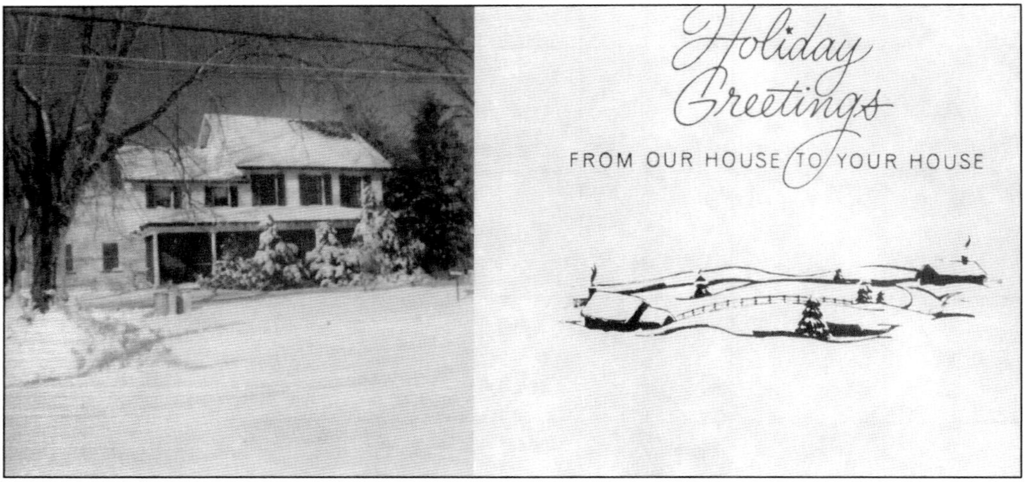

The "Casagrand House in Winter" Christmas card shows the c. 1890 home of George S. Casagrand and his wife, Mable, who were originally from West Orange, New Jersey. The house was located across from the Bay Avenue intersection. Their children included Alfred, Berkeley Township postmaster from 1958 to 1972; Robert, owner of Casagrand's General Store; Casey; George; Mable; and Joan. A root cellar for vegetables was under the kitchen. The floor beams were half trees with bark on the bottom side and were laid on tree stumps. It was demolished in 1991. Below, this 1880s home was located across from Station Road on Route 9. Occupants included both the Boyd family and later the Barden family. Note the little girl watching on the far right.

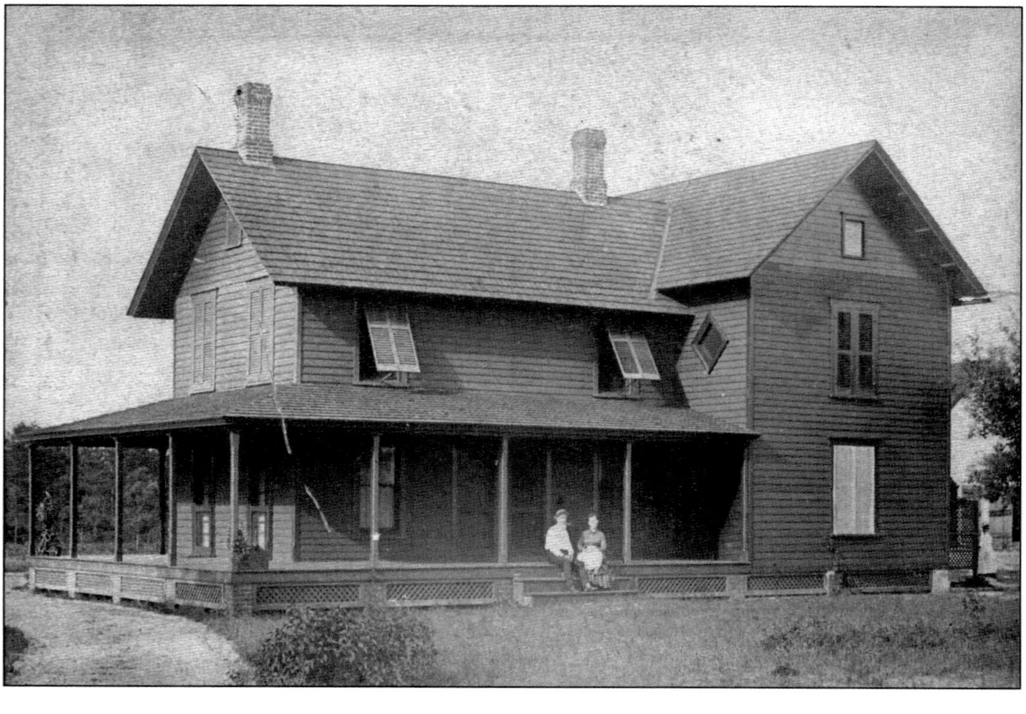

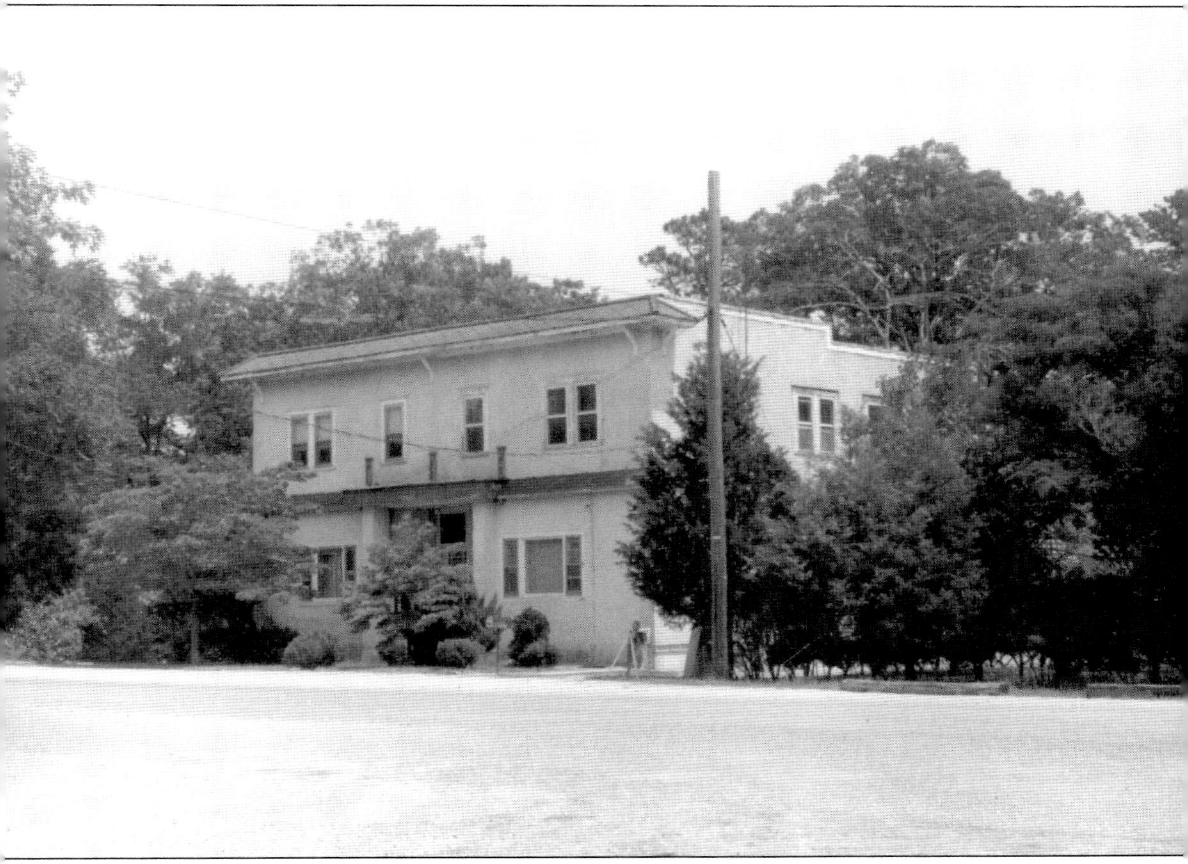

This stucco home with a parapet roof, c. 1920s, is located at Wheaton Avenue and Central Avenue across from the former railroad station. It originally was the Green Lantern restaurant owned and operated by Lillian A. Den Braven, who advertised "With All Home Cooking." It was popular with the potential customers of the Pinewald development. Today, it is a private residence. (Courtesy of the New Jersey Historic Preservation Office.)

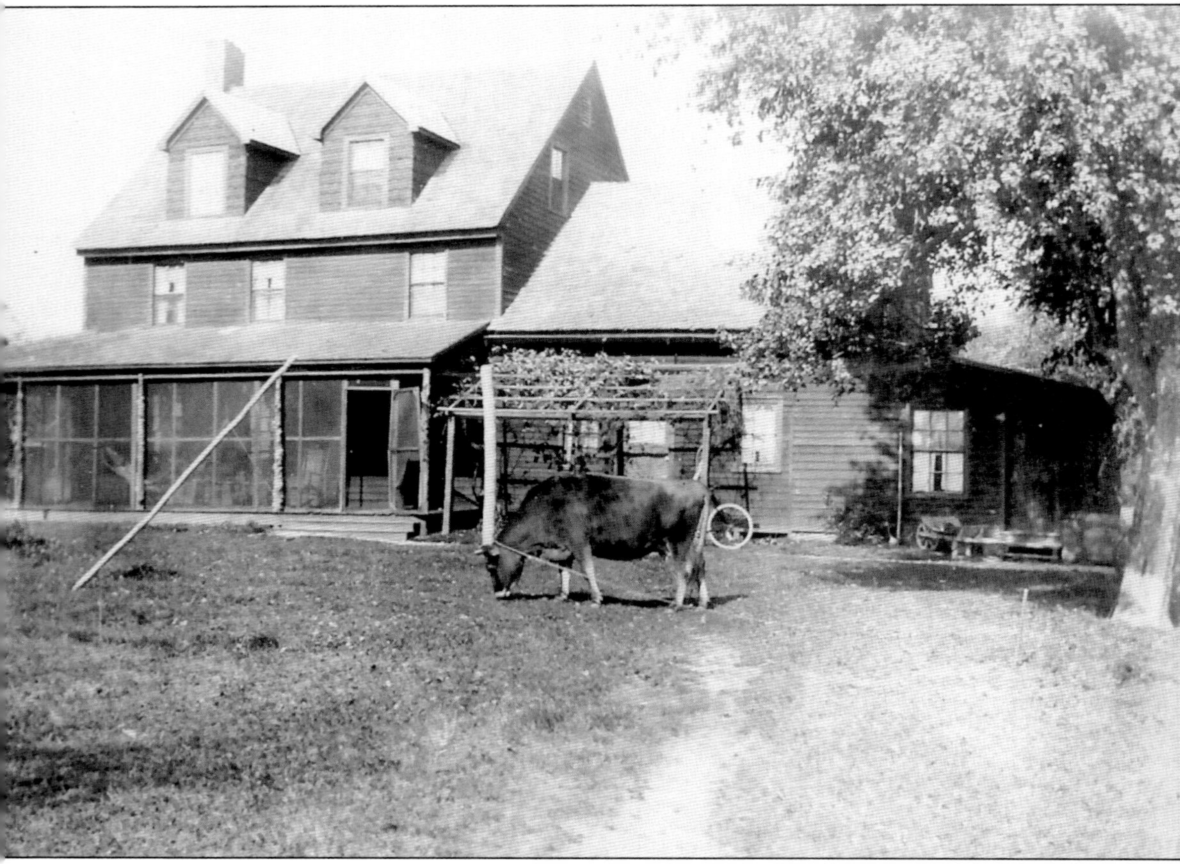

In 1996, the Anderson House on Sloop Creek Road was the oldest, continuously lived in homestead in Ocean County. Elias Anderson Sr. purchased the 262-acre farm from Gabrial Woodmansee on April 14, 1769. From 1867 to 1901, Elias Jr.; his wife, Penelope Rogers; and their 14 children lived there. Later, the Cornelius Lawrence family and the Veeder family occupied the property. Irving Nobles purchased it around 1952, and today, it remains in his estate. The Nobles Building Supply Company had operated its business from a large converted chicken coup behind the house. A local story has a Revolutionary War refugee, Dick Bird, being tracked by the local militia and then killed on the hearth of the huge fireplace. Today, the home remains abandoned, and the cow has moved on to greener pastures. (Courtesy of John Enggren.)

Benjamin Butler bought this property on Route 9, just north of Hickory Lane, in 1896 and later built this quaint homestead, shown here in 1903. Butler was also the proprietor of the general store and post office located on the left side of the home. The house and store were both demolished in August 2007. (Courtesy of John Enggren.)

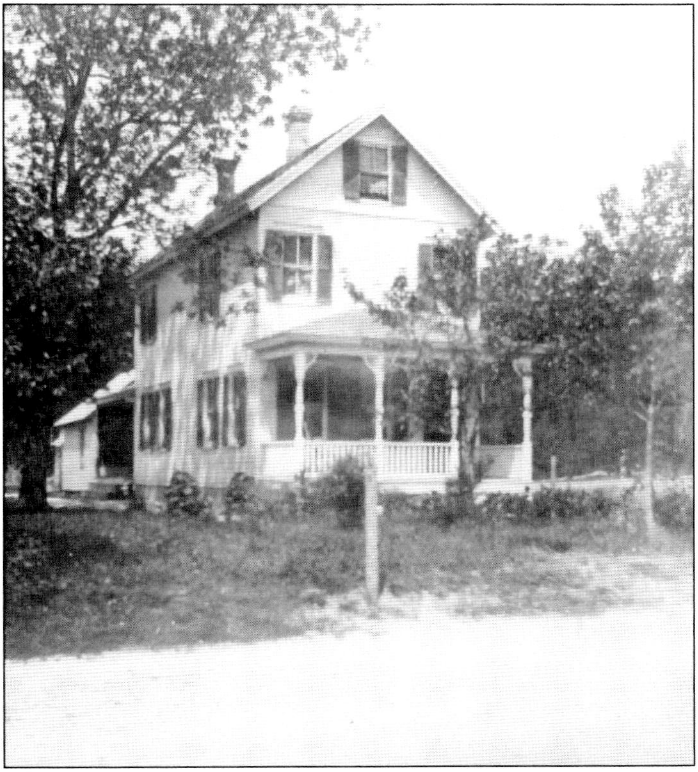

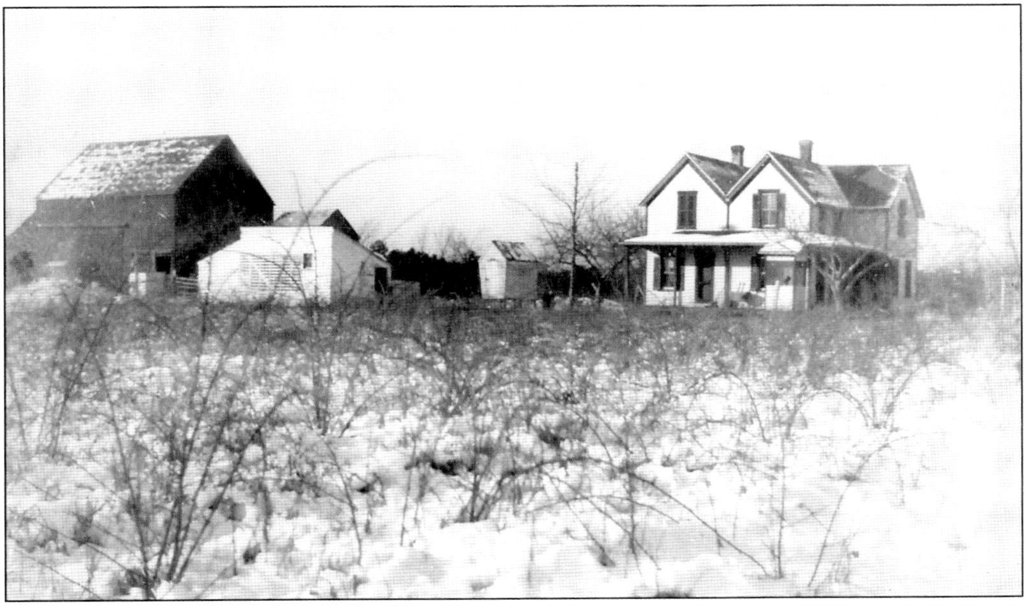

This 1905 wintry view shows the farmhouse built by Devine Butler in 1883 on Mill Creek Road. He was the father of the late mayor Marcus Butler. Butler also owned a grocery store in Seaside Park and raised much of the store's produce on this farm. The small corner building is an enclosed well. A little corncrib is in the center, and the white building was once a chicken coop. Today, the house remains a private residence, but the barn has since burned down. (Courtesy of John Enggren.)

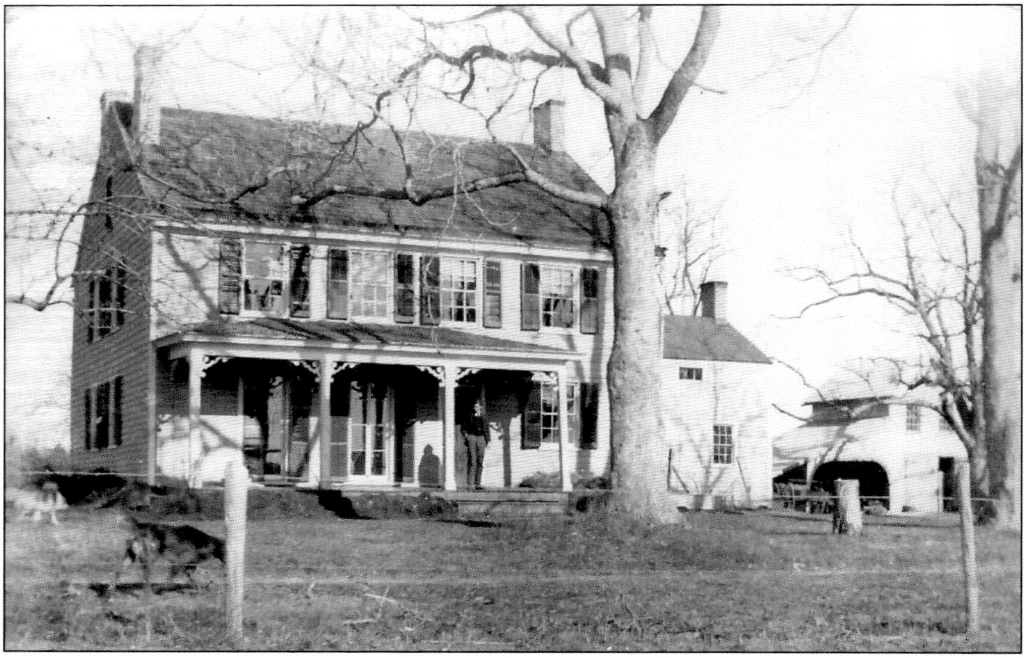

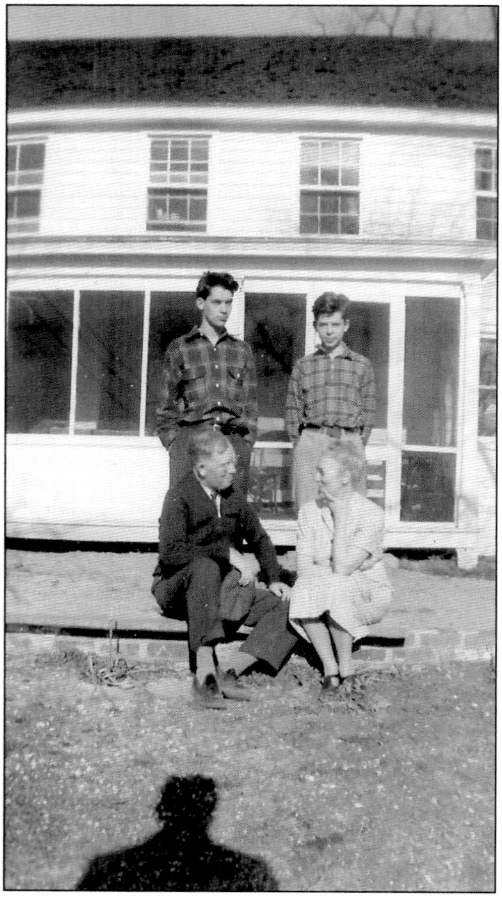

The Rogers Home at 2 Veeder Lane, as well as the accompanying 378-acre farm bordering Route 9, was purchased from John Imley in 1787 by the Rogers family; Imley and the Rogers family were some of the first settlers in Bayville. The house, built in 1772, was once occupied by a British raiding party during the Revolutionary War. The David Veeder family then took ownership in 1896. Young David, seen above, was an Ocean County court judge. The small saltbox on the right side of the house was the home's oldest section. The farm also included the Clover Cream Top Dairy. Most of the property was sold in 1958 for the Berkeley Shores housing development. Veeder family members, pictured at left around 1940, are, from left to right, (sitting) David and Edith; (standing) Bruce and Volkert. The home is still occupied today. Both the house and the nearby Rogers original cemetery on Bell Street are dedicated historic landmarks. (Both, courtesy of John Enggren.)

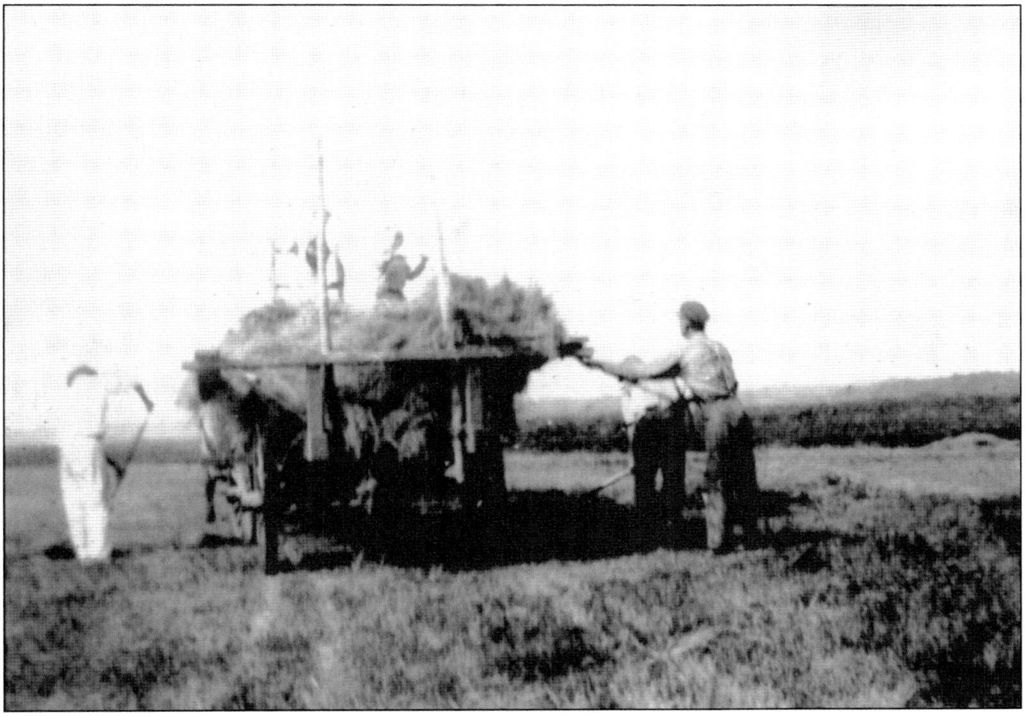

In 1933, the salt hay was cut from the meadows located between Good Luck Point and Cedar Creek. It was a summer ritual endured by the farmers of Bayville who either owned or rented this property. An empty hay wagon was brought to the meadows by a team of draft horses. The men forking the cut hay on the wagon are, from left to right, Don Stillwell, David Veeder, Bill Anderson, a hired hand, and Bert Jeffrey. The hay will now be stored in the barn for farm fertilizer and animal bedding. Below, the Veeder's Model A Ford hay wagon is being loaded to take to various businesses. Uses for the hay included ice storage, car seat stuffing, food insulation in transport, and the manufacture of brown bags. (Both, courtesy of Ron Stillwell.)

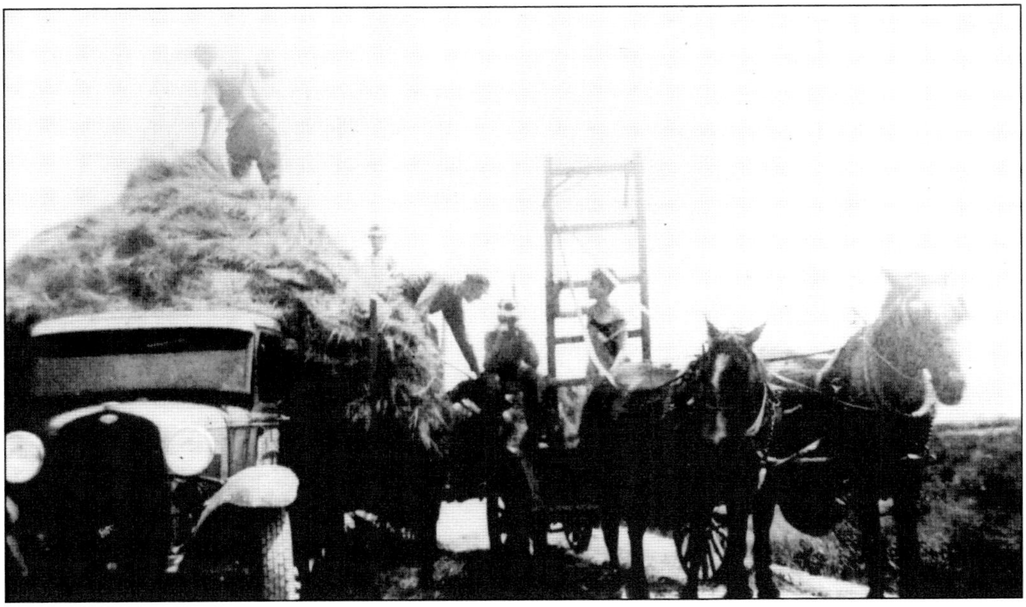

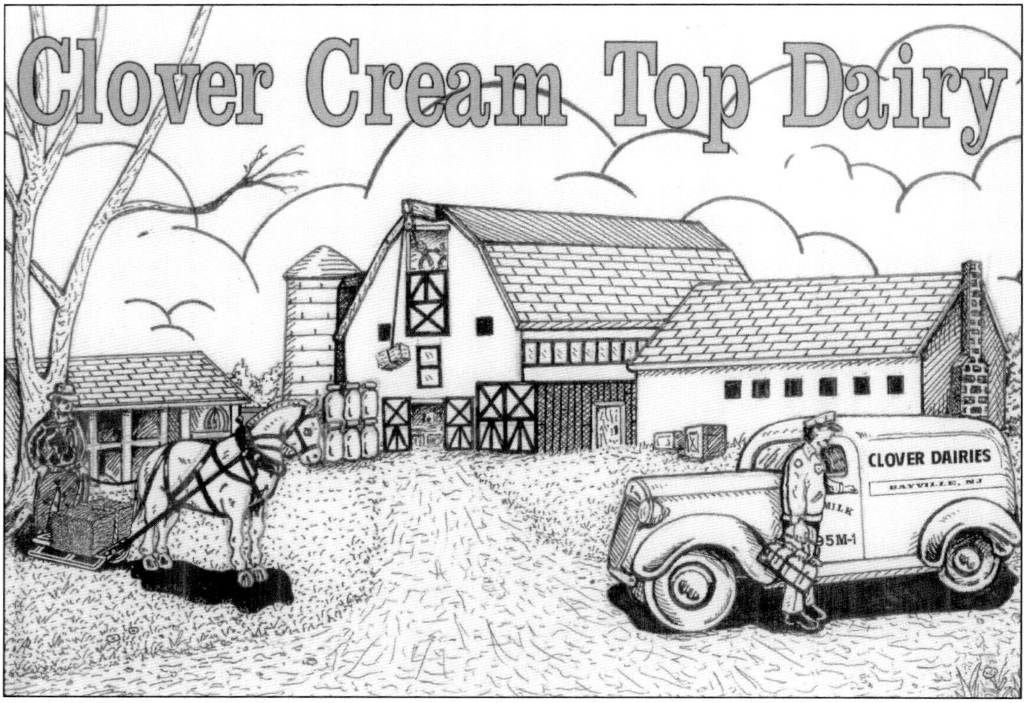

The Clover Cream Top Dairy was located on the south side of Veeder Lane across from the Veeder Homestead. It was originally operated by Ronald Stillwell in the 1940s and later by David Veeder in the early 1950s. The dairy had about 30 cows and two bulls. There were several delivery routes in central Ocean County. The barn was demolished in 1956, and the high ground was removed to fill in the nearby swamp area. Today, the site is part of the Berkeley Shores development. (Courtesy of Ron Stillwell and Volkert Veeder; drawing by Bob Coar.)

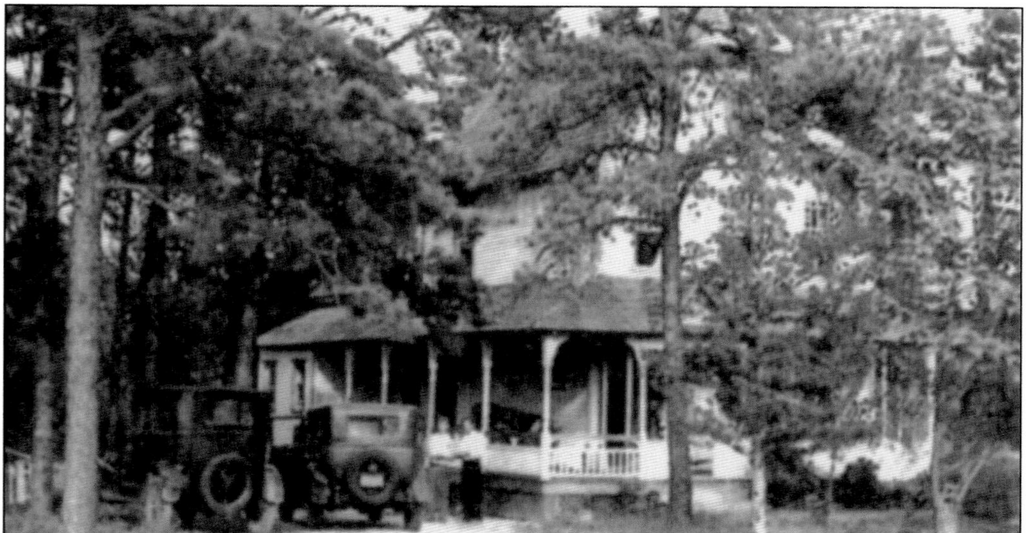

This early-1900s home was originally built on a lot in the Barnegat Park development started by Lieutenant Farrow in the 1880s. It is located on Schofield Avenue, now Coolidge Avenue. The first owner was M. Downing. The large porch adds a comfortable setting for relaxation and was typical for the times. Today, the house remains a private residence.

Two

By the Bay

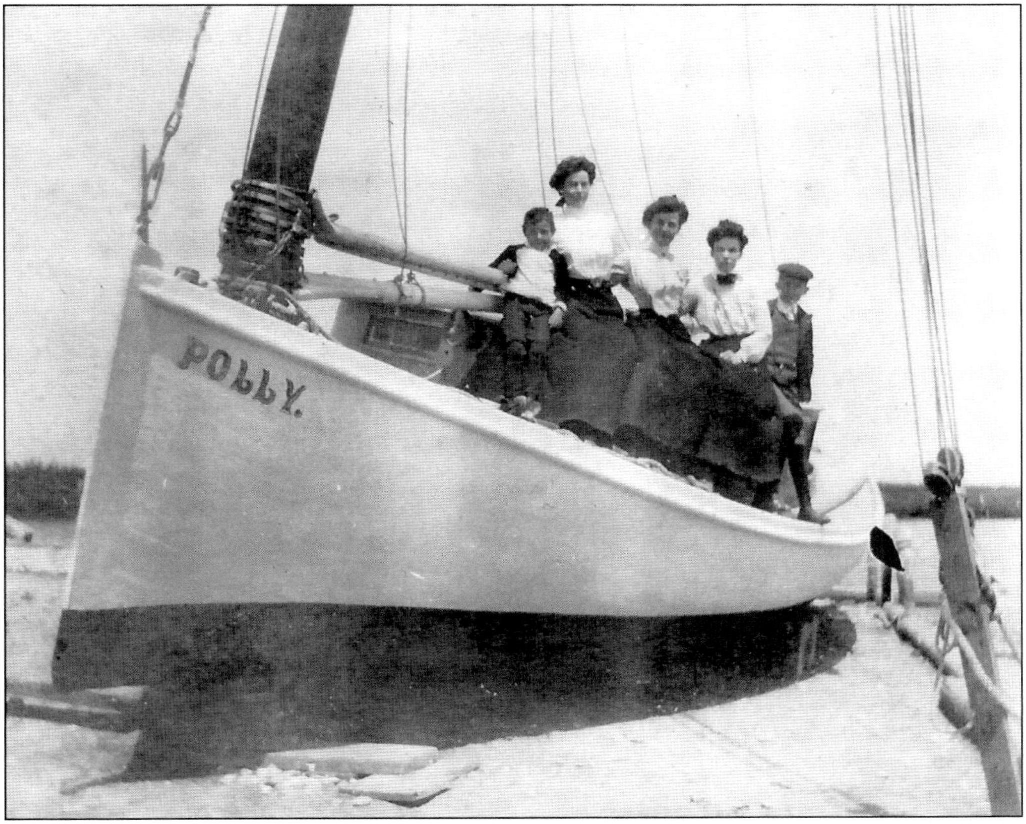

Three lovely ladies and two youngsters are enjoying a fine day in 1905. The craft *Polly* was hauled up on blocks on the Sloop Creek. The wooden sailboat was a 29-foot-long cat-rigged sloop. Newel Potter owned the boat and, in 1917, was issued license No. 23480 by the US Navy to operate in all waters included in the Third Navel District. (Courtesy of John Enggren.)

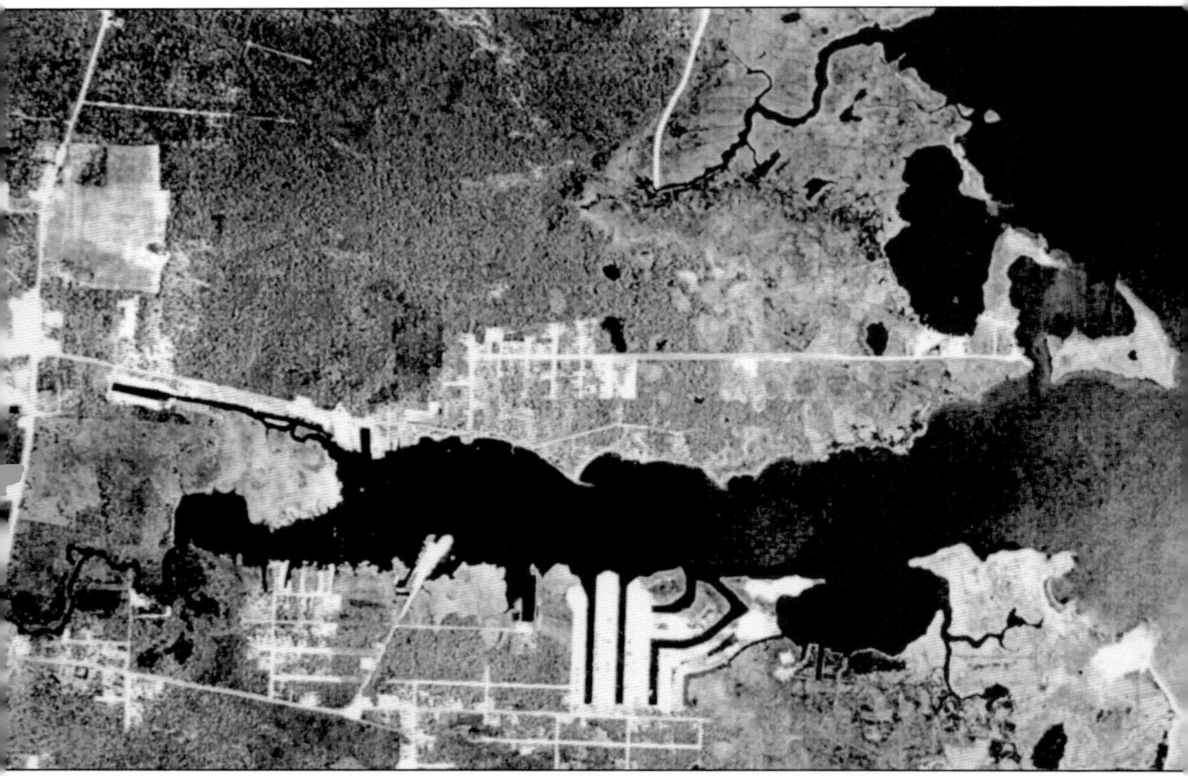

This 1955 aerial shows the early development of the Cedar Creek area. Route 9 is the vertical road on the left. The south shore is Lanoka Harbor in Lacey Township. Harbor Inn Road is on the north shore of the creek, leading to the Cedar Creek Marina. The road becomes Brennan Concourse going through Cedar Beach and ending at Bob Cuddy's Fishing Camp on the bay. In 1958, the road was extended out to the island to become Berkeley Island Park. In this photograph, the Sandpiper Beach lagoon dredging had just begun southeast of the Route 9 intersection. The development encompassed all the marshland from this point south to the Route 9 Cedar Creek Bridge. Just north on the east side of Route 9 is the Bernard and Julia Meinikheim Farm, which was sold in 1958 to become Bel Aire Park. Bayview Avenue, in the top center, ends at Maple Creek; it was extended south to Brennan Concourse in 1956. (Courtesy of Ocean County Library.)

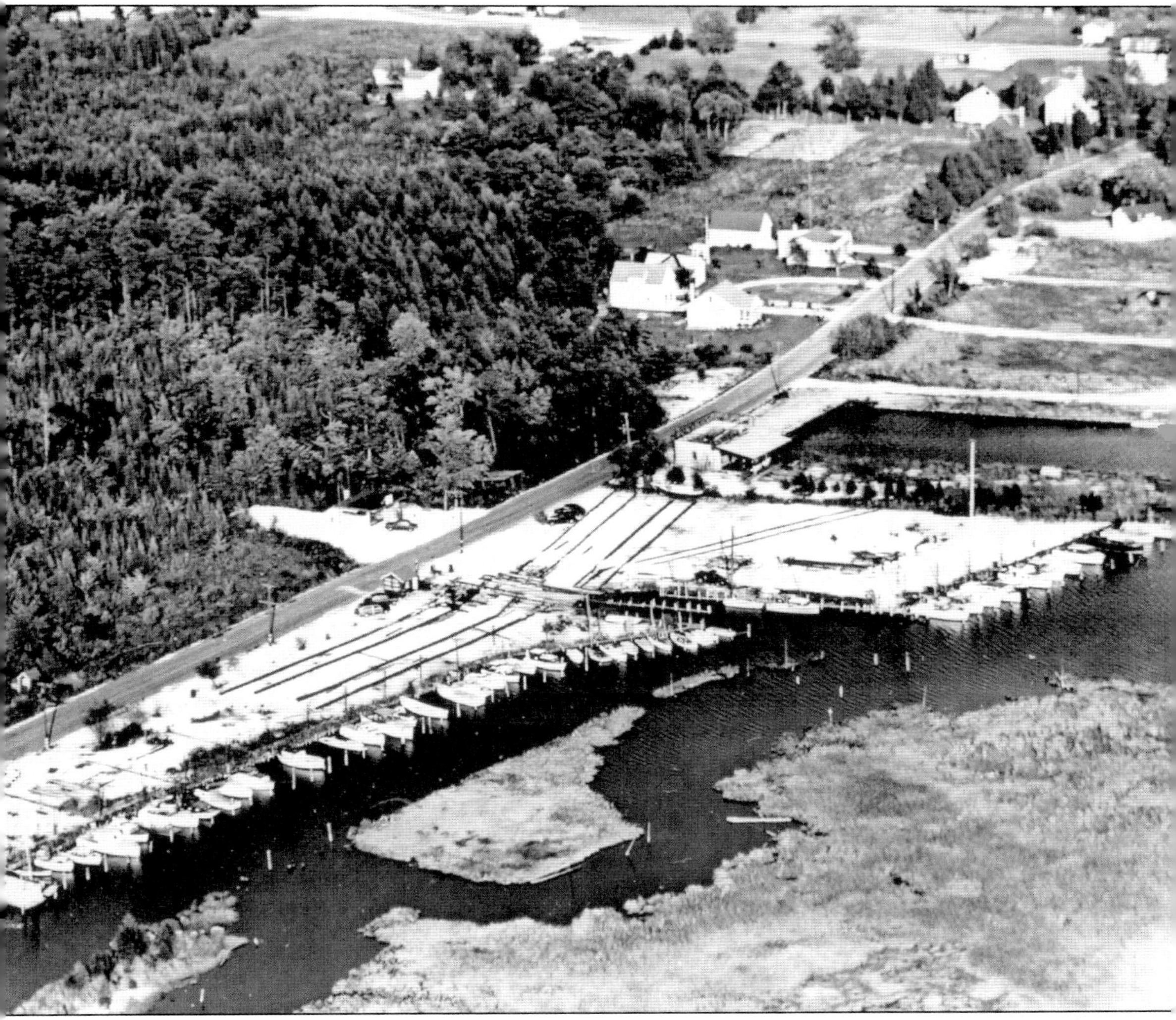

This 1953 aerial of the Cedar Creek Marina on Harbor Inn Road shows about 50 slips for small wooden recreational boats. A large truck engine pulled the boats out on a submerged rail for winter storage. The houseboat, shown at the far left, was occupied by Capt. Norman Hensel, who operated a local party fishing boat. Percy Grant, whose house, garage, and backyard garden are shown at the upper right, originally owned the boatyard. He previously had owned the Harbor Inn in the 1920s, seen at the top right. The Up the Creek Marina, with the large storage shed awaiting the roof, and lagoon are at center. Later Cedar Creek Marina owners were the Sergi Bros., Robert Connolly, and Bird Construction Company, which transformed it into a sailboat marina. In 1957, the marshland, shown at the bottom, became part of the Sandpiper Beach lagoon development.

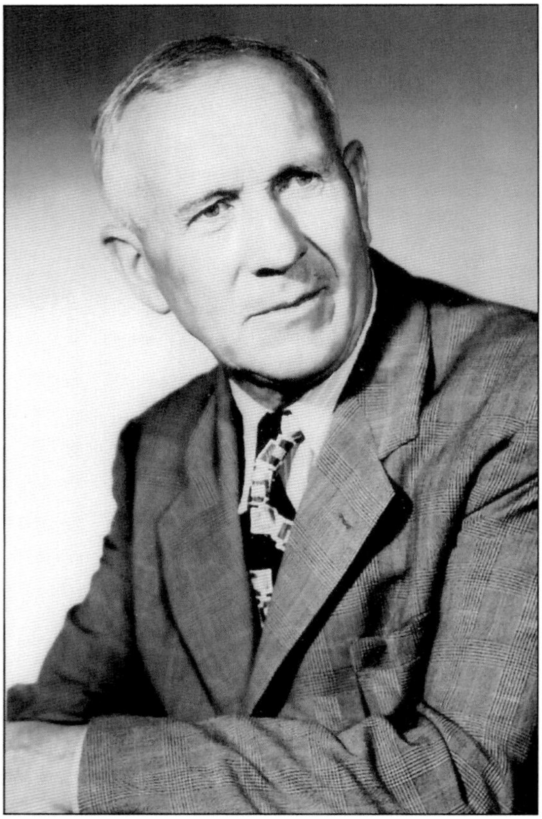

Thomas McIntyre, pictured here, purchased the Harbor Inn, as well as one mile of property along Neary Avenue and Brennan Concourse, in 1929. The Harbor Inn Corporation at 41 East Forty-second Street, New York, filed the subdivision as Cedar Beach on April 22, 1929. It proposed 18 one-block streets with 25-foot lots. In the early 1950s, about 70 small bungalows would be built. (Courtesy of Fran Casele.)

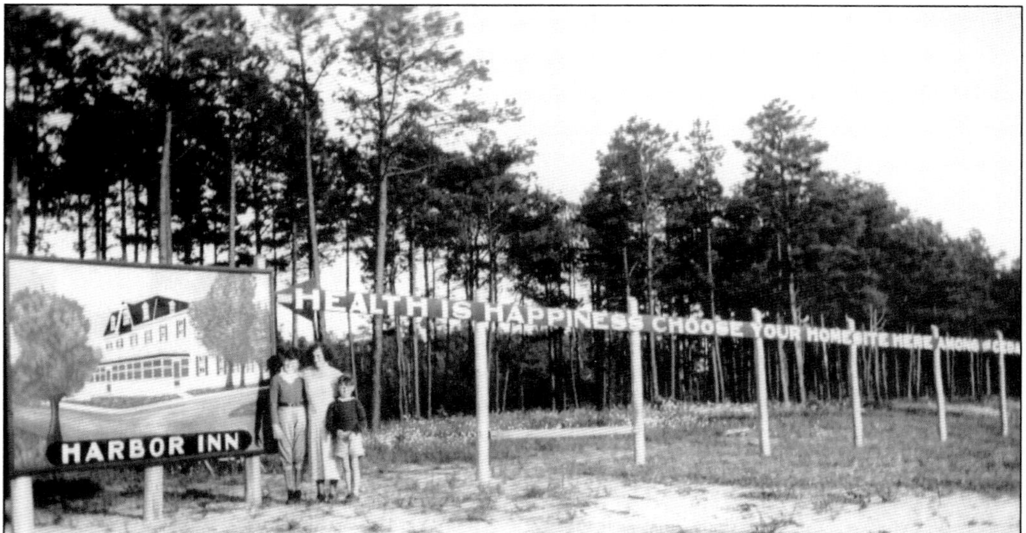

This long, unique advertising sign proclaims, "Health Is Happiness Choose Your Homesite Here Among The Cedars." The sign was placed by Thomas McIntyre to promote the early development of Cedar Beach. The Harbor Inn, pictured at left, served as the Cedar Beach Office. Standing next to the sign are, from left to right, son Edward, Margaret McIntyre, and son Thomas. (Courtesy of Marty McIntyre.)

In 1952, Marion Wick is sitting at Mac's Dock, located on the south side of the Harbor Inn. The dock was a summer meeting place for the young Cedar Beach crowd. Several small boats could dock here at a minimal rate. A Mr. Holmes owned the house in the far back center that originally was a houseboat. Commodore Percy Grant would relax on his waterfront property in the small, screened building on the right. (Courtesy of Marion Wick.)

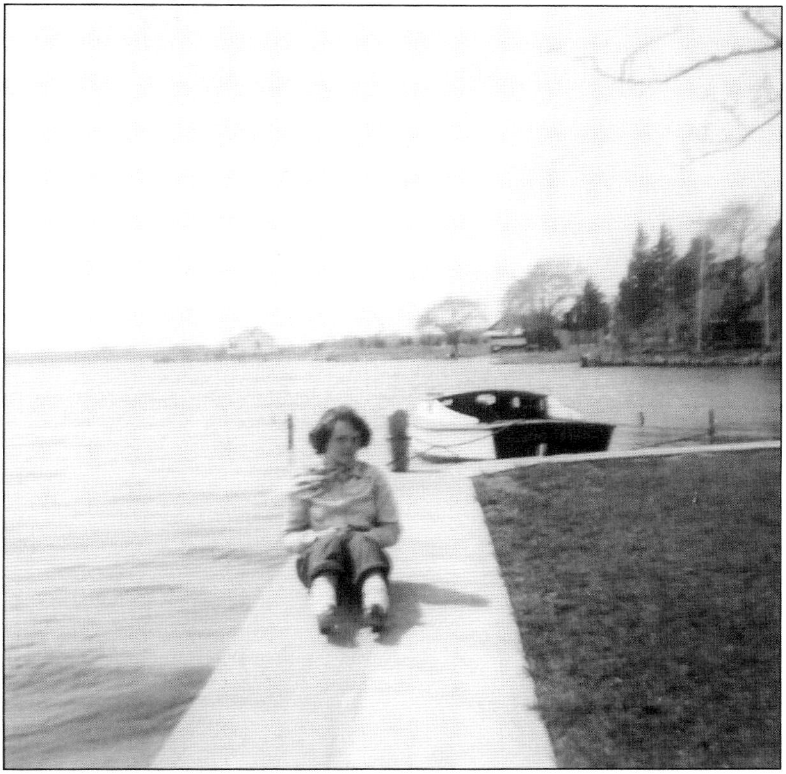

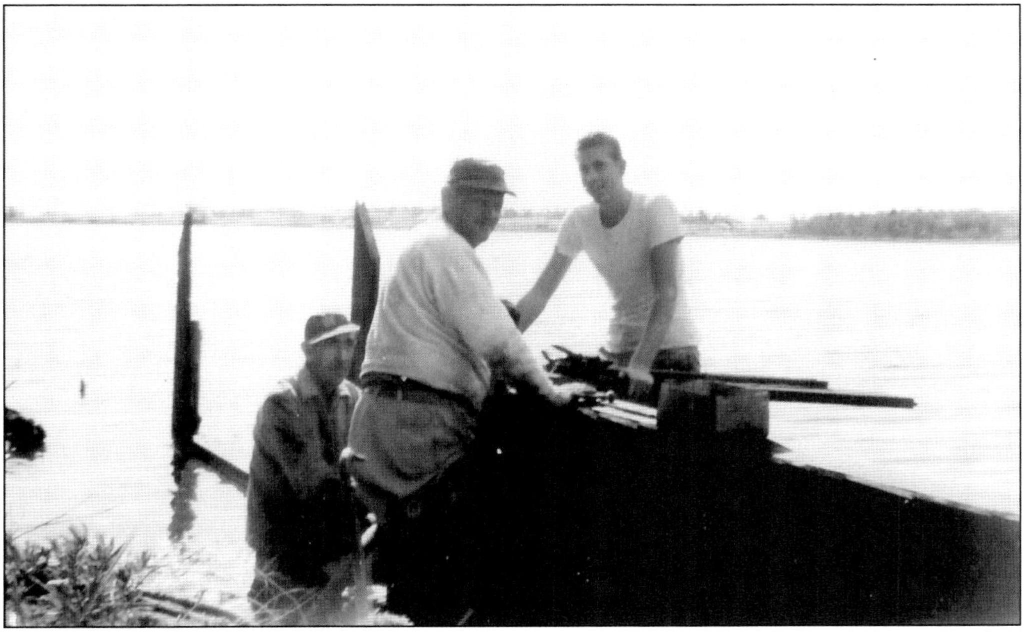

In the 1950s, three large lagoon developments were dredged along the Berkeley Township shoreline. These included Sandpiper Beach, Glen Cove, and Berkeley Shore Estates. This created a substantial increase in marine construction for boat slips, docks, piers, landfill, and bulkheads. This 1960 crew of the Bilt-Rite Bulkheading Company is working hard along the waterfront of Cedar Creek. From left to right are Fred Grant, Ed Stokley, and Al Stokley.

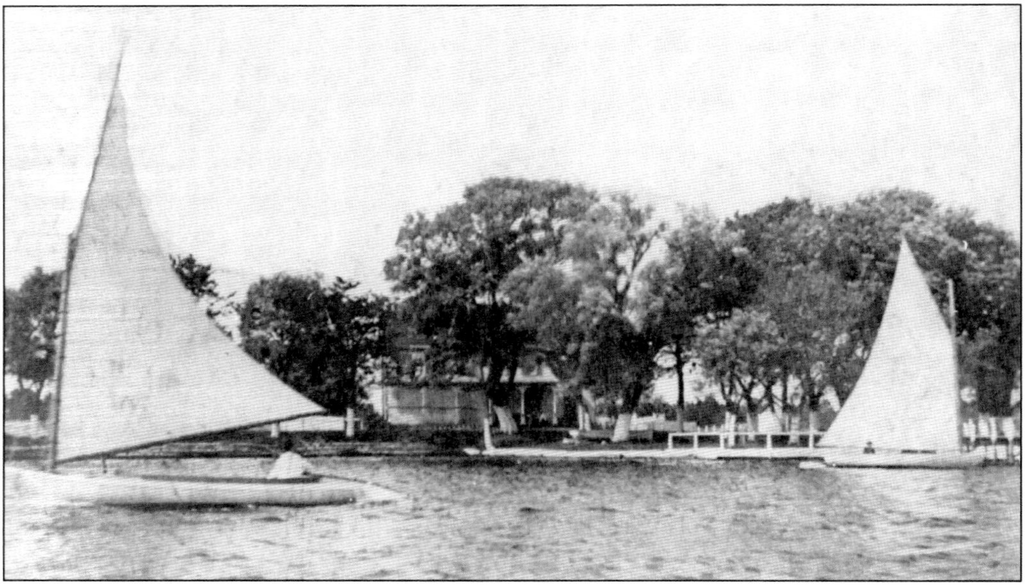

The Cedar Creek Sailing Association was formed in 1947 by several area sailors whose wooden boats were of various designs. The association was revived in 1962 by newcomers Al Stokley and Nelson Hall and continued until 1974. A perennial entrant was the *Ding Swat* sailed by Charles and Charlene Hall, who were longtime original members. The starting line was at Commodore Percy Grant's property just west of the Harbor Inn, shown above. Below, the sailors at the 1962 annual season end awards picnic are, from left to right, Russell Hall, Al Stokley, Nelson Hall, Commodore Percy Grant, Charles Hall, Bill Hayes, and Bill Catlow. The perpetual sailing trophy has the winners names inscribed and is on display at the Berkeley Museum. (Both, courtesy of Charles Hall.)

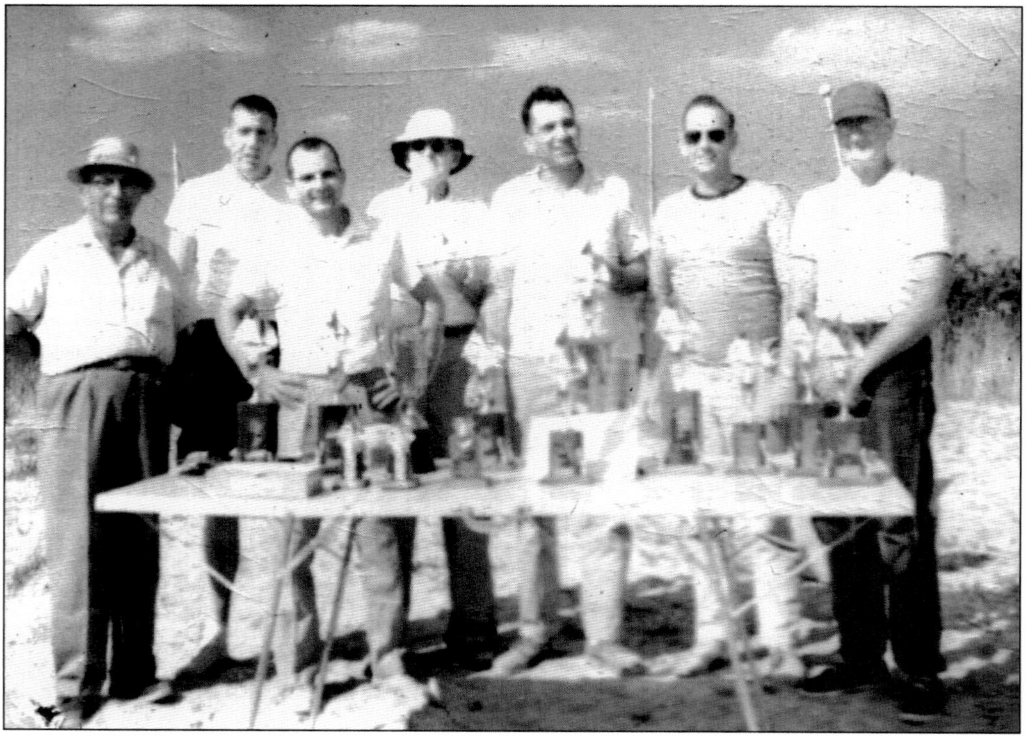

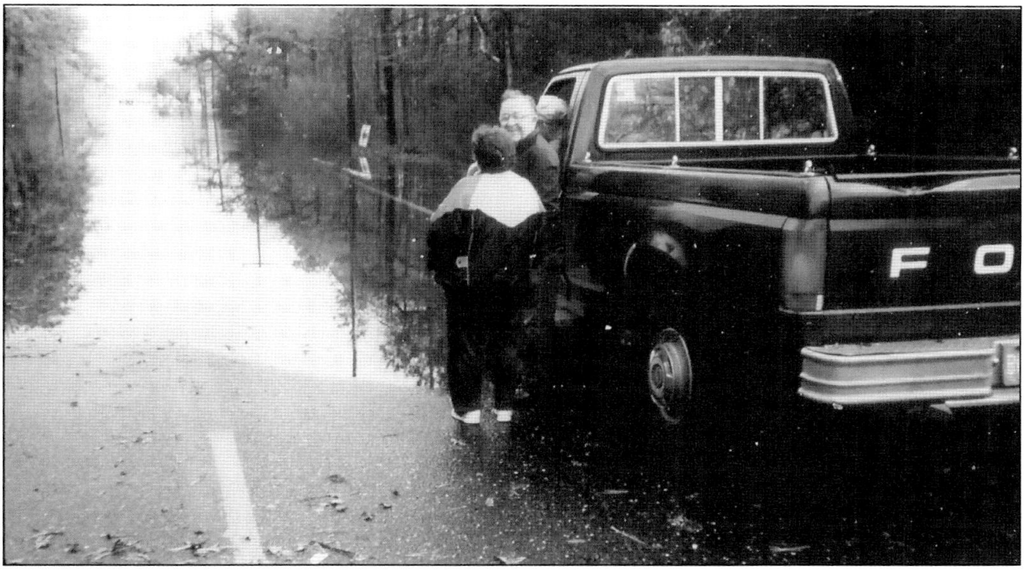

A northeast storm on December 12, 1992, was the second highest watermark on the Bayville shoreline in recent history. Brennan Concourse has a gradual one-mile incline from Berkeley Island Park west to Neary Avenue, which allows for an accurate comparison of water height. This flood reached Bayview Avenue. Victor Bergstedt Jr., known as "Trixie," is in his pickup opposite of Bayview Avenue wondering if he should risk trying to reach his marina or wait. The highest water level along Barnegat Bay in recorded history was during Hurricane Sandy on October 29, 2012.

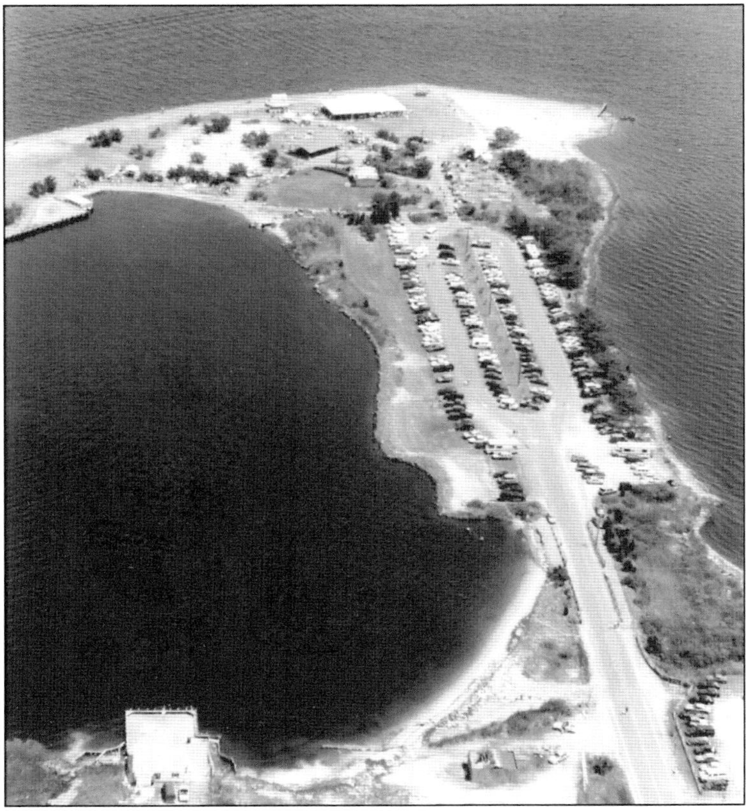

This is an early aerial view of Berkeley Island Park before it was damaged by Hurricane Sandy in 2012. It was one of the most popular waterfront parks on the Jersey Shore. The remains of the former Bob Cuddy's Fishing Camp house are shown at lower center right. Fred Stokley, the author's father, docked his shrimp boat and sold bait at the property shown at the far left. Today, that site is a private residence.

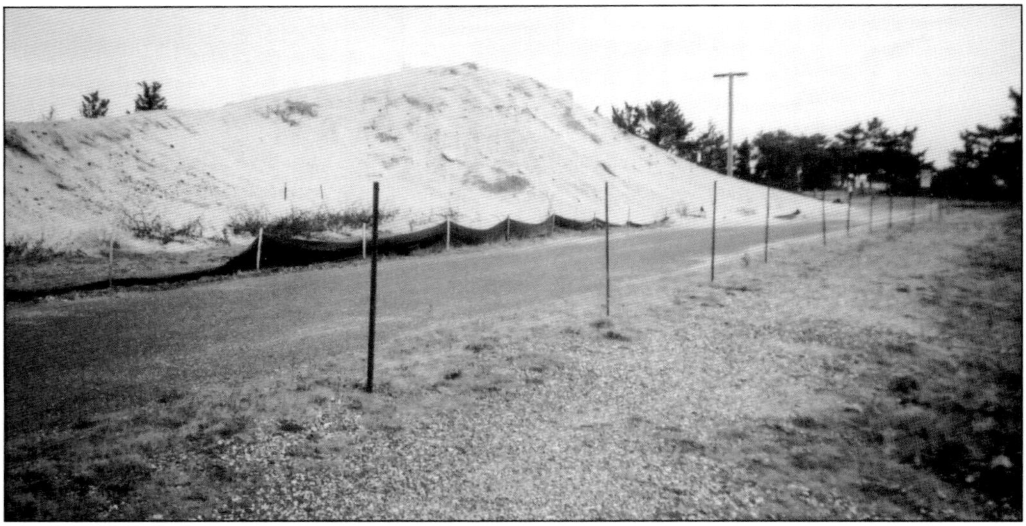

This large mound of dirt on Berkeley Island Park is the aftermath of Hurricane Sandy on the night of October 29, 2012. The huge water surge swept over the coastal area that night resulting in a record high tide for the Jersey Shore and leaving the park covered in sand. The once beautiful peninsula on Barnegat Bay is located at the eastern end of Brennan Concourse. The park was originally an island, and in 1955, it was filled in by dredging the surrounding waters. In 1958, the road was extended out to the island. In the 1980s, Ocean County acquired and developed the property. The park was temporarily closed afterwards but is scheduled to be restored in the near future.

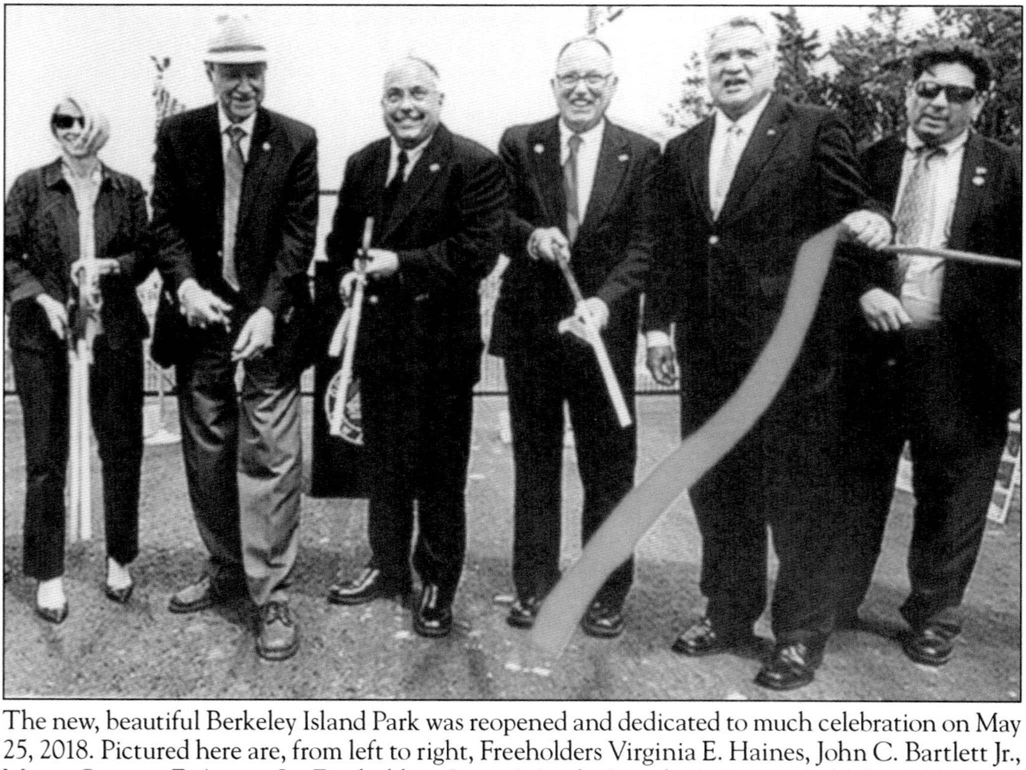

The new, beautiful Berkeley Island Park was reopened and dedicated to much celebration on May 25, 2018. Pictured here are, from left to right, Freeholders Virginia E. Haines, John C. Bartlett Jr., Mayor Carmen F. Amato Jr., Freeholders Gerry P. Little, Joseph H. Vicari, and John P. Kelly.

U-Drive-Em
Rowboats

Bait
Shrimp

BOB CUDDY'S FISHING CAMP

(New Mgr.—Russ Pensinger)

Harbor Inn Road
Cedar Beach
Bayville, N. J.

(7 Miles below Toms River on Route 9-4.)

Towing Service

Refreshments

This is Bob Cuddy's business card. Around 1940, the fishing camp was located at the end of Brennan Concourse on Barnegat Bay. Rowboats were rented for crabbing and fishing. A few private boat slips were also available. In 1954, it became Hen's Landing. Other owners followed.

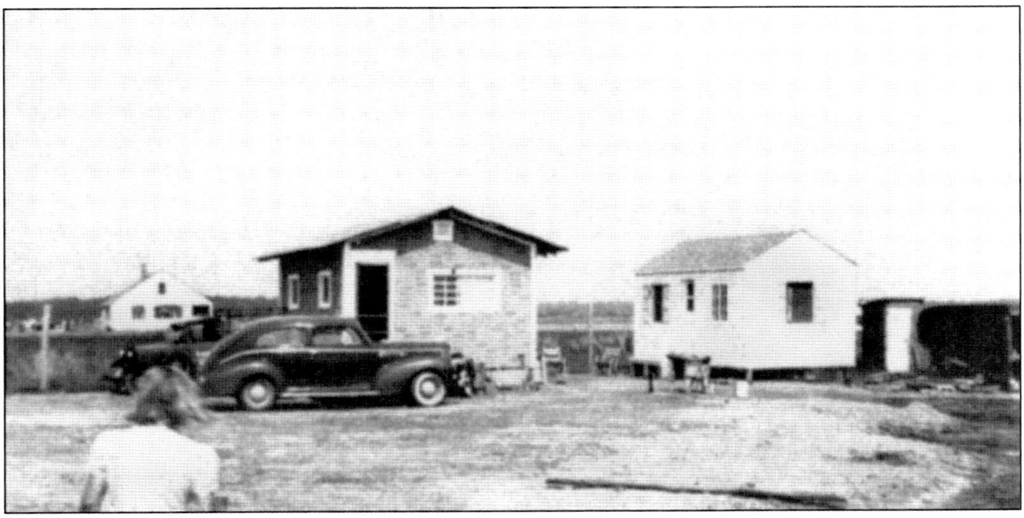

Bob Cuddy was the proprietor of this popular fishing camp from 1940 to 1949; it was located just west of Berkeley Island Park. Seen here are a storage shed, left, and a small bungalow, right. There were also three dockage piers and a refreshment stand. Trixie's house is in the distance at left. A rowboat rental was $2 with a tow or $5 with an outboard. Fred Stokley, the author's father, caught shrimp for both Cuddy's and Trixie's fishing camps. His house and shrimp boats were located next to Cuddy's, and today, it is a private residence. In the 1940s, Ernie Foster had a small cabin and shrimp boat located south of the camp. Today, both the Cuddy and Foster sites are vacant. (Courtesy of Chris Morley.)

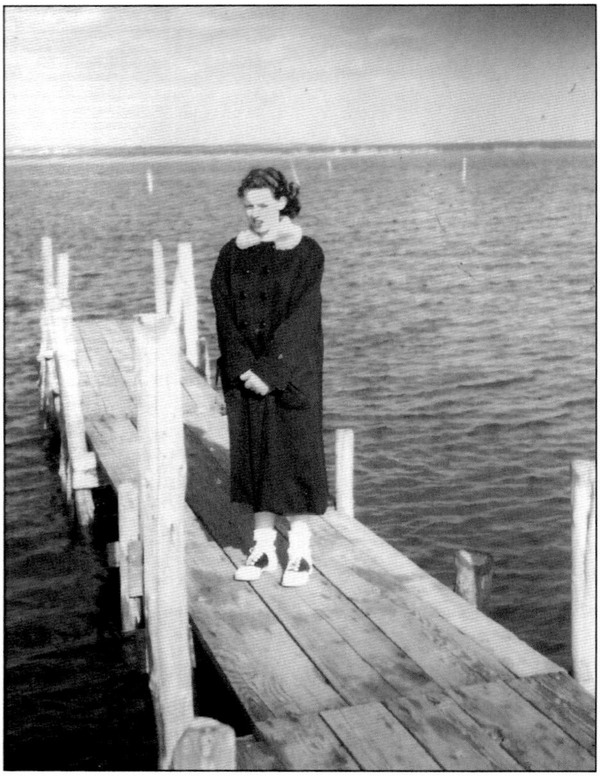

Pictured in 1952, Charlene Hall is standing on Bob Cuddy's Fishing Camp dock. Russell Pensinger, the proprietor, would tow rowboats from this pier out to the bay for fishing and crabbing. Elda, his wife, would later use binoculars to look for raised oars from the rowboats signaling their wish to return. It was a different era, and many families created fond memories on Barnegat Bay. (Courtesy of Charles Hall.)

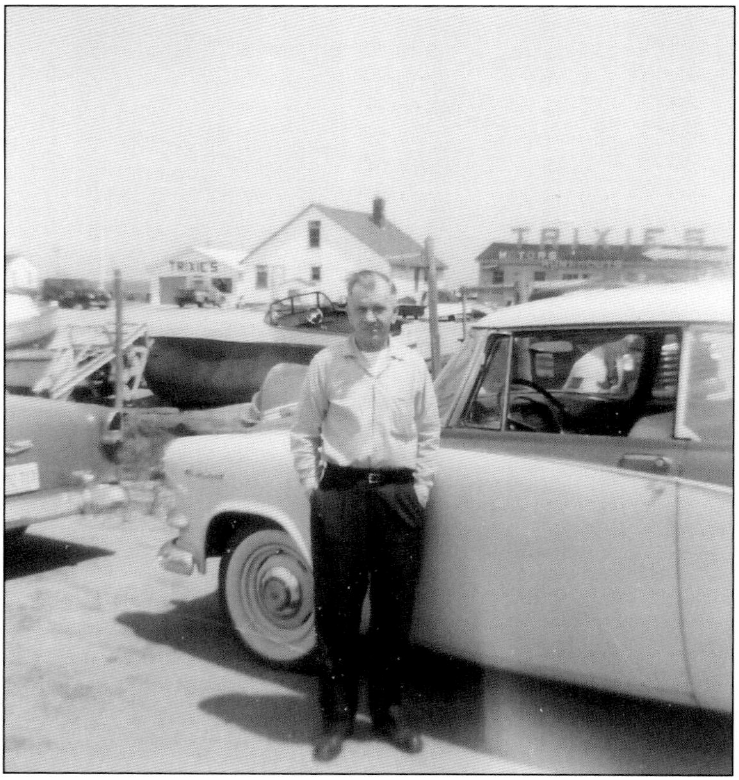

Russell Pensinger was the proprietor of the Bob Cuddy's Fishing Camp from 1949 to 1953. He and his wife, Elda, ran the business and lived in the small house on the site. He previously was employed as a milkman in Riverside, New Jersey, and after selling the fishing camp, he returned to his former job.

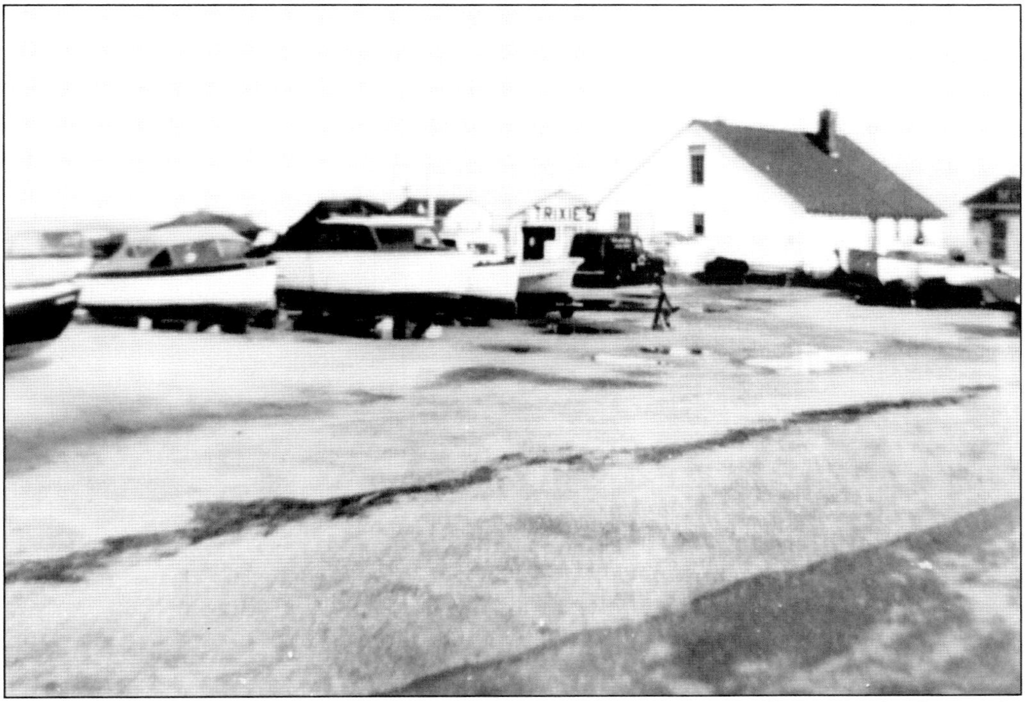

Trixie's Landing is located at 305 Brennan Concourse on a Barnegat Bay cove. In the 1940s, it originally was the home of the Bayview Gunning Club. The Bergstedt family purchased the property in 1948 and named it after "Trixie," whose real name was Victor Bergstedt Jr. Rowboat rentals, outboard motor sales, and private boat slips were offered. Robert Bergstedt, Trixie's son and an avid catamaran sailor, later took over the operation.

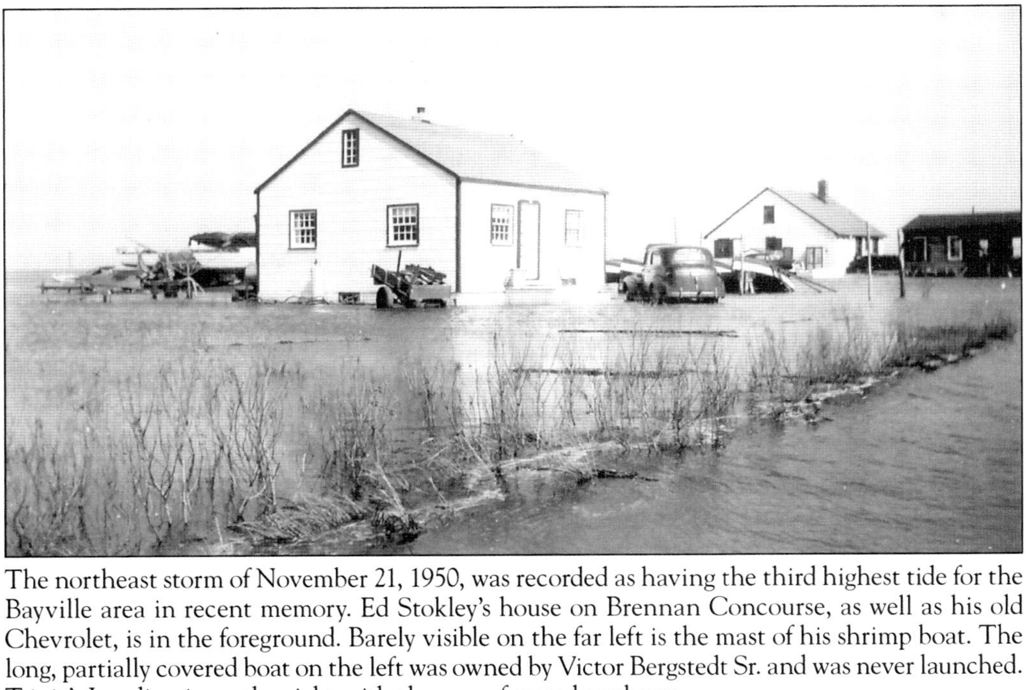

The northeast storm of November 21, 1950, was recorded as having the third highest tide for the Bayville area in recent memory. Ed Stokley's house on Brennan Concourse, as well as his old Chevrolet, is in the foreground. Barely visible on the far left is the mast of his shrimp boat. The long, partially covered boat on the left was owned by Victor Bergstedt Sr. and was never launched. Trixie's Landing is on the right with the row of stored rowboats.

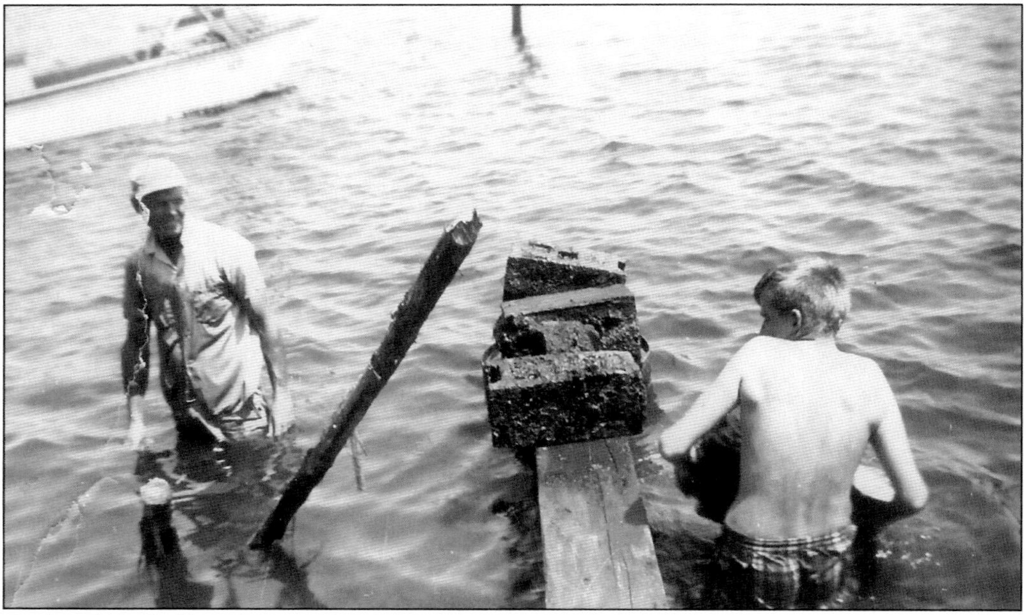

Fred Stokley (left) and Al Stokley (right) are removing debris to clear the way for easier dockage of Fred's shrimp boat seen in the upper left. The shrimp nets, which are typically dragged along each side of the boat, are seen here lying on the forward deck. The fast, garvey-designed boats, with one mast, plied the shallow, grassy waters south of Tices Shoal off Island Beach. The bait shrimp sold for $1 a quart. Other boat operators were Fred Grant, Ernie Foster, and Bernie Penn.

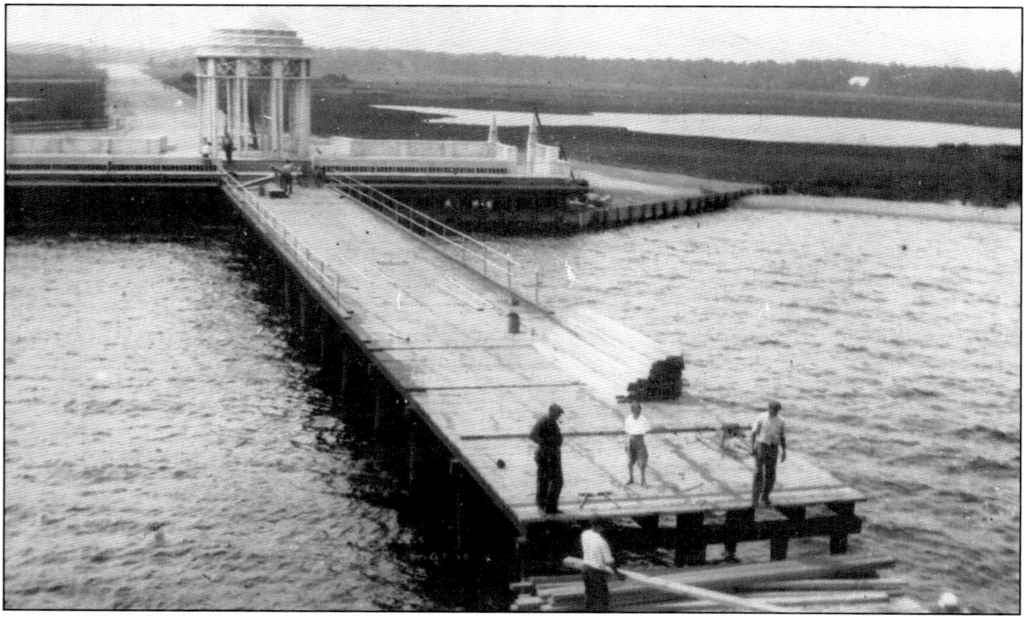

Seen in 1927, this ornate pavilion and pier are under construction by the B.W. Sangor Company on the beachfront of Butler Boulevard. It was hoped this extravagant structure would entice potential buyers to purchase property in Pinewald by offering access to the beach for waterfront recreation. The Sangor development failed by the 1930s, and the pavilion and pier were destroyed by fire in 1949. In the 1950s, this waterfront became known as Tijan's Beach and was used for public swimming.

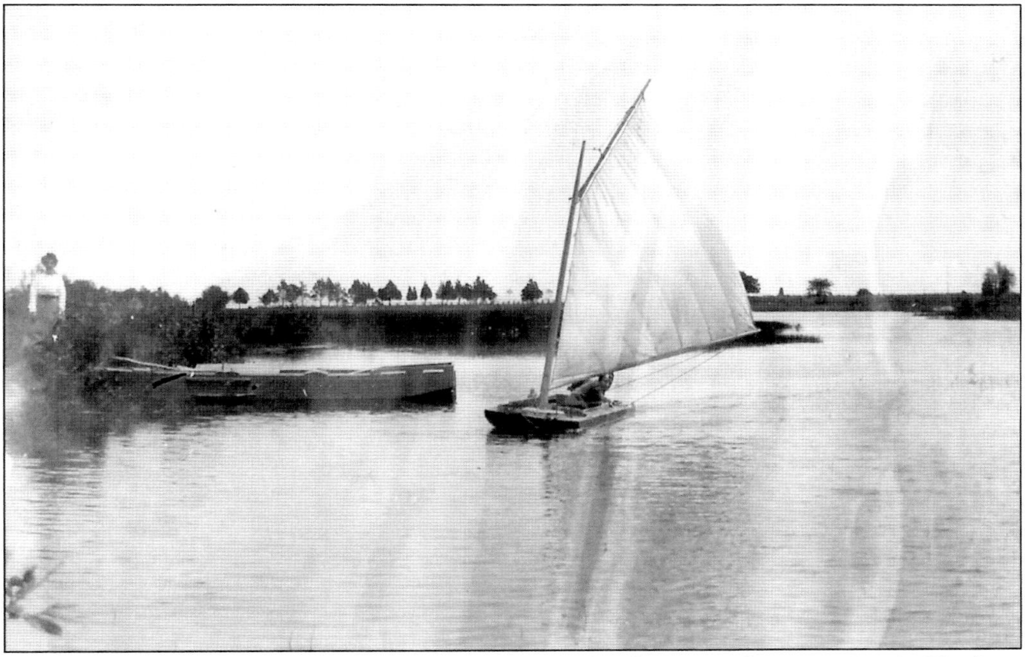

In 1903, Lucy Enggren is watching the small gaff-rigged sailboat on Clamming Creek. The boat pictured was similar to the Barnegat Sneakbox sailboat. It was suitable for both duck hunting and sailing along the shallow bay shoreline. The same craft could also be used as a rowboat when the sails and rigging were removed (Courtesy of John Enggren.)

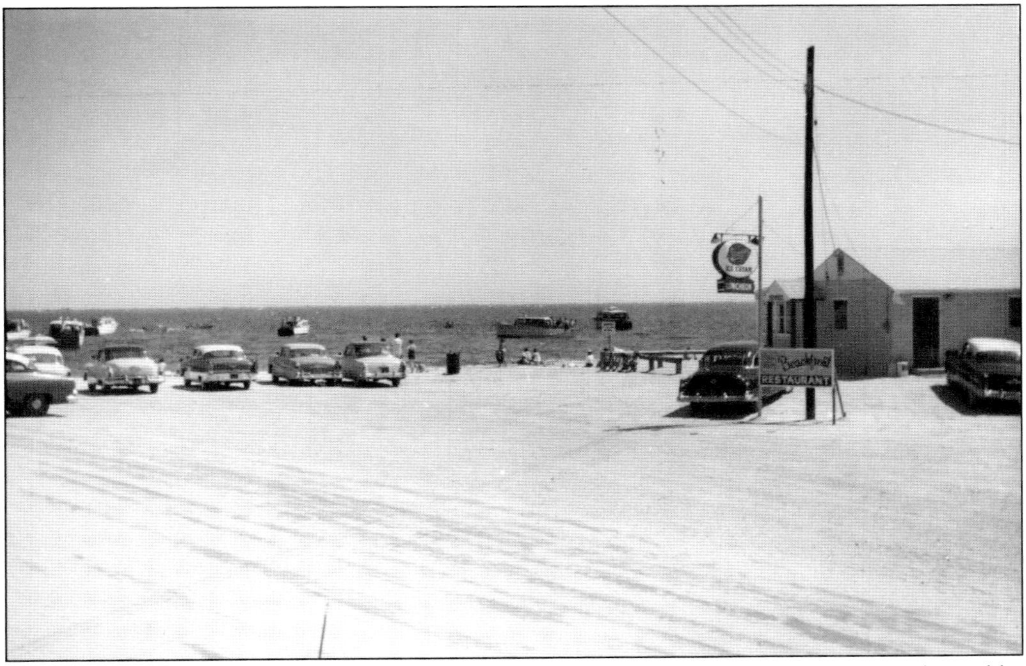

This is a 1957 view of Tijan's Beach, located at the end of Butler Boulevard. It was a popular, public bathing area with a scenic view of the bay. Several boating participants are also enjoying the fine weather. To the right is the Beachfront Restaurant that proclaims, "Food at It's Best." Today, only a small beach is available to the public on the north side. (Courtesy of Pat Hamilton.)

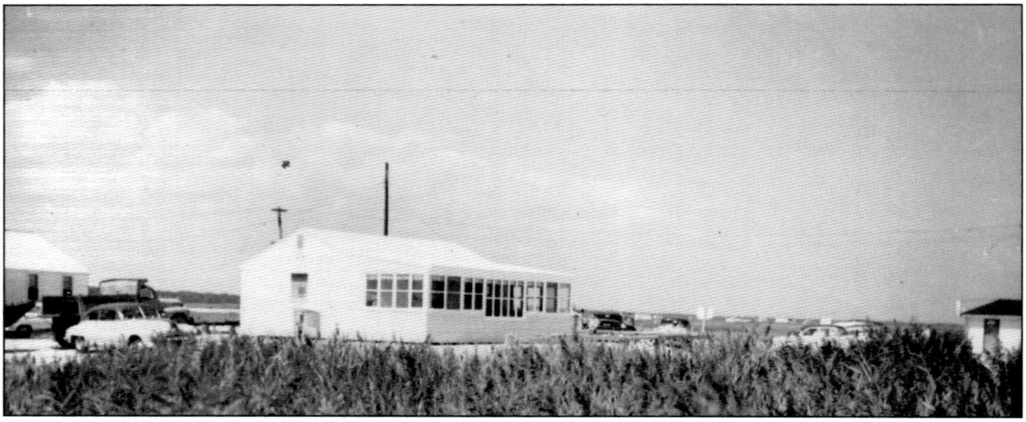

The Beachfront Restaurant, above, was owned and operated by Chef Henry "Sal" Salussolia from 1952 to 1960. The restaurant was located at the Glen Cove lagoon development started in 1953 by Enoch and Benjamin Mabie. It featured a counter service and an enclosed windowed dining room with a scenic waterfront view. Later, the restaurant became the Tijan Tonga Spa. Part of Whitey's Marina is shown here on the left. It was owned by Larry and Deb Thompson. The beach bathing facility is on the far right. (Courtesy of Pat Hamilton.)

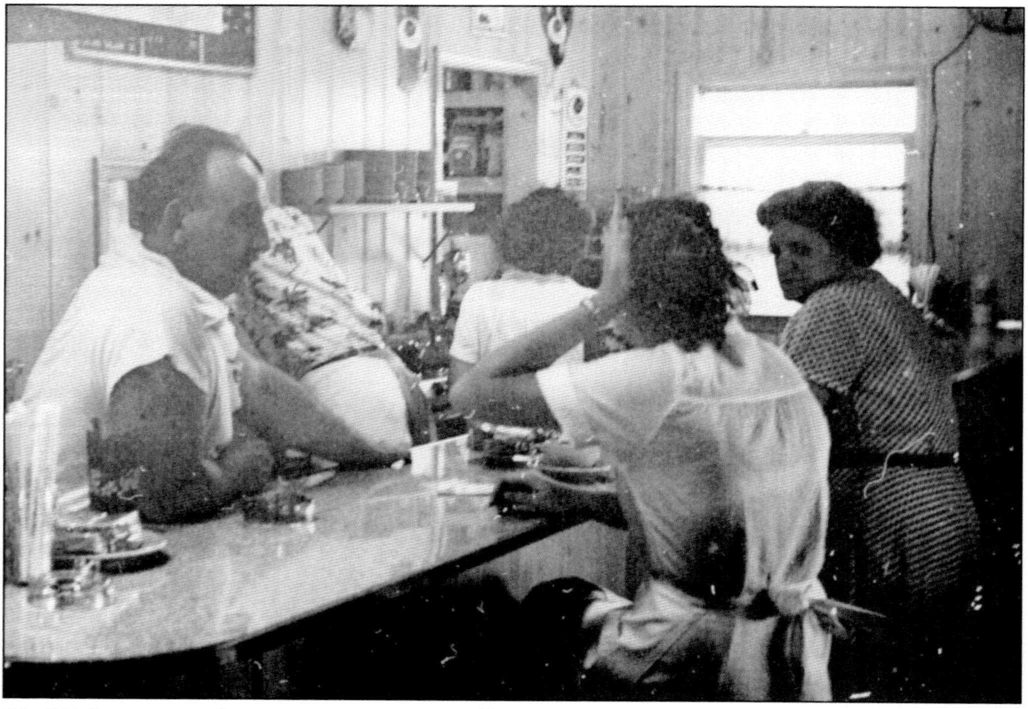

Chef Sal is seen at the restaurant counter talking to waitress Jean Stokley, at his right. He was always friendly and was an excellent cook of Italian food. Sal also drove a local school bus for many years. The restaurant has been demolished, and today, a large, private residence occupies the site. (Courtesy of Pat Hamilton.)

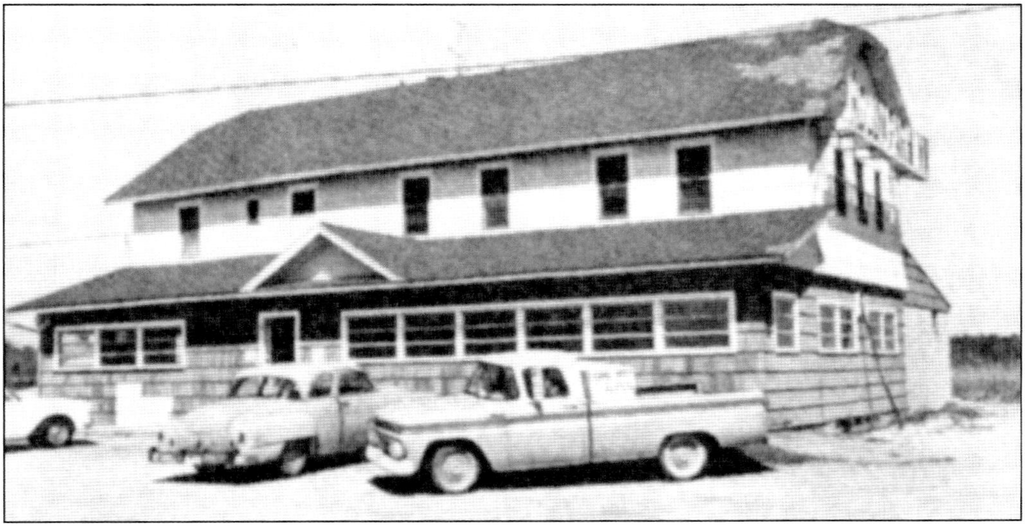

The Holly Park Inn (HPI) in the 1950s offered a restaurant, a large oval bar, and rooms for rent on the shoreline at the end of Bay Avenue. The friendly bartenders were Sam and Chris with entertainment provided by Frank McCabe at the organ. The HPI was a local landmark for years. Bill Leary, one of the earliest owners, ran the business mostly as a hotel with boat rentals. Later, other owners included Jack and Mickey Steele and the Hodulich family. The various name changes in recent years included Big Stosh's, Charley Nobles, P.J.'s, and Windows on the Bay. Today, it is named the Cove with the building having been substantially upgraded and expanded.

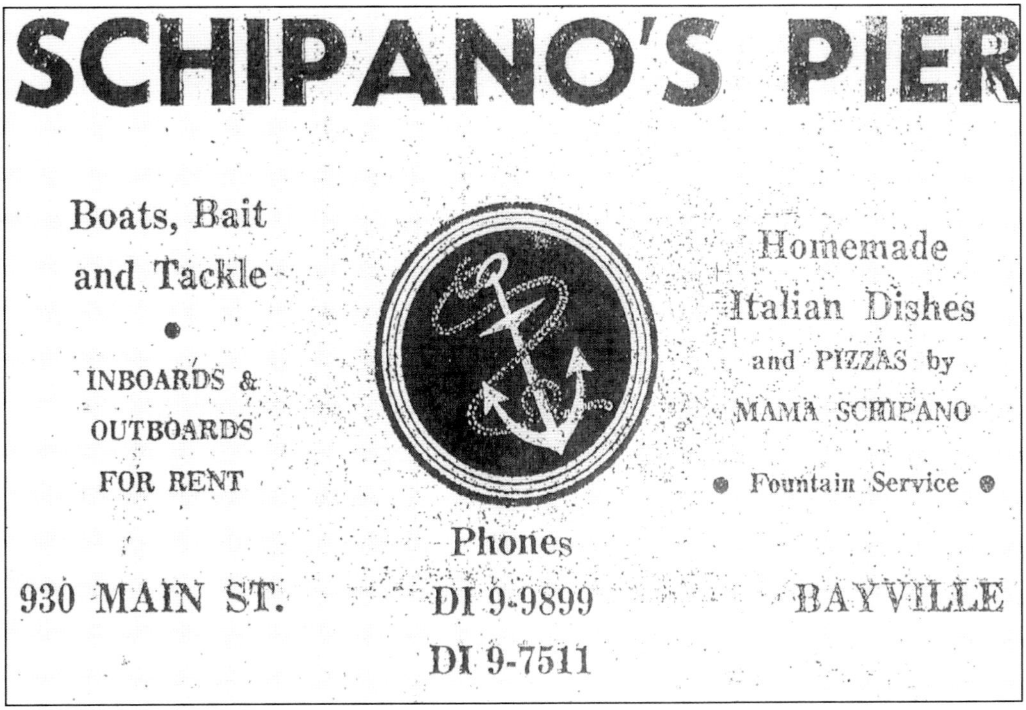

Schipano's Pier and restaurant was on the bay at the end of Main Street, in the Holly Park section of Bayville. It was a family-run business with "Mama" Schipano doing most the cooking. Today, the restaurant and pier are both gone. A private residence now occupies the waterfront property with just a small beach on the north side.

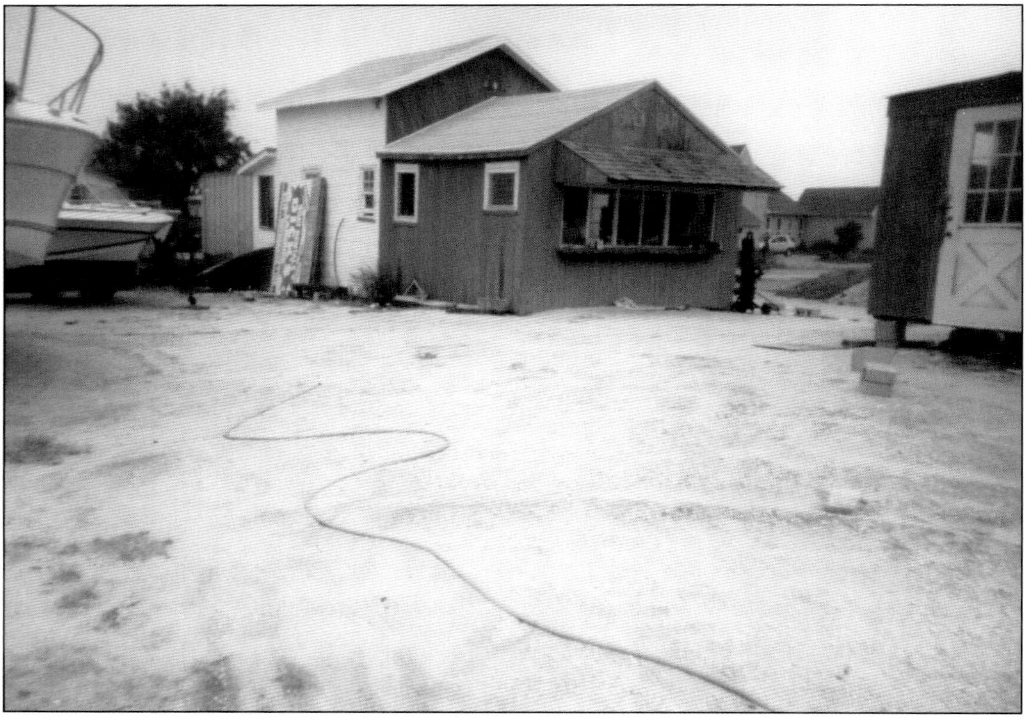

Dick's Landing was located on the bay east of Bayview on Balsam Road. It was owned and operated by Richard Baumgarten, who provided rowboat rentals and dock facilities. The site was previously known as Hibberds. Above is the former snack bar and storage facility. A large Dick's advertising sign has outlived its usefulness and has been placed next to the building. Today, the site is occupied by private residences.

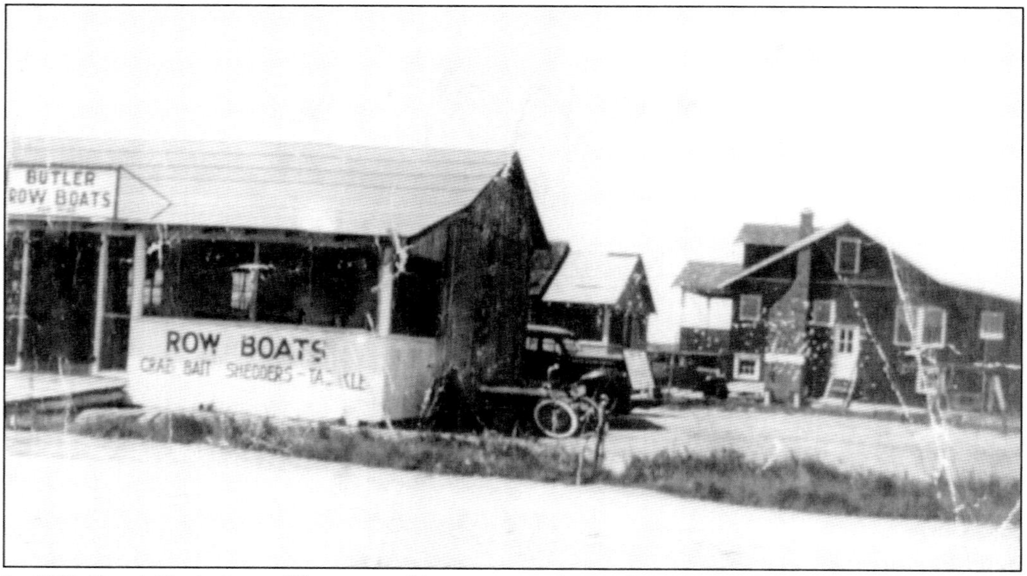

In 1939, Frank Butler's small boat rental business was located on the Great Sloop Creek at the foot of Sloop Creek Road. It was one of the earliest in Bayville and also provided private dockage. Frank was the son of Benjamin Butler, who owned a general store and post office near Hickory Lane on Route 9. The site later became the Harbor Lights Marina, and today, it is the C&C Marina.

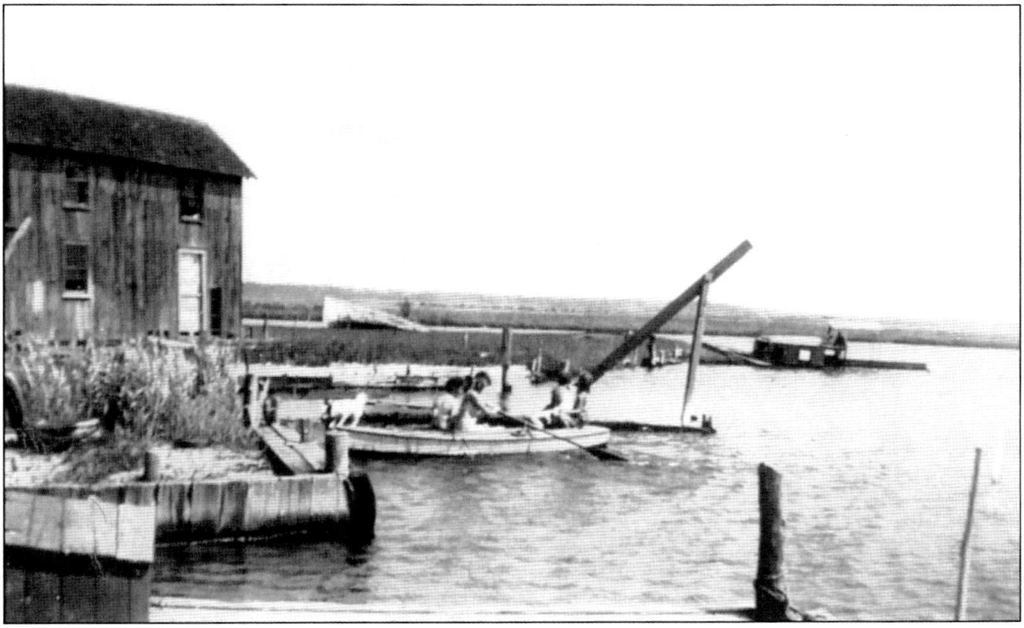

This view of the Sloop Creek is at the end of Naples Street looking north. The salt meadow in the background is now Allen Road with many homes. The lady rowers are, from left to right, Marie Vaeth and Shirley Leist. The two children watching the blimp overhead are, from left to right, Mickey Stoll and Arlene Pullen. Note the dog in the bow ready to jump ship with Shirley watching closely. The barn on the left was destroyed in the 1944 hurricane.

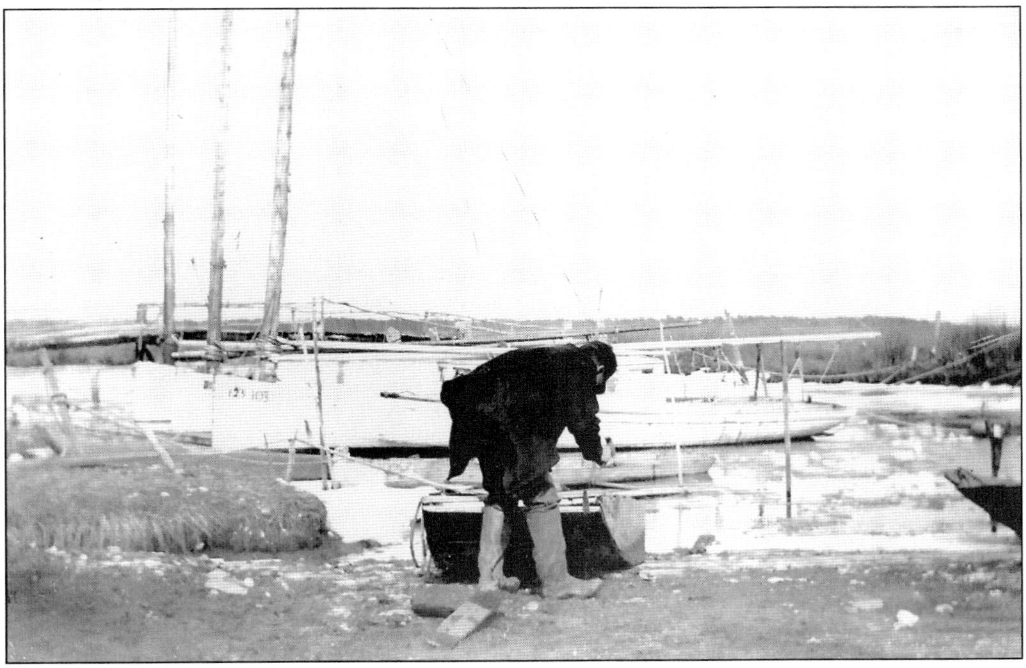

This winter scene appears to show a large bait box from Sloop Creek. Three large catboats lie peacefully tied to their mooring posts. The salt hay in the background was used by local farmers to feed their livestock. Remnants of the wooden bridge, seen here, that connected the mainland to the outer marshland are still in place. Today, the site is a public boat ramp.

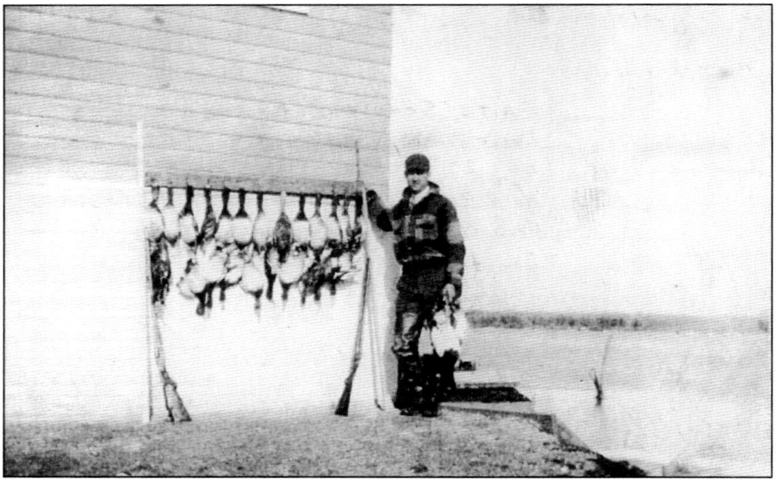

Fritz Schuler was a friend of the Leists; the Leist family had a home on the Sloop Creek. Here, Schuler is seen in 1926 at the Leist house with his take of 27 canvas-back ducks. The mostly undeveloped marsh meadows along Barnegat Bay at that time made an attractive setting for duck hunting.

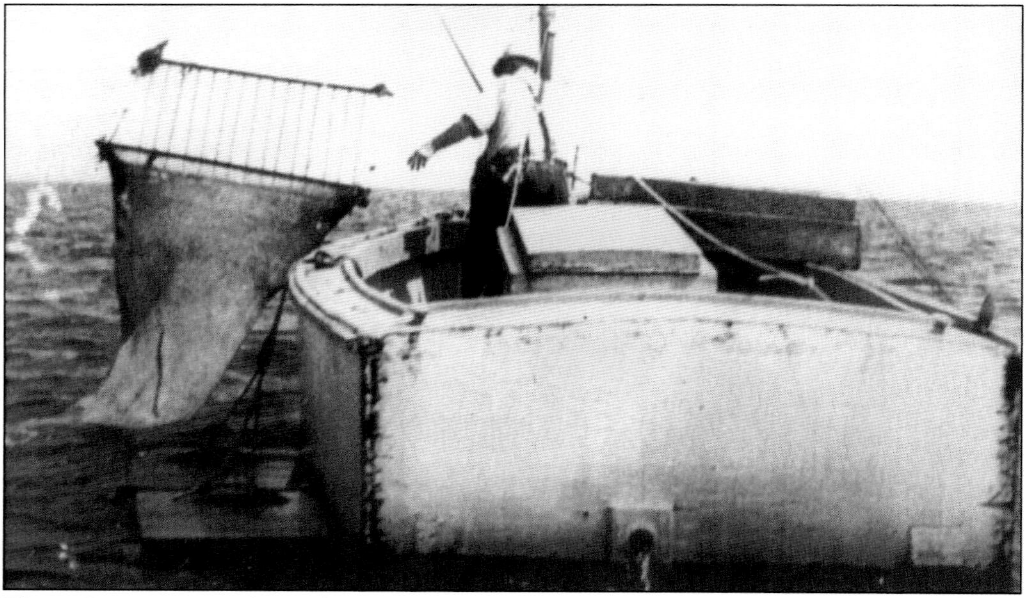

This is Bernie Penn's shrimp boat, from Forked River, on Barnegat Bay in 1960. His boat was of a typical 20-foot garvey design with one mast and two seine-like nets that were dragged on each side. These nets were often maintained on home sewing machines. The motor would be an automobile engine modified for high speed. These boats would later become the forerunners of the popular garvey bay boat races. There were several boats that would slowly cruise the shallow eel grass waters off Tice's Shoal near Island Beach State Park. Each net would be emptied, sorted out for shrimp, and then placed in a large box being towed on the side. This box was then pulled on board and returned to the fishing camps at high speed where the shrimp sold for $1 a quart. The author earned a hefty 50¢ a trip as the boat navigator. During summer weekends in the 1950s, there would be a large flotilla of happy fisherman and crabbers from Cuddy's, Trixie's, Downe's, and Whitey's fishing camps between Glen Cove and Cedar Creek. Fred Grant's shrimp boat would anchor nearby at channel mark 64 with a large shrimp sign at the top of the mast. Sportsman historically knew the bay for its superb fishing of weakfish, kingfish, and flounder. The Central Railroad would run a Fisherman's Special on several occasions. With the advent of lagoon development and the changing ecosystem, the Barnegat Bay shrimp boat would slowly sail off into the sunset. (Courtesy of Lacey Historical Society.)

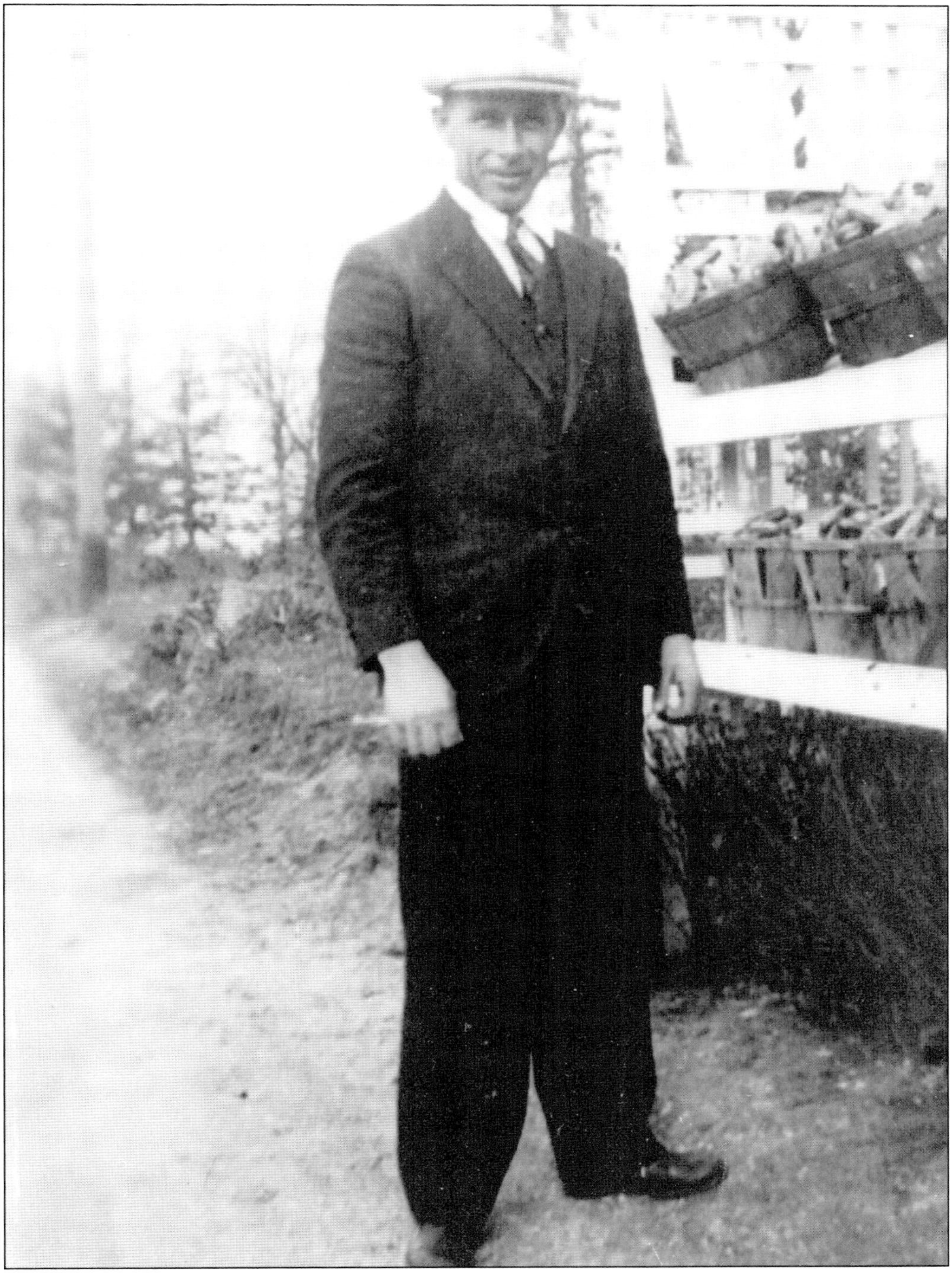

Clarence G. Cramer poses for his neighbor Marie Hauser Chamberlain at his roadside oyster stand in 1932. The stand was in front of his home, just south of Sloop Creek Road on Route 9. The oysters came from his oyster beds in nearby Barnegat Bay. In the 1950s, another popular oyster stand was at the Taylor residence located just north of Hickory Lane. (Courtesy of Betty Cramer.)

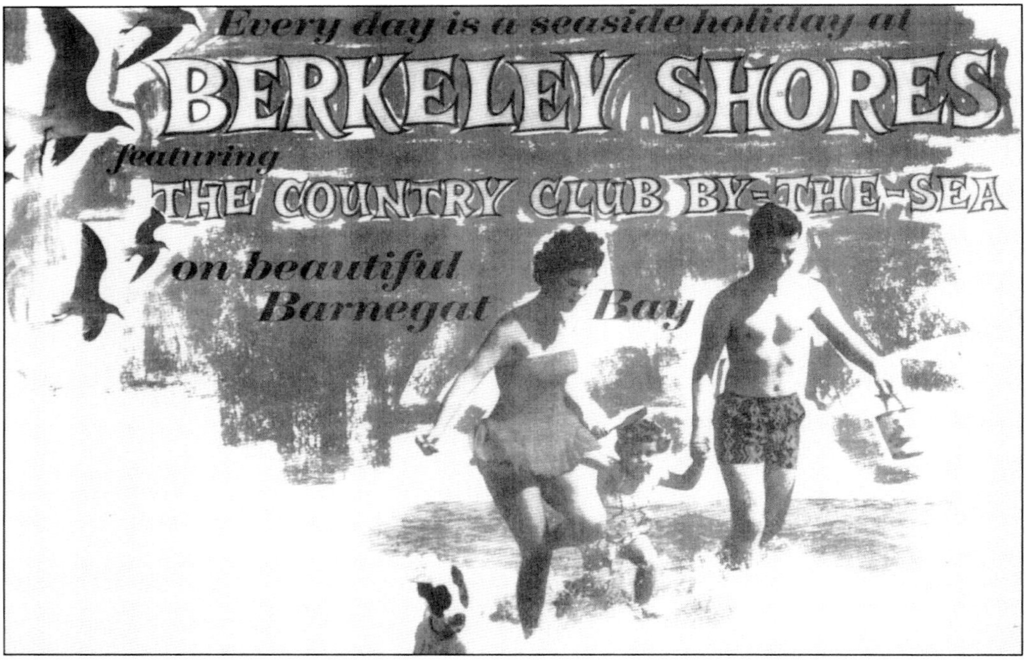

Hydrocarbon Chemicals of Newark, New Jersey, wholly owned Berkeley Shores Estates Incorporated. The lagoon development started in 1957 on both sides of Bayview Avenue and south of Veeder Lane. Houses on the west side of Bayview Avenue were not completed until several years later. Berkeley Shores was promoted as having a modern marina, a clubhouse with a pool, and lagoon homes starting at $11,990. Today, it remains an attractive waterfront community with several hundred homes consisting of five original models.

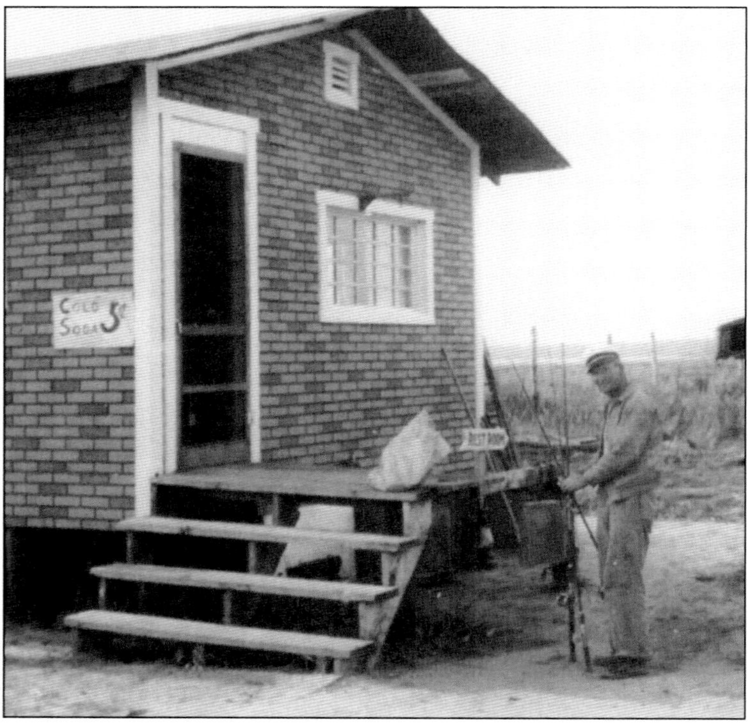

Pictured is Bob Cuddy sorting the fishing poles at his fishing camp in front of the storage shed in 1940. He purchased the property from Berkeley Township and would build a house and all needed docks and facilities for the camp near Berkeley Island Park. At that time, Brennan Concourse was a dirt road, and the site was all marshland. He lived here with his wife, Harriet, and children during fishing season renting rowboats. The property was sold in 1949.

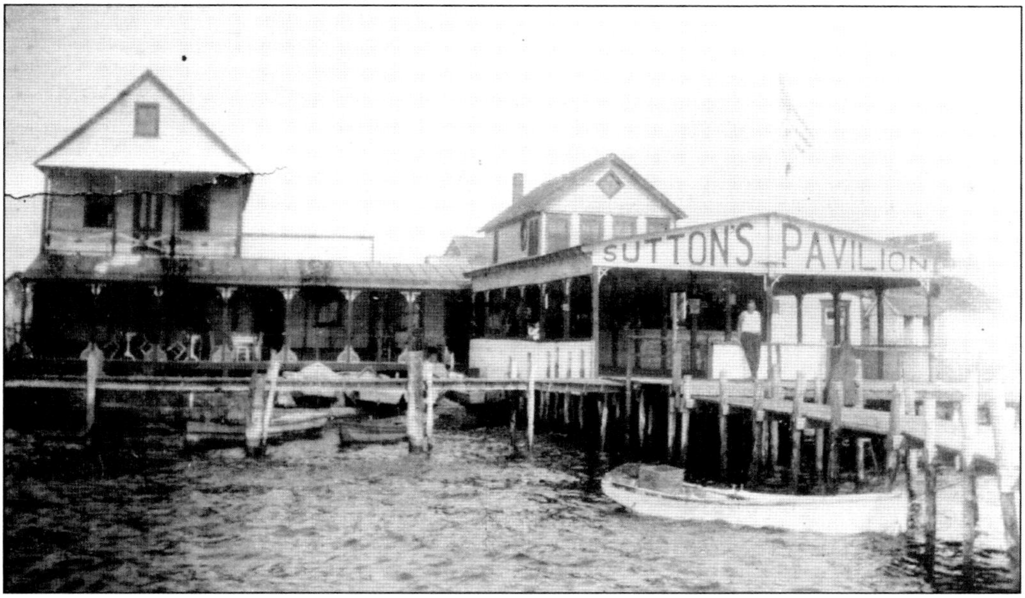

In 1905, Frank W. Sutton Sr. purchased this bay-front property from David Falkenburgh and opened Sutton's Pavilion. Frank W. Sutton Jr. later became chairman of the board of the First National Bank. This 1910 view reflects the site just south of the Philadelphia & Long Branch Railroad pier. The Barnegat Pier station and surrounding boating activity resulted in this becoming one of Bayville's earliest summer tourist retreats. In 1923, the business was sold to Anna E. Davis. (Courtesy of Pat Newman.)

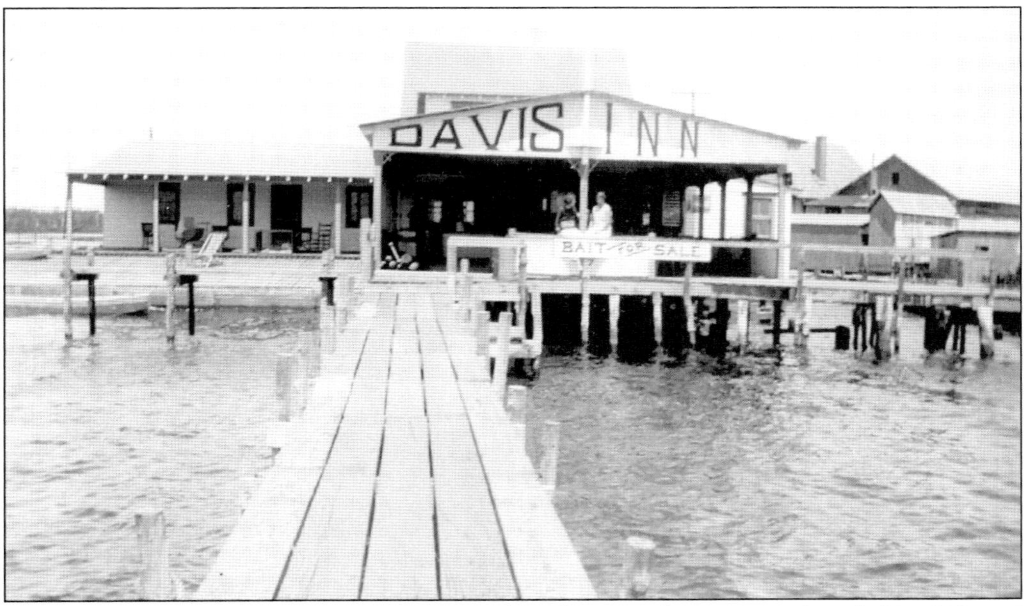

Anna Davis, a widow, purchased Sutton's Pavilion from Frank Sutton on March 28, 1923, and renamed it the Davis Inn. The modifications included painting the new name over the old and removing the two buildings that were behind the pier facade. The Davis Inn then continued as a popular fishing camp facility. Anna and her only daughter, Alice, are sitting inside the pavilion, perhaps discussing whether to place some crab lines off the dock on such a nice day. (Courtesy of Pat Newman.)

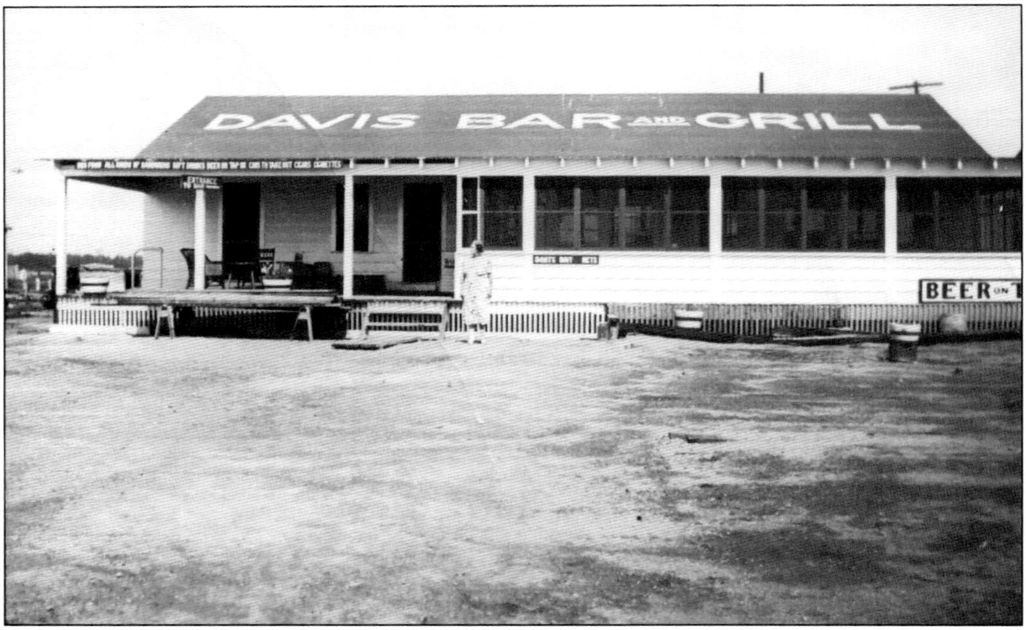

Anna Davis, proprietor, is standing in front of the Davis Bar and Grill in 1935. The site was a favorite, both as a restaurant and boat rental business, in the 1930s. The partially enclosed porch area lends itself for a fine-dining experience. The advertisement at left proclaims, "Sea food, all kinds of sandwiches, soft drinks, beer on tap or cans to take out, cigars, cigarettes." (Courtesy of Pat Newman.)

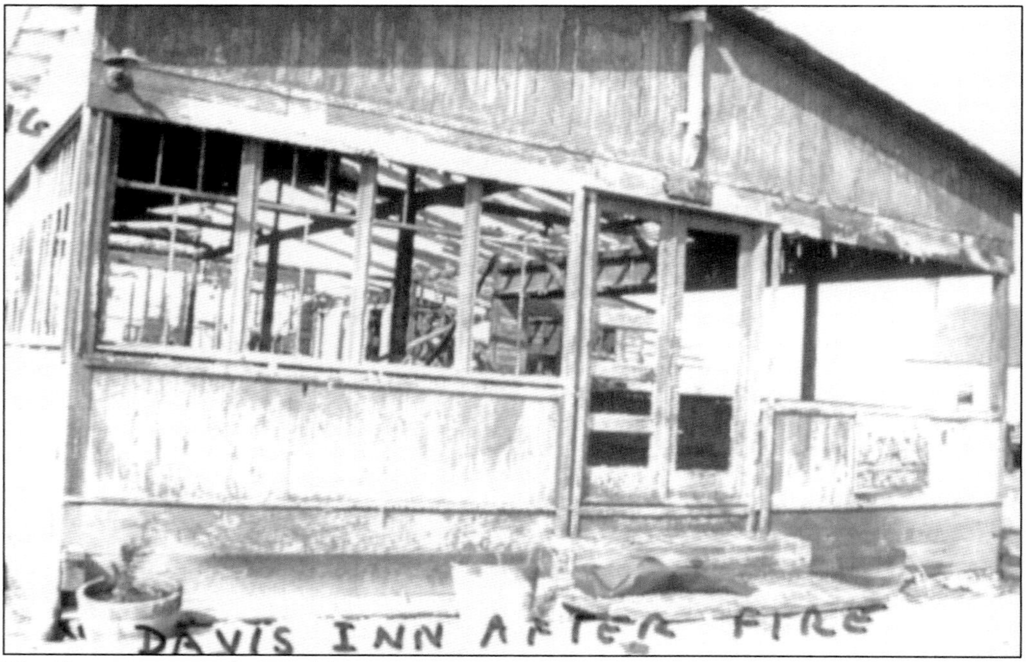

The Davis Inn was damaged by two separate fires over the years. The second was due to an explosion of unknown cause and is pictured here. This fire possibly prompted the sale of the inn and 17 rowboats on November 8, 1943, to Jennie D'Onofrio for $6,000. The pavilion continued as a restaurant with a dance floor, bar, and boating facilities. (Courtesy of Pat Newman.)

Anna Davis and her adopted daughter, Alice, are sitting near the Barnegat Pier railroad station around 1930. The station was adjacent to Anna Davis's restaurant and fishing camp facility. Alice would latter marry Arthur Newman, who had owned the Berkeley Machine Shop on Route 9 and was the namesake for the Arthur Newman Berkeley Industrial Park. Alice and Arthur would also become active in many Bayville civic activities.

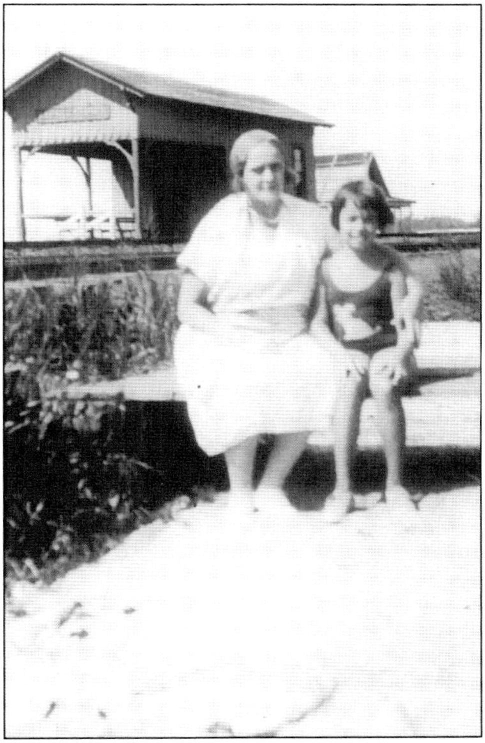

The Cedar Creek Life-Saving Station was in service from 1872 until 1938. It was originally designated Life-Saving Station No. 15 and later No. 111 when the US Coast Guard renumbered all the stations in 1915. It was formerly located between the two main bathing pavilions on present-day Island Beach State Park. At one time, there were 28 lifesaving stations along the New Jersey coastline between Sandy Hook and Cape May. The two men identified here in 1907 are Charlie Vanderveer, first row, seated at left, and Elwood Butler, second row, standing at right. They both resided in Bayville.

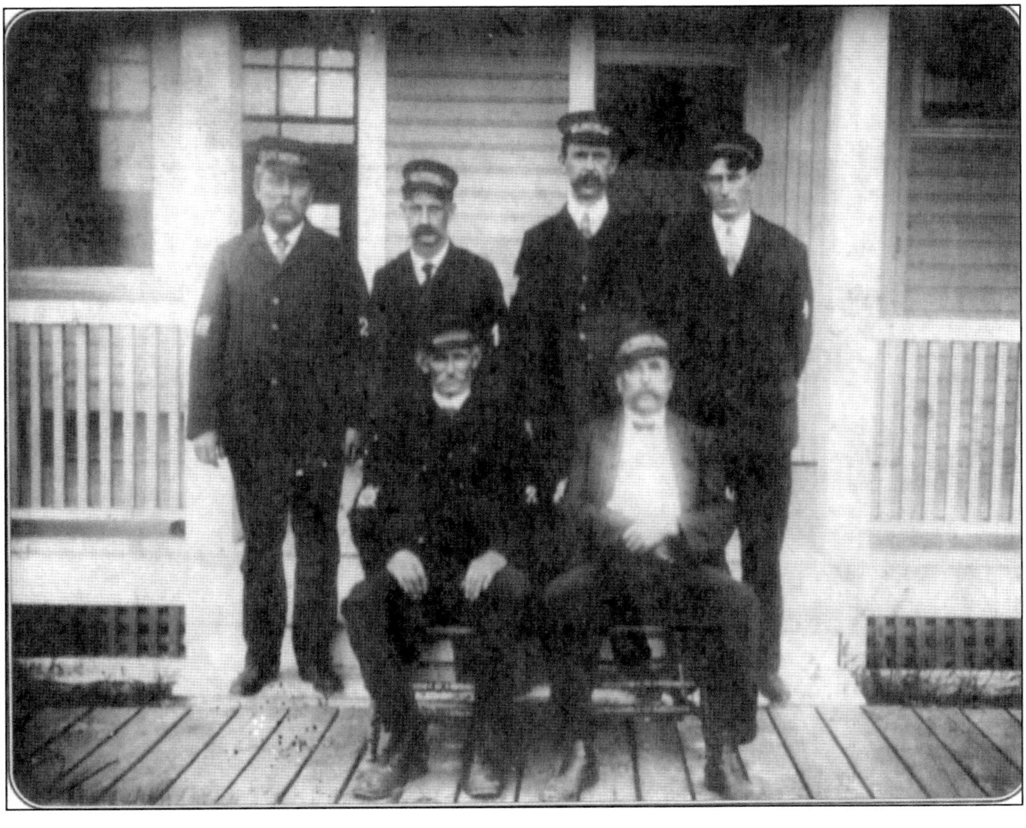

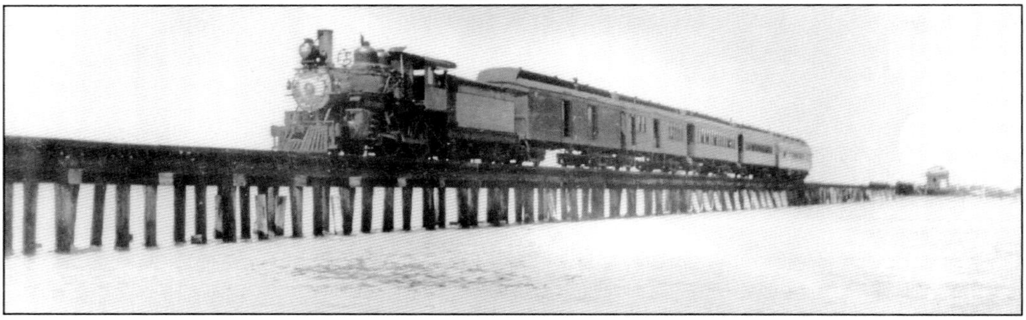

This train, with one baggage car, one combine, and three passenger cars, is heading east toward Seaside Park and Bay Head where it would then enter the New York & Long Branch Railroad. The Pennsylvania Railroad's 7,000-foot-long wooden trestle across Barnegat Bay was built in 1881. Over the years, it incurred damages from severe weather and ice flows. The swing bridge railing and the Barnegat Pier station can be seen in the distant background. (Courtesy of John Brinckmann.)

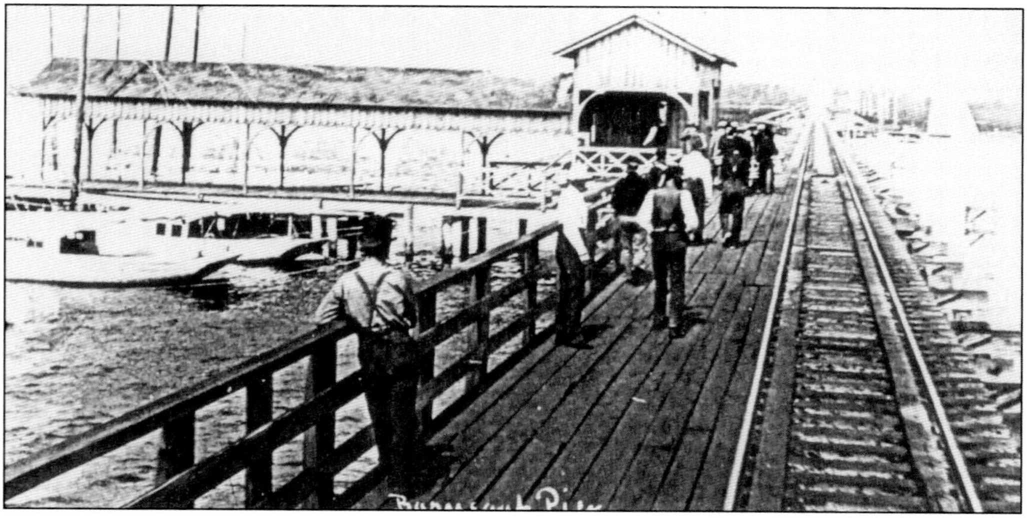

The boat pavilion and canopy dock on Barnegat Pier are featured in this 1920s view. The men are enjoying some relaxing time on the trestle. Everyone seems to be looking west, perhaps to catch a glimpse of an approaching train locomotive steaming across the meadows.

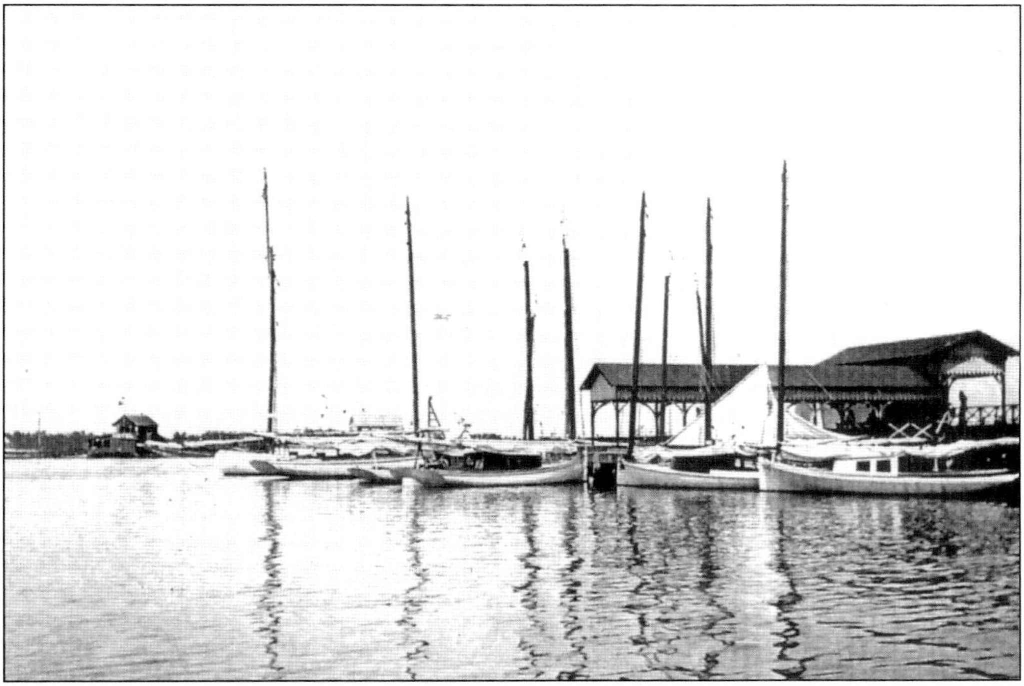

It is July 9, 1903, and several large catboats are moored at the Barnegat Pier canopied dock. The tranquil setting reflects a calm day on Barnegat Bay with little breeze and a clear sky. This pier dock was also used by transient boats that would make connections with the Tuckerton Railroad station at Barnegat Light.

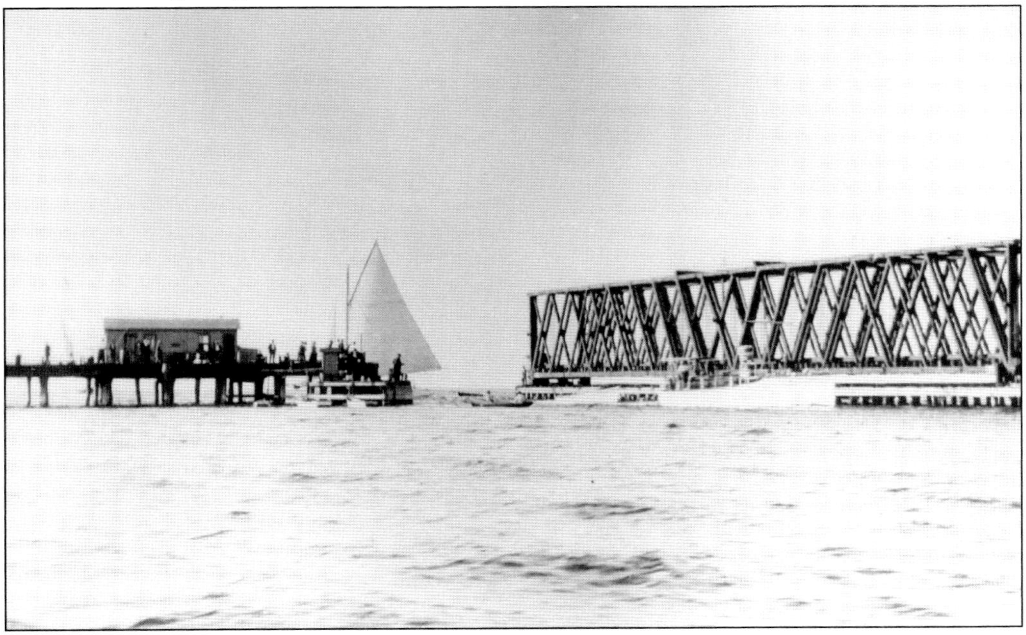

The swing bridge is open on the Barnegat Pier trestle to allow two large pleasure craft and a large sailboat to pass through. Several smaller boats are docked at the pier. The curious fishermen and vacationers are watching the intriguing scene from the pier's edge. (Courtesy of John Brinckmann.)

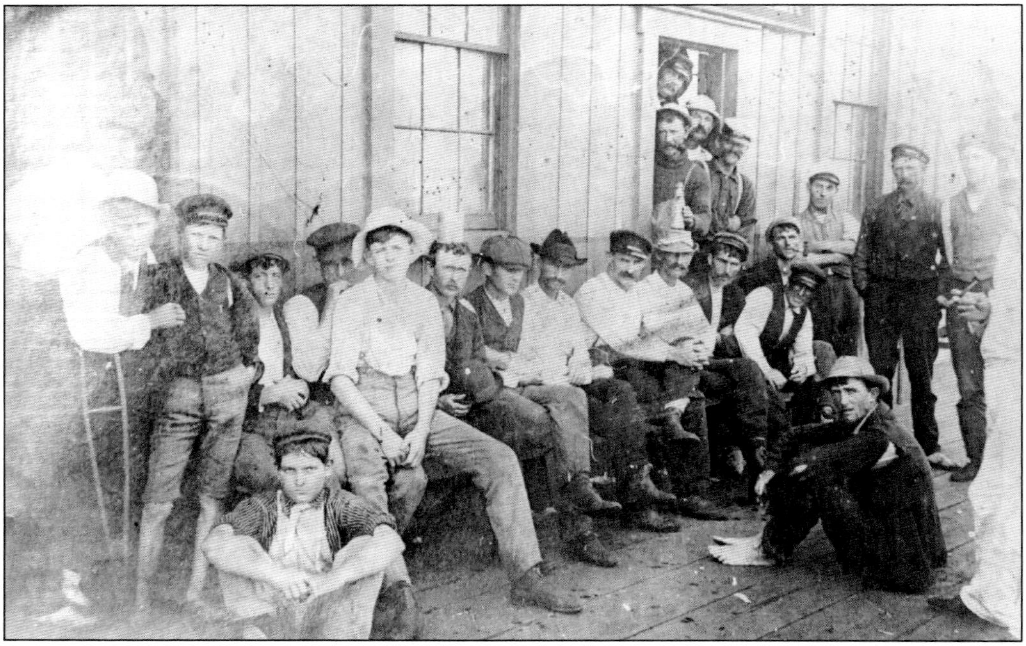

These are the Barnegat Pier baymen waiting for the boats to be docked and unloaded. The bay created the livelihood for many early residents of Bayville. The daily catch was either sold locally or packed in ice and shipped to city markets. One day in 1876 there were 29 oyster boats reported on the bay. There was an abundance of fish, crabs, oysters, clams, and shrimp until the ecosystem changed.

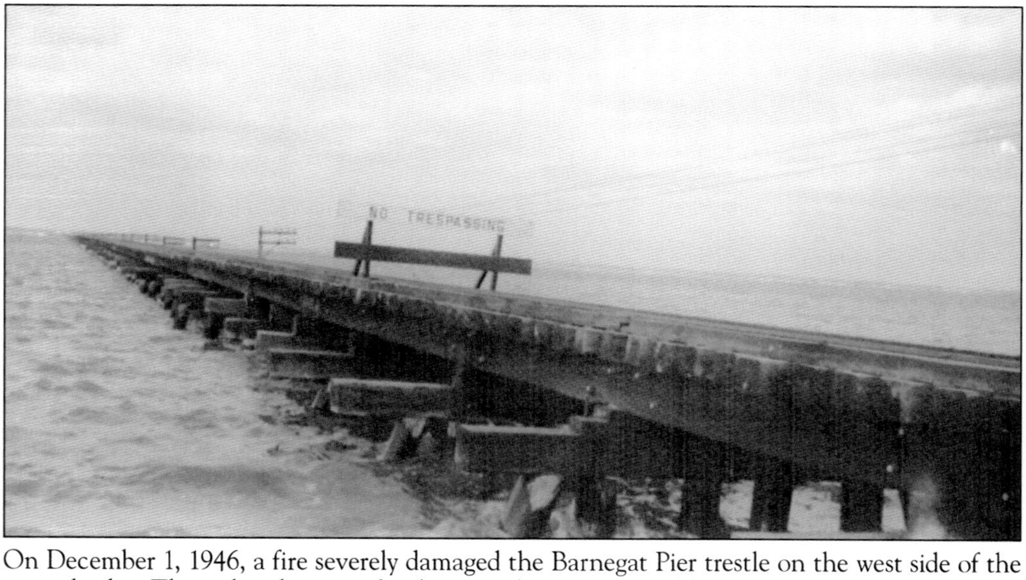

On December 1, 1946, a fire severely damaged the Barnegat Pier trestle on the west side of the swing bridge. The railroad service for the next three years would end at the Berkeley shoreline. Permission was later received to abandon the line, and in the summer of 1950, most of the bridge was removed, thus ending 65 years of adventurous train travel across the bay. (Courtesy of E.H. Weber, Ocean County Historical Society Collection.)

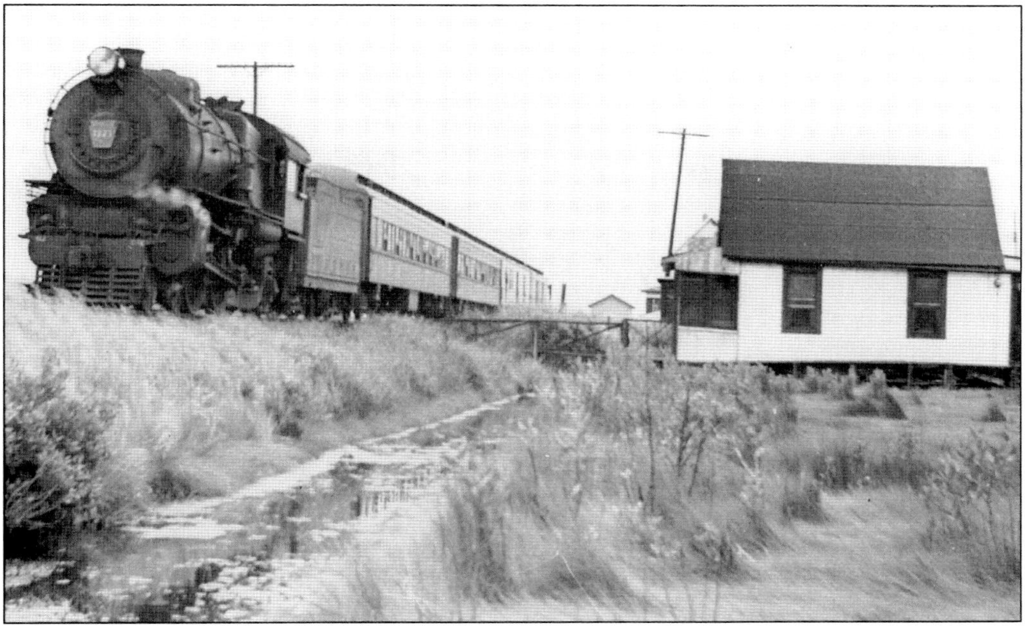

Train No. 996 is waiting to depart from Barnegat Pier on July 11, 1948. The bridge had partially burned two years earlier, requiring approaching trains to now start down the Island Heights spur and then back down to the bay. The temporary shelter with its rather crude walkway to the train is on the right. The top of the former Barnegat Pier station is in the distance. (Courtesy of E.H. Weber, Ocean County Historical Society Collection.)

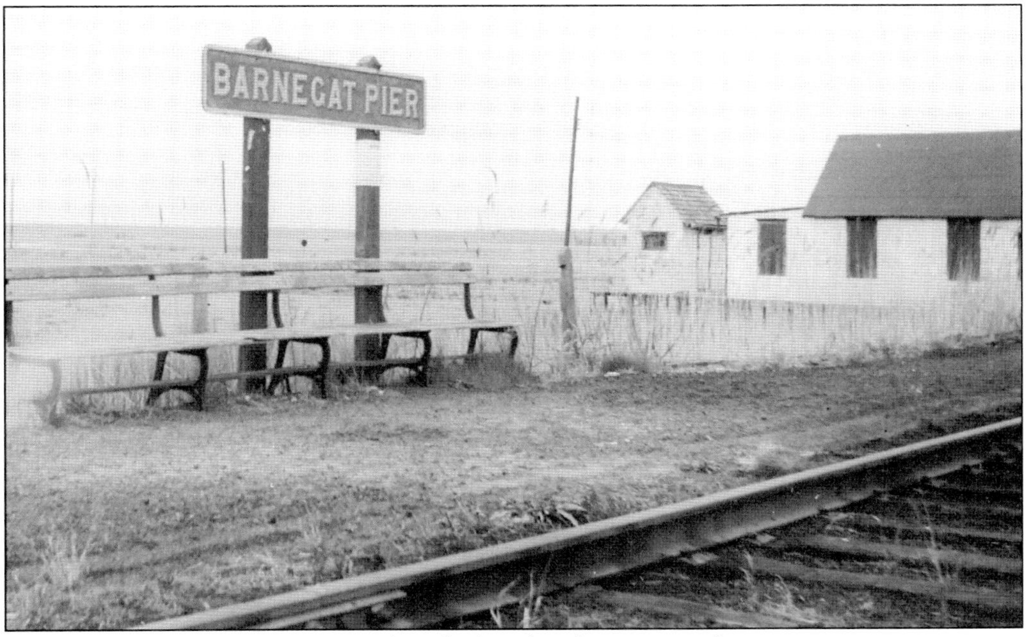

In 1948, the Barnegat Pier sign stood on the bay shoreline next to the temporary station seen on the right. The station name would continue to be used in the near future by the local population as the unofficial namesake for this area. The sparse wooden benches provided little comfort while waiting in such a desolate location. (Courtesy of E.H. Weber, Ocean County Historical Society Collection.)

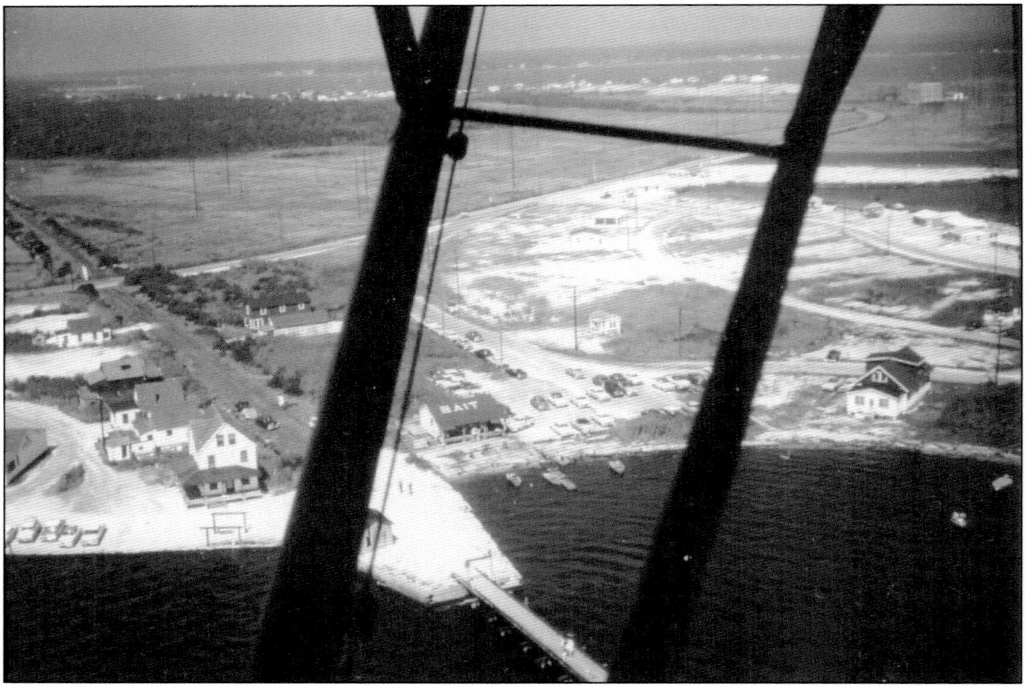

This unique 1960 blimp aerial view depicts the partial Waterfront Restaurant in the lower left; the old railroad shelter near to Bayview Avenue; the Wes Falkenburg Hotel on the beachfront; the abandoned Pennsylvania Railroad right-of-way with the remaining fishing pier at lower center; Don's Boats at mid-center; Mr. Lucky's house, which is now Lucky's Marina, at left center; and the telegraph building in the upper right. (Courtesy of Ron Stilwell.)

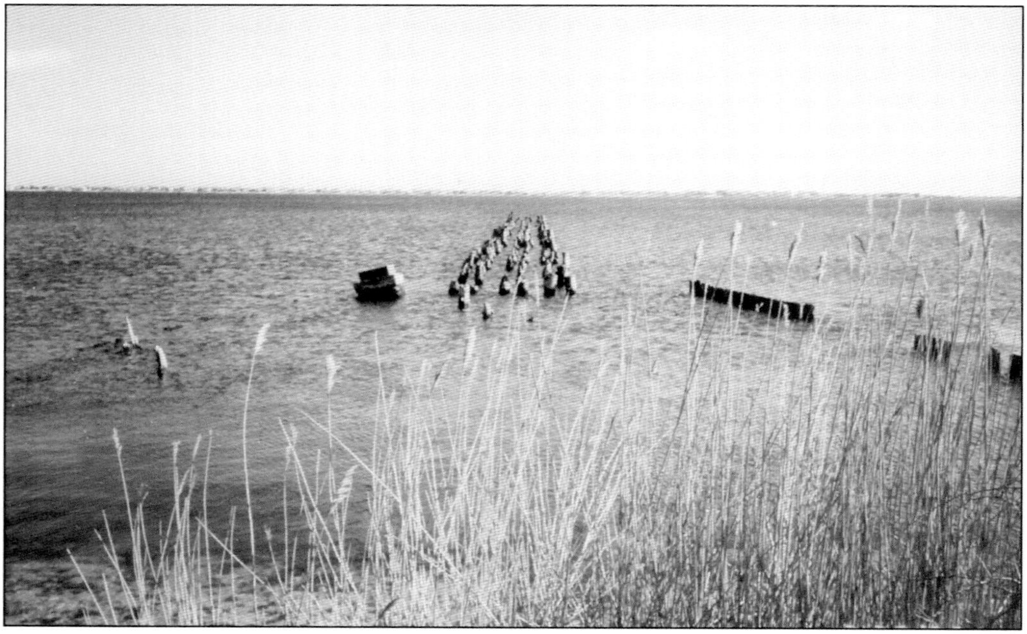

Today, these burned piling are the only visible testament on the Bayville shoreline to the narrow, wooden Pennsylvania Railroad trestle that once provided an exciting train ride across beautiful Barnegat Bay. A small segment of the trestle on the Seaside Park shoreline is now a public pier.

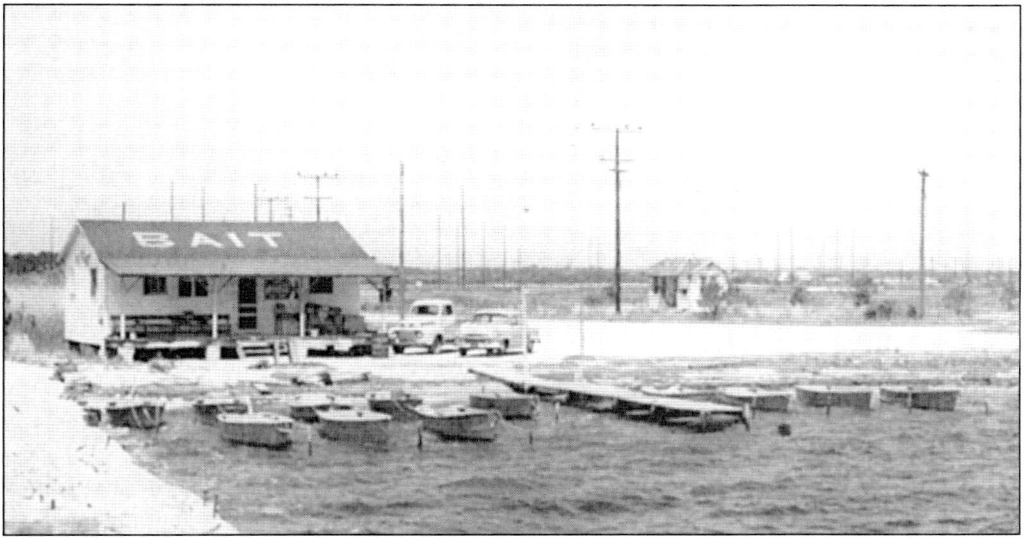

Don Stilwell rented rowboats and sold bait for fishing and crabbing at Don's Place, found just north of the Barnegat Pier, from 1948 until his death in 1958. Family members continued to run the business until it was sold in the mid-1970s. This 1950s postcard shows the 16-foot wooden rowboats that were available for just a few dollars a day. This site is currently occupied by a residential home.

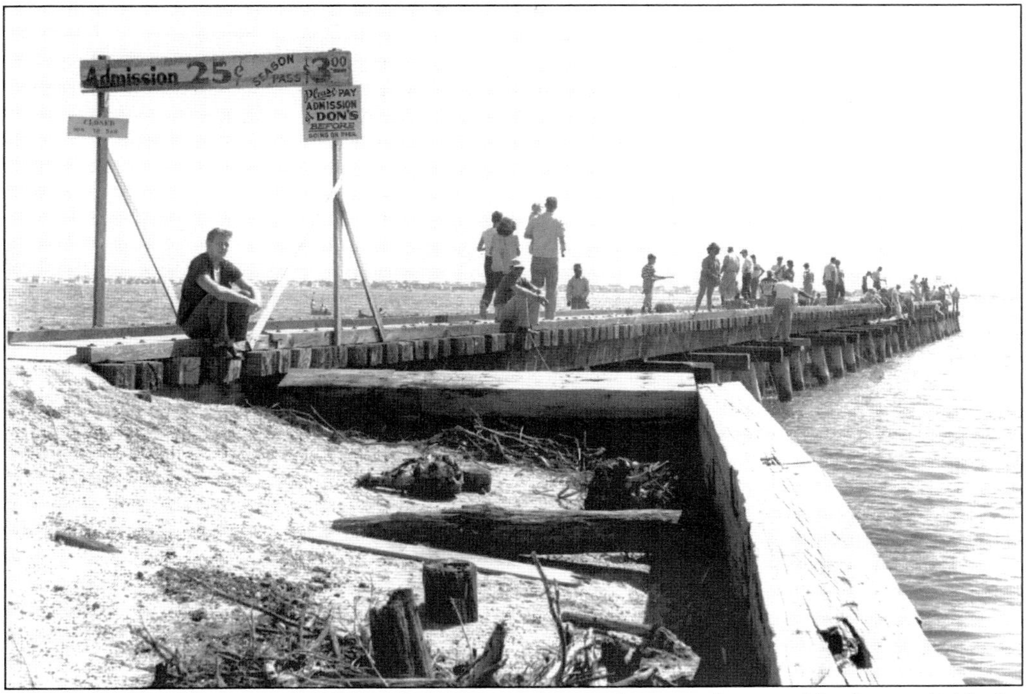

After the Pennsylvania Railroad Bridge across Barnegat Bay was destroyed by fire in 1946, the remaining section near shore became a popular fishing and crabbing pier for all ages (seen above). This classic photograph depicts the signs that all users are to pay at Don's Boats next door, either 25¢ a day or $3 for the season. These happy times all ended in 1962 when a fire swept through the waterfront area and burned this remaining section of the pier to the water level. (Courtesy of Ron Stilwell.)

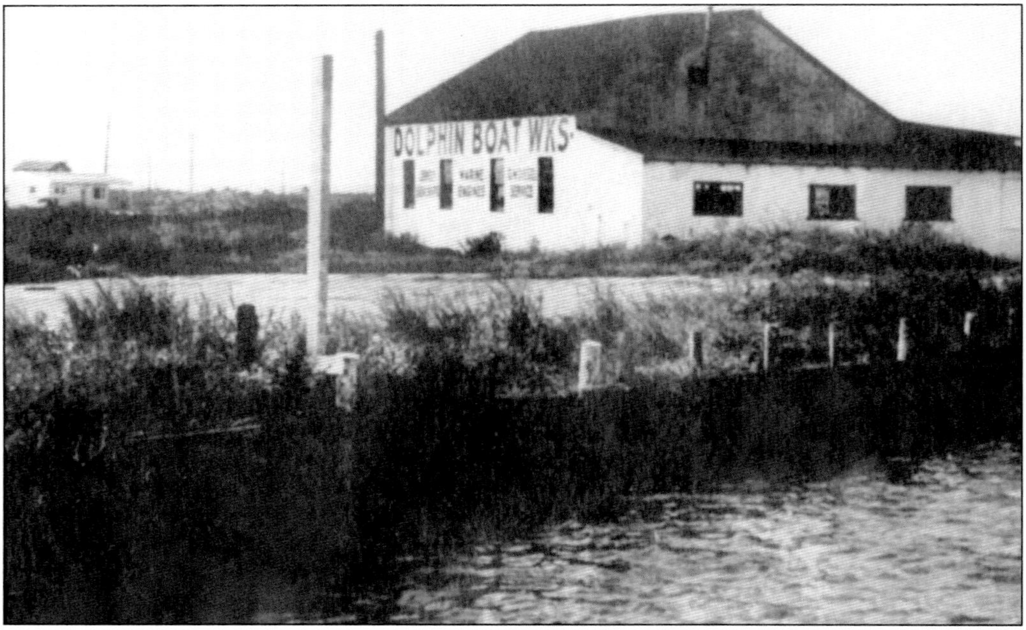

The Dolphin Boat Works was owned and operated by Bob Tracy from 1950 to 1955 and then by Davin Loizx until 1965. Dolphin manufactured the well-known Jersey Sea Skiffs and also serviced marine engines in this large warehouse-type building located on the bay at Good Luck Point. The business was sold in 1965.

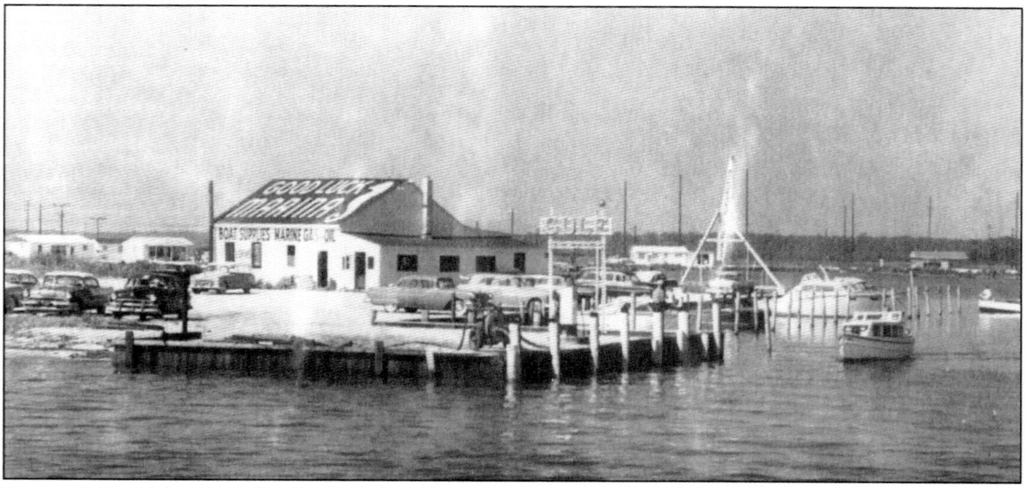

Roy and Gail Voss bought the Dolphin Boat Works in 1965 and changed the name to the Good Luck Marina. This 1970s view shows the early transition to the marina. The former manufacturing building now stores boat supplies and sports a seahorse on the roof. The marina was substantially upgraded over the years with 120 boat slips. Today, the facility remains a family-run business.

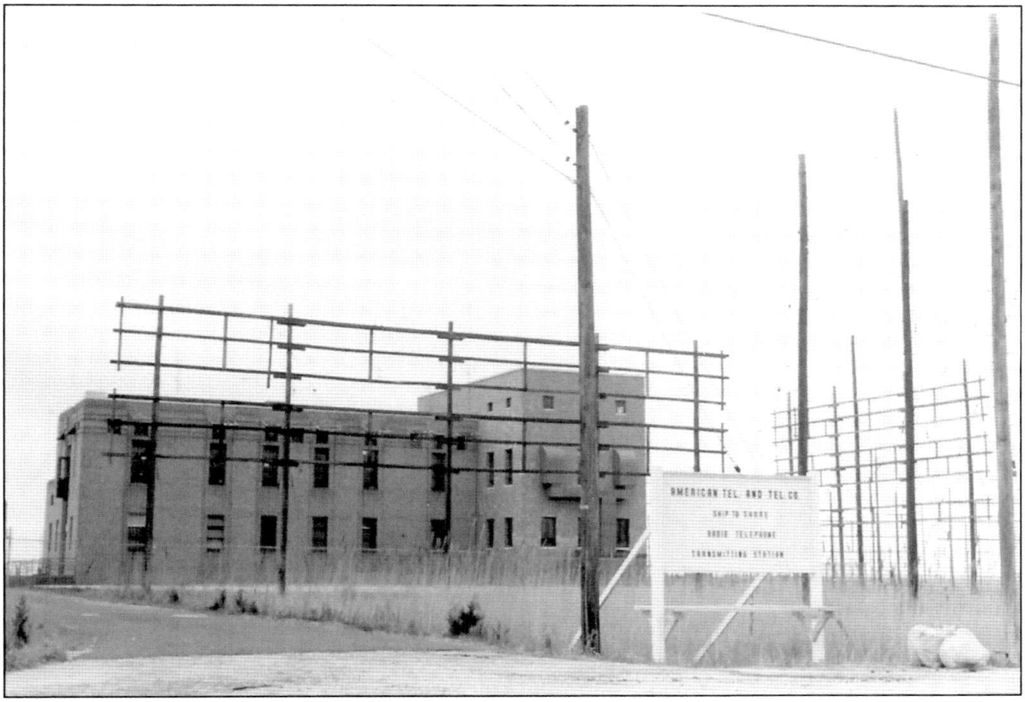

The American Telephone and Telegraph building and "pole farm," seen around 1930, was located at Good Luck Point. It served as a high-powered, short-wave, ship-to-shore radio transmitting station that linked Bell Systems telephones with ships at sea and strategic points in South America, Europe, and Africa. The call letters were WOO. The building was purchased by Berkeley Township for $1 on March 19, 2003, and today remains vacant. The federal government owns the surrounding preserved 161-acre meadowland. (Courtesy of Larry F. Casele.)

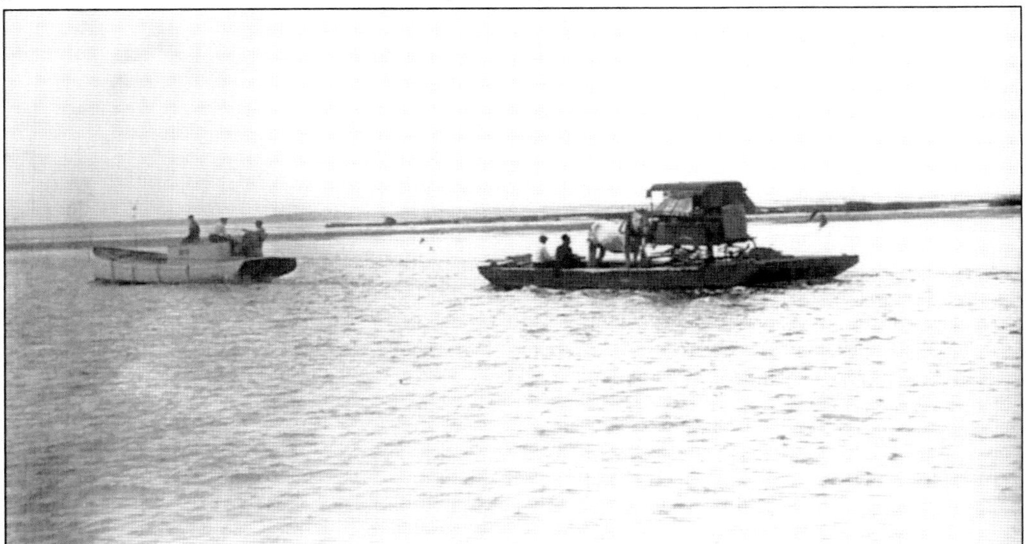
The original Seaside toll bridge opened in 1915. One way that people and goods were transported across Barnegat Bay before then was by the Good Luck Point ferry service in Berkeley Township. This horse-drawn wagon, pictured in 1900, is filled with commercial goods and is being towed across the bay to Seaside.

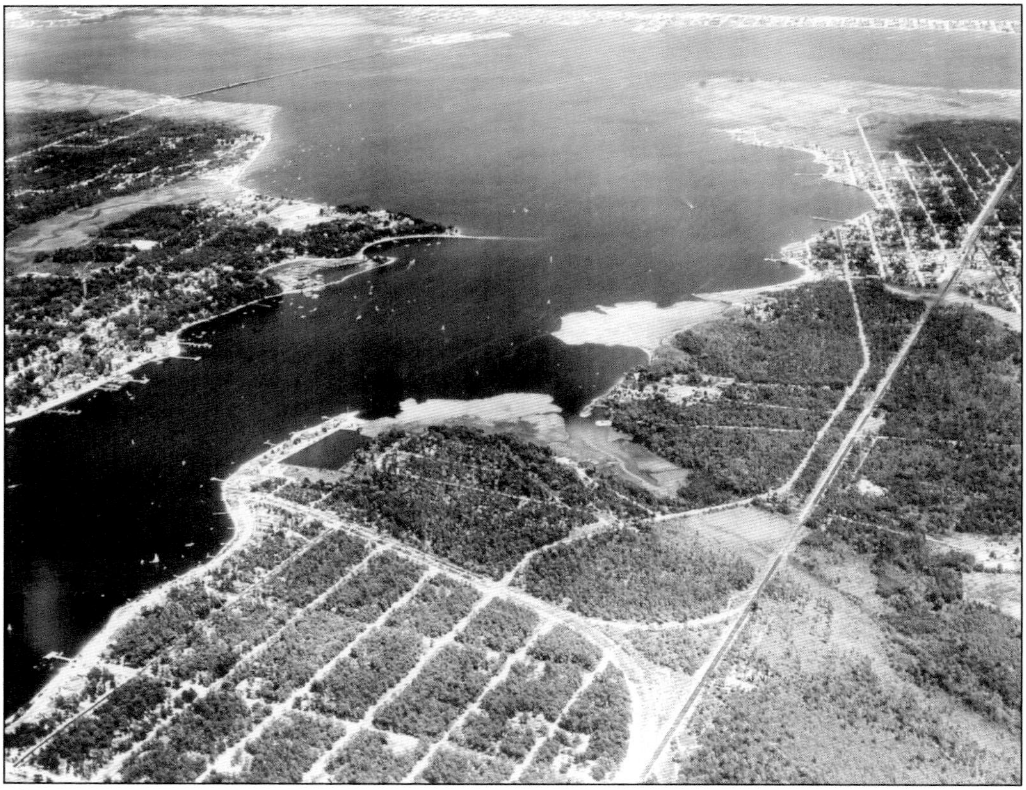

This early-1940s aerial depicts the one-mile-wide Berkeley Township boundaries along the south bank of the Toms River. Mill Creek is the large watershed in the center. The Pennsylvania Railroad runs diagonal across the lower right with Chelsea Avenue on the north side. The western boundary is the railroad spur, now Station Road. The eastern boundary is near the Jeffrey's Creek border with Ocean Gate, at center right. The Pelican Island section in Berkeley is in the upper left with the Seaside Bridge. (Courtesy of Larry F. Casele.)

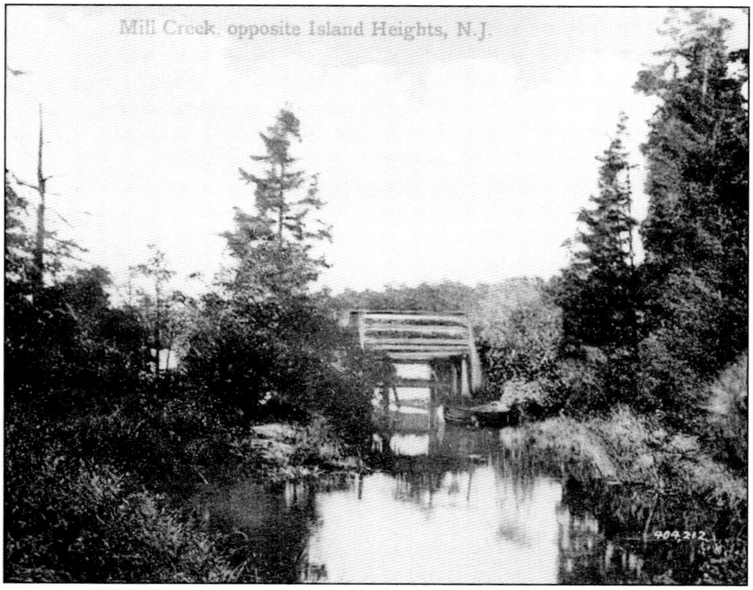

This scenic 1913 postcard is of the old Pennsylvania Railroad bridge at Mill Creek, constructed in 1881. The last passenger train to cross was on September 15, 1949, and the bridge was later dismantled. This crossing site eventually became part of the Florence T. Allen Conservation Area. (Courtesy of Larry F. Casele.)

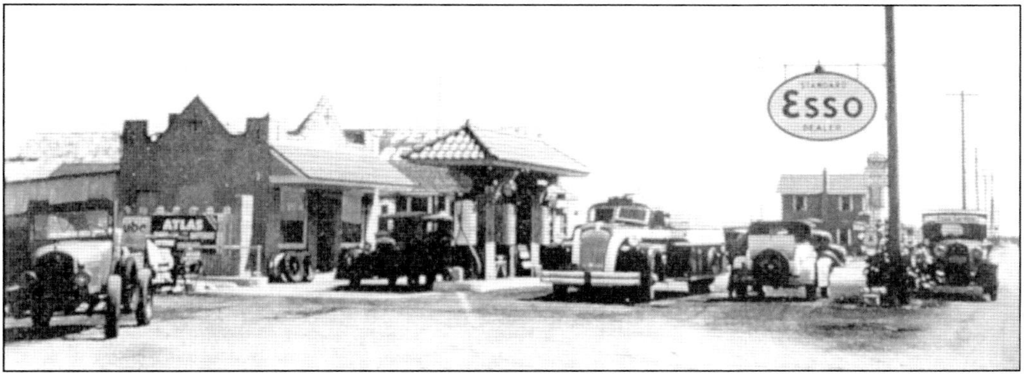

Malinda "Ma" Penn began serving the needs of the fishermen in the South Seaside Park section of Berkeley Township in 1920. Located at Twentieth Street and Central Avenue, the establishment included a gas station and later a bar. Ma kept the general store warm in the cooler seasons with a big potbelly stove. Penn's establishment was the center of the local community, and she would always extend a helping hand and credit when times were tough.

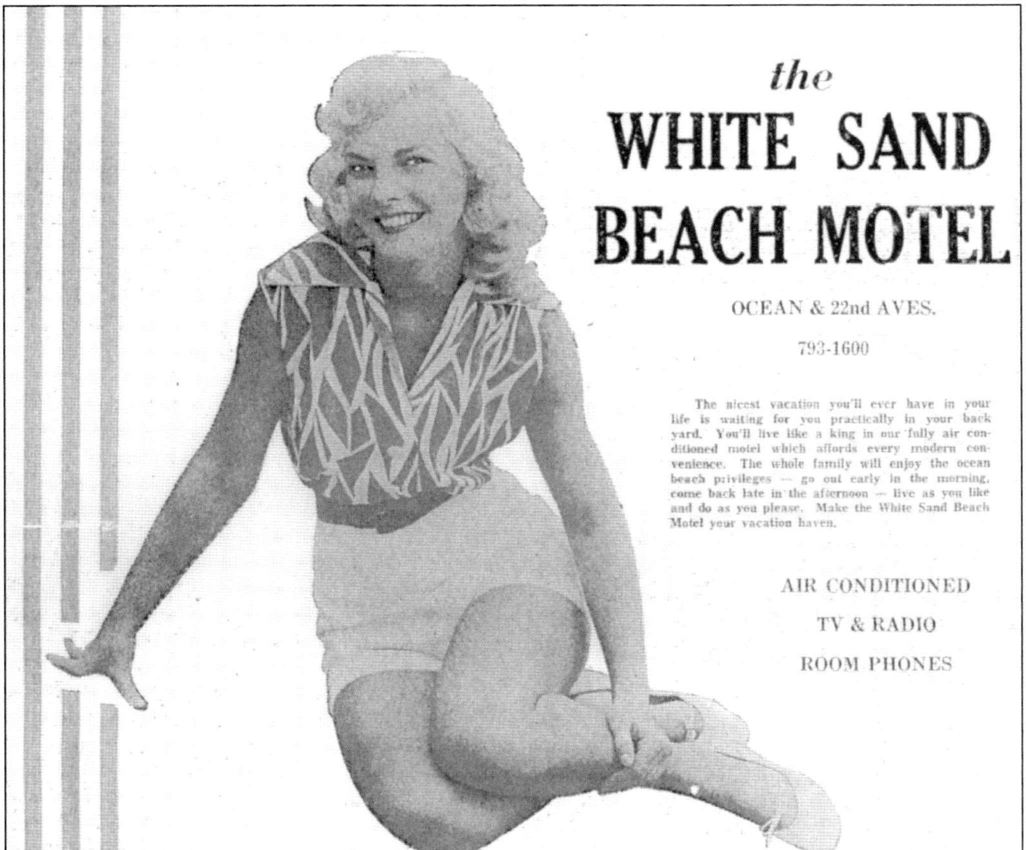

The White Sand Beach Motel was at Ocean and Twenty-second Avenues in South Seaside Park. Harry May and Ben Macler owned the 45-unit motel. May had previously leased the ocean beachfront to Berkeley Township in 1962. Later, he would also supply the motel patrons with beach badges for all beachgoers over the age of 12. The motel advertised that patrons would live like kings by having both a radio and a television.

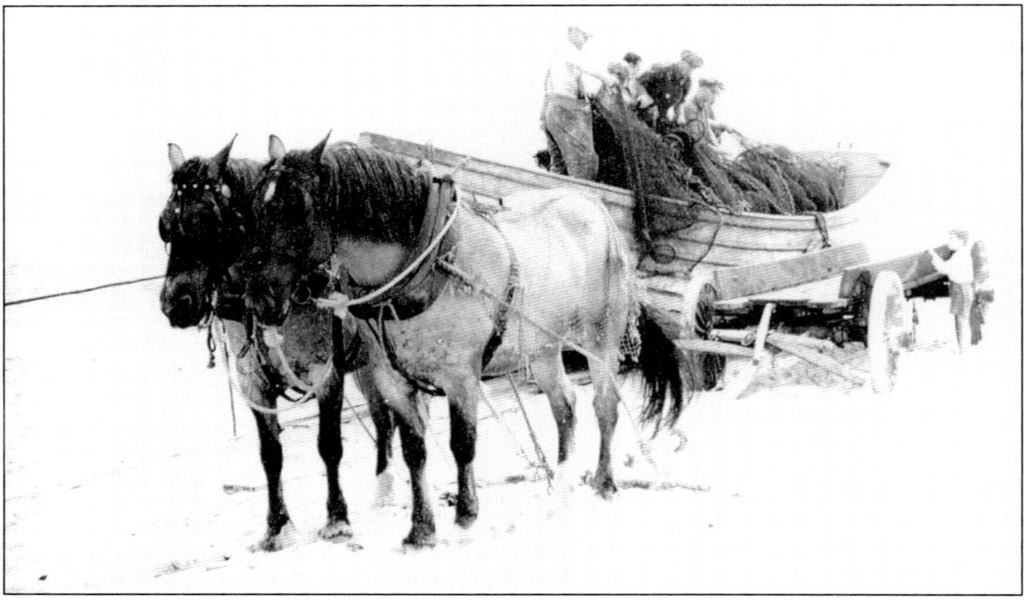

The South Seaside Park section of Berkeley Township had four pound fisheries between Twenty-first and Twenty-fourth Avenues between 1903 and 1953. They were the Seaside Fish Company, the Berkeley Fish Company, the Spring Lake Fishery, and the United Fishery. A pound net had five traps with about 30 pole supports and was located about a mile offshore. Teams of Clydesdale horses would pull the boats ashore until 1920, when tractors replaced the horsepower. The nets were loaded into the 33-foot-long boat as seen here. The season ran from March to November.

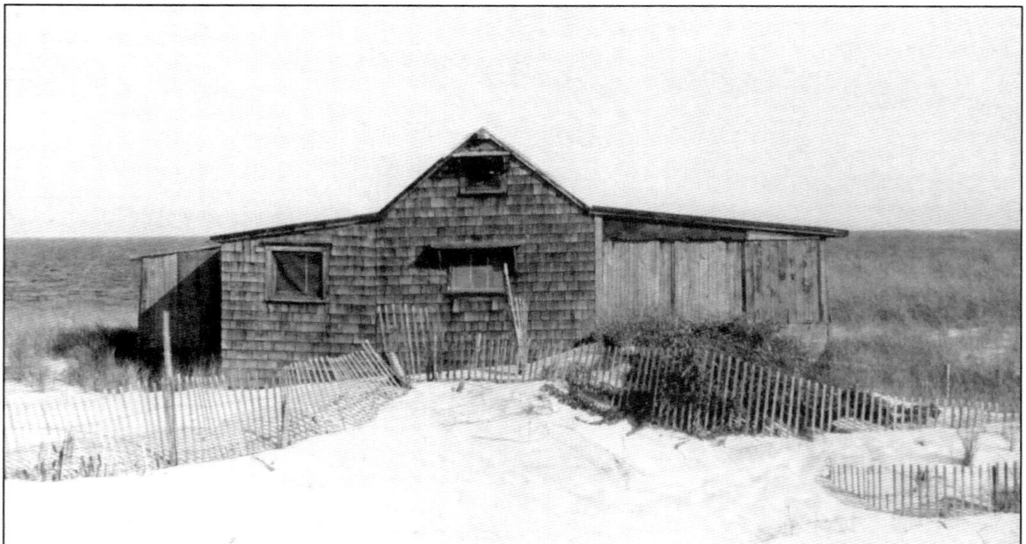

This was one of the oldest shanties near the beach on Island Beach State Park. The park is about 10 miles long or 3,000 acres. In 1926, Henry C. Phipps, a partner of Andrew Carnegie, bought it, and in 1933, the island became a borough. New Jersey bought it in 1953 for $2.7 million. At that time, there were about 100 shanties that were leased from the state without public utilities. In 1959, it became a state park, and in 1965, the area again became part of Berkeley Township. Today, it is New Jersey's most popular park, the Phipps Home is now the governor's summerhouse, and there are only a few shanties that still remain. (Courtesy of the New Jersey Historic Preservation Office.)

Three

PINEWALD

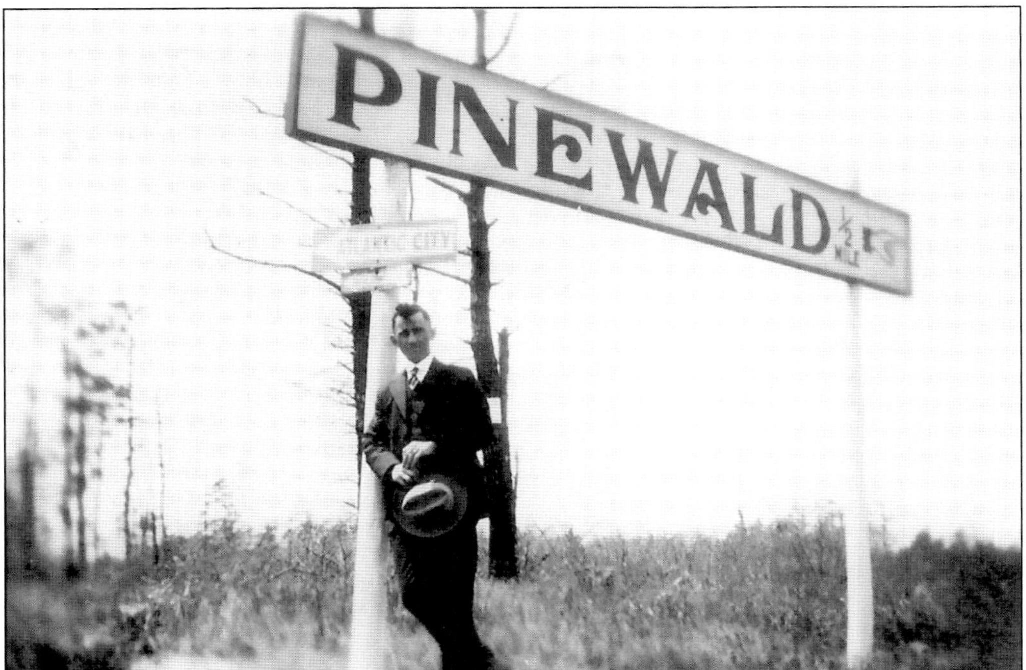

This Pinewald Road sign was placed on the west side of Route 9 near Serpentine Drive by the B.W. Sangor Company in 1926. It was part of a large advertising campaign to create public awareness of the expansive development. The smaller arrows point the way to Atlantic City and Wildwood.

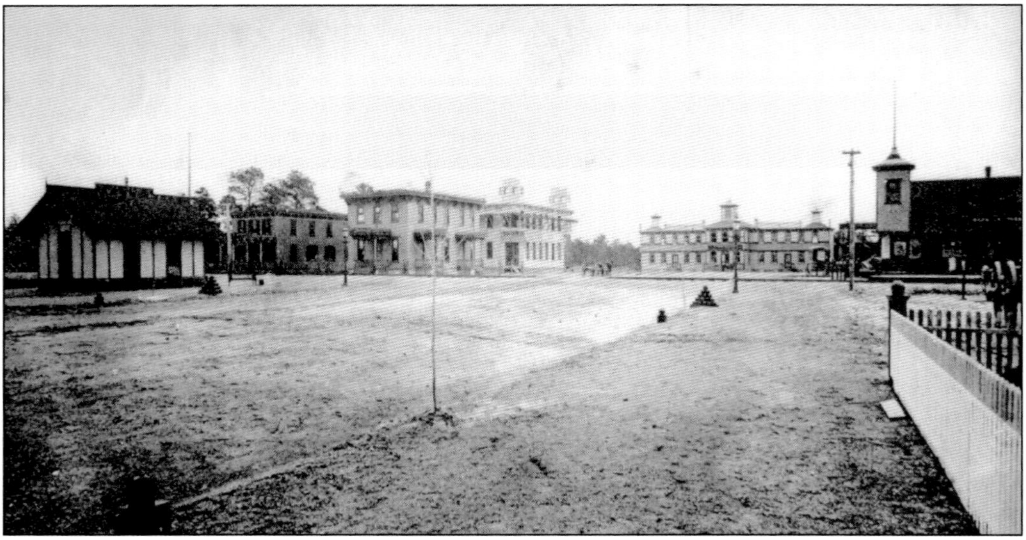

Lt. Edward S. Farrow conceived Barnegat Park as a retirement community for Civil War veterans. The initial subdivision map was filed in 1888. This 1891 view is looking east toward the intersection of Central Boulevard and Wheaton Avenue. The buildings are, from left to right, the land office, the post office, a state bank, a national bank still under construction, the commissary, and the railroad station. There were mortar balls, wagons, and caissons placed within the town square area for military effects. The development never succeeded economically and was mostly destroyed by three fires, the last on July 3, 1905. Pictured below is an 1889 assessment receipt that was issued for shares in the Barnegat Park Company. The company went into bankruptcy in December 1891 with only 12 homes being built prior to that time. (Below, courtesy of Larry F. Casele.)

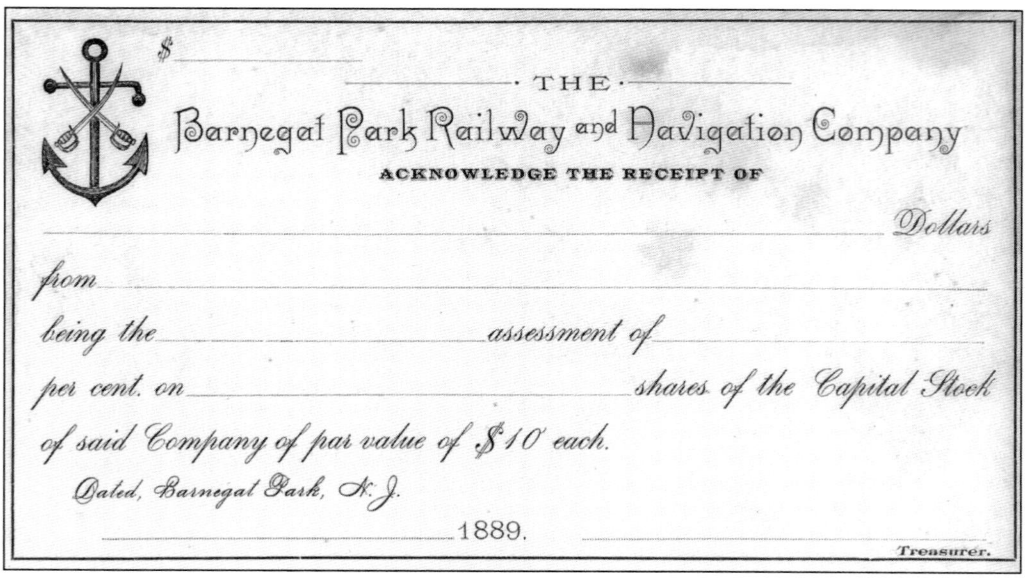

$ ________

THE

Barnegat Park Railway and Navigation Company

ACKNOWLEDGE THE RECEIPT OF

________ Dollars

from ________

being the ________ assessment of ________

per cent. on ________ shares of the Capital Stock

of said Company of par value of $10 each.

Dated, Barnegat Park, N. J.

________ 1889. ________

Treasurer.

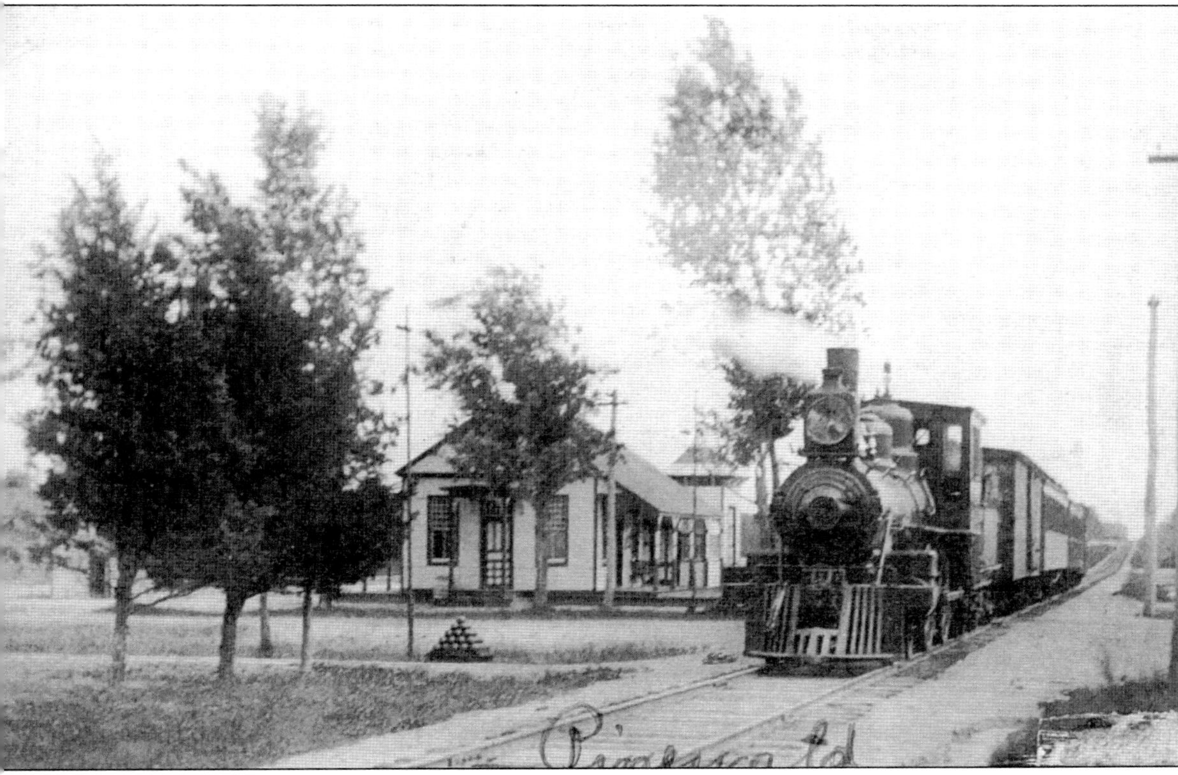

This train is at the Pinewald station in 1906 and is heading north on the Barnegat Branch of the Central Railroad. It was located at Wheaton and Central Avenues. There were three different stations here: Bayville, between 1872 and 1888; Barnegat Park, between 1888 and 1927; and Pinewald, between 1927 and 1974. The station name was Barnegat Park-Pinewald from 1912 to 1927. This station served Pinewald and most of the Bayville area.

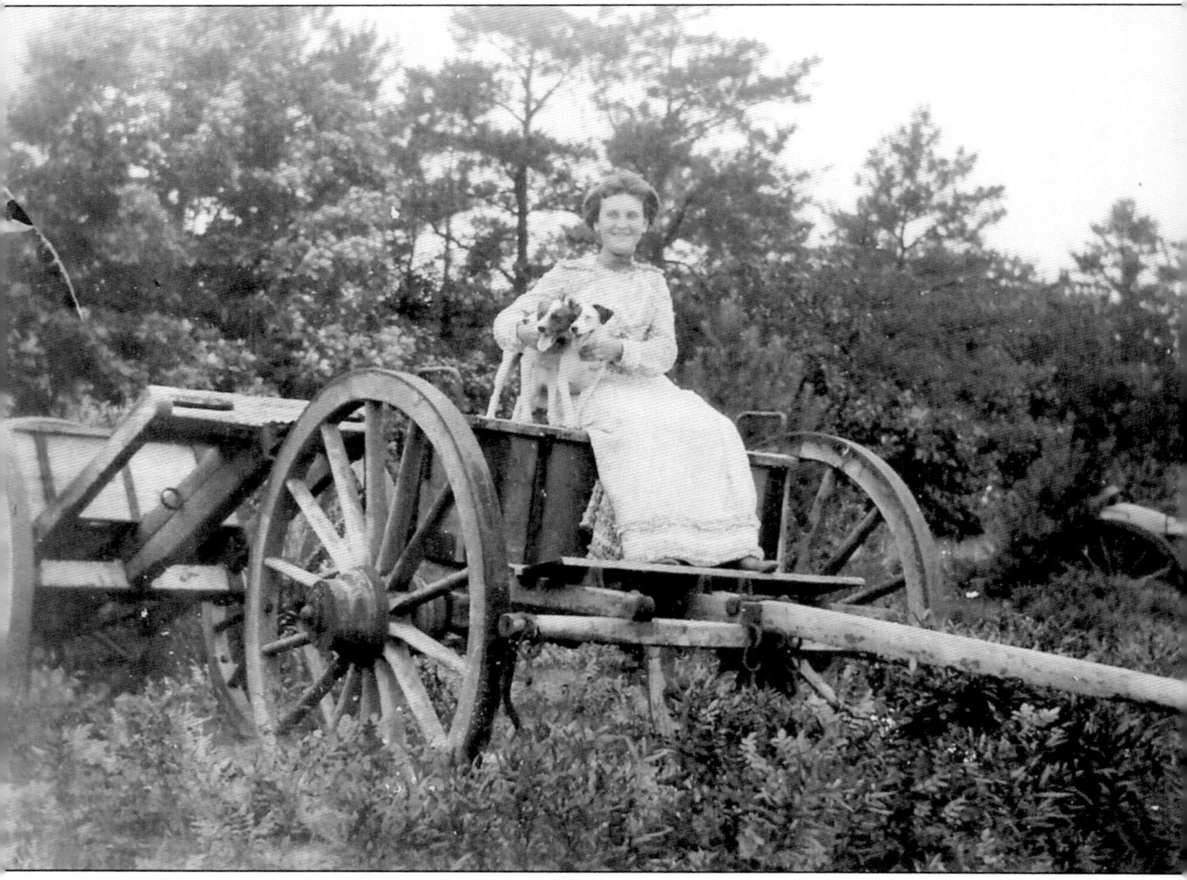

Lucy Enggren is pictured in 1905 sitting with her dogs on one of the many derelict caissons that had originally been placed near the railroad depot in 1889 by the Barnegat Park Company. Most all of these military effects were removed when the company failed. (Courtesy of John Enggren.)

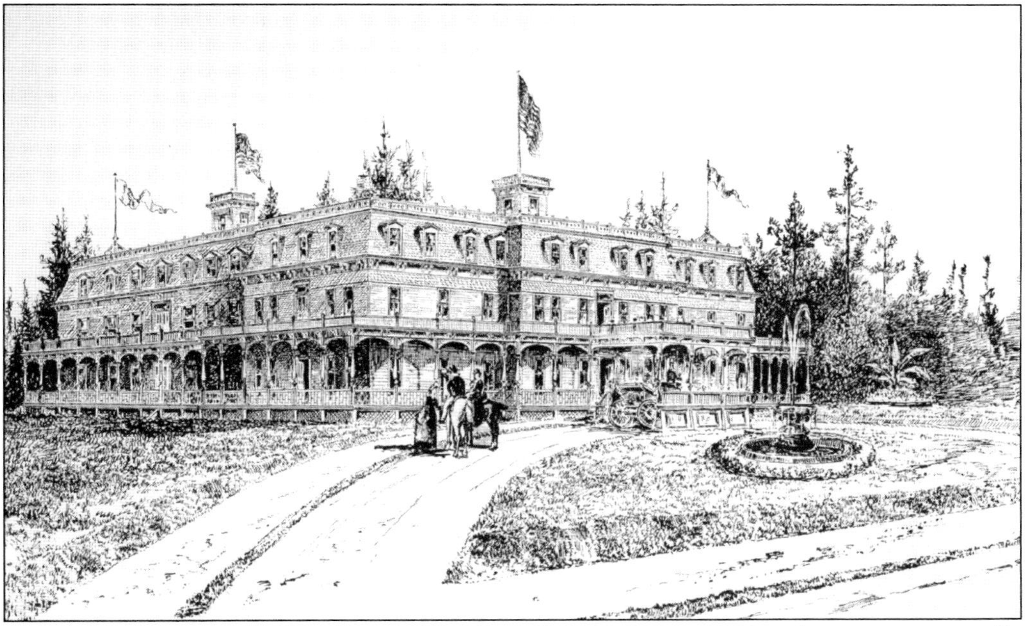

This artistic rendering of the Pines Hotel is the only indication as to what this structure actually looked like. It was built by the Barnegat Park Company in 1889 and opened in January 1891 to accommodate about 200 guests. It was built on six acres of land on the southeast corner of Central Boulevard and Nixon Avenue in Pinewald. The Pines burned down in 1895. Today, all that remains are parts of the foundation and various artifacts.

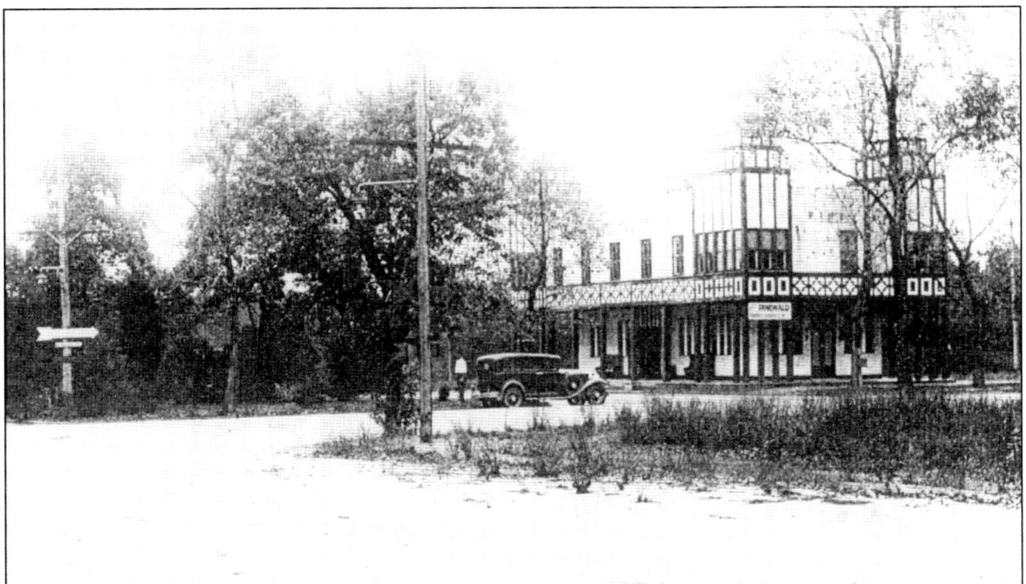

The B.W. Sangor Company constructed this administration building and railroad station in 1927 for its Pinewald development. It was located on the southwest corner of Wheaton Avenue and Central Boulevard. The arrows on the telephone pole point to the distant Royal Pines Hotel and the Forest Hills Inn in this 1930s postcard view. The tall flagpole is to the right of the arrows. The attached sign reads, "The Pinewald Property Owners Association," which later also utilized this building. (Courtesy of Larry F. Casele.)

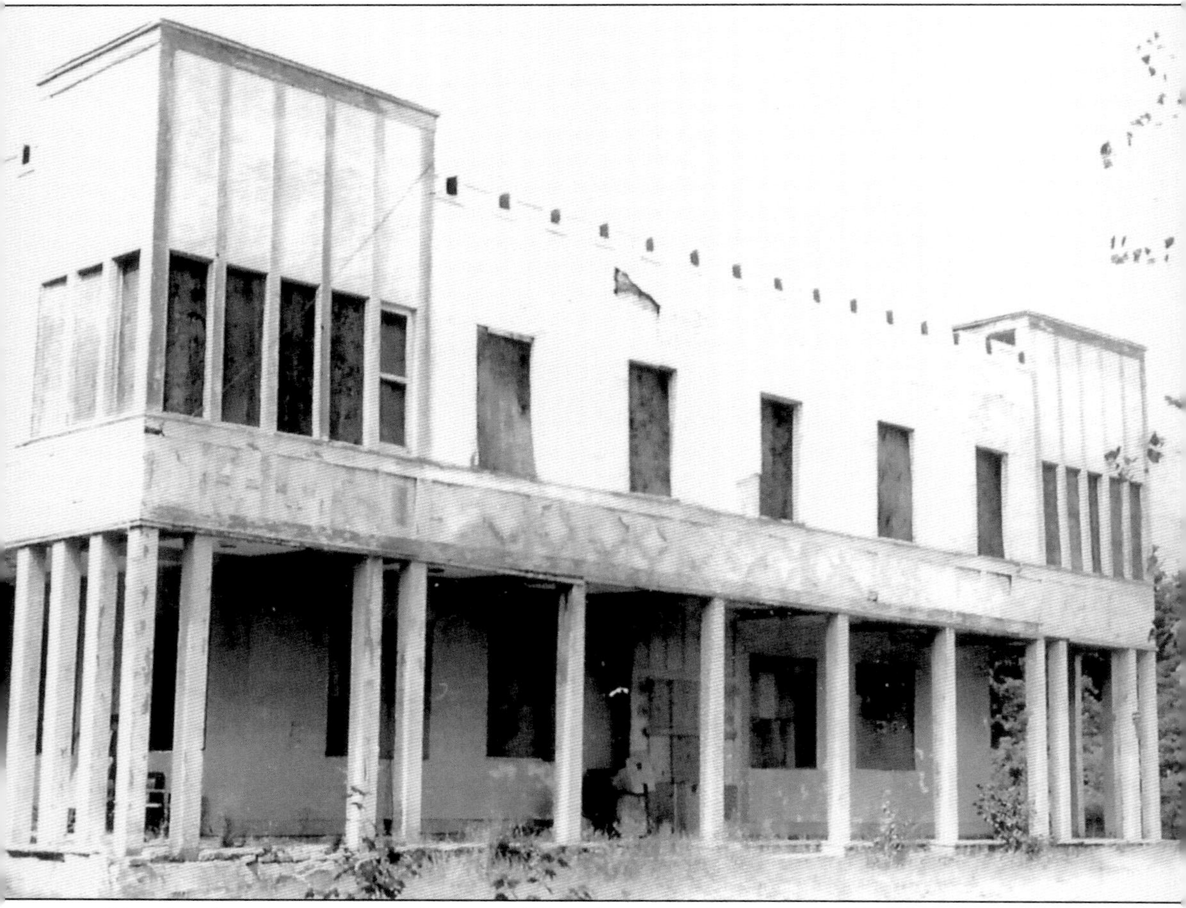

The abandoned station, seen here in 1974 with storage boxes stacked both inside and outside, indicates the end is only two years away and the station will be demolished. The last passenger train to stop here was in 1953, after 81 years of service. Later, it was briefly converted to a residence. Thus ended the final testament of the B.W. Sangor Company transporting hundreds of hopeful prospective Pinewald home owners in the 1920s.

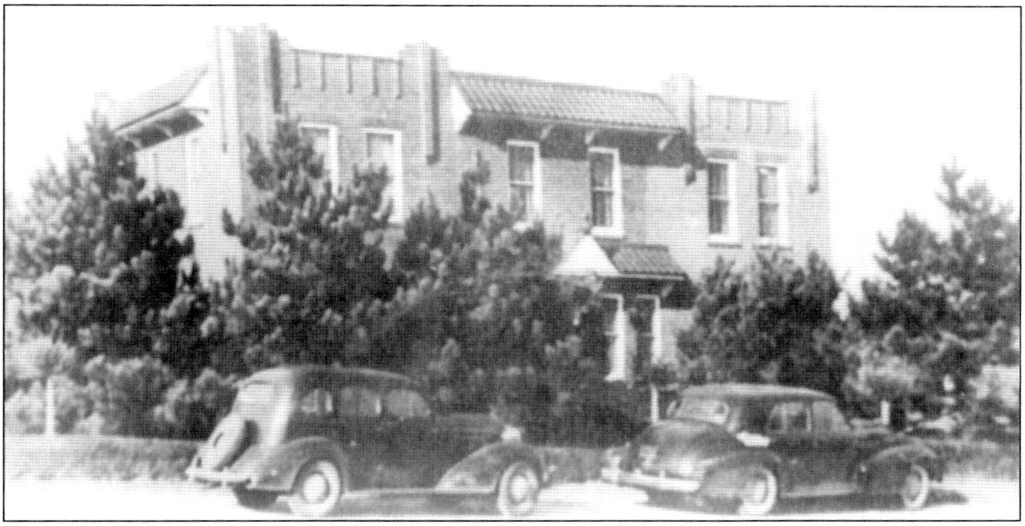

This 1937 postcard reveals the simple and pleasing lines that were the hallmark of the Forest Hills Inn located at the intersection of Lester Lane and Vanderbilt Avenue. In 1930, William Fritz constructed the redbrick inn in the Forest Hills subdivision of Pinewald, which was being developed by the B.W. Sangor Company. Fritz sold the business to William Hawkins of Ocean Gate, New Jersey, in 1938. Hawkins would operate a boy's military school there until the early 1940s. The building was demolished a few years later.

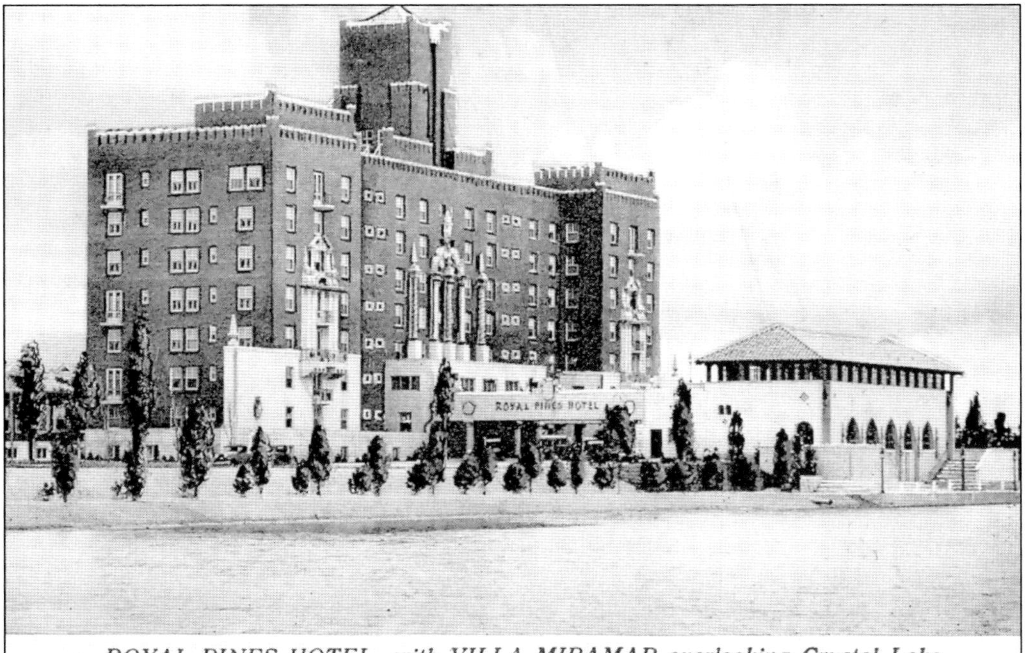

ROYAL PINES HOTEL, with VILLA MIRAMAR overlooking Crystal Lake

The Royal Pines Hotel, located on the west side of Crystal Lake, was designed by Russian architect W. Oltar-Jevsky and constructed by the B.W. Sangor Company between 1929 and 1930. It opened to the public in grand style on November 18, 1930, with 172 suites for 400 guests and was to be the focal point of the planned, residential community of Pinewald. Later, it would go through several ownerships and bankruptcies. It has served as Dennis Hospital and later as nursing homes, including Pinehaven, Bayview Convalesant Center, and Crystal Lake. (Courtesy of Larry F. Casele.)

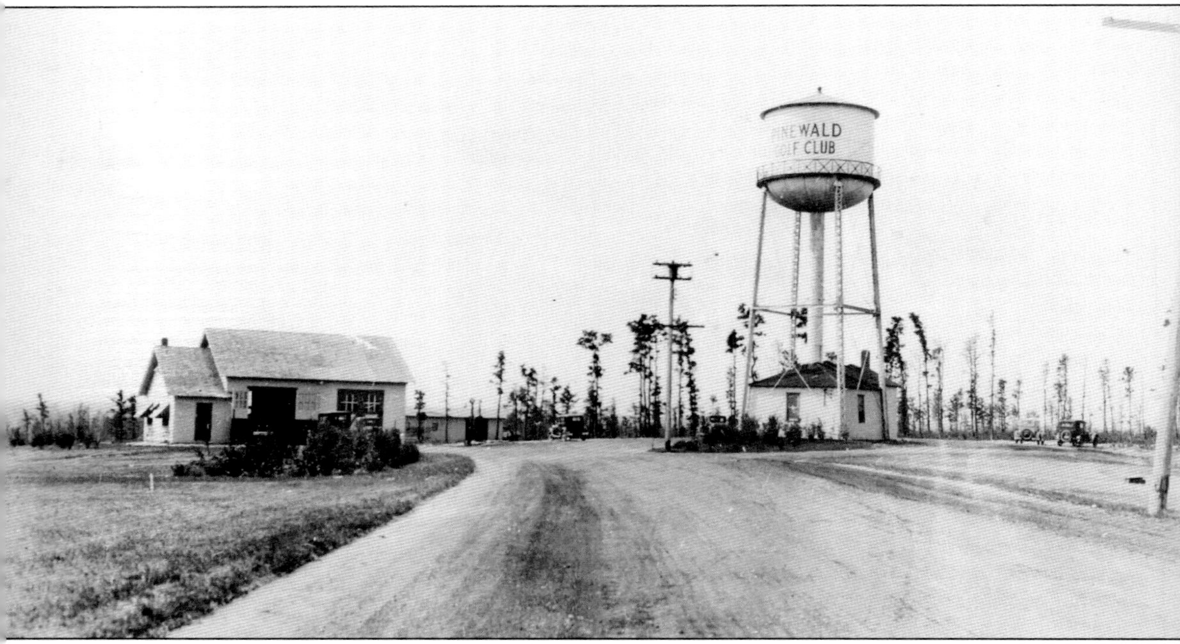

The Pinewald Golf Club Course was designed and built by the B.W. Sangor Company to entice potential purchasers to its development property. The course opened in 1930 on land that is presently part of the Cedar Creek Golf Course. The large water tank and pump house on the right were utilized to keep the fairways green.

Four

In the Pines

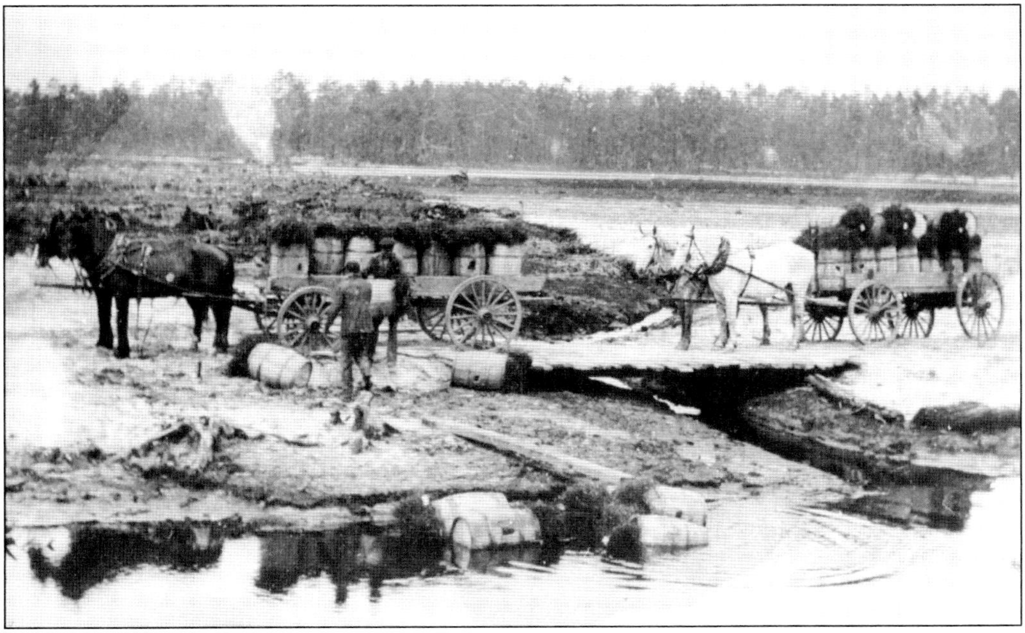

In 1909, a total of 225 acres of land was cleared in Double Trouble to place cranberry vines in the surrounding swamp area. These two men are unloading the barrels of vines for planting from the two horse-drawn wagons. Log bridges were also erected to cross the many irrigation streams needed to flood the bogs. This area had contained a large stand of Atlantic white cedars that had been cut for lumber.

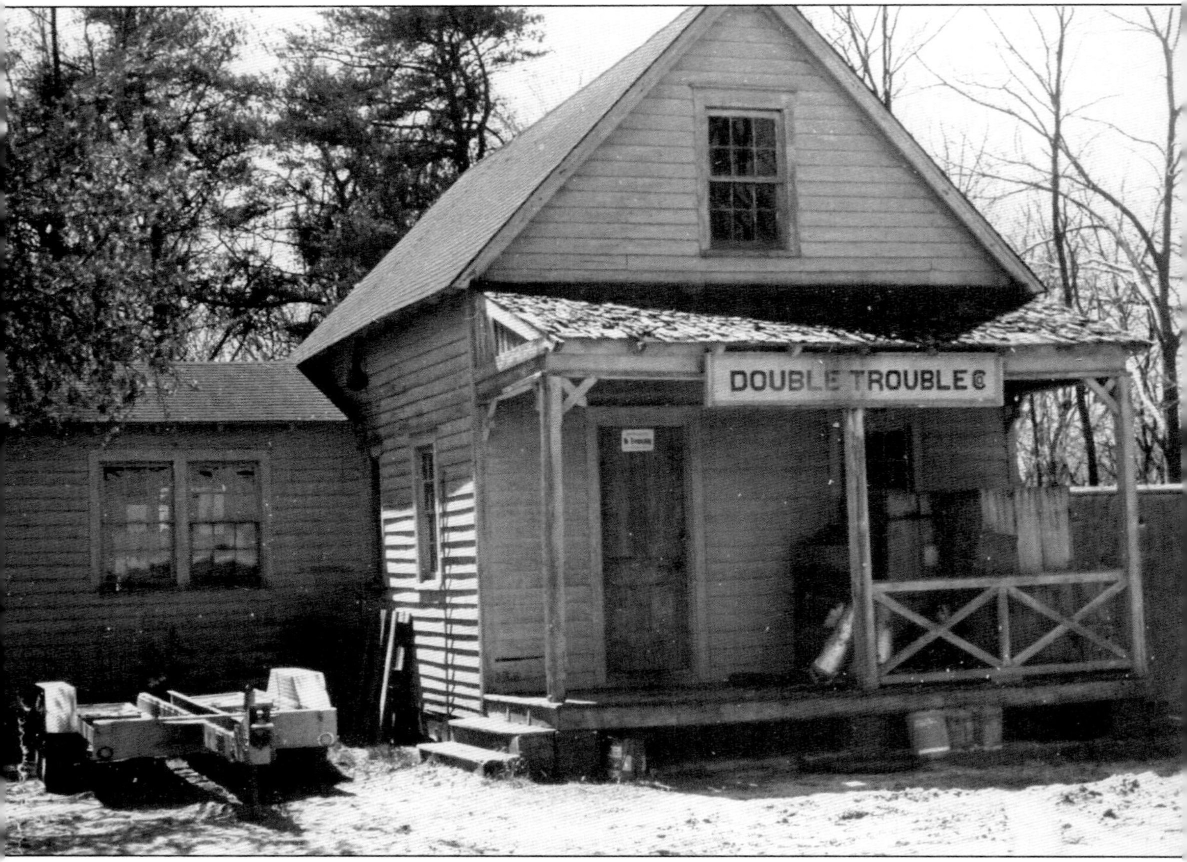

This general store served the year-round residents who worked and lived at the small community of Double Trouble until about 1930. The site is located along Cedar Creek about four miles west of Route 9. At one time, there also was a c. 1890 one-room schoolhouse located on the property for the workers' children. Thomas Potter Sr., one of Berkeley's earliest settlers, originally owned the tract. In 1903, the Edward Crabbe Company of Mays Landing, New Jersey, purchased the site from Mary Beatty, an heir of George Giberson, who had previously operated a large sawmill there. Commodore Crabbe (1872–1953) began a large cranberry farm while continuing the sawmill operation. A dam was built in 1909 to flood 400 acres of bog to grow the cranberries. It was 2,200 feet long and about 10 feet high with 12 control gates. In the 1970s, 129 acres were leased for cranberry production. The 2,000-acre site was acquired by the State of New Jersey in 1964, and the village placed it in the state historic register in 1977 and opened it as Double Trouble State Park in 1995.

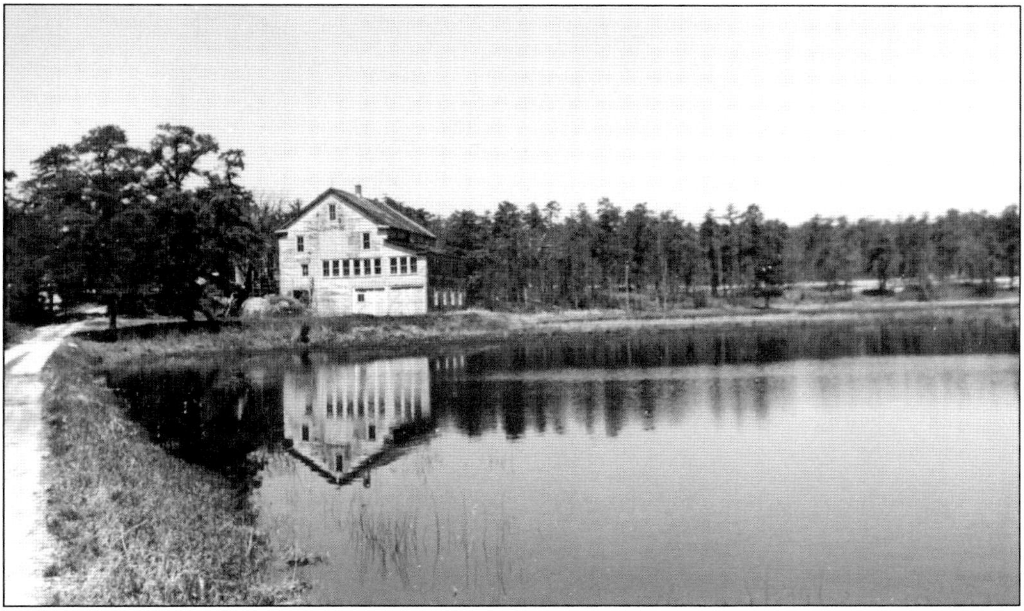

The Double Trouble sorting and packinghouse is located near the bogs on the east side of the park. In the early fall, the cranberries were originally picked by hand, but later, thrashing rotary machines would allow the berries to float to the surface and be loaded on trucks using vertical conveyer belts. The cranberries would then be washed and sorted on conveyer belts by the community workers, pictured below. The packaged deliveries were then shipped to distribution plants such as Ocean Spray. The packinghouse was restored in 1996 and today is one of the 14 buildings that are now part of the state park.

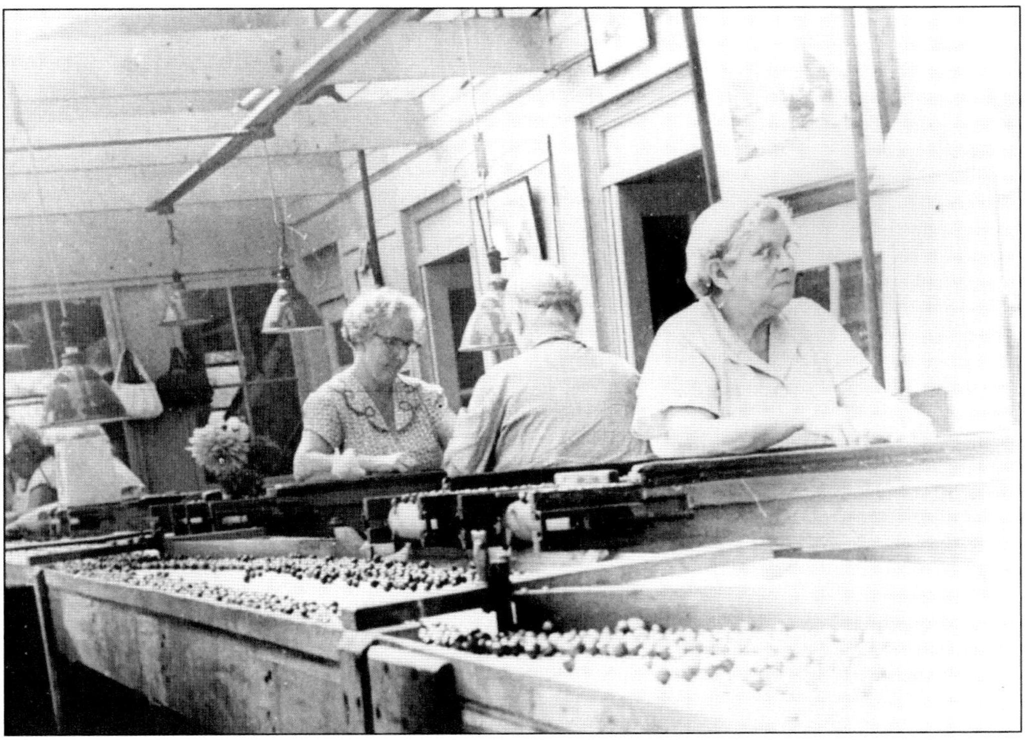

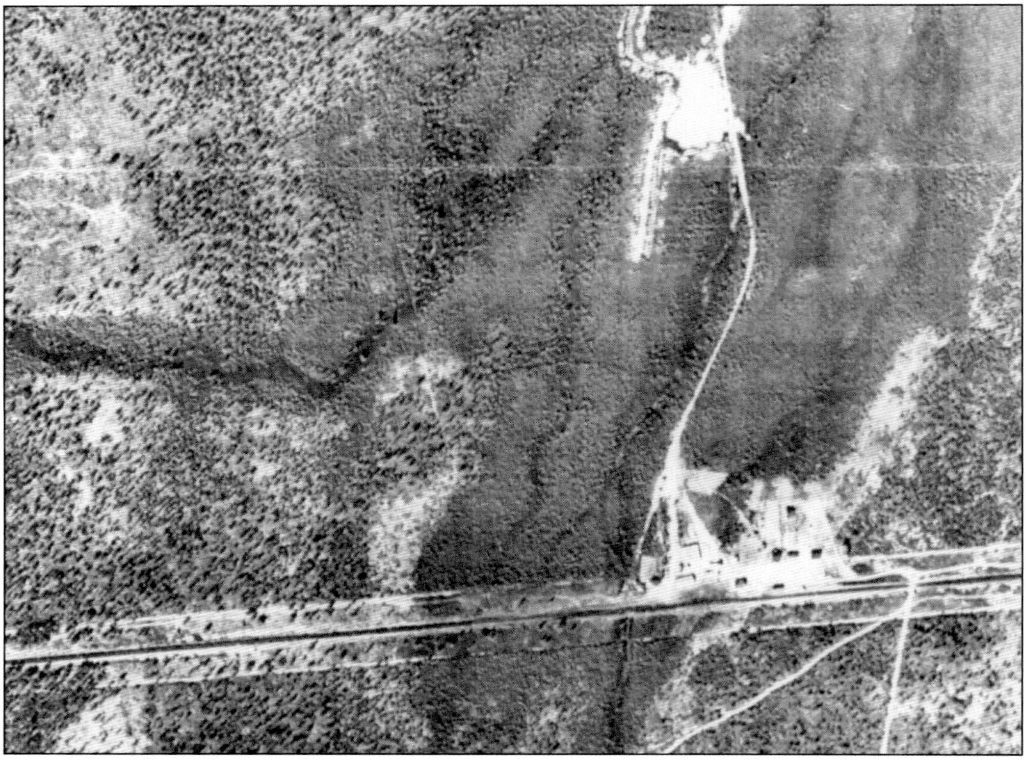

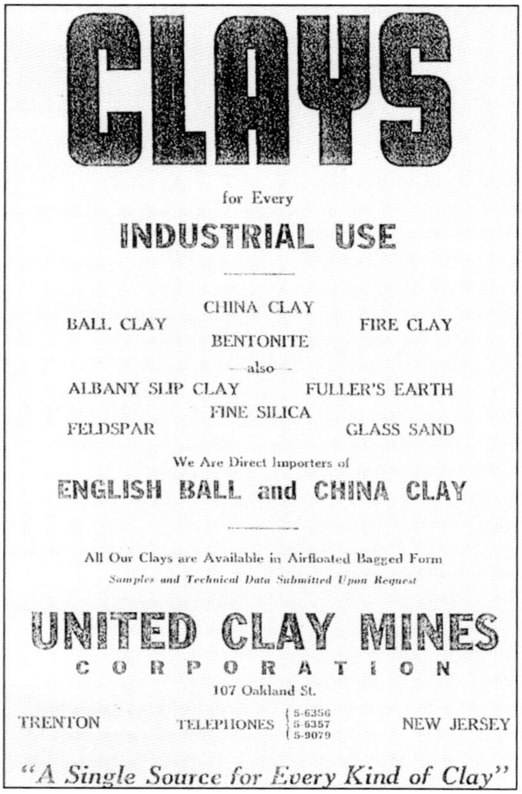

George C. Crossley of Trenton once owned the site of a clay mining operation between Toms River and Whiting from 1905 to 1950. Brick, pottery, and terra-cotta were manufactured from the clay. Over 100 workers worked here and lived in company houses. The children took the train to Whiting for school. The 1941 aerial shows the Pennsylvania Railroad across the bottom, several company buildings, and the rail line leading to the mining locations shown in white. In 1950, the property was sold to Cypress Mines Company, and in 1957, the last building was demolished. Today, it is a 497-acre Natural Lands Trust preserve with a self-guided walking trail. Seen at left in 1948, Crossley was owned by United Clay Mines at 107 Oakland Street in Trenton. The company would later become part of United Clays, Inc., which today has evolved into a worldwide mining operation. (Both, courtesy of Lois Morris.)

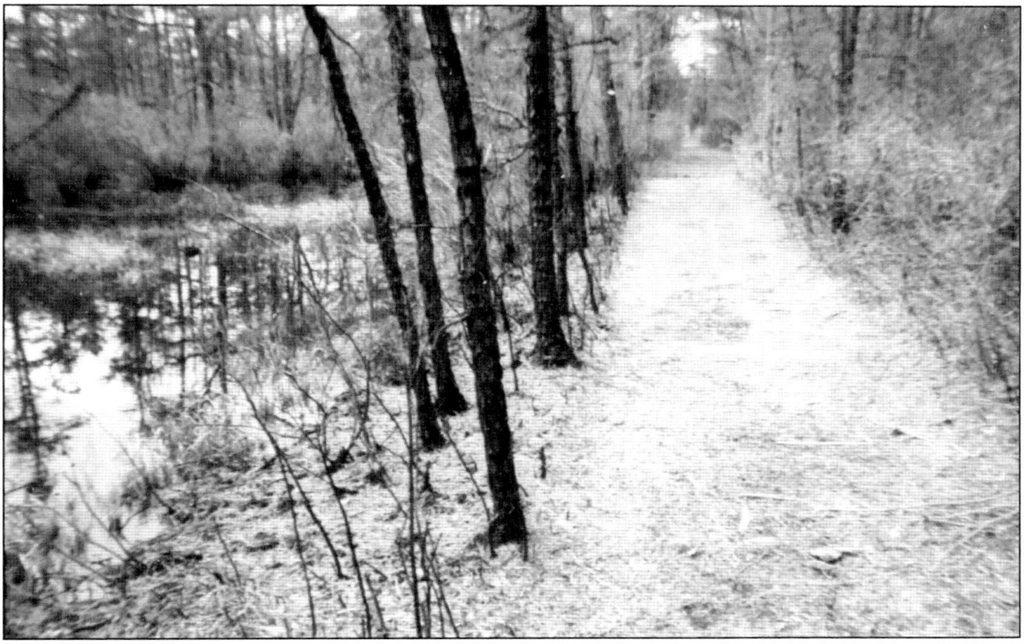

The loaded Crossley clay carts were pushed by hand on narrow-gauge rails that were built to transport the clay from the pits to the waiting train cars. Later, a small steam locomotive was utilized to pull the line of carts. The remnants of the railroad ties can be seen here next to the dug out clay pit area. The pits were initially dug by hand and later by a steam-powered crane.

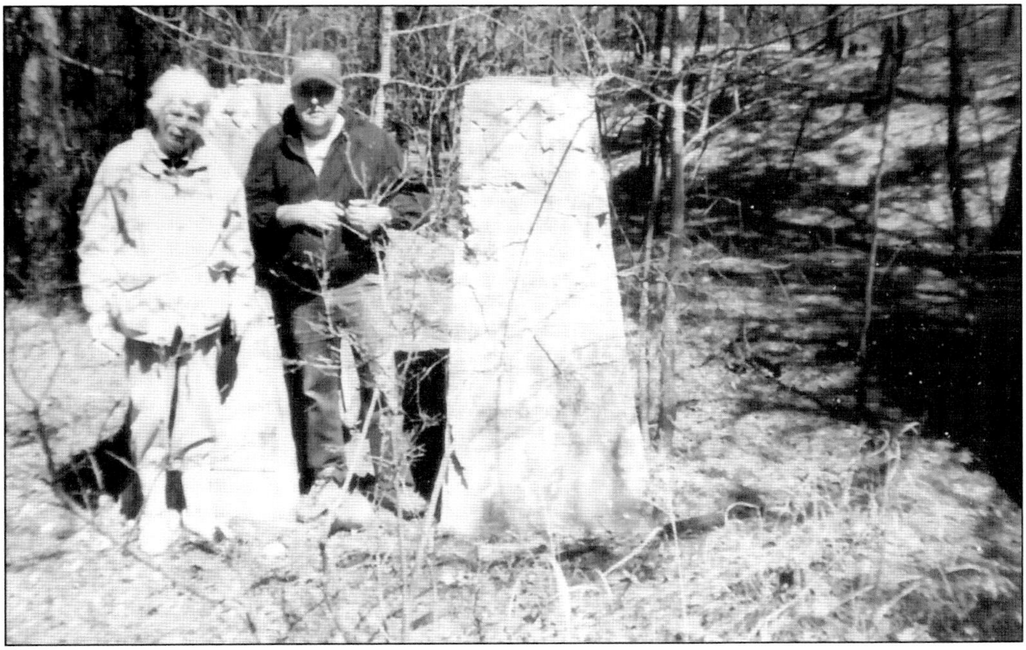

Lois Morris, Crossley historian, and Gary Madden, Ocean County railroad historian, are next to the platform pillars that supported the narrow-gauge railroad that transported the clay to the freight trains. The clay was shipped to the Perth Amboy processing plant to be made into brick, pottery, earthenware, tiles, and terra-cotta. The pillars are the only large artifacts remaining from the Crossley mining site.

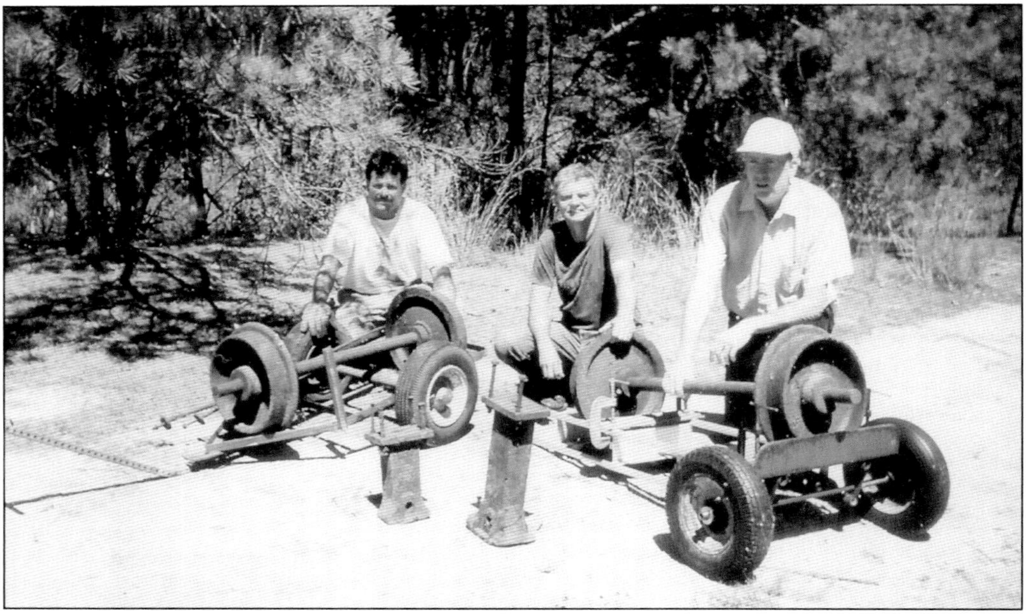

The wheels, chassis, and couplers shown here are the artifacts of a typical clay cart used at the Crossley clay mining site to transport the ball clay to the freight loading dock. They were found in a remote area of the preserve by Marty Rapp of the New Jersey Lands Trust. Members of the Berkeley Township Historical Society retrieved and reattached them to a wooden holding box to resemble an original cart and placed it in front of the Berkeley Museum, as seen below. Shown here are, from left to right, Dave Harrison, Jerry Beer, and Al Stokley.

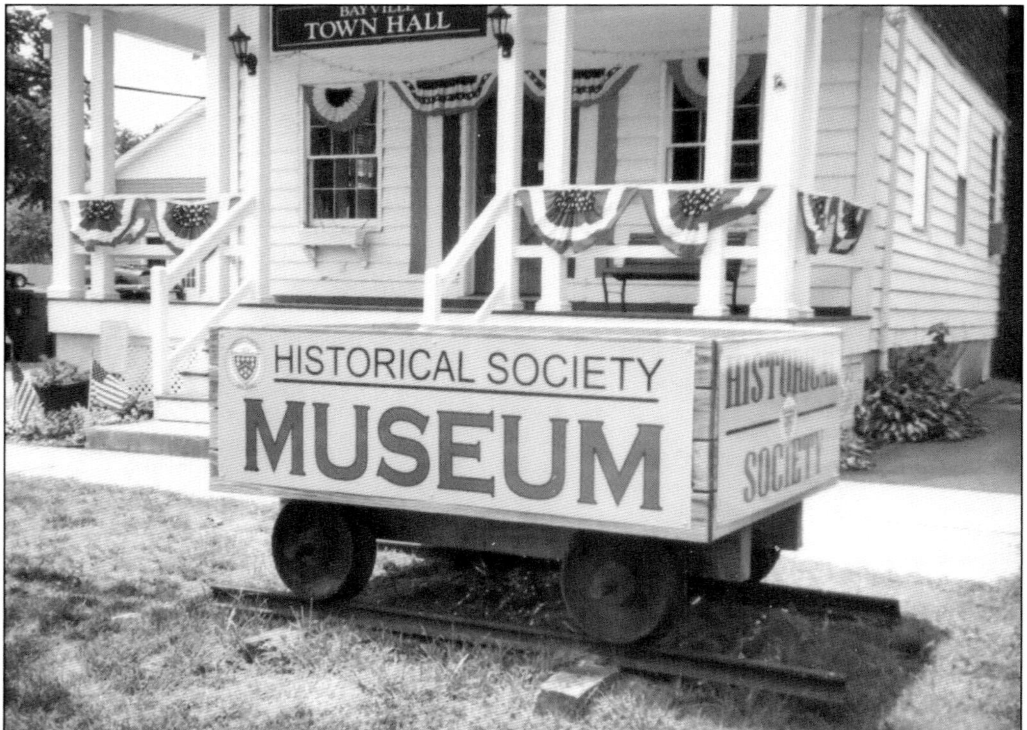

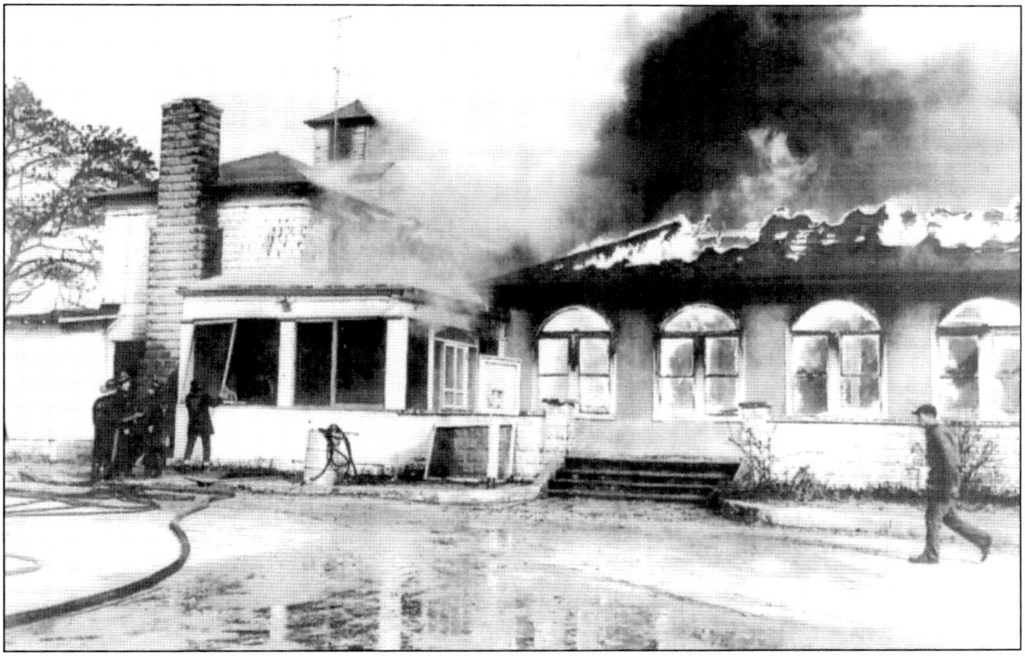

Marie and Maxmillian Hayden were the owners of Ma Hayden's Pinewald Villa, located on Central Avenue and started in the 1920s. Many banquets and special occasions were held there; it became the hot spot for dining and dancing. The last owners were Richard Korman, William Kubeck, and Milton Kovacafsky, who opened it as a taproom and later a roller-skating rink. After providing entertainment for almost 50 years, the end finally arrived in January 1960, when it burned to the ground. The fire was caused by a faulty gas heater in the restroom. The only fatality was Marshall Fuller, 38, a nearby resident worker. Today, all that remains is the front cement wall now overgrown with weeds. Below, this Pinewald Villa advertisement proclaims "a big time surely awaits you" when attending their many dances. This was true for over 30 years, as many popular social events were offered. (Below, courtesy of Barbara Britton.)

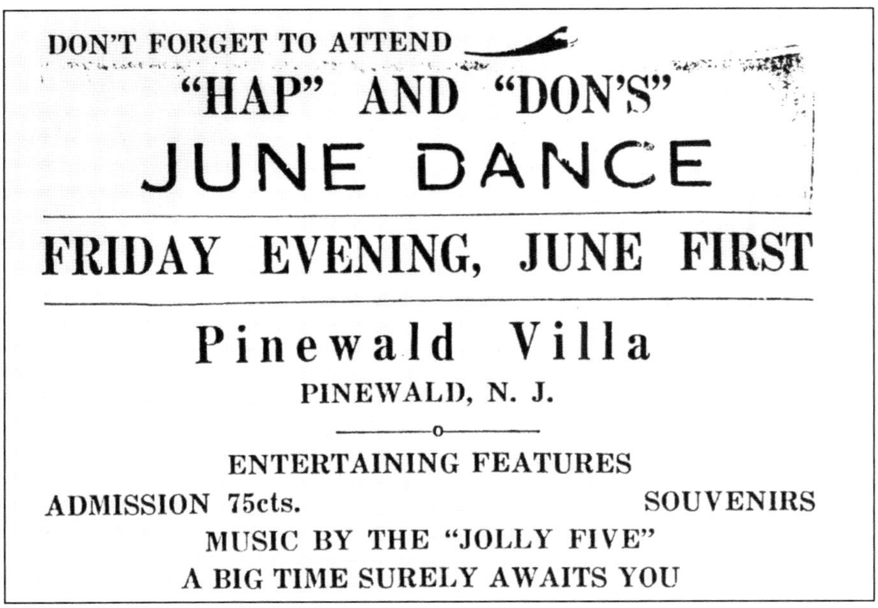

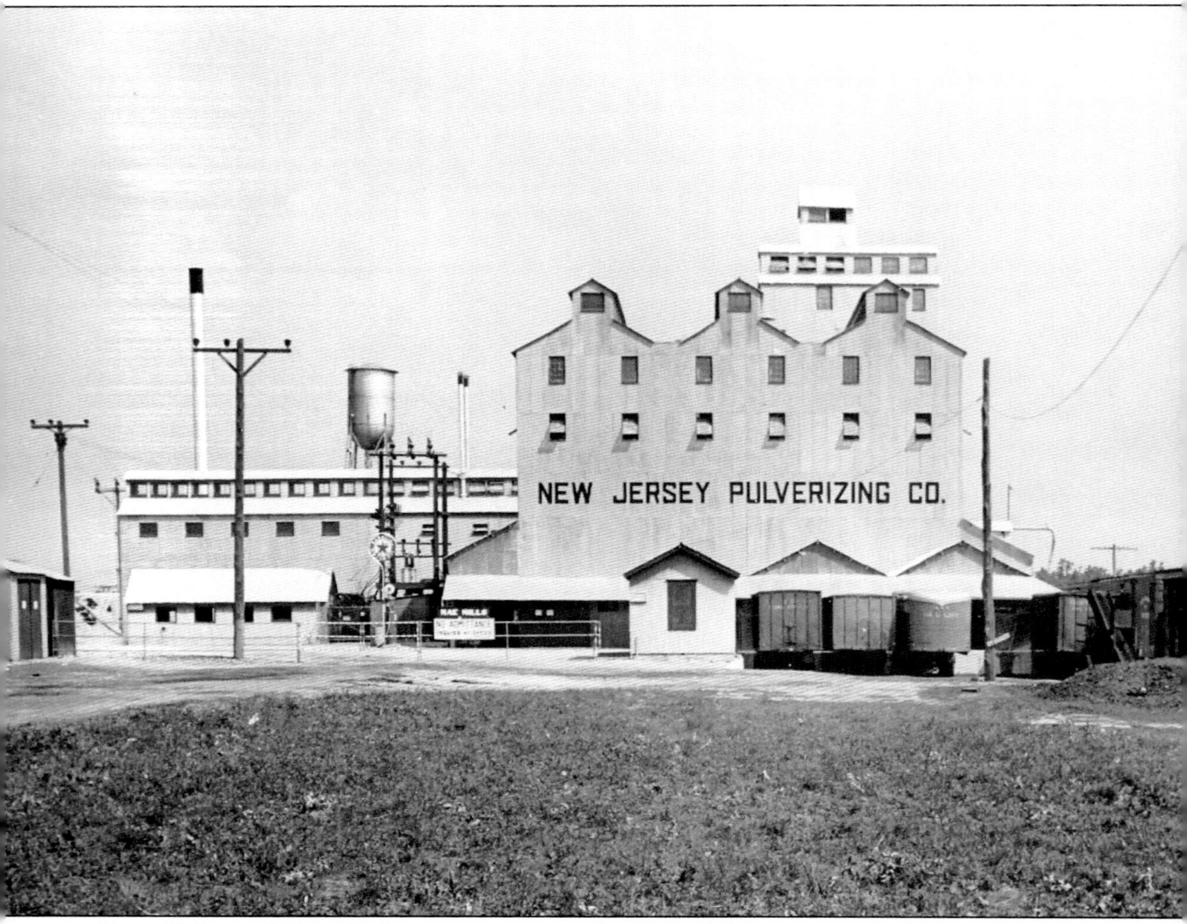

Ervin Fisher and Harry F. Spier were partners who opened the New Jersey Pulverizing Company's sand and silica processing plant in December 1925. It is located on the west end of Hickory Lane. Fisher and Spier previously had a similar sand operation in West Virginia, and many of their workers in West Virginia relocated to New Jersey. The plant was the largest shipper of freight on the Barnegat Branch Railroad for the next 30 years. Fisher Brothers Trucking business would also utilize the sand quarry to haul sand for local deliveries. Today, all the sand products are shipped out by truck. (Courtesy of Barbara Magahan.)

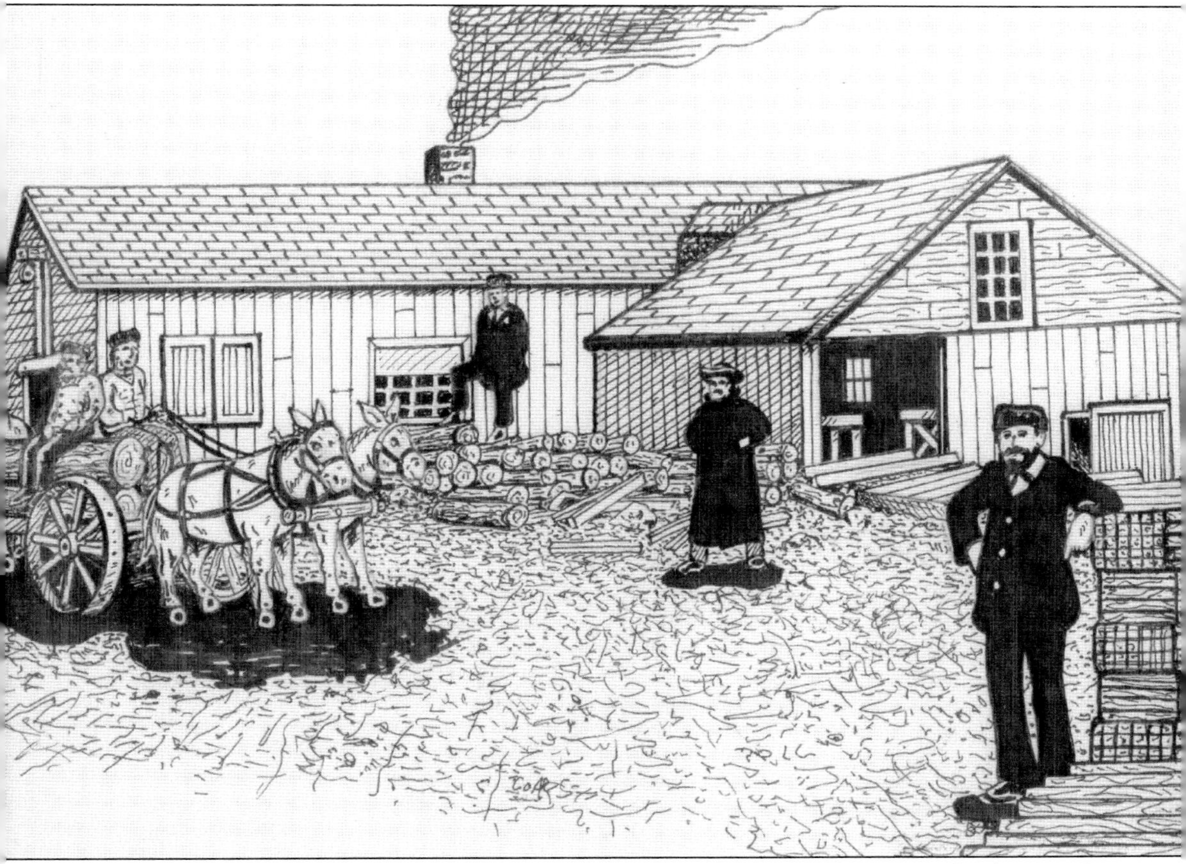

The Austin Sawmill was located on Cedar Creek near Bamber Lake. It was originally the site of Dover Forge, which made charcoal used by the seven foundries in Ocean County and was operated by Joseph Austin, who died in 1868. The forge was then demolished, and Nathan Austin, his son, built this sawmill on the site, which was later destroyed in a forest fire in the early 1900s. Nathan Austin is depicted here at far right. (Drawing by Bob Coar.)

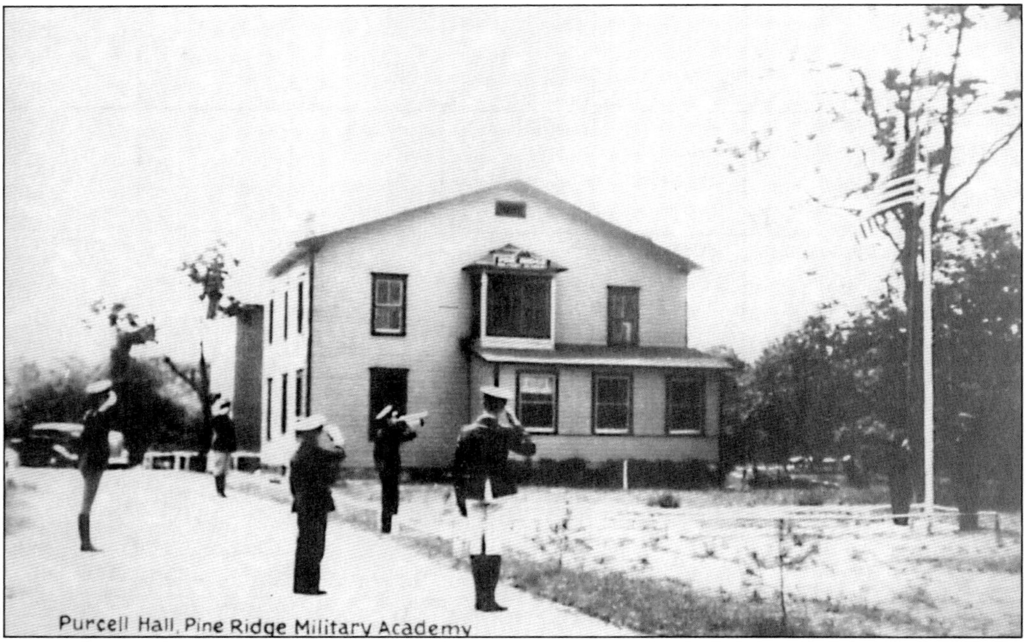

In the 1930s, the Pine Ridge Military Academy was a privately owned school for boys training for a future in the military. This view is of Louis Avenue adjacent to Ocean Gate Avenue. At Purcell Hall, the bugle is played as two students lower the flag to signal the end of another day. The academy would later move to the former Forest Hills Inn in Pinewald. Pine Ridge closed its doors by 1945. (Courtesy of Larry F. Casele.)

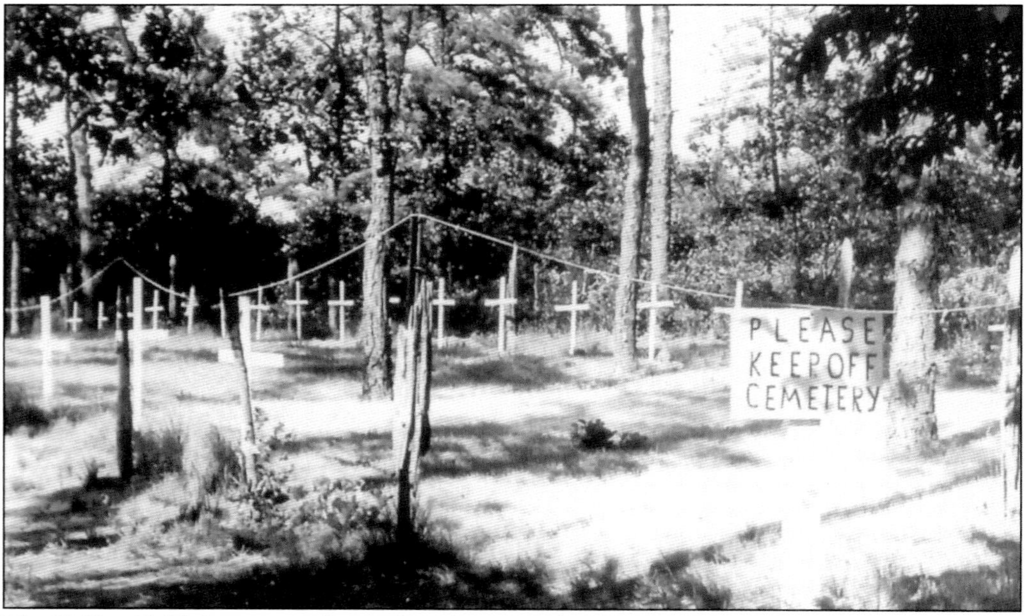

The Hollow Field Cemetery is located on the west side of Dover Road, east of Bamber. The burial plot has 31 gravesites, believed to have been the workers at nearby Dover Forge from 1809 to 1868. Oliver J. McGuire, a Toms River surveyor, discovered Hollow Field in 1952. In the 1970s, M.H. Septor of Toms River maintained it and erected crosses and created a bird sanctuary of houses and feeders there.

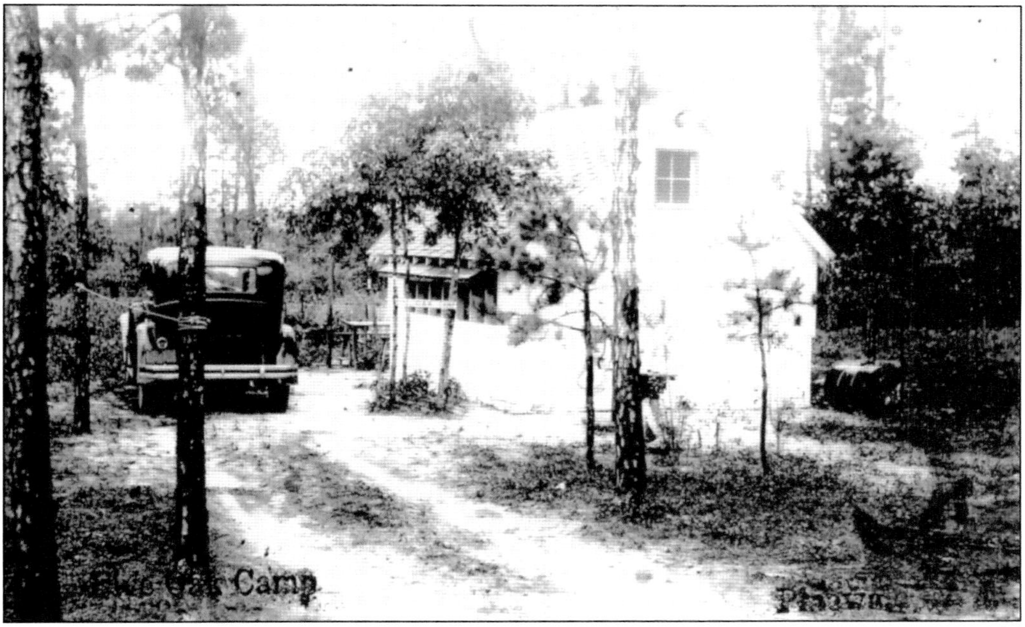

This 1934 postcard shows the small bungalow located at Five Oak Camp in the new Pinewald development. It was common for lot owners to initially stay in tents before these small homes were built. In 1931, these lot owners would also form the Pinewald Property Owners Association to lend assistance to their members. Note the clothesline on the left, the address board in the center, and the kerosene tank on the right. (Courtesy of Larry F. Casele.)

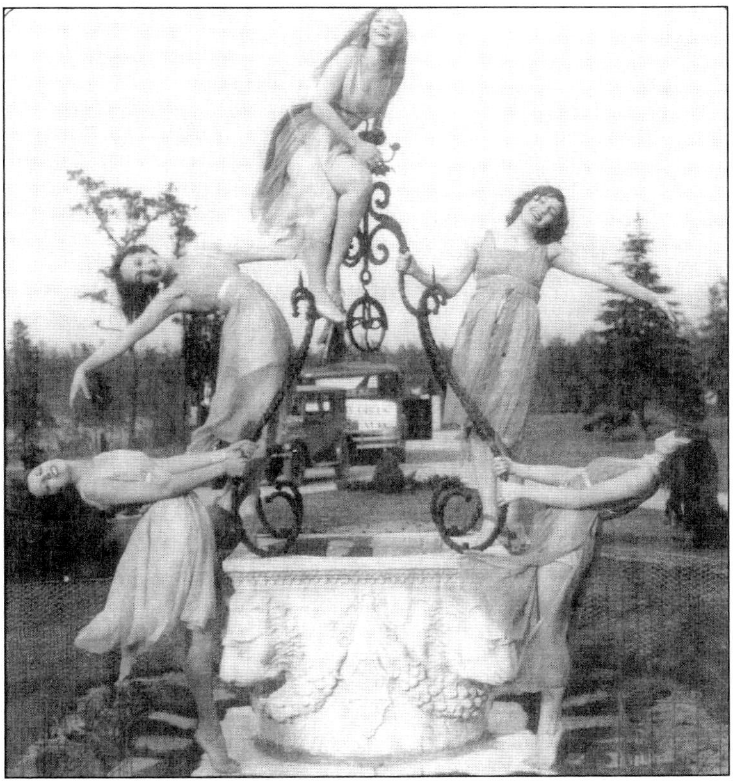

Pictured to promote the sale of lots for the B.W. Sangor Company, these young ladies are seen on a cold April 13, 1930, by Crystal Lake in Pinewald. The large, elaborate urn still resides at a home on Western Boulevard. The company's vision for a regal Royal Pines hotel and a modernistic town never materialized. These pretty models might as well have stayed warm in the old cars waiting for them in the background.

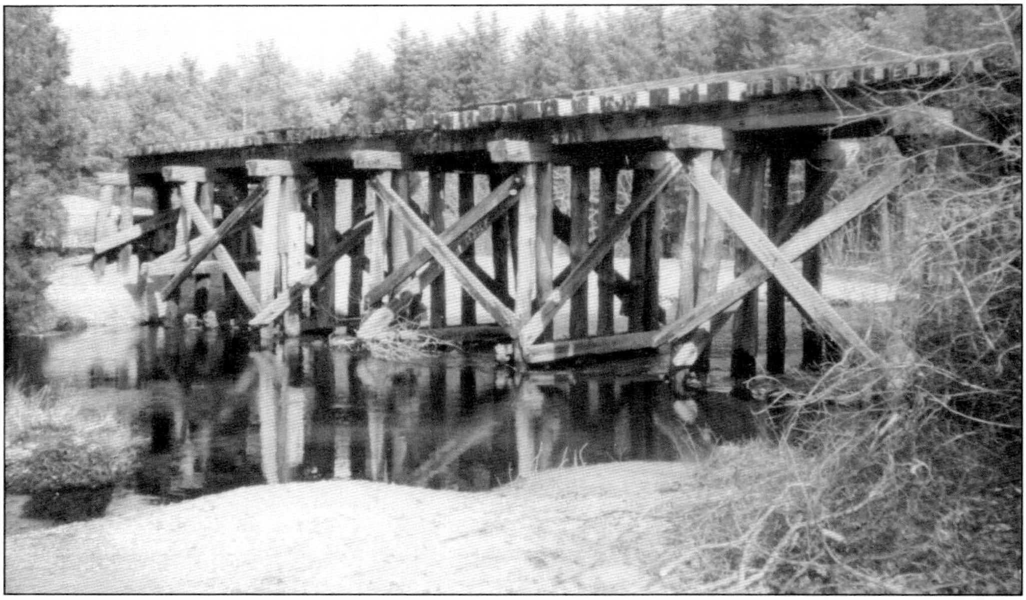

The wooden Cedar Creek trestle on the Central Jersey Barnegat Branch Railroad was built in 1871. The last freight train to go across was in 1970, and the rails were removed in 1974. The trestle is still standing and scheduled to be restored for the future Barnegat Branch Rail Trail. This location has become a recreational area for canoeing behind the present-day Cedar Creek Campground.

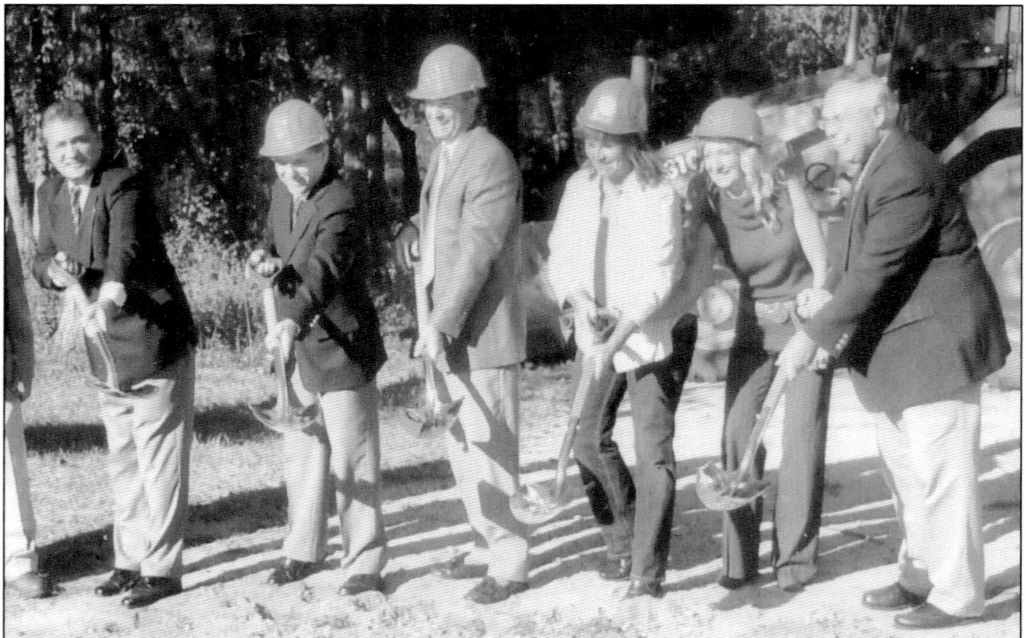

On October 15, 2007, the Barnegat Branch Rail Trail's ground-breaking ceremony was held on Burr Street in Barnegat. This linear park would be a 15.6-mile bike path from Barnegat to Toms River. Seen here are, from left to right, Ocean County freeholder Joseph Vicari, unidentified, Ocean County freeholder James Lacey, Lacey Rail Trail Committee members Donna Bahrle and Helen Henderson, and Ocean County engineer Ron Lotrecchio. Later, on June 30, 2011, construction also began on the 3.8-mile scenic Pinewald section in Berkeley.

Five

Along Route 9

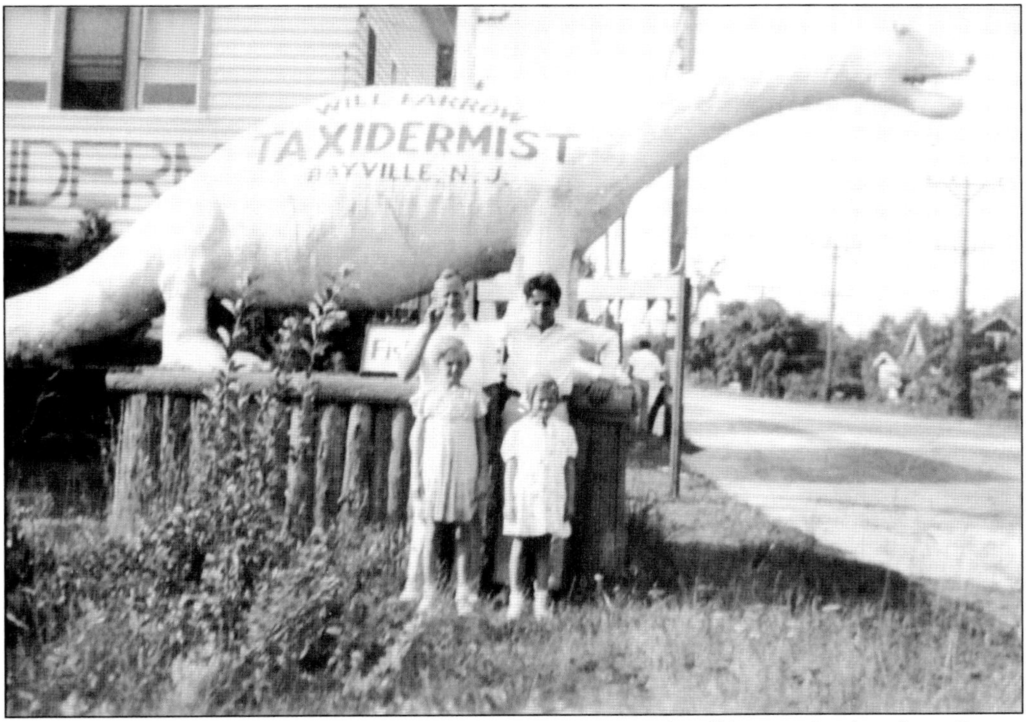

The 10-foot-high dinosaur is perhaps the most prominent and well-known landmark in Ocean County. It served as an advertisement for Will Farrow and his taxidermy business. In 1932, it was believed to have been moved from a Freehold Sinclair service station that used the dinosaur to mimic its company brand logo. A Mr. Geoghegan, who lived across Route 9 from Farrow's store, moved it to its current location. "Dino" has had several body changes over the years due to car accidents and general repairs. Today, he is still attracting attention from the passing motorists. Shown here are, from left to right, (first row) Ester and Lorraine Jones; (second row) George Jones and Frank Carrel.

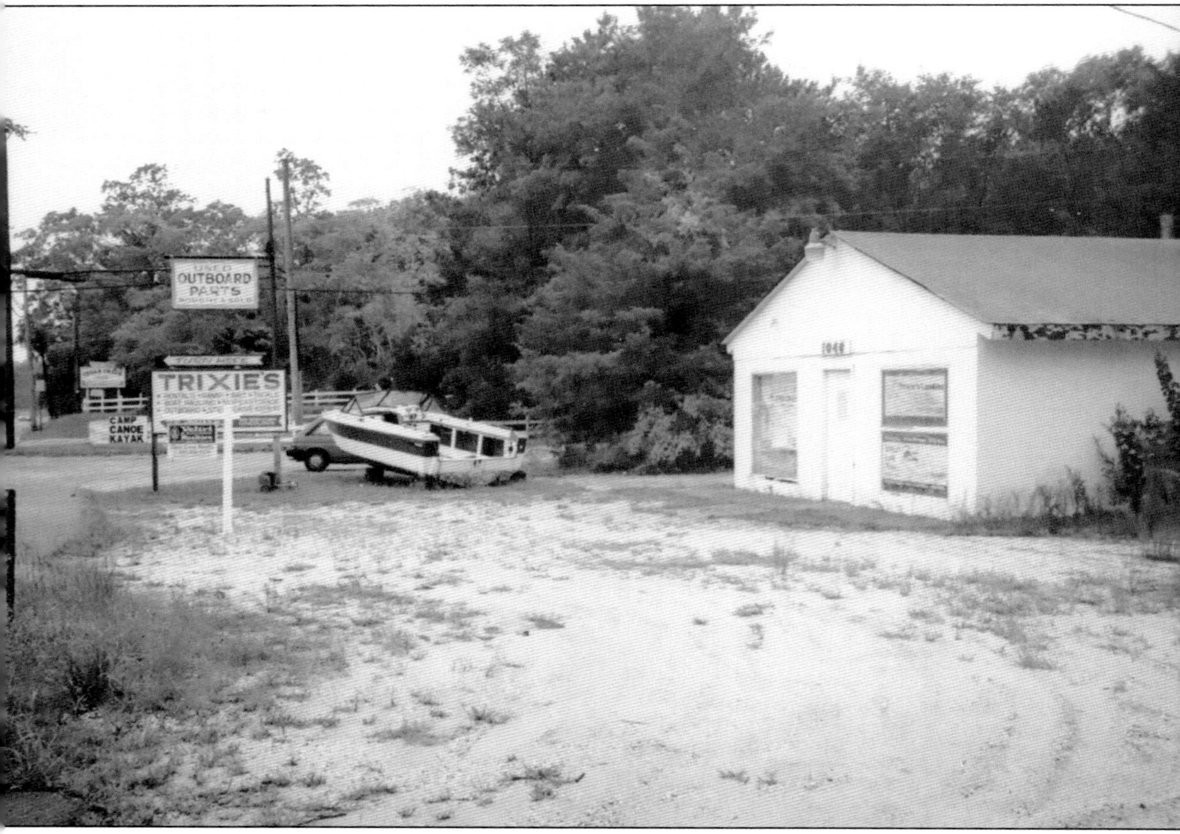

Trixie's was a marine business located at West Harbor Inn Road on Route 9 and also at nearby Berkeley Island Park. At this location, boats were offered for sale and outboard motors were both sold and serviced. The family residence was behind the store. The property was sold in 2013 and today is occupied by Green Mile, a housing repair business.

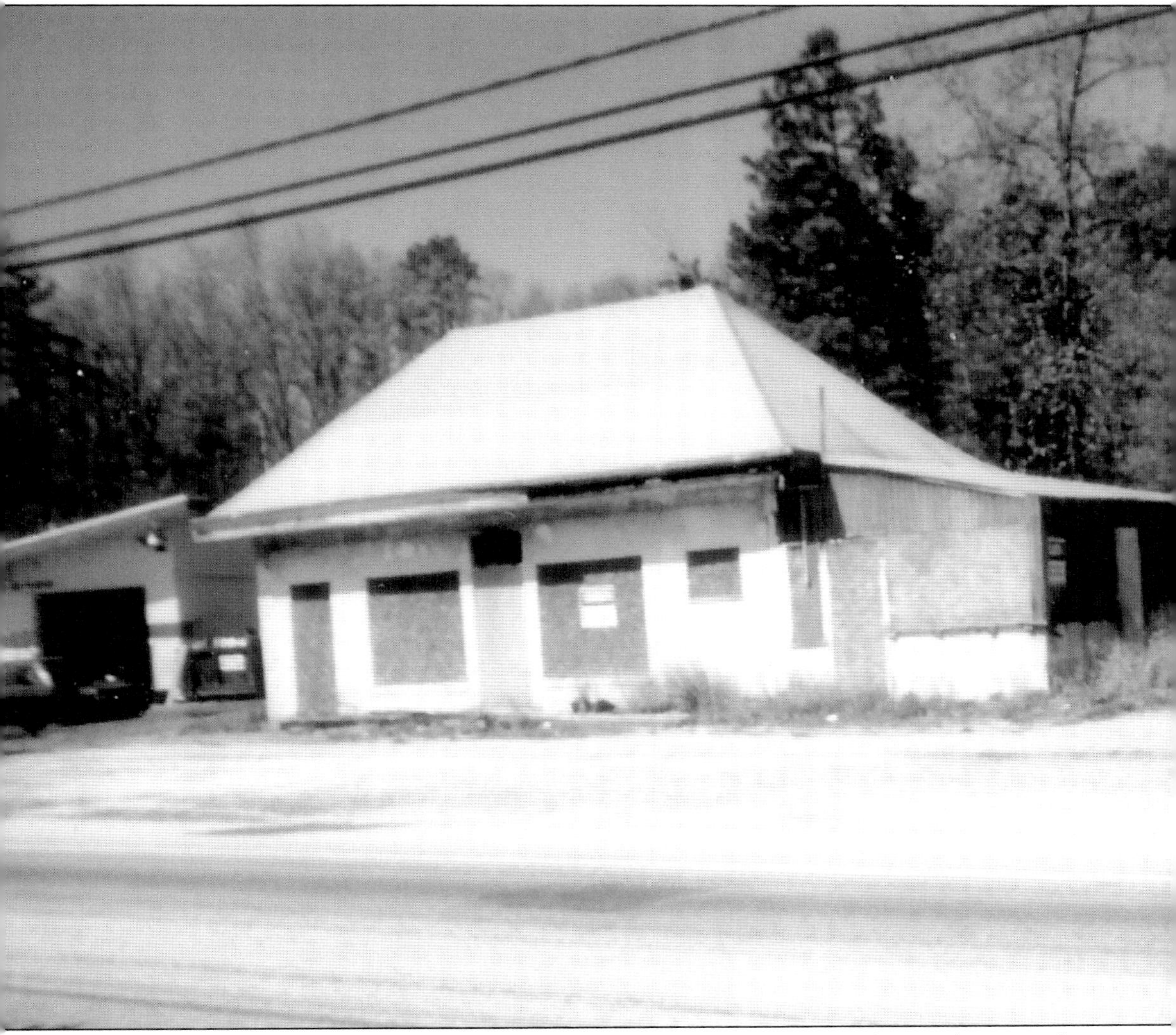

Buttermarks was a small refreshment stand and gas station located across from Bel Aire Park. There was an outside counter where a quick lunch and soda could be had. Jimmy Buttermark was the friendly proprietor and also a licensed electrician by trade. Quality Used Cars later occupied the property and restored the building as an office. This office was demolished in 2010 when the car lot was expanded.

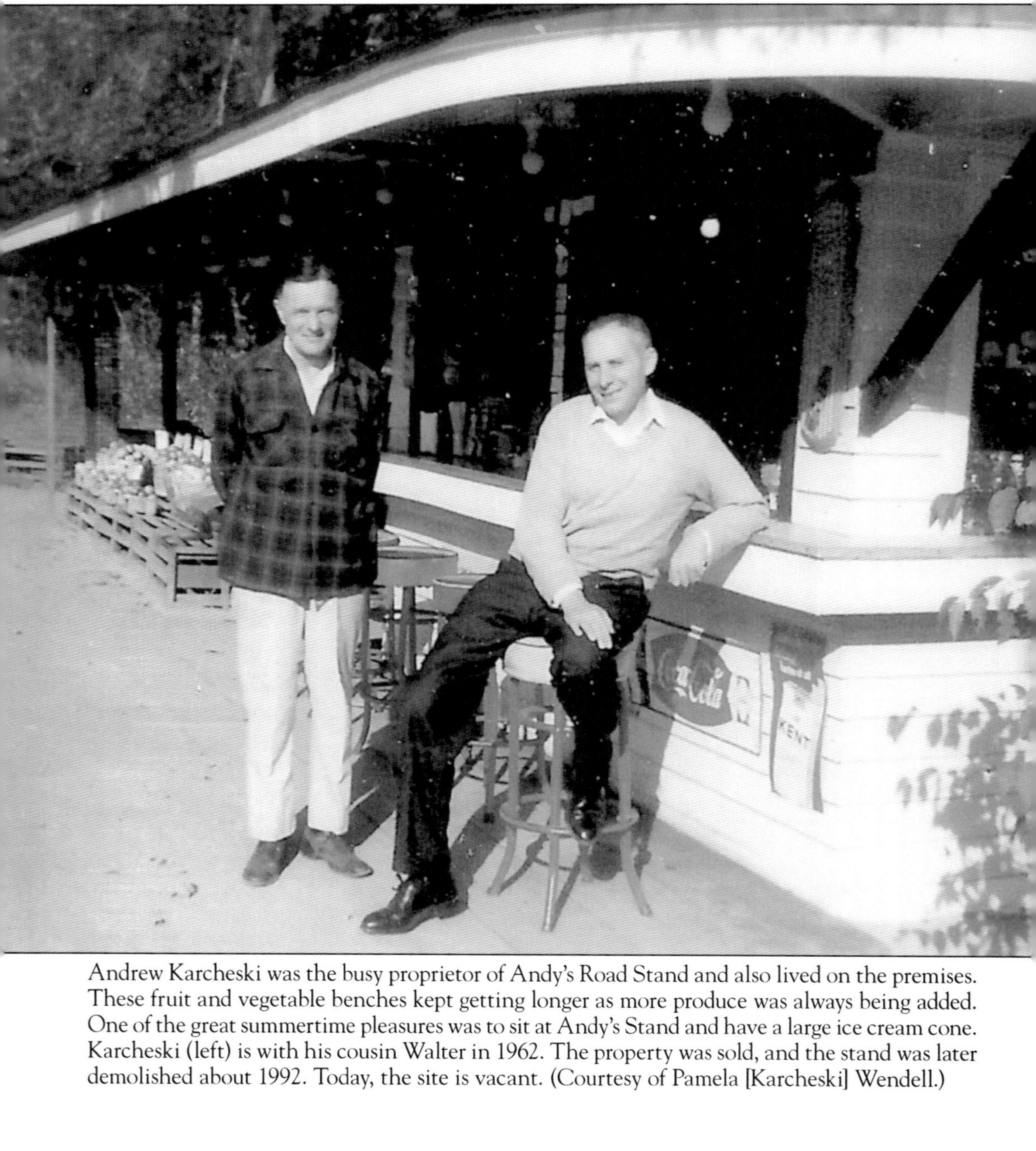

Andrew Karcheski was the busy proprietor of Andy's Road Stand and also lived on the premises. These fruit and vegetable benches kept getting longer as more produce was always being added. One of the great summertime pleasures was to sit at Andy's Stand and have a large ice cream cone. Karcheski (left) is with his cousin Walter in 1962. The property was sold, and the stand was later demolished about 1992. Today, the site is vacant. (Courtesy of Pamela [Karcheski] Wendell.)

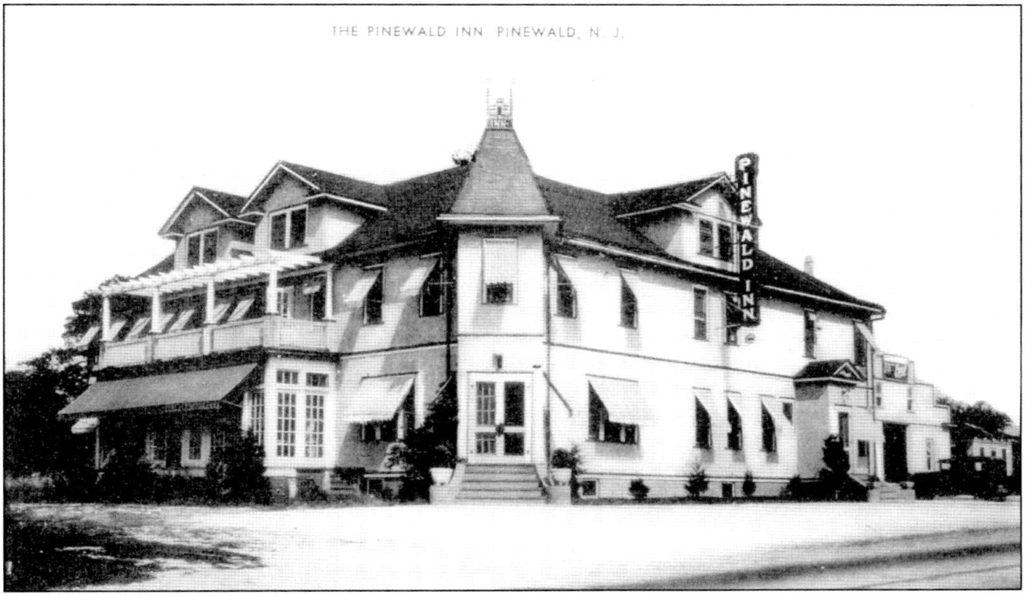

The Pinewald Inn, built in 1926, was owned and operated by the Lukowski family. This spacious structure was located on the corner of Floral Avenue and Route 9. Note the inn's name at the top of the front spire. In the 1950s, Tom Carroll and Dave Johnson, publishers of the *Ocean County Sun* newspaper, purchased the property; they were the last owners. (Courtesy of Larry F. Casele.)

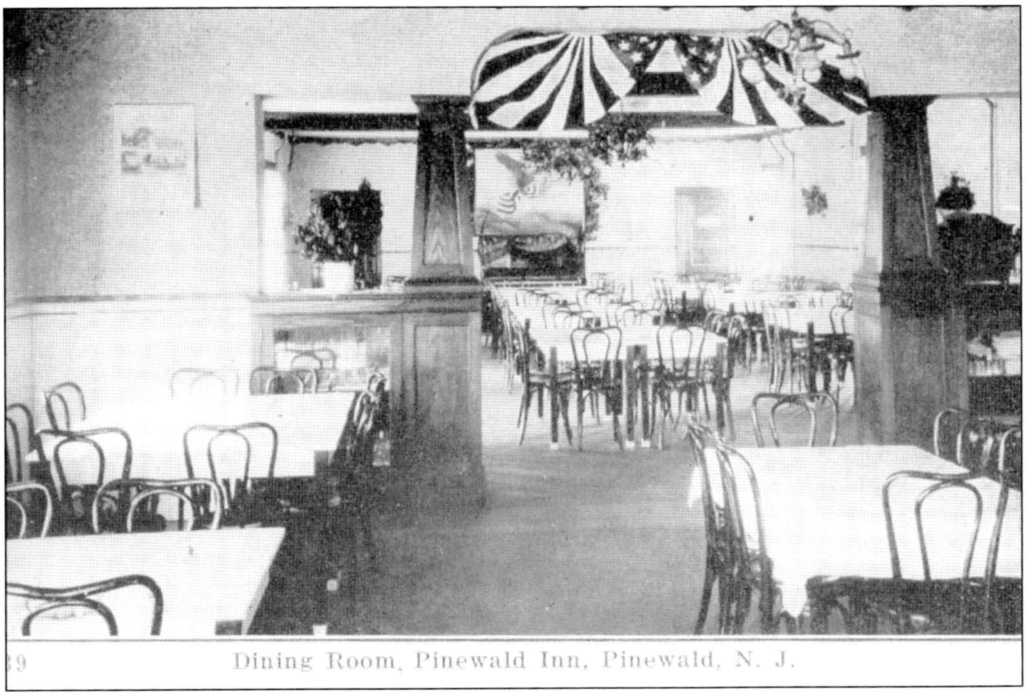

The Pinewald Inn's Coach 'n Four restaurant offered what was considered to be Berkeley's finest cuisine. It had a large glass-enclosed view extending from the south side creating a desirable dining atmosphere. The head chef was Joeseph Hoffrogge, a native of Essen, Germany. The inn burned down in 1964, but the two small storage buildings survived and are presently occupied by the Bayville Marine Center. (Courtesy of Larry F. Casele.)

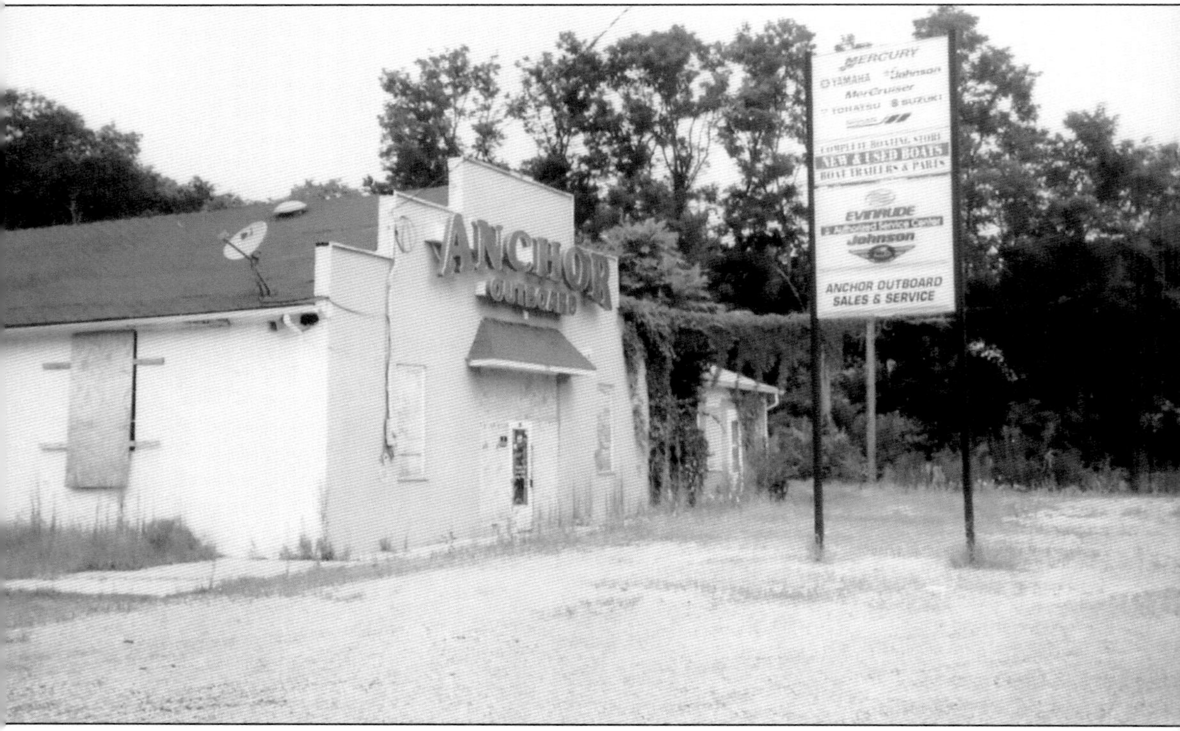

John Meeker started the Anchor Outboard in 1965 at 856 Route 9; Meeker's son William later operated it. The business utilized the two small buildings that previously were storage facilities for the Pinewald Inn. Both boats and outboards were on display to be sold or serviced. Anchor was the exclusive New Jersey dealer for Seaswirl boats. The property was later vacated, and today, it is occupied by the Bayville Marine Center.

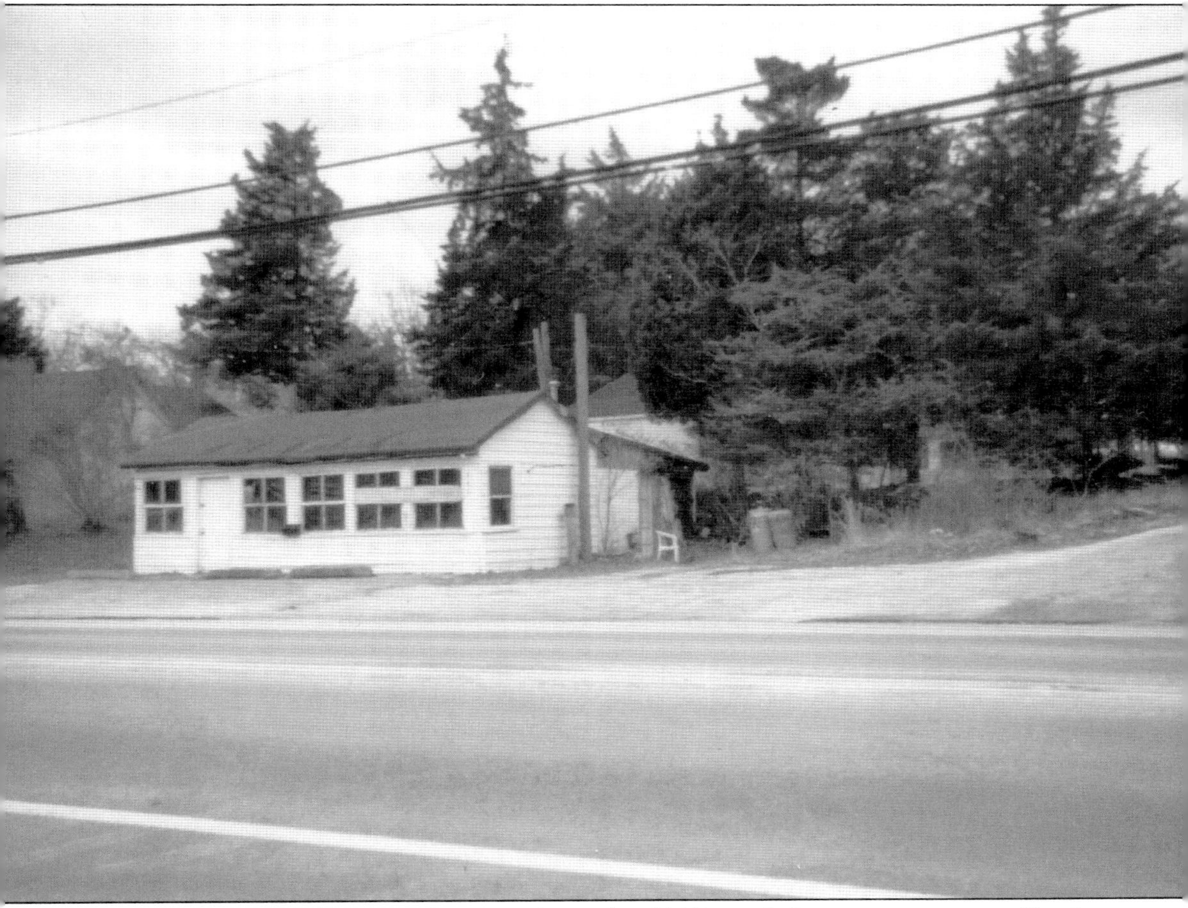

Ellen Leitch operated Ellen's Luncheonette, located at 846 Route 9. Counter service was offered, and there were a few small tables. In the 1970s, it was occupied by Vacuums Plus, which provided sales and service for all makes of vacuum cleaners. The several small rental cottages in the back of the property are still occupied today. The building was demolished in 2012, and today, the site remains vacant.

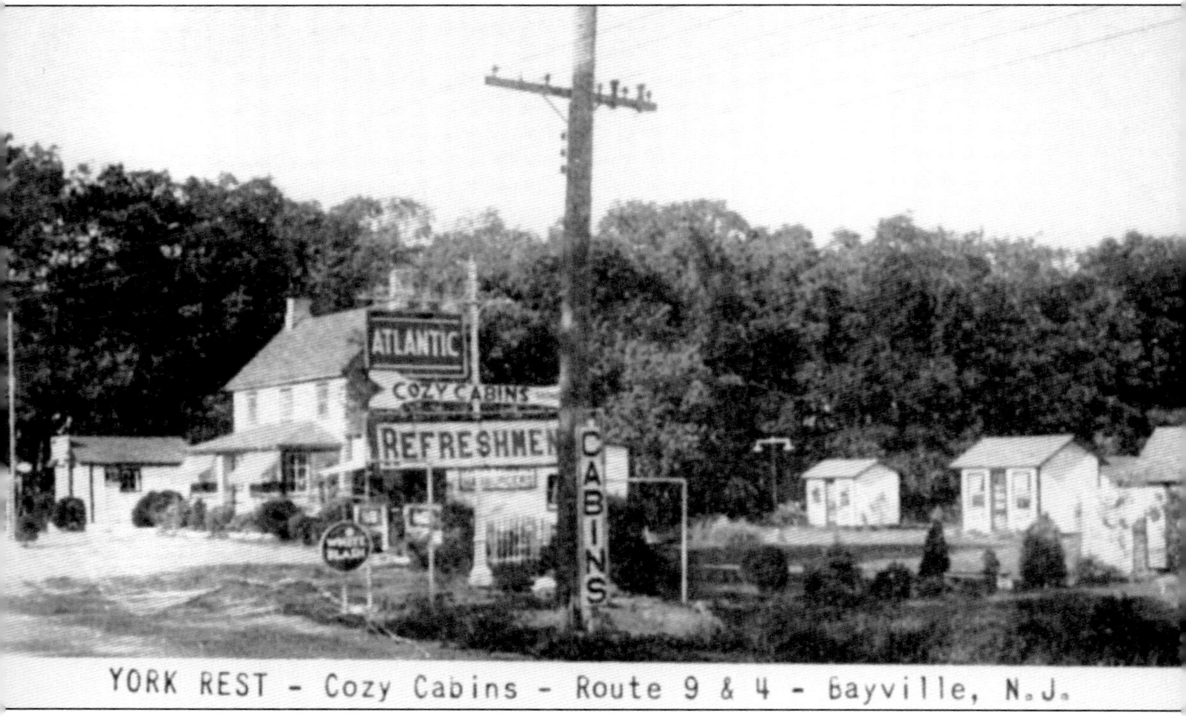

The York Rest was a welcome respite for early travelers on Route 9. It was located just south of the now Bayville Post Office. Several rental cabins were available, and a luncheonette was located in the front porch area of the stylish residence/office building. In the 1930s, the proprietors were a Mr. Freund and a Mr. Goudy. Anthony Kurnel Sr. and his wife, Lena, purchased the property in 1947. By 1957, a large repair garage had been added, the cabin rentals ended, and their son "Butch" Kurnel had taken over operations, until 1999. The business was then abandoned for several years, and the house was demolished. Today, the proprietors are E and L Extreme Automotive. (Courtesy of Larry F. Casele.)

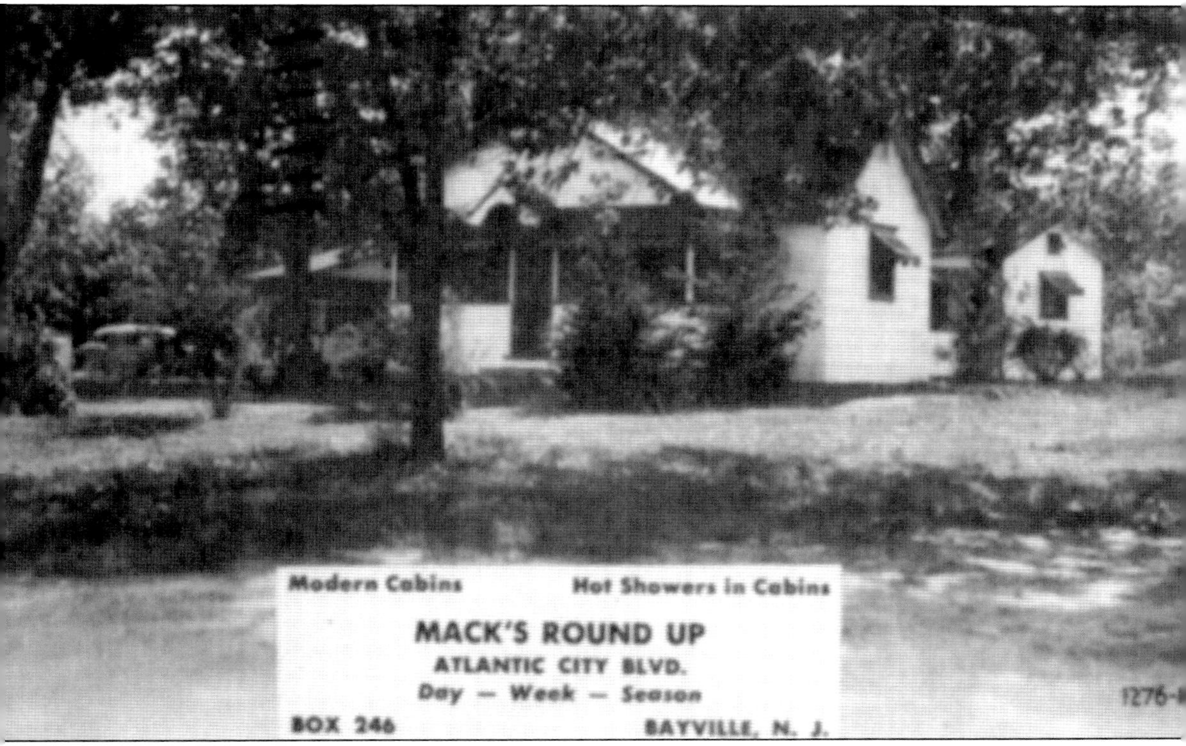

Thomas and Anne McDermott were the proprietors of Mack's Round Up Cabins. This 1940 postcard shows the stylish cabins, with their beach-like awnings, located where the Shady Rest Restaurant is today. The previous name was Jarry's Modern Cabins. In the 1950s, the proprietors were Kenneth and Lorelei Mather. Cabins could be rented by the day, week, or season. (Courtesy of Fran Casele.)

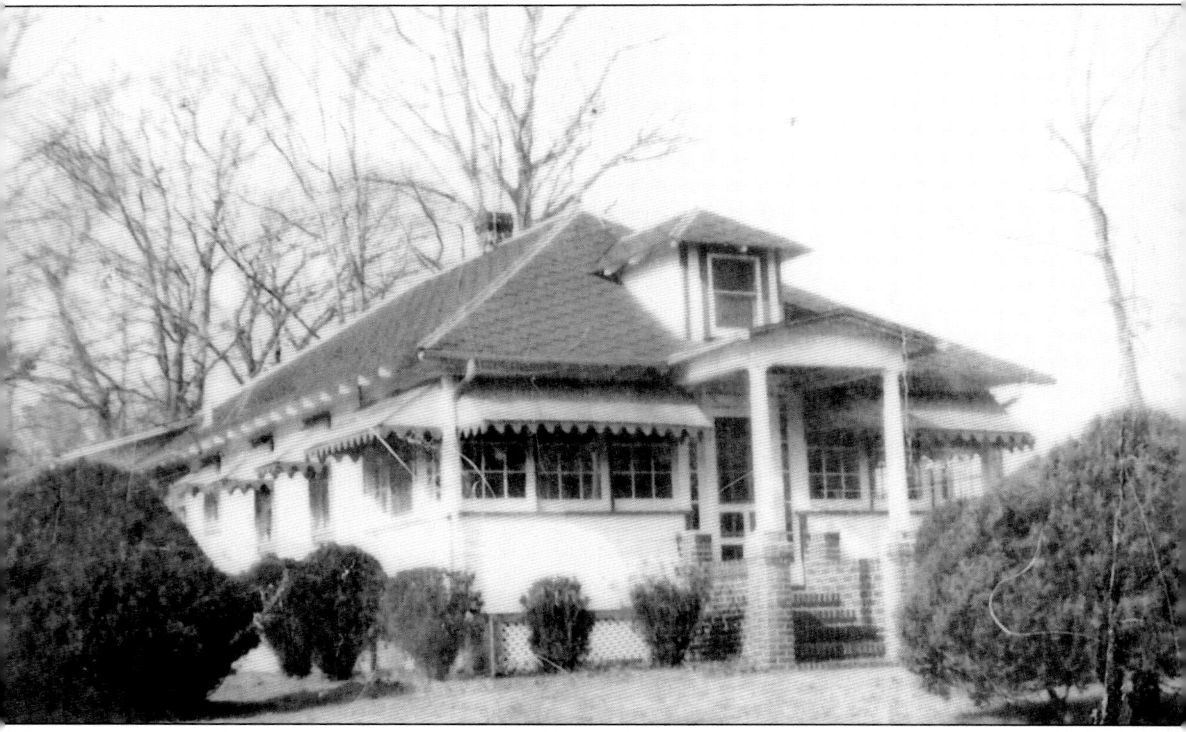

The neatly kept cottage seen above at 796 Route 9 formerly served as the main residence for the Mack's Round Up Cabins. In 1965, Robert and Alexis Popovics purchased the property. They then expanded the front area into a small restaurant that became the Pizza Parlor and Snack Bar. Additional modifications were made, and the business was renamed Shady Rest Pizza Parlor and Italian Restaurant. Later, the facade was enhanced with stone, and the cabins were replaced with a larger parking lot. In 1984, the Popovicses' son Stephen became the owner of the restaurant. Today, it remains one of Bayville's most popular year-round casual dining establishments.

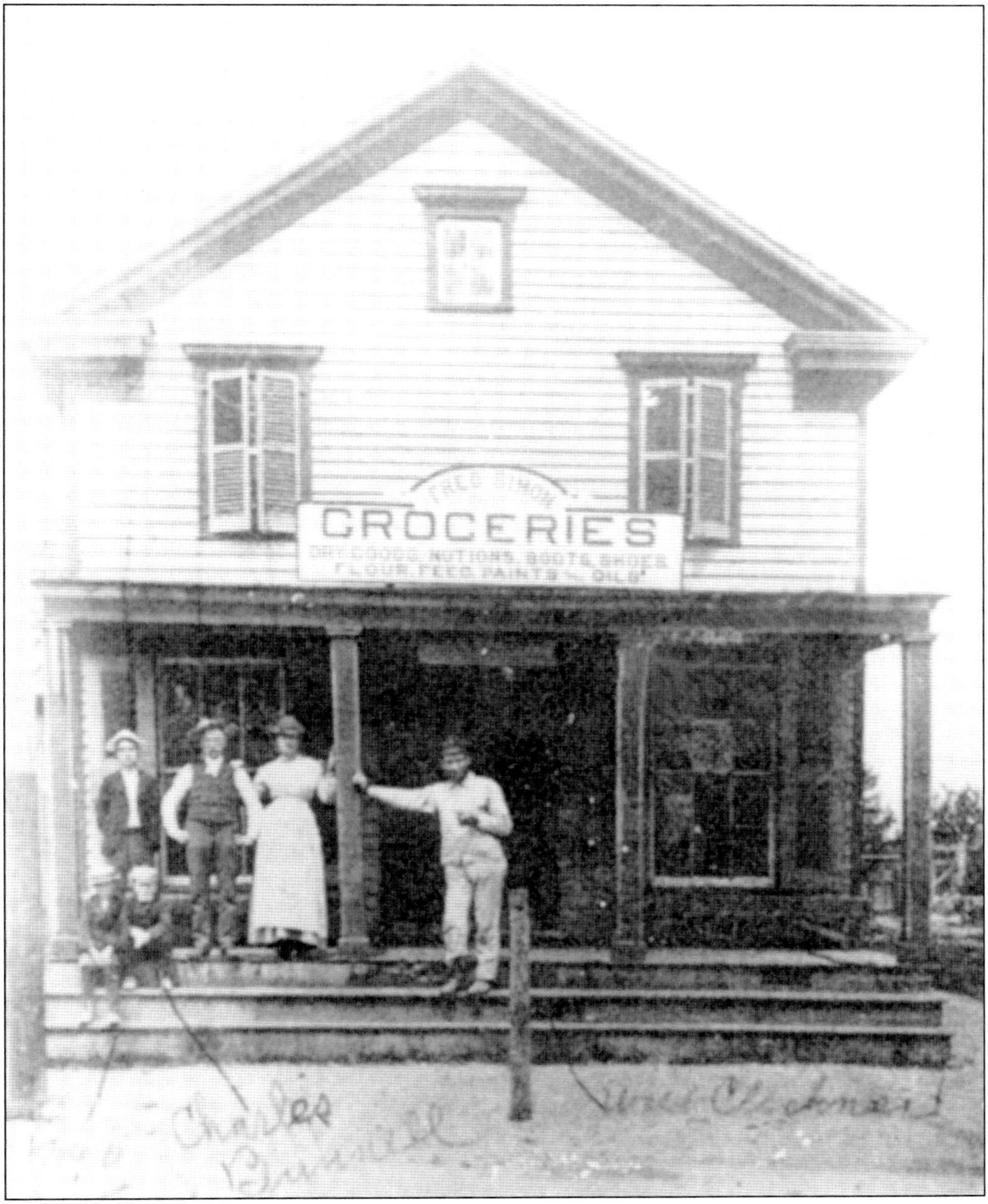

This was Fred Simon's house and grocery store in 1900. It was purchased in 1893 and located on Route 9 across from Bay Avenue. In 1906, the store burned down and was replaced by both a store and residence that was moved there from Barnegat Park, now Pinewald. The location served as Bayville's early post office from 1898 to 1914 with Fred Simon as postmaster. The store was later demolished, and Ryan's Funeral Home now occupies the site.

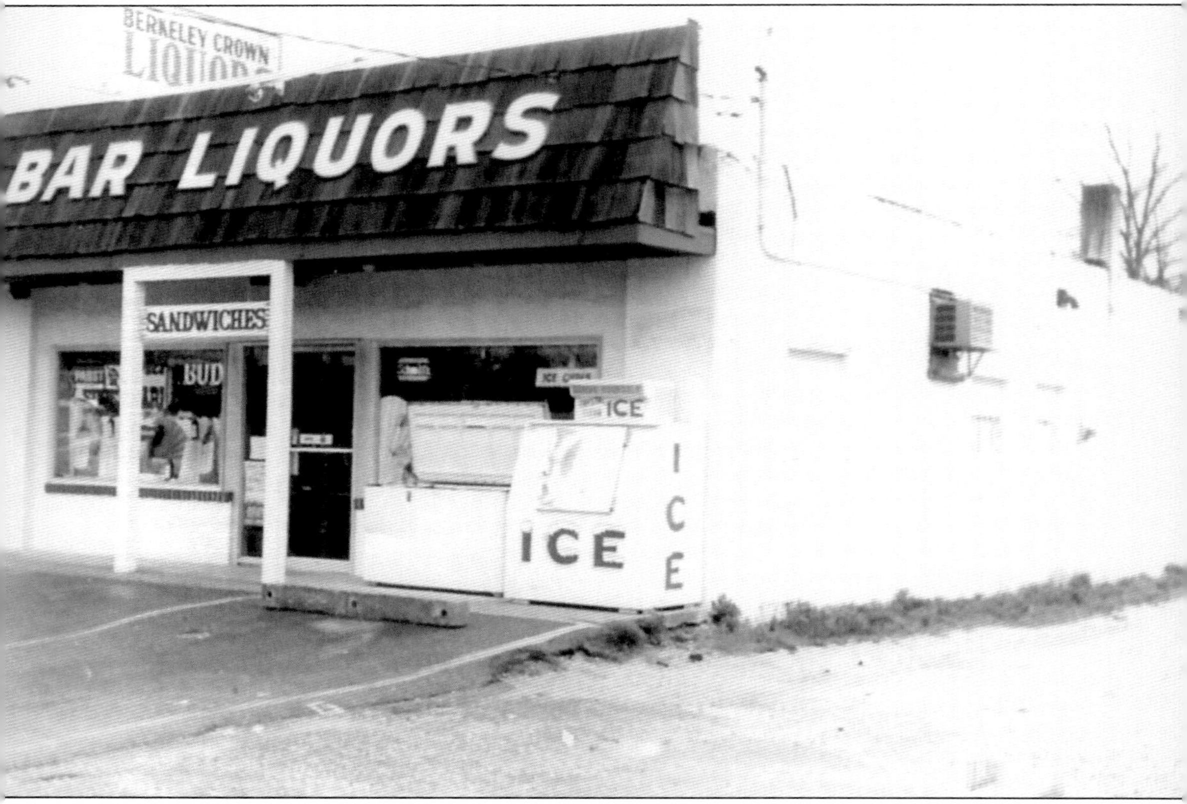

Hobby Lobby 2 first occupied this stucco building, located to the left of Friendly Furniture, about 1956. The store sold toy building kits, model trains, and even bait. For the next few years, it served as the Bayville Post Office with Alfred Casagrand as the postmaster. In 1962, Bob and Barbara Tholen became the proprietors of Berkeley Crown Liquors. The only addition made was a wooden-shingle facade. The store had a small bar and offered a light lunch menu of sandwiches. Berkeley Crown became part of the former Bayville Shopping Area, now known as Robert's Plaza. Today, the building is occupied by Conquest Comics.

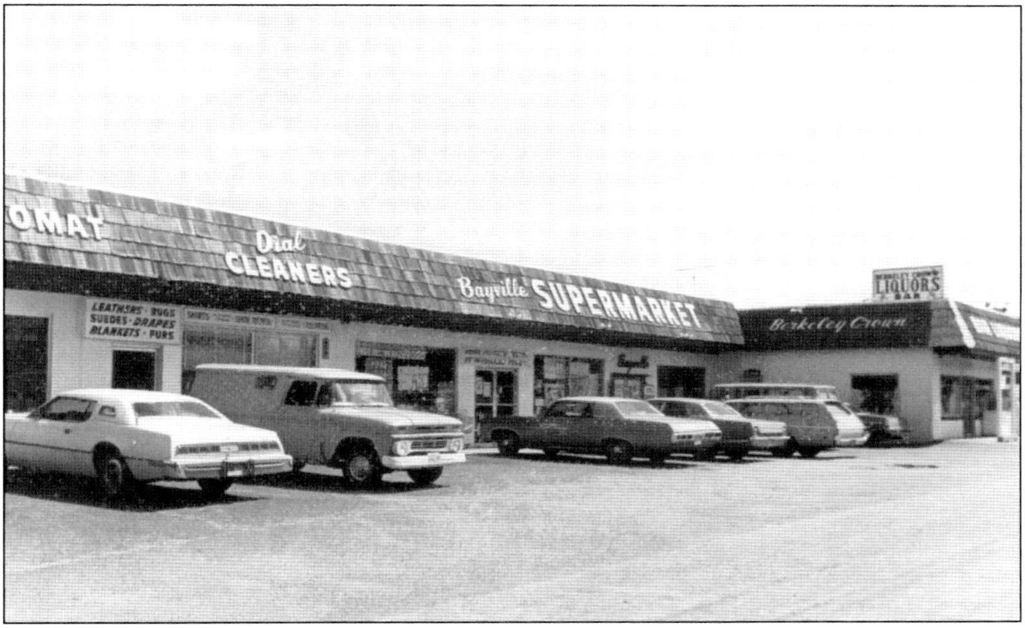

This supermarket was originally named IGA and owned by Willie Lahann and his wife. It opened in July 1959, and the building was expanded twice by 1962 to also include Dial Cleaners and Ernie Foster's Laundromat. The location was called the Bayville Shopping Area. Willie was previously a butcher with Koller's Market in Toms River. A special feature was cutting the fresh meats to a customer's satisfaction. Today, Robert's Plaza occupies it with several different stores.

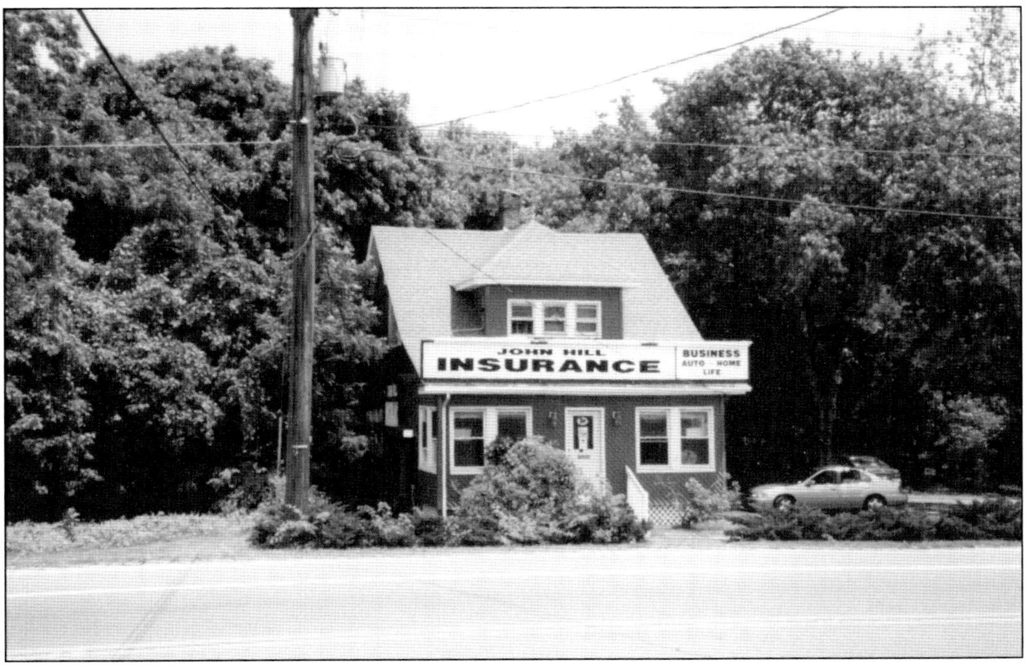

The John Hill Insurance Agency opened in 1961 on Buckley Lane, but in September 1962, it moved to 635 Route 9, shown here. Elwood Butler built this house in 1921. At that time, it was the only house in Bayville with a bathtub. The structure was torn down on May 24, 2007, and replaced with a modern office building. John Hill's son Michael presently operates the agency.

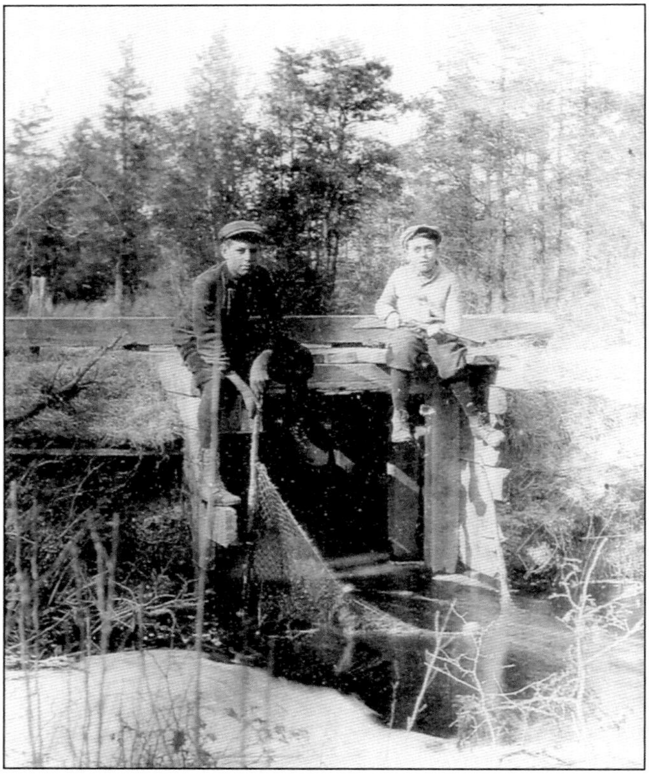

This iconic 1905 scene depicts George P. Vanderveer, left, and Hilbert Potter, right, seining for fish from Potter's Creek Bridge on Route 4, now Route 9. The bridge was upgraded in 1927 and again in 2010. Hilbert went on to be the township clerk and a school board member and held various other civic positions for over 42 years. He and his wife, Mildred, were honored in 1974 when the new H&M Bayville School was named in their honor. George lived just north of the bridge where Cedar Creek Gardens was located. He served in the Army during World War I, as seen below, and became the first military fatality from Ocean County. Today, the George P. Vanderveer, American Legion Post No. 129, Toms River, New Jersey, carries his name in honor.

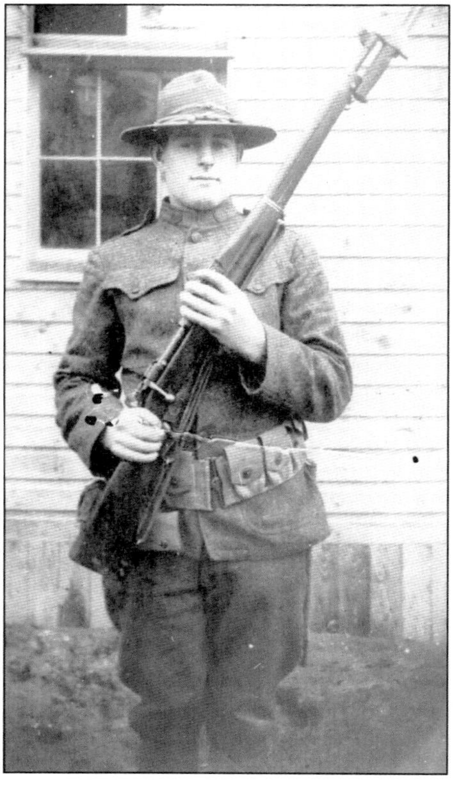

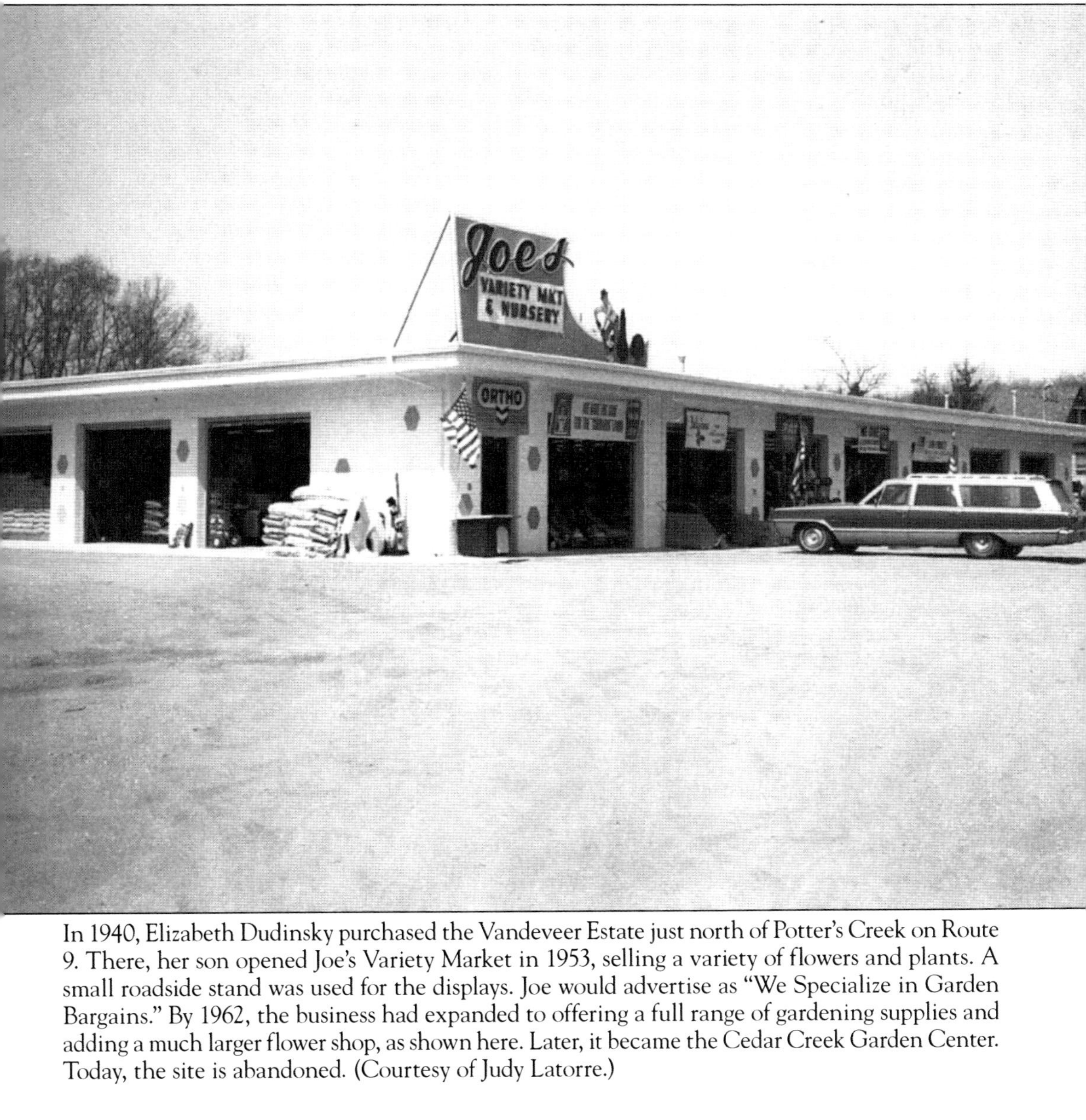

In 1940, Elizabeth Dudinsky purchased the Vandeveer Estate just north of Potter's Creek on Route 9. There, her son opened Joe's Variety Market in 1953, selling a variety of flowers and plants. A small roadside stand was used for the displays. Joe would advertise as "We Specialize in Garden Bargains." By 1962, the business had expanded to offering a full range of gardening supplies and adding a much larger flower shop, as shown here. Later, it became the Cedar Creek Garden Center. Today, the site is abandoned. (Courtesy of Judy Latorre.)

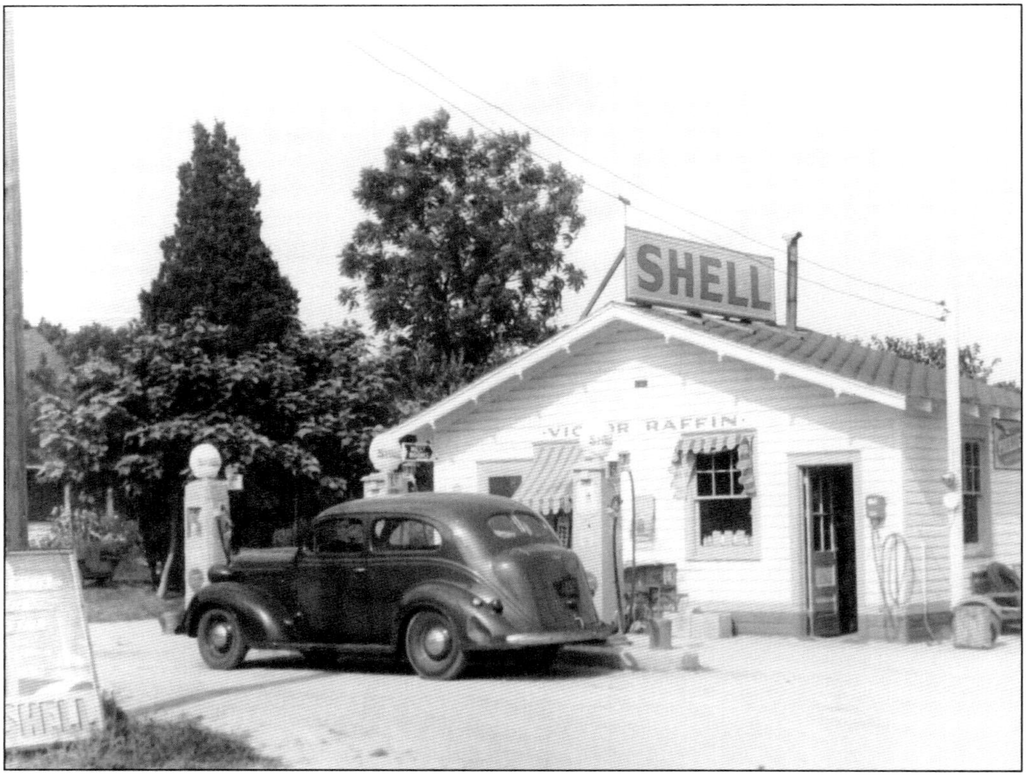

The Shell station was located on Route 9 opposite Hickory Lane. Victor Raffin purchased the property in 1931 and began an automobile service business. In 1948, he sold the property to Conrad and Dina Krause. They sold gas, cigarettes, newspapers, and baseball cards. The store was destroyed in an explosion in 1966, and today, the property remains vacant.

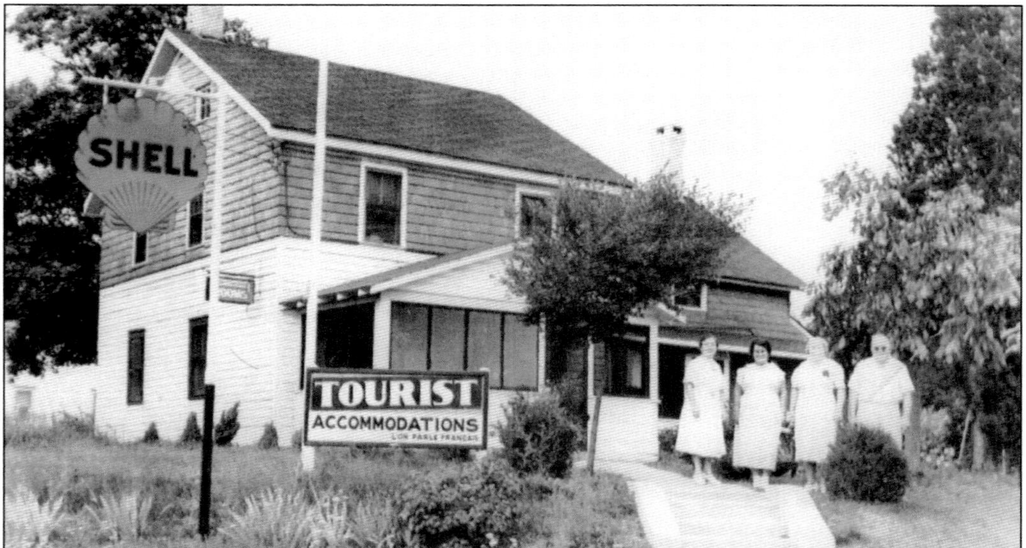

The Tourist House was located next to the Shell station on Route 9. Both were owned by Victor Raffin. It was an older house that also served as a bed and breakfast. The house was sold in 1948 and became a private residence. It was demolished in 1998, and today, the site remains vacant.

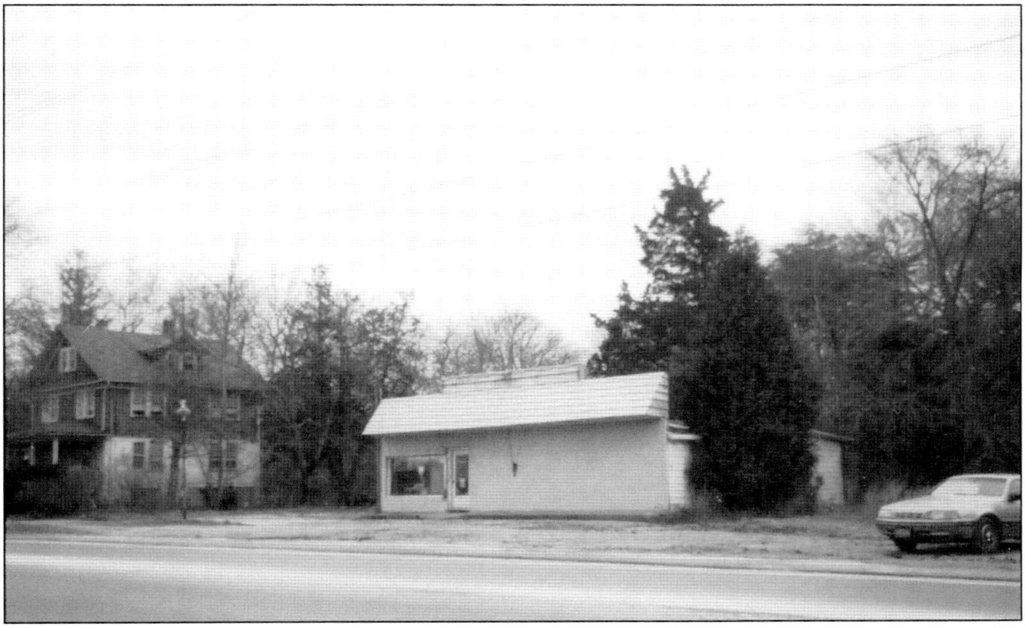

Casagrand's was known as Bayville's first convenience store and was located at 603 Route 9. The building was constructed in 1913 as a machine shop. Later, Clyde and Sara Eroh purchased it and opened it as a gas station. Bob and Noyla Casagrand rented it on October 1, 1950, and then purchased the property in 1964. Their advertisements read, "Pins to Bologna, Groceries, Clothing, Toys and String Band Records." They lived in the house on the left. The business closed in 1983, and the store was demolished in 1996. Today, the site remains vacant.

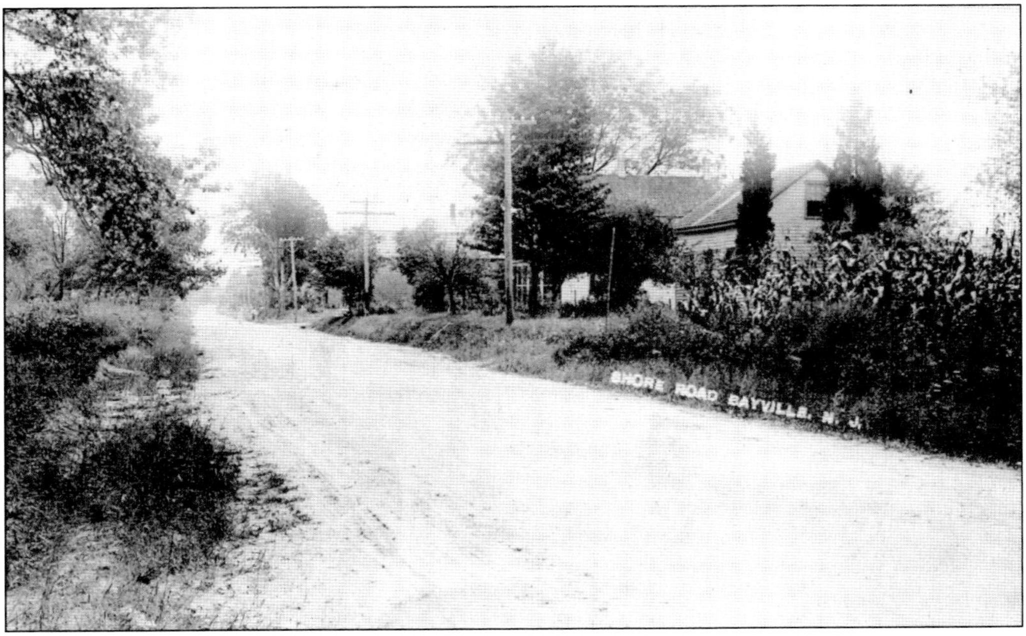

This rare 1913 postcard depicts a cornfield along the dirt road without a car or horse carriage in sight. The photographer set up his camera on the east side of Shore Road, now Route 9 near Buckley Lane. Hickory Lane is in the background on the right. The house barely visible on the left side is still standing. (Courtesy of Larry F. Casele.)

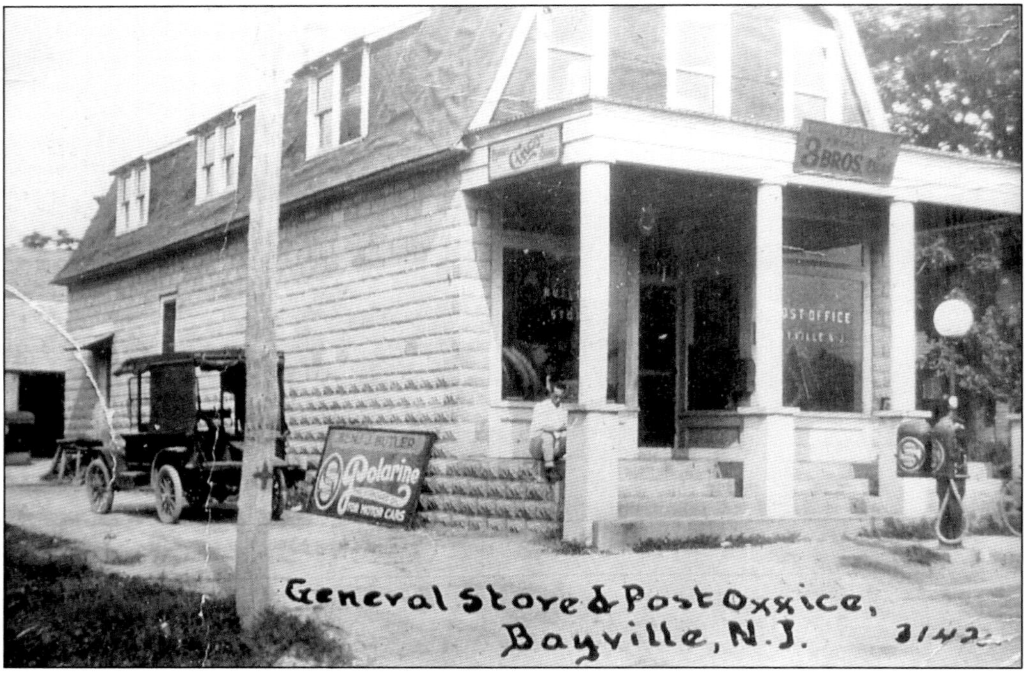

In 1925, Benjamin Butler's store was located north of Hickory Lane on Route 9. In 1852, James Butler purchased the property, and in 1896, he conveyed it to his son Benjamin. The store also served as the Bayville Post Office from 1914 to 1942 with both Francis and Benjamin Butler serving as postmasters. The upstairs was periodically used as a school classroom until 1926. It became Sheppard's General Store in the 1950s. It was then occupied by the Lord Berkeley Inn (below), which provided a catering service and had a banquet hall. It was last known as the Sand Dollar restaurant with the right side utilized as a Chrysler showroom. The building was demolished in 2007, and today, the property remains vacant.

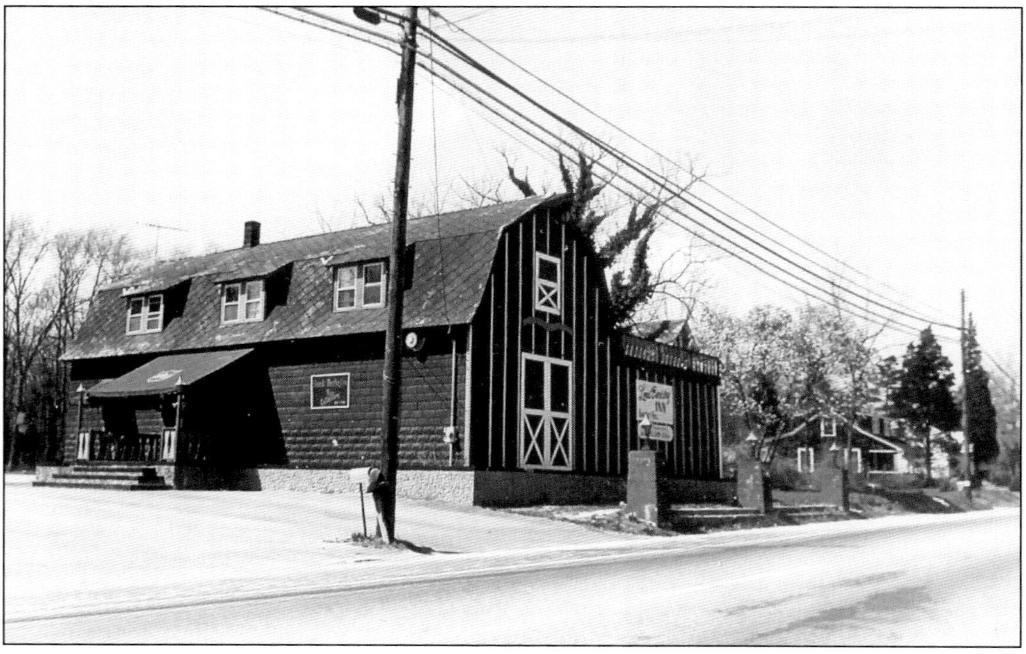

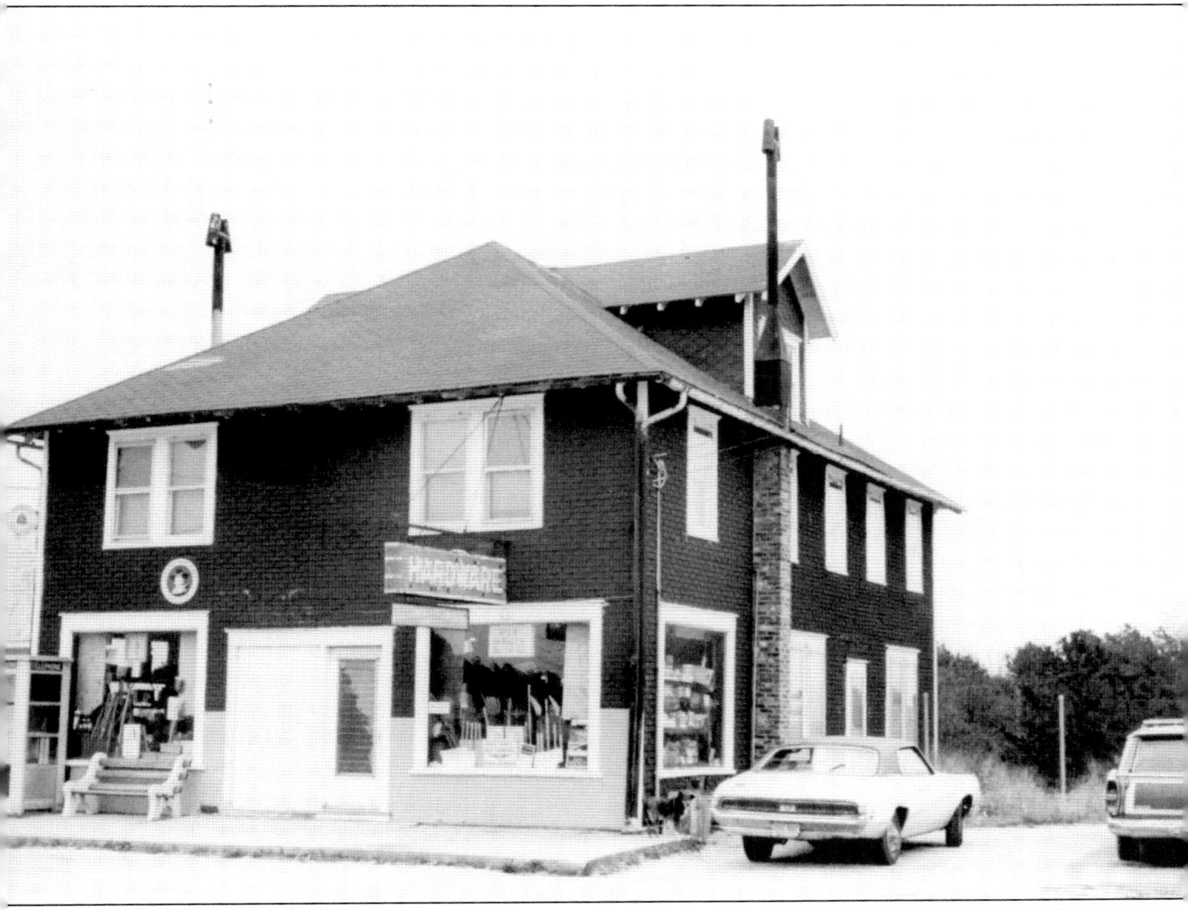

Fred and Grace Roe opened Roe's hardware in 1947. Located opposite the Trinity Methodist Church on Route 9, it served the community's hardware needs for over 30 years. The Roes lived upstairs in this two-story venerable old building that has become a town landmark. A pay phone, seen in the front, was also available. The left side served as the Bayville Post Office from 1942 to 1958 under postmaster Brad Coffey. Fred Roe was a charter member of the Bayville Volunteer First Aid Squad. The garage located to the rear of his store was used to house the squad's first ambulance, a 1949 Cadillac. Grace Roe was a member of the Bayville Ladies Auxiliary. The store had bins full of nails, shelves full of strange-looking tools, a variety of gadgets, and the ever present smell of paint and linseed oil. A fine selection of penny candy was always conveniently located next to the cash register. Today, the building is occupied by an antique store.

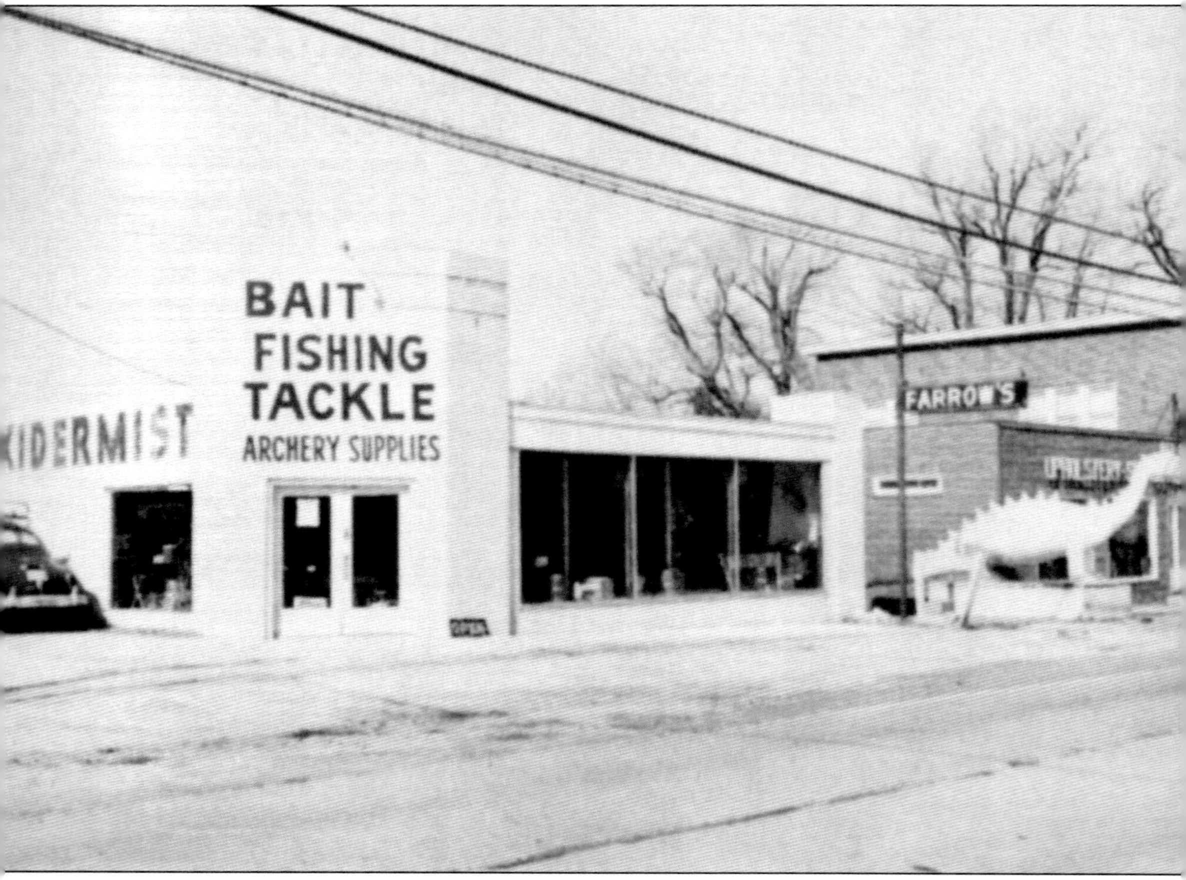

Many sportsmen would stop by the dinosaur in front of Will Farrow's taxidermy business between 1930 and 1965. Customers could get their favorite animal, bird, or pet prepared by Will for preservation and personal display. Recreational supplies were also offered for various sports. Will was the son of Lt. Edward S. Farrow, who conceived Barnegat Park, now known as Pinewald. Today, the building is unoccupied.

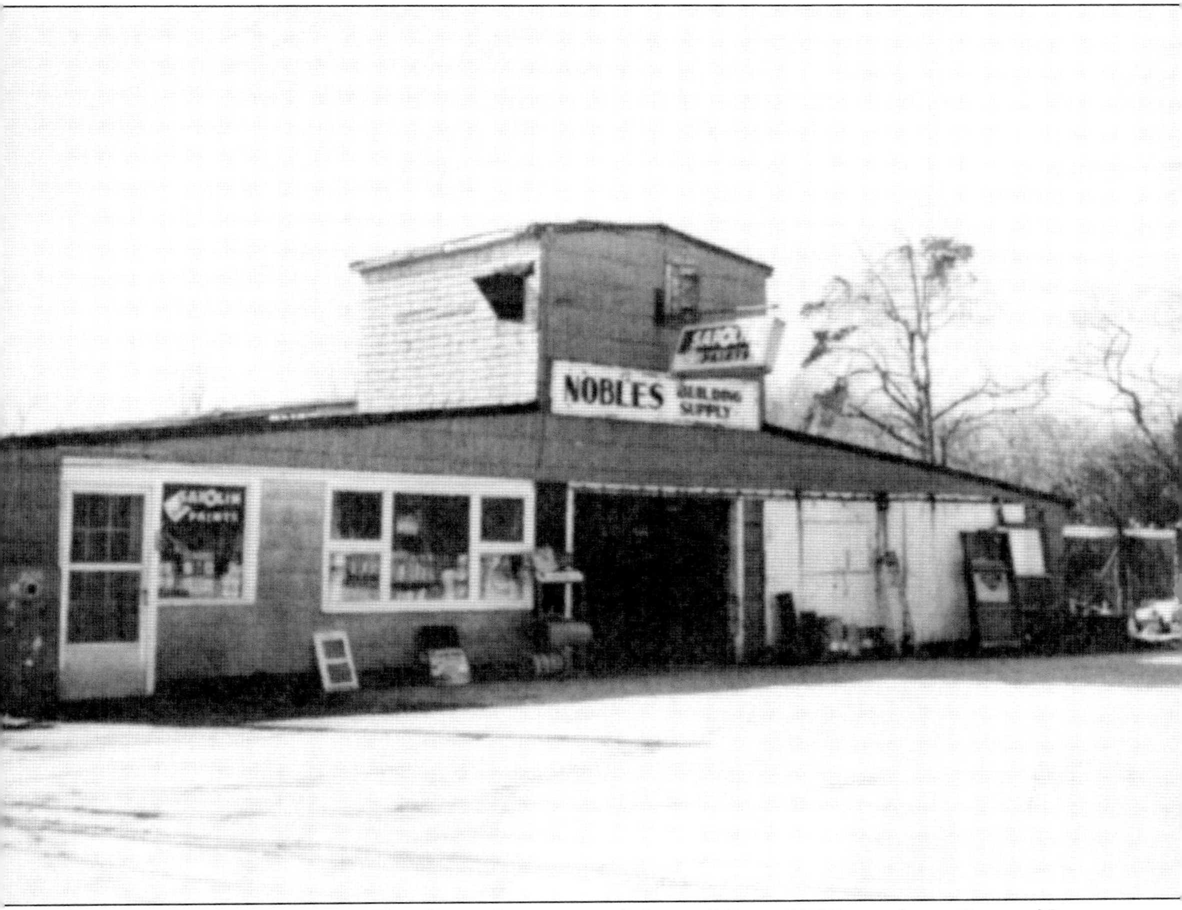

Nobles Building Supply was a family-run business with Irv and Betty Nobles and sons Jim and Joe. It was located behind the former Anderson house on 10 acres of land at 58 Sloop Creek Road. They purchased the property in 1964 from David Veeder and used a previously enclosed chicken coop for the business. Items sold included lumber, building supplies, paint, and hardware. Today, the business site is vacant.

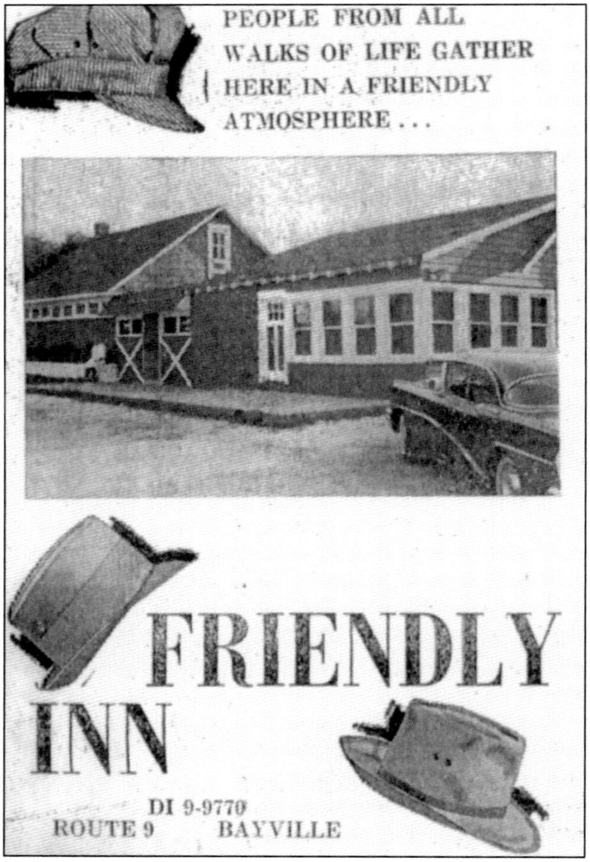

"Little" Joe Coccia, who was also active in public affairs, owned and operated the Friendly Inn, which was a bar and restaurant. The menu was mostly for a light lunch. In the 1970s, the business moved to the Berkeley Plaza Shopping Center as the Friendly Inn Liquors. The old building was demolished, and today, the site is occupied by TD Bank.

Ben and Tom's was a small Shell gas station in front of the old A&P supermarket. The very reasonable gas prices are reflected here in 1965. The station's owner was Jerry Keily, followed by others. It was demolished in 2005. Today, the property is vacant, allowing for a clear view of the present-day Berkeley Plaza Shopping Center.

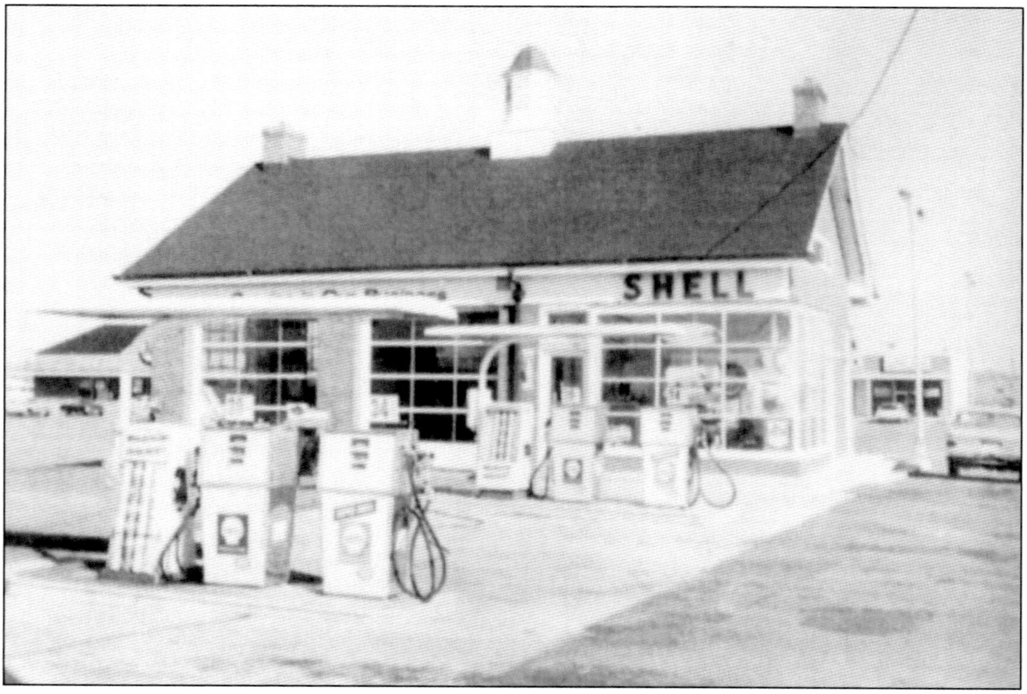

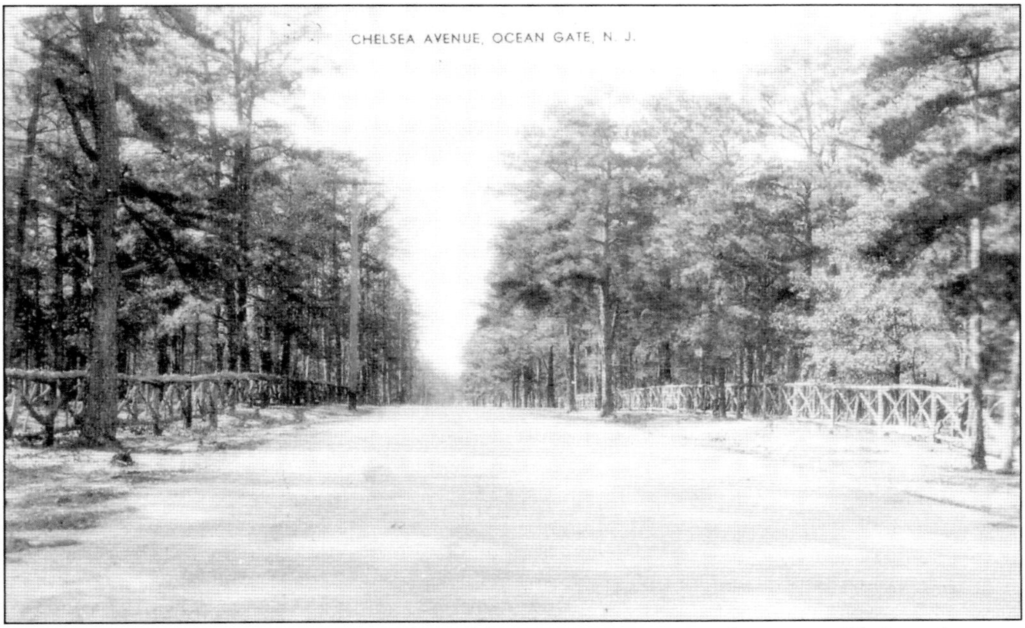

Berkeley Township provided the funds, and by 1922, construction began on Chelsea Avenue. This 1940 view is looking east from Jeffrey's Creek in Ocean Gate. It would be the connection between Ocean Gate and Beachwood along the scenic southern shore of the Toms River. The avenue goes through the Mill Creek, Riverbank, and Quail Run sections of Berkeley Township. Note the artistic craftsmanship in the wooden fence on both sides of the avenue. (Courtesy Larry F. Casele.)

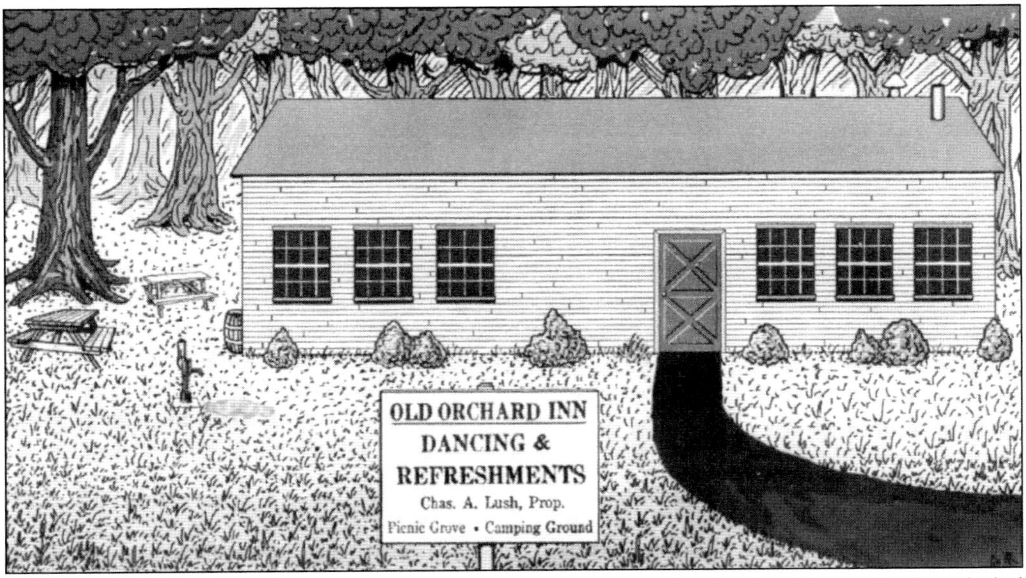

From 1930 to 1948, Charles A. Lush was the proprietor of the Old Orchard Inn, which included both a campground and a picnic grove area. It was known for its Lush's Ice Cream, a big favorite. There was a bar and a large dining area with a dance floor that was popular for banquets and special events. It was sold and then later demolished around 1949. Today, the site is occupied by a Rite Aid Pharmacy. Lush would go on to open another restaurant in Forked River. (Courtesy of Norma Farrow Rush and Bob Coar.)

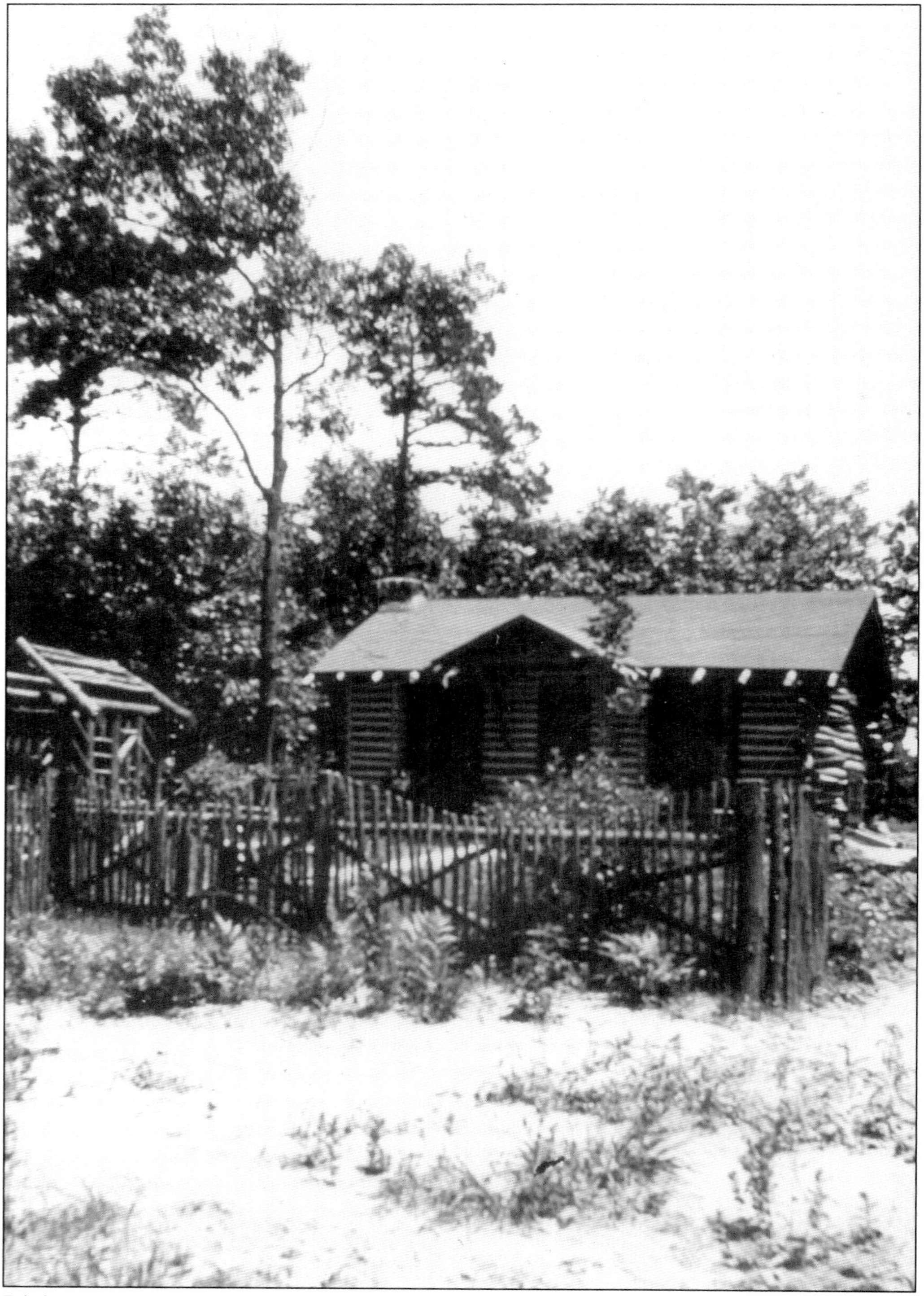

Edith Mulholland's rustic log cabin in 1932 was located where the Baywick Shopping Center is today. The small house was set back off the highway and had a sculpted, pole fence that enclosed the front yard. Many older residential properties, like Edith's, were demolished by the 1980s, allowing for Route 9 to then be rezoned to attract more commercial development.

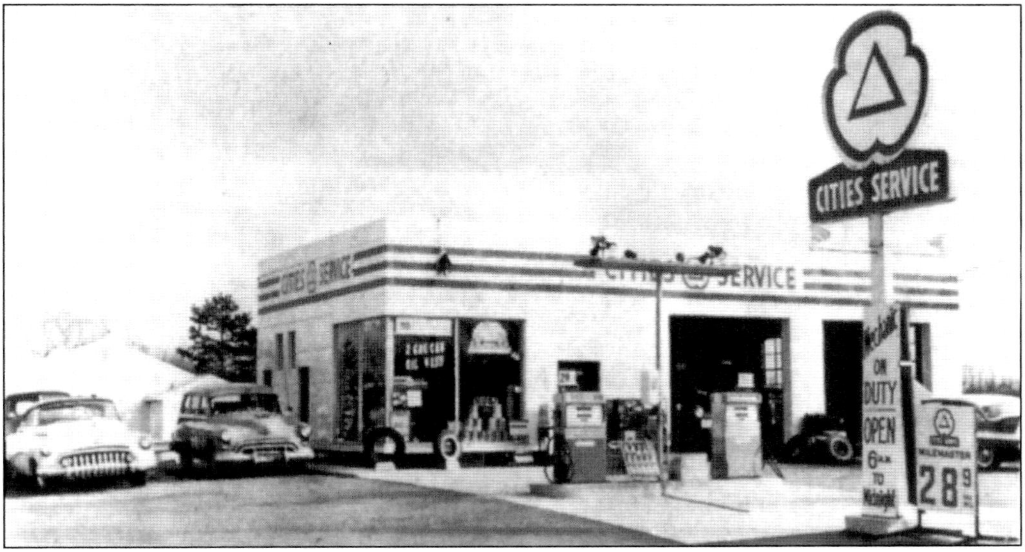

Pat's Service Station was located across from the dinosaur. It was originally owned by Pat Anastasio and S. Housewright. They sold a complete line of Cities Services products and did minor auto repairs. This view captures a look at the classic cars of the era. The price of gas shown here could only be bought in a dream today. Later, it would become Vic's Cities Services with a garage bay added on the right of the station. In the 1970s, the station was sold and the building remodeled to become the Royal Cake Box. Today, the building is shared by the Bayville Deli and Ocean Tactical.

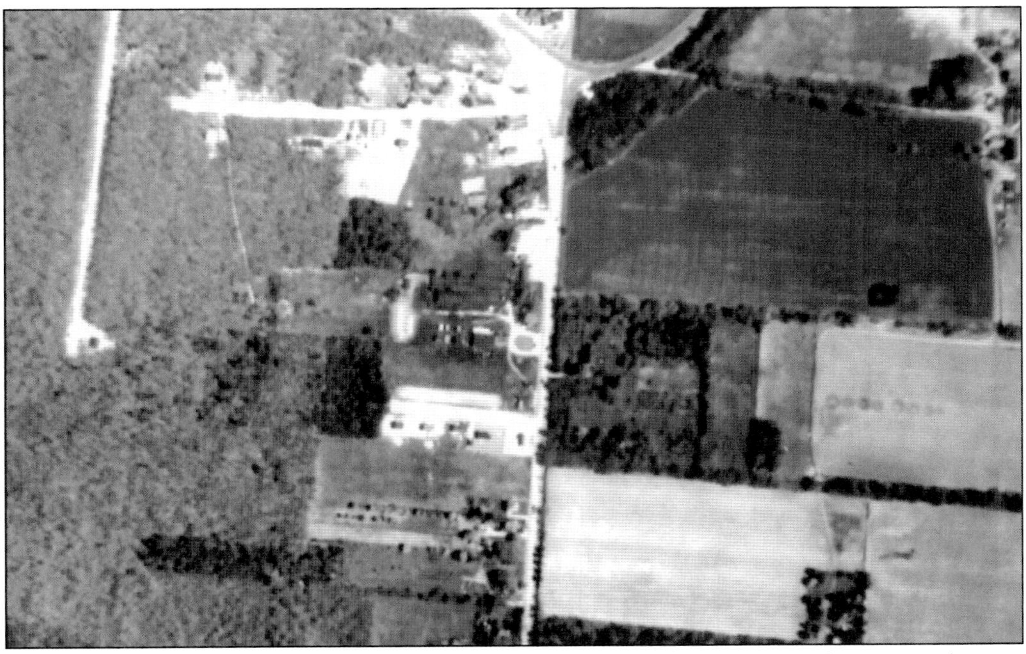

This is a 1955 aerial view of the 378-acre Veeder farm, located at Korman's Corner on the east side of Route 9 and Veeder Lane. The property and the Veeder Homestead are seen here at upper right. The Route 9 landscape was mostly rural with large undeveloped properties. The farmland was sold in 1958, and today, the site is mostly occupied by the Berkeley Plaza Shopping Center and McDonald's. (Courtesy of the Ocean County Library.)

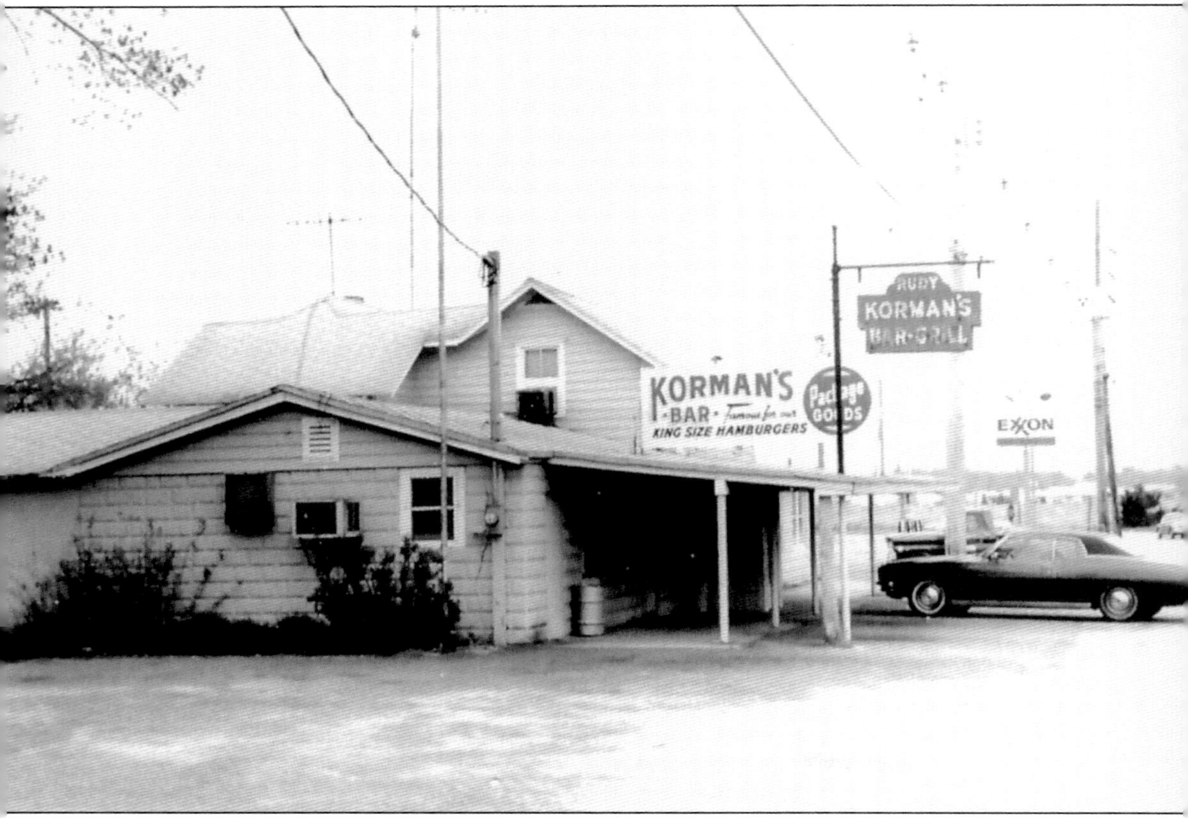

Rudy Korman opened Korman's Pine View Restaurant and Gas Station in 1928 at what was then Mott's corner on Route 9. A picnic grove was on the east side. In 1935, a liquor license was obtained, and it became Korman's Bar and Grill. In 1946, his son Rudy Jr. took over operations. In 1952, the picnic area was replaced with Korman's Exxon Service Station as seen on the right. By the 1950s, Korman's had become the center of entertainment for Bayville's rural residents. The restaurant now included a large dance floor with local bands performing regularly. The grill became "famous for our king size hamburgers." In the 1980s, the site became Vailsburg South and then Saints and Sinners. Today, it is occupied by Ace Outdoor Power.

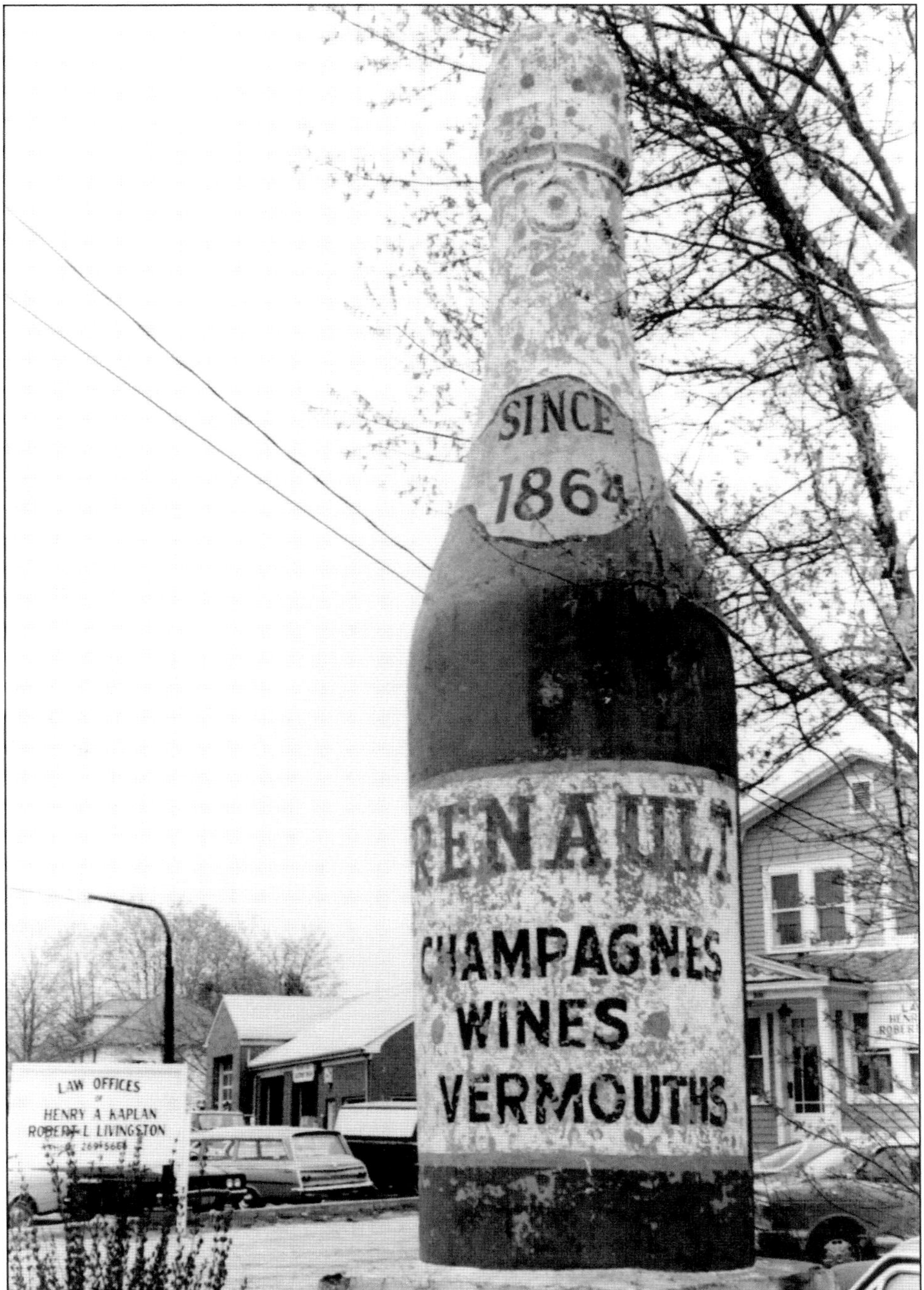

The large concrete champagne bottle, photographed here in 1979, is a Bayville icon. The Renault Winery of Egg Harbor, New Jersey, erected it in 1937. Renault contracted Luigi Portolupi, who had a cement lawn ornament business in Galloway Township, to erect the bottles on rented land. It is 25 feet tall and was originally on the east side of Korman's. Today, it has been moved to the west side of Korman's. In the 1960s, Renault could not maintain the bottles. In 1977, it was repainted to advertise "the Champagne of Propane" Ace bottled gas. In 2001, it took on a more artistic design, painted by John Spreen of Waretown. Today, it has been repainted all white.

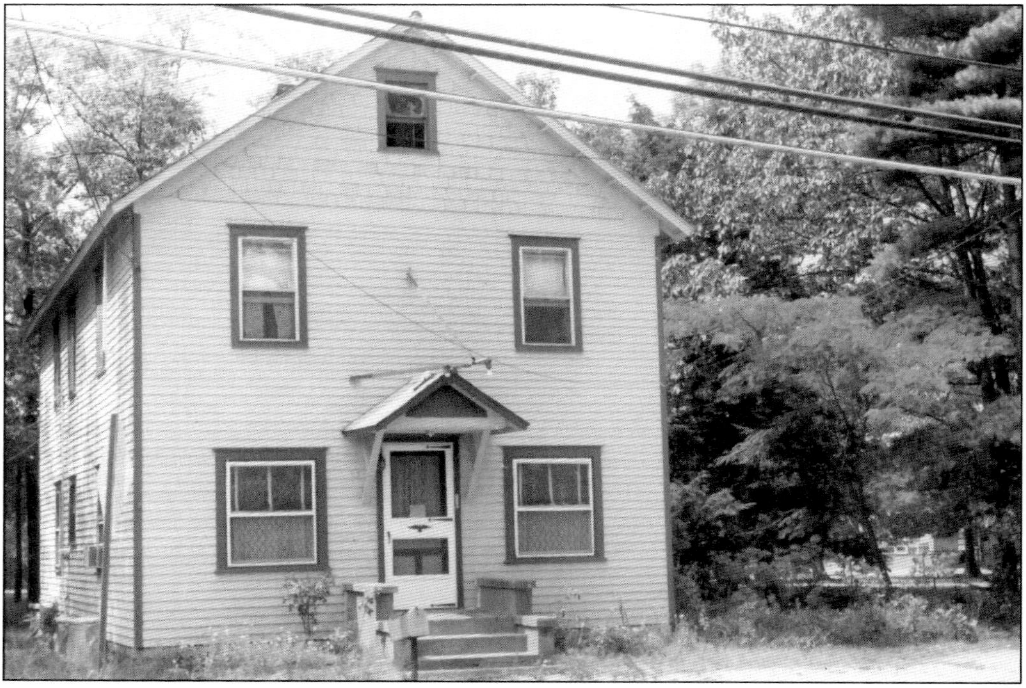

Bruno Nubbe and his wife were the proprietors of the Village Grove, located just south of the Bayville Grade School. Several small rental cabins were available for travelers. The two-story building above had a small store downstairs and the Nubbe's living quarters upstairs. This was truly a mom-and-pop candy store. The lucky schoolchildren could just take a short path to purchase their favorite treats. The author has fond memories of choosing what candy to buy for only small change. The Village Grove cabins, below, could not compete with the arrival of more modern motels. All the buildings were demolished by 1981. Today, the property is occupied by the Pinewood Plaza Shopping Center. (Both, courtesy of New Jersey Historic Preservation Office.)

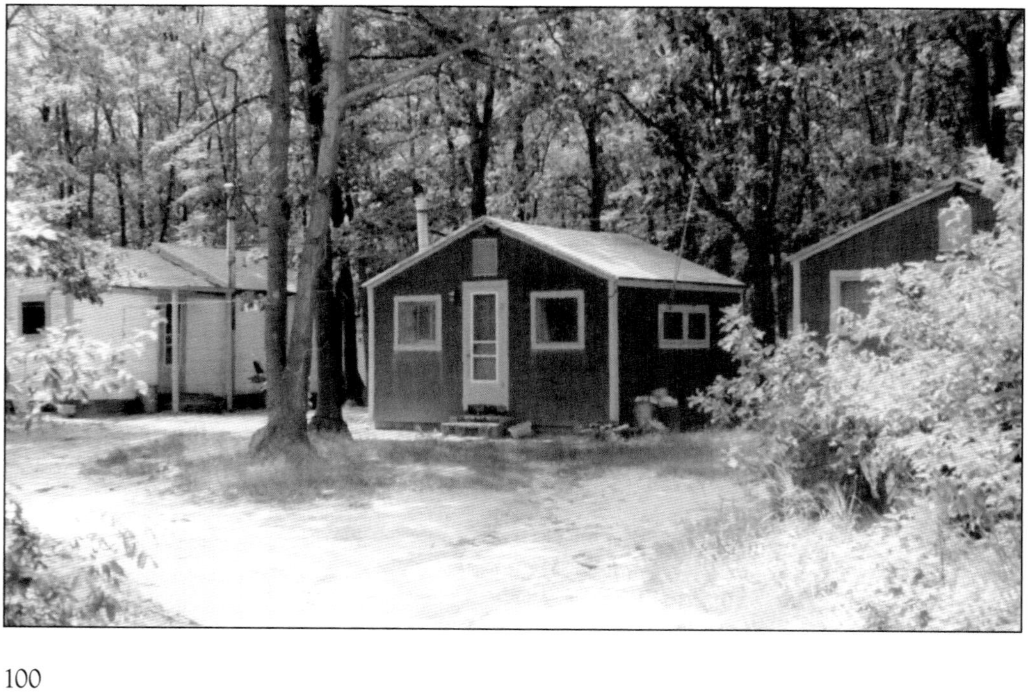

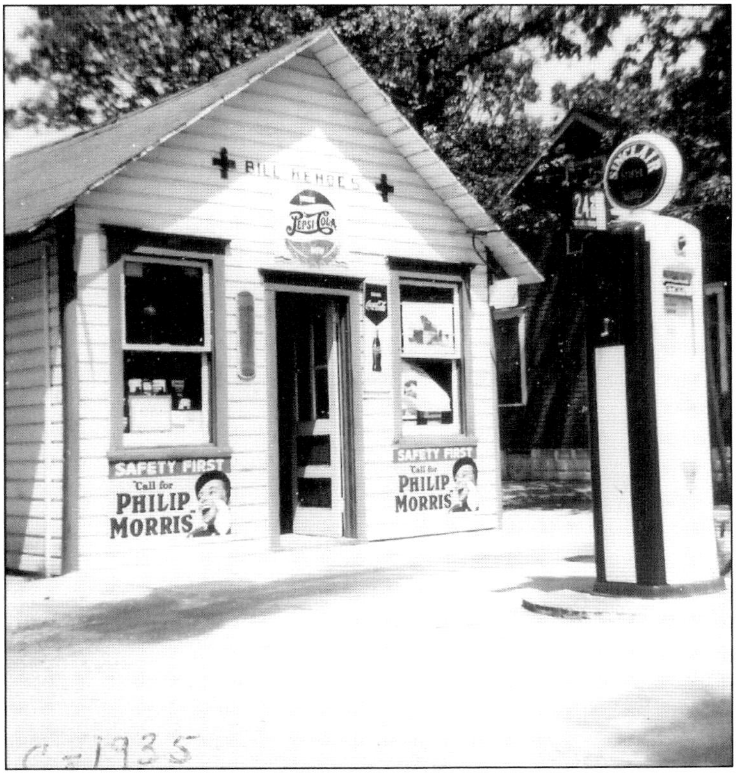

Bill Kehoe's Sinclair gas station was opened in the early 1930s. There was a small garage building in the back. This quaint little store sold motor products, cigarettes, and soft drinks. In 1953, Bill Jr. and his family moved into the house on the right and later rented out the business. In 1989, the buildings were demolished. Today, the Burger King located in the Baywick Shopping Center occupies the site. (Courtesy of Margaret Kehoe.)

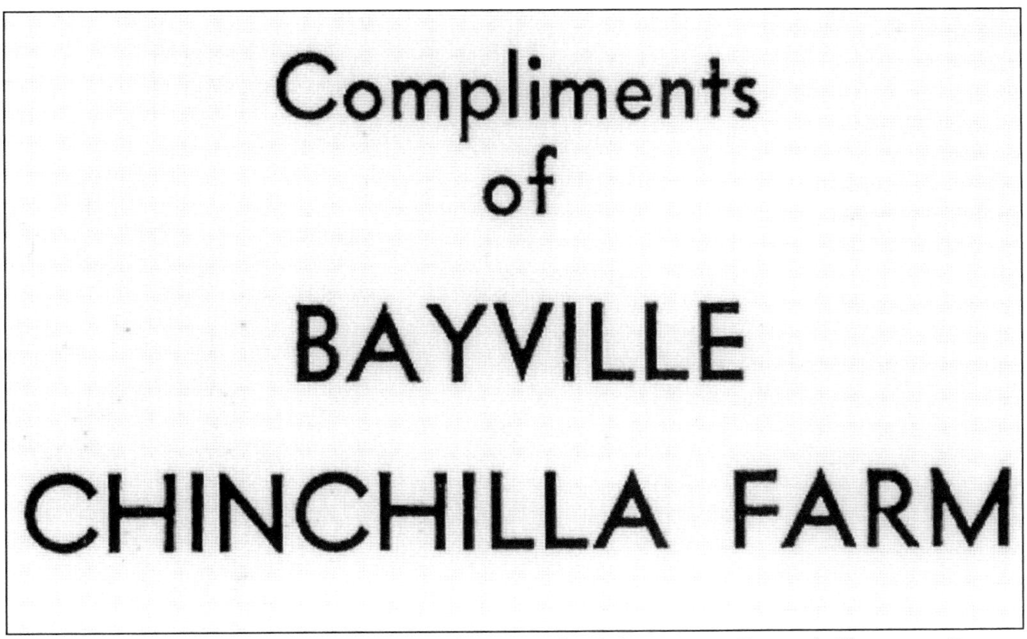

Compliments
of

BAYVILLE

CHINCHILLA FARM

The Bayville Chinchilla Farm was located just north of the current Baywick Shopping Center. The chinchillas were kept in cages in the basement of a Cape Cod–style house, which was also used as the proprietor's residence. These small rodents are indigenous to the Andes but are bred elsewhere for their expensive, soft, pal-gray fur. In the 1950s, raising chinchillas for profit was a popular fad. The house was demolished about 2004.

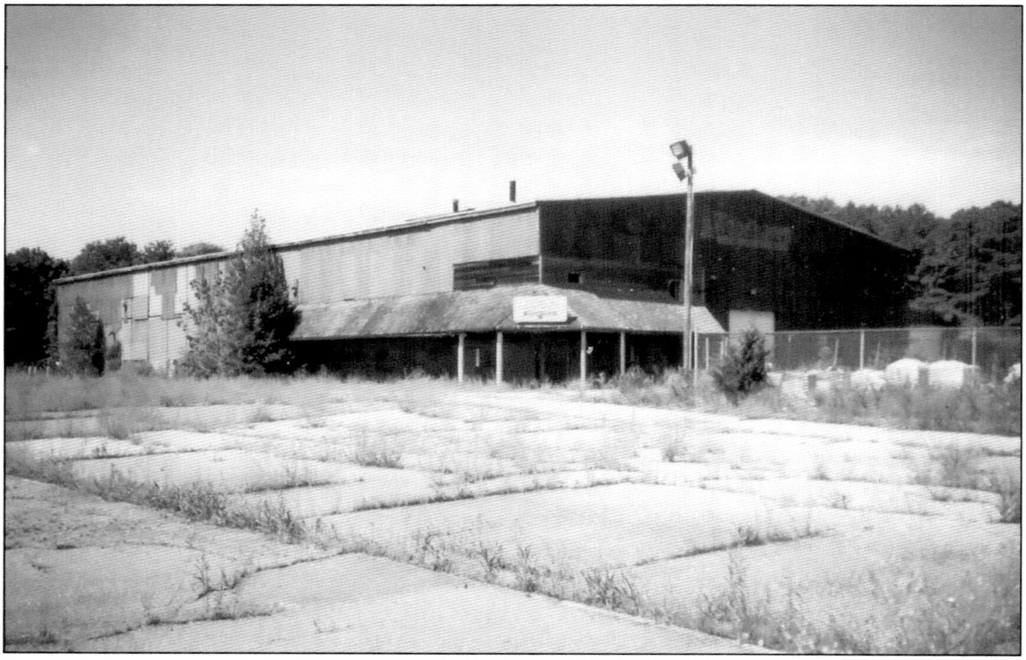

Seacraft Enterprises originally occupied this large building starting in the late 1950s. They provided inside boat storage, motor repairs, and dock service. A sailboat showroom was utilized for penguins, m-scows, prams, and sailing surfboards. Later, it was occupied by the Woodhaven Lumber Company, which sold all types of building products. In 2007, the property was vacated.

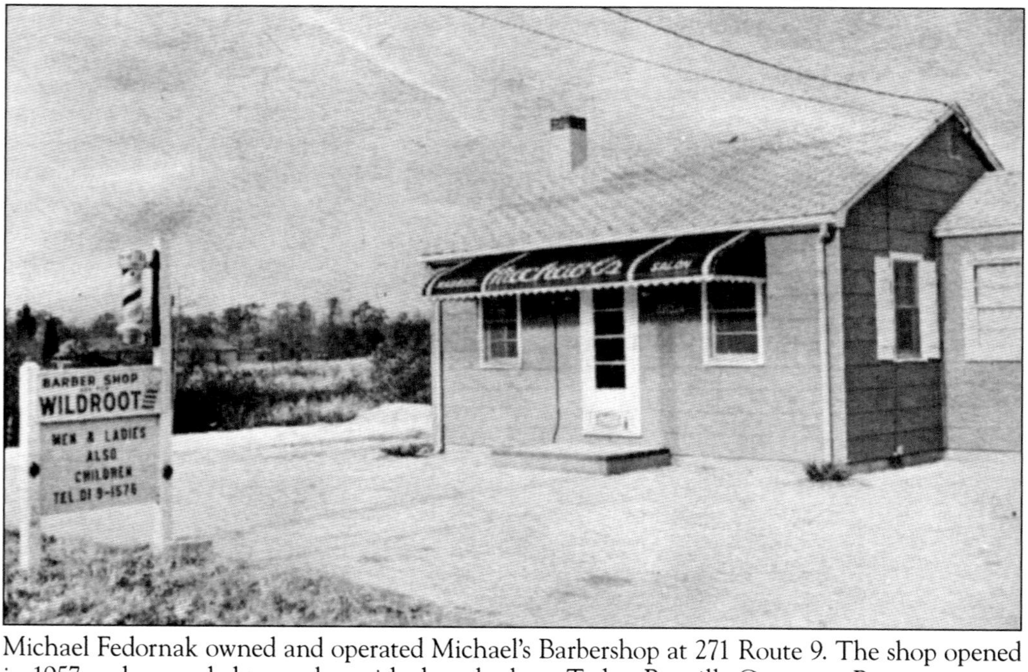

Michael Fedornak owned and operated Michael's Barbershop at 271 Route 9. The shop opened in 1957 and expanded to a salon with three barbers. Today, Bayville Computer Repair occupies the site. Later, Michael and Nick Grazio operated the M&N Barbershop in the A&P Shopping Center. In the 1970s, Michael was also president of the Municipal Complex Dedication Committee and the Berkeley Township Centennial Committee.

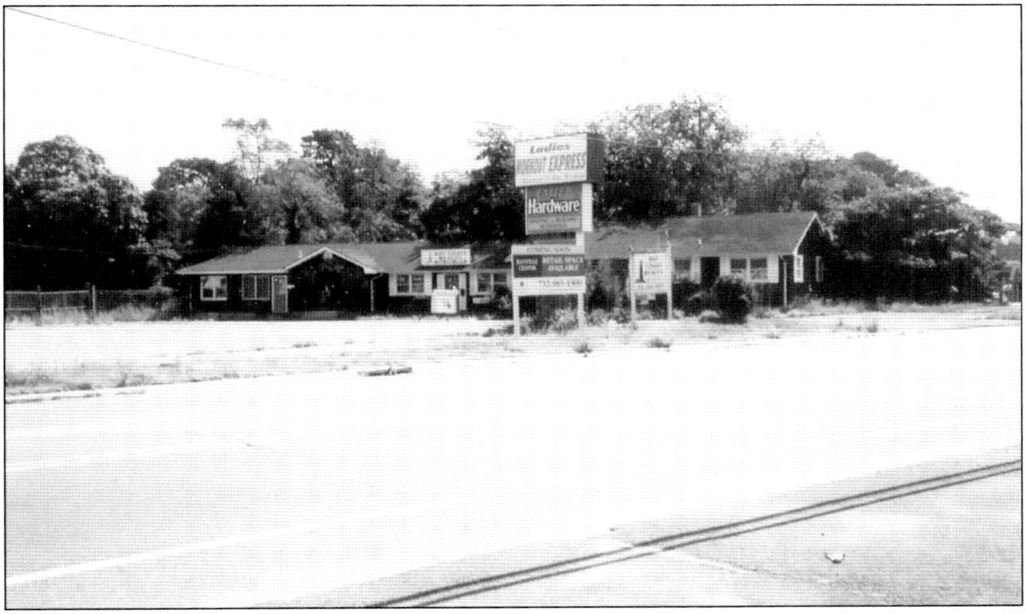

The Iaria Brothers' property at 295 Route 9 consisted of three partial model homes on the right side of the property. Joe Iaria was the president, Nick Iaria did the construction, and Bob Frizell was the salesman. In the 1960s, Iaria Brothers was a dealer for prefabricated-styled Ridge Homes. Bay Coast Realty would later occupy the premises. Today, the buildings remain vacant.

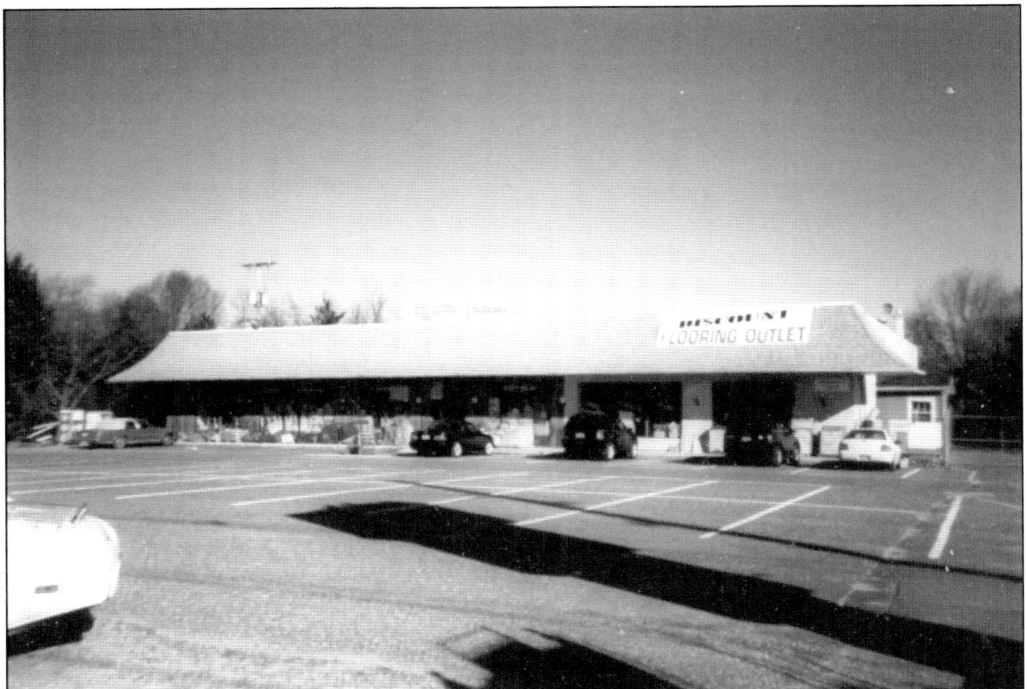

This retail center, started in the early 1960s, was Iaria Brothers United Building and Roofing. The company sold home construction products. Later, the building would host various other stores, including United Hardware, Discount Flooring Outlet, and Ladies Workout Express, which had a pink storefront. Today, the building remains vacant.

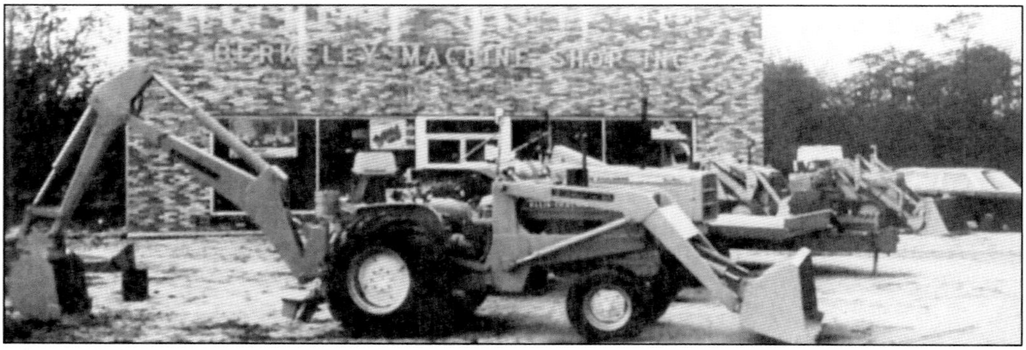

The Berkeley Machine Shop opened in 1959 at 259 Route 9. The owners were Art Newman, who was the namesake for the Berkeley Industrial Park, and Ernie Manuwald, the town mayor in 1962. They advertised that they kept the wheels of progress moving by handling maintenance and repairs for 95 percent of the area's industrial contractors. In 2010, Jersey Rents occupied it and constructed a new facade.

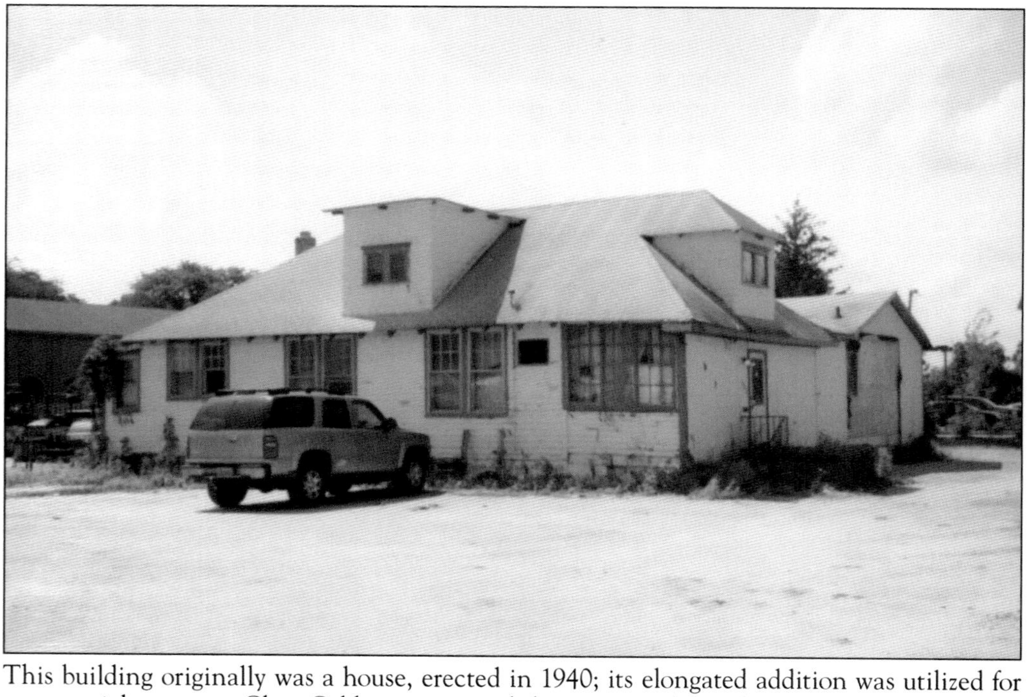

This building originally was a house, erected in 1940; its elongated addition was utilized for commercial purposes. Clear Cablevision owned this property located at 248 Route 9. The first cable company in Bayville was Adelphi, owned by Ernie Manuwald and Arthur Newman. In 2001, it was sold to Comcast. In 2006, the site became Finlay Hyrascreen, and the building was vacant for several years before being demolished in 2014.

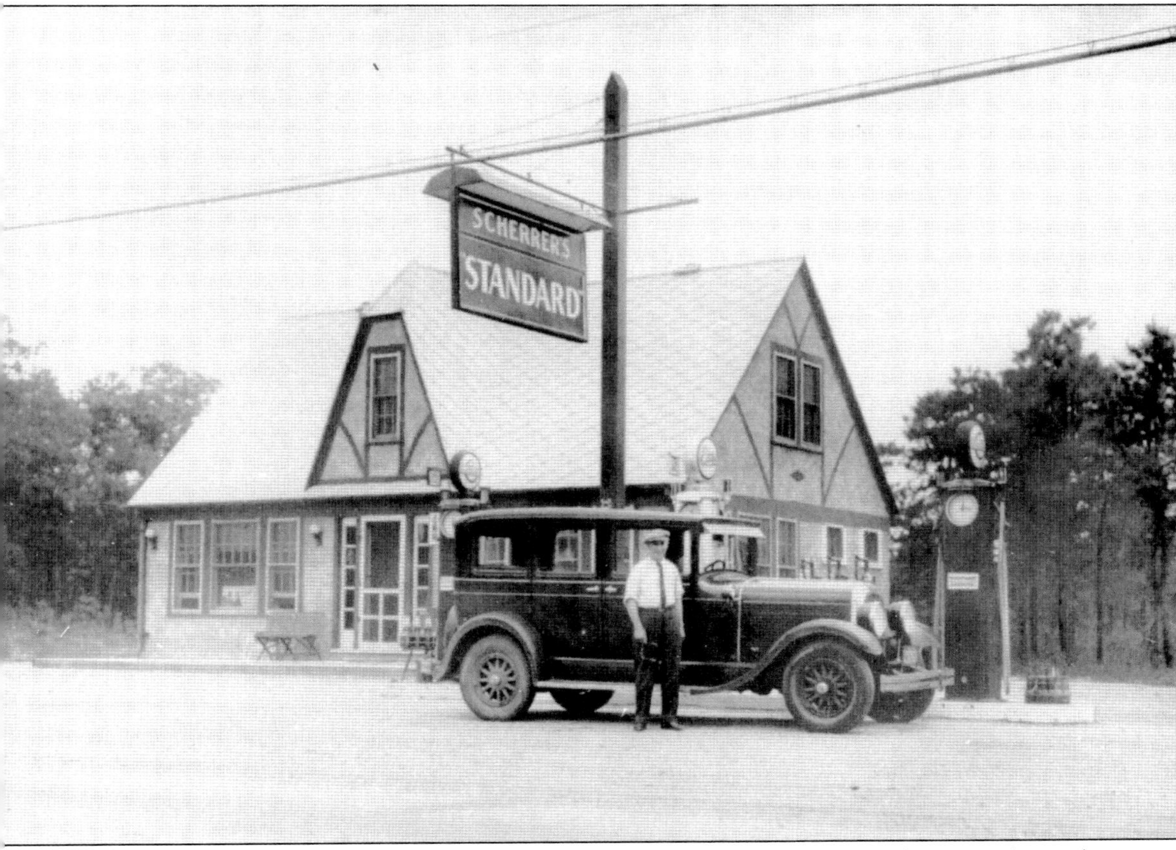

Adam Scherrer is holding his glasses to pose in front of his gas station and luncheonette, located at 267 Route 9, around 1935. The site originally was the Holy Park Rest. The last occupant was Mother Earth Farm Market and Flowers, which was in business until the late 1980s. The building was demolished about 1995, and today, the site remains vacant.

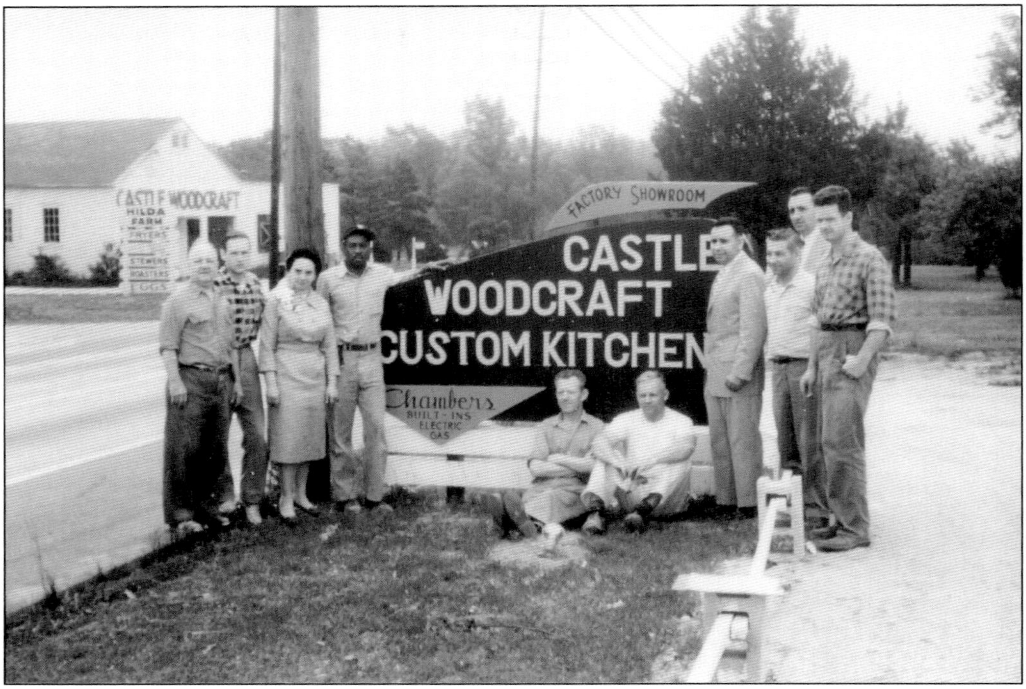

This Castle Woodcraft factory showroom was opened on Route 9 in the early 1950s. Pictured in 1954 with the company's employees are Ruth Guenzburger (owner, third from left), Edward Tolbert (public official, fourth from left), and Heinz Guenzburger (owner, fourth from right). The main factory can be seen across Route 9, with the Hilda Farm sign on the left. (Courtesy of Ernest Guenzburger.)

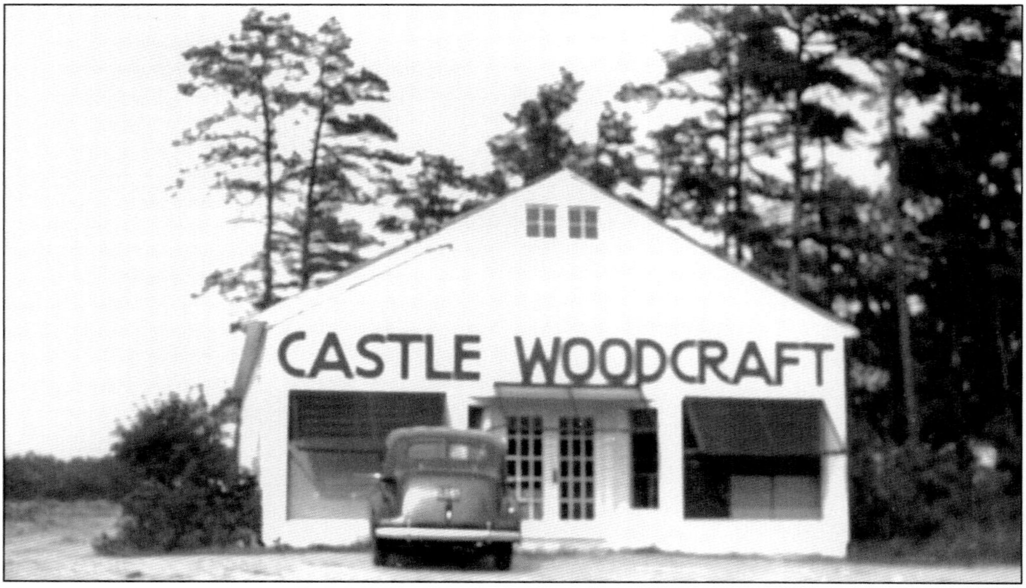

This early Castle Woodcraft factory opened around 1952 across from the company showroom on Route 9. It was expanded and remolded over the years to include a larger factory area, a showroom, and business offices. The original showroom building was then sold. (Courtesy of Ruth Guenzburger.)

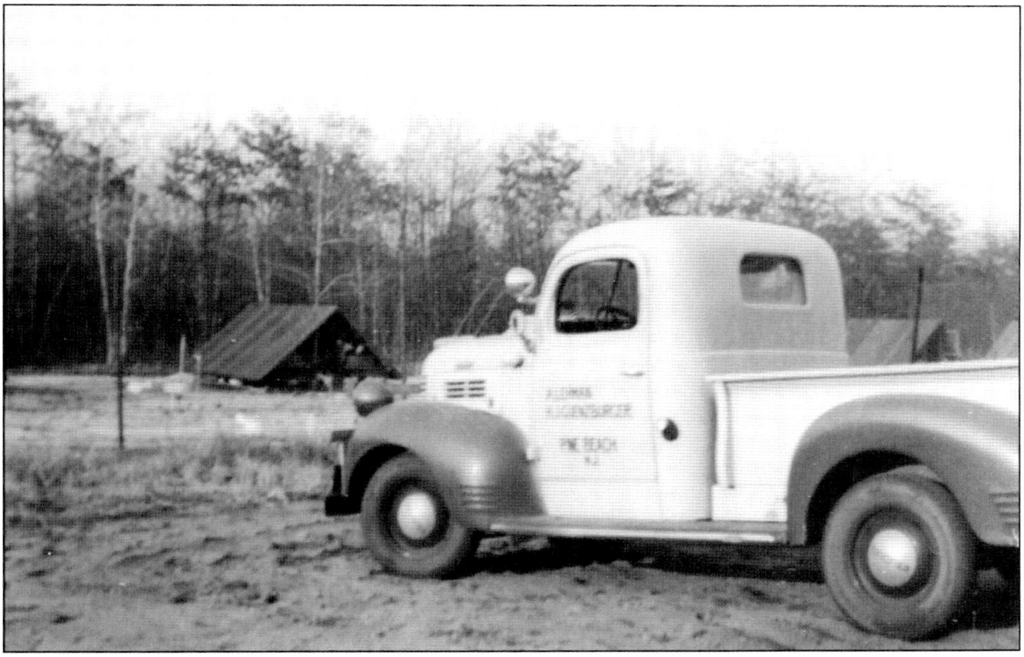

In 1952, Heinz Guenzburger and his sister Lottie (Guenzburger) Lehman would divide the family property on Route 9. Guenzburger would continue making custom kitchen cabinets, and the Lehman family would open Hilda Farm, named after their mother. The farm would sell both eggs and poultry. Guenzburger and his brother-in-law Arnold Lehman shared the same pickup truck, as seen here. Today, other commercial interests occupy the farm property. (Courtesy of Ruth Guenzburger.)

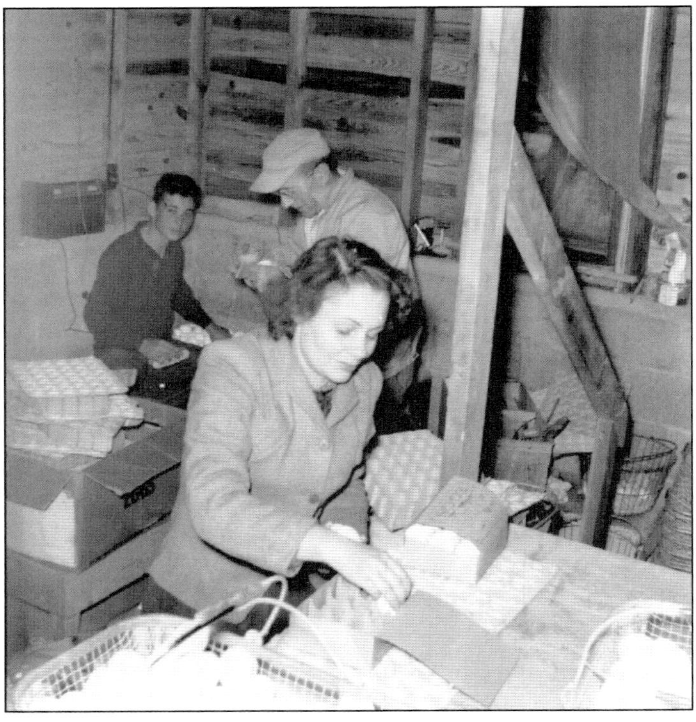

Lottie (Guenzburger) Lehman in 1954 is candling and packing eggs on the family-run Hilda Farm on Route 9. A large radio is available for music to be enjoyed by the workers and maybe even the chickens. Chicken farms were prevalent along Route 9 in the 1940s and 1950s between Toms River and Lakewood. (Courtesy of Ruth Guenzburger.)

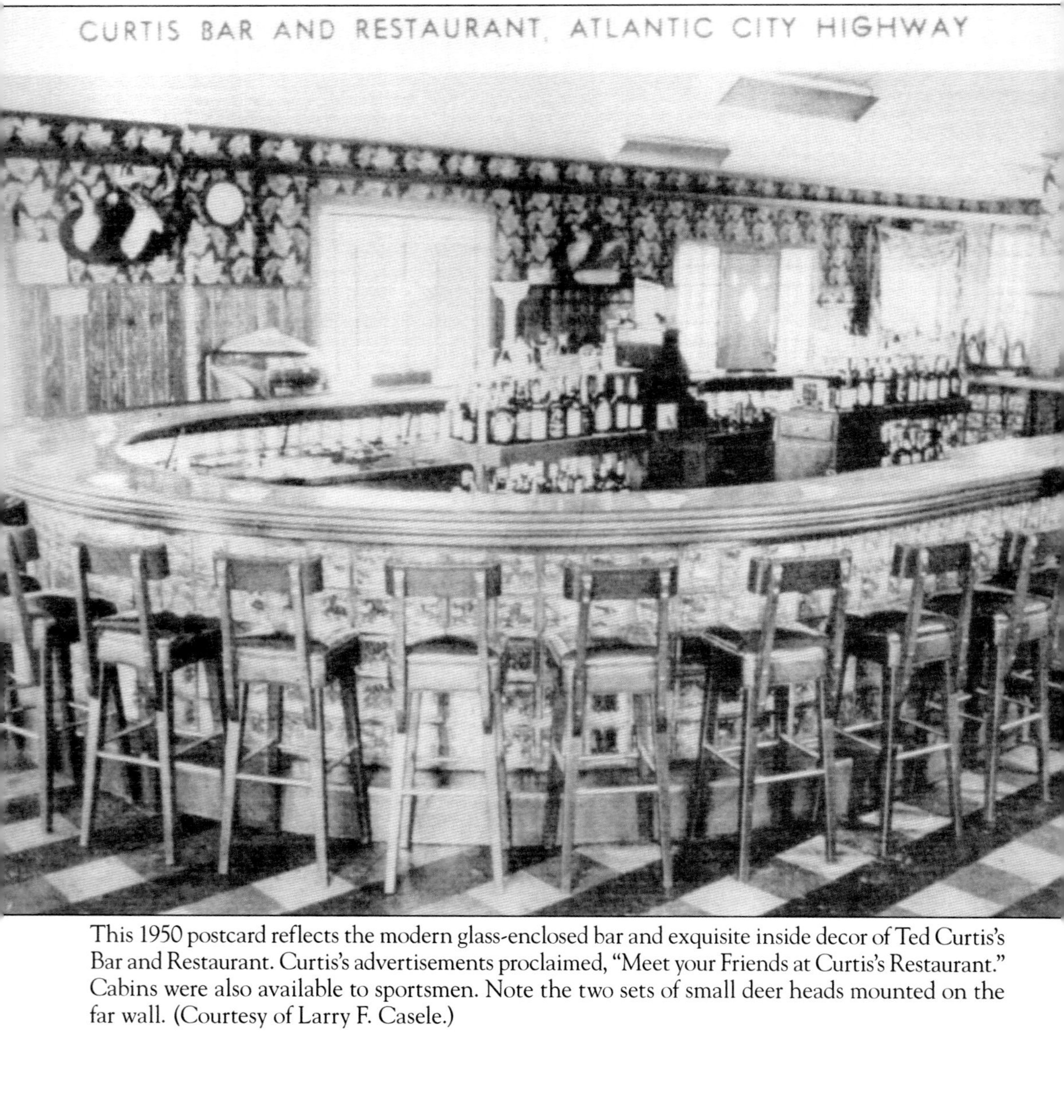

This 1950 postcard reflects the modern glass-enclosed bar and exquisite inside decor of Ted Curtis's Bar and Restaurant. Curtis's advertisements proclaimed, "Meet your Friends at Curtis's Restaurant." Cabins were also available to sportsmen. Note the two sets of small deer heads mounted on the far wall. (Courtesy of Larry F. Casele.)

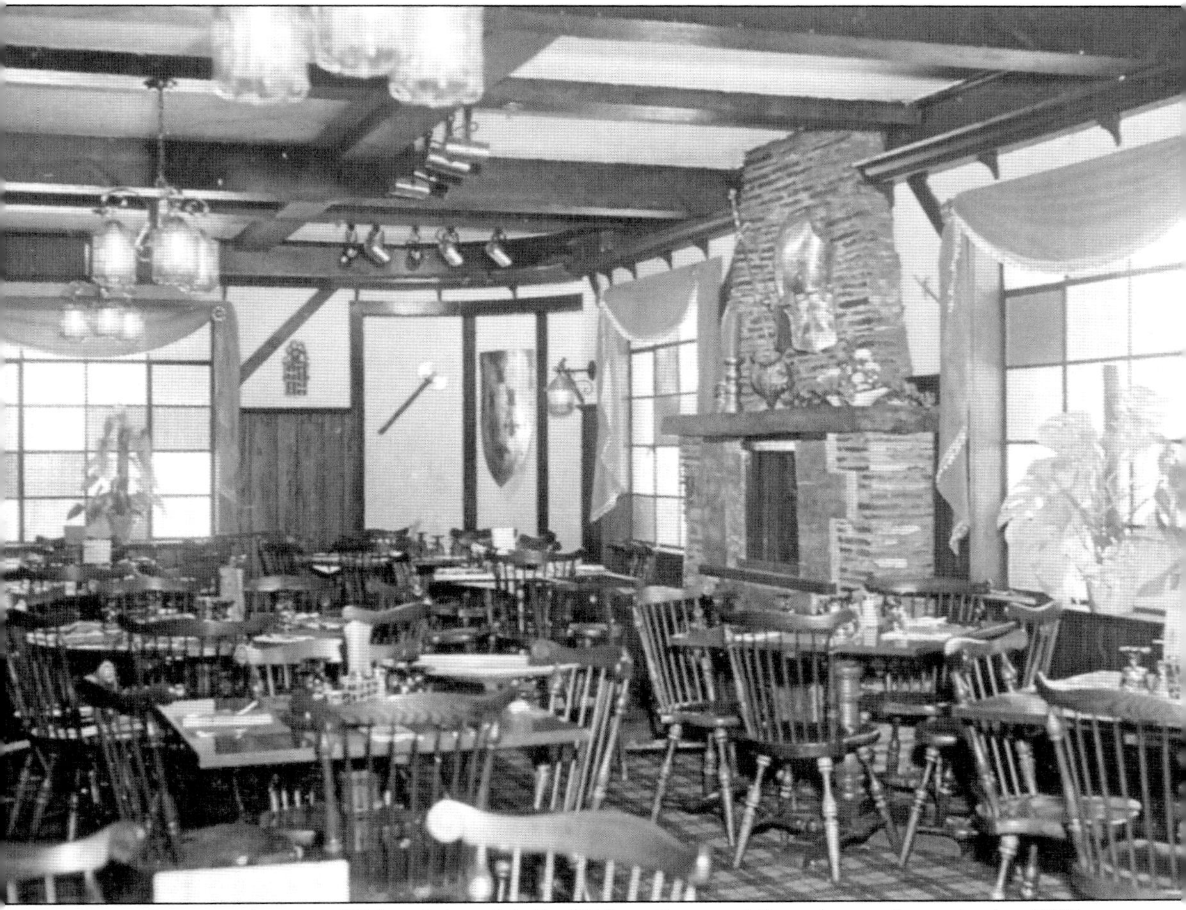

The Village Inn became Walter Schmidt's Sir Walters Pint and Pound, seen here, in the 1960s and offered "a new dining experience." It was styled as an old English castle motif with brightly colored pennants flying high from the rooftop. The dining area, as displayed here, was decorated with armor and weaponry pertaining to the middle ages. It also had an large fireplace original to the structure. Entertainment was offered nightly at the piano bar in the cocktail lounge. This unique restaurant closed in the 1970s. In 1985, C.B. Huntington's opened, and in 1989, Blackbeard's Cave Amusement Park was added adjacent to the restaurant. Both remain popular today.

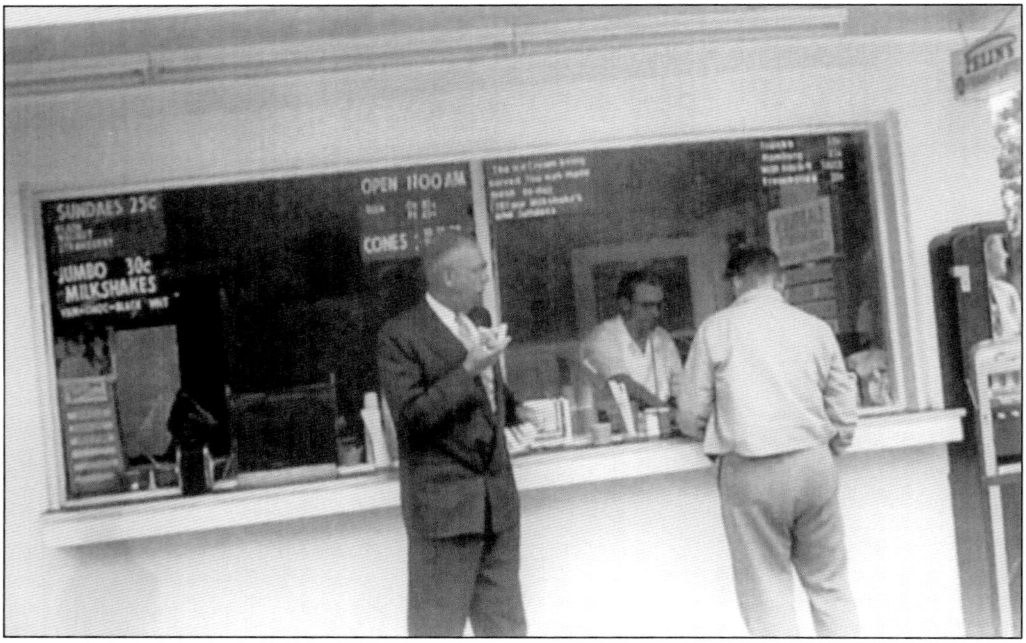

Walter Clifton Ladd, seen here behind the counter, was the proprietor of Laddies Ice Cream, located just north of today's Blackbeard's Cave Amusement Park. The small white stand opened in 1952. A Laddies milk shake made with homemade ice cream on a warm summer's night was always enjoyable and was only 30¢. In 1962, Laddies became Grady's Charpit, which was later demolished in the 1980s. Today, the site remains vacant. (Courtesy of Garry Castaldi and Jean Baldwin.)

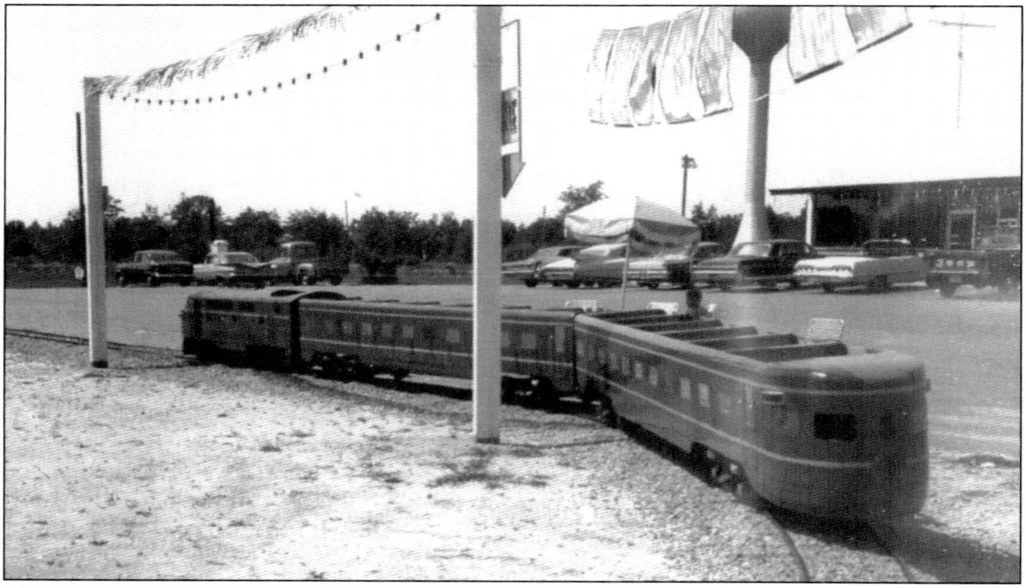

The Mergner family set up these small children's rides on Route 9 at Grady's Char Pit, right, in 1967. These rides would later be moved to the Seaside Boardwalk. This location was previously home to Laddie's Ice Cream Stand. Grady's Char Pit was owned by Jimmie Johnson, who also owned the Beachwood Shopping Center. The restaurant was demolished in the mid-1980s, and today, the site remains vacant. Note the Johnson Water Company Tower, right of center, which is still standing today. (Courtesy of Ken Mergner.)

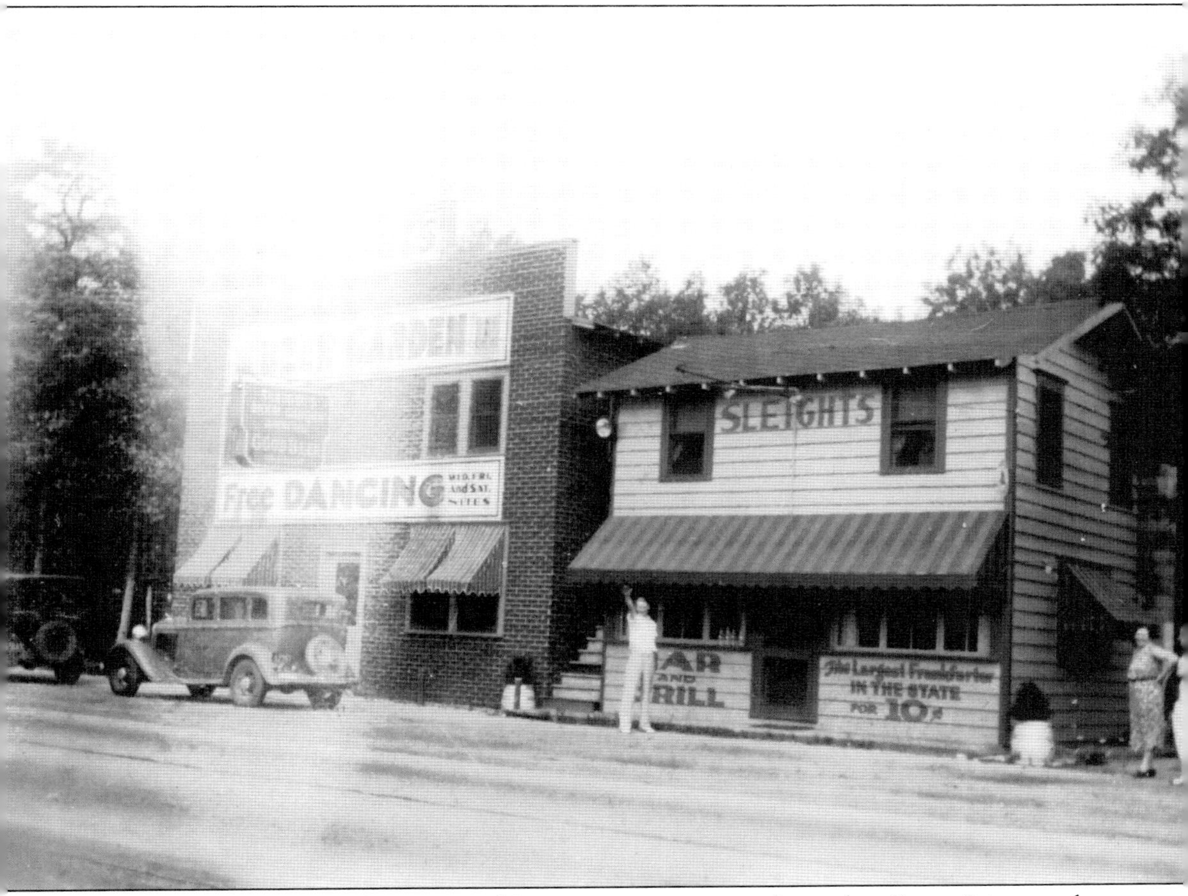

In the 1920s, Sleight's Luncheonette and Sunoco gas station were located on Route 9, just south of Pine Beach. During Prohibition, it was called the "shooting gallery," as William Sleight was rumored to make his own whiskey at that time. In the 1930s, Sleight's Beer Garden replaced the earlier shooting gallery in a new two-story brick building, with a staircase on the side. "Free Dancing" is now offered downstairs in the Royal Palm Room. William Sleight is pictured beckoning people to try his famous "foot-long" hot dogs—"the largest frankfurter in the state for 10¢." Later, it would become Mack and Bob's. The owners were Bernard "Tap" Mack with wife Edith and Bob Hummel with wife Gertrude Corrigan Hummel. The building has also been home to Edith Mack's Bar and Grille, Settimio's Restorante, Beach House Diner, Time to Dine, and Kokomos. (Courtesy of Mary Corrigan.)

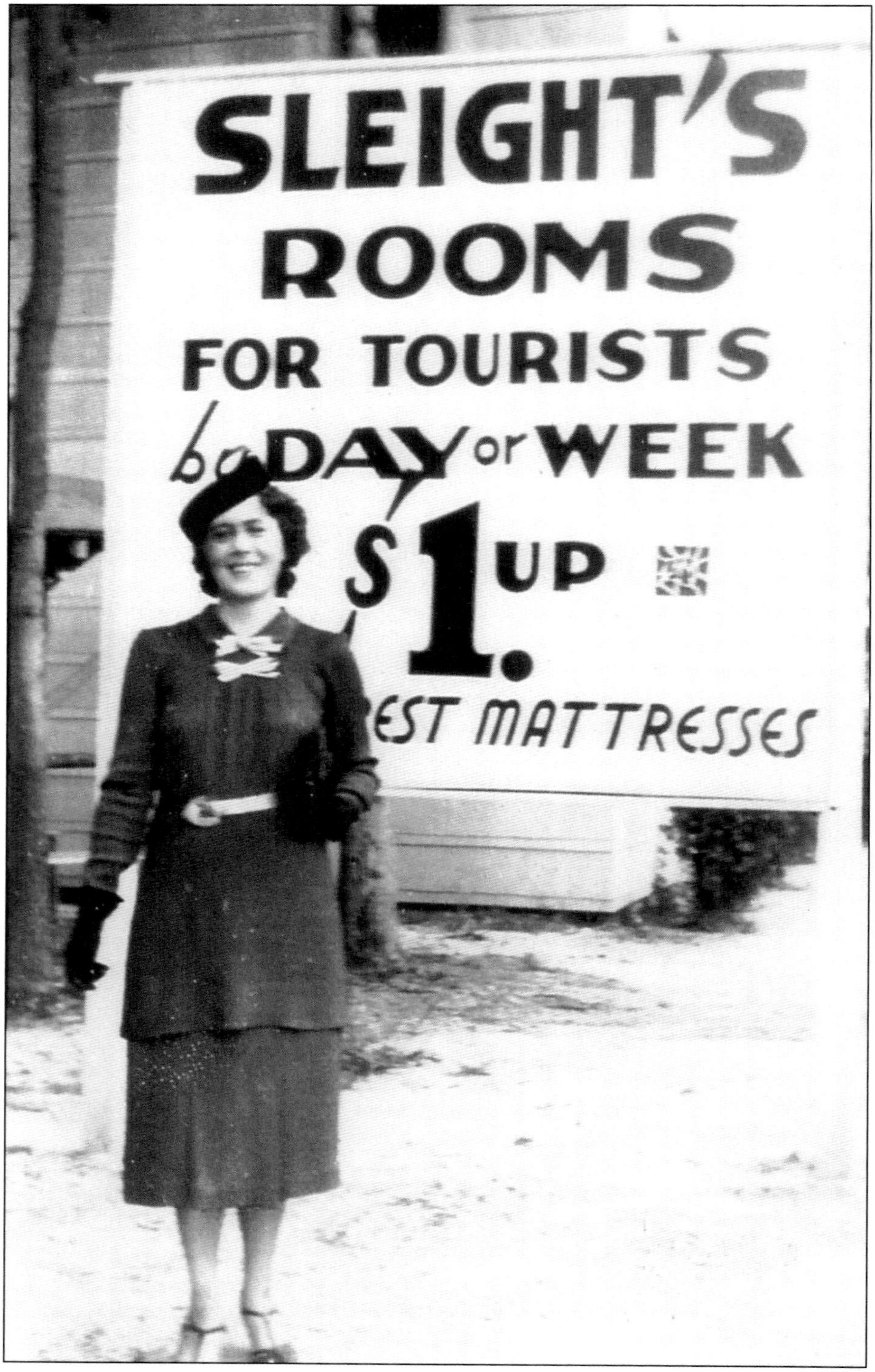

Madelyn Sleight is helping to promote the room rentals for daily or weekly rates starting at $1 a night. All the rooms had "finest mattresses." Sleight's was popular with the many New York tourists who were visiting Atlantic City or vacationing at the Bayville shore. (Courtesy of Mary Corrigan.)

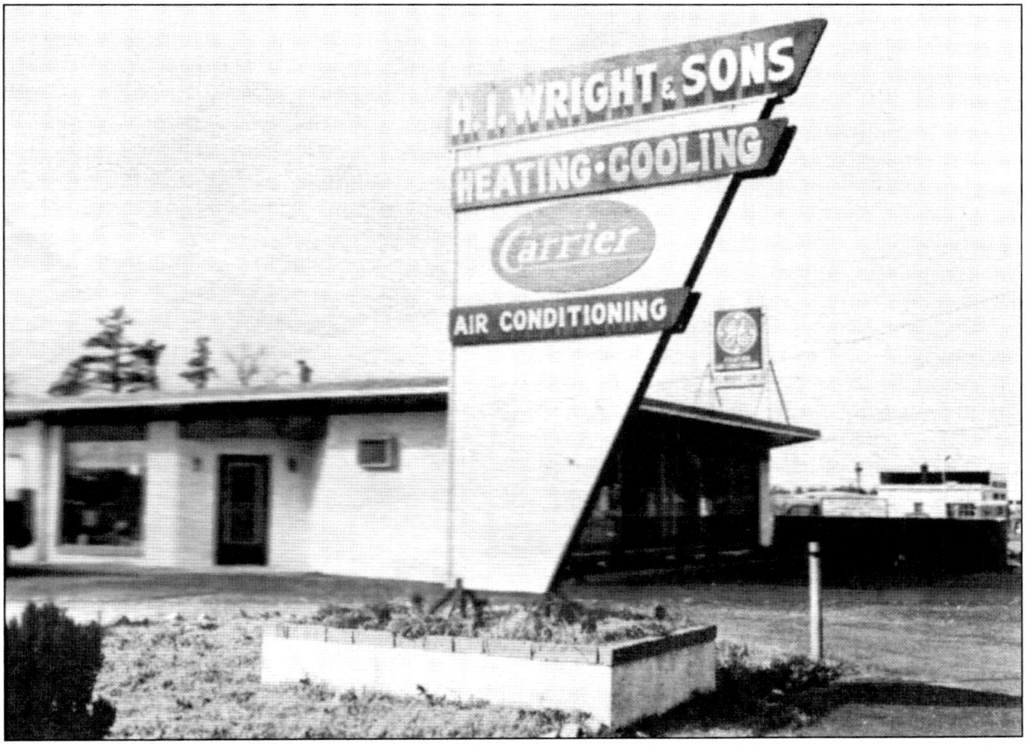

In the mid-1930s, Herbert and Violet Wright began a plumbing and heating business in their Holly Park home. By 1947, the company name became H.I. Wright and Sons when their five sons, Bert, Ed, Cliff, Jim, and Bill, entered the business. This c. 1950 building at Gladney Avenue and Route 9 was utilized for four decades by four generations of the Wright family. Today, Berkeley Auto Body occupies it.

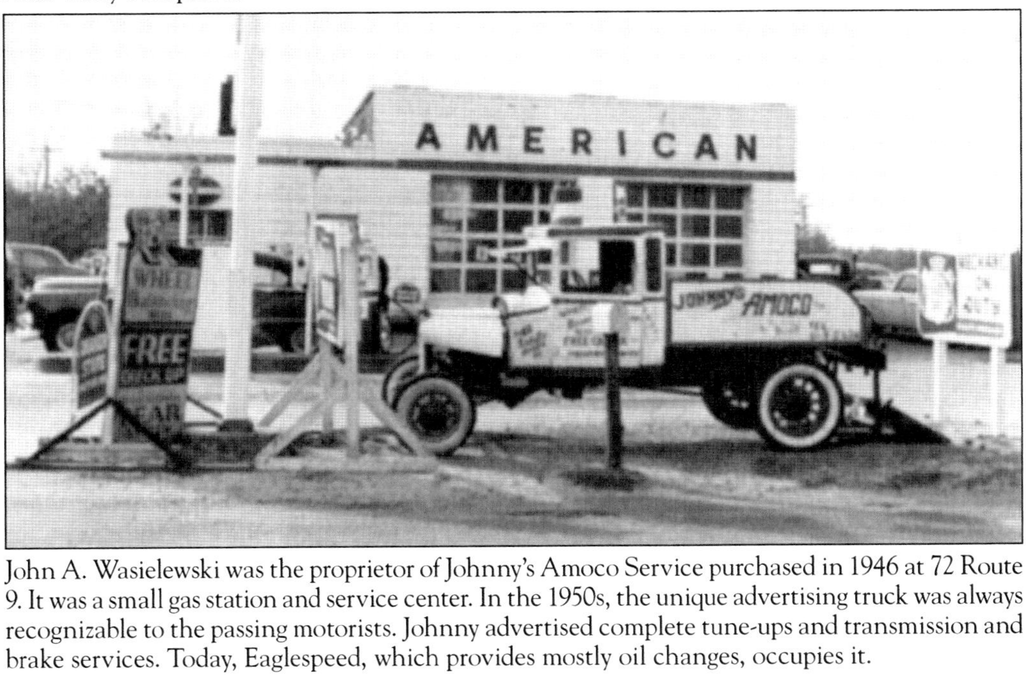

John A. Wasielewski was the proprietor of Johnny's Amoco Service purchased in 1946 at 72 Route 9. It was a small gas station and service center. In the 1950s, the unique advertising truck was always recognizable to the passing motorists. Johnny advertised complete tune-ups and transmission and brake services. Today, Eaglespeed, which provides mostly oil changes, occupies it.

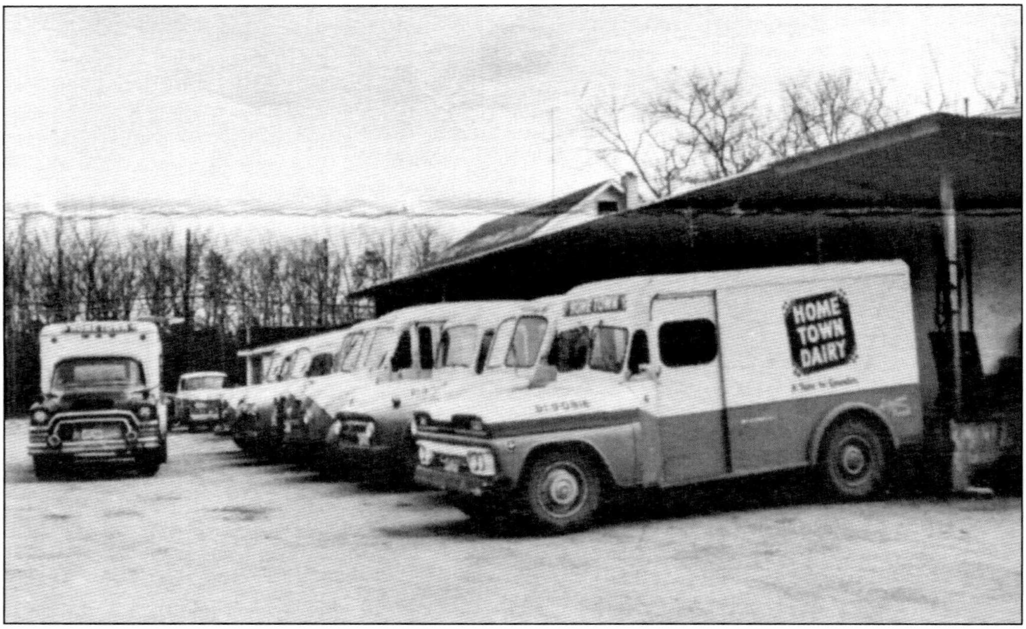

In 1946, Robert W. Davis founded Home Town Dairy on Route 9 with his two brothers, William R. Davis and Burton K. Davis. Robert initially made home deliveries by trading in his Plymouth for a new half-ton Ford pickup truck. In 1997, his grandson Robert A. Davis took over the business. Home Town Dairy served Ocean, Monmouth, Atlantic, and Burlington Counties. They delivered to 140 schools, 12 casinos, and various 7-Eleven stores. There were 3 buildings, 36 employees, and 20 vehicles. The property and buildings have remained basically unchanged since the business began. Below, in August 2011, a foreboding sale sign is revealed. The property was sold in 2012 after "Serving the Jersey Shore with Milk" for 66 years. Now, Home Town Dairy will serve no more. Today, Unique Photo occupies it.

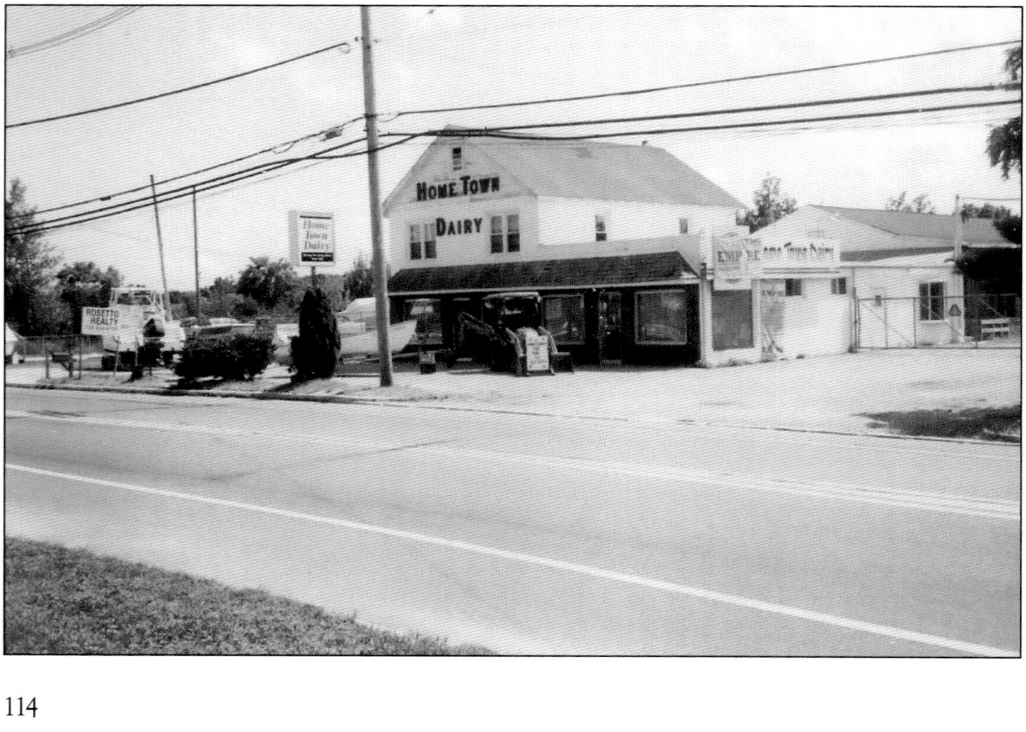

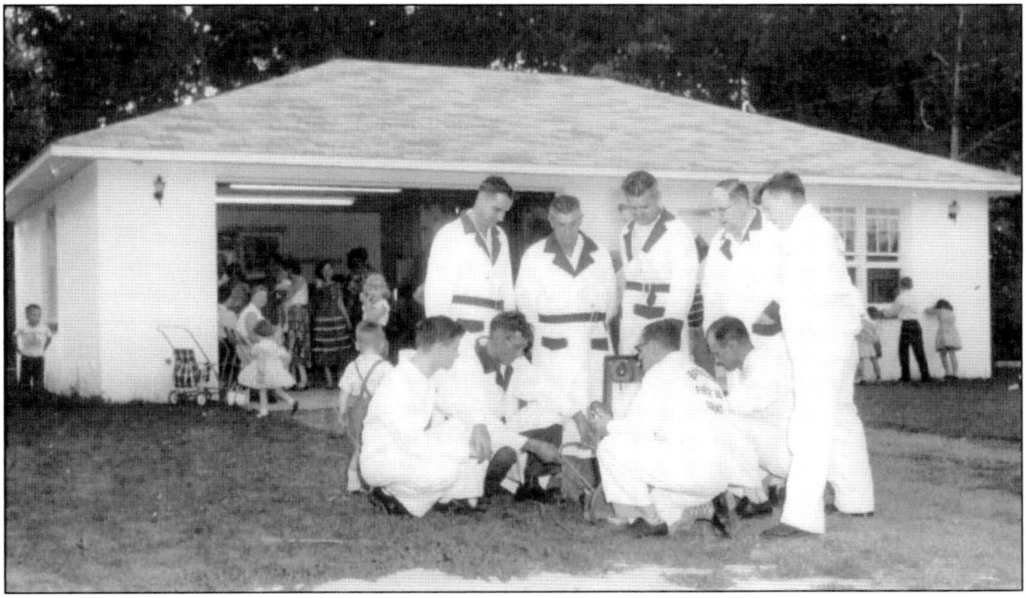

The Bayville First Aide Squad was founded in 1954 when a young boy was injured in a car accident and friends had to drive him to the hospital. This incident helped to start the squad. Clifford Wright was a founding member. Today, there are four squads in Bayville. Shown here in 1956, are members, from left to right, (kneeling) Cliff Wright, Charles Bunnell Sr., Bill Miller, and Guy Chamberlain; (standing) Ernest Manuwald, Clint Worth, Joe O'Neil, Fred Roe, and Jack Leddy. Note the small children playing hide-and-seek in the background.

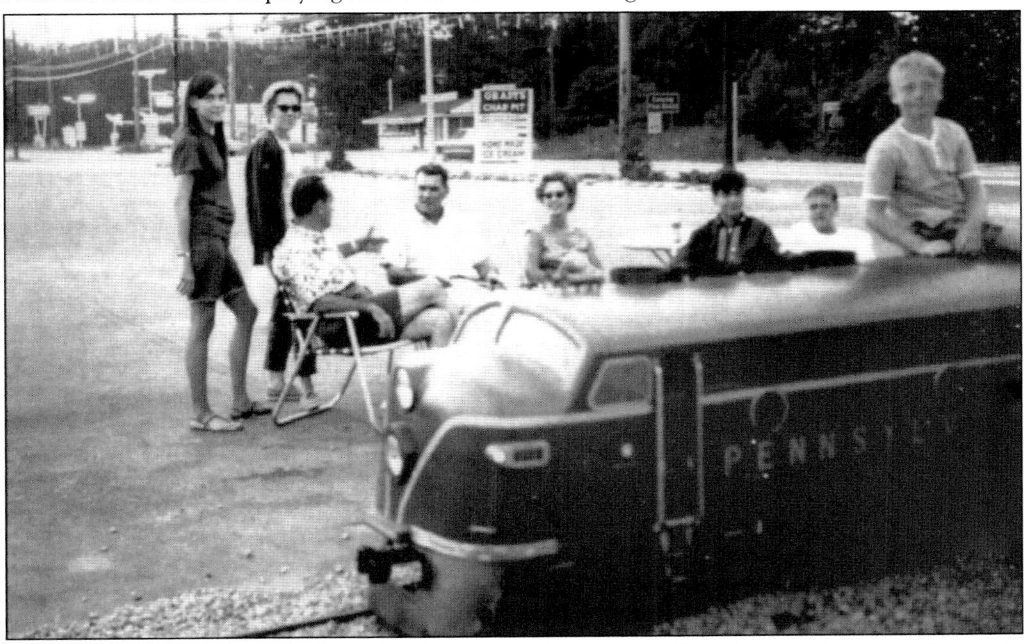

These families enjoyed attending the children's rides near the Beachwood Shopping Center in the mid-1960s. This view depicts a mostly rural background along Route 9. Mother Hubbard's restaurant is shown behind the Grady's Char Pit sign at top center. The proprietor was Eugenia Hubbard, who would serve a light lunch and dinner. This property was sold in 1968 and today is occupied by New Jersey Outboards. (Courtesy of Ken Mergner.)

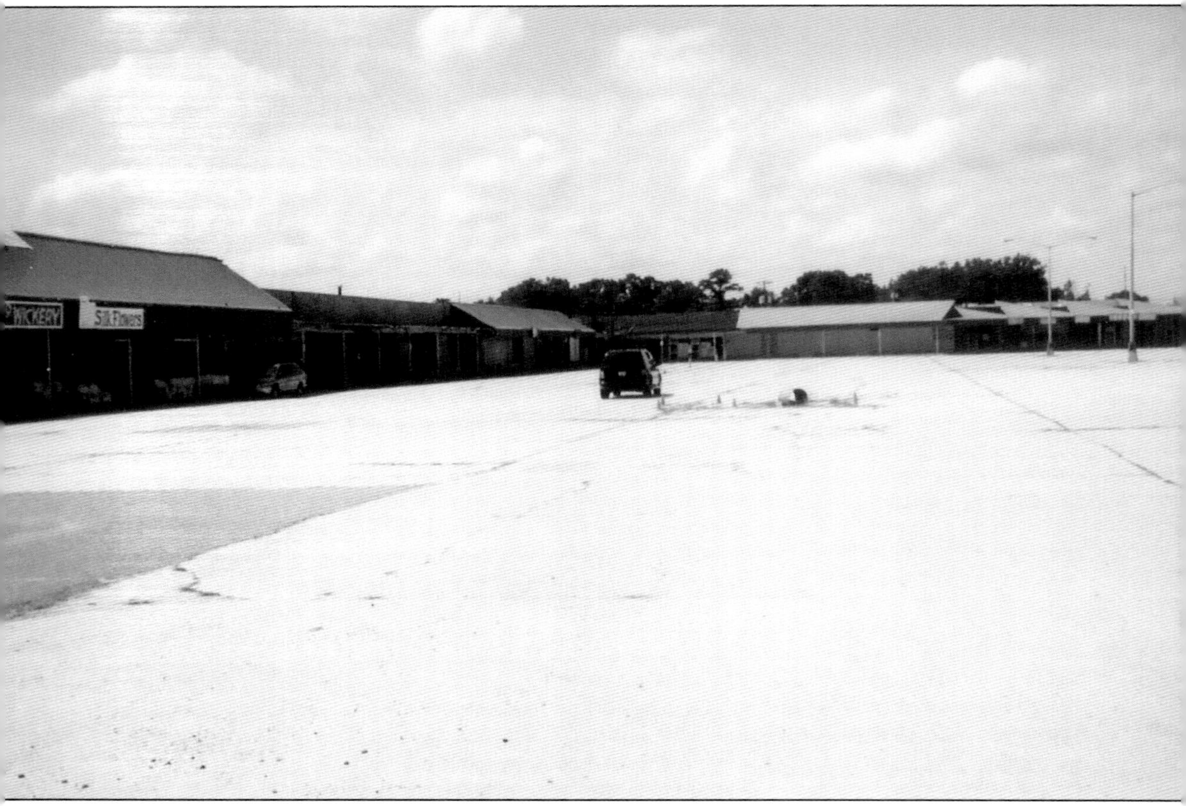

Jimmy Johnson owned and managed the Beachwood Plaza Shopping Center and opened it to much celebration in 1959. By the late 1960s, it had attracted about 20 popular stores, including Woolworths, Food Fair, Thrift Drugs, Lizabeth Brennan, Eagle Lumber, Berkeley Lanes Bowling Alley, and the Club Plaza. This site has deteriorated in recent years, and on August 6, 2011, the Wickery store on the left was the last active business. Johnson, a former blimp pilot, was originally from the South where he had many real estate investments. Later, in Bayville, he would own the Johnson Lumber Company, an asphalt plant, a water company, and an interest in the First National Bank of Toms River. He was elected to a local school board and in one election ran for governor of New Jersey. Today, the shopping center is vacant and fenced off from the public. Berkeley Township has had plans for the property to become the future town center.

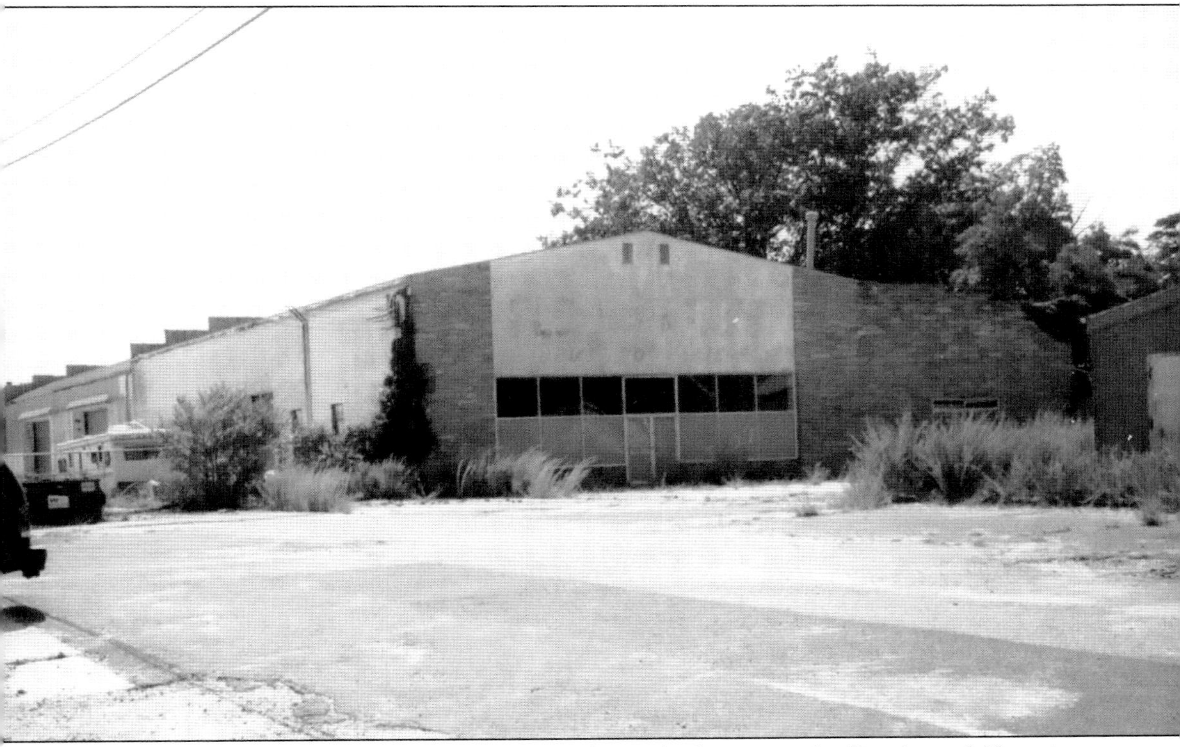

The Johnson Lumber Company warehouse was located adjacent to the Beachwood Shopping Center. Johnson would purchase large truckloads of lumber from down south and sell them at this building. He then bought commercial property along Route 9 in the mid-1950s. The front facade later read, "Flea Market with over 30 Vendors." Today, it remains vacant.

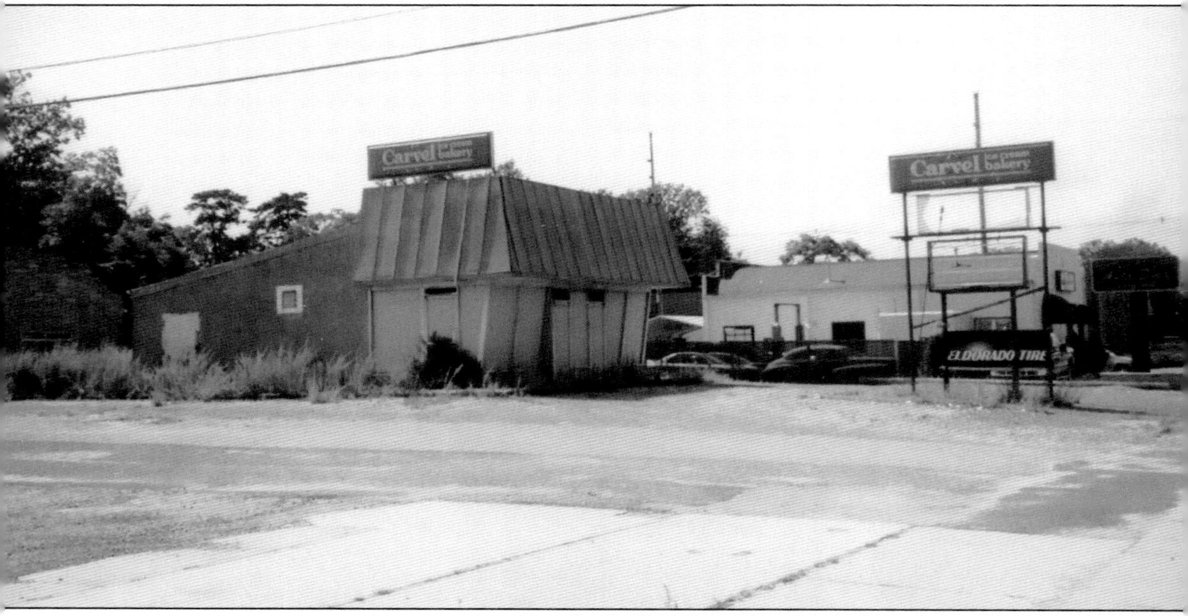

The Carvel store, located just north of the Beachwood Shopping Center, has been dormant for several years. Tom Carvel began with an ice cream truck in Hartsdale, New York, in 1929 and then founded the franchise in 1936. He became known for his folksy, gravel voice commercials. This Bayville store still proudly sports its colorful Carvel signs but remains boarded up.

Six

Community

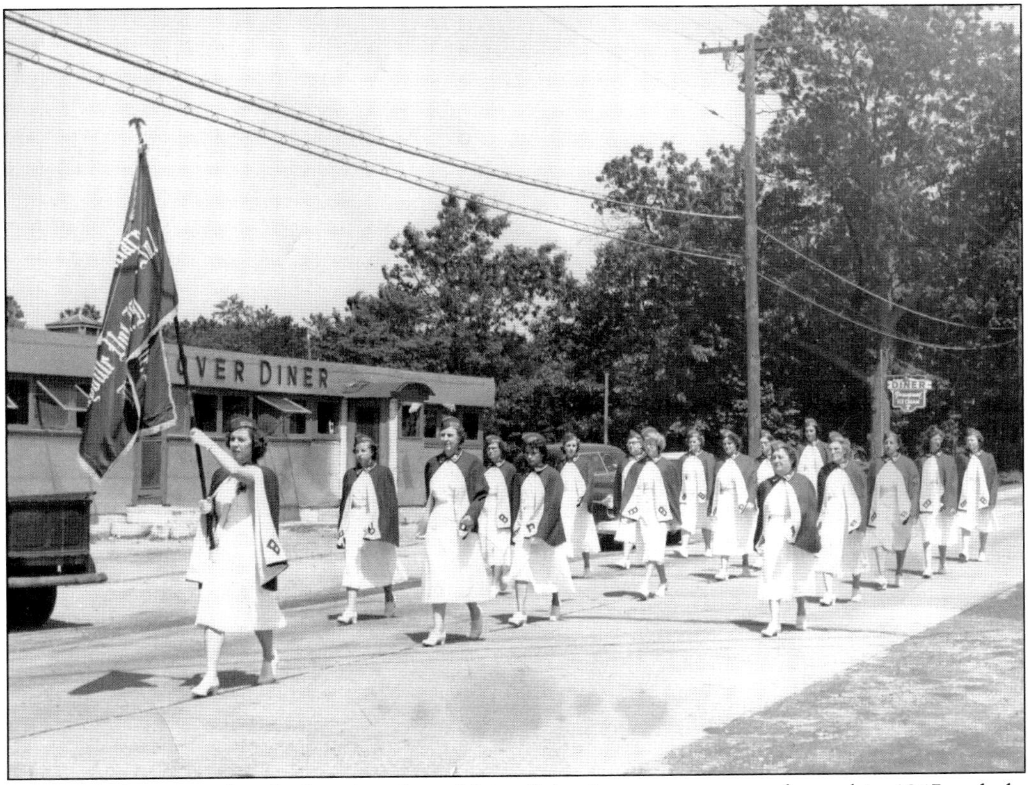

The Berkeley Township Ladies Auxiliary Unit of the fire company was formed in 1947 to help support Berkeley firefighters. The auxiliary is marching in a Toms River Parade around 1953. The flag bearer is Ethel Wright and the three ladies across the front are, from left to right, Charlotte Worth, Mildred Potter, and Grace Roe (far right). Other early members included Dora Rothfuss, Joan Veizer, Betty Brower, Nellie Harrigfeld, and Edna Chamberlain.

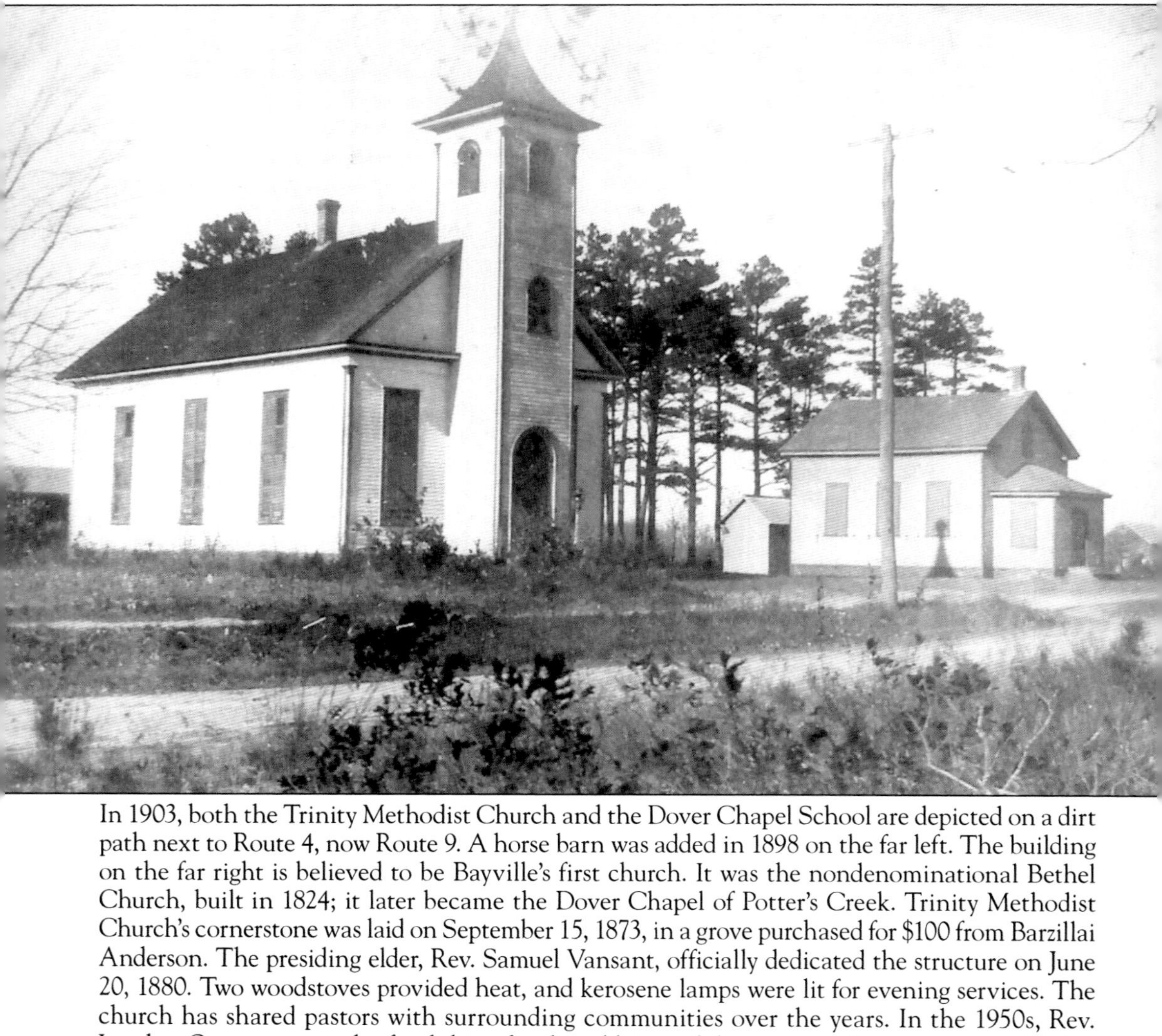

In 1903, both the Trinity Methodist Church and the Dover Chapel School are depicted on a dirt path next to Route 4, now Route 9. A horse barn was added in 1898 on the far left. The building on the far right is believed to be Bayville's first church. It was the nondenominational Bethel Church, built in 1824; it later became the Dover Chapel of Potter's Creek. Trinity Methodist Church's cornerstone was laid on September 15, 1873, in a grove purchased for $100 from Barzillai Anderson. The presiding elder, Rev. Samuel Vansant, officially dedicated the structure on June 20, 1880. Two woodstoves provided heat, and kerosene lamps were lit for evening services. The church has shared pastors with surrounding communities over the years. In the 1950s, Rev. Landon Owen promoted a fund drive for the addition of the present all-purpose room. Today, Faith Community Methodist Church is located in the building. The one-room chapel school is referenced as "Schoolhouse lot #12" in an 1848 deed. It closed in 1926 and then was replaced with the church's parsonage, which is utilized today. (Courtesy of John Enggren.)

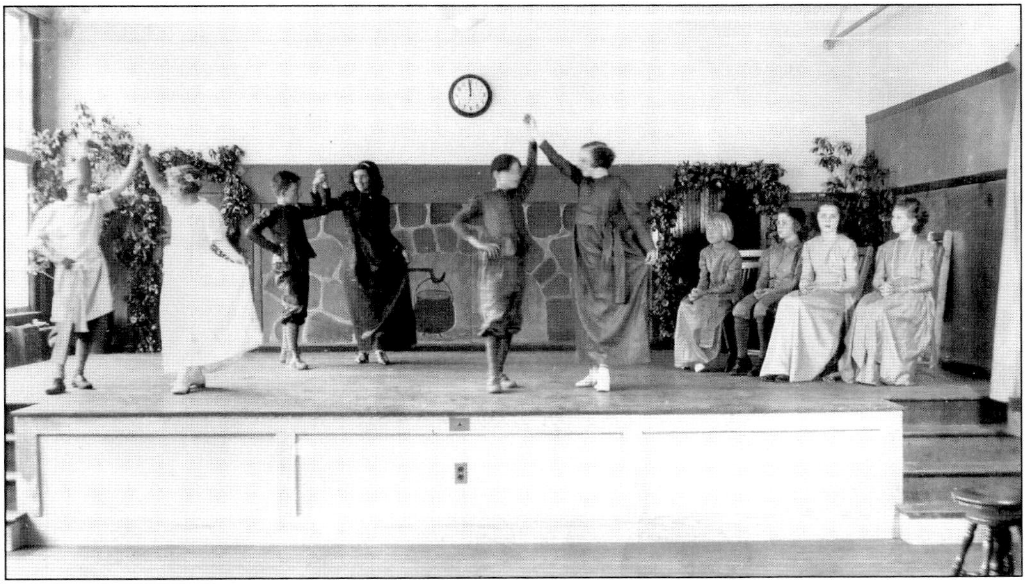

Cinderella is being performed at the Bayville Grade School in June 1938. Cinderella has only 12 hours and 1 minute left, according to the clock on the wall, until her carriage turns into a pumpkin. These show-stopping actors are, from left to right, Dick Hannis, Francis Gross, John Hertling, Betty Joy Cramer, George Flynn as the Prince, Hilda Harding as Cinderella, Emma Flynn, Billy North, Eleanor Manuwald, and Joyce Hart.

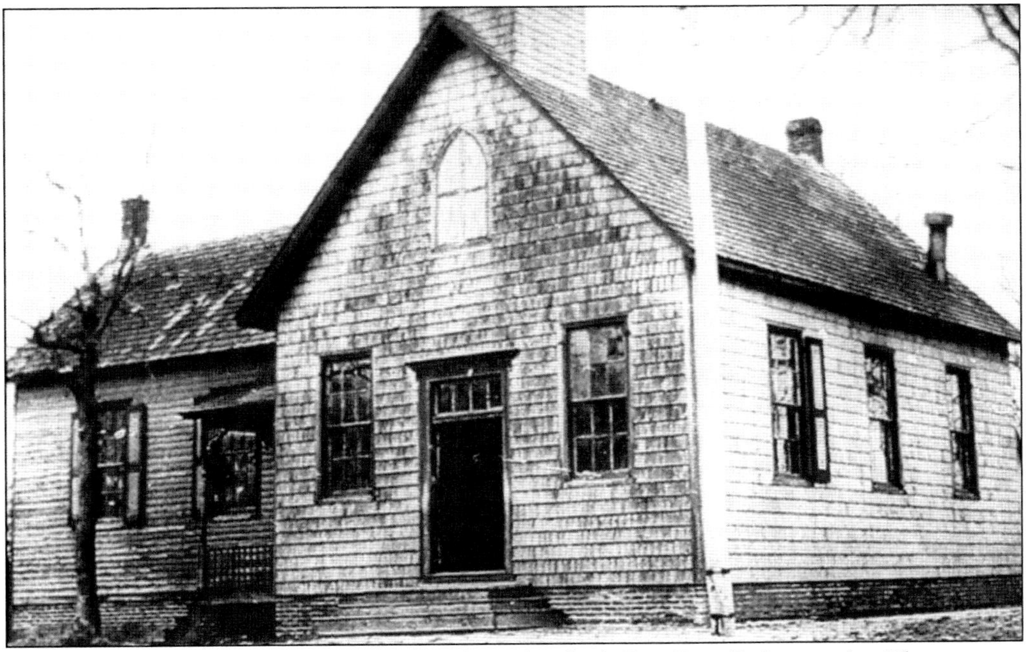

The Lower School was located on Route 9 where the Shady Rest Pizza Parlor is today. The property was purchased from Ruth Platt on March 13, 1869, by school district No. 1 for $75. The original one-room school was enlarged in 1897 by adding the wing seen to the rear of the building. Grades one through eight were taught here. The school was closed in 1926 when the new Bayville School opened farther north on Route 9. The Lower School was demolished in 1927 when the College Inn Store was built on the property.

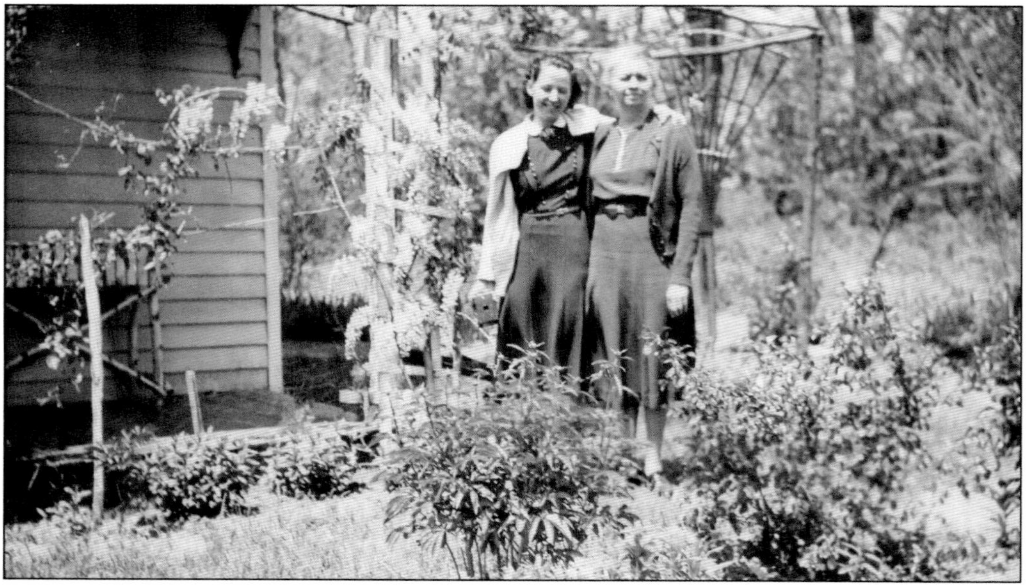

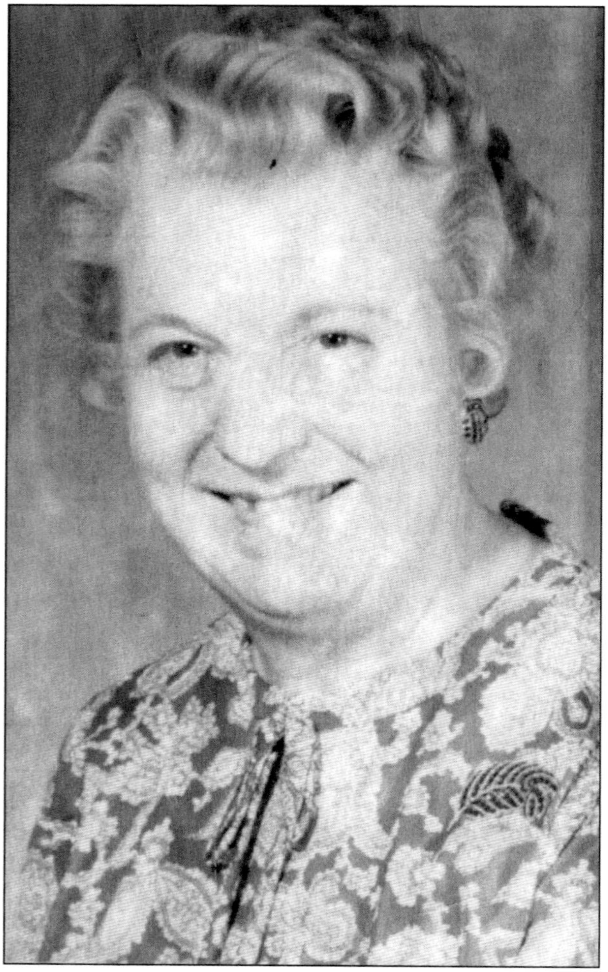

Clara B. Worth, right, is with her neighbor Daisy Wilhelm Endress, left. Clara began her career as a teacher and retired as a principal. She first worked at the Lower Bayville School in 1911 and later the Bayville Grade School in 1926. She retired after 45 years and was given a testimonial dinner on May 31, 1956. In 1963, the new Clara B. Worth Elementary School was named in her honor. On April 28, 1991, Worth was inducted into the Toms River Hall of Fame.

Mildred S. Potter, a native of Lower Bayville, was born on September 27, 1906, to Anna and Arthur Worth. Mildred's aunt Clara B. Worth was her teacher at the Bayville Grade School, which was where Mildred retired in 1967 after 42 years as both a teacher and principal. She lived on Route 9 at Potter's Sugar Hill until passing at age 101. The H&M Potter School on Veeder Lane is named for Mildred Potter and Hilbert, her late husband. She was inducted into the Toms River Hall of Fame in 1991.

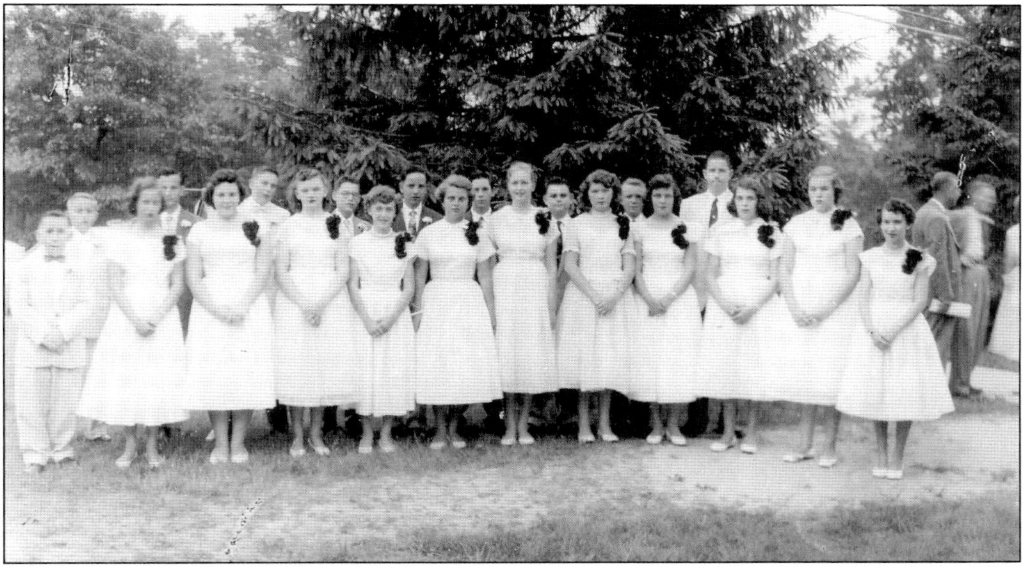

The 1956 Bayville Grade School eighth-grade graduation class was the largest and the last one from the school. The ceremony was held at the Bayville Methodist Church on June 20, 1956. The following school year, the new Central Regional High School would open for grades 7 through 12. From left to right are (first row) Eileen Kelly, Penny Sue McDowell, Sherrill Morrison, Janice Lyon, Eleanor Veals, Pamela Karcheski, Regina Decker, Helga Miller, Natalie Nobels, Jane Geisler, and Shiela Crane; (second row) Jim Lavery, George Petinbrinck, Ray ?, Alfred Stokley, Larry Worth, Carl Peterson, Scott Siddons, Ray Newman, Tom Page, and Gus Moran.

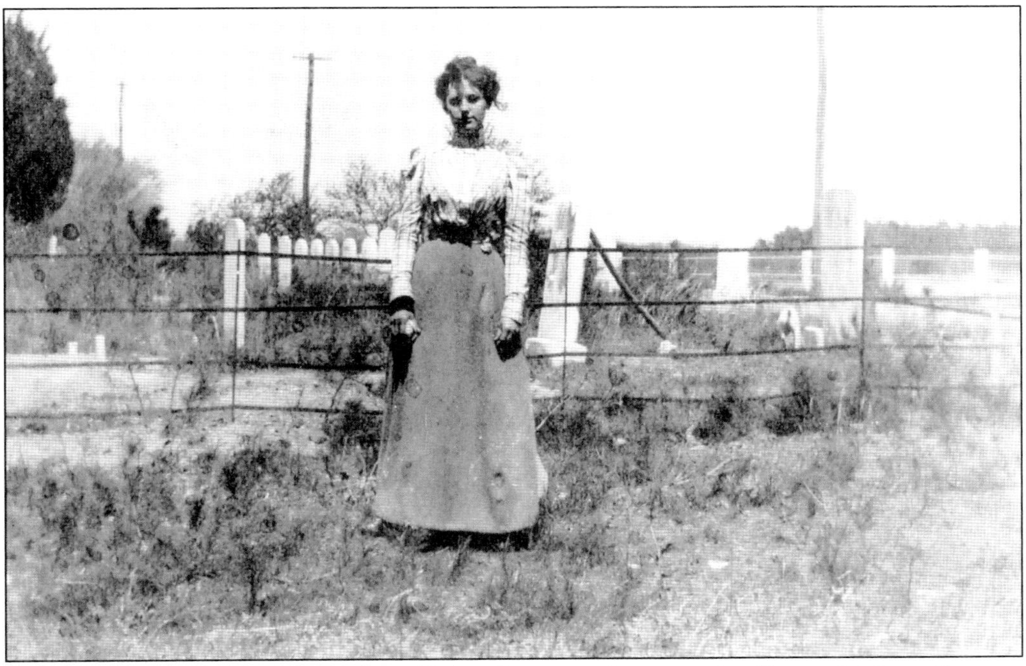

Standing adjacent to the Dover Chapel Schoolhouse on the west side of Route 9 is Lucy Enggren around 1903. Behind her is the Dover Chapel Cemetery. Note the propped up tombstone and her ubiquitous dog in the background. Today, the cemetery is adjacent to the parsonage for the Faith Community Methodist Church. (Courtesy of John Enggren.)

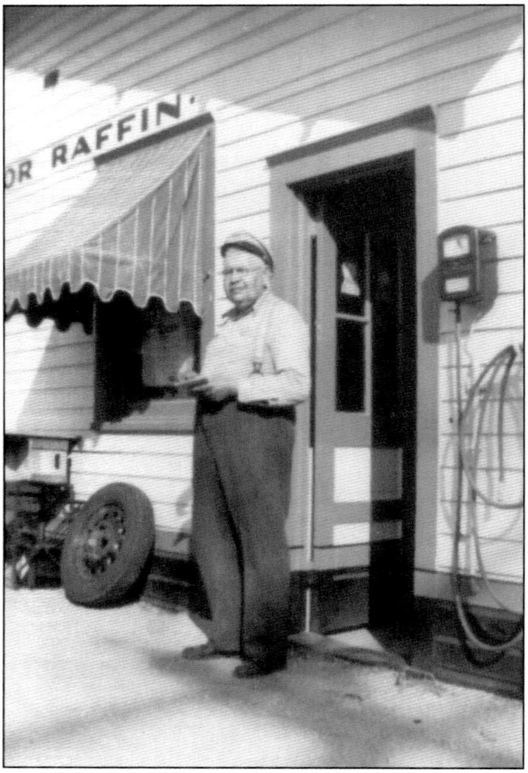

Victor Raffin was born in Lyon, France, and with his wife, Nellie, from Nottingham, England, they later moved to New York City. In 1932, he opened this small Shell service station across from Hickory Lane. He lived in the house next door and operated it as an early bed and breakfast. This home became known as the Tourist House and was one of the oldest in Bayville. In 1948, he sold the entire property to Conrad and Dina Krause, who also worked as a volunteer radio dispatcher for the First Aide Squad. Brother Fritz worked at the site as well. The house was demolished in 1998, and today, the site remains vacant. (Courtesy of Clare and Rosalie Cipriani.)

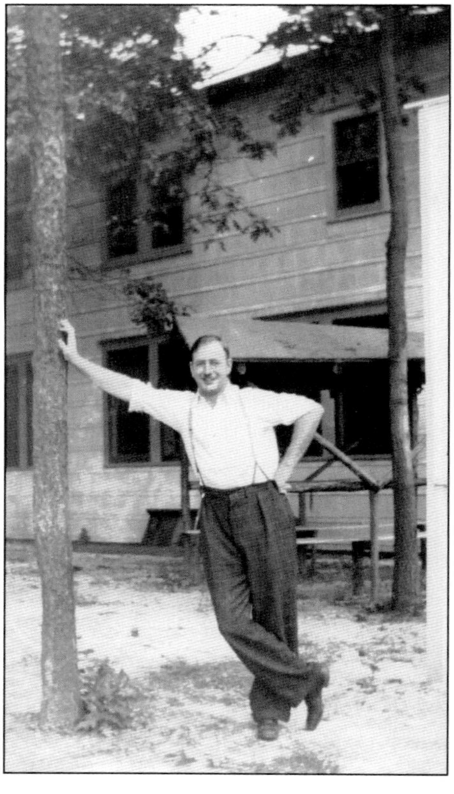

William Sleight, in 1937, is the happy proprietor of Sleight's Beer Garden on Route 9. This was perhaps the most popular meeting place in northern Bayville for dining and dancing. The business expanded over the years from a small stand to a two-story brick building with rooms to rent. Today, with new owners, it continues as a popular restaurant. (Courtesy of Mary Corrigan.)

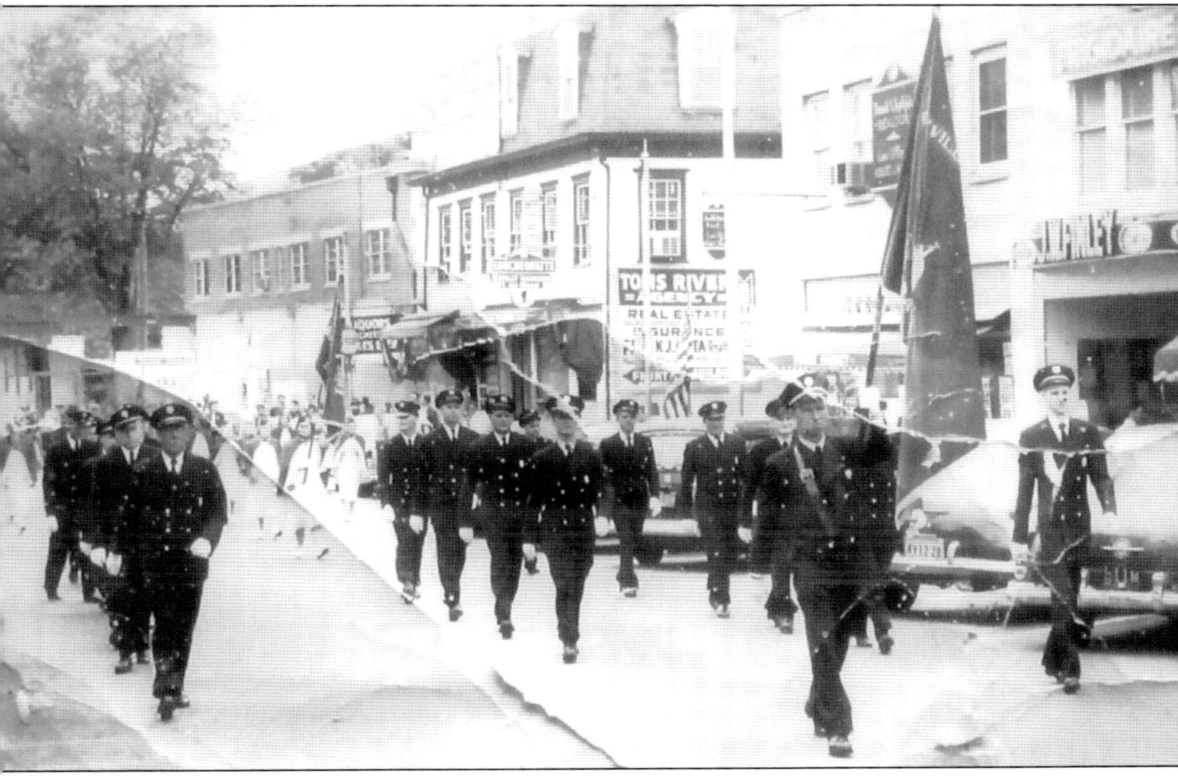

The Bayville firefighters are seen here proudly marching in a c. 1954 Toms River parade. Guy Chamberlain is the flag bearer, and Hilbert Potter, husband of teacher Mildred Potter, is to his right. The firefighters were organized in 1946 and had about 30 members at the time of the photograph. The Bayville Ladies Auxiliary is marching behind them

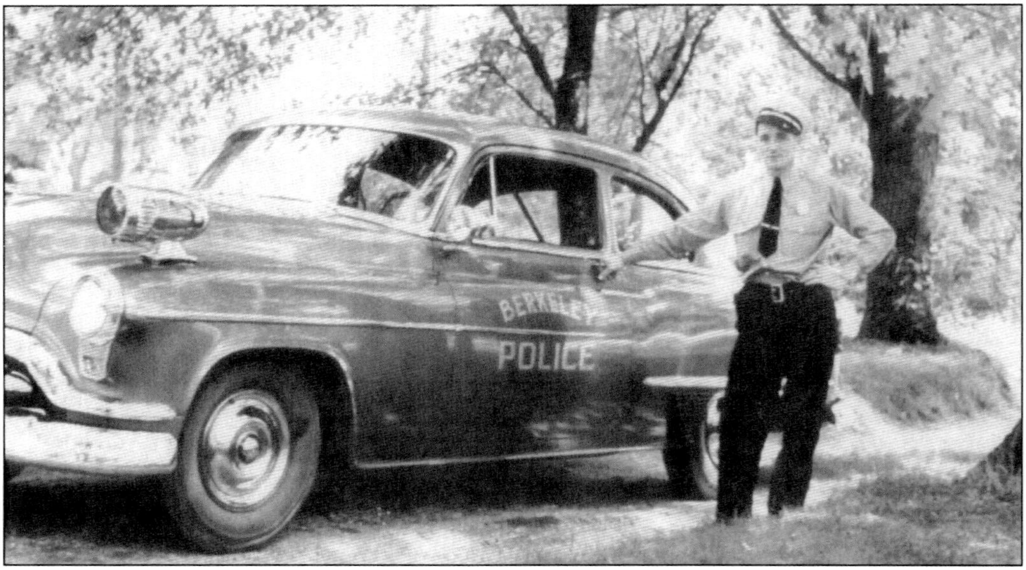

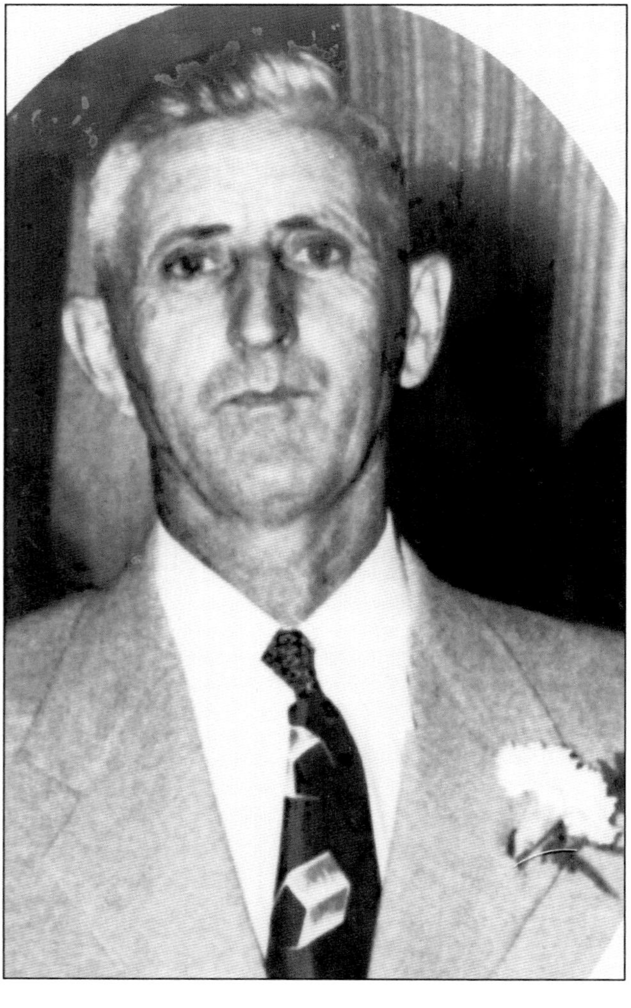

In 1952, Bayville resident Bob Casagrand became the chief of police for Berkeley Township. The police department at that time consisted of only two other part-time officers. Bob and his wife, Noyla, owned and operated Casagrand's General Store until 1983. Bob also drove a school bus and in 1954 helped found the Bayville First Aid Squad. Chief Casagrand is pictured here with his "hot" Oldsmobile patrol car.

Marcus C. Butler (1895–1986) served as the mayor of Berkeley Township from 1937 to 1958, the longest tenure in the township's history. He was the son of Devine and Hanna Butler, who had four sons and two daughters. Mayor Butler lived on Butler Boulevard, named for his family. He served in World War I and was a member the Methodist church for 62 years, a chairman of the planning board, and a bus driver for the Bayville Grade School.

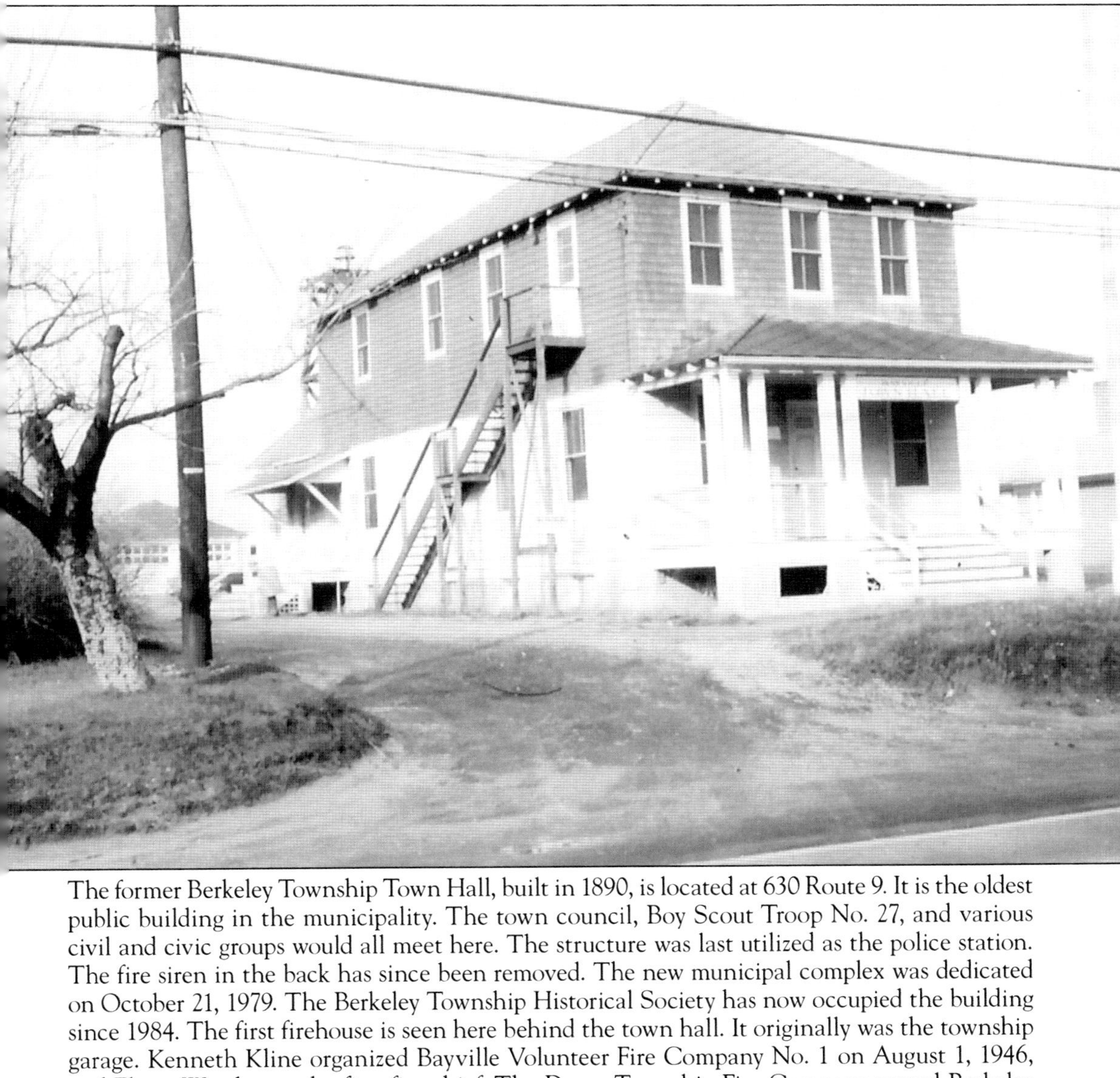

The former Berkeley Township Town Hall, built in 1890, is located at 630 Route 9. It is the oldest public building in the municipality. The town council, Boy Scout Troop No. 27, and various civil and civic groups would all meet here. The structure was last utilized as the police station. The fire siren in the back has since been removed. The new municipal complex was dedicated on October 21, 1979. The Berkeley Township Historical Society has now occupied the building since 1984. The first firehouse is seen here behind the town hall. It originally was the township garage. Kenneth Kline organized Bayville Volunteer Fire Company No. 1 on August 1, 1946, and Elmer Worth was the first fire chief. The Dover Township Fire Company served Berkeley Township prior to this time. In 1956, the fire company moved to the new firehouse across the street on Route 9. This old firehouse was demolished in 2006.